SECOND EDITION

The Theory and Practice of International Relations

William C. Olson
Associate Dean
School of International Affairs
Columbia University

Fred A. Sondermann
Professor of Political Science
The Colorado College

PRENTICE-HALL, INC., *Englewood Cliffs, New Jersey*

LIBRARY OF CONGRESS CATALOG CARD NUMBER: 66–19880

Printed in the United States of America C–91328

Current Printing (Last Digit):

10 9 8 7 6 5 4 3 2 1

PRENTICE-HALL INTERNATIONAL, INC. *London*
PRENTICE-HALL OF AUSTRALIA, PTY. LTD. *Sydney*
PRENTICE-HALL OF CANADA, LTD. *Toronto*
PRENTICE-HALL OF INDIA (PRIVATE), LTD. *New Delhi*
PRENTICE-HALL OF JAPAN, INC. *Tokyo*

Preface

Like the first edition of this book, this version of *The Theory and Practice of International Relations* is designed to meet the needs of two groups of readers. The first is the college or university student who is undertaking the study of international relations in a systematic way for the first time, whether early in his academic career or later on, perhaps even in his graduate years. The second is that member of what Gabriel Almond has termed "the attentive public" who, in his concern about foreign policy, finds that he needs to have a background within a broad framework before he can properly exercise his responsibilities as an informed participant in the democratic process. These two kinds of readers will find that our approach has been conceptual rather than factual, both in the introductions to the selected articles and in the selections themselves, which are the work of thoughtful analysts in political science and many other disciplines. We believe—and have tried to demonstrate in this book—that the study of world affairs is much too important to be left to one discipline or approach.

While we also humbly believe that greater understanding (by decision-makers) of the ideas set forth might result in more effective foreign policies, this is not primarily a book about foreign policy *as such*. After an introductory chapter on the field of study itself, the state system is analyzed, and the factors which go into the assessment of the ability of a state to achieve its objectives are identified. Various dimensions of policy are suggested, and the degree to which states have achieved an organizational and legal basis for working together is set forth. The final chapter stresses the responsibility of national leadership in foreign policy. Readers who seek in these pages the "inside dope" on "what is behind current events" will be disappointed, as will those who hope to find in a work with so ambitious a title any "magic key" or "short cut" to understanding or prediction.

Opinions will differ about our choice of selections on various topics, and indeed one of our most difficult editorial problems has been precisely that of determining what should be included and what should be left out. As the proverbial fisherman said, "you should have seen the ones that got away!" We can only hope that what is presented will meet the needs of those who make use of this volume, particularly in terms of opening up stimulating new avenues of creative thought about this most exciting—and risky—subject of international relations.

We wish to express our gratitude to those who have been so unfailingly cooperative in permitting us to reprint articles and portions of articles, including four of our own, which first appeared elsewhere. Both of us wish to acknowledge our continuing debt to Professor David McLellan of the University of California at Riverside, who joined us in producing the first edition.

Special thanks are due to two members of the staff of the Library of Congress, without whose assistance this second effort might never have been completed: Miss Marjorie Brown, indefatigable and knowledgable reference assistant in the Foreign Affairs Division, who can find a needle in a haystack; and Miss Elizabeth Anne Hodges of the office of the Deputy Director of the Legislative Reference Service, who so cheerfully and efficiently undertook the painstaking task of checking permissions, fees, biographies, citations, and textual materials for us.

In addition to our many professional colleagues across the country and abroad whose comments and suggestions have been so helpful, we want to give credit to the students who have studied international relations on the basis of the first edition of this book, and whose reactions have helped to produce what we hope is an improved second one. They have taught us more than they can ever know about our own field of study and research. One learns best by teaching, it is said, and we can testify that this is so.

But while we must share whatever credit is due this effort with many others, we cannot share the blame for its errors of omission and judgment; that is ours and ours alone.

W. C. O.
F. A. S.

Contents

Introduction

Part I
The Nature of International Relations

CHAPTER FOUR
Power and the Balancing Process, *79*

Part II
The Capability Inventory

CHAPTER FIVE
The Measurement of States' Capacities in Their Foreign Relations, *99*

CHAPTER SIX
The Impact of Geographic Considerations, *125*

CHAPTER SEVEN
Population and Economic Change, *148*

CHAPTER EIGHT
Economic Capability, *165*

CHAPTER NINE
The Military Dimension, *187*

CHAPTER TEN

Scientific and Technological Development, *205*

Part III
Ends and Means in Foreign Policies

CHAPTER ELEVEN

Intentions, Objectives, and Policy Aims, *227*

CHAPTER TWELVE

The Art of Diplomacy, *255*

CHAPTER THIRTEEN

Psychological Methods in Policy Implementation, *289*

CHAPTER FOURTEEN

Economic Aspects of Foreign Policy, *308*

The Theory and Practice of International Relations

Introduction

CHAPTER ONE

The Study of International Relations

One is naturally reluctant to classify his own special field of study as *the* most important among academic disciplines. This self-restraint is appropriate: given our present state of knowledge, none of us knows enough to claim with confidence that any one subject is more significant than another, except in terms of our personal inclinations. Yet most specialists manage to overcome their reluctance. The editors of this volume are no exception, and therefore advance, none too modestly, the proposition that if there is any truly crucial set of problems which confronts the student of the contemporary world, it is the set of problems generally spoken of under the heading "international relations." It is not too much to assert that the solution (or lack of solution) of problems in this area of human relationships will shape the design of our future. As a matter of fact, such solutions (or lack of solutions) may well determine whether there is to be a future at all for the kind of civilization we know. However much many of us might prefer to focus on private or intrasocietal problems, a precondition for continued existence is a profound understanding of, and wise and skillful participation in, world affairs on the part of national leaders, and in a democracy such as ours, on the part of at least a segment of the people.

National societies exist in a world in which there is a constantly growing number of other national societies, politically organized as states. These, and the governments which conduct their affairs, are the major participating units in international relations. Some of the states are not very powerful if measured on a world-wide basis, but they may be quite strong and effective within limited geographic regions. Others have sufficient power to implement their purposes on global scales. Each unit, however, commands some strength, some capacity to achieve its goals, if only in concert with others. Each organized human group has such goals, and the crucial point is that the goals of various groups are not necessarily complementary nor always easily reconcilable with those of other groups.

Although in many ways relations between states resemble relations between groups within states, there are important ways in which these relations differ. In contrast to the usual situation *within* states, there is no easily achievable consensus *among* the various groups which participate in international relations. Lacking common cultural, social, or historical backgrounds, they lack similar values for the present and common goals for the future. Within a state, order is maintained and violence is prevented through the presence of six conditions or institutions: 1) laws—written or unwritten—which reflect the moral judgment of the community; 2) political machinery to change these laws when change is needed; 3) an executive body to administer the laws; 4) courts to settle disputes in accordance with law; 5) superior public force which deters acts of individual or sub-group violence; and 6) "a state of public well-being sufficient that people are reasonable and prudent and are not driven by a sense of desperation to follow ways of violence."[1] One might add an additional factor, which is implicit in this particular listing, namely, an underlying consensus on acceptable goals and methods of achieving them among the members of such a society.

As one considers these preconditions for order and stability within a society, he finds that they are either absent from the international scene or, at best, exist there only in very rudimentary form. International relations thus take place in a special type of environment that the late Professor Frederick Sherwood Dunn once described as "one made up of autonomous units without a central authority having a monopoly of power."[2] A good, brief word for this is "anarchy."

It should be added that it is possible to draw the distinctions between domestic and international relations so rigidly as to make them unreal. Not all states contain all of the ingredients mentioned in the preceding list. The Congo comes to mind as an example where most of them have been conspicuously absent—with apparent consequences. On the other hand, not all international relationships lack a degree of consensus or institutions to ratify and operate that consensus—American-Canadian relations, relations among the Scandinavian countries, and the Benelux countries, are cases in point. One might, in fact, suggest that perhaps the study of relations within some societies can best be understood by using concepts from international relations, while the study of relations among certain states can profit from the use of concepts ordinarily employed in the study of domestic politics.

Yet the basic distinctions still do apply in most cases, and, given the nature of the international environment, the compulsions which operate on participants in international relations are extraordinarily complex and demanding. The problem of effective behavior in international relations has never been anything but difficult for the participating units and the men who make decisions on behalf of these units. In addition, a number of significant changes have taken place during the past half-century (some within the past two decades) that have fundamentally altered the traditional bases of international relations. One such change has been the shift of power from Western Europe to previ-

[1] John Foster Dulles, "The Institutionalizing of Peace," *Department of State Bulletin,* **XXXIV,** No. 880 (May 7, 1956), *passim.*

[2] "The Scope of International Relations," *World Politics,* **I** (1949), 143.

ously peripheral areas. In the immediate post-World War II period, this trend was reflected in the nearly complete bi-polarization of power, centering upon the Soviet Union and the United States. In the more recent past, other states and groups of states have assumed or reassumed considerable importance. There are continuing fluctuations in the power distribution among the states of the world, and it would be preposterous to contend that the process of change has come to an end. We also witness continuing changes in the nature of technology (particularly relevant in the weapons field), and it is by no means clear whether the precise impact of even past technological developments is as yet fully understood. The recent past has witnessed the downfall of long-established colonial empires and the emergence, at a bewildering pace, of new states which insist upon independence of action and freedom from entanglement in the conflicts between the Communist and the non-Communist states. In the areas where the new nationalism has expressed itself in the formation of dozens of new states, we also witness a simultaneous "revolution of rising expectations" —an unwillingness of peoples constituting more than half of the world's rapidly growing population to continue their long-accustomed patterns of misery and deprivation. These people and their leaders want improvements, they want them fast, and they may be prepared to subordinate certain preferences as to means to the overriding purpose of achieving their goals.

Their quest comes at a time when productive capacities and living standards in the more highly developed countries are increasing at a rapid pace, thus widening the gap that separates the countries of the world in terms of access to the benefits which a twentieth-century technical civilization could provide. Their problems are further complicated by the rapid population increases, falling with particular force on many countries which, at this point in their history, can least afford to support their additional peoples.

Finally, the last twenty years have witnessed the emergence of the Soviet Union as an immensely powerful nation, with thrust and purpose provided by history, leadership, and ideology. Our era is marked by the efforts of that country (and, increasingly, by the efforts of Communist China) to play an influential and, where possible, dominant part in the world. This goal is opposed by a coalition of states of which the United States is the most powerful member. The contest is referred to as the "cold war," although the term may be in the process of becoming outdated. In recent years, the respective coalitions—Communist as well as non-Communist—have demonstrated centrifugal tendencies, making both of them far less cohesive than they were in the period of the late 1940's and the 1950's. Whether or not the weakening of coalitions on both sides is a factor making for stability or instability is a question which is dealt with at various points in succeeding chapters.

All of these events and trends have profoundly changed the international environment. Change is the law of human life; but change with such speed (one is reminded of Stuart Chase's phrase, "an express-train out of control") poses most serious problems of understanding and adaptation. It is by no means clear that these problems have yet been met.

With an approximate understanding of some features of the environment in which international relationships take place, the problem of defining a particular country's part in that process now also should be clearer. A country's goals may be "reasonable"—by its own standards, though not necessarily those of others. Its capacities may be considerable, although there are always limits on what can be done. It is unrealistic for any country to expect that it can impose solutions which reflect only gain for its own position on all issues, at all times, and in all places. Indeed, the task of statesmanship is often to "cut one's losses" and accept the lesser of evils.[3] Within an environment tending toward anarchy, it is necessary for countries to coalesce with other countries in the pursuit of common goals. Such cooperation between legal equals imposes strains and tensions, just as does the opposition between contending states or groups of states.

There are only limited alternatives to the solution of international conflict: the ability to arrive at compromise settlements; the willingness to live with unresolved, ambiguous situations; or the employment of coercion. The first two alternatives are neither heroic nor glamorous, and the last is complicated by the nature of modern weapons that are too destructive to be used rationally in a total war situation.

Having thus set the stage with a brief description of the nature of international relations and the limitations imposed upon state action by the environment in which those relations take place, it becomes appropriate for us to proceed to a more specific introduction of international relations as a subject of study, to indicate the richness and variety of its material, and to acknowledge some of the many points of view from which the subject can be approached.

One faces, first of all, the problem of definition—not because a definition *solves* problems (in fact, it is a poor one if it does only that), but rather because it delineates the territory to be covered and hopefully gives rise to important questions that must be asked and answered. There are almost as many definitions of international relations as there are writers and teachers of the subject; yet, certain uniformities are apparent in the viewpoint held by many of its students. All definitions of international relations include not only political relations, but also others, such as cultural and economic ones. All definitions speak, explicitly or implicitly, in terms of individuals or groups (most frequently states and their governments) acting in pursuit of certain goals. And finally, all definitions stress the significance of locale: the study relates to activities *transcending national boundaries.* (A congressional decision to impose tariffs on imports is, from one point of view, a purely domestic decision; but it obviously affects the country's international relationships in important ways.)

While it is true, as Thompson points out in the article reprinted in this chapter, that the study of international relations has become closely linked to the study of *internal* aspects of participating states, this formulation is not fully comprehensive. Any social activity can be studied not only in terms of the participants' behavior, but also in terms of the context within which it takes

[3] A clear exposition of this point can be found in Charles Burton Marshall, *The Limits of Foreign Policy* (New York: Holt, Rinehart & Winston, Inc., 1954).

place as it affects the participants' behavior. A prominent writer on the study of international relations has written:

> Many theories (and texts) look at (international) relations from one angle only: the foreign policies of the units; the perspective is from below (the units), looking up. This is indispensable, but it is not enough. The situations created by the interaction of the units, whether their occurrence was expected by the units or not, have a logic of their own; the types of power configurations that result not only from the conflict, or convergence, of foreign policies, but also from the very structure of the world and from the operation of transnational forces, in turn reshape, condition, and often command foreign policies. Thus we also need another kind of perspective: from the top, looking down.[4]

Since it is obviously impossible to study everything that goes on across national boundaries, a widely employed limiting concept is that of "political" relations, or *international politics*. The most commonly accepted point of view is that in order for an action to qualify as "political," it must contain elements of actual or potential conflict and must, at some point, involve the governments of countries. These factors are no longer as limiting as they once may have been. It is difficult to think of an international relationship from which actual or potential conflict is wholly absent, just as it is difficult to think of relationships in which explicit or tacit cooperation is totally lacking. Also, many relationships formerly entirely private in character have become linked to government activities.

A question that causes some disputation is whether or not the study of international relations is a branch of another discipline, or can be considered a discipline in itself. To most people in the field, this does not seem to be a terribly important question. But students of the subject contend that questions in the field have an internal coherence and differ from questions in any other field of inquiry. One authority believes that the study of international relations is "a point of view, an outlook, a search for answers to questions in a way not now being utilized by the long-established disciplines."[5]

Recent studies have turned away from purely institutional and structural analysis, and towards utilizing materials from the behavioral sciences, especially sociology, psychology, social psychology, and anthropology. There is also considerable new emphasis on quantitative precision, insofar as the elusive subject matter permits. The student of international relations transcends traditional disciplinary boundary lines. In the past he has been linked most closely to historians and political scientists. These subjects remain indispensable to him; however, he also learns from sociologists about the group context of human behavior, and from psychologists about the behavior patterns of individuals. In addition, the anthropologist informs him of the variety of cultural systems and the need for comparative studies of men and societies. If one adds to all this the obvious contributions of such fields as economics, geography, demog-

[4] Stanley H. Hoffman, "International Relations: The Long Road to Theory," *World Politics,* XI (1959), 347. This point of view is more fully explored in the contribution by Professor Sondermann, Selection 3 below.

[5] C. Dale Fuller, *Training of Specialists in International Relations* (Washington: American Council on Education, 1957), p. 26.

raphy, technology, and strategy, one can feel a sense of the richness of the enterprise. No one can expect to know all there is to know in all of these fields; but it is important to know what questions to ask and where to look for the answers.

Let it be repeated that although the student of international relations can and must draw freely upon other disciplines, he performs a task which differs from that of other specialists. In his avowedly interdisciplinary endeavor, he studies the relations between units—individuals, groups, states, and governments—within the particular context of anarchy.

1

*The Teaching of International Relations in the United States**

William T. R. Fox and Annette Baker Fox

WILLIAM T. R. FOX, *Professor of International Relations at Columbia and Director of the Institute of War and Peace Studies, has long been a leader in the development of systematic international studies in this country. He is the author of a number of outstanding works in the field, including* The Super Powers (*1944*), *and* Theoretical Aspects of International Relations (*1959*).

His recent publications include, among others, "Theories as Forces in Modern World Politics," in The Role of Theory in International Relations (*Princeton: D. Van Nostrand Co., Inc., 1964*); *and a memorial to Frederick Sherwood Dunn in the October, 1962, issue of* World Politics.

MRS. FOX *is a Research Associate of the Institute of War and Peace Studies, and the author of* The Power of Small States (*1959*). *She has recently published "NATO and Congress"* (Political Science Quarterly, **LXXX**, *1965*) *and "The Small States of Western Europe in the United Nations"* (International Organization, **XIX**, *1965*).

The Foxes jointly authored Britain and America in the Era of Total Diplomacy (*1952*).

. . . The great transformations of twentieth-century world politics have drastically changed the focus and content of the typical international relations course without essentially modifying the reformist or, at any rate, meliorist attitudes of the teachers and writers.[1] It is now accepted that loss

[1] The key concept in a notable teaching experiment in international relations at San Francisco State College has been "transformations." Materials compiled and edited for this teaching experiment, and published as "Chandler Studies in International and Intercultural Relations," include three specifically dealing with transformations: Charles A. McClelland, *Nuclear Weapons, Missiles, and Future War;* DeVere E. Pentony, *The Underdeveloped Lands;* and Urban G. Whitaker, Jr., *Nationalism and International Progress,* San Francisco, Calif.: Howard Chandler, 1960.

World Politics,* **XIII (1961), 339–359. Reprinted by permission.

of insularity has taken away from the American people their freedom to choose to remain aloof from the politics of Europe, Africa, and Asia. There remains, however, the conviction that what the United States does or does not do makes a difference. American professors of international relations, no matter how little policy-oriented their intellectual interests may be, generally believe that deeper and more widespread knowledge of international relations will somehow result in better public policies and therefore in a better world for Americans to live in. They now know that even a superpower does not have unlimited choice,[2] but they by no means see the future as wholly predetermined.

A list of these great transformations would include: 1. the expansion of the European state system into a world system, with the superpowers peripheral to Europe playing unprecedented roles in a bipolar system; 2. the diffusion outward from Europe to the Afro-Asian world of nationalism and of demands for rising living standards and the dignity of participation in the political process; 3. the democratization of the control of foreign relations at the same time that the widened sphere of state activity has made the conduct of foreign relations ever more complex and difficult; 4. the sudden emergence of science and technology as great and semi-independent variables in the equations of world politics; 5. the drawing-together of the old states of Europe and the transoceanic states of European culture in varying forms of association, such as the European Coal and Steel Community, the British Commonwealth, and NATO; and 6. the new necessity, especially for the superpowers, to do things in peacetime which many states formerly did only in war—maintain a high level of defense mobilization, engage in coalition military planning, finance a massive foreign aid program, and develop a vigorous psychological strategy.

The study of international relations has been reshaped in an effort to clarify American choices as to how to counter, or adapt to, or give direction to these transformations.[3] The bipolar system and the concern for the new policy problems of the Far East, the Middle East, and Africa have caused a tremendous upsurge of area studies. Typical leading American universities have each developed programs for the intensive study of one or more areas formerly thought exotic.[4] There is new interest in regional organization and

2 Former members of the policy-planning staff of the Department of State have produced a series of books stressing the "realities" and therefore the limits of choice in American foreign policy. See Louis J. Halle, *Dream and Reality,* New York: Harper & Row, Publishers, 1959; George F. Kennan, *Realities of American Foreign Policy,* Princeton, N.J.: Princeton University Press, 1955; Charles B. Marshall, *The Limits of Foreign Policy,* New York: Holt, Rinehart & Winston, Inc., 1954.

3 See William Reitzel, Morton A. Kaplan, and Constance G. Coblenz, *United States Foreign Policy, 1945–1955* (Washington, D.C.: The Brookings Institution, 1956), for a survey which explicitly relates the relatively unchanging goals of American policy to changing American capabilities and transformations in world politics in order to clarify policy choices made in the decade surveyed and to be made in the years that followed. This was a logical development of Brookings Institution emphasis under Leo Pasvolsky on formulating problems for analysis so that the result would approximate a "position paper" such as might have been prepared inside the Department of State on one of these problems.

4 Columbia University, for example, has a Russian Institute, an East Asian Institute, and a Near and Middle East Institute. Each has meant a permanent expansion of the faculty by several professorships, and in each case one of the added professors has specialized in the international relations of the area.

the conditions under which the leaders of sovereign states most readily permit decisions to be made by regional organizations which the state has joined.[5] There is also an intensified interest in the international social forces which are operating in the turbulent half of the world now in a state of constitutional flux.[6] The inappropriateness of the new instruments of mass destruction for any socially acceptable purpose but deterrence has had two quite separate impacts: study by the civilian student of international relations of questions of military strategy and even of pure strategic theory,[7] and a renewed interest in finding technically well-founded bases for arms limitation which would lend added stability to the "balance of terror" and lessen the threat of the accidental or the catalytic war.[8] Finally, with the recognition of the importance of lengthened lead-times in arms production, the enhanced role of force in peace and of limited-war capabilities, and the need for military policies to be continuously coordinated with economic policies and information policies, there is sharply increased attention to national security policy, civil-military relations, and the interplay of domestic and foreign politics.[9]

[5] E.g., Ernst B. Haas, *The Uniting of Europe,* Stanford, Calif.: Stanford University Press, 1958; and Karl W. Deutsch, Sidney A. Burrell, Robert A. Kahn, Maurice Lee, Jr., Martin Lichterman, Raymond E. Lindgren, Francis L. Loewenheim, and Richard W. Van Wagenen, *Political Community and the North Atlantic Area,* Princeton, N.J.: Princeton University Press, 1957.

[6] Dankwart Rustow is, for example, . . . "professor of international social forces" at Columbia University. In the Columbia University Bulletin his course of lectures in that subject is described as "a comparative examination of cultural, social, and ideological forces of political change in their international setting. Modernization, nationalism, recruitment of political leadership, the multiplication of sovereignties, and the problems of new states."

[7] Cf. Bernard Brodie, *Strategy in the Missile Age,* Princeton, N.J.: Princeton University Press, 1959; William W. Kaufmann, ed., *Military Policy and National Security,* Princeton, N.J.: Princeton University Press, 1956; and Henry A. Kissinger, *Nuclear Weapons and Foreign Policy,* New York: Harper & Row, Publishers, 1957.

[8] Although the division of labor is not entirely logical, armament policies are usually analyzed in courses on "international politics," while arms limitation policies are dealt with in courses on "international organization." See Joseph Nogee, "The Diplomacy of Disarmament," *International Conciliation,* No. 526 (January 1960); and the symposium issue on "Arms Control" of *Daedalus* (American Academy of Arts and Sciences), Fall 1960.

[9] See, e.g., Samuel P. Huntington, *The Soldier and the State,* Cambridge, Mass.: Harvard University Press, 1957; and Walter Millis (with Harvey C. Mansfield and Harold Stein), *Arms and the State,* New York: Twentieth Century Fund, 1958.

2

*The Study of International Politics: A Survey of Trends and Developments**

Kenneth W. Thompson

KENNETH W. THOMPSON, *who is currently Vice-President of the Rockefeller Foundation, received his Ph.D. at the University of Chicago. Prior to joining the Rockefeller Foundation, he taught at the University of Chicago and Northwestern University. He is co-editor of* Principles and Problems of International Politics *(1950), author of* American Diplomacy and Emergent Patterns *(1962); and a frequent contributor to scholarly journals.*

The question was raised at the end of World War II as to whether or not international relations could stand as a separate field of study. Views were expressed by scholars and teachers in history and political science to the effect that in substance there was nothing peculiar to the subject matter of international relations which did not fall under other separate fields of social studies. At some universities and colleges there were dissenters to this prevailing viewpoint. Their particular philosophy manifested itself in attempts to create and establish integrated curricula under academic committees or departments dedicated to the broad generalized study of the subject matter of the field. It is still too early to pass judgment with any finality on the merits of these two points of view, the one viewing international relations as a mere duplication of the subject matter of many fields; the other insisting that there must be an ordering and integrative approach to the field. No serious student would presume to claim that the study of international relations had arrived at the stage of an independent academic discipline. However, there have been three significant developments within no more than a single generation which illuminate certain aspects of this problem. First we have witnessed the evolution and development of a point of focus or core in the field. Secondly, there have been the first faint and feeble beginnings of attempts to create a methodology appropriate for the field, or at least to determine those related methodologies in the social sciences whose methods and techniques could most usefully be appropriated for the study of persistent international issues. Thirdly, inventories have been drawn up by individual scholars, universities and institutes, of topics and concrete projects which would best serve in the development of general principles in the field and the validation of them through systematic inquiry.

1. THE CORE SUBJECT OF INTERNATIONAL RELATIONS

The movement in the direction of a focus or point of reference has its

* *Review of Politics,* **XIV** (1952), 433–443. Reprinted by permission.

origin in time primarily in the years immediately preceding and following World War II. To understand this development it is necessary to consider the four general stages through which the study of international relations has passed. While sometimes paralleling and supporting one another in time, these phases can be separated because of their particular implications. The first phase was the period in which the study of diplomatic history was prevalent. At this point the significant treatises and monographs, especially in England, dealt with concrete diplomatic events which had taken place over the past several centuries. For example, the studies of the conduct of British foreign policy by noted statesmen and diplomatists covering limited historical periods as, for example, the foreign policies of Palmerston, Castlereagh and Canning, represent the best and most fruitful studies in this period. Perhaps what most distinguishes this period is the high level of historical accuracy and the faithful attention to the canons of historiography and historical method by which it was characterized. Indeed, it is plain from the words and deeds of historians that they conceived their first duty to have been the foreswearing of every temptation to generalize about their observations. . . . Professor Samuel Elliot Morison in his address as retiring president of the American Historical Association in 1950 declared that the sole aim of any objective and scientific historian ought to be the full and complete reconstructing of a selected incident in history. The historian should avoid every temptation to generalize or dabble in universal principles in recording a story which it was his duty to portray in all its essential simplicity. Every effort to connect an event with what had gone before or to draw up lofty and ambitious principles could only weaken this first paramount undertaking. Indeed, we are given in capsule form in Professor Morison's address the prevailing philosophy which influenced most early studies in diplomatic history. In all fairness, the participants in this approach must be praised for their faithful adherence to principles of historical research and documentation.

The price which was paid for this rigorous, objective and nongeneralized approach to the field was the absence of anything corresponding to a theory of international relations. Because of the poverty of available documentary material on recent events, historians have shown themselves reluctant to face instant problems or to offer propositions about others in the recent past. Moreover, the criticism was voiced that this approach left public opinion and the general citizenry without leadership and without guides for understanding and action. As a consequence there grew up during the truce between the two wars an overriding concern for some means of exploring and studying the immediate present. In place of the detached and highly specialized techniques of history in general and diplomatic history in particular there developed an approach that we may designate the current events point of view. The "bible" for the study of international relations became *The New York Times*, and the role and function of the teacher of international affairs became one of interpreting and explaining the immediate significance of current events. This occasioned a flurry of popular interest in the field which, however, proved premature in that it rested on weak and unstable foundations. For this version of teaching and scholarship in international affairs, requiring as it did qualities on the part of the individual for performing the dual functions of pundit and advocate, made of specialists in the field little more than "special pleaders." In this sense, the areas which might have been exploited from the earlier study of diplomatic history were left essentially untouched. Since the study of the present was pursued without any reference to history, there were no ordering principles drawn from past experience. Instead each scholar became a spokesman for his own brand of international legislation or reform. Some discussed off the cuff free trade *versus* protectionism, others international monetary reforms, and others new ways and means of transforming international organization. But none attempted to relate the post-war political problems with comparable problems that might have existed at particular times in the past. To do so would have been antiquarian and proved that the scholar was at odds with his times.

President Wilson inveighed against the use of studies on the Congress of Vienna which the British proposed at the time of the Paris Peace Conference. From him any lesson or enlightenment which the methods of Talleyrand and Metternich might have thrown on the methods of Clemenceau or Lloyd George was ruled out of order. Therefore, the viewpoint of current events became a day-by-day exercise in proposing and disposing of each minor world problem as it presented itself. Furthermore, the absence of any firm methodological foundation for the study of these events led to a grand and extravagant conception of what international studies should encompass. It was said that all experiences and events which involved peoples of many lands should constitute the core of the field. Everything from the anthropology of the most primitive and pre-modern tribes to xenophobia was considered equally important. In these terms an informed discussion of the Olympic Games was as appropriate as an analysis of the latest move in German diplomacy. However engaging this appeared in theory and however appropriate for group discussion, it scarcely led to any carefully conceived approach to the most relevant international problems upon which war and peace might hinge. Someone has said, facetiously to be sure, that this was an era of letters to Congressmen, to editors, and to the public without more than a line or two of scholarly political or diplomatic monographs.

A third phase was inaugurated immediately following World War I.  Coming at this time, it paralleled and strengthened and indeed gave its own emphasis and meaning to the current events that students were discussing. The dominant viewpoint in international relations between the two wars was the viewpoint of international law and organization. Here again, the conception of scholarship which underlay this method of study was two-fold in nature. The mission of students in the field had been to discover the goals and objectives toward which international society ought to be tending. Once this step had been taken and the goal of an ideal world commonwealth accepted, the first explicit task of those engaged in this field of study was to bring about the necessary transformation of institutions and societies whereby these goals could be attained. In this way, the scholar became a crusader and reformer so that it was said by critics of this mode of thinking that in no other field had scholars become to such a degree captive of their own emotions and visions of the future.

. . . What inspired most of the thinking and a great deal of the writing in this period was a single belief. It was widely imagined that once an international organization had been established, all of the baffling and perplexing issues of international politics would disappear. International relations was defined as "the study of those related problems of law and . . . of ethics which were raised by the project of a League of Nations." Hence, the moral obligation of the scholar required that he preach and teach the urgent need for those actions by which an international organization could be established and made acceptable to all the world's peoples.

There are three characteristics of this period in international studies which are essential for considering its successes and failures. First, it was dominated by a spirit of unbounded optimism. Secondly, the research and academic interests, as well as the special competence and qualifications of men in the field, was concentrated primarily in the sphere of international law and organizations. Thirdly, a tendency to draw moral judgments in favor of all international ventures and developments at the expense of any national experience or action which might have its own peculiar international implication was always apparent. . . .

Secondly, the research of specialists in the field indicates the degree to which the study of international law and organization prevailed. The scholarship of individuals like Professors Berdahl, Colegrove, Fenwick, Garner, Hershey, Hyde, Potter, Shotwell, Wilson, and Wright was characterized in a positive way by great technical competence and a remarkable absence of parochialism and chauvinism. It is notable, however, that of the twenty-four scholars in the field who held the rank of professor by 1930, eighteen had devoted themselves exclusively to the study of international law and organization. Moreover a tendency persisted throughout these years of equating peace with government on the one hand, and war with power politics and the balance of power on the other. When international politics and its enduring practices and techniques was studied at all, it was studied by the diplomatic historian, but within the limits of his orientation. The experiences of the nineteenth century in the easing of international tensions were considered irrelevant as subjects deserving serious inquiry. Instead, technical and procedural problems and organizational reforms and improvements of international government preoccupied almost every scholar.

Thirdly, there was an implicit if unstated assumption which underlay the selection of almost every subject of inquiry. It was widely believed that everything international was good, and everything national was bad. Hence, those forms of international practice selected for study included such good and constructive international experiments as the League of Nations, and such questionable and dubious national issues and problems as imperialism and nationalism. The so-called bad or morally ambiguous international activities involved in the operations of the Third International were not discussed nor were examples of good national activities, such as the quest for national security by this country. Indeed, one of the illnesses from which the study of international relations still suffers is the cult of internationalism which places its own moral evaluations on the field of study in terms of the dichotomy of good internationalism and bad nationalism.

Following World War II, however, a tendency which has its inception in a period antedating World War II came to the forefront. The study of international politics replaced the study of international organization as the guiding concern and fundamental point of reference in international relations. An approach was made to recurrent world issues not with a view to praise or condemn but to understand them. Professor Grayson Kirk, . . . [now President] of Columbia University, in a survey of courses and students in the field immediately following the war found that international politics had become the basic introductory field of study almost everywhere throughout the country. In place of the examination of structure and organization in international society, students had turned to the study of underlying forces and trends which shape and mold the behavior of all nation-states. It became the objective of international politics to study the field in much the same terms that domestic politics had been studied for almost a generation. In the same way that American government has proceeded from the study of the American Constitution and the basic law to the examination of practical politics and pressure groups, so international studies became concerned with the study of trends in the foreign policies of separate nation-states and the forms and techniques through which the various national policies of states could be compromised and adjusted on the international plane. Instead of beginning with the *international* structure and society, the new line of inquiry has emphasized the urgency of examining *national* goals and objectives as a logical point of departure. Just as no one would imagine for a moment that national policy on the domestic scene is a quantity that is given at the outset but instead would expect that national policy derived from compromise and adjustment among the major political parties and pressure groups, so it has been argued that international policy, say, within the United Nations, must be studied as the resultant policy of the pressures and claims of many nations on the international scene. The practices and policies of international organization are from this viewpoint no longer comprehended as abstract considerations. Instead they are conceived in the framework of national aims and aspirations, the points of conflict of these aspirations and their areas of compatibility and incompatibility. In this way, the historic policies of England, the United States, or the Soviet Union become subjects of more vital interest than isolated studies of international government divorced from international politics as such. The international organization finds its proper and appropriate place if conceived of as a forum within which national rivalries are compromised and adjusted through novel political processes.

What this has done in practice has been to tie the study of international relations to political science as a primary unifying and integrating core. Without this core international relations had tended to ride off in all directions. With it the chances of discovering some relevant and general principles by which statesmen and citizens might be guided have become for the first time a reality. For political science assumes that the rivalry among groups and individuals for political power and the ways in which power and authority are exercised can be made a proper subject of inquiry and study. In the same way, international politics assumes that the struggle for power and influence on the international scene can be tested and examined on its own terms. . . .

In summary, then, the development of the study of international affairs has progressed through four relatively distinct stages or phases. Prior to and including World War I, diplomatic historians enjoyed what amounted to a virtual monopoly over this area. However, the imprint they made on the field by techniques of historical research still left crucial areas of inquiry outside of the range of international studies. Specifically, the analysis of recent events was hardly amenable to scientific history with its two-fold requirement of abundant documentation and the perspective of time. So the period between World War I and II found two distinct viewpoints vying for influence among teachers and scholars. There emerged, on the one hand, an energetic movement which aspired to examine the areas from which diplomatic history had excluded itself. Popularizers of international studies leaped boldly into the breach and a high-falutin' approach to everyday garden-variety current events grew up. The skills and techniques of the social sciences were used indifferently or not at all in this enterprise. Since the standard for embarking on research was the contribution a project would make to universal understanding and cooperation or to the encouragement of the aims and purposes of the League of Nations, it was hardly to be expected that any system for analysis could emerge at this time. Nor did the second viewpoint which prevailed during much of the interwar period mitigate these problems. Alongside the modish conception of international studies as the equivalent of current events, the prevailing point of reference was international law and organization. International relations were construed as moving along two different planes. One plane was the legal sphere in which nations were told how to act. The other was the sphere of actual conduct among states which had to be judged and evaluated in terms of conformity or divergence from the rules of international law. So exclusive an emphasis on law and organization had three consequences in practice. It led to research that was generally devoid of social and political analysis in so far as it stressed the form instead of the functions of international affairs. It invited the acceptance of a line of least resistance in the choice of areas of research. That is to say, official reports and publications in the field of law and organization poured across the desks of teachers in the field in streams that overpowered even those whose natural bent might have guided their studies along other lines of inquiry. It insured that the model for analysis would be a universal world state characterized by perpetual peace. The present tragic order of power politics among states was studied and assessed not by attempting to understand the underlying conditions which were responsible for its persistence among nation-states but through establishing the sharp deviation of this situation from the model of one world commonwealth.

The failure of this point of view to conform even accidentally with the facts of the interwar period ushered in the final stage in contemporary international studies. International politics has become the focal point of present-day research and teaching partly because of the march of events in the 1930's. For the crises which have followed one another in rapid succession from Mukden Bridge in 1931 to the present have found both teachers and students emotionally and intellectually unprepared for meeting each new challenge. The widespread belief which was engendered by claims that the new formal institutions would soon modify international behavior bore little resemblance to the events which followed. The relations of civilized nations which were to be modified by the operations of the League of Nations progressively deteriorated as the European balance of power was threatened by Germany and Italy. No minor constitutional defect of the League of Nations but the political conditions under which it operated was the primary factor which led to its breakdown. Yet only a realistic assessment of international phenomena could have anticipated and accounted for its decline and fall. The troublesome problem of assessing circumstances and conditions under which national interests could have been harmonized was subordinated to the study of form and structure of the novel international organization. The clue to the basic point of departure of international politics as distinguished from international organization may be found in the way that the current United Nations is evaluated. Formerly, the League had been at the center of the majority of recognized studies; now world politics is the milieu or setting in which every other subject is studied including the functions of the United Nations. International organization, law, trade, and finance are studied in a political instead of a constitutional context. And political scientists are accorded the task of asking questions covering problems which continue to vex our society. Inasmuch as the rivalries which occasion international tensions are now generally assumed to be political in character, this movement of the political scientist to the center of international studies is rooted in the facts of the situation. Today the threefold concern of international politics is with the forces and influences which bear on the conduct of foreign policy everywhere, the techniques and machinery by which foreign policy is executed, and both the novel institutions and traditional practices whereby the conflicts among nations are adjusted and accommodated. The fundamental and persistent forces of world politics such as nationalism, imperialism and the balance of power, however, have only belatedly become an appropriate subject for inquiry. The basic drives which determine the foreign policies of states, their desire for security and power, are the elemental facts with which international politics is fundamentally concerned. International politics is the study of rivalry among nations and the conditions and institutions which ameliorate or exacerbate these relationships.

. . . .

3

*The Linkage Between Foreign Policy and International Politics**

Fred A. Sondermann

FRED A. SONDERMANN *is Professor of Political Science and former Associate Dean of The Colorado College. His articles, which treat the linkage between the theory of international relations and the foreign policy process, have appeared in scholarly journals. Professor Sondermann is a past national president of the International Studies Association, and has taught at the Graduate School of International Studies at the University of Denver and the Claremont Graduate School.*

Presumably no social scientist is ever fully satisfied with the progress of his discipline. Yet few specialists seem more self-conscious about the state of their studies, more keenly searching for newer and better foci, concepts, data, and methods than those in the area of international relations. It seems painfully obvious to most of them that there is both need and opportunity for much further development of their field. . . .

The trend among specialists in the study of international relations is increasingly toward frank acceptance of their field as an interdisciplinary one; so much so, indeed, that more than one of them must have had melancholy occasion to agree with the definition of the student of international relations as "a person who regrets that he does not better understand psychology, economics, diplomatic history, law, jurisprudence, sociology, geography, perhaps languages, comparative constitutional organization, and so on down a long list."[1]

In consequence of this trend, the study of international relations has in recent years been characterized by increasing eclecticism with respect to data—traditionally taken from history, politics, economics, and geography, but more recently also from sociology, psychology, and anthropology. But such eclecticism raises as many problems as it solves, and the old troublesome questions continue to plague the specialist: what should he select? Where should he search?

The answer to these questions obviously hinges upon what one conceives to be the focal element, or elements, in the study of international relations. A focus provides clues to the questions of sources and content of data, concepts, and methods. The way in which a problem is posed shapes all further effort toward its solution, and thus affects the solution itself. The main purpose of the present paper is to discuss the formulation of an appropriate focus for the student of in-

[1] A. Zimmern, ed., *University Teaching of International Relations* (New York, 1949), p. 236.

* Paper presented at the Annual Meeting of the American Political Science Association, September 1958. This paper, in slightly altered form, was reprinted in James Rosenau, ed., *International Politics and Foreign Policy*.

ternational relations. For sake of simplicity and internal consistency, the question will be narrowed to the study of international *political* relations (international politics); the term "international relations," when henceforth used, will be deemed to *include* the term international politics.

One of the basic problems confronting the student of international political relations is the nature of the linkage between his own subject matter and that of certain other specialists. The related other fields of study are comparative government (which is more commonly pursued as the study of various foreign governments, with or without a comparative emphasis); and within this field, the study of foreign policies of various states.

We start with the assumption that the study of foreign policy is closely linked to the study of international political relations, but is not identical with it. This assumption, which will be discussed in detail below, is open to challenge, to be sure. Thus, Feliks Gross in *Foreign Policy Analysis* maintains that the two fields are identical, and that it is only in the non-political sphere that a separation of subject matter occurs.[2] Similarly, Russell H. Fifield writes that "International politics is really a study of the primary factors that enter into the politics of nations as reflected in current international developments."[3] The present paper proceeds from a different assumption, and while it presupposes a close linkage between the two fields of study, it attempts to distinguish between them—for sake of clarity, and in the hope that careful distinctions will contribute to the more orderly progress of studies in both fields.

If one wished to put the matter in extreme terms, it might be argued that the study of foreign policy, as a branch of the study of government, is in some respects quite similar to the study of governmental policies in such fields as, say, labor or education. The major distinction, of course, is that foreign policy is concerned with problems outside state boundaries and thus beyond a state's jurisdiction, while labor or educational problems are for the most part purely internal concerns, capable of being solved through domestic action. Nevertheless, all three activities do have certain elements in common. They are carried on in given ways by designated agencies of a national government, and are subject to constitutional, organizational, political, and other influences emanating from within the national society itself. The distinction between them lies in the strength of the influences emanating from sources outside the national society. . . .

Surely no student of labor or educational policies would pretend that if he studied such policies of a number of countries, either separately or comparatively, he would be a specialist in "international labor problems" or "international education." Another case, that of "international economics" is particularly instructive, since a field of study thus identified exists. Yet, specialists in it would certainly insist that they are concerned with *more* than the study of the economic policies, even the foreign trade policies, of various countries, and that much of their work deals with the analysis of an international system which is linked to, but not identical with, the various national economic systems and policies.

If these analogies are valid, there seems to be no ground for the *a priori*

---

[2] Feliks Gross, *Foreign Policy Analysis* (New York, 1954), pp. 4, 24, 49.

[3] Russell H. Fifield, "The Introductory Course in International Relations," *The American Political Science Review*, **XLII** (1948), 1190.

assumption that international political relations can be studied by merely investigating the foreign policies of various states. It would seem more appropriate to assume a close connection, rather than an identity, of subject matter. The nature of that connection presents problems which have not yet been explicitly faced by students of international politics.

There are a number of ways in which the ambiguity which characterizes this connection can be demonstrated. The one which was chosen for purposes of exposition here concentrates on the way in which various authors deal with the subject of international political relations: their definitions of the field, and the implications flowing from these definitions in terms of selection, coverage, organization, and treatment of materials. . . .

Quincy Wright has pointed out that the term "international relations" refers both to a condition and to the study of that condition,[4] but most authors merely define the condition itself; and one has to infer their concept of its proper mode of study from their actual treatment of the subject. Some authors, indeed, take the easy way out by not defining their subject at all—a solution with which anyone who has come to grips with the problem will have lively sympathy. Others define it in ways which are less than ingenious or challenging, and which multiply rather than reduce problems. Thus, to say that "international relations are the relations between sovereign states" or that "international politics consists of the political relationships of states" leaves a good deal to be desired in terms of clarity of thought and of real indication of the boundaries and the content of the phenomena to be studied.

Nevertheless, one does find similarities in most definitions, as well as in most treatments of the subject. In all definitions, the *locale* of the phenomena under investigation is stressed, i.e. one deals with activities which at some point cross boundary lines. Three additional ingredients which are explicitly or implicitly present in most definitions relate to the fact that the subject is conceived as *individuals or groups (actors)—acting—in pursuit of goals.*

Some brief comment about such definitions in general seems in order at this point. The difficulty with definitions of international relations or politics is not the term "international" or even the term "politics." As to the first, students of the subject generally realize that they do not really mean "international" at all, and use the term only as a convenient shorthand way of expressing something infinitely more complex, and as an elegant way of saying something which, if it were spelled out, would be most awkward. "Inter-powerful - individuals - or - groups - separated - by - boundary - lines" would certainly not be an attractive formulation, although it would be a good deal more precise than "international."

The term "politics"—in spite of much, and often highly complex, discussion of its meaning—is usually dealt with rather simply in the context of definitions by specifying that the activities under consideration are relationships in which, at some stage, governments or other groups exercising power and control are involved.

The really troublesome term is "relations." What does it mean? It is suggested that, minimally, it implies *contacts, connections,* or *associations;* and that it implies *action-and-reaction* (as a single concept) and the linkage between the two component parts. If this is the case, then one must con-

[4] Wright, *op. cit.*, p. 9.

clude that an "action" on the part of one group (government), even if directed toward another, is not of itself a "relationship"—although, and here is the difficulty, it is probably linked to a relationship in the sense that it was prompted by other actions and will in turn engender reactions on the part of others. But it is the burden of the present argument that, to qualify as a "relationship," such action must be considered within an "action-and-reaction" context. . . .

Kenneth Thompson has pointed out that international studies have become progressively more concerned with the investigation of foreign policies of separate nation-states. "Instead of beginning with the *international* structure of society, the new line of inquiry has emphasized the urgency of examining *national* goals and objectives as a logical point of departure." Thus the student of international politics really concentrates on the examination of motives and capacities of nations and statesmen.[5]

This emphasis has its advantages. . . . Some prominent scholars in the field believe that there should be much more concentration on the study of national societies and policies. Thus, Richard C. Snyder, in a major review of much recent literature in the field, expressed satisfaction at the increasing acceptance of policy-making as an analytic focus.[6]

On the basis of the discussion so far, three comments seem appropriate: 1. there is real confusion about the limits and contents of the study of international relations and about the relations between this field and that of foreign policy; 2. in practice, much more attention has been given to the study of foreign policies than to that of international political relationships; and 3. in order to construct more fruitful hypotheses in the field of international relations, it seems highly desirable, indeed essential, to indicate clearly both the limits of the two fields and the linkages between them.

There are three possible reactions to the third of these comments. One may hold 1. that the two fields are coterminous; 2. that the study of international politics is a generalized version of the study of foreign policy; or 3. that the field of international politics consists of *more* than the study of foreign policy. These three alternatives will now be examined in turn.

The implication which follows from the point of view that the two fields are, for practical as well as theoretical purposes, coterminous is that it is a matter of choice which label one wishes to attach to one's efforts. It would seem only reasonable, however, to say that in view of the preponderance of attention which has been centered on the study of foreign policy, this should be the name given to one's endeavors. This, in turn, would mean a recognition of the fact that, at this point in our studies, there scarcely is such a field, or subject matter, or discipline (actual or potential, developed or evolving) as "international politics" or "international relations."[7]

This position would undoubtedly not appeal to very many members of the profession. The reason for its rejection, however, should *not* be that so

[5] Kenneth W. Thompson, "The Study of International Politics: A Survey of Trends and Developments," *Review of Politics,* **XIV** (1952), 440, 458.

[6] Richard C. Snyder, "Toward Greater Order in the Study of International Politics," *World Politics,* **VII** (1955), 464–465, 473, 474.

[7] This, to be sure, is overstating the point for the sake of emphasis. As will be pointed out later, research efforts which focus on relationships do exist, albeit not in very large numbers nor of broad enough scope.

many people have for so long labored in the vineyard of "international relations" or "international politics" that they have acquired a vested interest in its status as a separate field of inquiry. All of them may have been in error in assuming that there was something to labor with or about—this has happened more than once in intellectual history.

The real reason for rejecting the proposition that the two fields are identical is that there do exist demonstrable environmental factors, processes, compulsions, and dynamics (the nature of which will be suggested below) in the field of international political relations which can neither logically nor conveniently be included in the study of foreign policy. The study of foreign policies of states is one of the important—quite possibly the most important—parts of the study of international political relations. But the latter is a broader field, which also includes inquiry into other problems.

The second alternative is that the study of international political relations is a generalized version of the study of foreign policy, and that the distinction between them is based on the level of generalization. This is apparently the point of view of those authors of texts who include a great deal of description and analysis of foreign policies of particular states; reflecting the preferences of many, perhaps most, teachers of international relations who believe that such discussions have a definite place in their courses.

The assumption on which this practice would logically seem to be based is that, while the study of the foreign policy of a single country may provide only clues as to the general situation in international relations, the study of the foreign policies of numerous countries (especially the states of major importance in the world) will provide an accurate picture of international relationships at given points in time. At a deeper level of assumption, this procedure of thinking, writing and teaching about international relations is based on the idea that any relationships, including those in the international field, can be studied only by focusing on the behavior of separate participants. This intellectual assumption corresponds to that of the psychologist, although its source for students of international relations probably lies in the study of history.

This is a serious, defensible assumption, and it deserves thorough examination. One way to arrive at generalizations is by induction: through the study of large numbers of isolated facts, which eventually are combined in propositions, hypotheses, theories, laws. From the practical point of view, furthermore, it is perfectly true that the moment one departs from generalized speculation, one must cite evidence; such evidence, in the form of examples, will almost invariably relate to actions of participants who behave(d) in given ways. Anyone who has taught a course in international relations, especially at the introductory undergraduate level, knows that he cannot remain for long at the level of generality, without constant use of referents in real life. Such referents, almost without exception, will come from, or relate to, the actual behavior (policies) of participants.

Even if the need for concreteness were not so great, there would be other good reasons for emphasizing the study of foreign policies. The outstanding ones are 1. that it is *possible*, i.e. it is a subject which can be investigated because much of the necessary evidence is available; and 2. pragmatically, it has contributed much to an understanding of international political relations. Thus, the attention given to this aspect of the subject is useful and productive. Studies in this area have contributed most of what we now know, and are bound to contribute more in the future.

The only *caveat* to be entered here relates to the assumption that the behavior of participants is the *only* fruitful point of departure for the study of international relations. The basic question, phrased somewhat awkwardly, is this: is the international environment at any given time what it is because the actors in it behave the way they do? Or do actors in international relations behave the way they do because of the nature of the environment in which they operate? The answer, obviously, is that both statements are possible; that there is no "either-or" dichotomy; but that, in practice, most students of international relations have assumed that the first proposition is more valid or in any event more useful. This is the only assumption which is called into question.

It is proposed that the subject of international relations can also be approached from the second point of view, and that such an approach may also be productive and may, because of its different focus, provide insights which differ from those contributed by the foreign-policy orientation. Even if such insights were to correspond to those gained by other methods, they would still serve a useful function by increasing the degree of assurance with which certain propositions can be advanced.

The possibility of such contributions leads to an examination of the third alternative, which holds that the field of international political relations consists of *more* than the study of foreign policies, and that different approaches than the ones hitherto emphasized may, in time, yield many important insights.[8]

Specifically, two alternative foci are suggested: 1. a study of interaction processes and situations as such, as distinguished from the study of interactors who behave in given ways; and 2. a study of the impact of the international environment on participants' behavior, as distinguished from a study of behavior as it affects the international environment. These alternatives do not entail the study of new phenomena, but rather suggest the investigation of the same phenomena which have always formed the core of international relations studies from a different point of departure and with a different focus of attention. . . .

One may focus, not on foreign policy decisions, nor on the dynamics of inter-action processes, but rather on the environment within which all international political relationships take place. One might take as one's point of departure the general international situation—"atmosphere" to use a term which is regrettably imprecise, but yet conveys information about environmental factors which are relevant to an understanding of an inter-action situation. Quincy Wright refers to this factor as "the condition of the entire field of international relations at the time," and specified the general level of tension and unrest in the world, the degree of economic, cultural, and po-

[8] For a statement on the need for a different focus, see Charles A. McClelland, "The Tasks of International Studies," SFIS, 58–6 (February, 1958), 10–11: ". . . an *international* perspective is something different from either a nation-centered or universal focus . . . the essential organization of international relations proceeds from a concentration on a *particular level of human activity*, 'above' the national plane and 'below' the universal. It is an awkward location. . . ."

litical interdependence among states, the general standards of value and law, and the conditions of population and resources, production and consumption, ideology, and world politics."[9]

The fact that the world is organized into separate nation-states, each with its own myths, traditions, cohesive and divisive forces, goals, capacities, and preferred methods of achieving aims, creates an *international system* which has profound impact upon the behavior of participants in that system's processes—and which exists, in a sense, separately from the behavior which it influences. The fact that we are in a period of rapid technological advance, accompanied by cultural lag, when territorial separations of units are maintained in spite of the fact that they have become largely irrelevant,[10] further creates tensions and uncertainties which profoundly affect all decisions in foreign policy. The concept of the "security dilemma" can be derived from the study of the foreign policies of various countries over a prolonged period of time; but it can also be derived from a study of the environment within which international relations in general take place.

One related point may easily be misunderstood and therefore deserves clarification: students of foreign policy and of international relations are not antagonistic competitors viewing each other suspiciously across (too much) *terra incognita* claimed by both. Rather, they are closely attuned to each other. Indeed, they may very well be the same person, in which case the only requirement must be that they should be aware which role they play at a given time. It is difficult to think of a student of foreign policy who is not concerned with the field of international political relations; it is altogether impossible to think of a specialist in international political relations who could neglect the information he receives from his colleagues in the field of foreign policy. . . .

The holistic approach here suggested would provide an opportunity to see the entire field of international political relationships in a perspective which eliminates the danger that intervening objects (including massive sets of data) will obscure the view. Present trends in the field, which lead to concentration on ever narrower and more specific subjects of study, make it likely that the student will be swamped by masses of un-integrated facts, and that the larger picture becomes lost in the process; or, at least, becomes progressively harder to envisage as more and more information demands absorption into a general formula. The question might well be asked whether, in the present stage of the evolving study of international relations, we need more data with which to construct theories; or whether we need more and better hypotheses which will guide our search for new data.

The danger of being overwhelmed results from the fact of starting one's inquiries—as students of international relations still must—without a broad body of theory which guides their search for evidence. Since this is so, one alternative lies in a broadly eclectic approach for sweeping dimensions. But if one casts one's net widely enough, one finds that practically everything in the world can in some manner be related to the study of interna-

[9] Quincy Wright, "Design for a Research Project on International Conflicts and the Factors Causing Their Aggravation or Amelioration," *The Western Political Quarterly,* **X** (1957), 265, 269–270.

[10] John H. Herz, "Rise and Demise of the Territorial State," *World Politics,* **IX** (1957), 473–493.

tional relations. We referred at the outset to the unfortunate student of the subject who regrets that he doesn't know everything; the sequel is his equally unfortunate colleague who either starves in the midst of plenty or dies of intellectual indigestion.

Another alternative lies in narrowing one's attention upon specific aspects of the field. This has been the predominant choice of students of the subject. But here the danger is that, in the process, one gets further and further away from one's core interest—the international relationship itself.

If, however, one can *concentrate* one's attention *without* shifting from the subject of international relations to another area of inquiry, one may perhaps evade both horns of the dilemma and hope, eventually, to register real progress in one's endeavors.

Part I

The Nature of International Relations

CHAPTER TWO

The International System and Its Participants

The term "nation" is an ethnic one, based upon a common heritage, language, culture, and sense of identity. A state is a body of people politically organized under one government with sovereign rights. Sovereignty refers to the exclusive jurisdiction that a state possesses within its territory and to its freedom to act in international affairs without subjection to the legal control of another state organization. From a number of perspectives, a state may encompass more, or less, than one nation; a nation may not possess statehood, but nations taken together make up the basic units and base of power in the international system in which we live. It is the organization of man's activity and loyalty into national communities, each possessed with that vital quality, "sovereignty," that gives international relations its distinctive character.

The contemporary state system dates roughly from the end of the Thirty Years' War. The temporal rulers of England, France, the German Reformation states, as well as the lesser princes and potentates of Europe, took advantage of the anarchy produced by the religious wars to assume and keep authority within their respective territorial domains. Earlier they had been obliged to bow to the authority of the Pope in religious affairs and to the Emperor of the defunct Holy Roman Empire in secular matters, and they had had to put up with the challenge of powerful feudal lords within their own kingdoms. But henceforth supreme authority, or sovereignty, came to be identified with the state, whose rights, independence, and power all derived from what Herz calls its "territoriality." Once established, sovereignty conferred upon each state the right to utilize the strength of its people and its resources in whatever way it wished, without regard for any political superior either inside or outside the national territory. This transformation created a world of sovereign, independent states, theoretically equal but varying widely in real power, each dependent for its survival upon its own ingenuity and resources. From then on, individual security, diplomacy, international law, war, commerce, and the development of culture and of civilization itself would derive their form and content from the nation-state as the highest sovereign political entity. That system, now extended to the far corners of the earth, prevails in its fundamentals right down to the present day.

States are neither equal in size nor in the resources they can command. Inequality in the distribution of real power profoundly affects the operation of a system theoretically based upon the equality of each sovereign state. In Samuel Grafton's words, "Even after you give the squirrel a certificate which says he is quite as big as any elephant, he is still going to be smaller, and all the squirrels will know it and all the elephants will know it."[1]

The Western state system (which in its essentials has become global) has always been dominated by a few powerful states whose unequal distribution of power has been expressed in terms of such classifications as "great powers" in contrast to "small powers." A great power has been defined by Martin Wight as "a Power with general interests, and with such strength that it can attempt to advance or protect those interests in every sphere," whereas by contrast small powers are "Powers with the means of defending only limited interests. . . ."[2] Wight also utilizes the term "Dominant Power," that is "one that can take on a combination of any other Powers."[3] An even less precise but perhaps more familiar term, "middle-class powers," presumably encompasses those too strong or ambitious to be classed as "small," but not strong or ambitious enough to be accorded "great" status. Some states are so weak, and so likely to remain so, that they are not "powers" at all—"power" presumably connoting the ability of a state to impose its will, by some means or other, on some other state.

At the top of this hierarchy of states is the "Super Power," a term suggested by William T. R. Fox to describe states possessing "great power plus great mobility."[4] In 1945 it looked as though there would be three superpowers, but postwar events soon revealed the weakness of Great Britain, leaving only Russia and the United States in this category. Perhaps China will one day merit this classification, although in terms of the development of an economy capable of sustaining power of this magnitude, it may be more likely that Europe, should it achieve effective integration, will sooner do so.

Being subject to no legal superior, nation-states are traditionally left to their own devices for regulating their foreign relations and guaranteeing their own security. The resulting process is often called "power politics," whereby each participant seeks to protect itself by employing whatever strength it has

[1] Quoted in William T. R. Fox, *The Super Powers* (New York: Harcourt, Brace & World, Inc., 1944) p. 3.

[2] *Power Politics* (London: Royal Institute of International Affairs, 1946) pp. 18, 27.

[3] *Ibid.*

[4] *Op. cit.*, p. 21.

to gain whatever advantage it can. However, in order to protect themselves against the worst dangers of such a Hobbesian "state of nature," states enter into alliance, whereby the strength of many is pooled to maintain a balance of power and to assure collective security against the power of the more menacing members of the system. In turn, other groupings emerge, made up of states which feel threatened by the collective power of the states allied against them.

Until the United States and Japan entered the international arena as the nineteenth century merged into the twentieth, the nation-state system was virtually limited to Europe. There a common culture and a common respect for the principle of dynastic legitimacy and (following the French Revolution) for the right of national self-determination, fostered a considerable measure of restraint in spite of power politics. Yet fundamentally, European security rested upon the essential autonomy and defensibility of each national territory. Each of the great states was both large enough to provide its people with living space and strong enough to deter potential invaders. There existed neither the necessity nor the opportunity for unlimited expansion, and the European states could regulate their relations by such methods as limited war and the balance of power. As a basic sense of security took hold in nineteenth-century Europe, it became less imperative for the leaders of its separate units to mobilize their people and their resources for defense. Just as today the expectation of war engenders the very conditions which precipitate war, the expectation of peace in those days fostered peace. But in assessing this period one must not overlook in the European system a "safety valve" in the form of overseas expansion. Nationalistic and economic pressures could exploit a less dangerous outlet, where even the sharpest conflicts could hardly be regarded as vital.

Thus, during the long period in which the international system afforded the major powers an opportunity to develop in comparative peace and prosperity, the nation-state served a most useful and constructive function. Beginning with the nineteenth century, however, certain trends began to undermine the principle of territorial impenetrability which underlay the ability of each state to exist alongside similar powers. These trends had to do in part with difficulties inherent in the application of the principle of self-determination, in part with the perfection of instruments of ideological–political penetration, and in part with the development of weapons of mass destruction.

But it was World War I that brought about the breakdown of the European order of powers. The League of Nations' principle of collective security—which sought to mobilize the effort and commitment of all to protect the system against any one of its more aggressive members—proved inadequate to the enormous task of combatting the anarchy engendered by the totalitarian nationalism of the thirties. Ethnic heterogeneity in Central and Eastern Europe had already rendered impossible the development of viable national states. Conflicts between new nation-states and their minorities soon became interwoven with the international ambitions of the revisionist powers—Fascist Italy and Nazi Germany. Hitler's Germany in particular was seized by a kind and degree of nationalism unlike any ever experienced in Europe. The deprivations and insecurity produced by industrialization, the dissatisfactions stemming from the Versailles settlement, the specter of Communism, the unworkability of the Weimar Republic: all combined to create a traumatic condition. Millions of Germans threw themselves into the arms of Der Fuehrer, who preached a doctrine of tribal nationalism resting on a vision of a mythical Aryan race, and promised to provide them a more rewarding social existence at home and a glorious identity in the world. As Germany became expansionist, Italy and Japan stepped up the tempo of their expansion. By the mid-1930's it was easier to see than to do anything about the handwriting on the wall on which the bankruptcy of an international system based upon nationalism was writ large. Just as World War I epitomized the collapse of the old order, World War II sounded the deathknell of the international system whose birth had come with the end of the "war to end wars."

Rivalry between the superpowers since World War II has demonstrated most dramatically the limits of the claims of most nations to equal political sovereignty. More conventional nation-states continue to play their role as actors on the inter-state stage, but their relative weakness reveals a disparity of power among them which has drastically modified the concept of a system composed of relatively equal sovereign entities. Even the strongest powers—the Soviet Union and the United States—are physically vulnerable to such devastating air-atomic attacks as to render the security function of their respective territorial states virtually meaningless.

Transformation of the balance of power system into a bipolar order—as an outcome of World War II inherent in the disparity of power between these superpowers and other nation-states—greatly increased the instability of the international system. Monolithic organizational principles throughout the Communist bloc and early postwar manifestations of Soviet expansionist intentions under Stalin quickly crystallized another bloc of powers around the United States. The inability or unwillingness of the superpowers to reach agreement on the terms for peaceful coexistence brought about such a high degree of bloc integration that in one leading work the term "bloc actors" is used rather than "nation-states" to explain the operation of the bipolar system.[5] Characteristic of the new system is the fact that many states—though by no means all—concluded that their security could be assured only by integrating their own systems and concerting their policies with those of the leading member of the bloc. If such integration (even though it may never become complete) were to reach a certain level, it would become extremely difficult for a bloc member to withdraw or to feel secure in doing so. In contrast to the gradualism and adjustment which are found in a flexible balance of power system, the bipolar system is characterized by a desperate struggle on the part of each bloc to acquire or maintain preponderant capability vis-à-vis its competitor. This engenders drives to enlist new members in each bloc. In such a loosely integrated bloc as the Western, the divergent national values of its members are often a

[5] Morton Kaplan, *System and Process in International Politics* (New York: John Wiley & Sons, Inc., 1957).

source of disagreement and tension. The Suez crisis of 1956 was a striking demonstration of this. Even within the Soviet bloc the vitality of the nation-state manifests itself in the varying experiences of Yugoslavia, Poland, and Hungary. Within both systems, these disintegrating tendencies have become more rather than less marked, particularly with the emergence of Red China as a great and potential superpower and the reemergence of independent French power under de Gaulle.

Two additional categories of states exist in the international system—the neutrals and the uncommitted. Neutrals like Switzerland and Sweden hope to preserve their independence by relying upon their internal strength and their relative international weakness (together with the interests that all antagonistic states have in preserving some "neutral" ground). If aggression cannot be rendered impossible, at least it can be regarded as irrelevant or unnecessary. Uncommitted and neutralist powers like Egypt, India, and Indonesia regard the "cold war" as a selfish struggle between the superpowers in which they do not need to be involved, except to take advantage of the situation to serve their respective interests. What is impressive is the extraordinary variety of relationships that can exist even in a world dominated by an encompassing bipolar rivalry.

A source of great potential revolutionary change in the nation-state system is the possession of nuclear weapons by additional powers. As this occurs, the concentration of the world's power (military and industrial) in the hands of two superpowers tends to give way to a system in which an indefinite number of lesser powers would exist on the basis of fundamental equality as possessors of the new weapons. Should such a development reach certain proportions, it would work a fundamental change in the present balance of power. It would accentuate the anachronistic nature of the nation-state as the basic unit in international relations and confront the world with the nightmare of uncontrolled and widespread atomic armaments.

Among the many ironies of contemporary power politics is the fact that the very possession of nuclear weapons of enormous capacity (which are unlikely ever to be used) may be a source of genuine weakness rather than undoubted strength for states and may make it less possible for them to act rather than increasing their capacities.

1

*Continuity and Change in International Systems**

George Liska

GEORGE LISKA *is Professor of Political Science at Johns Hopkins University and a Research Associate of the Washington Center of Foreign Policy Research. Among his many contributions to the literature in international relations are* The New Statecraft: Foreign Aid in American Foreign Policy *(1960), and* Europe Ascendant: the International Politics of Unification *(1964).*

I

What are the "distinctive features" of individual international systems and how can one proceed to identify them? There are two main ways of doing so. One can be sensitive to differences or one can search for similarities between individual international systems—that is, either stress more or less revolutionary transformations or stress continuities in function, even if not in form. The two viewpoints are as irreconcilable in principle as are any other set of basic differences in outlook on politics; they could provide the stuff of a vain debate just as easily, instructively, and in the last resort inconclusively as did the proponents of enlightened realism and realistic idealism. What is fundamental to the adherent of one outlook is superficial to the adherent of the other, and vice versa. The reduction of apparent differences to an underlying identity of form, function, or relation can be rejected as an exercise in abstraction that produces voids without relevance for either political reality or theory; and the emphasis on profound transformations in forces and unique configurations of facts and events can be dismissed as an exercise in inventory-taking that obstructs historical vision and buries the lessons of the past. One can agree with the proposition that to abstract is to seek the general in the historically unique. But there remains the question of what is historically unique, and how deep or in what direction one need probe to reach the level of the general without abstracting away the historical.

The change wrought by a new technology or by a new form of political and social organization and ideology is not a fixed quantity. It is less pronounced when the phenomenon is viewed in the context of relations among political units than when it is compared with analogous phenomena in other historical periods. The arrow

* *World Politics,* **XVI** (1963), 118–136. Reprinted by permission. This is a review of Richard N. Rosecrance, *Action and Reaction in World Politics: International Systems in Perspective* (Boston: Little, Brown and Company, 1963); and it also refers to some of the writings of Stanley Hoffman, namely, "International Systems and International Law," *World Politics,* **XIV** (1961), 205–237; "International Relations: The Long Road to Theory," *ibid.,* **XI** (1959), 346–377; and *Contemporary Theory in International Relations* (Englewood Cliffs, N.J.: Prentice-Hall, Inc., 1960).

differs more from the missile in the genealogy of weapons than inter-unit politics of the arrow age differs from that of the missile age. The same is true of relationships between dynasticism and mass society, and between parochialism and nationalism, for instance. To a disputable extent, transformations in particulars are neutralized as they are dispersed among parties to inter-unit politics and as they are complemented, possibly after a time-lag, by transformations in other, but interacting, spheres. The change wrought by the weapons of mass destruction in international politics is lessened when weapons are diffused among states, and when there has been a concurrent evolution toward mass society, a more dynamic economy, and transnational regional political organization. What matters, I shall try to suggest later, are the balances and margins, not the absolutes.

Neither Hoffmann nor Rosecrance denies the existence of continuities and recurrences in international politics, albeit they allow for these only in regard to very general patterns or categories. But when they actually delineate individual systems, they are led to give emphasis to transformations. One of the reasons for this is that they weight intranational and transnational factors and phenomena on a par with international (or interstate) ones, in reaction to the contrary emphasis of the so-called realistic school. They would restore full richness to international relations over against the view of international politics as a body of specialized action within the matrix of changing social and technological phenomena. The question is whether emphases that are useful for placing in relief the salient characteristics of a contemporary system are just as useful for attempting systematic comparison of many international systems over a longer period of time and across cultural boundary lines—in other words, whether a systematic identification of meaningful differences may not require a self-conscious preliminary effort to exhaust the fund of similarities in patterns and functions.

[The authors share] the inclination to see a fundamental difference in the international politics that preceded and those that followed the socio-political revolution initiated in 1789 and the technological revolution in weapons initiated in 1945. While the first revolution is said to have terminated the deliberate self-limitations allegedly practiced by the *ancien régime,* the latter infused international politics with an unlimited military capacity for material destruction.

It is probably fair to say that in the less than twenty years since Hiroshima we have been offered no coherent doctrine of the "new" thermonuclear international politics, as distinct from the development of its specific military-strategic concepts. Even a brief attempt to indicate the outline for such a doctrine discloses the difficulty. If the political realm actually reflected and followed the technological realm, we would witness a sharper than usual polarization between high politics and low-level politics. High politics would have been stalemated on the model of the stand-off in the strategic nuclear-weapons sector and reduced to occasional diplomatic communication designed to convey the meaning of ambiguous and doubtfully credible military-strategic demonstrations. And the stalemate of high policy would have depressed non-military contacts between adversaries to a subpolitical level of public propaganda and secretive inquisitions, analogous to subconventional warfare in the military sphere and practically merging with such warfare. Some such development was possible in the early postwar years, and such elements of international politics as were introduced into pre-atomic political methods are likely to persist. But this is a different proposition from admitting an anachronistic and presumably provisional survival of pre-atomic politics in the nuclear age, as a consequence of the territorial state becoming penetrable by nuclear missiles instead of merely by the marching phalanx and the tank column. There have been shifts in the respective functions of military and diplomatic activities, and many functional substitutes for military action have emerged; but that is as far as the change has gone and the trend seems to be backward rather than forward. It is permissible to attach greater long-range significance to such retrogressions than does Hoffmann and to differ still more from Rosecrance, who believes in the fundamental difference of the international system and constellations of the deterrent age from those of earlier, balance-of-power, periods and systems.

The obvious question is whether changes in intensity of relations, in outward forms of techniques, and in institutional superstructures add up to a transformation in international systems. One essential aspect—the way actors feel about each other and the things they would like to do for themselves and to each other at different levels of tension in comparably structured situations—has probably changed less over time than we think it ought when we compare the components of our predicament with the predicaments of earlier international systems. One reason for the limited nature of significant change is that the crucial balances have tended to remain relatively constant. Thus the greater power of destruction implicit in modern weapons has been offset by the greater capacity of modern societies to reconstitute themselves and reconstruct their economies. It took decades for the great European nations to recover from the exhaustion of hegemonic wars, and some of them never did; so-called economic miracles of a more recent past have been facilitated by previous destructions. Ideological and nationalist drives have tended to increase the range in fluctuations between pacific and bellicose dispositions; but countervailing transnational principles and sentiments have also grown in intensity, and (as Hoffmann notes) ideological and revolutionary drives have tended to be restrained by the perils implicit in revolutionary new weapons. And there has probably not been a substantial change in the politically relevant aspect of the relation between what the main powers would *want* to do to each other and what they actually *can* do—in the sense of the net margin of inflicted over received damage. Hostile powers normally want to do to each other more than they can, with the result that they must settle for much less most of the time.

Upon careful inspection, the differences between a unipolar imperial system, a multipolar competitive system without an acute hegemonic challenge, and a polarized system with pronounced hegemonic features may be found to be greater than are differences between the manifestations of the same type of system at different historical periods and at different stages of socio-political and technological evolution. The international system toward which we seem to be moving in the 1960's may already have more in common with the international system of the mid-eighteenth century and the mid-nineteenth century than it has with the system of the immediate post-World War II period.

II

The inclination to stress similarities in international politics over time is commonly correlated with the tendency to impute to the structure of the international system a controlling influence over the behavior of actors with different internal characteristics and different technical means of action. The most recent name for the ancient compound of necessity and foreign-policy primacy is dominance of the international system over subsystems; the opposite view is to regard international actors as essentially free to act in the international arena according to their predispositions and, if any, their intranational compulsions. The user of the historical-systems approach might be well advised to start out with a presumption in favor of the dominance of the international system under consideration, to be relaxed only after its explanatory power has been exhausted. By contrast [one may choose] to place great emphasis on intranational and transnational forces—notably, on internal political conditions and on transnational ideologies.

As regards the domestic determinant, it is not particularly revealing to assert that states disturb international stability by going to war when governing elites have an "insecure tenure" or when they are overconfident of their tenure. All governments seek success in foreign policy; and insecure governments may be more tempted than others to heed the death-bed advice of Shakespeare's Henry V to his successor: "to busy giddy minds with foreign quarrels." But the determination or desperation with which they do so is due to their position in the balance of rising and declining energies and power that is a primary given, not capable of satisfactory explanation, of the politics of international systems. It is possible to explain particular expansionist drives as the result of a desire to escape from internal tensions; but it is also possible to impute the intensification of internal tensions and controls to the fact that a nation is committed to an expansionist policy in the first place. The relative significance of internal and external determinants is as insoluble as is the question whether economic or political ones are more important. Even the Girondists . . . were partly drawn into expansionism by a combination of provocations and ineptitudes manifested by other powers that in turn are partly explainable by pre-revolutionary conflicts of interests among these powers and between them and the French state. The occurrence of the French Revolution itself is as inseparable from the international overexertions and failures of the French monarchy as the international politics of the succeeding era is inseparable from the French Revolution. *Mutatis mutandis,* similar connectedness has been evident in other, more recent imperialisms. In matters of this kind, a great deal depends on how far along in the chain of reciprocal determination one chooses to cut off further inquiry—a choice often governed by one's prejudices. It is arguable that a domestic determination is always temporary. When a regime with insecure tenure succeeds too well in transferring its insecurity to the international system, the resulting rise in tension tends to restore dominance to the international system over the behavior of other states and, eventually, over that of the original disturber of the peace himself.

2

*The Equality of States as Dogma and Reality**

Philip C. Jessup

PHILIP C. JESSUP *has served as the American judge at the International Court of Justice since 1961. Before that he occupied the chair of Hamilton Fish Professor of International Law and Diplomacy at Columbia University. As a frequent consultant to the United States government, he served from 1948–52 as U.S. representative to the General Assembly and in 1949 was appointed Ambassador-at-Large. His contributions to the study of international law include* A Modern Law of Nations (*1948*); Transnational Law (*1956*); *and* The Use of International Law (*1959*). *He is also a frequent contributor to scholarly journals.*

I. INTRODUCTION

The equality of states is one of the most familiar and frequently reiterated principles of modern international law. Equality ranks traditionally with sovereignty and independence as an inherent and unimpeachable attribute of the state. As an infant nation the United States asserted the equality of states; as a great world Power, the United States concedes it. "Russia and Geneva," said Chief Justice Marshall in 1825, "have equal rights." It has been argued that sovereignty, independence, and equality are absolutes; they exist or do not exist, just as a figure either is a circle or is not a circle. Nevertheless the terms "semi-sovereign" and "semi-independent" have a wide currency in the books which is not matched by any such term as "semi-equal." Dickinson, in his magisterial book on the subject, makes a useful distinction between "equality before the law" or "equal protection of the law" which is a matter of status, and "equality of capacity for rights." "Equality before the law is absolutely essential to a stable society of nations," according to Dickinson. "If it is denied the alternatives are universal empire or universal anarchy." But equality of capacity for rights is not in his opinion essential to the reign of law. "It has never been more than an ideal and among states its utility even as an ideal is limited. . . . Conceding that equality of capacity for rights is sound as a legal principle, its proper application is limited to rules of conduct and to the acquiring of rights and the assuming of obligations under those rules" of international law.

There was a period in which the doctrine of equality of states had to make its way as the national state emerged in Europe out of the collapse of the Empire; but for a century at least statesmen and international politicians have been able to assert the existence of the principle without fear of verbal contradiction but with some certainty that while equality is preached, inequality will be practiced.

* *Political Science Quarterly,* **LX** (1945), 527–554. Reprinted by permission from *Political Science Quarterly.*

The international problem of equality is the result of the coexistence of two facts: states are not factually equal, for their powers differ; states have "feelings" and the psychological factor cannot be ignored any more than the power factor.

Power may be overcome by superior power or checked by an equivalence of power. From this principle there has evolved, in the interest of maintaining the peace, the plan of the balance of power. Power may be surrendered and from this principle stem plans for disarmament, for an international police force, and for a world state. Power may be utilized by those who have it for the general advantage of the international community as a result of a conviction of self-interest. This is the theoretical basis of the United Nations Charter which recognizes the existence of power and entrusts its exercise, under agreed limitations, to those who possess it.

Just as within states the last hundred years reveal a growth of social consciousness and of a public conscience, so has it been, in lesser degree, in the international community. Contrasting the Congress of Vienna of 1815 and its aftermath with the Paris Peace Conference of 1919 and its aftermath, one finds in both situations the original dominance of the great Powers, but in the latter period, as the League of Nations developed, there is a growing participation and, comparatively, a growing influence of the middle and small Powers commanding a world audience through the Geneva forum. Moving on to the San Francisco Conference of 1945, one observes that the voice of the middle and small Powers is louder, more insistent, and, again comparatively, more productive of results. "We are prepared," King Haakon of Norway said in regard to the Dumbarton Oaks Proposals, "to let the great powers play the leading role . . . but we insist upon sovereign equality of the small nations in the sense that . . . we shall have the right to take care of our interests by taking part in the decisions."

The psychological factor may not unfairly be called the prestige factor. This is not universally true, as for example when the small riparian states on the Danube demand representation on a river commission with a view to exercising at least some influence over decisions which vitally affect them. But the insistence of certain diminutive states at the Hague Peace Conference of 1907, for permanent and equal representation on the bench of the proposed International Court of Arbitral Justice, was much less genuinely a reflection of real interest than of prestige considerations. In the field of power politics, every state likes to think that it decides its own destiny. Most of them do so to the same extent that you or I as voters determine individually whether the country will go to war. Theoretically, in the United States for example, I act through elected representatives and there is to be sure a cumulative effect of votes, but actually the single voter's voice has no more influence on keeping the United States out of war than the Norwegian or Panamanian Foreign Minister could stem the tide of events which swept those countries into World War II. Yet Norway, for example, may exercise real influence as one of a small international commission for regulating the fisheries of the North Sea, just as the individual American citizen may exercise influence as a member of a village board of selectmen.

As one examines the manifestations of the doctrine of equality of states in international relations, one seems to detect the emergence of a notion that it does no violence to the doctrine if unequal rights or privileges are accorded on the basis of a formula which fairly reflects a recognizable degree of interest. One is tempted to compare the American constitutional doctrine that a reasonable classification of persons affected saves a statute from doing violence to the constitutional guarantee of the equal protection of the laws. Examples of this notion are abundant in connection with various international organizations. For instance, in the International Institute of Agriculture, voting was determined by membership in one of five classes, members of Class I having five votes and members of Class V having one vote. Equality was admitted in the sense that each state was free to choose the class to which it wished to belong, but membership in Class I involved an assessment of sixteen units of the budgetary base and membership in Class V involved the assessment of only one unit. A comparable plan in the Bretton Woods Agreements led states to seek a large allotment of shares in the Fund in order to be entitled to larger credit facilities, and to avoid larger allotments of shares in the Bank with resulting larger obligations to subscribe capital.

There is a general, and quite human, tendency in international affairs for states to emphasize their rights rather than their duties. That is why the action of the United States was notable in its early history when it combined claims for respect of its neutral rights with acknowledgment of its neutral duties. Similarly in various historical discussions of demands for the extension of territorial waters in order to enjoy wider rights in the monopolistic control of fisheries, some statesmen were wise enough to point out that sovereignty over a wider zone of waters entailed an extension of neutral duties in time of war.

It is relatively easy to find formulae for inequalities in voting power and in representation in technical international organizations where interest can be measured by statistics or factual criteria. It is supremely difficult to find acceptable formulae in political organizations where the prestige factor and problems of national existence may be at stake. Great Powers have power because they are great and not because a skillful draftsman has invented an ingenious formula. The platform of the League to Enforce Peace in 1918 suggested that "The representation of the different nations in the organs of the League should be in proportion to the responsibilities and obligations they assume." This suggestion is not dissimilar to the actual basis of five-great-Power control of the Security Council of the United Nations. The provisions of the Charter on regional arrangements reflect in large part the wide concessions which the United States in pursuance of the Good Neighbor Policy has actually made to the principle of equality in the Americas. The United Nations Organization is affirmed by the Charter to be "based upon the principle of the sovereign equality of all its Members," but no one can deny that unequal rights, privileges and responsibilities are also recognized throughout the Charter. Some of the factual inequalities are based on the more readily measurable types of interest as in the composition of the Trusteeship Council. Some, as in the voting provisions of the Security Council, are based upon the inescapable fact of power differentials. It is true, as Woodrow Wilson said, that "all nations are equally interested in the peace of the world"; it is not true that all can make equal contributions to its maintenance. . . .

3

*Rise and Demise of the Territorial State**

John H. Herz

JOHN H. HERZ, *Professor of Government at the City College of New York, has also written* Political Realism and Political Idealism *(1951) and* International Politics in the Atomic Age *(1959).*

BASIC FEATURES OF THE MODERN STATE SYSTEM

Traditionally, the classical system of international relations, or the modern state system, has been considered "anarchic," because it was based on unequally distributed power and was deficient in higher—that is, supranational—authority. Its units, the independent, sovereign nation-states, were forever threatened by stronger power and survived precariously through the balance-of-power system. Customarily, then, the modern state system has been contrasted with the medieval system, on the one hand, where units of international relations were under higher law and higher authority, and with those more recent international trends, on the other, which seemed to point toward a greater, "collective" security of nations and a "rule of law" that would protect them from the indiscriminate use of force characteristic of the age of power politics.

From the vantage point of the atomic age, we can probe deeper into the basic characteristics of the classical system. What is it that ultimately accounted for the peculiar unity, compactness, coherence of the modern nation-state, setting it off from other nation-states as a separate, independent, and sovereign power? It would seem that this underlying factor is to be found neither in the sphere of law nor in that of politics, but rather in that substratum of statehood where the state unit confronts us, as it were, in its physical, corporeal capacity: as an expanse of territory encircled for its identification and its defense by a "hard shell" of fortifications. In this lies what will here be referred to as the "impermeability," or "impenetrability," or simply the "territoriality," of the modern state. The fact that it was surrounded by a hard shell rendered it to some extent secure from foreign penetration, and thus made it an ultimate unit of protection for those within its boundaries. Throughout history, that unit which affords protection and security to human beings has tended to become the basic political unit; people, in the long run, will recognize that authority, any authority, which possesses the power of protection.

Some similarity perhaps prevails between an international structure consisting of impenetrable units with an ensuing measurability of power and comparability of power relations, and the system of classical physics with its measurable forces and the (then) impenetrable atom as its basic unit. And

* *World Politics,* **IX** (1957), 473–493. Reprinted by permission.

as that system has given way to relativity and to what nuclear science has uncovered, the impenetrability of the political atom, the nation-state, is giving way to a permeability which tends to obliterate the very meaning of unit and unity, power and power relations, sovereignty and independence. The possibility of "hydrogenization" merely represents the culmination of a development which has rendered the traditional defense structure of nations obsolete through the power to by-pass the shell protecting a two-dimensional territory and thus to destroy—vertically, as it were—even the most powerful ones. Paradoxically, utmost strength now coincides in the same unit with utmost vulnerability, absolute power with utter impotence.

This development must inevitably affect traditional power concepts. Considering power units as politically independent and legally sovereign made sense when power, measurable, graded, calculable, served as a standard of comparison between units which, in the sense indicated above, could be described as impermeable. Under those conditions, then, power indicated the strategic aspect, independence the political aspect, sovereignty the legal aspect of this self-same impermeability. With the passing of the age of territoriality, the usefulness of these concepts must now be questioned.

Thus the Great Divide does not separate "international anarchy," or "balance of power," or "power politics," from incipient international interdependence, or from "collective security"; all these remain within the realm of the territorial structure of states and can therefore be considered as trends or stages *within* the classical system of "hard shell" power units. Rather, the Divide occurs where the basis of territorial power and defensibility vanishes. It is here and now. But in order to understand the present, we must study more closely the origin and nature of the classical system itself.

The Rise of the Territorial State

The rise of the modern territorial state meant that, within countries, "feudal anarchy" of jurisdictions yielded to the ordered centralism of the absolute monarchy, which ruled over a pacified area with the aid of a bureaucracy, a professional army, and the power to levy taxes, while in foreign relations, in place of the medieval hierarchy of power and authority, there prevailed insecurity, a disorder only slightly attenuated by a power balance that was forever being threatened, disturbed, and then restored. Such has been the customary interpretation.

It is possible to view developments in a somewhat different light. Instead of contrasting the security of groups and individuals within the sovereign territorial state with conditions of insecurity outside, the establishment of territorial independence can be interpreted as an at least partially successful attempt to render the territorial group secure in its outward relations as well. Especially when contrasted with the age of anarchy and insecurity which immediately preceded it, the age of territoriality appears as one of relative order and safety.

Indeed, the transition from medieval hierarchism to modern compartmentalized sovereignties was neither easy, nor straight, nor short. Modern sovereignty arose out of the triangular struggle among emperors and popes, popes and kings, and kings and emperors. When the lawyers of Philip the Fair propounded the dual maxim according to which the king was to be "emperor in his realm" (*rex est impera-*

tor in regno suo) and was no longer to "recognize any superior" (*superiorem non recognoscens*), it was the beginning of a development in the course of which, in McIlwain's words, "Independence *de facto* was ultimately translated into a sovereignty *de jure*."[1] But centuries of disturbance and real anarchy ensued during which the problems of rulership and security remained unsettled. The relative protection which the sway of moral standards and the absence of highly destructive weapons had afforded groups and individuals in the earlier Middle Ages gave way to total insecurity when gunpowder was invented and common standards broke down. Out of the internal and external turmoil during the age of religious and civil wars, a "neutralist" central power eventually managed to establish itself in and for each of the different territories like so many *rochers de bronze.*

The idea that a territorial coexistence of states, based on the power of the territorial princes, might afford a better guarantee of peace than the Holy Roman Empire was already widespread at the height of the Middle Ages when the emperor proved incapable of enforcing the peace. But territoriality could hardly prevail so long as the knight in his castle (that medieval unit of impermeability) was relatively immune from attack, as was the medieval city within its walls. Only with a developing money economy were overlords able to free themselves from dependence on vassals and lay the foundations of their own power by establishing a professional army. Infantry and artillery now proved superior to old-style cavalry, firearms prevailed over the old weapons.

As in all cases of radically new developments in military technology, the "gunpowder revolution" caused a real revolution in the superstructure of economic, social, and political relationships because of its impact on the units of protection and security. A feeling of insecurity swept all Europe.[2] Though a Machiavelli might establish new rules as to how to gain and maintain power, there still followed more than a century of unregulated, ideological "total" wars inside and among countries until the new units of power were clearly established. Before old or new sovereigns could claim to be recognized as rulers of large areas, it had to be determined how far, on the basis of their new military power, they were able to extend their control geographically.

The large-area state came finally to occupy the place that the castle or fortified town had previously held as a unit of impenetrability. But the new unit could not be considered consolidated until all independent fortifications within it had disappeared and, in their place, fortresses lining the circumference of the country had been built by the new central power and manned by its armed forces. If we contrast our present system of bases and similar outposts surrounding entire world regions with what are to-

[1] Charles H. McIlwain, *The Growth of Political Thought in the West* (New York: The Macmillan Company, 1932), p. 268.

[2] Ariosto expressed the feeling of despair which invaded the "old powers" of chivalry when gunpowder destroyed the foundations of their system, in terms reminding one of present-day despair in the face of the destructive forces loosed upon our own world:

> "Oh! curs'd device! base implement of death!
> Framed in the black Tartarean realms beneath!
> By Beelzebub's malicious art design'd
> To ruin all the race of human kind."

Quoted from *Orlando Furioso* by Felix Gilbert, in Edward M. Earle, ed., *Makers of Modern Strategy* (Princeton: Princeton University Press, 1943), p. 4.

day small-scale nation-states, perhaps we can visualize what the hard shell of frontier fortifications consolidating the then large-scale territorial states meant by way of extending power units in the age of absolutism. They became, in the words of Frederick the Great, "mighty nails which hold a ruler's provinces together." There now was peace and protection within. War became a regularized military procedure; only the breaking of the shell permitted interference with what had now become the internal affairs of another country.

In this way was established the basic structure of the territorial state which was to last throughout the classical period of the modern state system. Upon this foundation a new system and new concepts of international relations could arise. And as early as the second half of the seventeenth century a perspicacious observer succeeded in tying up the new concepts with the underlying structure of territorial statehood. . . .

The Territorial State in International Relations

From territoriality resulted the concepts and institutions which characterized the interrelations of sovereign units, the modern state system. Modern international law, for instance, could now develop. Like the international system that produced it, international law has often been considered inherently contradictory because of its claim to bind sovereign units. But whether or not we deny to it for this reason the name and character of genuine law, it is important to see it in its connection with the territorial nature of the state system that it served. Only then can it be understood as a system of rules not contrary to, but implementing, the sovereign independence of states. Only to the extent that it reflected their territoriality and took into account their sovereignty could international law develop in modern times. For its general rules and principles deal primarily with the delimitation of the jurisdiction of countries. It thus implements the *de facto* condition of territorial impenetrability by more closely defining unit, area, and conditions of impenetrability. Such a law must reflect, rather than regulate. As one author has rightly remarked, "International law really amounts to laying down the principle of national sovereignty and deducing the consequences."[3] It is not for this reason superfluous, for sovereign units must know in some detail where their jurisdictions end and those of other units begin; without such standards, nations would be involved in constant strife over the implementation of their independence.

But it was not only this mutual legal accommodation which rendered possible a relatively peaceful coexistence of nations. War itself, the very phenomenon which reflected, not the strength, but the limitations of impermeability, was of such a nature as to maintain at least the principle of territoriality. War was limited not only in conduct but also in objectives. It was not a process of physical or political annihilation but a contest of power and will in which the interests, but not the existence, of the contestants were at stake. Now that we approach the era of absolute exposure, without walls or moats, where penetration will mean not mere damage or change but utter annihilation of life and way of life, it may dawn on us that what has vanished with the age of sovereignty and

---

[3] François Laurent, as quoted by Walter Schiffer, *The Legal Community of Mankind* (New York: Columbia University Press, 1954), p. 157.

"power politics" was not entirely adverse in nature and effects.

Among other "conservative" features of the classical system, we notice one only in passing: the balance of power. It is only recently that emphasis has shifted from a somewhat one-sided concern with the negative aspects of the balance—its uncertainty, its giving rise to unending conflicts and frequent wars, etc.—to its protective effect of preventing the expansionist capacity of power from destroying other power altogether. But at the time of its perfection in statecraft and diplomacy, there were even theories (not lived up to in practice, of course) about the *legal* obligations of nations to form barriers against hegemony power in the common interest.

More fundamental to the conservative structure of the old system was its character as a community. Forming a comparatively pacified whole, Europe was set off sharply against the world outside, a world beyond those lines which, by common agreement, separated a community based on territoriality and common heritage from anarchy, where the law of nature reigned and no standards of civilization applied. Only recently have the existence and role of so-called "amity lines" been rediscovered, lines which were drawn in the treaties of the early modern period and which separated European territories, where the rules of war and peace were to prevail, from overseas territories and areas.[4] There was to be "no peace beyond the line"; that is, European powers, although possibly at peace in Europe, continued to be *homo homini lupus* abroad. This practice made it easier for the European family of nations to observe self-denying standards at home by providing them with an outlet in the vast realm discovered outside Europe. While the practice of drawing amity lines subsequently disappeared, one chief function of overseas expansion remained: a European balance of power could be maintained or adjusted because it was relatively easy to divert European conflicts into overseas directions and adjust them there. Thus the openness of the world contributed to the consolidation of the territorial system. The end of the "world frontier" and the resulting closedness of an interdependent world inevitably affected this system's effectiveness.

Another characteristic of the old system's protective nature may be seen in the almost complete absence of instances in which countries were wiped out in the course of wars or as a consequence of other power-political events. This, of course, refers to the territorial units at home only, not to the peoples and state units beyond the pale abroad; and to the complete destruction of a state's independent existence, not to mere loss of territory or similar changes, which obviously abounded in the age of power politics.

Evidence of this is to be found not only in a legal and political ideology that denied the permissibility of conquest at home while recognizing it as a title for the acquisition of territorial jurisdiction abroad. For such a doctrine had its non-ideological foundation in the actual difference between European and non-European politics so far as their territoriality was concerned. European states were impermeable in the sense here outlined, while most of those overseas were easily penetrable by Europeans. In accordance with these circumstances, in-

[4] See Carl Schmitt, *Der Nomos der Erde* (Cologne, 1950), pp. 60ff.; also W. Schoenborn, "Über Entdeckung als Rechtstitel völkerrechtlichen Gebietserwerbs," in D. S. Constantinopoulos and H. Wehberg, eds., *Gegenwarts Probleme des Internationalen Rechts und der Rechtsphilosophie* (Hamburg, 1953), pp. 239ff.

ternational politics in Europe knew only rare and exceptional instances of actual annihilation through conquest or similar forceful means.

Prior to the twentieth century, there were indeed the Napoleonic conquests, but I submit that this is a case where the exception confirms the rule. The Napoleonic system, as a hegemonial one, was devised to destroy the established system of territoriality and balanced power as such. Consequently, Napoleon and his policies appeared "demonic" to contemporaries, as well as to a nineteenth century which experienced the restoration of the earlier system. During that century occurred Bismarck's annexations of some German units into Prussia in pursuance of German unification. As in Napoleon's case, they appeared abnormal to many of his contemporaries, although the issue of national unification tended to mitigate this impression. Besides these, there was indeed the partition of Poland, and considering the lamentable and lasting impression and the universal bad conscience it produced even among the ruling nations in a century used to quite a bit of international skulduggery, again one may well claim an exceptional character for that event.[5]

What, in particular, accounts for this remarkable stability? Territoriality—the establishment of defensible units, internally pacified and hard-shell rimmed—may be called its foundation. On this foundation, two phenomena permitted the system to become more stable than might otherwise have been the case: the prevalence of the legitimacy principle and, subsequently, nationalism. Legitimacy implied that the dynasties ruling the territorial states of old Europe mutually recognized each other as rightful sovereigns. Depriving one sovereign of his rights by force could not but appear to destroy the very principle on which the rights of all of them rested.

With the rise of nationalism, we witness the personalization of the units as self-determining, national groups. Nationalism now made it appear as abhorrent to deprive a sovereign nation of its independence as to despoil a legitimate ruler had appeared before. States, of course, had first to become "nation-states," considering themselves as representing specific nationality groups, which explains why in the two regions of Europe where larger numbers of old units stood in the way of national unification their demise encountered little objection. In most instances, however, the rise of nationalism led to the emergence of *new* states, which split away from multinational or colonial empires. This meant the extension of the European principle of "non-obliteration" all over the world. It is perhaps significant that even in our century, and even after the turmoil of attempted world conquest and resulting world wars, a point has been made of restoring the most minute and inconsiderable of sovereignties, down to Luxembourg and Albania.[6]

This hypertrophy of nation-states presented new problems—above all, that of an improved system of protec-

[5] Except for these cases, we find only marginal instances of complete obliteration. The annexation of the Free City of Krakow by Russia eliminated a synthetic creation of the Vienna settlement. British conquest of the Boer Republics, if considered as an instance of annihilation of European polities in view of the European origin of the inhabitants, happened at the very rim of the world, as it were, remote from the continent where the practice of non-annihilation prevailed.

[6] Cf. also the remarkable stability of state units in the Western Hemisphere *qua* independent units; unstable as some of them are domestically, their sovereign identity as units appears almost sacrosanct.

tion. For by now it had become clear that the protective function of the old system was only a relative blessing after all. Continued existence of states as such was perhaps more or less guaranteed. But power and influence, status, frontiers, economic interests—in short, everything that constituted the life and interests of nations beyond bare existence—were always at the mercy of what power politics wrought. Furthermore, much of the relative stability and political equilibrium of the territorial states had been due to the extension of Western control over the world. When what could be penetrated had been subjugated, assimilated, or established as fellow "sovereign" states, the old units were thrown back upon themselves. Hence the demand for a new system which would offer more security to old and new nations: collective security.

I propose to view collective security not as the extreme opposite of power politics, but as an attempt to maintain, and render more secure, the impermeability of what were still territorial states. To an age which took territoriality for granted, replacing power politics with collective security would indeed appear to be a radical departure. From the vantage point of the nuclear age, however, a plan to protect individual sovereignties by collective guarantees for continuing sovereignty appears questionable not because of its innovating, but because of its conservative, nature. Its conservatism lies in its basic objective: the protection of the hard-shell territorial structure of its members, or, as the core article of the Covenant of the League of Nations put it, its guarantee of their "territorial integrity and political independence" against external aggression. The beginning of air war and the increasing economic interdependence of nations had indicated by the end of World War I that the old-style military barriers might be by-passed. If territorial units were to be preserved in the future, it would be accomplished less by reliance on individual defense potentials than by marshaling collective power in order to preserve individual powers.

But since the idea of organizing a genuine supranational force—an international police force—was rejected, the League had to cling to classical arrangements insofar as the procedures of protection were concerned. The guarantee to the individual states was to be the formation of the "Grand Coalition" of all against the isolated aggressor, which presupposed the maintenance of a certain level of armed strength by the member states. A member without that minimum of military strength would be a liability rather than an asset to the organization—in Geneva parlance, a "consumer" and not a "producer" of security. Thus classical concepts (the sovereignty and independence of nation-states) as well as classical institutions (in particular, hard-shell defensibility) were to be maintained under the new system.

Whether there ever was a chance for the system to be effective in practice is beside the point here. It is sufficient to realize how closely it was tied to the underlying structure as well as to the prevailing concepts and policies of the territorial age.

THE DECLINE OF THE TERRITORIAL STATE

Beginning with the nineteenth century, certain trends became visible which tended to endanger the functioning of the classical system. Directly or indirectly, all of them had a bearing upon that feature of the territorial state which was the strongest guarantee of its independent coexistence with other states of like nature: its hard shell—that is, its defensibility in case of war.

Naturally, many of these trends concerned war itself and the way in which it was conducted. But they were not related to the shift from the limited, duel-type contests of the eighteenth century to the more or less unlimited wars that developed in the nineteenth century with conscription, "nations in arms," and increasing destructiveness of weapons. By themselves, these developments were not inconsistent with the classical function of war. Enhancing a nation's defensive capacity, instituting universal military service, putting the economy on a war footing, and similar measures tended to bolster the territorial state rather than to endanger it.

Total war in a quite different sense is tied up with developments in warfare which enable the belligerents to overleap or by-pass the traditional hard-shell defense of states. When this happens, the traditional relationship between war, on the one hand, and territorial power and sovereignty, on the other, is altered decisively. Arranged in order of increasing effectiveness, these new factors may be listed under the following headings: (a) possibility of economic blockade; (b) ideological-political penetration; (c) air warfare; and (d) atomic warfare.

(a) *Economic warfare.* It should be said from the outset that so far economic blockade has never enabled one belligerent to force another into surrender through starvation alone. Although in World War I Germany and her allies were seriously endangered when the Western allies cut them off from overseas supplies, a very real effort was still required to defeat them on the military fronts. The same thing applies to World War II. Blockade was an important contributing factor, however. Its importance for the present analysis lies in its unconventional nature, permitting belligerents to by-pass the hard shell of the enemy. Its effect is due to the changed economic status of industrialized nations.

Prior to the industrial age, the territorial state was largely self-contained economically. Although one of the customary means of conducting limited war was starving fortresses into surrender, this applied merely to these individual portions of the hard shell, and not to entire nations. Attempts to starve a belligerent nation in order to avoid having to breach the shell proved rather ineffective, as witness the Continental Blockade and its counterpart in the Napoleonic era. The Industrial Revolution made countries like Britain and Germany increasingly dependent on imports. In war, this meant that they could survive only by controlling areas larger than their own territory. In peacetime, economic dependency became one of the causes of a phenomenon which itself contributed to the transformation of the old state system: imperialism. Anticipating war, with its new danger of blockade, countries strove to become more self-sufficient through enlargement of their areas of control. To the extent that the industrialized nations lost self-sufficiency, they were driven into expansion in a (futile) effort to regain it. Today, if at all, only control of entire continents enables major nations to survive economically in major wars. This implies that hard-shell military defense must be a matter of defending more than a single nation; it must extend around half the world.

(b) *Psychological warfare,* the attempt to undermine the morale of an enemy population, or to subvert its loyalty, shares with economic warfare a by-passing effect on old-style territorial defensibility. It was formerly practiced, and practicable, only under quite exceptional circumstances. Short periods of genuine world revolutionary propaganda, such as the early stages of the French Revolution, scarcely affected a general practice under which dynasties, and later governments, fought each other with little ideological involvement on the part of larger masses or classes. Only in rare cases—for instance, where national groups enclosed in and hostile to multinational empires could be appealed to—was there an opening wedge for "fifth column" strategies.

With the emergence of political belief-systems, however, nations became more susceptible to undermining from within. Although wars have not yet been won solely by subversion of loyalties, the threat involved has affected the inner coherence of the territorial state ever since the rise to power of a regime that claims to represent, not the cause of a particular nation, but that of mankind, or at least of its suppressed and exploited portions. Bolshevism from 1917 on has provided the second instance in modern history of world revolutionary propaganda. Communist penetration tactics subsequently were imitated by the Nazi and Fascist regimes and, eventually, by the democracies. In this way, new lines of division, cutting horizontally through state units instead of leaving them separated vertically from each other at their frontiers, have now become possible.

(c) *Air warfare* and (d) *nuclear warfare*. Of all the new developments, air warfare, up to the atomic age, has been the one that affected the territoriality of nations most radically. With its coming, the bottom dropped out—or, rather, the roof blew off—the relative security of the territorial state. True, even this new kind of warfare, up to and including the Second World War, did not by itself account for the defeat of a belligerent, as some of the more enthusiastic prophets of the air age had predicted it would. Undoubtedly, however, it had a massive contributory effect. And this effect was due to strategic action in the *hinterland* rather than to tactical use at the front. It came at least close to defeating one side by direct action against the "soft" interior of the country, by-passing outer defenses and thus foreshadowing the end of the frontier—that is, the demise of the traditional impermeability of even the militarily most powerful states. Warfare now changed "from a fight to a process of devastation."[7]

That air warfare was considered as something entirely unconventional is seen from the initial reaction to it. Revolutionary transition from an old to a new system has always affected moral standards. In the classical age of the modern state system, the "new

[7] B. H. Liddell Hart, *The Revolution in Warfare* (New Haven, Conn.: Yale University Press, 1947), p. 36. Suspicion of what would be in the offing, once man gained the capacity to fly, was abroad as early as the eighteenth century. Thus Samuel Johnson remarked: "If men were all virtuous, I should with great alacrity teach them all to fly. But what would be the security of the good, if the bad could at pleasure invade them from the sky? Against an army sailing through the clouds, neither walls, nor mountains, nor seas, could afford security" (quoted in J. U. Nef, *War and Human Progress* [Cambridge, Mass.: Harvard University Press, 1952], p. 198). And Benjamin Franklin, witnessing the first balloon ascension at Paris in 1783, foresaw invasion from the air and wrote: "Convincing Sovereigns of folly of wars may perhaps be one effect of it, since it will be impracticable for the most potent of them to guard his dominions. . . . Where is the Prince who can afford so to cover his country with troops for its defense, as that ten thousand men descending from the clouds, might not in many places do an infinite deal of mischief before a force could be brought together to repel them?" (from a letter to Jan Ingelhouss, reproduced in *Life Magazine*, January 9, 1956).

morality" of shooting at human beings from a distance had finally come to be accepted, but the standards of the age clearly distinguished "lawful combatants" at the front or in fortifications from the civilian remainder of the population. When air war came, reactions thus differed significantly in the cases of air fighting at the front and of air war carried behind the front. City bombing was felt to constitute "illegitimate" warfare, and populations were inclined to treat airmen engaging in it as "war criminals." This feeling continued into World War II, with its large-scale area bombing. Such sentiments reflected the general feeling of helplessness in the face of a war which threatened to render obsolete the concept of territorial power, together with its ancient implication of protection.

The process has now been completed with the advent of nuclear weapons. For it is more than doubtful that the processes of scientific invention and technological discovery, which not only have created and perfected the fission and fusion weapons themselves but have brought in their wake guided missiles with nuclear warheads, jet aircraft with intercontinental range and supersonic speed, and the prospect of nuclear-powered planes or rockets with unlimited range and with automatic guidance to specific targets anywhere in the world, can in any meaningful way be likened to previous new inventions, however revolutionary. These processes add up to an uncanny absoluteness of effect which previous innovations could not achieve. The latter might render power units of a certain type (for instance, castles or cities) obsolete and enlarge the realm of defensible power units from city-state to territorial state or even large-area empire. They might involve destruction, in war, of entire populations. But there still remained the seemingly inexhaustible reservoir of the rest of mankind. Today, when not even two halves of the globe remain impermeable, it can no longer be a question of enlarging an area of protection and of substituting one unit of security for another. Since we are inhabitants of a planet of limited (and, as it now seems, insufficient) size, we have reached the limit within which the effect of the means of destruction has become absolute. Whatever remained of the impermeability of states seems to have gone for good.

What has been lost can be seen from two statements by thinkers separated by thousands of years and half the world; both reflect the condition of territorial security. Mencius, in ancient China, when asked for guidance in matters of defense and foreign policy by the ruler of a small state, is said to have counseled: "Dig deeper your moats; build higher your walls; guard them along with your people." This remained the classical posture up to our age, when a Western sage, Bertrand Russell, in the interwar period could still define power as something radiating from one center and growing less with distance from that center until it finds an equilibrium with that of similar geographically anchored units. Now that power can destroy power from center to center, everything is different.

CHAPTER THREE

Motivation in the Nation-State System

In endeavoring to explain or account for the way nations behave, the social scientist often encounters such simplistic arguments as those which attest that Germans periodically go to war because they are a militaristic people, or that Pearl Harbor resulted solely from a wily scheme in Washington, or that the Cold War was brought on just because of Stalin's lust for power. So great is the variety of explanations that the social scientist seeks a common denominator, or theory, grounded in the uniformities of international life and the constants of human behavior that will enable him to order, and hopefully to predict, the results of a wide and confusing range of variables. But sometimes he is tempted to conclude, as someone did, that "history teaches that history does not teach."

One of his most difficult problems is to ascertain whether there are any rules of conduct that motivate, or especially that restrain, states in their relationships with one another. Analysis is complicated by the fact that, while part of the world appears to be moving toward a consolidation of nations into larger and larger units, dozens of new states are just beginning to play their roles on the world stage. Many of these newer states are at an earlier and less well-defined stage of development than were some of the Western nations when the modern state system emerged three centuries ago after the Thirty Years' War. Their norms are not the same as those upon which, in the West, some degree of moral or ethical consensus has been developed (albeit with such outrageous exceptions as the Nazis) over a three hundred year period in which world politics were for all practical purposes European politics.

As Georg Schwarzenberger, professor of International Law at King's College (London), has observed, theories on international morality, and particularly its effects upon state politics, tend to separate into three principal categories.[1] According to one school of thought, there is no connection at all between morals and politics. These people deny the existence of any sort of ethical restraint upon the policies of states in a world of "dog-eat-dog" and "survival of the fittest." The only restraint thus is power, and many who hold this view of politics have compared the contemporary world with the lawless environment of

[1] *Power Politics* (New York: Frederick A. Praeger, Inc., 1951), pp. 219 ff.

renaissance Italy, in which that crafty analyst of political reality, Niccolò Machiavelli, advised that

> . . . a prudent ruler ought not to keep faith when by so doing it would be against his interest, and when the reasons which made him bind himself no longer exist. If men were good, this precept would not be a good one; but as they are bad, and would not observe their faith with you, so you are not bound to keep faith with them.[2]

A second viewpoint is that there is a connection between morals and politics. It is argued that since this is apparent in the development and acceptance of codes of behavior for individuals, and since states are made up of individuals, states must behave as men do. They identify international morality with individual morality. Colonel House, President Wilson's principal adviser, when drawing up a draft for the Covenant of the League of Nations, argued that the same standards of honor and ethics should apply internationally and in the affairs of nations as in other matters. Social morality—the moral order—is based upon the relations of individuals, and, therefore, both in an empirical and a normative sense, should be governed by the same rules. States are the highest expression of social organization in our time, pending the eventual development of a true world order. This is not a new idea—Kant expressed it in *Perpetual Peace* in 1795:

> Hence the mechanisms of nations working through the self-seeking propensities of man . . . may be used by reason as a means of making way for the realization of her own purpose, the empire of right, and as far as it is the power of the State, to promote and secure in this way internal as well as external peace . . . . it is the irresistible will of nature that right should at last attain supremacy.[3]

A third position, that stands in sharp contrast to the other two, is that there are two quite different kinds of morality: one reserved for individual persons in their relations with one another, and the other appropriate for states. This perspective found its expression in Fascism, which regarded war as the highest achievement of mankind. Readers of William L. Shirer's description of Nazi Germany[4] will recall how insistent the mass murderers of Jews were to have people understand that they were really "quite decent fellows" even though they committed terrible deeds in the name and in the presumed interest of the state. Even in its less extreme form, this approach sees the state as having its own ethic: to serve its own ends—its "vital interests"—by whatever means are appropriate or necessary. Rules which restrain persons do not and should not restrain the nation. When the state goes to war, its citizens are honored and glorified for doing what in civil society is regarded as the most heinous of crimes—taking the lives of others.

[2] *The Prince,* 18: "In What Way Princes Must Keep Faith" (New York: Mentor Books, 1952), pp. 101–102.

[3] Cited by Schwarzenberger, *op. cit.*, p. 219.

[4] *The Rise and Fall of The Third Reich* (New York: Simon and Shuster, Inc., 1961).

There are variations on each of these three points of view, as for example, the view that very high ethical principles must be observed in dealing with *some* countries, but not with others, or that the state should observe such principles only up to a certain point, then the gloves are off. Another version seems to be that "anything goes" if the other side starts the fight, but a "moral" nation should not itself start the fight; it is morally acceptable to resist aggression but not to undertake it. But as United Nations investigators have discovered in attempting to assign blame in the Israeli-Arab conflict, it is very difficult to ascertain, after years of blows and counter-blows, just which side is guilty of aggression.

In practice, two things seem to be apparent. One is that morality in foreign affairs is talked about a good deal. Indeed, as Professor Schwarzenberger has phrased it, it is "the universal reference." Even Stalin is said to have referred to "the necessity of there being a minimum moral standard between all nations. . . . Without such a minimum moral standard nations could not co-exist."[5] And the second is that moral restraints do seem to have little effect upon the struggle for power among nations in an international system without a recognized authority, without common norms, and, above all, without security. As the late Nicholas J. Spykman, Director of the Yale Institute of International Studies, put it, "it is the so-called sovereign independence of states, the absence of higher authority, and the freedom from external restraints that give to interstate relations their peculiar character of anarchy."[6]

Unquestionably a theory of motivation postulating power for the sake of survival and security, based upon the realities of the international system, helps us to understand the intensity and persistence of conflict. A more humanistic but equally valid formulation of this theory would be to start with the fact that the great majority of people in every nation-state believe that the security and integrity of their country is the condition of the good life, and that a threat to its independence is a threat to their way of life—their private values. In a sense, then, the function the state performs in giving its members peace of mind and prosperity makes them reluctant to trust their fate to other people.

But to believe that the conditions imposed by the system constitute the sole explanation for nation-state behavior is to leave unexplored several other sources of motivation. In view of the pathological intensity of the hostility that has existed between Russia and America, there is a widespread disposition to believe that differences of political and economic organization and beliefs are the most important causes of international conflict. Nation-states appear to be influenced in their behavior by the antipathy that an alien ideology arouses in the minds and emotions of another people. Some observers have raised the question of whether ideology has not transformed the national conflicts of the past into "international civil wars," such as "those recently fought in Korea and

[5] In a conversation reported by Harry Hopkins, cited by Schwarzenberger, *op. cit.*, p. 223.

[6] *America's Strategy in World Politics* (New York: Harcourt, Brace & World, Inc., 1940), p. 16.

Indochina that partake of the character of international and civil war simultaneously."[7] From this perspective the "cold war" is a struggle between two competing moral philosophies. In contrast to this interpretation, Hans Morgenthau argues that ideologies are only moral justifications of what is essentially the pursuit of power for its own sake. "In other words," he writes, "while all politics is necessarily pursuit of power, ideologies render involvement in that contest for power psychologically and morally acceptable to the actors and their audience."[8]

However, Clyde Kluckhohn, the Harvard anthropologist, takes exception to this summary dismissal of conflicting moral values as a source of tension: "Values are something more than 'epiphenomena,' verbal rationalizations of existing conditions. Values influence and, on occasion, determine action."[9] In fact, no one is more emphatic than Professor Morgenthau in stressing that the intensity and totality of the power conflict in our day is due to the changed moral climate: "Nations no longer oppose each other as they did from the Treaty of Vienna to the First World War, within a framework of shared beliefs and common values, which imposes effective limits upon the ends and means of their struggle for power."[10] Historically—at least in the period following the Napoleonic Wars—it is probably true that the policies of the European states were less influenced by ideological factors than other issues; but in our day conflicting systems of belief deny the existence of any basis for peaceful coexistence.

There should be nothing mysterious about this phenomenon. Ideologies or belief systems respond to one of the deepest intellectual and psychological needs of men—to know where they are going and to believe that what they are doing is right. To challenge belief systems is to challenge something that has the deepest meaning to human beings—thereby to thwart the desire for moral certainty and security. Foreign policy is no more immune than other social activity from the values which a people hold, and it is even argued that people or states do not have interests apart from their moral or ideological convictions. This may be especially true when the foreign policy and international conduct of one of the superpowers is dominated by the doctrine that, because of the inescapable dynamics of capitalist society, conflict is inevitable, and that it has the historical task of assisting every attempt by non-Communist peoples to "free" themselves by revolutionary means from the existing status quo.

Whether ideological values are the ultimate determinant of foreign policies or not, their influence poses an extremely difficult dilemma for statesmen and diplomats. No statesman can afford to ignore the values held by a significant portion of his countrymen; similarly, no theory of international relations

[7] Arnold Wolfers and Laurence W. Martin, *The Anglo-American Tradition in Foreign Affairs* (New Haven: Yale University Press, 1956), p. xviii.

[8] *Politics Among Nations*, 2nd ed. (New York: Alfred A. Knopf, Inc., 1954), p. 61.

[9] Elting E. Morison, ed., in *The American Style* (New York: Harper & Row, Publishers, 1958), p. 146.

[10] *Op. cit.*, p. 230.

would be realistic that fails to treat seriously the force of contending value-systems.

Nor can one comprehend what motivates nations in their competition with each other unless he perceives the economic and political interests of influential groups or elites within each society. In every society there are many people whose loyalties and interests are influenced as much, if not more, by their identification with a business firm, a labor union, or a patriotic or religious organization as by their responsibilities as citizens. Despite their customary claims that they are pursuing objectives consistent with the national interest, the motives of such groups are sufficiently different to require examination in terms of a distinctive theoretical analysis. There are political leaders and chiefs of departments of government who, in quest of prestige or a larger share of the national budget, assert their personal or bureaucratic preferences to be the expression of the national interest. Theodore Roosevelt is a striking example of an American President whose conception of the national interest prompted him to conduct foreign policy so as to antagonize Latin Americans for many years thereafter. Within most societies there are many groups or elites whose values and interests can only be achieved by the extension of their state's power and authority. A paradox of the modern industrial society is that while economic and technological organization now necessitates the pursuit of vital interests at the world level, the political structure of the state cannot be extended indefinitely because it is based upon the loyalty of a unique national group rather than upon the shared loyalties of a supra-national or universal community.

In his *Imperialism: The Highest Stage of Capitalism,* Lenin attempted to construct a theory of nation-state behavior on the basis of the need of monopoly capitalism for safe investment outlets for surplus capital that can no longer find a profitable outlet within the developed home market. Although Lenin's theory hardly constitutes a comprehensive or scientific explanation of imperialism, it does focus upon the peculiar need of modern industrial and banking institutions to transcend the limits of national boundaries and to secure access to the resources and markets of the world. Lenin failed to account for the fact that Russia and the United States were active imperialists at a time (1900) when both were net capital importing countries, but his explanation does serve to remind one that within any nation there are groups and individuals whose peculiar interest or beliefs in the virtue of extending their own state's authority over the land, lives and resources of another people may have a telling effect on the motivations of their own government in its selection of foreign policy options.

To anyone genuinely interested in seeking the deeper causes that underlie the sequence of international developments, it becomes increasingly apparent that there is as yet no single theoretical explanation for the behavior of States and their leaders. So vast and complex is the process that no one has seen it whole. Taken together, the selections which follow suggest that the intensity of modern tension and conflict stems from man's inability or unwillingness to abandon his primary loyalty to the state at a stage in history when his social and economic needs have begun to transcend the state itself.

1

*National Images and International Systems**

K. E. Boulding

Kenneth Ewart Boulding *is Professor of Economics at the University of Michigan. Winner of the John B. Clark Medal of the American Economics Association, his scholarly contributions include* Economics of Peace (*1945*); Principles of Economic Policy (*1958*); Conflict and Defense (*1962*); *and* Disarmament and the Economy (*1963*).

An international system consists of a group of interacting behavior units called "nations" or "countries," to which may sometimes be added certain supra-national organizations, such as the United Nations.

Each of the behavior units in the system can be described in terms of a set of "relevant variables." Just what is relevant and what is not is a matter of judgment of the system-builder, but we think of such things as states of war or peace, degrees of hostility or friendliness, alliance or enmity, arms budgets, geographic extent, friendly or hostile communications, and so on. Having defined our variables, we can then proceed to postulate certain relationships between them, sufficient to define a path for all the variables through time. Thus we might suppose, with Lewis Richardson,[1] that the rate of change of hostility of one nation toward a second depends on the level of hostility in the second and that the rate of change of hostility of the second toward the first depends on the level of hostility of the first. Then, if we start from given levels of hostility in each nation, these equations are sufficient to spell out what happens to these levels in succeeding time periods. A system of this kind may (or may not) have an *equilibrium* position at which the variables of one period produce an identical set in the next period, and the system exhibits no change through time.

Mechanical systems of this kind, though they are frequently illuminating, can be regarded only as very rough first approximations to the immensely complex truth. At the next level of approximation we must recognize that the people whose decisions determine the policies and actions of nations do not respond to the "objective" facts of the situation, whatever

[1] See Anatol Rapoport, "Lewis F. Richardson's Mathematical Theory of War," *Journal of Conflict Resolution,* I (September, 1957), 249, for an excellent exposition.

* *Journal of Conflict Resolution,* **III,** No. 2 (June, 1959), 120–131. Reprinted by permission. This paper was presented to a meeting of the American Psychological Association in Washington, D.C., on August 30, 1958.

that may mean, but to their "image" of the situation. It is what we think the world is like, not what it is really like, that determines our behavior. If our image of the world is in some sense "wrong," of course, we may be disappointed in our expectations, and we may therefore revise our image; if this revision is in the direction of the "truth" there is presumably a long-run tendency for the "image" and the "truth" to coincide. Whether this is so or not, it is always the image, not the truth, that immediately determines behavior. We act according to the way the world appears to us, not necessarily according to the way it "is." Thus in Richardson's models it is one nation's image of the hostility of another, not the "real" hostility, which determines its reaction. The "image," then, must be thought of as the total cognitive, affective, and evaluative structure of the behavior unit, or its internal view of itself and its universe.[2]

Generally speaking, the behavior of complex organizations can be regarded as determined by *decisions*, and a decision involves the selection of the most preferred position in a contemplated field of choice. Both the field of choice and the ordering of this field by which the preferred position is identified lie in the image of the decision-maker. Therefore, in a system in which decision-makers are an essential element, the study of the ways in which the image grows and changes, both of the field of choice and of the valuational ordering of this field, is of prime importance. The image is always in some sense a product of messages received in the past. It is not, however, a simple inventory or "pile" of such messages but a highly structured piece of information-capital, developed partly by its inputs and outputs of information and partly by internal messages and its own laws of growth and stability.

The images which are important in international systems are those which a nation has of itself and of those other bodies in the system which constitute its international environment. At once a major complication suggests itself. A nation is some complex of the images of the persons who contemplate it, and as there are many different persons, so there are many different images. The complexity is increased by the necessity for inclusion, in the image of each person or at least of many persons, his image of the image of others. This complexity, however, is a property of the real world, not to be evaded or glossed over. It can be reduced to simpler terms if we distinguish between two types of persons in a nation—the powerful, on the one hand, and the ordinary, on the other. This is not, of course, a sharp distinction. The power of a decision-maker may be measured roughly by the number of people which his decisions potentially affect, weighted by some measure of the effect itself. Thus the head of a state is powerful, meaning that his decisions affect the lives of millions of people; the ordinary person is not powerful, for his decisions affect only himself and the lives of a few people around him. There is usually a continuum of power among the persons of a society: thus in international relations there are usually a few very powerful individuals in a state—the chief executive, the prime minister, the secretary of state or minister of foreign affairs, the chiefs of staff of the armed forces. There will be some who are less powerful but still influential—members of the legislature, of the civil service, even journalists, newspaper

[2] See K. E. Boulding, *The Image* (Ann Arbor: University of Michigan Press, 1956), for an exposition of the theory on which this paper is based.

owners, prominent businessmen, grading by imperceptible degree down to the common soldier, who has no power of decision even over his own life. For purposes of the model, however, let us compress this continuum into two boxes, labeled the "powerful" and the "ordinary," and leave the refinements of power and influence for later studies.

We deal, therefore, with two representative images: 1. the image of the small group of powerful people who make the actual decisions which lead to war or peace, the making or breaking of treaties, the invasions or withdrawals, alliances, and enmities which make up the major events of international relations, and 2. the image of the mass of ordinary people who are deeply affected by these decisions but who take little or no direct part in making them. The tacit support of the mass, however, is of vital importance to the powerful. The powerful are always under some obligation to represent the mass, even under dictatorial regimes. In democratic societies the aggregate influence of the images of ordinary people is very great; the image of the powerful cannot diverge too greatly from the image of the mass without the powerful losing power. On the other hand, the powerful also have some ability to manipulate the images of the mass toward those of the powerful. This is an important object of instruments as diverse as the public education system, the public relations departments of the armed services, the Russian "agitprop," and the Nazi propaganda ministry.

In the formation of the national images, however, it must be emphasized that impressions of nationality are formed mostly in childhood and usually in the family group. It would be quite fallacious to think of the images as being cleverly imposed on the mass by the powerful. If anything, the reverse is the case: the image is essentially a mass image, or what might be called a "folk image," transmitted through the family and the intimate face-to-face group, both in the case of the powerful and in the case of ordinary persons. Especially in the case of the old, long-established nations, the powerful share the mass image rather than impose it; it is passed on from the value systems of the parents to those of the children, and agencies of public instruction and propaganda merely reinforce the images which derived essentially from the family culture. This is much less true in new nations which are striving to achieve nationality, where the family culture frequently does not include strong elements of national allegiance but rather stresses allegiance to religious ideals or to the family as such. Here the powerful are frequently inspired by a national image derived not from family tradition but from a desire to imitate other nations, and here they frequently try to impose their images on the mass of people. Imposed images, however, are fragile by comparison with those which are deeply internalized and transmitted through family and other intimate sources.

Whether transmitted orally and informally through the family or more formally through schooling and the written word, the national image is essentially a *historical* image—that is, an image which extends through time, backward into a supposedly recorded or perhaps mythological past and forward into an imagined future. The more conscious a people is of its history, the stronger the national image is likely to be. To be an Englishman is to be conscious of "1066 and All That" rather than of "Constantine and All That," or "1776 and All That." A nation is the creation of its historians, formal and informal. The written word and public education contribute enormously to the stability and persistence of the national images. The Jews, for instance, are a creation of the Bible and the Talmud, but every nation has its bible, whether formed into a canon or not—noble words like the Declaration of Independence and the Gettysburg Address—which crystallize the national image in a form that can be transmitted almost unchanged from generation to generation. It is no exaggeration to say that the function of the historian is to pervert the truth in directions favorable to the images of his readers or hearers. Both history and geography as taught in national schools are devised to give "perspective" rather than truth: that is to say, they present the world as seen from the vantage point of the nation. The national geography is learned in great detail, and the rest of the world is in fuzzy outline; the national history is emphasized and exalted; the history of the rest of the world is neglected or even falsified to the glory of the national image.

It is this fact that the national image is basically a lie, or at least a perspective distortion of the truth, which perhaps accounts for the ease with which it can be perverted to justify monstrous cruelties and wickednesses. There is much that is noble in the national image. It has lifted man out of the narrow cage of self-centeredness, or even family-centeredness, and has forced him to accept responsibility, in some sense, for people and events far beyond his face-to-face cognizance and immediate experience. It is a window of some sort on both space and time and extends a man's concern far beyond his own little lifetime and petty interests. Nevertheless, it achieves these virtues usually only at the cost of untruth, and this fatal flaw constantly betrays it. Love of country is perverted into hatred of the foreigner, and peace, order, and justice at home are paid for by war, cruelty, and injustice abroad.

In the formation of the national image the consciousness of great *shared* events and experiences is of the utmost importance. A nation is a body of people who are conscious of having "gone through something" together. Without the shared experience, the national image itself would not be shared, and it is of vital importance that the national image be highly similar. The sharing may be quite vicarious; it may be an experience shared long ago but constantly renewed by the ritual observances and historical memory of the people, like the Passover and the Captivity in the case of the Jews. Without the sharing, however, there is no nation. It is for this reason that war has been such a tragically important element in the creation and sustenance of the national image. There is hardly a nation that has not been cradled in violence and nourished by further violence. This is not, I think, a necessary property of war itself. It is rather that, especially in more primitive societies, war is the one experience which is dramatic, obviously important, and shared by everybody. We are now witnessing the almost unique phenomenon of a number of new nations arising without war in circumstances which are extremely rare in history, for example—India, Ghana, and the new West Indian Federation, though even here there are instances of severe violence, such as the disturbances which accompanied partition in India. It will be interesting to see the effect, if any, on their national images.

We now come to the central problem of this paper, which is that of the impact of national images on the relations among states, that is, on the course of events in international relations. The relations among states can be described in terms of a number of different dimensions. There is, first of all, the dimension of simple geographical space. It is perhaps the most striking single characteristic of the national state as an organization, by contrast with organizations such as firms or churches, that it thinks of itself as occupying, in a "dense" and exclusive fashion, a certain area of the globe. The schoolroom maps which divide the world into colored shapes which are identified as nations have a profound effect on the national image. Apart from the very occasional condominium, it is impossible for a given plot of land on the globe to to be associated with two nations at the same time. The territories of nations are divided sharply by frontiers carefully surveyed and frequently delineated by a chain of customs houses, immigration stations, and military installations. We are so accustomed to this arrangement that we think of it as "natural" and take it completely for granted. It is by no means the only conceivable arrangement, however. In primitive societies the geographical image is not sharp enough to define clear frontiers; there may be a notion of the rough territory of a tribe, but, especially among nomadic peoples, there is no clear concept of a frontier and no notion of a nation as something that has a shape on a map. In our own society the shape on the map that symbolizes the nation is constantly drilled into the minds of both young and old, both through formal teaching in schools and through constant repetition in newspapers, advertisements, cartoons, and so on. A society is not inconceivable, however, and might even be desirable, in which nations governed people but not territories and claimed jurisdiction over a defined set of citizens, no matter where on the earth's surface they happened to live.

The territorial aspect of the national state is important in the dynamics of international relations because of the *exclusiveness* of territorial occupation. This means that one nation can generally expand only at the expense of another; an increase in the territory of one is achieved only at the expense of a decrease in the territory of another. This makes for a potential conflict situation. This characteristic of the nation does not make conflict inevitable, but it does make it likely and is at least one of the reasons why the history of international relations is a history of perpetual conflict.

The territorial aspect of international relations is complicated by the fact that in many cases the territories of nations are not homogeneous but are composed of "empires," in which the populations do not identify themselves with the national image of the dominant group. Thus when one nation conquers another and absorbs the conquered territory into an empire, it does not thereby automatically change the culture and allegiances of the conquered nation. The Poles remained Polish for a hundred and twenty-five years of partition between Germany, Austria, and Russia. The Finns retained their nationality through eight hundred years of foreign rule and the Jews through nearly two thousand years of dispersion. If a nation loses territory occupied by disaffected people, this is much less damaging than the loss of territory inhabited by a well-disposed and loyal population. Thus Turkey, which was the "sick man of Europe" as long as it retained its heterogeneous empire, enjoyed a substantial renewal of national health when stripped of its empire and pushed back to the relatively homogeneous heartland of Anatolia. In this case the loss of a disaffected empire actually strengthened the national unit.

The image of the map-shape of the nations may be an important factor affecting the general frame of mind of the nation. There is a tendency for nations to be uneasy with strong irregularities, enclaves, detached portions, and protuberances or hollows. The ideal shape is at least a convex set, and there is some tendency for nations to be more satisfied if they have regularly round or rectangular outlines. Thus the detachment of East Prussia from the body of Germany by the Treaty of Versailles was an important factor in creating the fanatical discontent of the Nazis.

A second important dimension of the national image is that of hostility or friendliness. At any one time a particular national image includes a rough scale of the friendliness or hostility of, or toward, other nations. The relationship is not necessarily either consistent or reciprocal—in nation A the prevailing image may be that B is friendly, whereas in nation B itself the prevailing image may be one of hostility toward A; or again in both nations there may be an image of friendliness of A toward B but of hostility of B toward A. On the whole, however, there is a tendency toward both consistency and reciprocation—if a nation A pictures itself as hostile toward B, it usually also pictures B as hostile toward it, and the image is likely to be repeated in B. One exception to this rule seems to be observable: most nations seem to feel that their enemies are more hostile toward them than they are toward their enemies. This is a typical paranoid reaction; the nation visualizes itself as surrounded by hostile nations toward which it has only the nicest and friendliest of intentions.

An important subdimension of the hostility-friendliness image is that of the stability or security of the relationship. A friendly relationship is frequently formalized as an alliance. Alliances, however, are shifting; some friendly relations are fairly permanent, others change as the world kaleidoscope changes, as new enemies arise, or as governments change. Thus a bare fifteen or twenty years ago most people in the United States visualized Germany and Japan, even before the outbreak of the war, as enemies, and after Hitler's invasion of Russia, Russia was for a while regarded as a valuable friend and ally. Today the picture is quite changed: Germany and Japan are valuable friends and allies; Russia is the great enemy. We can roughly classify the reciprocal relations of nations along some scale of friendliness-hostility. At one extreme we have stable friendliness, such as between Britain and Portugal or between Britain and the Commonwealth countries. At the other extreme we have [had] stable hostility—the "traditional enemies" such as France and Germany [used to be]. Between these extremes we have a great many pairs characterized by shifting alliances. On the whole, stable friendly relations seem to exist mainly between strong nations and weaker nations which they have an interest in preserving and stable hostile relations between adjacent nations each of which has played a large part in the formation of the other.

Another important dimension both of the image and of the "reality" of the nation-state is its strength or weakness. This is, in turn, a structure made up of many elements— economic resources and productivity, political organization and tradition, willingness to incur sacrifice and inflict cruelties, and so on. It still makes some kind of sense to assess nations on a strength-weakness scale at any one time. Strength is frequently thought of in military terms as the ability to hurt an opponent or to prevent one's self from being hurt by him. There are also more subtle elements in terms of symbolic loyalties and affections which are hard to assess but which must be included in any complete picture. Many arrays of bristling armaments have been brought low by the sheer inability of their wielders to attract any lasting respect or affection. No social organization can survive indefinitely unless it can command the support of its members, and a continuing sense of the significance of the organization or group as such is much more durable a source of support than is the fleeting booty of war or monopoly. The Jews have outlasted an impressive succession of conquerors. These questions regarding the ultimate sources of continuing strength or weakness are difficult, and we shall neglect them in this paper.

In order to bring together the variables associated with each nation or pair of nations into an international system, we must resort to the device of a matrix, as in Figure 1. Here the hostility-friendliness variable is used as an example. Each cell, a_{ij}, indicates the degree of hostility or friendliness of nation I (of the row) toward nation J (of the column). For purposes of illustration, arbitrary figures have been inserted on a scale from 5 to -5, -5 meaning very hostile, 5 very friendly, and 0 neutral.[3] A matrix of this kind

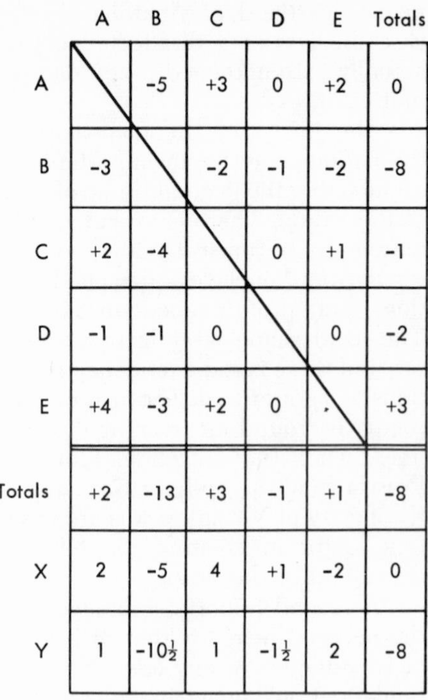

	A	B	C	D	E	Totals
A		-5	+3	0	+2	0
B	-3		-2	-1	-2	-8
C	+2	-4		0	+1	-1
D	-1	-1	0		0	-2
E	+4	-3	+2	0		+3
Totals	+2	-13	+3	-1	+1	-8
X	2	-5	4	+1	-2	0
Y	1	$-10\frac{1}{2}$	1	$-1\frac{1}{2}$	2	-8

FIGURE 1

[3] The problem of the measurement of hostility (or friendliness) is a very interesting one which we cannot go into extensively here but which is not so hopeless of solution as might at first sight appear. Possible avenues are as follows: (1) A historical approach. Over a period of years two nations have been at war, threatening war, allied, bound by treaty, and so on. Each relation would be given an arbitrary number, and each year assigned a number accordingly: the average of the years' numbers would be the index. This would always yield a symmetrical matrix—that is, the measure of I's relation to J would be the same as J's relation to I, or $a_{ij} = a_{ji}$. (2) An approach by means of content analysis of public communications (official messages, newspaper editorials, public speeches, cartoons, etc.). This seems likely to be most immediately useful and fruitful, as it would give current information and would also yield very valuable dynamic information about the *changes* in the matrix, which may be much more important than the absolute figures. The fact that any measure of this kind is highly arbitrary is no argument against it, provided that it is qualitatively reliable—that is, moves generally in the same direction as the variable which it purports to measure—and provided also that the limitations of the measure are clearly understood. It would probably be advisable to check the second type of measure against the more objective measures derived from the first method. The difficulty of the first method, however, is the extreme instability of the matrix. The affections of nations are ephemeral!

has many interesting properties, not all of which can be worked out here but which depend on the kind of restraints that we impose on it. If we suppose, for instance, that the relations of nations are reciprocal, so that *I*'s attitude toward *J* is the same as *J*'s toward *I*, the matrix becomes symmetrical about its major diagonal—that is, the lower left-hand triangle is a mirror image of the upper right-hand triangle. This is a very severe restriction and is certainly violated in fact: there are unrequited loves and hates among the nations as there are among individuals. We can recognize a *tendency* however, for the matrix to become symmetrical. There is a certain instability about an unrequited feeling. If *I* loves *J* and *J* hates *I*, then either *J*'s constant rebuff of *I*'s affections will turn *I*'s love to hate, or *I*'s persistent wooing will break down *J*'s distaste and transform it into affection. Unfortunately for the history of human relations, the former seems to be the more frequent pattern, but the latter is by no means unknown.[4]

The sum totals of the rows represent the over-all friendliness or hostility of the nation at the head of the row; the sum totals of the columns represent the degree of hostility or friendliness *toward* the nation at the head of the column. The sum of either of these sums (which must be equal, as each represents a way of adding up all the figures of the matrix) is a measure of the over-all friendliness or hostility of the system. In the example of Figure 1, *B* is evidently a "paranoid" nation, feeling hostile toward everyone and receiving hostility in return; *D* is a "neutral" nation, with low values for either hostility or friendliness; *E* is a "friendly" nation, reciprocating *B*'s general hostility but otherwise having positive relations with everyone. In this figure it is evident that *A*, *C*, and *E* are likely to be allied against *B*, and *D* is likely to be uncommitted.

In the matrix of Figure 1 no account is taken of the relative size or power of the different nations. This dimension of the system can easily be accommodated, however. All that is necessary is to take the power of the smallest nation as a convenient unit and express the power of the others in multiples of this unit. Then in the matrix we simply give each nation a number of places along the axes equal to the measure of its power. Thus in Figure 2 we suppose a system of three

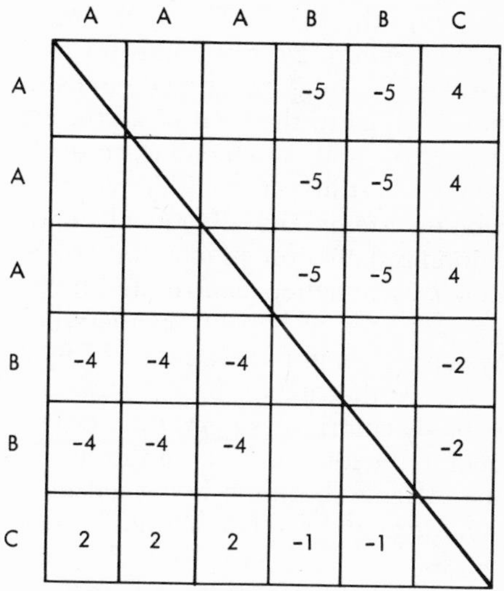

	A	A	A	B	B	C
A				-5	-5	4
A				-5	-5	4
A				-5	-5	4
B	-4	-4	-4			-2
B	-4	-4	-4			-2
C	2	2	2	-1	-1	

FIGURE 2

nations, where *B* is twice as powerful as *C* and *A* is three times as powerful as *C*; *A* is then allotted three spaces

[4] George F. Kennan once said: "It is an undeniable privilege of every man to prove himself in the right in the thesis that the world is his enemy; for if he reiterates it frequently enough and makes it the background of his conduct, he is bound eventually to be right" ("The Roots of Soviet Conduct," *Foreign Affairs,* July, 1947). If for "enemy" we read "friend" in this statement, the proposition seems to be equally true but much less believed.

along the axes, *B* two, and *C* one. The analysis of the matrix proceeds as before, with the additional constraint that all the figures in the larger boxes bounded by the lines which divide the nations should be the same, as in the figure.

The difference between the sum of a nation's column, representing the general degree of support or affection it *receives,* and the sum of a nations row, representing the sum of support or affection it *gives,* might be called its *affectional balance.* This is shown in the row *X* in Figure 1. It is a necessary property of a matrix of this kind that the sum of all these balances shall be zero. They measure the relative position of each nation in regard to the degree of support it can expect from the international system as a whole. Thus in Figure 1 it is clear that *B* is in the worst position, and *C* in the best position, vis-à-vis the system as a whole. Another figure of some interest might be called the *affectional contribution,* shown in the line *Y*. This is the mean of the column and row totals for each nation. The total affectional contribution is equal to the total of all the figures of the matrix, which measures the general hostility or friendliness of the whole system. The affectional contribution is then a rough measure of how much each nation contributes to the general level of hostility of the whole system. Thus in the example of Figure 1 we see that nation *B* (the paranoid) actually contributes more than 100 per cent to the total hostility of the system, its extreme hostility being offset to some extent by other nations' friendliness.

One critical problem of an international system, then, is that of the *dynamics* of the hostility matrix. We can conceive of a succession of such matrices at successive points of time. If there is a system with a "solution," we should be able to predict the matrix at t_1 from the knowledge we have of the matrix at t_0 or at various earlier times. The matrix itself will not, in general, carry enough information to make such predictions possible, even though it is easy to specify theoretical models in which a determinate dynamic system can be derived from the information in the matrix alone.[5]

The difficulty with "simple" systems of this nature is that they are very much more simple than the reality which they symbolize. This is because, in reality, the variables of the system consist of the innumerable dimensions of the images of large numbers of people, and the dynamics of the image are much more complex than the dynamics of mechanical systems. This is because of the structural nature of the image; it cannot be represented simply by a set of quantities or variables. Because of this structural nature, it is capable occasionally of very dramatic changes as a message hits some vital part of the structure and the whole image reorganizes itself. Certain events—like the German invasion of Belgium in 1914, the Japanese attack on Pearl Harbor in 1941, the American use of the atom bomb at Hiroshima and Nagasaki, the merciless destruction of Dresden, and the Russian success with Sputnik I—have profound effects and possibly long-run effects on reorganizing the various na-

---

[5] As a very simple example of such a system, let $(a_{ij})t$ be a cell of the matrix at time t and $(a_{ij})t + 1$ be the corresponding value at time $t + 1$. Then if for each cell we can postulate a function $(a_{ij})_{t+1} = F(a_{ij})_t$, we can derive the whole $t + 1$ matrix from the t matrix. This is essentially the dynamic method of Lewis F. Richardson, and in fairly simple cases it provides an interesting way of formulating certain aspects of the system, especially its tendency toward *cumulative* movements of hostility (arms races) or occasionally of friendliness.

tional images. The "reorganizing" events are hard both to specify and to predict; they introduce, however, a marked element of uncertainty into any dynamic international system which does not exist, for instance, in the solar system!

In spite of this difficulty, which, oddly enough, is particularly acute in short-term prediction, one gets the impression from the observation of history that we are in the presence of a true system with a real dynamic of its own. We do observe, for instance, cumulative processes of hostility. If we had some measures of the hostility matrix, however crude, it would be possible to identify these processes in more detail, especially the "turning points." There is an analogy here with the business cycle, which also represents a system of cumulative stochastic processes subject to occasional "reorganizations" of its basic equations. Just as we can trace cumulative upward and downward movements in national income, the downward movements often (though not always) culminating in financial crisis and the upward movements often leading to inflation and a subsequent downturn, so we can trace cumulative movements in the hostility matrix. We have "prewar" periods corresponding to downswings, in which things go from bad to worse and hostility constantly increases. The total of all the hostility figures (e.g., —8 on Fig. 1) is a striking analogue of the national-income concept. It might be called the "international temperature." Just as there is a certain critical point in a deflation at which a financial crisis is likely to ensue because of the growing insolvency of heavily indebted businesses, so there is a critical point in the rise of hostility at which war breaks out. This critical point itself depends on a number of different factors and may not be constant. Some nations may be more tolerant of hostility than others; as the cost of war increases, the tolerance of hostility also increases, as we see today in the remarkable persistence of the "cold war." A deflation or downturn, however, *may* reverse itself without a crisis, and a "prewar" period may turn into a "postwar" period without a war. Indeed, in the period since 1945 we might identify almost as many small international cycles as there have been business cycles! The "upturn" may be a result of a change of government, the death of certain prominent individuals, or even a change of heart (or image!) on the part of existing rulers. The catharsis of a war usually produces the typical "postwar" period following, though this is often tragically short, as it was after the end of World War II, when a "downturn" began after the revolution in Czechoslovakia. The downturn is often the result of the reassertion of a persistent, long-run character of the system after a brief interlude of increasing friendliness. There seems to be a certain long-run tendency of an international system toward hostility, perhaps because of certain inescapable flaws in the very concept of a national image, just as there also seems to be a long-run tendency of an unregulated and undisturbed market economy toward deflation.

In considering the dynamics of an international system, the essential properties of the image matrix might be summed up in a broad concept of "compatibility." If the change in the system makes for greater compatibility the system may move to an equilibrium. The "balance-of-power" theory postulates the existence of an equilibrium of this nature. The record of history, however, suggests that, in the past at least, international systems have usually been unstable. The incompatibility of various national images has led to changes in the system which have created still greater incompatibility, and the system has moved to less and less stable situations until some crisis, such as war, is reached, which represents a discontinuity in the system. After a war the system is reorganized; some national units may disappear, others change their character, and the system starts off again. The incompatibility may be of many kinds, and it is a virtue of this kind of rather loose model that the historian can fill in the endlessly various details in the special situations which he studies. The model is a mere dress form on which the historian swathes the infinite variations of fashion and fact.

In the model we can distinguish two very different kinds of incompatibility of images. The first might be called "real" incompatibility, where we have two images of the future in which realization of one would prevent the realization of the other. Thus two nations may both claim a certain piece of territory, and each may feel dissatisfied unless the territory is incorporated into it. (One thinks of the innumerable irredenta which have stained the pages of history with so much blood!) Or two nations may both wish to feel stronger than, or superior to, each other. It is possible for two nations to be in a position where each is stronger than the other *at home,* provided that they are far enough apart and that the "loss of power gradient" (which measures the loss of power of each as we remove the point of application farther and farther from the home base) is large enough. It is rarely possible, however, for two nations each to dominate the other, except in the happy situation where each suffers from delusions of grandeur.

The other form of incompatibility might be called "illusory" incompatibility, in which there exists a condition of compatibility which would satisfy the "real" interests of the two parties but in which the dynamics of the situation or the illusions of the parties create a situation of perverse dynamics and misunderstandings, with increasing hostility simply as a result of the reactions of the parties to each other, not as a result of any basic differences of interest. We must be careful about this distinction: even "real" incompatibilities are functions of the national images rather than of physical fact and are therefore subject to change and control. It is hard for an ardent patriot to realize that his country is a mental, rather than a physical, phenomenon, but such indeed is the truth! It is not unreasonable to suppose, however, that "real" incompatibilities are more intractable and less subject to "therapy" than illusory ones.

One final point of interest concerns what might be called the impact of "sophistication" or "self-consciousness" on national images and the international system. The process of sophistication in the image is a very general one, and we cannot follow all its ramifications here. It occurs in every person in greater or less degree as he grows into adult awareness of himself as part of a larger system. It is akin almost to a Copernican revolution: the unsophisticated image sees the world only from the viewpoint of the viewer; the sophisticated image sees the world from many imagined viewpoints, as a system in which the viewer is only a part. The child sees everything through his own eyes and refers everything to his own immediate comfort. The adult learns to see the world through the eyes of others; his horizon extends to other times, places, and cultures than his own; he learns to distinguish between those elements in his experience which are universal and those which are particular. Many grown people, of course, never become adults in this sense, and it is these who fill our mental hospitals with themselves and their children.

The scientific subculture is an important agency in the sophistication of images. In the physical world we no longer attribute physical phenomena to spirits analogous to our own. In the social sciences we have an agency whereby men reach self-consciousness about their own cultures and institutions and therefore no longer regard these as simply given to them by "nature." In economics, for instance, we have learned to see the system as a whole, to realize that many things which are true of individual behavior are not true of the system and that the system itself is not incapable of a modicum of control. We no longer, for instance, regard depressions as "acts of God" but as system-made phenomena capable of control through relatively minor system change.

The national image, however, is the last great stronghold of unsophistication. Not even the professional international relations experts have come very far toward seeing the system as a whole, and the ordinary citizen and the powerful statesman alike have naïve, self-centered, and unsophisticated images of the world in which their nation moves. Nations are divided into "good" and "bad"—the enemy is all bad, one's own nation is of spotless virtue. Wars are either acts of God or acts of the other nations, which always catch us completely by surprise. To a student of international systems the national image even of respectable, intellectual, and powerful people seems naïve and untrue. The patriotism of the sophisticated cannot be a simple faith. There is, however, in the course of human history a powerful and probably irreversible movement toward sophistication. We can wise up, but we cannot wise down, except at enormous cost in the breakdown of civilizations, and not even a major breakdown results in much loss of knowledge. This movement must be taken into account in predicting the future of the international system. The present system as we have known it for the past hundreds or even thousands of years is based on the widespread acceptance of unsophisticated images, such as, for instance, that a nation can be made more secure *merely* by increasing its armaments. The growth of a systems-attitude toward international relations will have profound consequences for the dynamics of the system itself, just as the growth of a systems-attitude in economics has profound consequences for the dynamics of the economic system.

If, as I myself believe, we live in an international system so unstable that it threatens the very existence of life on earth, our main hope for change may lie in the rapid growth of sophistication, especially at the level of the images of the powerful. Sophistication, of course, has its dangers also. It is usually but a hair's-breadth removed from sophistry, and a false sophistication (of which Marxism in some respects is a good example) can be even more destructive to the stability of a system than a naïve image. Whichever way we move, however, there is danger. We have no secure place to stand where we are, and we live in a time when intellectual investment in developing more adequate international images and theories of international systems may bear an enormous rate of return in human welfare.

2

*The Basis of National Loyalty**

Morton Grodzins

MORTON GRODZINS *was a member of the Political Science Department of the University of Chicago and the author of several outstanding books, including* Americans Betrayed (*1949*), *and* The Loyal and the Disloyal: Social Boundaries of Patriotism and Treason (*1956*).

It is a contradiction in terms to speak of a man without loyalties. He does not exist. The human qualities that differentiate man from other mammals are the products of his social life. One with all the attributes of man, including his brain, is in isolation not a man. He is a beast.

This only says that when you scratch man you touch loyalty. For man means society. And society—social structures of every sort—rests upon loyalties: upon systems of mutual rights and duties, common beliefs, and reciprocal obligations. To accuse one of being devoid of loyalty can have only one meaning. His loyalties are antagonistic to your own.

The basic objective of this article is . . . to show how factors of life situation tend to bind men's loyalty to their *nation* . . . .

FUNCTION OF LOYALTIES

Loyalties are a part of every individual's life because they serve his basic needs and functions. They are a part of his indispensable habit patterns. Loyalties provide him with a portion of that framework through which he organizes his existence. In the absence of such a framework, he could establish no easy, habitual responses. He would be faced with the endless and hopelessly complicated task of making fresh decisions at each moment of life. He would soon degenerate into wild and random inconsistencies or into a brooding state of confusion and indecisiveness, conditions that soon merge into the psychotic.

The propensity of man to organize the structure of his activities is apparent in every phase of his life. His very perceptions are so organized. Even what a man sees or smells or hears is determined in very large part by predisposing frameworks. This has been demonstrated in laboratory experiments, and the experiments are duplicated daily in ordinary life situations. Drivers of cars which have collided have very different stories to tell. Two readers of the same book derive from it support for widely divergent points of view. Chinese music and Mohammedan paintings are displeasing or unintelligible to those who have not acquired the framework necessary to make them beautiful and meaningful.

This "structuring" of life's enormous range of potentialities begins from the very moment of birth. For

* "The Basis of National Loyalty" by Morton Grodzins is reprinted with permission from the December 1951 issue of the *Bulletin of the Atomic Scientists*. Copyright 1951, by the Educational Foundation for Nuclear Science, Inc.

the first years of life, when the plasticity of individuals is very great, the family is the dominant molding agency. Later, play groups, school, church, job, social class, government, all take important, sometimes parallel, sometimes conflicting, roles in shaping an individual's career, attitudes, and personality.

These groups that so crucially affect existence are the groups that demand and receive loyalty. They become the eye-pieces through which a person views his life and its relation to society. They actually and literally determine what he does and does not see, what he does and does not like, what he does and does not consider his life goals. Without the aid and comfort of these group ties, an individual would find existence impossible.

Loyalties are thus the source of great personal gratification. They contribute to making life satisfying. They protect the individual, reducing the area of his uncertainty and anxiety. They allow him to move in established patterns of interpersonal relations with confidence in the action expected of him and of responses that his action will evoke. By serving the group to which he is loyal, he serves himself; what threatens the group, threatens the self. There is no self outside group activity. "In so far as one identifies himself with a whole, loyalty to that whole is loyalty to himself; it is self-realization, something which one cannot fail without losing self respect."[1]

Complete identification between individual and group does not often exist. Totalitarian governments attempt to accomplish this end by destroying all intermediary loyalties, or by fusing the activities of all other groups with those of the state.

In the Western democracies the case is different. Except in periods of extreme crisis, freedom to form and maintain group ties is cherished and encouraged, and individuals preserve strong loyalties to numerous non-national groups. These loyalties are given to family, friends, neighborhood, church, ethnic society, job, class, and to a host of other institutions, groups, and idea systems. They exist most frequently in situations that bring the individual face-to-face with others who share his views and situation; they may also exist where this immediate human contact does not exist. The relative strength and weakness of these numerous loyalties change with age, with shifts in life situation, with new experience, and especially under stress of crisis. They change as old relationships no longer serve biological needs or as they no longer supply satisfaction and security to the individual in the total network of his social existence.

TWO STRANDS OF NATIONAL LOYALTY

Individual satisfactions are related to *national* loyalty in an infinite number of ways. Almost the entire social structure is organized to promote and sustain this relationship. One of the prime reasons for the strength and universality of national loyalties is the virtuosity and deftness with which the connection between nation and happiness can be established. For convenience, one can distinguish between two broad strands which together tend to bind human satisfaction to national welfare.

DIRECT NATION-PERSON TIE

Patriotism as a religion

On one plane the relationship between individual and nation is direct. Satisfaction springs from immediate

[1] C. H. Cooley, *Social Organization: A Study of the Larger Mind* (New York: Charles Scribner's Sons, 1909), p. 38.

identification with nation, from the acceptance of national symbols, the internalization of national ideals. There is delight in attaching oneself to a larger cause. Inner doubts are dissipated: the cause gives purpose and direction to life. The meanness and pettiness of everyday existence become unimportant; the nation is the dominant power unit in the modern world and it is involved in enterprises of grandeur. In this way, the nation acts to dissipate actual and imagined discontents and weaknesses; it simultaneously crystallizes the common faith which philosophers and politicians, sociologists and seers have argued is essential to any successful group life.

The world is organized territorially, and to some extent functionally, into national units. This very organization permits a complex flow of simple emotions to be woven into the sentiment of national loyalty. National states and the institutions within them conspire to promote and to sustain this loyalty.

Ethnocentrism: death to the porpoises

The tendency of man to prefer the familiar to the unfamiliar is a universal social phenomenon. The search for new experience and delight in the exotic must largely be understood in terms of the reassurance of the familiar and the habitual. As the world is presently organized, the familiar and the habitual are principally equated with the national. In this way affection for the scenes and experiences of childhood becomes identified with the nation. The familiar language, the familiar food, the familiar humor, the familiar interpersonal responses—including, as Kipling wrote, the familiar lies—all are affectionately related to the nation.

Familiar misery is frequently more attractive than promised or actual, but unfamiliar, bliss. This is a function of what social anthropologists call ethnocentrism, the practice of judging foreign customs by familiar standards. Even the mean and savage regard their own way of life as the best and all others as sub-human or at least distinctly inferior. This mechanism has been described and documented in many ways. A classic example is in Anatole France, whose Penguin cottager affirms:

> He who says neighbors says enemies. . . . Don't you know what patriotism is? For my part there are two cries that rise to my lips: Hurrah for the Penguins! Death to the Porpoises!

The modern network of worldwide communications and other technological factors tend to weaken the force of ethnocentrism. But it remains potent because it lives on difference, real or imagined. It is strengthened by the structural qualities of the nation-state system. The great hostilities generated within nations are suppressed to every extent possible; they find outlets in bursts of patriotic fervor directed against other national units.[2] Man's love of community—his aim-inhibited libido, in Freud's term—is thus encouraged to stop at national boundaries. The ills of one's own person and one's own culture are projected outward: we are peaceful, they are aggressive; we are kind, they cruel; we aim for justice, they for conquest.

These mechanisms prompted the sardonic Sumner to comment that "the masses are always patriotic." They inspire the antagonisms and animosities that are basic to most patriotic en-

---

[2] See Talcott Parsons, "Certain Primary Sources and Patterns of Aggression in the Social Structure of the Western World," *Psychiatry*, **X** (May, 1947), 167–81.

deavor. The process is self-generating and circular. National boundaries and patriotism to the nation establish convenient ethnocentric battle lines; the belligerencies so evoked add to patriotic fervor; the heightened patriotism produces new belligerencies. Thus patriotism can pour meaning into otherwise empty lives. The price may be individuality itself; but this seems cheap to those glorying in and suffering for great causes.

The conspiracy of institutions

The nation is not the only focal point for mass loyalties. Just as loyalty to a nation competes with loyalty to family, job, and friends, so it must compete with loyalty to race, religion, and class. The nation's advantage is based not only on the psychological processes just described: to some degree those energies are also available to other causes. The strength of national, rather than other, loyalties is also partly the result of objective facts: common language, common historical traditions, a definable territory. Finally, national loyalty is built strong as the result of the active role taken by social institutions in building a firm direct tie between individual and nation. The institution of government is of first importance in this effort.

Government is a powerful agency in setting up norms of behavior. By laws establishing limits of freedom and control, government defines general guidelines for life activities. Through control of the schools, government has a crucial lever for inculcating habits of thought, for encouraging some character traits and discouraging others, and for molding individuals to standards of thought and action. Through its multitude of substantive programs, the state purchases conformity and allegiance. By enforcing service in the armed forces, the state transforms citizens into soldiers and in the process brings about similarly striking changes in attitude and outlook. As the source of major news developments, government commands a large portion of the words and symbols transmitted to the public by press, radio, television, and film. By the encouragement of national holidays and festivals, government pounds home myths of national might and images of national glory. By fostering patriotic organizations and activities, government enlists citizens in active demonstrations of patriotism.

There are tremendous variations in the extent and manner that governments utilize the power they possess for building patriotism. There are even greater variations in the size and composition of the groups to which governments are responsible and thus in the final ends for which patriotism is utilized.

Democratic values and traditions do not countenance the ruthless exploitation of people by the state for the state. The power structure within democracies makes such exploitation impossible; it occurs only at the price of changing the character of the state itself. And in the United States, government power is further dispersed as the result of the federal system. Nevertheless, even in the United States, the patriotic theme is an essential ingredient of all public activity, even that at the state and local level.

Public education, for example, has been least affected in the United States by the insistent trend toward national financing and supervision. Yet, as the studies of Charles Merriam and Bessie Pierce have shown, the themes of patriotism and national service are consistently and insistently pursued.[3]

---

[3] Charles Edward Merriam, *The Making of Citizens* (Chicago: The University of Chicago Press, 1931); Bessie L. Pierce, *Civic Attitudes in American School Textbooks* (Chicago: The University of Chicago Press, 1930).

The total impact of the schools is designed certainly, if unwittingly, to conform to Rousseau's dictum: that education should direct the opinion and tastes of men so that they will be "patriots by inclination, by passion, by necessity."

This is true for all nations. Naturally enough, the truth has been demonstrated most graphically and most bleakly by the totalitarian governments. The Nazis showed that a state-operated educational system could be even more powerful than the family as a molder of attitudes and personality, supplanting or destroying the family's influence to a large measure.

The Nazis attempted to create a situation in which individuals received all their cues for action from a state or party agency. They did this by capturing or destroying all other institutions and groups—religious, professional, and social—that guide and control human action. The terrible efficiency of this fully mobilized state-controlled education cannot be doubted. It drastically altered the direction of the culture and the temper, the very personality of the people.

In the United States and other Western democracies, one does not find this total mobilization of state resources and state institutions for the purpose of constructing strong national allegiance. Yet state activities, with minor exceptions, move strongly toward cementing loyalty to the nation. Only a small portion of these activities aim at building direct emotional ties between individual and state. School programs illustrate this attempt, as do bond drives, ceremonies dramatizing the might of armed forces, the display and symbolic care of the flag. But in the democracies, unlike the totalitarian nations, the major impact of state activities is an indirect one: it strengthens national loyalties by strengthening the numerous voluntary groups through which so much of the life and politics of democratic people is organized and directed.

The effects of these programs do not, of course, stop with the voluntary groups. The groups have a vitality of their own. They, in turn, direct the emotions of group members toward the nation. In this circular fashion, virtually all groups contribute to national allegiance. Their members minimize or efface any antagonisms between their own group and the nation. They identify group and national welfare. "What is good for business is good for the nation," trumpets the National Association of Manufacturers. "High wages mean national health," responds the Congress of Industrial Organization.

The voices and forces all pushing in the same direction produce the religious quality of patriotism. It is a quality for which totalitarian nations strive continuously but which is known to democracies largely in periods of crisis—"an element of worship, of willing sacrifice, of joyful merging of the individual in the life of the nation."[4] Here the direct nation-individual linkage is most graphically expressed.

Indirect Nation-person Tie

Non-national loyalties as filters of national loyalty

The second strand relating individual to nation is an indirect one. Here satisfactions are experienced in the face-to-face relations of everyday living, in pleasurable interpersonal experiences, warm friends, sympathetic neighbors, the achievement of expectations in marriage and career. One's relationships to the nation are transmitted, or filtered, through these ex-

4 Bertrand Russell, *Why Men Fight* (New York: The Century Company, 1917), p. 55.

periences. To the extent that they produce a satisfactory life situation, the individual's identification with his nation is positive. His loyalty may be presumed, though it is a loyalty different in kind from the loyalty fostered by direct ties with the state. Where a life situation does not produce a balance of gratifications, the individual's identification with the nation wavers. His loyalty may be more easily eroded.

Until the advent of modern totalitarianism, it is doubtful if the direct nation-person tie could have been built strong enough to sustain national loyalties over long periods of time. It involves, ultimately, the destruction of all privacy. Only with the techniques of modern political exploitation does this seem possible.

For the Western democracies, at least, patriotism cannot be maintained over long periods of time by the direct tie to the nation alone. No one has expressed this idea more clearly than George Washington, who wrote from Valley Forge in April, 1788:

> Men may talk of patriotism; they may draw a few examples from ancient story, of great achievements performed by its influence; but whosoever builds upon it, as a sufficient Basis for conducting this Bloody war, will find themselves deceived in the end. . . . I do not mean to exclude altogether the Idea of Patriotism. I know it exists, and I know it has done much in the present Contest. But I venture to assert, that a great and lasting War can never be supported on this principle alone. It must be aided by a prospect of Interest or some reward.

Washington's concept of "interest" was largely a commercial one. The definition need not be so narrow. But Washington's point is basic.

Democratic nations cannot exist unless the "interests"—the life goals—of its citizens are at least approximately achieved. And these achievements are in areas where there is little or no direct nation-person relationship. National loyalty here becomes a by-product of satisfactions achieved in non-public spheres of activity.

Indeed, from this view a generalized national loyalty is a misnomer. It does not exist. Loyalties are to specific groups, specific goals, specific programs of action. Populations are loyal to nation only because the nation is believed to symbolize and sustain these values.

Leon Trotsky once remarked that revolutions were not caused by the poor. If they were, he said, there would be revolutions going on all the time. This is one way of expressing the important fact that "life expectations" or "life goals" are not fixed or static concepts. Individuals define these terms in various and divergent fashions; their definitions are influenced in many ways, not least of all by parents, profession, sex, and social class.

To say that loyalty is dependent upon the achievement of life satisfactions is therefore not to say that the poor are the disloyal, the rich, loyal. The individual's own definition of satisfaction is of crucial importance. The fat men who do not make easy converts are those fat in satisfactions, not necessarily in body or other material possessions. A subtle tool to measure these satisfactions would be an index of the discrepancy, if any, between life expectancy and life achievements, as defined by the individual. Where the spread is a big one, deprivations are experienced and loyalty to the nation (not considering direct nation-person ties) is presumably less strong than where expectations are actually or approximately achieved.

This variety in definition of life satisfactions is crucial to understanding the interplay between those satisfactions and national loyalty.

A second general consideration is also of great importance. Life goals are achieved and life satisfactions are pursued within the framework of groups. The happy man in isolation does not exist. He may—and most frequently does—take his terms of reference, his cues for action, his definitions of the good and desirable from the small face-to-face groups with which he comes into most intimate contact: family, friends, business associates, professional colleagues, fellow-workers. Or these cues for life may be influenced by larger, less visible groups with which he identifies himself: social class, the universal church, the international workers. In these latter cases and even in those cases where frames of reference are derived from such apparent abstractions as "the good of mankind," there is usually a face-to-face group in existence, functioning to define and to clarify abstract goals in terms of day-to-day activity.

The principal loyalties of men in democratic states are directed toward these non-national groups and interests. Their very existence provides possibilities for sharp clashes between national and other loyalties. But these other loyalties are also the most important foundation of national loyalty.

Why this is so has already been suggested. The nation is the most important group with which all persons in a given geographic area are associated. It gives all citizens a common point of reference. It sustains their groups. A threat to a nation is interpreted as a threat to all groups within the nation and to the gratifications derived from those groups. The satisfactions springing from smaller groups are thus related to the nation and to national loyalty.

But in times of crisis, the national demands may easily conflict with the demands of non-national groups. Family welfare, professional status, career and job stability may be threatened or thwarted by governmental policy. In such circumstances, clean choices need not always be made. When they do, national loyalty may mean family or professional disloyalty. Where loyalty to family or to career or to profession is held foremost, then the result is national disloyalty.

The total configuration is a fine paradox: non-national loyalties are the bricks from which national loyalty is constructed; they are also the brickbats by which national loyalty is destroyed.

3

*Forms and Variations of Nationalism**

William C. Olson

WILLIAM C. OLSON, *presently Associate Dean of the School of International Affairs at Columbia University, served for four years as Chief of the Foreign Affairs Division of the Legislative Reference Service in the Library of Congress. Among the numerous institutions at which he has lectured are the Air War College at Maxwell Field, the University of California, and the School of Advanced International Studies in Washington. As a research associate of the Institute of War and Peace Studies, his current research interests center upon foreign policy and the legislative process, particularly its informational base.*

. . . [I]t is over thirty-five years now since Carleton J. H. Hayes contributed his great *Essays on Nationalism,* and much has been written on the subject since then. Therefore we need only remind ourselves briefly of what the term *nationalism* connotes. As a more recent authority, Hans Kohn, puts it, nationalism is "a state of mind in which the supreme loyalty of individuals is felt to be due to the nation-state. . . . It recognizes the nation-state as the source of all creative energy and economic well-being." To some it is analogous to patriotism; to others, like Hayes himself, it is better thought of as a combination of patriotism and nationality.

The elements or features of nationalism have been variously described, but it seems clear that the following are characteristic of most manifestations of this, the central political phenomenon of our time, which to historically minded people like me means the past three centuries. There is, of necessity, some territorial identification, some land or soil, either possessed or coveted. There are shared cultural qualities, such as language, customs, literature, the general mores of the group, and of these language, as the vehicle of communication, is perhaps the most pervasive. Some dominant social or economic institution, such as Hinduism or socialism, is normally present. Belief in a common historical tradition—especially one which combines intense pride in the achievement of one's own people, or more particularly its heroes, with profound sorrow or even bitterness in the tragedy of its defeats and frustrations—ties the nation together. This is bound up with the conviction, or at least the hope, that the nation has a glorious future to look forward to, occasionally even encompassing some conception of a destiny for world mastery. If the nation happens not to have a government, if it does not possess that most precious of political properties, sovereignty, then there is a dogged determination to get it as soon as possible.

The state thus involves the nation, and the nation involves the state. If

* *Proceedings of the Institute of World Affairs,* **XXXVI** (1961), 32–41. Reprinted by permission. Originally titled "Centrifugal Forces in World Order: The Flame of Nationalism."

the nation loses its quality of statehood, if it loses sovereignty, this is regarded as but an unfortunate temporary aberration that is to be overcome, as shame and defeat are overcome, as quickly as possible and by whatever means may be at hand. The old pronouncement, "The King is dead; long live the King," meaning that the young prince has at once replaced his deceased father as monarch, has in more recent times become "The state is dead; long live the nation." For even if the state dies, the nation lives on in the expectation that the state will one day be restored to life. If on the one hand, there is love or esteem for one's fellow nationals (though not necessarily as individuals, as Boyd Shafer has pointed out), there is on the other a whole gamut of feelings from discomfort with, to disdain of, to downright hostility toward other nationals, taken as a group. Nationalism tends to doubt the possibility of real friendship with neighboring states, and in its extreme form it may even glorify combat. "What this country needs," said one of America's nationalists at the turn of the century, "is a good war," just as by contrast one of its most ardent internationalists once claimed that America was "too proud to fight."

Now what is the effect of all this upon world order? . . . One may, without offending anyone, rail against the evils of abstract nationalism, and one may even go as far as a prominent American historian did when he said, "If nationalism is not mitigated, it will be an unqualified curse to future generations." But substitute the word *patriotism* and imply that love of one's country might be anything less than an unqualified blessing, and all manner of good citizens become indignant. As I have already indicated in citing Hayes, it is the peculiar combination of love of country (which is patriotism) with the nation (which is an ethnic term), and in turn the combination of the nation with the state (which involves government), that has created the profound political problem which thwarts the growth of international order today.

A distinction also needs to be made between the internal and the external dimensions of our problem. When speaking of the centrifugal forces at work in contemporary world politics and trying to relate them to the nature and working of nationalism, one must of course make clear that it is primarily in the external sense that he uses the term *centrifugal*, for what tears apart outside the state, binds together within. Within the state, nationalism is, almost without exception, a centripetal force. It draws people together; it overcomes their differences; it produces one nation; it rests upon a sense of belonging; it creates unity; it rejects any disintegrative force within its borders; it has a cohesive impact upon society. It may even force into a conforming mold every facet of life in such a way that the only values that have any meanings are national values. From the internal perspective, such transnational forces as the church, the scientific community, communication, the arts, the desire of people to see the world beyond their own narrow confines, all tend to break down the exclusive control of the centralized nation-state. In fact, these forces have an effect exactly the opposite to nationalism, that is, they contribute to the growth of international cohesiveness; they cement the ties of world order.

There appear to me to be only two ways in which nationalism can operate as a centrifugal force *within* the state, and both of these involve situations in which the cultural boundaries of the nation do not correspond with the geopolitical boundaries of the state. One occurs when there is more than one nation within the compass of the state, as in the notable case of Austria-Hungary, where the problems presented by this anomaly were not solved, or as in the case of Canada. . . . The other way involves just the opposite kind of problem, where the boundaries of the nation exceed those of the state, producing what the Fascists used to call *Italia irredenta*, the unredeemed, living outside the secure borders of their true and only legitimate national home. The shoe is of course on the other foot now, with the German-speaking south Tyroleans trying to get themselves, with generous encouragement from Vienna, back into their Austrian *Vaterland*. But except for these two kinds of situations —and of course there are a good many of these—nationalism as an internal phenomenon is centripetal, not centrifugal, that is, it draws together and holds a people: it does not split them apart. Thus it is in the international sphere that our problem really presents itself, despite the romantic hopes of such nationalists as Theodore Roosevelt, who tried to square the circle by a world-minded patriotism which postulated an international order that was made up of a large collection of nation-states of varying degrees of power and influence, which would somehow be more loyal to their collective values and mutual welfare because of the intensity of their national fervor. But actually what is good for one's own nation may not be good for mankind, although in the long run the opposite may very well be true.

To bring our discussion to a head, I should like to suggest that there are at least eight ways in which nationalism acts as a disruptive, disintegrative, centrifugal force in world order. This is not to say that its influence is entirely negative or undesirable; one need only cite its utility in bringing to an end, albeit too abruptly in some situations, the outdated policy of imperialism, and its undoubted value in acting as a non-military deterrent force, as against the expansion of Communist ideology.

First, and perhaps most important, is the emotional content of nationalism. This is expressed in terms of its fundamental irrationality, particularly in its intense and virulent forms. Implicit in the whole concept of order, at whatever level, is the necessity of rationality. If order is rational, then disorder is irrational. World order, and whatever tendency there may be toward it, is discouraged and frustrated by any force that depends for its existence and survival upon emotional fervor and the rejection of rational thought. Spectacular displays of nationalistic symbols, the whipping up of crowds in response to appeals to unreason, the stimulation of feelings of unthinking loyalty and blind devotion to the nation and its exclusive interests, the artificial manufacture of all manner of emotion-packed paraphernalia, all represent the psychology of nationalism. They all resist, often explicitly, any tendency, or movement, or inclination to think in terms of world values, or, indeed, even to think. One reason that this is so is that the facts of international life deny the validity of the "exclusivism" of nationalism; therefore the practitioners of virulent nationalism resort to the emotional and reject the rational. The more intense the nationalism, the more irrational it is. For a nation to live sensibly in the second half of the twentieth century is for it to qualify and to modify its fervency.

A second element which makes nationalism a centrifugal force in world affairs is its stress upon differences and its resultant inability or reluctance to concede similarities between peoples.

While the fabric of world order may accommodate patches of many different colors, there must obviously be enough likeness of material to permit the whole cloth to be woven. Nationalism tends to deny this. Nationalism stresses, accentuates, encourages, may even artificially create differences between its people and others. It makes distinction a virtue and a source of pride. To be like a foreigner is not only to be subject to rebuke, it is a cause for suspicion, and in some languages the word for *foreign* is the same as the word for *enemy*. To define one's own nationhood often begins with an indication that it is unlike another's. "We are not like them" is one of the commonest and most prideful of human expressions. The highest consciousness of which most people seem capable is not social consciousness, or world consciousness, but national consciousness.

Similar to this is a third element of nationalism, but it has a quality of a different dimension. I speak of national conscience. Whereas national consciousness is psychological, national conscience is ethical. It has a moral quality. It is of course true that belief in world order, particularly if it has its foundation in such religious ideas as the brotherhood of man, has a moral quality too. But the state, and especially the nation-state, has the ability to demand and receive a dimension of loyalty denied to the world at large. This is because people accept the *rightness* of the claims of the state. Contrast the degree of belief in the nation and its cause with the relative lack of concern for the welfare of all mankind which exists today. When Norman Cousins asks "Who Speaks for Man?" does anyone answer? The national ethic, resting upon the very existence of the nation, in its past, in its future, often its extension and greater glory, stands out in sharp distinction to the absence of any such ethic at the international level. As de Maistre said many years ago, "I have seen, in my time, Frenchmen, Italians, and Russians; I even know, thanks to Montesquieu, that one may be a Persian; but as for *Man*, I declare that I have never met him in my life; if he exists, it is without my knowledge." The state never admits that it is wrong. It tends to justify all its actions as serving what it calls the "national interest," which even as practiced an historian as Charles Beard never succeeded in defining. One is struck by our own old tendency to make diplomatic blunders, but even more by our new tendency to regard them as victories. But there is no more reason to be surprised by this than there is for an Indian to be surprised when his government, so pious in its pacifistic internationalism at the time of its inception, behaves just as any other nation-state might in the Kashmir crisis, defending its actions on the basis of morality. It was George Kennan who lamented the legalistic-moralistic bias of the approach of the American people to foreign policy, but are we really so different from any other nation in regarding our own particular set of policies as having a moral validity and justification which those of other states seem to lack? Implicit in the very idea that one's own nation-state is always right is the suspicion that therefore one's enemies (and perhaps even one's friends) in the arena of world politics are wrong. Against such an ethic, the growth of a truly world ethic must be a slow one.

All of these elements—irrationality, differentiation, and moralization—become more pronounced in their negative effects upon world order when the state and the nation, for whatever reason, fail to coincide. When Woodrow

Wilson opened the Pandora's box of self-determination, little did he dream that he was contributing to world disorder. He was soon made painfully aware of it by the motley parade of spokesmen who came pleading to Versailles with their claims for statehood for this or that little ethnic group. (For a time it looked as if every crowd with an accent had to have a government to go with it!) This failure of the nation and the state to coincide may be the result, of course, of other things than new claims, such as the loss, partial or complete, of territory in a war (as in the case of Germany after World War I or of Estonia after World War II). It may be brought on by the gradually more intense development of national feeling by a group not hitherto conscious of a desire for statehood (as is occurring all over the African continent now), or by the division of the nation into two or more states, especially when each of these may contain large groups of other nationals (of which the most notable example perhaps is Poland), or by the attempt of the state artificially to create a sense of nationhood within its borders (of which Belgium is a not altogether happy example.) Sometimes the problems created by such divisions are successfully overcome, as in the case of the development of the Czechoslovakian state after the First World War. . . . But more often this is a source of tension and strife, of revolution and war. Had the accidents of geography and history contrived to put all the Russians in one place, and all the Malays in one place, and all the Peruvians in one place, the world of nation-states might have been a more orderly one. Even then, unhappily, there would be many justifications for boundaries; nationhood is only one.

The fifth element of nationalism to which I wish to draw attention may be termed "variation in form." Nationalism may be economic. It may be ideological. It may be historic. It may be administrative or political. It may be cultural. All of these forms exist in the world at the same time, though not all in the same state at the same time. Many observers, for example, those who see in such organs as the Economic and Social Council the real value of a United Nations whose political and security functions have been frustrated, feel that the most practical route to world order is through economics rather than diplomacy. World order grows out of world economy; countries learn to do business together by doing business together. Yet look at the devices created to control international trade by nation-states pursuing exclusive, short-term, and often contradictory policies: import quotas, export licenses, special commodity surtaxes, blocked currencies, exchange controls, retaliatory tariffs, imperial preferences, export bonuses, quarantine restrictions, and on down the list. In the long run, of course, such practices hurt everyone, including the states which imposed the restrictions in the first place. Economists understand this—a fact that perhaps reveals why politicians seldom seem to listen to economists.

Politicians have further contributed to our dilemma by producing still another form of nationalism, an artificial variety based in the first instance upon administrative convenience. This is something fairly new, and can be seen most vividly in the emergent nation-states of Africa (if indeed the term *nation-state* is really appropriate at all in that region), where sovereign states stand where colonial administrators used to tread. The criteria for drawing boundaries between imperial holdings are only by chance the criteria for drawing the configuration of a new state in the age of nationalism. Just what is a Mauretanian, for example? Or an Upper Voltan? Or, for that matter, a Congolese? Is he a national of a former French colony or of a former Belgian colony? Or neither? Or both? Yet if these administrative subdivisions fail to provide a viable basis for statehood, what will? Tribal organization? And if an inhabitant of a place like West Irian does not want to be an Indonesian just because his homeland used to be in the vast colony of the Dutch East Indies, what then?

Still another form of nationalism—the ideological variety—is perhaps best illustrated by Yugoslavia today. That used to be the kingdom of the Serbs, Croats, and Slovenes; now it is a Communist state based upon its own particular brand of Marxism. . . .

Gaullist France is representative of still another form of nationalism—the historic, having as its principal foundation the restoration of the new Fifth Republic to the nation's former glory and to its place (always called "rightful") in the family of nations. So far the new French claim is not territorial, quite the contrary, but whether it is primarily mystical or atomic is hard to say. Historic nationalism can provide an especially difficult threat to world order, because if every country were to become aware of its former position in the balance of power to such a degree that it wanted to restore it, chaos would result, since at least in Europe almost every bit of soil has at one time or another fallen under the control of several different states.

A less threatening form of nationalism is the purely cultural variety, and it may be that in this category nationalism is in fact more of a centripetal than a centrifugal force. While art and music and literature are international and while each nation takes pride in its own cultural achievements, it is usually willing to concede with good grace the claims of other nations. Cultural nationalism becomes a threat to world order whenever a state claims superiority over others because of its own cultural greatness and attempts to base political influence upon it. The trend toward world order is thwarted by all these forms of nationalism, and it is not enough to devise means of dealing with only one of them at a time.

A sixth factor of nationalism is variation in the stage of its development that is to be found at one and the same time. To illustrate: The constitutions of the Benelux countries are written in such a way that their governments can merge their sovereignty with others on a broader political base, and serious discussions take place on the practicalities of European integration. In the Old World the age of nationalism, which began with the conclusion of the Thirty Years' War over three centuries ago, seems to be drawing to a close. But in the New World—and that term now applies better to Africa than it does to our own hemisphere—the age of nationalism is just beginning, as it has very recently begun in the Middle East and the Orient. If the mood in Accra and Jakarta were the same as in Brussels and the Hague, then world order might be on the threshold of realization. But what we seem to be entering, however, is not a period of world integration at all, but at best an era of regional integration, and that only in some regions. One reason that the world is in such a confused state just now is, not only that the degree of virulence of national feeling differs from country to country, but that it changes from time to time, often rapidly, within a given state. A country which produced a distinguished international lawyer yesterday may produce a nationalist movement today and an aggressor tomorrow. We live in several stages of the development of nationalism simultaneously, and while this makes for an exciting world, it hardly makes for an orderly one.

The seventh element—also a variation—involves what might best be termed ambivalence. It has internal as well as external connotations. In democratic states, at least, different groups within the state possess different degrees of nationalistic feeling at any given point in time. One need not go far afield to demonstrate this: within the past few weeks I have seen or heard every kind of appeal from one demanding far greater sacrifice on the part of the American people for less privileged peoples overseas to a plea that all patriotic Americans refuse to receive United Nations Children's Fund Christmas cards. On World Brotherhood Sunday a politician advocates drastic cuts in foreign aid. During the Suez crisis in England, opinion clashed between every viewpoint from shame and horror that Britain had ever attacked at all to frustration and disgust that she failed to go ahead and "smash the wogs" altogether. When such differences are reflected in the party structure of a country, and the ascendancy of one party over its foes may mean a much more or a much less nationalistic policy, world order becomes very remote indeed.

The complexity of this factor becomes even more clear when we examine the external connotation of ambivalence. Someone once said that the trouble with Europe during the inter-war years lay principally in the failure of the swing of the political pendulum —left right, left right—in each of the key countries to synchronize with the swing in other countries. When the left came into control of the House of Commons, the right took over the *Popolo d'Italia.* When the Wilhelmstrasse was advocating concessions, the Quai d'Orsay was most insistent in its demands for French security. Only once, when Briand and Stresemann happened to be in office at the same time, did the pendulums swing together, and that produced the brief period known as "the sunshine of Locarno." The remainder of the twenty years lay under the shadow of blackening storm clouds. A similar failure to synchronize may be seen on a world scale today, though happily the Europeans seem to be getting along quite well together in the face of the Soviet threat. Here Indonesia becomes more nationalistic; there Japan becomes less so. Here Cuba adopts Fidelismo, there Argentina discards a dictator. Here Turkeys commits itself to a military pact, there Iraq (its capital having given the pact its very name) pulls out. And so it goes.

The last element of nationalism to which I wish to draw attention is perhaps the most fundamental: it is denial of the facts of interdependence. Only a primitive society can be self-sufficient; the more complex a society the more its members require one another, not just as individuals, but more especially as groups, or nations, in the world society. Yet self-sufficiency is nevertheless the goal of every unsophisticated nationalist. Politics denies what economics requires, just as history teaches that history does not teach. Nationalism refuses to accept any international control (or indeed even any influence) from the outside world if it can be avoided. It resists the adjustment and accommodation that an interdependent world demands. It is suspicious of negotiation, for negotiation may mean concessions, and to concede anything is to suffer a defeat. The "other" side's gain is "our" loss, and there is no recognition of the possibility that through negotiation both sides may gain more than they lose. International organization serves no purpose which the nationalist would concede is useful; he is not only hesitant but fearful about placing too much reliance and dependence upon it.

One hears a great deal these days about world public opinion—the appeal to world public opinion, the force of world public opinion, the necessity to listen to world public opinion—and even about "the conscience of the world." It may be, as Max Beloff has so forcefully argued on numerous occasions, that there is really no such thing as world public opinion. But to deny that there is such a thing as world communication would be to deny one of the most apparent and exciting and dangerous facts of contemporary international reality. How hackneyed the phrase about the world getting smaller all the time! But if this is so, does it not follow that in the nature of smaller places, things are getting more crowded all the time, and that in the nature of crowded places, there is more tension all the time, despite what the philosophical idealists and the travel agents may say about understanding and good will resulting from this? If there is more understanding, it is because people work at it, and not because of any automatic result of some new world-wide "togetherness." More communication may indeed simply make the competing voices seem more strident, demanding, and incompatible. What seems to be an automatic consequence of the increased ability, technically, of people to communicate with one another is an increased tendency on the part of the nation-state to block communication and restrict contacts across its borders, lest its people hear something that is not in accord with the image of reality which it is trying, through its monopoly of propaganda, to engender. Thus, as the techniques of sharing opinion, of encouraging contact, of promoting thought, of broadcasting ideas are improved, so also is the ability of the bureaucracy of nationalism to frustrate them. Jamming the radio waves is but one of the techniques utilized.

To summarize briefly, we have endeavored to show how nationalism, through its emotionalism, its stress upon differences, its narrow ethic, through its variations in form, its ambivalences, the different though simultaneous stages of its development, its necessity to forge a union between nation and state, and, above all, its denial of the reality of interdependence, operates as a centrifugal force in world order. Nationalism seems still to be, despite advances toward cooperation being made among the more mature states and despite the transnational character of communism, the most compelling characteristic of world politics in our time. The age of nationalism may be coming to an end, but if the end is in sight, it hardly promises to be a peaceful one. How curious—and how tragic—it would be if the final verdict of history were to be that Man so exaggerated his love of nation that he lost his world. Most of us could not share the coldly objective view ascribed to a cynical astronomer who, upon realizing that the earth was about to blow itself up, mused, "Oh, well, it was just a minor planet."

CHAPTER FOUR

Power and the Balancing Process

Confronted with a possibility of interstate conflict—a possibility that is seldom very remote—each government must constantly be concerned not only with its own economic, military, and political strength and influence, but that of others as well. The power of states in international relations is relative; hence their leaders must at all times be concerned with their own state's comparative position vis-à-vis that of other states. The studied attempt on the part of statesmen, in light of these realities and of their perception or understanding of them, so to adjust their country's power position as to serve its greatest advantage is often referred to as the pursuit of "balance of power policies," though, as the selection by Haas below indicates, this is not the only definition of that term. The ongoing adjustment of the various factors of power, both as conscious acts of decision-makers and as an "automatic" sequence of events, has been characterized by Professor Fox and others as "the balancing process." This kaleidoscopic process, which is taking place all the time in our dynamic world of shifting power relationships, is seen as a basic feature of the international system in which we live.

Several variations of meaning and usage of the term "balance of power" exist, but fundamentally there seem to be two: balance may connote an equal (or essentially equal) distribution of power between two sides, as a scale is "in balance," i.e., *equilibrium;* or it may mean *preponderance,* in a manner analogous to having a "balance in the bank," in the sense of possessing a surplus of assets over liabilities.[1] Yet neither of these conceptions covers one of the historically most effective applications of balance of power principles, that is, by Britain over a period of many decades when she endeavored to "hold the balance" by placing the weight of her strength and influence on the scales of European politics. By standing against the stronger powers in the scale, Britain sought to bring about the equilibrium between her potential enemies that would leave her safe and secure; once asked in a mid-Western American city to explain British foreign policy, Winston Churchill is reported to have risen

[1] For an instructive treatment of the balance of power in theory and practice, based upon examples drawn from historical situations, see especially Hans J. Morgenthau's discussion in any of the editions of *Politics Among Nations* (New York: Alfred A. Knopf, Inc.).

to the platform, said "support the weaker power on the Continent," and sat down.

As we have seen, the international political scene is characterized by the presence of an increasing number of autonomous units, each of which pursues certain self-defined (and sometimes ill-defined) goals, restrained as little as possible by others and apparently not at all by abstract moral principles. While the power and position of one's own state must be placed in the context of the power and position of various other states within the evolving international environment, there is no assurance that the goals, and particularly the means and options selected by the leaders of the respective governments in pursuit of those goals, will always harmonize. Indeed, it is precisely because disharmony frequently occurs that so much potential or actual international conflict exists.

For many states, an uneasy equilibrium may be all they can aspire to with any hope of achievement. Even this is beyond the capacities of some, who can only hope that a more powerful opposing neighbor may be engaged elsewhere or be otherwise unprepared to bring its whole power to bear upon their weak defenses. This common situation often explains why certain smaller and weaker states can "get away with so much" in their relationships with larger and stronger powers. Just as the United States benefited from this kind of situation—Europe's preoccupation with her internal balance of power throughout the 19th century—weak states benefit today from balance of power policies and uncertainties between the Soviet Union, the United States, and other major powers.

Occasionally the leaders of a state either can, or think they can, acquire the capability successfully to threaten and dominate its neighbors, so that they can altogether ignore the balancing process. Conversely, such statesmen as Woodrow Wilson have condemned the whole idea of the balance of power and have sought to create a new kind of world system, based upon law rather than upon power politics. Whatever the reasons for the failure of the League of Nations, statesmen after the Second World War nevertheless endeavored once again to establish a new kind of world system. For a time it appeared that the United Nations, including at least in its early years all of the Great Powers (as the League had not), might succeed, but whether international politics will *continue* to be dominated by the Cold War remains to be seen. While certain observers profess to discern the beginnings of the emergence of a quadri-polar balance, with Europe and China joining America and Russia on the scales, others regard the enhancement of Chinese and European strength as refinements and complications of an international system still bi-polar in its fundamental character. In contrasting the present configuration with that of the inter-war period, Hugh Seton-Watson has observed:

> Between the world wars there were seven Great Powers—five in Europe (Britain, France, Germany, Italy, Russia), one in Asia (Japan), and the United States of America. Since 1945 there have been two giant Powers, the United States and the Soviet Union. Admittedly the old Great Powers of Western Europe are still factors to be reckoned with, and in Asia there are two countries of vast population, China and India, which are capable of reaching giant power status within

a few decades. But the two giants of today overshadow the world in a manner that is new in human history.[2]

Historically, the more frequent manifestation of the balance of power has taken the form of a multiple balance, in which a larger number of states, fairly evenly matched, have shifted their alignments to correspond with their changing interests and their changing perceptions of the intentions of others. The operation of this balancing process has over considerable time resulted in the prevention of conflicts which might well have destroyed one or more of the participating states. Each state involved is interested, not only in maintaining or improving its own power position in absolute and relative terms, but also in preventing other states from becoming so strong that they might at some future time become dangerous. Participants in such a multiple balance of power system thus tend to coalesce against stronger members and come to the aid of weaker states which are threatened. Since coalitions are flexible, all participants proceed with caution and circumspection, lest the impression of unreasonable ambition on their part antagonize other members of the system and bring about a coalition between them. At least this is the theory of the multi-polar balance; critics of the theory and especially of the practice in the form of balance-of-power policies argue that, far from preserving peace and protecting the participants, it has always—sooner or later—brought on war, defeat and mutual destruction. It may be that the key to the argument lies in whether, without the application of the balancing principle, wars would have come *sooner* or *later;* no one has professed lately to see in it the formula for permanent peace.[3] But one must ask whether a state, especially one that lies in proximity to states "playing the game" and that has a relevant degree of strength of its own, can "opt out," or whether it has to be involved in the balancing process whether it endeavors to carry out a balance of power policy or not.

As in some previous historical periods, the contemporary situation is seen by some as a relatively simple balance, or a bi-polar distribution of power. But a bi-polar balance is usually regarded as being inherently even more brittle, unstable, and dangerous than a more complex system. The apparent simplified bi-polarity of the immediate postwar era may be giving way to a new configuration in which a growing number of states refuse to commit themselves to either side. Close attention to foreign office pronouncements and to propaganda claims and threats reveal that both systems, if not actually breaking up, are at least facing basic internal challenges. The Americans have been frustrated by French intransigence; the Russians have seen the initiative if not the control of world Communism pass from Moscow to Peking; and both blocs are rejected, resisted, or used by new states determined to join neither one.

Yet no new true Super-Power seems likely to appear very soon. Were

[2] *Neither War nor Peace* (London: Methuen & Co., Ltd., 1960), p. 9.

[3] Kenneth Thompson has observed that "it is a sobering fact that the nineteenth century was perhaps the most peaceful of modern centuries; the twentieth, by contrast, has been an epoch of unparalleled bloodshed," and that what characterized the earlier, more peaceful century was a "system of old-fashioned balance of power." "Collective Security Re-examined," *American Political Science Review,* **XLVII** (1953), 413.

Europe to unite, and were a United Europe to decide to make a bid for nuclear parity with America or Russia, it would probably have the industrial and technological capacity to do so. But nothing like this seems to be happening. Not only do many Europeans seem unwilling or unable to unite, but they seem to be content (or at least resigned) indefinitely to remain secure under the American nuclear umbrella. Like Britain, France is a member of the so-called nuclear club, but any ambition she may seem to have of becoming a contender with the Super-Powers by dominating Europe is clearly unrealistic. Germany, divided as a result of defeat, remains divided as a function of balance of power considerations. Its reunification seems impossible so long as America and Russia insist on remaining in the heart of Europe; yet, reunification also seems essential if a new Super-Power in Europe is to emerge. Despite what must be conceded to be giant strides toward becoming a modern state, the Chinese have far to go before attaining the technology a Super-Power requires. China lost prestige when she threatened India during the Kashmir crisis; she lost reputation for power when she failed to make good on her threat. Hence, eventually there may be four Super-Powers where there are now only two, but that day does not appear to be imminent.

Outside the Communist and NATO blocs, any challenge to the Super-Powers by the emergence of entirely new claimants seems even less possible than it may have a few years ago. India, while possessing many of the basic factors of great power, has difficulty managing them. Japan, though clearly a mature economic state performing its second miracle of industrialization, shows no sign of wanting a second try at regional or world domination, and could only acquire Super-Power status in league with China—a most unlikely combination. If Brazil possesses certain of the factors of great power, those she lacks would appear to deny her any significant power role in the years ahead. Therefore, what seems to be in prospect as we enter the last third of this breathtaking century is a continuation of modified bi-polarity.

States have employed a variety of methods to establish or maintain either a fairly equal power distribution with other states or a situation of preponderance. One of these has been termed "compensation," which consists in giving a state the equivalent of something of which it has been deprived. A recent example is the manner in which the Soviet Union undertook to compensate Poland for the loss of territorial claims on its Eastern frontier by extending its Western frontier into territory historically claimed by Germany. Another method involves a division of weaker states among much stronger states, so that the underlying power ratio among the dividing powers is essentially maintained; e.g. the various divisions of Poland in the eighteenth and twentieth centuries. Also instructive in this regard was the division of Africa among contending European colonial powers during the past century. As a method for keeping power relations constant (for everyone, that is, except the unfortunate victim), this has proved quite effective, provided the dividers are in fact interested in preserving a balance; in the case of the Munich agreement of 1938, four European states truncated a fifth without its consent, but instead of preserving peace, this only served temporarily to postpone war. A third method takes the form of agreements to establish buffer zones or states between actual or potential antagonists—areas over which both parties exercise agreed-upon degrees of influence. Persia (Iran) has been an example of this, and recent proposals for "disengagement" contemplate this type of solution to the conflict between the Soviet Union and the anti-Soviet coalition. Still another approach is represented by attempts within a state to strengthen its own power base relative to others by increasing or improving social cohesion, industrial and economic productivity, economic self-sufficiency, and armaments. This internalized approach is normally easier and hence more common than attempts to weaken the other side through the use of economic, psychological, political, or particularly military means, for such attempts may have to take the form of trying to split up existing coalitions, or reverting to the extremity of war. Finally and most frequently, states conclude alliances and even construct interlocking systems of alliances (if, as in the case of the United States today, a sufficient number of other states possess similar interests, intentions, and especially, security requirements). Such alliances may be purely defensive—to protect and preserve a given power position; or they may be offensive—designed to exert pressures to alter a given power situation and construct a new one.

In the balancing process, states may have opportunities for "equilibrium plus" in power contests with others. Such contests take place for two reasons. First, any power position is difficult, even impossible, to measure with any degree of precision, as will be seen in the discussion of "The Capability Inventory" below. Hence, since there is always a chance for error, each state tends to want to ensure that *its* error is on the side of safety and accordingly tries to acquire more than enough of the factors of power needed to guarantee its security. Second, a surplus of power, if attainable, is (like a surplus of funds) desirable, even if there are no immediate plans for its use. It provides psychological satisfaction, and, more significantly, it constitutes a reserve which can be drawn upon should there be necessity or opportunity to do so.

In assessing the viability of the balance of power, one must not forget the basic purposes which underlie the pursuit of power policies. First of all, the objective is to prevent another state or group of states from becoming so powerful as to threaten one's own security (however defined), or even one's own system of basic values, or possibly continued existence as a viable society. Second, any statesman wishes to see his own state powerful enough to withstand demands that others may make upon it. Third, he may hope to make certain demands upon others and have those demands honored.

The entire concept of balance of power, as a stabilizing force in international politics, has been criticized for its unreality, its imprecision, and its inherent danger. Despite such criticism, balance of power policies continue and will continue to be pursued. In terms of the processes which actually do exist in interstate relations, the balance of power is among the facts of international life. Regardless of one's value preferences (and recognizing the inappropriateness, suggested by Haas, of picturing balance of power policies as the sum total of *all* international politics), it seems evident that sophisticated policymakers of all countries really have no choice but to pursue some type of balance of power policies in order to protect and advance the interests of their state in a context in which these interests are constantly subject to challenge.

1

*Power Politics**

Martin Wight

MARTIN WIGHT *is Dean of the School of European Studies and Professor of History at the University of Sussex. He is a member of the Royal Institute of International Affairs and the author of* Power Politics (*1946*); British Colonial Constitutions (*1952*); *and co-author of* The World in March 1939 (*1952*).

The central principle in what we might call the "mechanics" of power politics is that of the Balance of Power, which describes the way Powers group themselves in a state of international anarchy. The Balance of Power is a phrase with two distinct meanings. It can be used either objectively or subjectively—to describe either a "law" or principle of international politics (a general statement of how Powers in fact behave), or a policy which may be adopted by a particular Power.

In the first sense, as a principle of international relations, the Balance of Power is an application of the fundamental law of self-preservation. If there are three Powers, of which the first attacks the second, the third cannot afford to see the second so decisively crushed that it becomes threatened itself; therefore if it is far-sighted enough it supports the second. When one Power grows dangerously strong, other Powers combine against it. The Balance of Power thus comes into play each time that a Dominant Power has tried to gain mastery of the world. The Dominant Power usually has a small entourage of vassal-states which are more frightened of defending their independence than of collaborating, and of jackal-states which have private local interests to pursue; but arrayed against them there arises a grand coalition of superior strength which finally wins. This is the extreme illustration of the Balance of Power.

The Balance of Power develops through various phases. First there can be a *multiple* balance, i.e. a balance similar to a chandelier. This was the normal state of Europe in the eighteenth century. In Western Europe and overseas there was the balance between Britain, France and Spain; in Central and Eastern Europe there was the balance between Austria and Prus-

* *Power Politics,* "Looking Forward" Pamphlets, No. 8 (1949), published by the Oxford University Press under the auspices of the Royal Institute of International Affairs. Reprinted by permission.

sia, Russia and Turkey. The balances interacted, and were completed by the smaller Powers. The Great Powers changed partners when their interests shifted as in a quadrille. . . . The multiple balance broke down, first with the War of American Independence and then decisively with the Revolutionary and Napoleonic War. The Vienna Settlement tried to restore it. . . . But the multiple balance can only last so long as there is international tranquillity and no vital issues arise to split the Great Powers. When this sooner or later occurs, the Great Powers divide into opposite camps, and the multiple balance is replaced by a *simple* balance: it is no longer a chandelier but a pair of scales. This was what happened in Europe with the creation of the Franco-Russian Alliance of 1893 against the Triple Alliance of Germany, Austria-Hungary and Italy; and again with the creation of the Berlin-Rome Axis in 1935 against the League Powers. The period of the simple balance is marked by heightened tension, a race between the two groups in armaments, and uneasy oscillations which we know as *crises.* Mr. Churchill has brilliantly described a crisis, writing of the pre-1914 Balance of Power:

> The great Powers marshalled on either side, preceded and protected by an elaborate cushion of diplomatic courtesies and formalities, would display to each other their respective arrays. In the forefront would be the two principal disputants, Germany and France, and echeloned back on either side at varying distances and under veils of reserves and qualifications of different density, would be drawn up the other parties to the Triple Alliance and to what was already now beginning to be called the Triple Entente. At the proper moment these seconds or supporters would utter certain cryptic words indicative of their state of mind, as a consequence of which France or Germany would step back or forward a very small distance or perhaps move slightly to the right or to the left. When these delicate rectifications in the great balance of Europe, and indeed of the world, had been made, the formidable assembly would withdraw to their own apartments with ceremony and salutations and congratulate or condole with each other in whispers on the result.

It was the same with the crises of the 1930's, except that the courtesies had worn thinner and the power was more naked. . . . And in due course the maneuverings for position cannot be prolonged, and the Balance of Power overbalances into war.

But there is not only the distinction between a multiple and a simple balance. We must also consider the confusion arising from the fact that the word balance itself has two meanings: it can mean *equilibrium,* and it can also mean *preponderance,* as when we say we have a balance in the bank—i.e., a plus, not an equality between assets and debits. This is the distinction between the objective and the subjective view of the Balance of Power. The historian will say that there is a balance when the opposing groups seem to him to be equal in power. The statesman will say that there is a balance when he thinks that his side is stronger than the other. And he will say that his country *holds* the balance, when it has freedom to join one side or the other according to its own interests. . . . The earliest known use of the phrase Balance of Power in English is, very appropriately, in a book dedicated to Queen Elizabeth in 1579: "God hath put into your hands the balance of power and justice, to appease and counterpoise at your will the actions and counsels of all the Christian kingdoms of your time." Since the day when Elizabeth broke the Anglo-Spanish alliance and threw

England on the side of France and the Dutch rebels against the Dominant Power of Spain, the Balance of Power has been the traditional British foreign policy. . . .

The Balance of Power is as nearly a fundamental law of politics as it is possible to find: it is easy to see from history that it is the way most Powers have pursued self-preservation in most cases. But rulers often make mistakes in their forecasts of power, and sometimes have other motives besides the interests of the state they rule. A good example of bungling the Balance of Power is provided by Italy in 1940. The German conquest of Western Europe immediately put Italy, like Britain, in mortal danger. In that crisis Italy might have chosen to throw itself on the side of Britain and the other resisting states, in order to preserve a balance against the Dominant Power. It did the reverse, because Mussolini was so fettered by his previous policy and by his hatred of Great Britain that he gladly anticipated its defeat. But it is unlikely that he had any illusions about the nature of his voracious ally. By not combining with Great Britain to form a real balance, he was driven into the futile policy of trying to establish a private balance between Italy and Germany. He accordingly made his ridiculous and contemptible invasion of Southern France, in order to buy prestige with as many casualties as he could manage before France surrendered, and thus to be able to meet Germany more as an equal. The result was that while Great Britain survived, Italy was occupied and ruined. This has been the usual fate of jackal Powers; . . . For we may notice that the law of the Balance of Power is the more true of states according to their strength, confidence and internal cohesion. Weak and corrupt states, and especially those ruled by an unrepresentative despotism or clique, tend to gravitate *towards* the Dominant Power; it is popular states without deep social cleavages (whether their governments be parliamentary democracy or a mass-party dictatorship) that tend to gravitate *away from* the Dominant Power.

* * *

Compensation

There are three chief ways in which the Balance of Power operates: by compensation, by intervention, and by the establishment of buffer states. . . .

In its simplest form compensation means giving a state the equivalent of something of which you deprive it: as when Russia takes from Poland the territory east of the Curzon Line and offers it most of East Prussia, Pomerania and Upper Silesia instead. This applies, of course, only to victorious Powers and their satellites; defeated Powers are usually deprived of territory without compensation. But in its more developed form, compensation means that one state cannot afford to see another increase its power without obtaining a proportionate increase, i.e. equality of aggrandizement. This was the principle on which, in the nineteenth century, the Great Powers approached the Eastern Question, partitioned Africa, and established spheres of influence in the Far East. . . .

By the principle of compensation, a Power can be forced to take part in an international transaction against its will. The classic example is the First Partition of Poland in 1772. Frederick the Great of Prussia and Catherine the Great of Russia had agreed on the partition; Maria Theresa of Austria could not afford to be left out. She opposed it on moral grounds, but her ministers did not, and reasons of state were paramount. "Elle pleurait, et prenait toujours," said Frederick cynically. A similar thing occurred when in August 1918 America joined the Allies in intervention in Russia. Wilson had steadily opposed intervention; but Britain, France and Japan forced his hand by sending troops themselves. America could not afford to allow the Japanese a free run in Siberia; Wilson at once reversed his policy and dispatched American troops, at the same time issuing a statement of the moral objections to intervention which was the Wilsonian equivalent of Maria Theresa's tears. It is the principle of compensation that made Russia join in the Second World War against Japan after the defeat of Germany; whatever the Russian desire for rest and recuperation, Stalin could not afford to see his allies settle the Pacific without an equal say himself.

Intervention

Intervention means interference by a Power in the internal affairs of another Power. We may classify it as either defensive or offensive, according to whether it aims at preserving or at altering the Balance of Power. The principle of defensive intervention might be stated thus: no Power can allow the Balance of Power to be decisively altered in its disfavour by a change of regime or policy in another state. Allied intervention in Russia in 1918–20 was of this kind; British intervention in Iraq in 1941 in order to frustrate Rashid Ali's coup d'etat provides a more dramatic and compelling instance. British intervention in Greece in 1944 probably also comes under this head. Offensive intervention is a technique of penetration and expansion, aimed at provoking a change of regime in another state or even at destroying its independence altogether. . . . It was the method used by . . . Germany and Italy to overthrow the government of Spain in the Spanish Civil War (1936–39). Russia's use of the Communist International in the early nineteen twenties and Nazi Germany's use of the fifth column represent the organization of this technique to an extent previously unknown. . . .

There is also non-intervention. Non-intervention, like neutrality, requires unassailable confidence and strength to be an effective policy, and a non-intervening Power is liable to have its hand forced if it cannot make other Powers follow non-intervention as well, as we have seen in the case of Wilson in 1918. Thus non-intervention is itself usually a positive, not a negative policy: a holding of the ring with a subtle bias in favour of one of the combatants. . . . Hence the truth of Talleyrand's sardonic remark, that "non-intervention is a political term meaning virtually the same thing as intervention." The Non-Intervention Committee during the Spanish Civil War gave a crowning and tragic illustration.

Intervention is frequent in the relations between a Great Power and its satellites. The classic example is the relations between the United States and Latin America. The United States proclaimed the Monroe Doctrine in 1823 to prevent intervention by the European Powers in Latin America; but as it grew in strength it turned the Doctrine inside out to justify intervention in Latin America on its own part. . . .

Intervention is the point at which domestic and international politics intersect, and there are particular opportunities for it in a period of conflicting ideologies; vertical national loyalties, so to speak, are then confused by horizontal loyalties. Most of the general wars have had a national civil war as a principal feature.

Buffer Zones

A buffer zone is an area occupied by a weaker Power or Powers between two or more stronger Powers. It will be the vital interest of each stronger Power to prevent the other from controlling the buffer zone, and each will pursue this interest in one of two ways, according to its strength: either by seeking to establish its own control over the buffer zone, transforming it into a protectorate or a frontier province, or by maintaining its neutrality and independence. Buffer states can therefore be roughly divided into neutral states and protectorates. Neutral states are states without an active foreign policy at all; protectorates are states whose foreign policy is controlled by another Power.

* * *

Each of the Dominant Powers in Europe at the height of its power has absorbed a buffer state, whose independence has been re-established as vital to the general interests of Europe after the Dominant Power has been defeated. . . .

The most important buffer zone in the world is that dividing Russia from the British Empire. Russia lies in the long curve of the British Empire rather like an egg in a spoon, but the two are separated by a layer of weak states stretching from the Near to the Far East. Britain's great anxiety throughout the nineteenth century was to keep this layer intact. . . .

It is broadly true that politics, like nature, abhors a vacuum; and buffer states cannot achieve stability and security on their own. This was the great weakness of the belt of East European Powers between Germany and Russia under the Versailles Settlement—the Middle Zone. It came into existence while Germany and Russia had temporarily ceased to be Great Powers, but it could not be maintained without relation to them; least of all could it be, as the Allies seem to have hoped, a wall to hem them both in. As soon as the two had resumed their strength they moved into this vacuum again, as the prelude to conflict between themselves. But the Second World War, by destroying Germany, France, and Italy as Great Powers, has turned the whole of Europe into the buffer zone between Russia and Anglo-America. In Eastern Europe Russia is building up a frontier belt of friendly and satellite states, a glacis against invasion; the West European seaboard, with Britain as the great outpost, is equally vital to America. In between lies the vacuum of defeated Germany; and it is in its partition into spheres of influence, its neutralization, or its movement into the orbit of one or other of the victorious Great Powers, that we shall trace the shifting or stabilization of the Balance of Power in the next twenty or thirty years.

2

*The Balance of Power: Concept, Prescription or Propaganda**

Ernst Haas

ERNST HAAS, *Professor of Political Science at the University of California (Berkeley), is the co-author of an outstanding text,* The Dynamics of International Relations (1956). *His* The Uniting of Europe: Political, Social, and Economic Forces, 1950–1957 (1958), *is an original study of the underlying problems and forces working for and against European unity. He is a frequent contributor to journals in the field of international relations and organization, and has recently published* Beyond the Nation-State: Functionalism and International Organization (1964), *a theoretical study of functionalism and a specific case study of the International Labor Organization.*

NOTE: *In preceding sections of this article, not reprinted because of lack of space, Professor Haas discusses the following possible meanings of the term "balance of power": 1. distribution of power; 2. equilibrium; 3. hegemony; 4. stability and peace; 5. instability and war; 6. power politics; 7. a universal law of history; 8. a system and guide to policy-making. He now addresses himself to the task of analyzing the meanings and intentions of those who use the term.*

. . . .

BALANCE OF POWER AS DESCRIPTION

Forswearing any theoretical or analytical purpose, writers commonly have recourse to the term "balance of power" in discussing international affairs. Current references to the balance of power by journalists and radio commentators most frequently fall into this category. And in most instances the meaning to be conveyed to the audience merely implies "distribution" of power, rather than "balance" in anything like the literal sense. . . .

On other occasions, however, the descriptive use of the term implies more than a mere distribution of power. It may then come to mean "equilibrium" or even "hegemony" or "preponderance" of power, still without implying more than a descriptive intent. It is quite possible that the political motivations of the particular user may make their entrance at this point. Thus Lisola, writing in the seventeenth century, saw in the balance of power the equilibrium between Hapsburg and Bourbon interests. But he used his description to counsel war on France in order to maintain that very equilibrium. Austrian writers again invoked the balance of power principle during the wars of the Polish and Austrian Succession in order to secure allies against France and Prussia, represented as seeking hegemony. During the preceding century, French writers had used the equilibrium connotation of the term to demand war on

* Excerpt from *World Politics,* V (1953), 459–474. Reprinted by permission.

Austria. And it might be pointed out parenthetically that during the Seven Years' War British officials frowned on the use of balance of power terms to justify British aid to Prussia, since it was Frederick II who had "disturbed the balance" with his attack on Austria. In all these writings and statements the term "balance of power" is used and abused as a descriptive phrase, connoting the existence or non-existence of equilibrium and the actual or threatened hegemony of some state or alliance. The same easy transition in meaning from "distribution" to "equilibrium" and finally to "hegemony" can sometimes be detected in contemporary references to the balance of power. These usages are rarely kept in their separate compartments. And, when the users' intentions go beyond that of mere description, clarity of thought and purpose may be seriously jeopardized.

Balance of Power as Propaganda and "Ideology"

A precise understanding of the verbal meaning of the term "balance of power" becomes especially important when it is used as a propagandistic slogan or as an ideological phrase. . . . The meanings of "balance" as being identical with either "peace" or "war" fall into this category. Obviously, while it might be correct to speak of a state of balance or imbalance *implying* or *engendering* either war or peace, the balance as such cannot logically be equated with conditions which might arise as a consequence of the balance, i.e., war or peace. In the cases in which the authors employed it to mean "peace" or "war," "balance of power" then became no more than a convenient catchword to focus individual aspirations into a generally acceptable mold; and there can be no doubt that at certain times the concept of balance was an extremely popular one, whether it was used for policymaking or not. If used in a patently forced manner, the term becomes indistinguishable from plain propaganda. . . .

(*Professor Haas cites some examples of the usage of the term for propaganda purposes. Ed.*)

It is apparent that . . . the balance of power was invoked in such a way as to serve as the justification for policies not *ipso facto* related to balancing anything. In some instances it was used to cloak ideological conflicts, in others to sanctify the search for hegemony over Europe, and in still others to "justify" the continued strength and size of a defeated state. The significance of this invocation, then, lies not in any theoretical belief, but in the fact that the users of the term felt so convinced of its popularity as to make its conversion into a symbol of proper policy propagandistically profitable.

Propaganda assumes the dishonest use of facts and the distortion of concepts devised on intellectually sincere grounds. It implies conscious and deliberate falsification.[1] Ideology, as defined by Mannheim, however, postulates belief in a set of symbols which, even though they may be "false" ob-

[1] My conception of propaganda may be expressed in Leonard W. Doob's definition: "International propaganda is a systematic attempt by an interested individual (or individuals) to control the attitudes of groups of individuals through the use of suggestion and, consequently, to control their actions." *Propaganda* (New York: Holt, Rinehart & Winston, Inc. 1935) p. 89. It is clear that this postulation does not assume that the propagandist himself accepts the material or shares the attitudes he attempts to disseminate. I cannot accept the definition of propaganda offered by Doob in *Public Opinion and Propaganda* (New York: Holt, Rinehart, & Winston, Inc., 1948), p. 240, since it seems almost indistinguishable from the more general concept of ideology.

jectively, still characterize the total myth system of social groups and are essential to the spiritual cohesion of a ruling group which would lose its sense of control if it were conscious of the "real" state of affairs. It is therefore possible to raise the hypothesis that the balance of power may have served such "ideological" purposes. It may have been used to explain policies in terms of natural laws, in terms of moral rightness, or in terms of historical necessity if the symbol chosen to "put it over" was a sufficiently widely accepted one; indeed, if it was a symbol —even a metaphorical one—which the ruling groups themselves tended to accept. In this sense, the term "balance of power" would not serve a strictly propagandistic purpose, since the element of falsification yields to the element of self-deception.[2]

In a remarkable eighteenth-century essay the whole concept of the balance of power was criticized in these very terms. In his *Die Chimäre des Gleichgewichts von Europa,* Justi concluded that the balance of power theory is nothing but the ideological justification adopted by statesmen eager to hide their real motives, motives usually described by the term "aggression." . . .

* * *

. . . he urges what he considers the real *raison d'être* of the usage, thus, incidentally, coming perilously close to characterizing the balance of power as a purely propagandistic device:

When a state which has grown more powerful internally is attacked . . . in order to weaken it, such action is motivated least of all by the balance of power. This would be a war which is waged by the several states against the strong state for specific interests, and the rules of the balance of power will only be camouflage under which these interests are hidden. . . . States, like private persons, are guided by nothing but their private interests, real or imaginary, and they are far from being guided by a chimerical balance of power. Name one state which has participated in a war contrary to its interests or without a specific interest, only to maintain the balance of power.[3]

The distinction between the propagandistic and ideological uses is thus a tenuous one. The "camouflage" is ideological only if the actors on the international stage are themselves convinced, to some extent, of the identity of "private interest" with a general need for balancing power *qua* power.

BALANCE OF POWER AS ANALYTICAL CONCEPT

At the opposite pole of the propaganda-oriented application of the term "balance of power" lies the user's intention to employ the term as a tool of analysis. It is in this area of intentions that the term rose to the status of a theory of international relations during the eighteenth and nineteenth centuries, no less than it has in our own era. It is also true, however, that in

[2] For a masterful analysis of this aspect of the balance of power, see Alfred Vagts, "The Balance of Power: Growth of an Idea," *World Politics,* I (October, 1948), 88–89, 100ff. I have explored the ideological significance of the concept with respect to European diplomacy in the 1830's in my doctoral dissertation, *Belgium and the Balance of Power,* Columbia University Library.

[3] J. H. G. von Justi, *Die Chimäre des Gleichgewichts von Europa* (Altona, 1758) p. 65. Albert Sorel's estimate of the invocation of balancing terminology by statesmen is a similar one. Since he denies that balancing policies are deliberately chosen by diplomats and since he urges that only the search of unilateral hegemony motivates policy, he argues in fact that the use of the term by statesmen implies a disguised hankering for superiority and no more. Albert Sorel, *L'Europe et la Revolution française* (Paris, 1908), p. 34.

this area as well as in the other fields of intentions analyzed so far, not one but several of the verbal meanings of the term find application. Even as a tool of scholarly analysis the term has been used to mean "power politics," "equilibrium," "hegemony" and, finally a "universal law" of state conduct.

"The basic principle of the balance of power," wrote Réal de Curban, "is incontestable: the power of one ruler, in the last analysis, is nothing but the ruin and diminution of that of his neighbors, and his power is nothing but the weakness of the others."[4] And in a Hobbesian state of nature which was presupposed to exist among sovereign states no other conclusion seemed possible. This reasoning has led numerous writers to equate the balance of power with power politics or *Realpolitik* generally. The struggle for self-preservation in the state of nature implies the formation of alliances and mutually antagonistic blocs which in turn make negotiations in "good faith" a contradiction in terms. Power politics are the only discernible pattern in which balancing is an inherent process. As such, it is not separate from but identical with competitive power struggles. Consequently, in dispassionate analyses of international affairs the "balance" of power carries no significance other than that usually associated with "power politics," unrefined by any conception of equilibrium or deliberate balancing measures.[5]

Furthermore, the concept of evenly balanced power, or "equilibrium," finds frequent application as a tool of analysis. In the preceding discussion the equilibrium concept found application merely as a descriptive phrase implying no generalized behavior patterns in international relations. In the present context the reverse is true. Lasswell, in speaking of the "balancing process," for instance, assumes that under conditions of expected future violence—domestic as well as international—any increase in the coercion potential of one power unit will lead to a compensatory increase in the competing unit or units. Further increases on the part of one side will always bring corresponding increases on the part of its competitors, so that in effect a rough equality of power potential will always prevail, a factor which may make for either open conflict or induce fear of refraining from hostilities, depending on circumstances, the nature of the elites in question, and the accuracy of intelligence reports concerning the degree of "balancing." The analytical application of the equilibrium-meaning of the balance of power, in short, generalizes the basic assumption of the absence of international consensus and the consequent inherent presence of conflict into a pattern of balancing.

Carrying the equilibrium-meaning one step further results in the application of the balance of power concept as implying the search for hegemony. This application again finds its counterpart in the intentions of detached analysts striving for a generalized understanding of phenomena rather than for description. Spykman, . . . clearly sets forth the assumptions of this approach. His argument is that the search for power by sovereign states is an end in itself, since conflict—actual or potential—is the only consistent pattern in relations between state units. While the search for power originally implied the desire for self-preserva-

[4] Gaspard de Réal de Curban, *La science du gouvernement* (Paris, 1764), VI, 442.

[5] See, e.g., H. N. Brailsford and G. Lowes Dickinson, as quoted in Georg Schwarzenberger, *Power Politics,* London, 1940, p. 123, and also the author's own comments, which also tend to equate power politics with power balance.

tion, a generalized desire for power-seeking over a long period of time converts this process into an end in itself. On this level, the discussion of the balance of power is identical with power politics generally. As in the case of Lasswell's balancing process, however, the generalized process of competitive power-seeking must result in equilibrium if war is avoided—temporarily. But statesmen, as indicated above, seek a margin of safety in superiority of power and not in equality of power. Hence the search for equilibrium in effect is the search for hegemony, and the balance of power as an analytical concept becomes another term for the simultaneous search for preponderance of power by all the sovereign participants. No wonder Spykman exclaims that

> He who plays the balance of power can have no permanent friends. His devotion can be to no specific state but only to balanced power. The ally of today is the enemy of tomorrow. One of the charms of power politics is that it offers no opportunity to grow weary of one's friends. England's reputation as *perfide Albion* is the inevitable result of her preoccupation with the balance of power.[6]

In this refined analysis, the balance of power comes to be considered as a special case—either in its equilibrium or its hegemony connotation—in the general pattern of power politics, though Spykman in the passage just cited again tends to use the two terms interchangeably.

The supreme attempt to use the balance of power as an analytical concept arises in the case of those writers who make the balance the essence of a theory of international relations. It is here that the balance attains the quality of a "law of history," . . . Professors Morgenthau and Schuman, for instance, in giving the balance of power this extended meaning, go beyond the characterization of equilibrium and hegemony. They develop the thesis that it is inherent in the nature of a multi-state system based on sovereignty to engage in mutually hostile policies, for whatever motives. In this process the search for balanced power, the need to form blocs and counterblocs to prevent the feared attainment of hegemony by one or the other of the participants in the conflict is a natural, if not instinctive, choice of policy. A group of revisionist states always lines up against a group of states devoted to the maintenance of the status quo in such a way that approximate balance results. So general is this pattern that it attains the quality of a historical law. And the characteristic feature of this law is that it does not necessarily assume a conscious intention on the part of statesmen to "balance power with power" in a sense which would imply the official acceptance of a balance of power theory by governments. Statesmen, to be sure, may be consciously motivated by balancing notions. But, if they are not, the policies which they would most logically adopt would be those consistent with the balance of power. As Professor Morgenthau indicates, if they fail to do so, they do not make "logical" policy and thereby violate historically proven and generalized modes of conduct. The distinctive feature about the balance of power applied as a tool of analysis, then, is its possible separation from the motivations of governments.

BALANCE OF POWER AS PRESCRIPTION

While the analytical application of the term does not imply conscious ac-

---

[6] Nicholas J. Spykman, *America's Strategy in World Politics* (New York: Harcourt, Brace & World, Inc., 1942), pp. 1–21, 103–4.

ceptance of balancing rules by governments, there is a large body of thought—historical and contemporary—which does insist that the balance of power is—or should be—a guiding principle for decision-making on the part of governments. It is this application of the term which makes use of the meaning defined above as "guide-and-system." Once more international relations are pictured, in one version, as being in the Hobbesian state of nature, so that survival dictates the formation of alliances among those states committed to "preserving the balance" against the onslaught of the state(s) allegedly seeking world or regional domination or, as the eighteenth-century writers put it, "universal monarchy." In this sense, the balance is a conscious guide dictating the rules of survival. In another sense, however, the world (or Europe, in the earlier writing) is represented as a "system" of states tied together by mutual interdependence, common institutions, and a common system of law (the law of nations), and the search for hegemony of a single member of this "system" was then represented as an attack upon the whole organic unit. The system was based on the continued independence of all members and their common will to resist the search for hegemony by any one of their number. The balance of power was inherent in the very system itself and also acted as a body of rules dictating the proper policies for preventing the attainment of hegemony, i.e., it acted as a "guide."

That Metternich subscribed in principle and in considerable detail to the theory of the balance of power as a guide to foreign policy-making is beyond any doubt. Consistent with his over-all political philosophy of the value of historically sanctioned social and political traditions, of the need for preserving what the historical process had created and for protecting it against the fanaticism and stupidity of misguided men, i.e., the liberals, Metternich considered the balance of power as another of these time-hallowed doctrines, and as an international institution vital to the preservation of the total institutional status quo which he so cherished. As he wrote:

Politics is the science of the life of the state, on its highest level. Since isolated states no longer exist . . . it is the society of states, this important condition of the contemporary world, which has to be watched carefully. Thus each state, in addition to its particular interests, has certain common interests, either with the totality of the other states or with certain groups among them. The great axioms of political science derive from the understanding of real political interests, of all states; the guarantee for their existence rests in these general interests, whereas particular interests . . . only possess a relative and secondary value. History teaches that whenever the particular interests of one state are in contradiction with the general interest and whenever the latter is neglected or misunderstood, this condition . . . is to be regarded as exceptional and pathological. . . . The modern world is characterized, in distinction to the old world, by a tendency of states to approach one another and to enter into the bonds of society in some manner; so that the resulting bond rests on the same foundations as the great society which developed in the shadow of Christianity. This foundation consists of the command of the Book of Books: "Do not do unto others what you would not have others do unto you." Applying this basic rule of all human associations to the state, the result is reciprocity, politically speaking, and its effect is . . . : mutual respect and honest conduct. In the ancient world, politics sought pure isolation and practiced absolute egoism, without any control save common sense. . . . Modern history, however, shows us the application of the principle of solidarity and the balance of power offers us the drama of the unified efforts of several states in restraining the hegemony of a single state and limiting the expansion of its influence, and thus forcing it to return to public law.[7]

This formulation of international relations in general as necessary and close rapport between the states of Europe, which he regarded in the then customary manner as so many atoms in a universe held together by Christian moral rules and the dictates of international law, and of the balance of power as the *ad hoc* regulating mechanism of this system, is in almost all respects identical with the formulation of Ancillon, of Castlereagh, of Brougham, and of Gentz. Thus Ancillon, Prussian court chaplain in the 1820's, tutor to Frederick William IV, and State Secretary for Foreign Affairs from 1832 until 1835, argued:

All forces are similar to the nature of expanding bodies; thus, in the society of large states in which law does not enjoy an external guarantee, we take as our point of departure the possible or even probable misuse of force. What will be the result? Mutual distrust, fear and restlessness, always recurring and always effective. Each state can have no other maxims in its external relations than these: whoever can do us damage through an excessive balance of power in his favor, or through his geographical position, is our natural enemy, but whoever in view of his position and forces is able to harm our enemy, is our natural friend. These simple maxims which the need for self-preservation has given to man, are and have been at all times the anchors on which all of politics rests.[8]

Nor was Castlereagh's understanding of the balance of power much different, even though he indicated that "my real and only object was to create a permanent counterpoise to the power of France in peace as well as in war." The Concert of Europe through its regular conferences was merely to be the consultative mechanism whereby the *ad hoc* balance could be maintained through timely negotiations.[9] However, the likelihood of the guide-and-system version of the balance implying different "rules" for different states is here betrayed.

Gentz's theory of the balance of power was stated in his *Fragmente aus der neusten Geschichte des politischen Gleichgewichts in Europa* (1806), the purpose of which was to give the Austrian and British governments an excuse for unleashing a new war on Napoleon without having been attacked first. Gentz, it might be added, was in the pay of the British cabinet to produce writings of this type. He rejected the arguments that an exact equilibrium is impossible and that power cannot be measured as irrelevant to the system, since all the system requires is eternal vigilance that no state acquires enough power to overawe all of Europe.[10] Also, he thought that the certainty of a strong counterforce being mustered against the hegemony-

---

[7] Metternich, *Aus Metternichs Nachgelassenen Papieren* (Vienna, 1882), I, 32ff., a section entitled, "Maxims on Which the Actions of My Political Career Have Been Based."

[8] Paul Haake, *J. P. F. Ancillon und Kronprinz Friedrich Wilhelm IV, von Preussen* (Munich, 1920), p. 40. Of Ancillon's own works, see his *Ueber den Geist der Staatsverfassungen und dessen Einfluss auf die Gesetzgebung* (Berlin, 1825), pp. 16–19, 313–314, 317–331, and *Tableau des révolutions du système de l'Europe* (Paris, 1806), IV, 5–19.

[9] Sir Charles Webster, *British Diplomacy, 1813–1815* (London, 1921), pp. 62, 218; and Castlereagh's memorandum of October 30, 1814, for Alexander I, cited in Angeberg, *Les traités de Vienne* (Paris, 1864), pp. 399–401.

[10] Gentz, *Fragmente aus der neusten Geschichte des politischen Gleichgewichts in Europe* (St. Petersburg, 1806), pp. 1–8.

seeker was a sufficient deterrent and that actual war would usually be unnecessary. And

> Only when one or the other state, with open violence, invented pretexts, or artificially concocted legal titles undertakes enterprises which, directly or in their inevitable consequences, lead to the enslavement of its weaker neighbors, or to the constant endangering, gradual weakening and eventual demise of its stronger neighbors, only then there will come about a breach of the balance, according to the sound conceptions of the collective interest of a system of states; only then will the several states combine in order to prevent the hegemony of a single state, through a timely contrived counterweight.[11]

Yet Gentz opposed policies of partition and compensation as violating the true conservative character of the theory. Moreover, there could be no such thing as indifference to a given issue, since under the power rules all issues had to be of equal interest to all states in the system.[12] His comments on the right to intervene in the domestic affairs of other states are of the highest interest. Gentz urged that ideological distastes for internal changes elsewhere did not in themselves constitute a ground for balance of power intervention and war. But as soon as such changes had the necessary consequence of upsetting the balance of power, i.e., as soon as the new ideology seemed to suggest the search for hegemony, then the right to intervene existed, as in 1793.[13]

The case of Lord Brougham is a fascinating one for the study of the theory of the balance of power. In his essay on "The Balance of Power," written in 1903, he urged that the balance was the only tenable theory of international relations. He defined it in the same terms as Gentz and Ancillon and added:

> Had it not been for that wholesome jealousy of rival neighbors, which modern politicians have learned to cherish, how many conquests and changes of dominion would have taken place, instead of wars, in which some lives were lost, not perhaps the most valuable in the community and some superfluous millions were squandered! How many fair portions of the globe might have been deluged in blood, instead of some hundreds of sailors fighting harmlessly on the barren plains of the ocean, and some thousands of soldiers carrying on a scientific and regular and quiet system of warfare in countries set apart for the purpose, and resorted to as the arena where the disputes of nations might be determined.

The old argument of the tacit federation of Europe, the common system of law and morals, and the need for the regulating mechanism of the balance to keep one of the "federated" states from absorbing the others is restated in full.[14] The principle, as well as the detailed application of the theory in its guide-and-system form, were stated by the young Brougham in the classical manner, and with unsurpassed and brief lucidity:

> It is not then in the mere plan for forming offensive or defensive alliances; or in the principles of attacking a neighbor in order to weaken his power, before he has betrayed hostile views; or in the policy of defending a rival, in order to stay, in proper time, the progress of a common enemy; it is not in these simple maxims that the modern system consists. These are indeed the elements, the great and leading parts of the theory; they are the maxims dictated by the plainest and coarsest views of political expediency: but they do not form the whole system;

[11] *Ibid.*, pp. 10–14.
[12] *Ibid.*, ch. II.
[13] *Ibid.*, ch. IV.
[14] Brougham, *Works* (London, 1872), VIII, 4–12.

nor does the knowledge of them . . . comprehend an acquaintance with the profounder and more subtile parts of modern policy. The grand and distinguishing feature of the balancing theory, is the systematic form to which it reduces those plain and obvious principles of national conduct; the perpetual attention to foreign affairs which it inculcates; the constant watchfulness which it prescribes over every movement in all parts of the system; the subjection in which it tends to place all national passions and antipathies to the views of remote expediency; the unceasing care which it dictates of national concerns most remotely situated, and apparently unconnected with ourselves; the general union, which it has effected, of all the European powers in one connecting system—obeying certain laws and actuated, for the most part, by a common principle; in fine, as a consequence of the whole, the right of mutual inspection, now universally recognized among civilized states, in the appointment of public envoys and residents [sic]. This is the balancing theory.[15]

Intervention in domestic developments of other states, of course, is legal if the balance of power is really and truly threatened by these changes. The superiority of the balance to all ideological considerations, so plainly stated here, is especially striking. This principle he repeated in his "General Principles of Foreign Policy" (1843) in most emphatic terms:

But the mere circumstance of our preferring a democratic to an aristocratic or a monarchical to a republican scheme of government, can never afford any good ground for uniting with others who have the same preference, against a community or a league of states, whose views of national polity are of a contrary description.[16]

[15] *Ibid.*, pp. 12–13, 33–38.

[16] *Ibid.*, pp. 70–71, 77, 79–80, 80–83.

Hence the Holy Alliance—or the Western bloc against it after 1832—was not consistent with the rules of the balance. Not only is ideological intervention condemned, but Brougham urged that

It is the bounden duty of all rulers to discourage sentiments in their subjects leading to national enmities; and when a popular cry arises against any foreign people, a general clamor of war, there is no more sacred duty on the part of the government than to resist such a clamor and keep the peace in spite of it.[17]

In short, any manifestations of public opinion had to be rigorously excluded from policy-making under balancing rules, a sentiment heard more and more frequently in our present epoch.

Whether the balance of power is regarded merely as a set of rules to be applied to the preservation of the state or whether it is expanded into the defensive mechanism of some "system"—and by analogy the United Nations system might today be considered the successor to the European system postulated by the earlier writers—the rules laid down by Gentz and Brougham remain the same. The statesman who is anxious to preserve his state must have recourse to balancing principles in averting the hegemony of his rival. The perusal of the contemporary literature on this subject confirms this conclusion. George F. Kennan's *American Diplomacy* is merely the latest and best-known example of the continuing importance ascribed to balancing in rules international relations. And the fact that the examples cited concerned statesmen conscious of the balance as a motivating force underlines the possible importance of the concept as prescription.

[17] *Ibid.*, pp. 91–93, 100–102.

Part II

The Capability Inventory

CHAPTER FIVE

The Measurement of States' Capacities in Their Foreign Relations

One of the most important, and yet one of the most difficult, tasks for the student and practitioner of international relations deals with the analysis of the capability of states to formulate and implement their policy objectives.

The task is important because this analysis helps to comprehend facets of the relations among states which might otherwise remain incomprehensible. On one level we can say that since force and the threat of force constitute the ultimate recourse regulating international relations, states can neither afford to neglect the elements which make up their respective arsenals of force, nor can they neglect to consider and compare these with those of other states. This is true, even if the force itself is never used. In fact, force that is *not* used may be more effective (as a deterrent) than force that is in use or that has been used. But a discussion of state capabilities must not be confined, as it has too often been in the past, to elements of, and capabilities for, physical coercion. "Capability" has many sides—and such aspects as resources, productive capacity, scientific inventiveness, technological "know-how," diplomatic skill, governmental efficiency and stability, cohesiveness, confidence, ideological commitment, and morale may in many instances be more relevant to the understanding of an international relationship than the coercive forces at the disposal of the governments involved. Sprout defines the "political potential" of states in terms of the *combined* coercive power and noncoercive influence which states can bring to bear on other states.

In analyzing state capability, it is useful to caution against the temptation to think in deterministic categories. These appear all too easily in thought and discussion. A country's geographic position, its economic potential, or its military capability, for example, will undoubtedly affect its policies, but the relationship is usually not a direct, automatic, causal one. Professor Jones places this matter into proper perspective by relating capabilities to strategies, and the excerpt from Professor Sprout emphasizes the same point by advocating the use of the term "political potential" instead of the term "power." This is sound advice, not only because of the coercive and military connotations of the term "power," but also because the term "potential" draws attention to the fact that men in positions of influence and control can *choose* whether or not, and if so in what ways and to what extent, to transform potentialities into actualities.

In fact, with the advent of weapons systems of unprecedented destructive capacity, we may well have reached a terminal point in traditional capability analysis, because the very power of these systems renders them useless in practice. Their use can scarcely be contemplated in pursuit of any legitimate and rational objective. Hence, we are in the presence of a "new fact" in the study of international relations, in the face of which we may have to make provision in our power calculations for those instruments of force that, because of their magnitude and potency, are in practice unusable.

Some authorities have proposed that environmental factors (capacities, political potential) become important and relevant only as they are perceived and taken into account by policy-makers; that the way in which they become important is closely linked to the decision-making formula; that the analysis of state capability consists of calculating the opportunities and limitations which are implicit in the environment of the state under consideration, and that capability calculations are always carried out within the framework of assumptions regarding the objectives and strategies of the state concerned.[1] The latter point is extremely important to bear in mind in the study of this and succeeding chapters. The question whether or not a given country is "powerful" can never be answered except in conjunction with a statement of the situation, objectives, and relationships within which the power or capability is to be exercised. This draws attention to the fact that capability involves not only the country which attempts to exercise its power and influence, but also the country or countries over which such power and influence are to be exercised. The best situation, of course, is one in which interests are (or can be made to appear to be) in harmony, so that coercion does not have to be contemplated in the first place. It also implies that such ingredients of international relationships as reputation and prestige may be among a country's most important capabilities.

In attempting to measure capability, it is useful to keep certain considerations clearly in mind:

1. The student of international relations should never forget that the ingredients in the comparative analysis are *multiple*—and, further, that these

[1] Harold and Margaret Sprout, *Foundations of International Politics* (Princeton: D. Van Nostrand Co., Inc., 1962), Chap. 4, "Power, Political Potential, and International Capabilities."

various ingredients interact with one another. Calculations of the capacity of a given society are almost never soundly based if they are based on only a single factor—be that factor geography, demography, economics, or even military capacity. What is needed is a type of "grand estimate," involving all the elements which may, for the particular purpose at hand, be relevant.

2. The ingredients which one must study are *dynamic;* they are always subject to change. Given the present state of research and technological capabilities in many countries, some of these changes may come about with extreme rapidity. This means that evaluations once made must be constantly renewed. Any change in any of the components affects the capability of one society vis-à-vis another. Countries rise and decline in their capacity to achieve objectives. The cause for either rise or decline may be internal or external, within or beyond the competence of a country to regulate or control. The student of international relations must be sensitive and alert to all changes in the capability constellation; above all, he must never take the permanency of any given situation for granted.

3. The various elements which constitute a given country's "capability arsenal" must be studied on a *comparative* basis with similar elements—or "mixes" of elements—in specific other countries. It is very tempting—and relatively easy—to compare a given country with itself at a previous time or stage. This type of auto-comparison is not without value or relevance, because it can provide information about the direction and speed of trends within a society. But the student of international relations is, by definition, concerned with relations *between* societies, and hence with comparisons between them. The more specific one is about the comparisons to be made, the more useful the analysis will be. Professor Jones is entirely correct in suggesting that the *margin* of power between two countries is more important than the absolute power of either country. Being specific in these matters also permits the student to discriminate more carefully between a variety of possible situations. A country may, for example, be deficient in one aspect of capability as compared with another country, but may make up for this deficiency in other ways. Country A may be militarily (or economically, or politically) "weak" compared with country X, but at the same time quite "strong" when compared with country Y. This simple example also draws attention to the fact that in many cases one must attempt to compare not only single countries, but combinations, coalitions, alliances, groups of countries—a task further complicated by the fact that, in addition to performing the necessary calculations for a number of countries, one must then also estimate the cohesiveness of the groupings involved.

4. Given the complexity of the task, there is considerable temptation to look for short-cuts in evaluating a country's capabilities. One cannot say that such short-cuts are never useful; but the conscientious student should not be carried away with trying to resolve complex problems by overly simple means. Professor Jones cautions against such short-cuts as comparisons of national income or gross national product. Similar cautions can be cited against comparisons of steel production, of the production or consumption of energy, and

so forth. In the long run, there seems to be no substitute for the type of "grand estimate" spoken of above. One of the reasons is that most short-cuts tend to overlook what Professor Jones has called "modifiers" of a power inventory—such factors as quantity, availability, sustaining capacity, substitution capacity, qualitative differences, and the like. They also tend to disregard the *uses* to which the item in question is being put.

5. Let us assume for the moment that all necessary information was readily at one's disposal (a most unrealistic assumption, to be sure). Another problem would yet confront us—namely, how to *weight* the various ingredients; as they are composed of different qualities and types, one cannot simply add them together. It is at this point that assumptions about possible uses of capabilities must enter the analysis. For example, does one assume relatively stable and peaceful relationships? Or does one posit the probability of coercive types of relationships? Does one envisage an active policy on a localized, on a broad regional, or even on a world-wide basis?

6. What all of this adds up to is the fact that evaluations of power—"grand estimates"—can in the nature of things not be precise. In view of the limitations upon accurate measurement of national power, it is best visualized as a matrix in which the ingredients are always in flux both in relation to one another and in relation to the power matrices of other countries. All one can hope for is that the questions that are asked be defined as precisely as possible, that the data provided to answer these questions be as complete as possible, and that the assumptions which are made be as explicit as possible. Then, if either questions, data, or assumptions are found to be deficient, the necessary corrections can be made. The unavoidably unsatisfactory nature of this type of analysis must not, however, be a reason to abandon the effort altogether. While much of international relations is uncertain, there is no need to glory in this uncertainty. Rather, there is every reason to attempt to reduce it as much as possible and to substitute as much certainty as the subject matter permits.

1

*Geopolitical Hypotheses in Technological Perspective**

Harold Sprout

HAROLD SPROUT *is Bryant Professor of Geography and International Relations at Princeton University and a Fellow of the Royal Geographic Society. In collaboration with his wife, Margaret Sprout, he has written such outstanding works as* Foundations of National Power (*1945*)*;* Man-Milieu Relationship Hypotheses in the Context of International Relations (*1956*)*; and* Foundations of International Politics (*1962*).

. . . I prefer *political potential* to the term *power.* This preference derives from the overriding military connotation that *power* has acquired in recent years, and that probably cannot be altered significantly now. Political relationships unquestionably include a large element of coercion or threat thereof. But no such concept of power comes anywhere near to expressing the totality of political relationships. Neither hostility (in either a legal or a psychological sense) nor violence (in a military or a quasi-military sense) is a necessary ingredient of relationships universally regarded as political; that is, relationships that exhibit some conflict of purpose or interest, and some exercise of coercion or non-coercive influence. Conflicts of interest divide friends and allies as well as those who regard each other as present or prospective enemies. Governments employ a wide range of tools and techniques to gain their ends, many of which exhibit no property realistically describable as coercion or threat thereof.

It has long seemed to me that a term other than *power* is needed to cover both the military and non-military aspects of political interaction and relationship. For this purpose I have come to favor the term *political potential,* defined in a manner somewhat analogous to the meaning of *potential* in the physical sciences.

In non-scientific discourse, the noun *potential* commonly denotes something that is possible though not yet achieved. This idea of latency is expressed, for example, in the familiar concepts of military potential and industrial potential, terms that refer generally to the magnitude of a community's capacity to mobilize or redirect resources for military or industrial purposes. The idea of latency, or capacity for future achievement, would be more precisely expressed by the noun *potentiality* or the adjective *potential:* for example, the military potentiality of China is so-and-so; or the potential coal reserves of Britain are such-and-such.

In the vocabulary of physical science, the noun *potential* carries a different meaning, a meaning just the

* The passage reproduced from *World Politics* **XV** (1963), 188–189 is derived from a fuller statement of the same ideas in *Foundations of International Politics,* copyrighted in 1962 by D. Van Nostrand Company, who join in the permission granted by Princeton University Press.

opposite of latency. About the closest one can come to expressing it verbally is to define potential as the measure of pressure, or pull, or attraction, or simply effect that one body exerts on another. This concept of potential is also expressed in physical systems by such terms as *voltage* and *gravitation.* This concept is manifestly not strictly transferable to social systems, but it does seem to suggest a fruitful analogy. By this analogy one may think of the combined coercive power and non-coercive influence of a state over other states in the international system as constituting its political potential: that is to say, its pressure, or pull, or attraction, or simply effect on their behaviors. To express this idea I prefer *political potential* to *power,* with its strong connotations of coercion and violence.

The reverse of political influence is political deference. Deferential behavior may be compliance with specific demands. Or it may be reflected in recognition of leadership or superior capabilities in the absence of specific demands. Potential and deference also embrace the idea of political prestige, defined as the attractive, or influential, impact of extraordinary achievements in sports, industry, the arts, science, engineering, etc.

Through time, relationships of influence and deference exhibit patterns that are more or less precisely describable. Many familiar terms of international politics denote such patterns: for example, alliance, coalition, sphere of influence, orbit, satellite, protectorate, command of the sea, bipolarity, Monroe Doctrine, Communist bloc, Atlantic community, European community, neutralism, and many others. . . .

2

*The Power Inventory and National Strategy**

Stephen B. Jones

STEPHEN B. JONES, *Professor of Geography at Yale University, is among the outstanding American authorities on political geography. He is the co-author of* Geography and World Affairs *(1962) and recently conducted a study of the changing function of political areas in Europe and Asia which involved numerous meetings with geographers in Japan, Malaya, Lebanon, Austria, England, and other countries.*

But, alas, what man does know and measure himself, and the things that are round him;—else where were the need of physical fighting at all?[1]

[1] Thomas Carlyle, *History of the French Revolution,* II, Book 5, ch. 5.

A familiar sight in the newspapers and weekly magazines is a world map (often, I regret to say, on the Mercator projection) on which population, oil production, or similar information is shown by rows of small men, barrels,

* *World Politics,* VI (1954), 421–452. Reprinted by permission. This paper has been prepared as part of a research project on national power sponsored by Yale University and the Office of Naval Research. All views expressed are the responsibility of the author, not the sponsors.

includes two categories of resources. One might be called "area resources," including the size and the shape of the country and immobile resources like landforms, soils, and climates. The other is the mobile mineral and biological resources. Location, sometimes considered an attribute of land by economists, will be treated later in another manner.

The factor of labor is perhaps better called "human resources." There are likewise two parts. First is population, considered as to number, age structure, and so forth. Second is what might be called "mental resources," the social, political, economic, and military systems of a country and the stock of skills, leadership, and patriotism.

Capital is better called "equipment resources," since it includes not only economic capital goods but also military equipment and the material apparatus of government. An additional item is supplies or stockpiles of consumable materials and goods—foods, metals, merchandise, munitions, etc.—and the financial stockpile of precious metals and credit.

There is of course a high degree of relationship among the items mentioned. Equipment is produced by organized skill operating on mobile natural resources. In turn, it may be used to extract further natural resources. Whether an ore deposit of marginal tenor is usable or not depends on skill, organization, and equipment. Leadership and patriotism are like enzymes in metabolism. In the final analysis, without them there is no power.

The foregoing paragraphs list resources as tangible as soil, as intangible as leadership, as measurable as population, as difficult to measure as patriotism. There is no common unit and no statistical summation is possible. Cost has been suggested as a measure of tangible items. Because of the importance of the budget in national housekeeping, there is a tendency to express many problems in terms of cost, but even as a measure of armaments it has its limitations. That a carrier might cost twenty times as much as a destroyer does not mean that twenty destroyers equal one carrier, in the operational sense. "Power value" rather than cost would be the significant figure if it could be measured, as sales value rather than cost is the real criterion for the inventory of a store. The Maginot line was costly, but its power value turned out to be nil. Cost is therefore not an adequate index of power. It does have its use as a "modifier" of inventory items, as will be discussed on a later page.

Even though one must give up the seductive hope that the power inventory can be summed up in dollars, kilowatt hours, or some other common unit, there remains the possibility that some key items may be used as rough indices of the probable total. The hope, of course, is to find measurable items that will so serve. Manpower of military age or the output of fuels, steel, or all heavy industry are some of the possibilities. Such data unquestionably are basic and under some conditions give a correct estimate of relative power. The longer a war lasts, the more likely are such data to be significant. They are particularly applicable when a country has limited access to external supplies. One could write a history of World War II in terms of supplies, with a measure of truth. But with far less than the whole truth: equally important is what was done with the supplies. Poverty of resources correlates with the weakness of Italy but does not explain the military failures against Greece or, for that matter, against the British at sea and in North Africa. Too little oil and too much intuition were long-run handicaps for Hitler, and it would be difficult to say which was the greater. Had his long-range strategy been sounder, he might have created a sufficient synthetic oil industry. Even in estimating potentials one must consider the strategic ray. To be sure, our analogy does not imply that the strategic ray is the more important, but only that *both* rays are important.

National income and its close relative, gross national product, have been considered possible indices of national power. They are operational in nature, rather than being inventory items, but this would be no disadvantage if they measure what can be done with a given inventory. For one thing, they give an idea of the dislocations to be expected from the diversion of resources from civil to military purposes. Their chief value is as tools, not as indices, however. Sherman Kent has commented adversely upon the search for indices of national power, and upon this use of national income data in particular.[10] He stresses the importance of fat, slack, and flexibility in the national economy.

That quantifiable items like manpower or the output of heavy industry or economic aggregates like national income cannot serve as indices of national power does not, of course, mean that quantification is useless. Much of science consists of efforts to narrow the range of guessing. Since there is, inevitably, a large element of guesswork in an estimate of national power, quantitative information is highly desirable for all items for which it is obtainable. But, for the same reason, there is no use refining quantitative data to a high degree.

[10] Sherman Kent, *Strategic Intelligence for American World Policy* (Princeton, 1949), p. 51 and n.

Modifiers of the Power Inventory

If the power inventory is thus essentially a check-list, with some quantifiable items, it becomes desirable to run through the concepts that must be kept in mind when the check-list is used. If we take any item of the list of power resources, we find that a chapter or a book or possibly a shelf of books can be written about it. It can be qualified almost without limit. We might start with population, for example, and find ourselves many pages later discussing the rate of training of civil defense workers in the use of Geiger counters. Such thoroughness may be necessary and desirable for some purposes—for a detailed mobilization program, for example. For general thinking about power, more generic concepts are desirable. These generic concepts we shall call "modifiers" of the power inventory. Not all the modifiers are applicable to every item of the power inventory, though with some imagination most of them can be applied. It may seem absurd to apply "motivation" to petroleum, for instance, but the motivation of the investors, management, and workers determines whether oil is produced or not. To return to the earlier attempt to distinguish between an element and a factor, motivation is essential to the petroleum industry as a factor of power.

One of the most obvious modifiers of the power inventory is quantity. In some commentaries on national power, quantity is the only modifier considered. That the United States produces three times as much steel as the Soviet Union closes the argument for some people. But quantity is a whole family of modifiers. Its principal genera are availability and change. Availability has two subdivisions, the space and time aspects. Spatial availability is summed up in the term "location." The effect of location on steel supplies is shown by the fact that the United States during World War II needed a third more steel for shipbuilding than for ordnance and other direct military uses.[11] Location has two subspecies, accessibility and mobility. To illustrate, Mackenzie River oil is highly inaccessible but highly mobile. The Canol pipeline (another non-combatant use of steel) did not improve the accessibility until after the need had passed. "Tonnage" ores like iron are less mobile than ores that can usefully be measured in pounds. Labrador iron ore probably could not have been made accessible during World War II even had the need arisen. Manpower is relatively mobile and with a man move his skills, but the mobility of manpower varies with culture. Aboriginal natives need fewer supplies than do more civilized troops and workers, but at the same time they may be more essential to the economy of their villages, which have no labor-replacing machinery.

The time aspect of availability appears in the familiar phrase "lead-time," which stands for the period required to convert plans into production.[12] Lead-time is a phase of the problem of potential power. That there is a difference between actual and potential power is obvious, but these two terms are too vague to be of much service. A geographer is likely to think of ore and fuel reserves when he hears the word "potential." An economist is likely to think of factories convertible to war production. A military man may think of the reserve corps or of mothballed ships. A fivefold classification of states of availability is here proposed: 1. power resources available immediately; 2. power resources available after activation; 3. power resources available after conversion; 4. power resources available after development; and 5. power resources available hypothetically.

Immediately available resources include such things as armed forces in being, munitions in depots, money or credit at hand. (There is of course a locational immediacy as well. A division in Germany and one in Texas are not equally immediate in availability for a given emergency.) Resources available after activation include such things as reserve troops and officers, mothballed ships, money and credit requiring legislation before use. Resources available after conversion include such things as factories suited for war production, and manpower untrained but adaptable to military or industrial service. This category is one that the United States has banked on heavily in the past, thanks to Britain, France, and the Atlantic Ocean. Resources available after development form another group that has given much comfort to Americans in the past but which is less comforting now. Such things as minerals known to exist but not in production and products known to be practical but not available in quantity, like synthetic rubber in 1942, are included. Hypothetical power resources remind one of the story of the diplomat who spoke most feelingly of his country's claims to some tropical territory. "It is full of rich resources," he exclaimed, "all undiscovered!" But hypothetical power

---

[11] American Iron and Steel Institute, *Steel Facts* (October, 1952).

[12] Lead-time has a range of meanings. An artilleryman might think of it as the interval between placing an order and receiving the ammunition. An airman is more likely to think of the longer interval between conceiving a new airplane and the mass production of the final model. There is a different lead-time for each of the availability states discussed in this article, *infra*.

should not be laughed at. The atomic bomb was hypothetical until 1945.

These availability states are of course not rigidly separated pigeonholes, but they do differ in kind as well as in degree. They should permit sharper thinking than do "actual" and "potential." A given power resource is not confined to one category. Many exist in all five states. Oil, for instance, may be immediately available in storage tanks. Idle wells and refineries may be activated. Non-essential use can be curtailed—this would be conversion. New wells may be drilled in proven fields—this is development—and favorable structures may be wildcatted on the hypothesis that oil exists in them. Intangibles like leadership can exist in all five states. How power resources are distributed through the availability series reflects the national strategy. The United States traditionally has left as much of its power as possible in the convertible and developable states. The trend is to push many items into higher states and to step up the pace of conversion and development.[13] Not even the most spartan of nations could keep all its resources in a condition of immediate availability, but simple trust in "the power and potential of American mass production" goes the way of the faith that a million Americans would spring to arms overnight if their country were attacked.

The term "potential" has another connotation than that of availability. It also implies the maximum sustainable rate of production, or, more precisely, of expenditure, of a given item of power. Maximum sustainable rates follow different rules, depending upon the nature of the resource, the time element, and national strategy. Where natural resources are ample and the rate of production depends largely upon capital and labor, long-continued increases are possible, though perhaps at the cost of diverting capital and labor from other items. American steel production, for example, is capable of much further growth, if low-grade and foreign ores are utilized. In other cases, the maximum sustainable rate may vary with the period of time involved. The expenditure of manpower, if in excess of natural replacement, is an obvious example. To estimate the maximum sustainable rates of power expenditure therefore requires knowledge of both resources and their probable strategic use.

The availability states discussed above are closely related to three aspects of the national economy discussed by Sherman Kent: fat, slack, and flexibility.[14] Kent defines these terms as follows:

> By *fat*, I mean such things as some of the things Britain had at the start of World War II: extensive external assets, a large merchant marine, access to necessary raw materials and the credits to buy them without going into current production, a large and up-to-date supply of capital equipment, a large inventory of finished goods, a national diet of three to four thousand calories per day, etc. Important elements of German fat may be said to have existed in the excess capacity of machine tools, a large amount of brand new plant and new housing. The Italians had practically no fat, indeed little enough lean.
>
> By *slack*, I mean such things as the 40-hour week, twelve to sixteen years of education for youth, small proportion

---

[13] It has been remarked that conscription was adopted during the Civil War, upon entry into World War I, before entry into World War II, and now appears to be a permanent institution. In another sphere, the *New York Times*, March 8, 1953, mentioned the opening of a watch factory so designed that it could shift without pause to the making of fuses.

[14] *Loc. cit.*

of women in the labor force, unemployment of both labor and capital, only partial utilization of equipment, etc.

By *flexibility,* I mean the capacity of the economy to beat plowshares and pruning hooks into swords, and that in jig time. I mean the ability of technicians to make typewriter factories over into machine gun factories, and put the manufacturers of dry breakfast food into the shell-fuse business. I mean the ability to make synthetics from scratch where the natural sources have dried up.

"Fat" and "slack" correspond to "resources available after activation." Steel production, for example, is expansible in several ways. Plants may be operating below capacity. To activate this unused capacity would be taking up slack. Or they may be operated temporarily above capacity by postponing repairs. This would be using up fat. "Flexibility" covers the two concepts of "conversion" and "development." The quotation from Kent illustrates both. Making war goods in typewriter and cereal factories is conversion. Making synthetics from scratch (if the basic processes are known and not hypothetical) is development. The difference is significant because the lead-time of change is likely to be greater for development than for conversion and the investment of money, manpower, and materials larger. The expansion of steel production by building new mills is development, and involves the temporary diversion of steel from other uses.

These terms can be applied to persons as well as to commodities or plants. The conversion of clerks into soldiers, of housewives into welders, is familiar. The longer process of producing physicians, physicists, or general officers is more appropriately called development. The population factor as a whole can be developed, as by the importation of labor, alliances, and public health measures. The long-term effect of pro-natalist policies on the birth rate is still somewhat hypothetical.

The importance of change in relation to quantity needs no emphasis. Change has two aspects, rate and range. Rates of production, mobilization, conversion, expansion, etc., need no discussion. Changes of rates, or accelerations and decelerations, are also important, and one may need to consider changes in the changes of rates. The higher derivatives of change are significant in demography, where one wishes to know not only the death rate, for instance, but whether it is rising or falling and how the rate of rise or fall is changing. Rates of resource accumulation or wastage are important. Secular changes of vast consequence may be taking place almost unperceived by untrained observers, such as soil erosion, climatic alteration, or the aging of the population. The range of change obviously applies to fluctuating quantities like temperatures or harvests. Better knowledge of the range of Russian winter temperatures would have aided Hitler in 1941–1942. Range may also apply to rates. There is an upper limit to the rate of oil production from a given field, for instance, beyond which recovery declines and salt water may intrude.

Rates and ranges of expansion are major considerations in estimating power. The expansion of American production during World War II surprised even optimists, though whether time will be available in a future conflict for similar expansion is debatable. Soviet recovery after World War II was also surprisingly rapid. Expansion has its converse, contraction. The ability to do without may be important in war. Many contractions are effected for the purpose of expanding or maintaining supply or effort in other lines or places. Rationing of gasoline to civilians permitted expanded military consumption. But expansion without concomitant contraction is of course possible, as in the activation of unused plants. Use of the electrolytic process of tinplating instead of the dipping process gave more plate from less tin, so that a reduced supply of a raw material was not reflected in an equivalent contraction of the product.

Substitution is another modifier of quantity. Substitution can be looked at from two sides. One can ask if an item in short supply can be replaced by a more abundant or a synthetic product, or one can ask if some item which is abundant may have other uses. We usually think of the former—glass for tinplate, synthetic for natural rubber—but the latter may be significant when weighing the power resources of other countries. An American thinks of potatoes as food, primarily, but they are an important source of industrial alcohol in the Soviet Union. Substitution of machines for men is a favorite American occupation. The high degree of automation possible in peace may be deceptive as to the possibilities in war, when destruction and disruption may make muscle-power indispensable. The reverse substitution of men for machines has its limitations also.

The doctrine of limiting factors in biology means, for example, that a plant needing nitrogen is not helped by an excess of phosphate. Man's ingenuity in finding substitutes makes this doctrine only loosely applicable to human affairs. Nevertheless, limiting factors do appear, particularly in war and under conditions of blockade and attrition. Substitution very often requires time and imports, which may not be available. The limiting factors may be rates. For instance, there was no doubt that the United States could create a synthetic rubber industry adequate for its needs. The question was whether it could be created in time.

The Quality Modifiers

Quality is a second family of modifiers. The two main branches of the quality family are the quality of materials and goods on the one hand, and of operation on the other. These terms are meant to apply very broadly. American schoolboys or African natives are materials in the present sense, having certain qualities in that condition. Trained as workers, soldiers, professional men, etc., they might be called goods, their qualities in that state depending not only on inherent vigor and intelligence and childhood environment but upon specific training. Operation is also used broadly, to include business management, military organization, and government.

Quality of course connotes the question, "How good?" For our study, the question really is, how well does something serve its strategic purpose? An example of the distinction is the use by the Communists in Korea of obsolete wooden-frame airplanes for night bombing, because these old planes give poor radar echoes.

Quality is often placed in opposition to quantity, the ideal of "the mostest of the bestest" being difficult to attain. It is not necessarily unattainable, however, and quality often has been improved while quantity was being increased. The *a priori* opposition of quality and quantity possibly dates from handicraft days. The Battle of Britain is often cited as a triumph of quality over quantity, British planes, pilots, and operations being considered superior to the German. Because of these qualitative superiorities and the fact that fighting took place over British soil, the Royal Air Force sometimes obtained local quantitative superiority.[15] A different relationship of quality and quantity can be illustrated by a famine-struck area. The difference between high- and low-grade wheat would mean little. Quality would be negligible in comparison with quantity and availability.

Change of quality must also be considered. This has three aspects, durability, obsolescence, and variation. Durability and obsolescence might be lumped as life expectancy of materials or goods. The significance of durability needs little elaboration. The United States was able to get through four years of war with its initial stock of private automobiles, in part because the cars proved durable beyond customary expectation. (Gasoline and tire rationing of course lengthened car life by reducing use.) The durability of railroad equipment, machine tools, and the like was important. Materials and labor needed for maintenance and replacement of non-combatant equipment of course must be drawn from the supply available for military use. Durability can be obtained at excessive cost and can be offset by obsolescence. Military equipment, however, is subject to very hard usage, and expenditures to increase its durability usually are justified. Breakdowns are likely to occur at the worst possible time and place when the equipment is overworked during an emergency.

High durability and low rate of obsolescence are major criteria of materials and goods that are to be stockpiled or mothballed. To judge when obsolescence has so reduced power value that goods should be scrapped requires something like clairvoyance. Brodie argues cogently against prematurely scrapping obsolescent naval ships, on the grounds that quantity may offset a modern qualitative inferiority.[16] The destroyer-for-bases deal of 1940 is a supporting illustration. Whether the great stock of slow Liberty ships is a real or an illusory asset in event of war is a question currently debated. Rommel repeatedly refers to the gradual obsolescence of his tanks relative to those of the British.[17] Rommel's victories actually increased his problems, for the Germans came to think him a miracle worker who could win with any weapons, while the British were compelled to replace lost equipment and had fewer competing demands for their best tanks. There is perhaps more danger that obsolescent items will be rated too highly in terms of power than that they will be scrapped prematurely, but pruning the power tree of its fading branches does not strengthen it unless there is concomitant new growth. In the inorganic world of ships, tanks, and the like, new growth does not come spontaneously.

Variation in quality may involve the familiar phenomenon of "the weakest link." Ships in line of battle can steam no faster than the slowest vessel. One defective shell can jam a gun. All troops in combat may have to fall back if one unit gives way. In the first battle of El Alamein, Auchinleck directed major counter-attacks at Italian divisions, forcing the Germans to limit their own drives.[18] On the other hand, the phenomenon of "the strongest link" sometimes is encountered. Rommel's crack Afrika Korps saved many critical situations and kept the Italian

---

[15] Chester Wilmot, *The Struggle for Europe* (London, 1952), pp. 51–53.

[16] Bernard Brodie, *Sea Power in the Machine Age* (Princeton, 1943), pp. 203, 334, 442–445.

[17] B. H. Liddell Hart, ed., *The Rommel Papers* (New York, 1953), p. 245 and elsewhere.

[18] *Ibid.*, pp. 252–254.

army in battle long after it would otherwise have collapsed.

Variations in the quality of leadership—economic, political, military—are important modifiers of the power inventory and of course are difficult to assess. A change of leaders may change the power value of a military unit almost overnight. Even pushbutton warfare will require not only a man to push the button but, more important, a man to say when to push the button. This ineluctable individual factor may be overlooked in the power inventory because it cannot be treated statistically. It is apt to be neglected in the economist's or the geographer's approach to the study of power. Uncritical historians, on the other hand, may give too much attention to individuals. "The Gauls were not conquered by the Roman legions but by Caesar," said Napoleon, whose own history showed the potency of genius, but also that manpower, weather, and nationalism were not to be ignored.

Operation: Focus of Inventory and Strategy

When we speak of operation and of the quality of operation, we are at or near the common focus of the inventory and strategic beams of our opening analogy. We use "operation" in the broad sense of "the way things work."[19] How well things work is a major modifier of the power inventory. We can apply this concept of working quality to items in wide variety—a squad of soldiers, a mine, a factory, an army, the whole of an economic or political system. This aspect of quality may be illustrated by Russian experience in the first five-year plan, when modern factories were built but sometimes nothing came off the assembly lines.

Operation has two main parts, motivation and organization. Motivation—involving reward, punishment, loyalty, leadership—is essential even for the most prosaic effort. To return to the example of petroleum as a factor of power, the motivation of the seamen on tankers may be a critical matter. Motivation for the long-haul usually demands pecuniary or other material rewards. But material motivation is not enough; it has proved insufficient for high quality of work even in purely economic activities. In this respect, however, states may go to the other extreme. As has been said, without patriotism there is no power, but one cannot expect patriotism to replace pay checks year after year. Americans seem particularly reluctant to admit that political and military operation really works from the top down, though checked and criticized (in both senses of criticism) from below. Patriotism, luck, or *le bon Dieu* may not provide administrators of high quality if pay is inadequate.

Organization may be divided into control and integration. Control is essential in government, industry, or battle. Loss of control is a nightmare of the military commander and all sorts of communication devices are used to provide a mechanical guard against it. Control involves motivation. A General Patton might control where a weaker man might lose control. Control is necessary for a rationing system and for maintaining secrecy in government and the armed forces. Integration means how the parts of an organization mesh together. One

[19] "Operation" has the narrow military meaning of "a military action" and the broader one of any strategic, tactical, service, training, or administrative action. "Administration" was considered as a substitute for "operation" in the present paper, but was rejected because of its bureaucratic connotation and because, in military usage, it does not apply to strategic or tactical activities.

aspect is illustrated by the integration of Negro troops into white units in the United States Army. This step multiplied many-fold the power value of the Negro soldiers and removed from them the stigma of "the weakest link." The operations of alliances are generally hampered by imperfect integration. The faulty integration of American railroads early in World War I led to intolerable congestion. The converse of congestion—shortages—may also arise from faulty integration, even when ample materials or goods are available.

The pace of operations is an important aspect of their quality. Equipment of high quality is necessary but not sufficient for fast pace. Whittlesey has pointed out that the time-dimension of human activities has three derivatives, velocity, pace, and timing.[20] A jet airplane may have a velocity near the speed of sound. The pace of air operations depends on many other velocities than those of airplanes. It depends, among other things, on the rate at which intelligence reaches the commander, on the rapidity with which plans are formulated and orders issued, upon the speed of servicing and repair. Pace—"the average tempo of trajections in a specified area"—may thus be more significant than velocity. The sluggishness of bureaucratic pace is notorious. Fortunately, it is also world-wide, though this does not permit us to be complacent about it. One purpose of war games is to step up the pace of operations that may some day be performed in the face of the enemy. Perhaps all branches of administration should hold war games.

Operational quality is roughly synonymous with some meanings of "efficiency" but not necessarily with that which relates output to input, if we measure output and input in conventional ways. Diplomatic operations of high quality are not necessarily economical of time or money. It is debatable whether the decision of 1953 to concentrate war production in the most efficient factories was wise or unwise as a long-run policy, since dispersal among more plants not only might decrease vulnerability but might permit faster acceleration of production in event of war.

Vulnerability and Cost

Vulnerability is a modifier of the power inventory that of course now affects the innermost parts of the home front. The power value of two factories may depend, after war begins, more on their vulnerability than on their efficiency.[21] The vulnerability of Britain to air attack weakened Chamberlain's hand at Munich. Theoretically, the states with atomic weapons have the power virtually to blow each other to bits. Whether they will do so is debatable. Atomic warfare might resemble the strategy of the fleet-in-being, the threat of atomic weapons being used to tie up the resources of the opponent. Vulnerability will nevertheless be a factor, for the side that has attained the best defense against atomic weapons can make the most aggressive threats. Distressingly little attention has been paid to the reduction of vulnerability during the period of rapid construction since World War II. Some records have been stored in underground vaults, but little has been done to safeguard the really essential resources of labor and equipment, without which records have little meaning.

---

[20] Derwent Whittlesey, "The Horizon of Geography," *Annals of the Association of American Geographers*, **XXXV** (March, 1945), 23–24.

[21] To be somewhat facetious, one might list a sixth availability state, "available after bombardment."

Simplicity is one of the classical principles of war. A major reason is the vulnerability of complicated operations, especially in the face of an active enemy. Simplicity is difficult to attain in industrialized war, in spite of modern methods of communication and control. Simplicity in plan may be obtainable only through complexity of control, as in assembly-line manufacturing. In industry, simplicity is not sought for itself but only if costs can be reduced or sales increased. In fact, the search for cheaper supplies or more extensive markets often results in complicated cross-hauling of materials and goods[22] and in duplication of delivery and marketing systems. Much of this complexity, efficient though it may be in a capitalistic economy in peace, would have to be eliminated in time of war, especially if the home front were heavily bombarded.

Cost as an index of power or a measure of power value has been discussed on an earlier page. In spite of its limitations in these respects, it remains a significant modifier. In part, this is because of the subjective importance given to the cost of national defense by taxpayers and their Congressional representatives. There is a persistent clamor for social security and insurance sells steadily, but that national power is the most basic form of social security and insurance, without which the others are illusory, is commonly forgotten in time of peace. The subjective importance of cost is of course greatest in the democracies where public opinion is most effective in government.

Cost has objective as well as subjective importance. Cost, in relation to national power, implies the question, "How much of our resources are required to increase our supply of a given item, or its readiness for use?" Japan, for example, could build warships with cheaper labor than could the United States, but the cost in terms of available steel was proportionately greater to Japan. Japan could man a warship for a small part of the payroll of its American counterpart, but the oil for fuel came from a much more limited resource. World War II showed that most nations can sacrifice living standards for war to a degree hardly thought possible and that national bankruptcy can be staved off for years. Nevertheless, drain on resources is a reality, if replacement does not keep up with use. The attrition on manpower is perhaps the most obvious form, but drain on equipment, if there is insufficient reinvestment to maintain or replace it, may be serious.

The Strategic Beam

The power inventory has now been provided with a set of modifiers —a check-list for a check-list, so to speak. A question may arise: Are the modifiers so numerous and so indeterminate that they reduce the inventory to a pulp? This thought can be dismissed with little comment. So long as there is politics among sovereign states, there will be estimation of power. Even though the best estimates are only rough, they are better than reliance on intuition or emotion. It is true that the modifiers are warning signs rather than guideposts, that they point out traps rather than show where the path lies. Nevertheless, insofar as they conform to realities they should be useful. . . .

One of the most serious of the problems that beset the student of national power is how to avoid encyclopedism. The modifiers of the power inventory are no protection against this. In fact, the mechanical applica-

[22] Edward L. Ullman, "The Railroad Pattern of the United States," *Geographical Review,* **XXXIX** (April, 1949), 254–255.

tion of a check-list to a check-list would yield compound encyclopedism. Encyclopedism is likewise a problem in basic intelligence research. What facts to collect, in how much detail to present them, how far to go in evaluation without treading on the sacred ground of policy-making? These and similar questions plague the intelligence research worker. Roger Hilsman has challenged the encyclopedic method in intelligence and calls for workers to be "manipulative, instrumental, action-conscious, policy-oriented."[23] In terms of our analogy, what Hilsman appears to desire is that the intelligence worker get more light from the strategic beam and not work only by the inventory beam, where he is forever stepping into shadows. The aptness of this analogy will be attested by many who have worked in intelligence, though they may not be optimistic about the practical solution of the problem.

If one looks at power along the inventory beam, one is asking, "What have I?" If one looks along the strategic beam, one is asking, "What do I need?" Each question of course connotes the other, but most will agree that, as in personal finances needs run ahead of funds, among nations it is strategic needs rather than love of statistics that sets us counting our power resources. This analogy can easily be strained, however. In the first place, neither the power inventory nor strategic needs can be expressed completely in monetary or even statistical terms. Second, the public purse is much more elastic than the personal one. A nation does not live on a fixed income, and it is production rather than the budget that really counts. Third, it is not so much a case of shifting one's line of sight from the inventory to the strategic beam as of looking along both. It takes binocular vision, so to speak, to see national power in full relief. What one can do is influenced by what one has, but what one has is influenced by what one does, in world politics at least.

This paradox, if it is one, will be discussed under four heads: 1. the harmony of resources and national strategy; 2. the augmentation, or reduction, of resources by national strategy; 3. the allocation of resources in relation to national strategy; and 4. the relativity of power in the light of national strategies.

Harmony of Inventory and Strategy

That national strategy must be in harmony with national resources may seem like a truism, but the statement is true only in a very general sense. It can be a very misleading doctrine if resources are considered to be a fixed sum and if national strategy is conceived in strictly military terms and only in isolation. The doctrine has been used by some isolationists, who argue not that the United States *can* isolate itself (by means of some wonder-weapon, perhaps), but that it *must* isolate itself because it cannot afford a broader strategy. One possible answer, of course, is to say that the broader strategy may be the cheaper in the long run. Walter Lippmann took a different tack: he held that a state must balance its commitments and its power,[24] but he goes on to say of the "true statesman": "Having determined the foreign commitments which are vitally necessary to his people, he will never rest until he has mustered the

---

[23] Roger Hilsman, Jr., "Intelligence and Policy-making in Foreign Affairs," *World Politics*, V (October, 1952), 44.

[24] Walter Lippmann, *U.S. Foreign Policy: Shield of the Republic* (Boston, 1943), pp. 9–10. He adds, "with a comfortable surplus of power in reserve."

force to cover them." In other words, if two strategies appear equally good, we may choose the cheaper, but if it is penicillin we need, aspirin will not do.[25]

Harmony of resources and needs may be all very well, but what if a state cannot muster the force to cover its vitally necessary commitments? One answer, too popular with Americans, is to recalculate the risks and cut the commitments. Another answer, popular with Americans and justifiably so if the limitations are realized, is to turn to science. The development of wonderful new weapons is much in mind, but should the brunt of war remain on the shoulders of the ground forces, even more important may be the use of science to augment natural resources. A kinder deity might have given this country limitless high-grade iron ore and never-failing oil wells, but we know of other ways to meet our needs, such as beneficiation of lean ores and the distillation of oil shales. But such expansion of resources does not come about automatically or with the ease of comic-strip art. It requires research, capital, labor, and time, all of which must be comprehended in the long-term national strategy.

Import and stockpiling programs are of course another way of augmenting a state's resources or of conserving domestic supplies. Since the United States has traditionally discouraged imports and since large stockpiles are uneconomic, in a business sense, such programs require a consciously strategic viewpoint.

A state may augment its resources through the acquisition of colonies or the formation of alliances. An alliance may be the only resort of a small state, short of outright annexation to a great power, by which it can "muster the force to cover its vitally necessary commitments." In estimating the power of an alliance, due consideration must be given to strategic aspects. The power of an alliance is never the simple sum of the power inventories of its members. The total may be much less than the sum if organization is weak or if the members cannot easily support each other. On the other hand, the joint power of the United States and Canada is potentially more than the sum of their separate resources, because together they form a coherent block of North America reaching into the Arctic instead of splitting the continent along a long, weak boundary.

A state may augment its power by building up the power of its allies or, without an alliance, of its presumptive friends. This of course is an objective of American foreign aid programs. The motivation of foreign aid programs ranges from pure humanitarianism through the belief that sound independent nations are "safe" to the strictly military desire to build up foreign facilities and sources of supply. This last is sometimes called "geologistics" and augments resources by cutting down "transmission losses" and taking advantage of lower wages and prices.

Power resources can be reduced instead of augmented if the national strategy is unsound or obsolete. Clumsy diplomacy or a speech or act that is stupid in relation to foreign policy may cut national power or, looked at another way, may require an increased use of resources to achieve a given end. Wishful thinking plays a role in national strategy. A state's resources may be as effectively reduced by it as by the drainage of an oil field

[25] This analogy, while sound in principle, is difficult to apply. The choice of strategies may be more like the choice among medicines of uncertain therapeutic value for a disease not definitely diagnosed.

or a drop in the birth rate. Two ingrained American habits of mind are faith in machinery and a desire to pull back from overseas commitments. Any strategic theory that embodies or seems to embody these ideas is sure to find advocates. The popular enthusiasm for wonder-weapons finds support in these mental habits. Wishful thinking is by no means confined to the man-in-the-street and the professor-in-the-tower. The fateful conferences of Munich and Yalta show that statesmen are not immune.

THE PROBLEM OF ALLOCATION

One of the knottiest problems of national strategy is the allocation of resources, between private and governmental demands and among the various branches of the government. In a democratic country, such allocations are strongly influenced by habits, moods, and political pressures held or generated by the public. Certain clichés crop up. For instance, it becomes said that the civilian economy can bear only so much military or foreign aid expense. At bottom, this is a rationalization of American hedonism. Pushed to the test, a state must pay the price of victory or lose. If there is sufficient solidarity, spontaneous or enforced, civilian consumption can be pared to the bone.

The division of resources among the armed forces may bring up the cliché of "balance," which usually means that increases and cuts in the budget shall be equally shared.[26] Certain criticisms of "balance" are, however, not without clichés themselves. The argument is heard that air power has the greatest inherent capabilities of any arm, because of the velocity of its vehicles and their global, three-dimensional medium of operation; the air arm should therefore receive the lion's share of appropriations. The conclusion may be true, but it does not follow from the premise as stated in general terms. Capability, like balance and allocation, is a vague word unless we are told, capability for *what*. Even within an armed service we find arguments about allocation of resources. Hitler's navy was torn between the submariners and the advocates of a balanced fleet, with each side claiming that the war would be lost if its counsels were disregarded.

Allocation of resources therefore can be discussed rationally only in the light of given national strategies. National strategy is to the power inventory as management is to the materials inventory of a factory. What is produced, and when, depends on the judgment of the management. The decisions of course are not free or unlimited. They depend not only on the resources of the factory but upon the milieu—the cultural and natural environments offering possibilities and imposing limitations.[27] It hardly needs to be said that national strategy usually is less logical and consistent than industrial management. The play of interests makes the national strategy a sort of vector sum of ideas that are often divergent and sometimes diametrically opposed. The struggle between isolationists and interventionists in the United States in the interwar period is an obvious example. The single vote in the House of Representatives that renewed the selective service act might be called the vector sum in that case.

The strategy of industrial manage-

[26] Cf. an article in the *New York Times*, November 11, 1953, p. 17, headed "Wilson Hints End of Arms Balance."

[27] Cf. Stephen B. Jones, "Possibilism and Strategic Thought," abstract to be published in the *Annals of the Association of American Geographers* in June 1954.

ment is tested promptly. The statement of profit and loss gives the answer. There is no such easy test for national strategy. That a state has survived thus far may be all that we can claim, and we may not know for sure whether this is because of, or in spite of, its national strategy. Even the lessons of war are not conclusive. Witness the different conclusions that have been drawn from strategic bombardment in World War II.[28]

Generally speaking, there are two philosophies of resource allocation. . . .

Neither the "one-basket" nor the "flexibility" philosophy of resource allocation can guard against obsolescence. As cavalrymen loved horses, so sailors love ships and airmen love airplanes. Whether anybody but a scientist can love an intercontinental rocket is a question, yet conceivably it might make other military implements obsolete. Steel and oil are sinews of war, as everyone knows, but one can imagine a titanium-hulled, uranium-powered missile that would make no great demand for steel or oil even in the manufacturing stage. This is of course dream-stuff today, but it shows that the projection of the inventory ray into the future must be checked against possible projections of the strategic ray.

National power must constantly be re-evaluated in terms of the methods and instruments available to national strategy. If Lower Slobbovia plans war on Upper Denturia, relative power is not determined solely by the fact that the former has bigger piles of rocks and more men to throw them. Can it bring its power to bear? If a wide, swift river separates these two countries, does Lower Slobbovia have the needed vehicles for crossing? Is its organization good enough to land its rock-throwers en masse, not in driblets? Are its emissaries loud braggarts who infuriate the Denturians or shrewd operators who may settle the dispute without fighting? All this bears on such questions of allocation as whether the Slobbovian *Führer* should put some of his rock-gatherers to canoe-building and send some of his rock-throwers to a school of diplomacy.

Allocation in Space and Time

Power resources exist in space and time. This may seem an obvious statement, yet it is an aspect that may be neglected. In the language of physics, there are space and time dimensions of the field of power.[29] Strategy is the art of movement in such a field.

In a sense, space and time are resources. The nation that has them can adopt strategies that would be suicidal without them. Space consumes more than time; it consumes fuel, supplies, and manpower. Yet trading space for all of these is generally a sign of unpreparedness rather than of wisdom. But space and time are more than resources. They are conditions of resource allocation and use. Here, again, the strategic ray of the power triangle is valuable. Space and time aspects may be left out of an inventory. They are integral parts of national strategy.

[28] E.g., Alexander de Seversky, *Air Power: Key to Survival* (New York, 1950); and Marshall Andrews, *Disaster Through Air Power* (New York, 1950). There were divergent opinions in the Strategic Bombing Survey (*Summary Report, Pacific War*, Washington, 1946, and *Air Campaigns of the Pacific War*, Washington, 1947).

[29] This may be mere jargon. The reader may judge after considering Whittlesey, "The Horizon of Geography," *Annals of the Association of American Geographers, op. cit.*, pp. 1–36, and Stephen B. Jones, "A Unified Field Theory of Political Geography," published in the same journal in June 1954.

The Sprouts made use of space as a strategic condition when they compared British sea power, based on an island close to the continent where the main rivals lay, with American sea power, facing two broad oceans.[30] Whittlesey, we have said, lists three derivatives of time: velocity, pace, and timing.[31] Velocity and pace have been touched on above, under operational quality. Timing was implicit in the discussion of the five availability states. Availability is strategically meaningful only in terms of how long it takes to bring a given item to the state of "immediately available." Locational availability also can be translated into terms of time and timing. Thomas' discussion of the "railway revolution" in war shows that even a century ago mobilization was not something that just happened.[32] In the Battle of Britain, radar helped the British get their planes to the right place at the right moment. One might say that radar gave the RAF a complete picture of the space-time field which helped offset the fact that the Luftwaffe was the larger force and held the strategic initiative.

THE PROBLEM OF RELATIVE POWER

That national power is always relative is almost axiomatic. In the eyes of Lichtenstein, Switzerland is a great power. A superficial approach to the relativity of power has been to compare the power inventories of the states or alliances under discussion, with emphasis upon actual or potential power according to the purpose or leanings of the writer. Such a simple method has of course long been rejected by those more deeply concerned with the problem. No substitute formula, simple or complex, will come from the present paper. The emphasis upon the interplay of the inventory and strategic beams leads only to greater uncertainties, when two or more states are considered.

Emphasis upon the strategic aspect of relative power does not render the power inventory useless. Basic data on such fundamentals as manpower, steel production, and the like are indispensable, and it is generally true in world politics as in pugilism that a good big man is better than a good little man. What the strategic approach does is to ask how good the man is, as well as how big. If strategic considerations make the estimation of relative power more complex, they may compensate by making it less fatalistic. It is less necessary to kneel before statistical superiority, unless the margin be great. The free world has had no reason to fear the Soviet Union—statistically. But generally the Soviet Union has held the initiative in world affairs. If the statistically weaker country has often called the tune for the statistically stronger, a reversal of roles is at least theoretically possible.

The simplest statement above relative power is that the margin of power between A and B is more significant than the absolute power of A or B. Unfortunately, we cannot express a margin of power statistically any more accurately than we can measure absolute power. We must make the best informed guess possible.

Relative power is sometimes discussed as if a state had only its own resources. But tight blockade is rare. Alliances, trade with neutrals, conquests of territory, scientific substitution, all may increase relative power.

---

30 Harold and Margaret Sprout, *Toward a New Order of Sea Power* (Princeton, 1940), pp. 14–15 and 19–22.

31 "The Horizon of Geography," *op. cit.*, pp. 23–24.

32 Thomas H. Thomas, "Armies and the Railway Revolution," in *War as a Social Institution* (New York, 1941), pp. 88–94.

On the other hand, we cannot assume that a state necessarily commands all its own resources. Some may be highly vulnerable (like the French coal fields in both world wars); some may be withheld by public unwillingness to sacrifice; administrative clumsiness may prevent full employment of resources. In short, the modifiers we have discussed apply to the calculus of relative power.

Power relations are never simply between A and B. They take place in the configuration of international politics. Even in the so-called bipolar world of today, many states are involved. The shift of China from the non-Soviet to the Soviet camp profoundly affected the relative power of the United States and the Soviet Union, without changing the absolute power of either of these countries by itself. The relative power of the United States and Communist China in Korea was profoundly affected by the mere existence of the Soviet Union in the background. Even weak states affect relative power if they influence when or where competitive crises arise. The weakness of the states of the Eurasian rimland is the despair of the American strategist.

If it is the margin of power that really counts, one must ask for how long a period the margin must be maintained and what sort of competition is taking place. In a short war, margins of skill and readiness may count for more than relative potentials. There are some who hold that a little more skill (especially in handling Soviet minority peoples) and a little more readiness (for Russian winters) might have given Germany military victory over the Soviet Union. In long wars, relative potentials obviously become more significant, if the disparity in skills is not too great. In short crises not leading to war, relative diplomatic skill may be decisive. The long-term competition called the Cold War has demanded skills and other resources in combinations of unusual nature. The Cold War is a competition for entire peoples. Diplomacy is no longer merely the communing of diplomat with diplomat but a problem of mass communication of many kinds. Skill in communicating ideas and methods on a wide range of topics—government, subversion, farming, birth control, etc. —may tip a country like China or India to an extent that military power is almost incapable of offsetting.

Relative power, considered item by item, must be evaluated differently if the given item is scarce or abundant. If some element is scarce, the margin between just enough and not enough may be very significant. If both parties to a competition have some item in plenty, some derivative factor may be significant. Both the United States and the Soviet Union have large coal reserves, for instance. Whether they will last four hundred or four thousand years makes no immediate difference; they suffice for the present. Much more important are such derivatives as the rate of production, how much it could be increased, the manpower requirements of coal-mining in the two countries, and the speed with which a hydrogenation industry might be developed if liquid fuels run short.

Our opening analogy stated that the power inventory must be triangulated by national strategy. To extend the analogy to relative power, not only a state's own inventory and strategy must be considered but also the inventories and strategies of the other state or states involved in the political configuration. Theoretically, in this age of global competition, this would mean sixty or more strategic beams sweeping the international skies—with an effect more dazzling than illuminating. And, actually, it is in such a spider-web of beams that we are caught, when Germany and China, Iran and Guatemala, Indochina and British Guiana may hit the headlines the same day. The speed of communication and reaction in world politics, as well as the global scope, calls for more background in strategic thought than has been the American custom. Otherwise we are repeatedly surprised, "for, to the blind, all things are sudden."[33]

The complicated interrelationships of national strategies and relative power may be somewhat simplified if we consider national strategy to have two aspects, one of which we may call "autonomous," the other "responsive." There is not a dichotomy between these but, rather, a gradation. For example, England was not forced to adopt sea power as its principal weapon. In fact, there was little attempt to employ sea power independently until the reign of Henry III. Insularity permitted the British to rely on sea power but did not command it. Similarly, the decision of Britain to maintain a fleet equal to the two closest rivals was an autonomous decision, for Britain was free to adopt a smaller or greater ratio, limited only by the willingness to risk and the willingness to sacrifice. The location of the principal British naval bases was less autonomous; it depended on the probable enemy of the period and that enemy's resources and possible strategy. The distribution of British ships among the fleets and bases was also not fully autonomous; it was responsive to the political changes and the moves of the opponents.

A state faced with rising unemployment might make autonomous decisions on combating it. It might widen military training, thus tightening the labor market by removing young men and increasing economic activity by orders for military equipment and supplies. Or it might pay men for raking leaves or expand unemployment insurance. One policy enhances available power, the other doesn't, though the theoretical potentials remain unchanged. If, having failed to train its men, the second state is attacked, it is forced to make a convulsive responsive effort. Enemy power must be matched if possible, when and where and however it is used.

The autonomous aspects of national strategy are extremely important. They are the main aspects about which decisions are made in advance of conflict. These decisions are likely to be swayed by factors extraneous to the true problem. These decisions may weigh heavily in the scales when one comes face to face with an opponent and must respond to his moves. The decision of the Truman administration to take a stand on immigration to Palestine was autonomous. Extraneous factors of domestic politics played an important part. The effect of this and subsequent decisions on American power in the Middle East was and continues significant.

The last aspect of relative power that we shall discuss might inelegantly be called "historical peristalsis." In both politics and technology, change is endless but not continuous. Nor is the phase always the same from one country to another. The peristaltic changes in naval technology, the political responses to such changes, and the relative power relations resulting from both are so well brought out in Bernard Brodie's *Sea Power in the Machine Age*[35] that no discussion here is needed. Similar processes take place in diplomacy, propaganda, and all the

[33] Carlyle, *History of the French Revolution*, I, Book 7, chap. 8.

[35] *Op. cit.*

other implements and methods of national strategy. To use a more refined but less apt analogy, the light of the strategic beam fluctuates. Hence the evaluation of the power inventory must change.

Thought is subject to many kinds of distortions, many of them quite unintentional. One common distortion is polarization. One polarization that is germane here is the tendency to place in opposition the long and the short views. The phenomenon of "historical peristalsis" indicates that both long and short views are necessary and complementary. A statement about national power really should carry a date.

Another form of polarization also is germane: The "and/or/versus" distortion. If one mentions, for example, "the spirit and the sword," it takes the merest twist of the tongue to change it to "the spirit or the sword" and but an intonation to give "or" the meaning of "versus." When we have spoken of power inventory and national strategy, *and* means *and,* not *or* or *versus.* Especially is it not intended to polarize material and imponderable aspects of power. There are non-material as well as material items in the power inventory and national strategy requires the availability of both. Even a national strategy of complete pacifism requires for inventory a stock of Grade A martyrs, as complete militarism requires a stock of Grade A brutes. Though a sound national strategy should reduce the wastage of resources, strategy is not a substitute for resources but is the art of using them.

CHAPTER SIX

The Impact of Geographic Considerations

Among deterministic theories of national power, few have exercised a more seductive and persistent appeal than geography. Until a half century ago, the relationship of geographical position to national power appeared to be one of the most stable and predictable factors in international politics. Europe in particular was endowed with such a favorable combination of climate, population, and resources that its economic, technological, and social organization appeared destined to give it unlimited supremacy over the rest of the world. In fact, with the exception of North America, the rest of the world appeared to be hopelessly limited by geographic and climatic conditions.

The only significant transformation that anyone seems to have perceived was that envisaged by Halford MacKinder, who foresaw in the increasing efficiency of rail transportation a geographically predetermined struggle between the landpower of the Eurasian "heartland" (designated as the "Pivot Area" in 1904) and the seapower of the inner or Marginal Crescent.[1] MacKinder believed that the marked improvement in land transport would eventually enable one central authority to control the region from roughly central Europe to the Siberian wastelands, and that such control would offset the greater capacity and flexibility of movement by sea and thereby put the historically dominant Western European powers at the mercy of whoever controlled Russia and the North European Plain. MacKinder's views, as well as the studies of Friedrich Ratzel, inspired a whole host of geographic determinists, of whom the German geopoliticians were the most notorious with their claim that geographic factors entirely determine the growth and decline of nations. Most analysts are now highly conscious of the relativity of geography, and agree that geography is not *the determining* but merely one of the many *conditioning* factors that shape the patterns of a state's behavior. Nor do contemporary geographers hold to any preconceived notions of what a nation is capable of achieving. The concept generally accepted today is "that the physical character of the earth has different meaning for different people: that the significance to man of the physical environment is a function of the attitudes, objectives, and technical abilities of

[1] Halford J. MacKinder, "The Geographical Pivot of History" (a paper read before the Royal Geographic Society in 1904).

man himself. With each change in any of the elements of the human culture, the resource base provided by the earth must be reevaluated."[2]

Harold and Margaret Sprout have elaborated the concept of "environmental possibilism," a term calling attention to the fact that geography, far from being immutable, is capable of being molded to man's purposes. As they point out, it is to be hoped that by achieving a more accurate conception of the man-milieu relationship, the student of international relations will avoid the deterministic pitfalls that have beset geopolitics. Above all, it should become clear that the mere analysis of data regarding geographic position, topography, resources, population, climate, industry, and so forth, has no intrinsic political meaning apart from the purposes for which men intend to exploit these geographic and related aspects of their environment. Geography becomes part of the analysis of international relations as a function of the "attitudes, objectives, and technical abilities of man himself." As men are able to view and control their environment in different ways, the relationship of geography to international relations changes.

The Sprouts call our attention to the relationship between "capability" and "intention." The question is: Will countries do whatever they are capable of doing? Or will they, under given circumstances, be content to try to achieve less? The dominant tendency on the part of practitioners of international relations has been to equate the two. It seems difficult to escape from the dilemma, and while the academic student of international relations may legitimately criticize the tendency to equate capability and intention, and deplore the policies to which this tendency gives rise, he should also attempt to empathize with the policy-maker who may feel that he has no alternative but to act on this assumption.[3]

In spite of the relativity with which its role must be viewed, geography *is* related to national power and strategy in many specific ways. The successive technological revolutions of the last half century have changed, but they have not eliminated, the importance of location, topography, climate and size. For purposes of clarification, Stephen B. Jones, in the article "Global Strategic Views," suggests that we look at the influence of geography upon international relations from the two perspectives of "inventory" and "strategy"—terms which were already referred to in the introduction to the previous chapter. "Inventory" is Jones' shorthand term designating the power potential which a nation possesses by virtue of its size, population, resource endowment, and industrial base. What is important in "inventory" is the optimum combination of size, development, and aggregate wealth—widely diversified as to type of commodities produced, and distributed in such a manner as to permit a relatively high proportion of expenditure on capital and military goods. Thus Switzerland may have a high standard of living, but it does not possess the massive geographic

[2] P. E. James, *American Geography, Inventory and Prospect* (Syracuse: Syracuse University Press, 1954), pp. 12–13.

[3] *Man-Milieu Relationship Hypotheses in the Context of International Policies,* Center of International Studies, Princeton, 1956.

and economic base upon which great power ultimately rests. "Strategy," as the term is here used, refers to the implications that geographic position plus technology hold for international relations. The fact that the United States is separated from the Eurasian continent by several thousand miles of open sea and by the frozen Arctic Ocean still counts for something in the calculations of American and Soviet strategists. Similarly, size has positive and negative strategic consequences for a country as large as the Soviet Union, depending upon the location of its resources and the efficiency of its transportation system.

In this connection, it may be relevant to note the idea, elaborated by some students of international relations, that there are great technical difficulties involved for a country which attempts to operate far from its home base, regardless of the fact that new means of communications have come to the fore. "There are . . . limits to the effective radius of political power from any center of the world," writes George F. Kennan, surely one of the most perceptive observers of international relations, adding that

> There is no magic by which great nations are brought to obey for any length of time the will of people very far away, who understand their problems poorly and with whom they feel no intimacy of origin or understanding. This has to be done by bayonets, or it is not done at all. What I am asserting is that universal world dominion is a technical impossibility, and that the effectiveness of the power radiated from any one national center decreases in proportion to the distance involved, and to the degree of cultural disparity.[4]

The analytical value of the distinction between "inventory" and "strategy" becomes clear if we consider the historical record of the last century. The unification and rapid industrialization of Germany in the last third of the nineteenth century enormously increased its economic, demographic, and industrial "inventory." This enabled Germany to resort to war twice within a generation in the confident expectation of achieving a position of hegemony in Europe. From the standpoint of "strategy," unification and industrialization enabled Germany to transform the disadvantages of a geographically vulnerable position into the advantages of a centralized power. Belgium and Switzerland afford additional examples of the strategic consequences that location may have upon a country's existence. Belgium, because of its location at a point strategically vital to three great powers (Britain, France, Germany), found itself unable to remain neutral. Switzerland, located just off the main strategic axis of Western Europe, escaped involvement in two successive World Wars. The United States and the Soviet Union are accounted the world's major powers in large part because they enjoy the geographic advantages of both a favorable inventory of national assets and a strategic location. It was this combination of advantages that a century ago evoked from de Tocqueville a prophetic observation that both Russia and America would one day hold within their hands "the destinies of half the globe" and that early drew MacKinder's attention to the potential of the Eurasian Heart-

[4] *Russia and the West Under Lenin and Stalin* (Boston: Little, Brown and Company, 1961), p. 276.

land which the Soviet Union now controls. And though MacKinder did not foresee the strategic importance that the arctic region would assume with the development of air power, his concepts are so solidly rooted in geographic realities that the Rimland, that great belt or crescent of land that runs from the North Cape through Western Europe, the Middle East, and South East Asia to the Kamchatka Peninsula, is still the main arena of world conflict.

The favorable conditions of climate, topography, resources, and communications by inland seas and overland routes that combined to make Europe and Southern Asia the oldest centers of civilization and power still give them a key position in international politics. Western Europe possesses the resources, social organization, industrial capacity, and trained manpower which in the hands of the Soviet Union would represent a dangerous accretion of power. Climate has not dealt as favorably with the Middle East, Africa, and Asia as it has with Europe; this fact, combined with an excess of population has prevented Africans and Asians from effectively developing their rich resources.[5] As a result, those regions remain power vacuums more than power centers. Thus geography establishes the foundations upon which capacity, interdependence and conflict are based, and its importance should not be underestimated. However, as the authors of the two selections in this chapter suggest, it is the perception, will, and creativity of men that ultimately determine the influence that geography will have upon international politics.

[5] George H. T. Kimble, "Handicap for New Nations: Climate," *New York Times Magazine*, September 29, 1963, p. 37 ff.

1

*Geography and International Relations**

Jean Gottmann

Jean Gottmann, *former Research Director, Study of Megalopolis, for the Twentieth Century Fund, is currently a professor at the Ecole des Hautes Etudes in Paris, France. He is an honorary member of the Royal Netherlands Geographic Society and the author of* A Geography of Europe *(1950) and* Megalopolis *(1961).*

The world we live in happens to be a diversified, highly partitioned space. The surface of the earth is partitioned in a great many ways; politically and physically, economically and culturally. The political divisions are the *raison d'être* of international relations; the variety of the different parts of the earth's surface is the *raison d'être* of geography. If the earth were uniform—well polished, like a billiard ball—there probably would not be any

* *World Politics,* III (1950), 153–173. Reprinted by permission.

such science as geography, and international relations would be much simpler. Because the general principles of geology, geophysics, botany, or economics do not apply in the same way throughout the different compartments existing on the earth, geographical studies appeared and were useful, cutting across the abstraction of the topical disciplines and attempting a scientific analysis of regions and their interrelations.

The belief is, therefore, very old and quite natural that geography is a potent factor in international relations. At a moment when international organization is beginning to play an outstanding part in the daily affairs of every nation, when the advance of the techniques of transportation would seem to make every event global, every country shrinking, every old partition crumbling—at such a period of history it may be worth while to attempt a brief analysis of this geographical factor. The question has a profound meaning to geographers as well as to political scientists dealing with international affairs. No one would argue against the usefulness of geographical data for the study of a problem localized in or moving through an area on the earth's surface. One would not speak of a geographical factor, however, if geography could contribute only such data of a statistical or descriptive nature. The belief concerning geography as a determinant element carries a different meaning; to appraise it we may have to formulate a definition of the methods and aims of geography itself.

ENVIRONMENT AND THE BEHAVIOR OF NATIONS

Let us first glance at what the discussion has so far covered. The debate is an old one and seems to stem from the logical search for some stable elements in the ever shifting and subtle pattern of international relations. These relations develop amidst a complicated interplay of many factors, few of which are endowed with any degree of stability; but the most stable of all is certainly the physical environment, most fully described by geographers. The "geographical conditions" of a political phenomenon seem not only stable but also rather easily surveyable and measurable, at least in many of their components. The temptation has been great and often has triumphed to reduce the geographical environment to the best measured and defined physical components.

The environment seems to provide the permanent material foundation both of nationalism, insofar as the nation is defined and affected by the territory it occupies, and of power, for a nation depends much on the resources obtainable within its territory for the upbuilding of its status among other nations. International relations have always been concerned with a certain order to be maintained or improved, over the whole or a part of the earth's surface. Geography studies the existing order, registers it in the simplified but convenient form of maps, explains the interplay of the physical factors (meteorology, topography, hydrography, vegetation, etc.), and describes the distribution of the population and the forms of settlement. History is a much more turbulent process. If it could be explained by geography, some stable principles could be worked out helping to understand the past and to forecast the future.

The temptation thus arises to establish a "cause and effect" link between the permanent geographical conditions and the more stable aspects of international relations. Power, after all, needs some basic resources and geography seems just the thing to give an appraisal of the potential. Further application of such logic carries down a steep slope: geographical conditions are given a determining influence on the behavior of nations and governments. In the story of international relations, where a number of nations may harbor some feelings of guilt because of past deeds, such grievances can be relieved by an "environmentalistic" or, in simpler terms, a "geographical" explanation: responsibility is shifted to those physical, cosmic forces that play with helpless peoples. Even some of the emotional components of nationalism can be brought down to geography as stemming from the native soil.

This simple and all the more impressive relationship between geography and international affairs can be traced back as far as historical records go. Ancient navigators exploring far away areas found strange peoples living in strange climates. The connection was quickly established between ethnic and climatic features. Many facts made this basic relationship obvious: colored peoples lived in other than European and Mediterranean areas; Negroes were found in tropical territories, and yellow races under monsoon climates. Weather is, of all conditions outside our control (at least to date), the one every individual feels the most directly in his daily life. Beliefs as to the influence of climatic conditions on the behavior of peoples and on the consequent distribution of political systems and power are found not only in the writings of early political scientists, such as Montesquieu, for instance, but they are still widespread in the common man's opinion of many a civilized country.[1]

A fundamental flaw in this reasoning appears as one tries to co-ordinate the stability of the physical maps with the instability of the political pattern of the world. Some geographers tried to save what they considered to be the basis of their prestige by assuming changes in the climatic map. If the site of the leading powers of the world had shifted from the Middle East to Atlantic shores, it could be explained by a migration of climates: the optimum climate for power would have migrated from the Valley of the Nile, where it was achieved at the time of the Rameses, to Greece, Rome, western Europe, and finally to the eastern United States. Such a brilliant theory lacked only the proof of any substantial change in the climatic regime of Egypt during the historical times. Desiccation took place in the Middle East before the great empires arose there. The rules of water conservation set forth in Hammurabi's Code refer to a situation much worse than any water shortage in New York City or Washington, D.C.

The paradoxical point in such theories is that, starting from the stability of the environment in the search for the permanent laws governing international relations, geographers came to an emphasis on the possible instability of these physical conditions. The trend of investigation ought to be enough to demonstrate that it took the wrong path. Climate has been carefully studied by biologists; and the further their knowledge of human nature advances, the surer they are that heredity rather than ambient climatic conditions determine the human type. Even such an enthusiastic "sun worshipper" as the late Ellsworth Huntington came at the end of his career to recognize the importance of many

[1] Montesquieu has many references to climate in his *Spirit of Laws*. Earlier Jean Bodin, and others, linked State and Soil in an environmentalistic way. The same trend is found in very recent works, especially by the late Ellsworth Huntington.

other factors.[2] There is no optimum climate for power or civilization.

The oversimplified relation between a nation's character and its physical environment has been only one of the aspects of the discussion we are concerned with. It was, however, a critical one, because it was basic. Once we admit that no climatic regime is an obstacle that could not be overcome by a stubborn and organized national endeavor, then the eventual part of the environment in international affairs is reduced to a small lot indeed. We have harbored for a long time prejudice against the tropical, i.e., the humid and hot climates. India has shown at various times in its history, and again at present, that a tropical country can rise to an eminent place among powers. Brazil may well be on the way to another demonstration of a determined nation's command over a tropical environment. Cold climates in the subarctic area would seem the most difficult to conquer. No major power has ever risen that was based entirely in the very cold areas of the globe; but many powers have had a substantial part of their territory in such areas without being definitely weakened thereby. Arid deserts have been cradles of powerful or advanced nations many times. Neither mountains nor plains could claim greater concentration of either power or political weakness throughout history.[3] Thus neither climate nor topography could indeed be held determinant for a country's position in the world, especially in our epoch of sweeping technological progress.

All this does not mean that physical geography is not important to the daily detail of international relations. It is easy to compile a list of physical features that have to be reckoned with: the distribution of land and sea, the topography, the hydrographic network, the size of the territory, and its aptitudes to produce.

. . . If modern technology and economics could be put into a brief formula for the use of geographers, it may be as follows: "Nature does not produce; nature only reproduces." Production is an economic not a natural function. It carries with itself the connotation of being aimed at something. This results from the human activities that have inserted themselves inside the great cycles (vegetative and mineral) of nature, and have somewhat disrupted them, in order to serve ambitious men driving toward certain goals. Even mining, often described as the type of the most destructive use of resources, does not destroy, scientifically speaking, the extracted ores or metals: it only displaces them. The gold taken out of South African soil could be found generations later in the teeth of Europeans or in the fountain pens of Americans. The iron found in concentrated form in Swedish mines and extracted a long time ago may still be in some engine or railroad car, or it may have been returned to the earth one way or another. This displacement by man of natural elements from their "normal" physical order,

[2] See his *Mainsprings of Civilization* (New York: John Wiley & Sons, Inc., 1945) where heredity plays a part. The danger for the geographer of studying the impact of physical conditions on human behavior is to be sucked into biological problems such as the chromosomes' or the genes' reactions to changes in environment. This is not the geographer's field and, moreover, the modern trends of biology ought to induce the geographer to more and more caution in such an approach.

[3] Arnold Toynbee's theory of "challenge and response" is, in a way, inverted environmentalism. Some statements in the early volumes of his *Study of History* worried us as granting far too much influence to physical forces, at the expense of other relations of the civilization considered.

through mining, agriculture, forestry, or waterworks, has been developed on a larger scale and for an increased number of elements as the population grew and as the techniques of applied chemistry and physics improved. Recent advances in nuclear physics have again opened wide possibilities of transposing elements by human decision. They may render economic self-sufficiency for a country easier but less profitable.

The numbers of the people and their technological level are determinant factors in putting to use potential "natural" resources or in substituting some organization for the lack of some desirable resource within the area considered. The size of the area here again plays a part. It may be easier to "organize" a smaller than a bigger space. This again depends on the density and on the quality of the population—and in the final resort on the social and political organization that makes it difficult or easy to put things and people to work. We come, therefore, to consider the organization of national or regional groups in their relation with the physical environment they are set in. Many times geographers have expressed the belief that government is a factor in political geography and in the use of resources. That seems today an obvious truth but needs more digging in the search for the roots of the matter.

What seems to us important is that men and things are different from one region to another, from one country to another. There is a natural variety in the space inhabited by men. This natural diversity is much less varied than the political one, and the two do not coincide on the map. The pattern achieved as a result of human action and organization is the most complicated but also the important one to international relations and to the daily life of men. Geography has aimed at a survey of "what is where"; it has not been very successful in explaining why it was so, how and why the present order was evolving. To achieve a better understanding of these momentous questions it may be helpful to look at them through the eyes of the doers: human groups do not all see the same thing in the same environment. Each group does to the environment what they think they should do. They do not all think alike. In a space differentiated already by nature, this diversity of people's minds, of the spirit of the nations, creates more differentiation. The differentiation of the space accessible to men appears to be the *raison d'être* of both geography and international relations.

The Organization of Differentiated Space

International relations have always been complicated because the *spirit* of each nation is so different from the spirit of the other nations. This is especially true of neighbor-countries: boundaries between them exist because each country *feels* it is different from the other. This national, or regional, spirit is always made of many components: a historical background, and its interpretation, common to the members of the community, but alien to those beyond the border. The common link is preserved and often reinforced by the education that family and school give the younger generations. The local environment always plays a part among the foundations of such national or regional spirit, but the important thing is what the people are *taught to see* in the physical and social conditions they live in. We know that the highlands of the vast island of Madagascar were quickly deforested and converted into a poor, low-growing steppe, after the conquest and reorganization of the land by a people of cattle herders coming from the Indian area. Trees and agriculture did not mean much to them. Madagascar today still exports beef. Even more striking changes have happened within the last five centuries throughout the Americas. . . .

To be distinct from its surroundings, a region needs much more than a mountain or a valley, a given language or certain skills; it needs essentially a strong belief based on some religious creed, some social viewpoint, or some pattern of political memories, and often a combination of all three. Thus regionalism has some *iconography* as its foundation. An icon, a symbol slightly different from those cherished by its neighbors, was cared for in each region of the Old World, adorned with whatever jewels and riches the community could supply, until it either broke up or became a sound economic investment. Economic interests have been a great motive, perhaps overrated even in international affairs, but popular emotions have been more often aroused by other motives.[4] So many problems would have been easier to settle if nations were less attached to their pride, their past, their way of life, their culture—all that we round up in the term "national spirit." But would life be worth living if we did not have those values to care for? A great many people have been asking themselves this question, recently and also many generations ago. History teaches us that people often preferred leaving the soil of their ancestors to giving up their beliefs or their way of life. The latter may have been substantially reformed afterwards as a result of the displacement, but it remained different from that which they did not wish to be imposed upon them.

To be different from others and proud of one's own special features is an essential trait of every human group. No group greatly resents its example being followed, but none likes to follow another's lead. This basic character, inherent to human psychology and sociology, makes every unit of space inhabited by man essentially a human unit. The most stubborn facts are those of the spirit, not those of the physical world. This is so true that international law has struggled for some time with a confusion between the "natural" and the "rational" laws—nature, as described by us, is what we believe it ought to be. And while history shows how stubborn are the facts of the spirit, geography demonstrates that the main partitions observed in the space accessible to men are not those in the topography or in the vegetation but those that are in the minds of the people. Nations like to tame nature, and everyone in its own way.[5]

Any space in which men penetrate becomes partitioned in some way. A long battle, much more complicated than the history of shipbuilding, has been fought for the freedom of the high seas. Certain national flags still hold the monopoly of transportation by sea between certain points although the route passes through the high seas —the United States flag between San Francisco and New York, or the French flag between Le Havre and Fort de France. An involved legislation rules about the right of access to

[4] See the remarkable analysis given by Jacob Viner, "The Economic Problem," in *New Perspectives on Peace*, ed. by G. B. de Huszar (Chicago: University of Chicago Press, 1944), pp. 85–114.

[5] Gilbert Chinard in his book *L'homme contre la nature* (Paris, 1949) gives interesting examples from American history. We have also come to similar conclusions in our studies of Old World regions; see Jean Gottmann, *A Geography of Europe* (New York: Holt, Rinehart & Winston, Inc., 1950).

mineral riches as far as human action can go underground. Another legislation has sprung up in the atmosphere. Since men fly, air space has been partitioned: it is much easier to enter the stratosphere, although its structure is a very special one, than to cross (unless authorized by the proper authorities) the vertical and imaginary boundary-plan separating the air spaces over two different national territories.[6]

All of these cultural and legal patterns have obvious consequences in economics. Economists also deal with space and are much concerned about its organization. But space is for them little differentiated: they formulate its essence for their own purposes as costs of transportation, distances, and the partitions as customs tariffs and regulations—all things that can be changed by a stroke of the pen. The reality is more complex because it is geographical, i.e., differentiated. In fact, every unit of territory, regional or national, is individualized. Its own spirit gives it a certain individuality. A distinguished economist, Edgar M. Hoover, has attempted in his book on *The Location of Economic Activity* to formulate the principles of the distribution in space of these activities.[7] This is an important book for geographers as it formulates a number of interesting abstractions; but as Mr. Hoover works his way ahead closer to the actual facts, he comes up against elements less and less reducible to general terms and of a different nature than quantitative area: he cannot avoid emphasizing the importance of economic and social structure of communities, of technological changes, of political boundaries, of national defense considerations, etc. His chapters grow thinner as the complexity of the factor grows. The economist comes up against all those accidents which differentiate and make the quality of the space we live in. There is an organization of space. The economist is interested in it because it is *organization*, the geographer because it is *space* which for him is a limited, differentiated unit, endowed with problems of accessibility, sovereignty, evolution, and finally "personality," if that term could be applied to entire communities.

The differentiation arising between compartments of space is the very foundation of any study in international relations. Evolution of that differentiation has long been a major concern of political geography. About half a century ago, the French geographer, Paul Vidal de la Blache, wrote that there should be no problem more important in that field than to trace how "elements of a general life infiltrate through the multiplicity of local cases."[8] He was then studying how the many parts of what became France came together to form a separate and unified nation. His sentence defines the geographical analysis of empire-building or of the processes forming those vast zones of civilization that still weigh so heavily on human relations. His problem is also the problem of international organization. But what is the importance of geography

[6] See John C. Cooper, *The Right to Fly* (New York: Holt, Rinehart & Winston, Inc., 1947). It will probably be difficult for the laws of the air to remain in their present state. It seems hard to avoid putting a "ceiling on sovereignty" in the atmosphere, at some altitude, if some actual freedom to air navigation is to be instituted.

[7] Edgar M. Hoover, *The Location of Economic Activity* (New York: McGraw-Hill Book Company, 1948).

[8] Paul Vidal de la Blache, *Tableau de la géographie de la France* (Paris, 1902) (the first volume of the monumental *Histoire de France* edited by Ernest Lavisse). The first chapters of this volume are a masterpiece and should be better known by geographers and political scientists.

in all these delicate problems, would ask the reader, if the determinant causes of spatial differentiation are in the spirit, the culture, the history of the communities? Why shouldn't the historian, the sociologist, the psychologist, and the cultural anthropologist be the people to study the problems of differentiated space? Having always been against the worshipping of labels and artificial partitions, we do not doubt that a historian well trained in geography could do as good a job as a geographer well trained in history. They could do still a better job probably by working together on the problem, but such debates are beside the main point. The problem raised is that of the original scientific contribution of geography to its own field. Is geography merely a method for filing, for classifying data provided by many natural and social sciences, or does it have something of its own besides? We think it has a very definite and original role, only it is a complex one that has rarely been clarified. We shall attempt to define that role in terms of the formula already stated that geography studies the organization of differentiated space accessible to man.

How can the *differentiated quality* of a spatial unit—let us call it a *region* for brevity—be defined? Chiefly by a method stressing the differences from other regions. But a region is not a dead, crystallized body; it is an ever changing one; so are the other regions. How can we express such an unstable relationship between a number of moving elements? By stressing the relationship geographers apply often the comparative method. They record the *pluses* and *minuses,* the *mores* and *lesses,* and measure what is measurable with common units. This method supplies statistical data but does not operate satisfactorily in spatial matters. Then the cartographical method is brought in: maps save long phrases and say it with more precision.[9] A good geographer can map almost anything, but the more clever his drawing grows the less people can read on it what the author intended to get across.

A map expresses a network of relations and that is what geography treasures. It is not simply a network of relations between functional phenomena integrated in a given place. It is much more a set of relationships between things that do not coincide in space but are scattered in space and still related. The world would be a pretty simple organization if, selecting a locality, you could explain what happens there by local conditions only. The point is that you never can explain a thing entirely by local developments. Let us take a tree: can we explain its growth, its shape by the conditions of the space it occupies? Never. First of all, the tree needs water; it is brought by rainfall. But the rain is not generated right there, nor just above our tree. It comes from a distance; so does the wind that curves the branches; so does the warmth that makes the tree live: it comes from the sun. Had another, higher tree grown to the south of ours, it would throw some shadow over it, so that stronger limbs would have extended eastwards or northwards, looking for the light and heat. The growth of the roots underground is another important factor. It may be limited by other roots of trees growing at some distance. And the roots will have to develop according to the pattern of underground water circulation; as a matter of fact, our tree may grow even without any local rain if a spring mur-

[9] See S. Whittemore Boggs, "Geographic and Other Scientific Techniques for Political Science," *American Political Science Review*, **XLII**, No. 2 (April, 1948), 223–238.

murs at some distance. The tree depends on a complex network of relations with the surrounding areas, some of them not being very close; it depends also on the timber policy of state authorities.

Nobody would dare compare modern man, and even less a whole community, to a tree. The example of an immobile plant shows simply that the physical environment itself, even in small details, is not locally determined. Climate in a given territory results from a play of forces usually centered far away. The weatherman in New York is concerned about the Caribbean highs and the Newfoundland lows, and so it goes all around the world. Topography is important in relation to what is beyond it: the structure of local strata belongs to geology, but the ability of a valley to be a route or of a mountain to be a barrier belongs to geography. Route and barrier are notions involving the outside world; they mean traffic, transportation, communications. The function of a river at a given point depends on the sea to which it flows and on what happens at the mainsprings from which the water comes. The physical environment is definitely a matter of interregional relations as much and perhaps more than of regional conditions.

How much more true the same principle would be in the field of cultural and economic geography. No culture has been entirely developed on the spot; it was always moulded by influences and pressures from other areas. If the region considered is entirely landlocked, these influences came mainly (but not exclusively) through the neighbors. In the case of a maritime situation some influences may have come directly from the antipodes or any other strange country. The distribution of land and sea thus reappears, but it can be corrected in several ways: for instance, a landlocked country bordering on a vast desert may have been affected by influences from strange lands across that desert. Like the sea, the desert can be either an easy route or a barrier; it is not densely occupied by men and offers more freedom to traffic. The sea, like the desert, may also discourage traffic for those who lack the spirit for spanning it. The physical environment is there, important insofar as it channels relations and helps to shape the network of communications, but this importance diminishes as civilization devises better means of transportation by land, sea, and air.

The network of cultural relations must be the most delicate and complicated to trace; mapping it is not an easy job. Vidal de la Blache once compared a country's civilization to a clock —it needs action from the outside to wind it up, otherwise it stops and does not show the right hour any more. He was defining France as constantly affected by the mingling of two different elements: the one continental, truly European; the other maritime, Mediterranean, bringing in influences from overseas.[10] In recent times the Atlantic element has become at least as important as the Mediterranean was. Maritime and continental simultaneously, by the shape of her territory as well as by her spirit, France has constantly participated in two patterns of development. It did not make her history more stable or simple, but it certainly enriched her. Today again her position in relation to what is happening on the oceans and on the main land masses both increases her importance and sharpens her problems.

It may be argued that to be maritime a country needs a "window on the open sea" and that a nation's des-

[10] Vidal de la Blache, *op. cit.*

tiny cannot be entirely emancipated from the impact of its territorial setting. The intercorrelations in the field of geography are intricate, and no factors can be said to be totally ineffective. Every one of them is important by its relation to others. The geographical position of a country is always defined with respect to some landmarks situated at a distance, for instance the equator and the meridian zero when latitude and longitude are given. But it is a much more complex and much less stable network of relations that the geographer must survey in order to serve practical purposes that interest the student of international relations.

When President James Monroe set forth the famous doctrine that bears his name, he was not simply following some general lines of geography and stating the dividing power of oceans between continents. The non-interference of European Powers in American affairs and the respect of the status quo were both conclusions based in fact on the study of all the relationships of power and of intention making up the political geography of the time. Commenting upon the declaration, Thomas Jefferson wrote to James Monroe on October 24, 1823:

> Our first and fundamental maxim should be, never to entangle ourselves in the broils of Europe. Our second, never to suffer Europe to intermeddle with cis-Atlantic affairs. America, North, and South, has a set of interests distinct from those of Europe, and peculiarly her own. She should therefore have a system of her own, separate and apart from that of Europe. . . . But we have first to ask ourselves a question. Do we wish to acquire to our own confederacy any one or more of the Spanish provinces? I candidly confess, that I have ever looked on Cuba as the most interesting addition which could ever be made to our system of States. The control which, with Florida Point, this island would give us over the Gulf of Mexico, and the countries and isthmus bordering on it, as well as all those whose waters flow into it, would fill up the measure of our political well-being. Yet, as I am sensible that this can never be obtained, even with her own consent, but by war; and its independence, which is our second interest, (and especially its independence of England) can be secured without it, I have no hesitation in abandoning my first wish to future chances, and accepting its independence, with peace and the friendship of England, rather than its association, at the expense of war and her enmity.[11]

Jefferson's comments provide a beautiful analysis of the interpenetration of the geographical position with international politics. It helps us to understand how much the natural, social, and political status of a region, with the population inhabiting it, is dependent on the network of relations that has been slowly elaborated in the past by geological and historical sequences. The geographical environment should not therefore be taken as the whole of local conditions. Every territory has some internal environment—physical, economic, and social. But this is under the impact of the *external* environment, formulated through a network of relations, situating the region considered amidst other differentiated units of the global space it participates in. The network itself is so complicated because every corner of space accessible to men is strongly differentiated, owing to the variety of human minds and the original spirit of communities.[12]

---

[11] *The Writings of Thomas Jefferson*, ed. by P. L. Ford (New York: G. P. Putnam's Sons, 1899), X, 277–278.

[12] In a recent article, David Mitrany ("Evolution of the Middle Zone," *Annals of the American Academy of Political and Social Science*, Vol. 271 [September 1950], pp. 1–10) observes that the present "iron curtain" follows a ribbon of territory in

It thus appears that the same difficulties stand in the way of the geographer and of the student of international relations. The two fields are very closely connected, although there has been some mutual ignoring of one another. Geography has often developed as a discipline in research and in teaching as a result of wars. In Europe, the geographer was looked upon in the nineteenth century as a technician who knew how to draft maps on which military brains could plan their campaigns and diplomats agree, or disagree, about boundaries. Without underestimating the importance of war in history, it may be argued that geography should contribute much more to the organization of peace. The geographers who created modern geography at the dawn of the twentieth century, mostly between 1895 and 1910, were all impressed by the importance of the network of relations affecting regional problems though having its roots and limbs stretched far outside the region concerned. Vidal de la Blache in France, MacKinder in Britain, Ratzel in Germany—all contributed to establish the authority of their skill. Most of their students, however much they admired the great men who traced on a broad scale, went into the sharpening of analytical techniques. Geography went into microanalysis, breaking up some of its unity, losing sight of its original aim: to contribute a system to the general human understanding of the world as a whole. It became "unscientific" to use the "broad scale," and geography got less and less useful to the other social sciences, and to international relations especially.

Some of Vidal de la Blache's students attempted to carry on along the path he opened. Jean Bruhnes and Camille Vallaux wrote a *Géographie de l'Histoire,* which reveals already an environmentalistic slant (in the narrow sense of the word). Albert Demangeon remained closer to his teacher's lead. In his well-known book on Picardy, the model of the French regional monographs, he stated that "the most productive farm was not the one striving at the highest yields, but the one adapting itself best to the conditions of competition and marketing."[13] Few geographers, alas, have kept in mind the importance of the network of relations. A recent volume published in Britain on *Geography Behind Politics,* although quoting abundantly both Vidal de la Blache and Demangeon, still states as the basic problems of political geography: the analysis of the relationship between community and physical environment (taken as the local conditions) and of the susceptibility of States to change.[14] This is still an approach leading to ecology, which Ratzel may have brought into geography from botany, his original field.

In 1750 a young and bright student of the Sorbonne, majoring in history, had the feeling that the historical studies ought to lead to some conclusions of practical value. Young Turgot, later one of the great French economists and reformers, wrote a brief, somewhat dim, and ambitious paper, which he entitled *La Géographie Politique.*[15] He suggested a full program

Central Europe which has been a curtain stopping many streams in history: the Romans, Western Protestantism, and the industrial revolution could not expand much east of it; the Turks and the Eastern Church remained behind it. Such stubborn divides should be investigated thoroughly by geographers for whom they set interesting problems.

13 Albert Demangeon, *La Plaine Picarde* (Paris, 1906).

14 A. E. Moodie, *Geography Behind Politics* (London, 1947).

15 The political geography of A. R. J. Turgot is to be found in *Oeuvres de Turgot,* ed. by Dupont de Nemours (Paris, 1844), II, 611–626.

for political science divided in three parts to which he claimed he gave their "real titles": "1. a reasoned history of the world; 2. a political geography that would follow from it; 3. a treatise of government, which would contain what I call the theory of political geography." In his political geography Turgot wanted to give "a profile of history" at a given moment. He did not complete this work and was soon oriented toward theoretical economics, so revolutionary his ideas appeared to his teachers. Two centuries after his attempt, it may seem possible to pick up his project again and expect some principles and theories to come out of a thorough study in the organization of differentiated space.

The theory of international relations deals with very abstract notions, such as sovereignty. It is through law and history that such problems are usually analyzed. The idea is very old, of course, that sovereignty ought to be related with space, for how could it apply without some spatial frame? Linking sovereignty to the local soil and sky is an old oversimplification, perhaps responsible for some of the less desirable features of usual nationalism. Linking sovereignty to the right to regional differentiation, to a freedom of ways of life, may perhaps help formulate a "spatial" principle of sovereignty; it may help to understand why lasting sovereignty on very vast areas seems to require a federal form of government, more respectful of regional variety. Sovereignty may well be the legal tool through which people attempt to preserve their right to differentiate themselves from their neighbors.[16] It is to national groups what private property and privacy are to individuals. The organization of differentiated space, to achieve any kind of stable form, has to provide for such security. Peoples, being suspicious of one another, do not take as "secure" conditions in which freedom for differentiation is not granted.

What could be the contribution of geographical thought to the study of international relations has been only hinted at as yet by a few geographers. A great many students in other fields have felt an urge for such a contribution. As international organization develops in the texts and in the facts, it may be found that the differentiation of human groups and therefore of accessible space is a major obstacle in applying too generalized abstractions. Geography should help solve the difficulty, if correctly interpreted. Differences can be organized without being suppressed. The multiplicity of regional ways of life can be maintained and even improved by general co-operation. We need to know about them,

---

[16] Recent technological developments have given rise to very complicated but most interesting new problems in the field of the law of the air. How far up does a national sovereignty extend in the space *above* its territory? . . . [S]pace available to men has changed from a bi-dimensional to a tri-dimensional problem. Law has almost seemed to ignore the third dimension or, more exactly, has extended it to the infinite. If the column of space above a given territory belongs to that territory without restriction in distance, the moon's sovereignty changes as it circles around the earth, and so would any satellite of the earth. . . . [B]ut how could this be left open when men get to be actively sending rockets to the moon or creating new satellites. . . . The problem of guided missiles passing over "neutral" territory is a different immediate problem in this same line, and the possibility of rain-making has recently shown in the vicinity of New York how disputed the control of the air is going to be. It has got to be both partitioned and governed according to laws based on permanent moral principles rather than on a changing "power politics" situation.

See especially Cooper, *op. cit.* Several discussions of these matters with Mr. Cooper have greatly helped us to elaborate our own view of these matters.

to understand their spirit and respect them, to study what relations have existed and still exist between all these ways of life. Without such a multiple net of relationships there probably would not have been such a multiplicity of regions. The ways and means of evolution, once known, could be put to the service of international relations. A great soldier, Marshal Lyautey, once defined warfare as "an organization on the march." Such should be peace.

2

*Global Strategic Views**

Stephen B. Jones

When Mackinder's "The Geographical Pivot of History" was printed in the *Geographical Journal,* the comments made by members of the audience were, according to the usual practice, printed also. Many readers have noted that one auditor, Amery, called attention to the airplane as possibly upsetting the assumptions on which Mackinder's theory was based—this in 1904, only a few weeks after the Wright brothers had made their first flight.

Mackinder, we have seen, wrote of the seaman's and the landsman's points of view. The basic pattern of the physical world was of course the same for both, but the strategic forecast hinged on the belief that land transportation was overtaking sea transportation as a vehicle of power. We have also seen that putting, or seeming to put, seaman and landsman in strong contrast may have been a disservice to clear thinking. Now we have the airman. Must we add the airman's point of view? Or would that only increase the confusion?

For one thing, there is a wide range of thought about air power. Experience with air power is limited, and the pace of technological change has been extraordinary. We find variation from the "all-out" school, exemplified by such men as Douhet and Seversky, through moderate but firmly "air-first" men to the conservatives who hold that the main function of air power is to assist surface operations.

The conservative group holds that the surface battlefield remains the locus of decision. Sea power is vital to the supply of the battle front. Air power is vital to the security of sea routes, for observation and rapid transportation, and as long-range artillery to interdict enemy movements. Strategic bombardment, to this group, should be related to surface operations. Such a view of air power leads to no very new view of the globe. A third dimension has been added to the Mahan or Mackinder world, but its surface features have not been erased, and the travel-time scale has not been greatly altered, since surface movement dominates.

For an example of the air-first moderates, we may take Slessor, who holds that the strategic air force, with nuclear bombs, is "the Great Deterrent" which may prevent another gen-

* *The Geographical Review,* **XLV** (1955), 499–508. Reprinted by permission.

eral war.[1] But local wars are still possible, with ground forces bearing much of the load. Slessor sees a need for armies and navies and even for a special "semi-static" force or militia for local and civil defense. Slessor does not describe his global view, as we use that term here, but manifestly it must combine something like the Rimland—the locus of local wars—with a disbelief in heartlands. His views on heartlands seem like an echo of Amery's, amplified by half a century of aeronautical development:

> Meanwhile do not let us be distracted by geopolitical talk about heartlands, which was all very well in Mackinder's day but ceased to be relevant with the advent of the long-range bomber. Russia's central position has some tactical advantages, vis-à-vis her neighbours, but in a world air war she would be at a decisive disadvantage. Air power has turned the vast spaces that were her prime defence against Napoleon and Hindenburg and Hitler into a source of weakness. In these days of near-sonic speeds, the depth of penetration necessary to reach some of her vital centres is offset by the size of the area to be defended and the fact that it can be attacked from almost all round the compass.[2]

In Slessor's view, the virtues of the Heartland—size, centrality, and inaccessibility—have become either of no advantage or disadvantageous. Have *Raum und Lage* gone into reverse, so to speak, in the air age?

In order that the Soviet power base be penetrable "from almost all round the compass," it is essential that the non-Communist powers maintain a strong position in the Rimland and in what Spykman called the "off-shore islands" of Great Britain, Japan, Africa, and Australia. If these areas come under Communist domination, it will be the Americas that are penetrable "from almost all round the compass."

Whether centrality in Eurasia gives the Soviet Union a commanding position or only a strong one [has been discussed above].[3] The relative value of land power and sea power in the Rimland was held undecided. What of air power? It is incomparably fast, of increasing capacity, and less and less restricted by weather and surface features. But the very speed of the airplane may offset some of the advantages of position. At near-sonic speeds, to fly, say, from Tashkent to Delhi would take less than two hours. But from Singapore to Delhi would take only four. Would the difference be critical? Would not what Whittlesey calls "pace"[4]—the average tempo of operations—and timing be more important than the velocity of flight, at such speeds? Fuel remains a great problem until atomic energy is adapted to aircraft, but could not Singapore be supplied as readily as Tashkent? If one is ready and resolute, need one be despondent over geographical position? For that matter, may not the Battle of the Rimland be decided by politics rather than by war? Was Vietminh lost by war, or by French delay in freeing and arming Vietnam and American unwillingness to enter the fray?

How do nuclear weapons affect these matters? One may readily agree that in an all-out nuclear war, with cities blasted from the face of the earth and even the countryside polluted with radioactive fall-out, "Heartland," "Rimland," "land power," and "sea power" are words with little signifi-

[1] John Slessor, *Strategy for the West* (New York: William Morrow & Co., Inc., 1954), especially Chapters 3 and 4.

[2] *Ibid.*, p. 34.

[3] In a section omitted from the present selection.

[4] Derwent Whittlesey, *The Horizon of Geography, Annals Assn. of Amer. Geogrs.*, **XXXV** (1945), 1–36; reference on p. 24.

cance. But we hear much of the tactical use of nuclear weapons. Just what "tactical use" means is not clear. Should it be stretched to include use against docks, bridges, and freight yards, it comes perilously close to "strategic bombardment," involving or inviting the destruction of cities. If, however, it is possible to confine nuclear weapons to tactical uses, it is not certain that either land power or sea power is favored or that the Heartland-Rimland relationship is altered. Much depends on the relative improvement in methods of attack and defense and on the alertness of the belligerents and the astuteness of their commanders.

Seversky's View

If there is a unique "airman's global view," it probably is essentially that of Seversky, and the azimuthal equidistant projection centered on the North Pole is its cartographic expression (Fig. 1).[5] The popularity of North Polar projections has been a valuable corrective to the overuse of the Mercator. The equidistant form, however, has the serious defect of stretching the latitudinal scale in the Southern Hemisphere, and this in turn has the visual effect of greatly exaggerating the width of the southern oceans.

Seversky definitely subordinates the army and navy to the air force. He believes that virtually complete air supremacy, not just local or temporary air superiority, is possible. The side that obtains air supremacy holds the other at its mercy. He does not expect this to come without enormous effort and losses, but he feels that a country such as the United States, with advanced technology but limited manpower, can better pay the price of air supremacy than that of superiority in three media.[6] Since he wishes the United States to avoid surface, and particularly ground, combat, he regards overseas bases as undesirable, probably untenable, and, in an age of intercontinental flight, unnecessary. Besides the Soviet Union and the United States, Britain alone has the potentialities of great air power. Only in the vicinity of Bering Strait does orthodox warfare seem justified. Latin America, within the circle of American air dominance, becomes the main reserve of American industry. Much of Africa and all of Southeast Asia are within the ellipse of Soviet air dominance. The overlap of the American circle and the Soviet ellipse is the "area of decision," where Seversky thinks the mastery of the air will be decided. Seversky's global view thus swings us back to the concept of Western Hemisphere defense, with a north-south rather than an east-west emphasis.

A number of American habits of mind favor acceptance of "the airman's view." A sort of "air isolationism" appears possible, the Western Hemisphere is revived, faith in machines and in American know-how is a string touched, the all-out air strategy seems economical in dollars and men. On the other hand, the conservatism of the Army and Navy and their civilian supporters is aroused. Dislike or disregard for "the frozen north" and habitual east-west thinking are strong. "The suggestive map" that speaks to most Americans is still likely to have the equator across the middle.

The choice among the conservative, moderate, and all-out air views is one of the most critical in the American future. The decision will determine the allocation of manpower and re-

[5] A. P. de Seversky, *Air Power: Key to Survival* (New York: Simon and Schuster, Inc., 1950).

[6] *Ibid.*, p. 11.

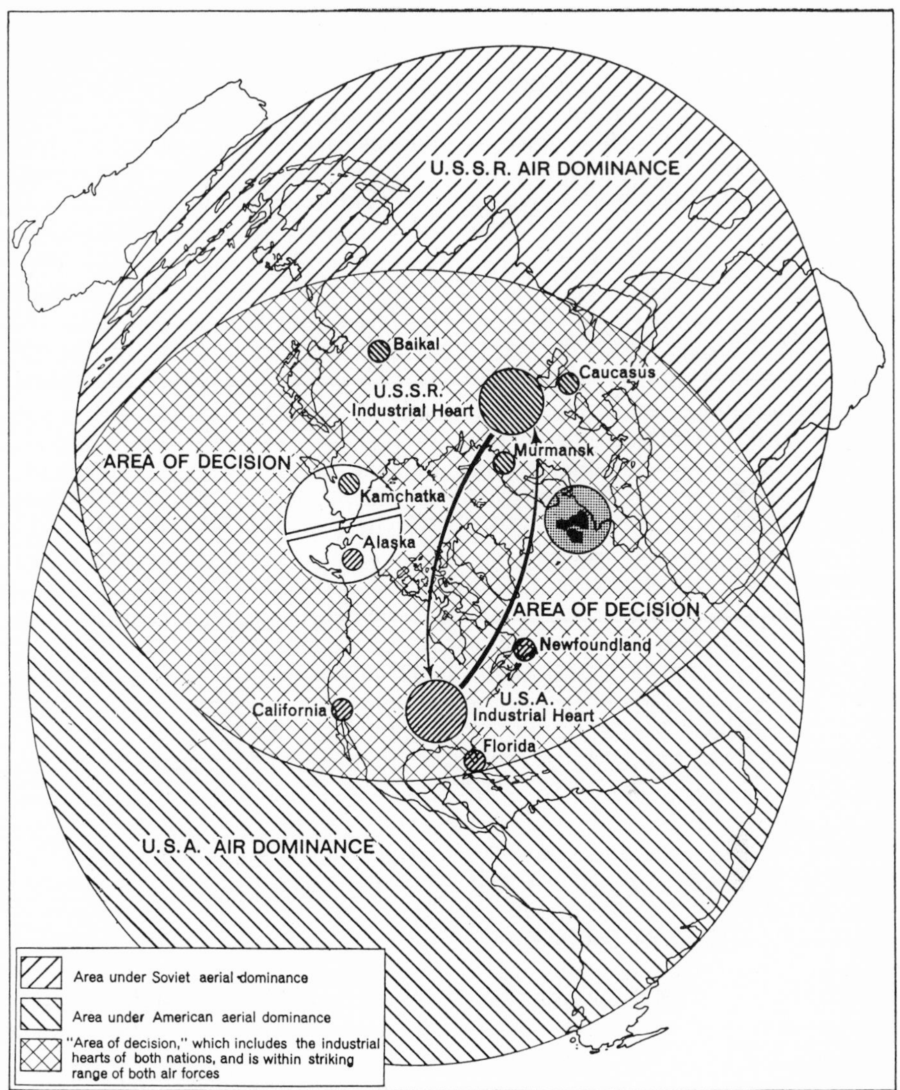

FIGURE 1.–The power equation between the American and Eurasian continents. Map by Alexander P. de Seversky, reproduced in black and white from colored insert map in his book *Air Power: Key to Survival* (New York: Simon and Schuster, 1950), facing p. 312. An adaptation of this map also accompanied an article by Major de Seversky in *This Week* magazine, February 13, 1949. The dotted circle "denotes the British Isles, our only tenable overseas base. . . . The white circle embraces Alaska and Kamchatka, where land-sea-air teams will have valid application in an attempt at mutual neutralization as strategic bases."

sources, the location of bases, policies toward Rimland countries and Latin America, and many other matters. It is beyond the reach of this paper to settle such weighty affairs. All we can do is to propound a few questions that bear on the evaluation of "the airman's view."

The first question concerns the reality of the Western Hemisphere and its self-sufficiency and defensibility. A report of a Senate subcommittee on strategic and critical materials says, as if it were axiomatic, "We belong in the Western Hemisphere."[7] The report demonstrates the present American dependence on sources of strategic and critical materials outside the Western Hemisphere but maintains that through stockpiling, exploration, subsidization, and scientific research the Americas could be made self-sufficient for a period of war. It is held that sea lanes to South America could hug the shore and be protected from enemy aircraft or submarines. "In the last analysis land transportation can be improved."[8] If we grant, if only for the sake of the argument, that the Americas could be made self-sufficient for a period of war, we must still question their complete defensibility by the strategy envisioned. Soviet planes in Central or even East Africa, beyond the circle of American air dominance, would be approximately as near the most vital parts of South America as planes based on Florida. South American cities, and particularly the influential metropolises of Brazil and Argentina, would be vulnerable unless their defenses were virtually perfect. American ability to retaliate, or to "neutralize" African airfields after a blow had fallen, would offer little solace. If substantial parts of Africa should come under Soviet control, it is not certain that Latin America would remain steadfast in support of the United States. We may thus have to defend large parts of the Rimland in order to protect Latin America, which the Senate subcommittee, possibly influenced by the polar projection, calls "our own backyard."[9]

Another question is that of defense against intercontinental bombardment. Perfect defense on both sides would cancel out the offense. In that case, intercontinental bombardment would not even be "the Great Deterrent." True, perfect defense is improbable, but if defense is less than perfect, retaliation is to be expected, and thus to launch an intercontinental air attack entails great risks. Nevertheless, if a nation places all its defensive bets on this strategy, it must be prepared to use it.

The foregoing questions can be reduced to one: When, and under what circumstances, does a nation that adopts the all-out intercontinental strategy launch its aircraft? One choice would be preventive war, a choice that the United States is unlikely to make. Another would be to use the intercontinental air force in the event of any further aggression across the Iron Curtain. This would be containment by intercontinental means. It might succeed—even the threat might be enough—but it would require unlimited fortitude for an American commander in chief to stand ready to give the signal, risking retaliatory destruction of American cities, to halt, for example, Communist expansion in some country of southern Asia. Third, there is "air isolationism." A defensive perimeter, to use that unhappy term, might be drawn around the Americas, perhaps including some overseas areas considered particularly important. Intercontinental air war would be used or threatened only if this perimeter were

[7] "Report of the Minerals, Materials, and Fuels Economic Subcommittee of the Committee on Interior and Insular Affairs," *83rd Congr., 2nd Sess., Senate Rept. No. 1627* (1954), p. 12.

[8] *Ibid.*, p. 28.

[9] *Ibid.*, p. 23.

crossed. Such a stand would require as much fortitude as the other. In fact, we have seen that large parts of the Rimland might have to be included within the defensive perimeter if Latin America were to be secure. Thus "air isolationism" approaches "containment."

The nub of the matter is that strategy and foreign policy are complementary and inseparable. This is particularly true of the key question of when to resort to armed defense.[10] Moreover, they are continuing processes and cannot be redirected overnight. If a state adopts a rigid strategy keyed to a single kind of war, its foreign policy is made rigid in major ways. This is not necessarily evil if the rigid view is sound, but history does not encourage the belief that man can foresee the precise course of future events. Some flexibility in strategic view seems wise. "Flexibility" should be forward-looking, however, not patterned on the past.

Recipe for a Composite View

We have examined . . . a series of global views of politics and strategy. None of them, taken singly, is an adequate picture of the world. None can unhesitatingly be called "the best" or even "the best yet." There is no simple system of political geography, no single thought filter through which to strain all geographical information. We need a series of filters, a composite or an eclectic global view.

* * *

. . . The "recipe for a composite view" that we give here makes no pretense to completeness or finality, nor does it contain anything that a geographer does not already know. It is merely an attempt to list the elements of a global view based on the concept of national power. No map of it is presented. This may be cowardice, engendered by our own warning . . . that mapping an idea is likely to reveal its fuzziness. But much of the material in our list is already on maps, and for other items data are incomplete.

National power, as has been elaborated elsewhere,[11] has two components that may be called "inventory" and "strategy." The former is what one has, the latter what one does with it. The inventory component can largely be subsumed, we believe, under Mackinder's old term "man settling," the strategic component largely under his "man travelling."[12]

I. Man Settling
  A. Population
  B. Culture
  C. Material Base
II. Man Travelling
  A. The Atmosphere
  B. Oceans and Islands
  C. Continental Interiors and Peripheries
  D. The Northern Region

This list probably needs little explanation. What is left out may be more surprising than what is included. For example, climate, landforms, and mineral resources are not specifically mentioned. They are, however, implied under other headings and would appear in the higher orders of subdivision.

No one is likely to question the place of population or material base in a global view of national power. Population has been mapped many times,

[10] Cf. W. W. Kaufmann, *The Requirements of Deterrence: Princeton Univ. Center of Internatl. Studies Memorandum No. 7* (1954).

[11] S. B. Jones, "The Power Inventory and National Strategy," *World Politics,* **VI** (1953–1954), 421–452.

[12] H. J. Mackinder, "The Physical Basis of Political Geography," *Scottish Geogr. Mag.,* **VI** (1890), 78–84.

and its elements have been carefully outlined by Trewartha.[13] Among the more significant subdivisions are trends, in relation to total numbers and age groups, and urbanization. Urbanization is an indication of the kind of economy and of the tempting targets for nuclear bombs. The material base of course includes sources of food, energy, and essential raw materials. Although maps of such items have been attempted, adequate and commensurable data for recent years are hard to find.[14]

The inclusion of culture as a major heading in a list based on the concept of national power may require some defense. But one element of culture is government, and the common political map is therefore a cultural map. The political interpretation of general culture is difficult and still in the experimental stage; thus it is perhaps faith that leads us to give culture so prominent a place. Culture has been placed between population and the material base because it is through culture that men make the material base economic, turn sources into resources, so to speak.

In subdividing "Man Travelling" our guiding principle has been that, for the immediate future at least, air, land, and sea movement are all of importance as means of projecting power. This is especially true because "projecting power" includes economic as well as military action. The relative importance of the three media varies for different kinds of action and in different parts of the world. The atmosphere, because of its global spread, its vertical extent, and the speed of the vehicles that use it, is of first and increasing importance. This is true whether or not "heartland operations" by strategic air forces are the pattern of future conflict. Every globe and relatively undistorted map gives an airman's view, but it takes imagination to see on them the useful and fearful canopy of air, so that emphasis is justified.

With the oceans we include the islands found in them. Every island is moated to a certain extent, and the defense of Britain in the Second World War and the delay the Formosa Strait imposed on the Chinese Communists show that the moating is still of some significance. But air power, and not just ships or water, is needed to make the moat effective. Not all islands or parts of the oceans are of equal importance. The islands and narrow seas off the Eurasian coast are of first importance today, those off the North American coast of second.

It is hardly news that the peripheries of continents differ from the interiors in ease of maritime access. In the age of nuclear weapons, peripheral location carries increased vulnerability from sabotage, ship- or submarine-launched missiles, and underwater explosion. It usually means a greater

13 G. T. Trewartha, "A Case for Population Geography," *Annals Assn. of Amer. Geogrs.*, **XLIII** (1953), 71–97; reference on pp. 88–89.

14 M. K. Bennett, in his book "The World's Food" (New York: Harper & Row Publishers, 1954), Chapters 12 and 13, subjects published data on national diets to considerable criticism. Excellent maps of energy production, consumption (1937, with estimates for 1948), and reserves accompany the study of "Energy Resources of the World" prepared under the direction of N. B. Guyol for the Department of State (*U.S. Dept. of State Publ. 3428,* 1949). The energy data in the *Statistical Yearbook* of the United Nations unfortunately do not include major Communist countries. The pending importance of atomic energy in industry further complicates the picture. Rapid strides in the beneficiation of lean iron ores make unreliable many published studies of the distribution of this basic metal.

dependence on sea-borne supplies. But it also means wider economic contacts by the most capacious and economical of carriers. Only in Eurasia does the division into interior and periphery have great political significance, as Mackinder showed long ago. In the Americas the interior has been absorbed by the coastal states, with minor exceptions. Nearly all of Africa today is controlled from the shores, though its future political pattern is obscure.

The final item of our composite view is "the northern region," based on the nature of the Arctic Sea and the northern parts of North America and Eurasia and their relation to the great centers of power that are certain, for a long time at least, to lie in the Northern Hemisphere. In the northern region surface movement meets resistance for much or all of the year whereas air movement is relatively easy. The northern region may be, as we have said, an aerial "pivot area." There are other parts of the world where air movement is much easier than surface movement, such as the rain forests and the deserts, but these either are smaller than the northlands or offer less serious obstacles. The deserts, for instance, are traversed more easily than the northlands by conventional vehicles, and the Amazon and Congo basins have their immense, never-frozen rivers.

The global view just outlined is merely what the mythical German scientist is supposed to have written, *eine Einführung in das Leben des Elephanten,* though measurable in pages rather than in volumes. The whole elephant is too big for us to see in detail, but we are not blind, only myopic, and we can discern its outlines. And we can and do pursue it, though the path of our safari is beset by pitfalls. On one side is the flood of unfiltered information that rushes endlessly. On the other are the quicksands of oversimplification. To remain still is to be stung by the scholar's conscience. But hazards and discomforts are inevitable accompaniments of adventure, and the pursuit of the global view is the geographer's intellectual adventure.

CHAPTER SEVEN

Population and Economic Change

There was a time, not too long ago, when the student of international relations studied population trends almost exclusively as an index of national power. The population profile, meaning the proportion of men and women in each age bracket, is still important because it tells us what proportion of the population is available for military service and for the labor force (although different countries vary in their policies of utilizing women for such purposes). Forecasts and projections inform us what these proportions are likely to be twenty or thirty years hence.

Yet it has become increasingly apparent that population does not automatically determine a nation's power position: the huge and growing populations of India and China, for example, have been and may continue to be sources of weakness rather than strength to those states. Almost all students of international relations agree that population is but one of the many variables that account for a nation's power and prosperity. In this sense, therefore, the population element is no different from geography or from any of the other ingredients of national capability which are examined by the student of international relations, and we return to the proposition advanced earlier: that the ingredients of a country's capability arsenal are always multiple.

If there is any one factor which distinguishes our age from previous eras, it lies in the unprecedented population growth throughout the world, falling with particular impact upon the economically less-developed areas that for the most part can least afford to support their rapidly growing numbers. If the size of a country's population exceeds the capacity of the existing productive resources to support it, or if it hinders the efficient exploitation of those resources, then it is a source of weakness rather than of strength. There must be some balance or equilibrium between population and resources which permits a society to generate an economic surplus over and above the subsistence level before a state can start on the long road to economic development. Before we can properly assess the relationship of a state's population to that state's capacity to formulate and achieve foreign policy goals, we must know what proportion of the national wealth is available for capital investment, education, scientific research; what proportion of the population is actually educated, in what fields and at what levels; and what capacity a population possesses for adapting to technological change.

The serious and growing imbalance between population and resources is one of the most intractable problems in the field of international relations. There was a time when the swollen populations of India and China could be treated as strategically unimportant. The United States and the European powers with the climate and resources conducive to industrial development were also those which had most successfully mastered the processes of population control. Beginning in the eighteenth and continuing through the nineteenth century, the European and North American resource base expanded more rapidly than the population, thereby providing a surplus for investment, education, and science. As a result, the United States, Great Britain, and Germany emerged as leading industrial powers. By the end of the 1930's, the Soviet Union was ready to join the select circle. The case of Japan's early development is instructive, because that development was achieved in the face of great population pressures. This indicates once more that population is not the only relevant factor to be taken into account in predicting development trends. More recently, Japan has been in the forefront of countries taking active measures to control their population growth.

These countries have developed the social organization, capital, skills, science, and technology necessary to exploit their own resources and those of the rest of the world. As a result of their superior technology, much of the mineral wealth and raw materials of the rest of the world flows unceasingly towards these several centers. Meanwhile, underdeveloped countries are experiencing great difficulties in controlling their population growth. So marked are the advantages accruing to the industrially developed countries that, in spite of large scale aid and development programs, their economic lead relative to the underdeveloped countries is actually increasing.

However, unlike in the past, the plight of the less developed countries can be ignored no longer. As Kingsley Davis points out in his article—and as we know from scenes of mob violence in Latin America, the Middle East, Africa, and Southeast Asia—the urban masses have become conscious of both their deprivation and their power. Political independence has brought a rising demand for economic development and better standards of living. Some of the implications of population growth for political viability are traced in the article by Sondermann below. As populations continue to grow, and as the inequalities of wealth, income, and education persist, we can expect dissatisfactions to lead to grave political unrest. Thus, population pressures in underdeveloped countries become a threat to world stability, and even if the West were prepared to deal with those problems with intelligence and moderation, we must expect a long period of revolutionary unrest and political instability.

In this connection, many Western students of international relations have failed to take sufficient account of what one Soviet theorist has called "the role of the popular masses in international relations."[1] We are so accustomed to thinking of states and governments as the only legitimate international actors that the role of the street mobs in Cairo, Bagdad, Caracas, and Havana tends

[1] Y. Arbatov, "The Role of the Popular Masses in International Relations," *International Affairs* (Moscow), September, 1955, pp. 54–67.

to take us by surprise. The Soviet Union, unlike Western governments, frankly identifies itself with the explosive aspirations of the street mobs in the hope of harnessing them to the chariots of world revolution. The Soviets and the Chinese believe that dissatisfaction, unrest, and rebellion in Africa, Asia and Latin America will benefit the long-term aspirations of Communist parties and states.

The population problem, then, is not a figment of the imagination or of the "Cassandra-complex" of scholars. It exists; it is grave; it is bound to become worse because even the most effective current program of control would not make itself felt for 20 to 30 years. Ideally, therefore, any program should start at least two decades ago! The problem is an extraordinarily touchy one to deal with. The sanitary-medical revolution which, by prolonging life expectancy, has brought about the population increases cannot—and should not—be undone. In fact, it is likely to continue in extending lives and thereby increasing populations. When penicillin, other antibiotics, DDT, and the like are available to cure, at minimal cost, such age-old enemies of life as tuberculosis, malaria, and a host of other diseases, no one can responsibly advocate, or realistically expect, that these means will not be used. Efforts at population control must therefore be directed toward the other end of the life-cycle, the control of births—or, more properly, of conception. This is surely the most private matter imaginable, in which considerations of public interest and benefit hardly intrude. Governments have been understandably reluctant to address themselves to the problem. One can see indications in a growing number of countries that the seriousness of this problem is being recognized, and that steps are being initiated to cope with it. But most of these programs are woefully inadequate.

States have traditionally equated a large population with national power; the thought-patterns of centuries are hard to break. The Western powers are confronted with the particular problem that the less developed, newer societies are the ones most affected. These societies and their governments tend to suspect that Western interest in population limitation in their countries is engendered by the calculation of continued dominance, and these suspicions are carefully fanned by Communist parties in these countries. Under these circumstances, it is very difficult for a country such as the United States, or her Western allies, to pursue policies vis-à-vis less developed countries other than to let them know that we would be willing to render assistance in handling the problem, if requested to do so.

In the unlikely event that anyone should still imagine that the problem is far removed from us, let it be added that even for the industrially developed countries, all is no longer clear sailing. As early as 1952 the report of the President's Materials Policy Commission, *Resources for Freedom,*[2] pointed out that civilian and military consumption was so great that even a country as rich as the United States faced severe shortages of important resources. According to this report, we had completed our transition from a raw materials *surplus* na-

[2] *Resource for Freedom,* Summary of Vol. I of a Report to the President's Materials Policy Commission (Washington, D.C.: U.S. Government Printing Office, 1952).

tion to a raw materials *deficit* nation, and our dependence upon overseas sources of supply was bound to increase. The countries of Western Europe were and are in an even more difficult position. The Soviet Union, a relative newcomer to industrial maturity, has only begun to exploit its potential resources and is unlikely to face major resource problems for some time. Therefore, though the United States enjoys a large industrial lead over the Soviet Union, it faces the need to establish economic and trade relations with resource-rich underdeveloped countries in order to guarantee a continued supply of basic materials.

Since World War II, American companies have acquired large holdings in Latin America, Africa, the Middle East, and Southeast Asia, now threatened by the rising tides of nationalism, spurred on by the deprivations occasioned by the population increases. The United States government has pursued enormous stockpiling programs. These activities can only prosper if the underdeveloped peoples believe that they are getting a fair deal. Thus, far from being unrelated problems, the quest for economic development among the underdeveloped countries and the Western resource position upon which our security and prosperity depend, are but two sides of the same coin.

1

*Political Implications of Population Growth in Underdeveloped Countries**

Fred A. Sondermann

I

The problem of the world's expanding population can be studied from various points of view. We can approach it first in terms of quantity, in which case we are confronted by sobering statistics. For example, the present annual increase (surplus of births over deaths) in world population approximates 50 million per year. Each day the world's population grows by over 130,000 people— . . . Each year, a "Great Britain" is added; in less than four years a "United States," in less than eight years an "India." If it takes one half hour to read this article, close to 3,000 additional people will have been added to the population of the globe during that time! [Editors' note: These figures have further increased since the article was written.]

The rate of increase is itself increasing. Thus, only fifteen years hence, according to the United Nations medium estimates, the earth will contain one billion more people than it has now; in forty years, it will have nearly four billion more. Another recent study indicated that world popu-

* *The Colorado College Studies,* No. 5 (1961), pp. 12–24. Reprinted by permission.

lation, which doubled in the last sixty years, can be expected to double again in the next forty. Perhaps more important, the shifts will vary in different areas of the world. It is predicted that between 1950 and 1975 the population of Latin America will increase by 86 per cent, that of Asia by 60 per cent, of Oceania by 59 per cent, Africa by 52 per cent, North America by 43 per cent and Europe, including the Soviet Union, by 31 per cent. Put in somewhat different terms, it is expected that by the year 2000 A.D., Asia will contain almost 62 per cent of the world's population (compared to the present 55 per cent); Latin America close to 10 per cent (compared to 6.5 per cent); while Africa's share will remain relatively stable at 8 per cent. But North America's share will decline from 6.7 per cent to 5 per cent, and Europe's from 23 percent to 15 per cent. If the share of the world's population living in underdeveloped countries is 65 per cent today, it is estimated that it will be over 75 per cent forty years hence.[1]

These are conservative figures, which set the framework within which discussion of the population problem must proceed. They project a shift of unprecedented magnitude in the balance of world population. In light of such figures it is hardly reassuring to note that a recent Gallup Poll showed 69 per cent of Americans "unworried" about the facts of population increases.

Second, we can discuss the problem from the moral-theological point of view—a useful and necessary task, because in the final analysis the many questions raised must be resolved by policies based on value judgments.[2] Thirdly, we can approach the situation as a problem in food supply, although this presents a somewhat narrow, if vital, focus. Literally as well as morally, man does not live by bread alone—he also needs energy, resources, science and technology, and productive facilities.[3] Hence the population situation can, and must be considered

[1] These figures were gathered from the following sources: "World Population Review: Projections to 2000 A.D.," *Population Bulletin,* **XV** (March, 1959), 18–19; *ibid.,* **XV** (December, 1959), 145; "Population Trends and Related Problems of Economic Development," prepared by UN Economic Committee for Asia and the Far East, cited in *New Republic,* **CXLI** (December 7, 1959), 6; Kingsley Davis, "The Other Scare: Too Many People," *New York Times Magazine,* March 15, 1959, p. 13.

[2] For an excellent discussion of this facet of the problem see Richard M. Fagley, *The Population Explosion and Christian Responsibility* (New York, 1960).

[3] Whether or not enough food for the expanding population can be produced is a question on which experts differ, although most of them seem to feel that, while great advances in food production may be forthcoming, problems will remain: (1) If the past decade is a guide, the outlook is far from bright, as increased food production has barely kept pace with population growth; (2) more than half of the present population of the world subsists on a subminimal intake of calories; (3) some of the possible increases in production will be enormously expensive to achieve; (4) the distribution system will have to be greatly revised, especially since additional food production will be most difficult to achieve in those areas where it is most needed; and (5) there *is* a limit to productivity. For details, see Warren H. Leonard, "World Population in Relation to Potential Food Supply," *Scientific Monthly,* **LXXXV** (September, 1957), 113–125; Harrison Brown, James Bonner, and John Weir, *The Next Hundred Years* (New York, 1957), pp. 66–67; W. S. Woytinsky, "World Resources in Relation to Population" in Philip M. Hauser, ed., *Population and World Politics* (Glencoe, Ill., 1958), pp. 46–75; Morton Clurman, "Will Births Outstrip Mankind's Resources?" *Commentary,* **XIII** (March, 1952), 282–290; B. R. Sen, "For Freedom from Hunger to Assure the Triumph of Human Dignity," *United Nations Review,* **VI** (April, 1960), 6–9; and Karl Sax, *Standing Room Only: The World's Exploding Population* (Boston, 1960), Chapter 4.

more broadly as a problem in economic development of presently underdeveloped countries. All of these are vital aspects of the problem, and it is difficult to separate the various approaches except for purposes of analysis.

I submit, however, that the world's rapidly expanding population also entails political as well as economic consequences and implications, in addition to, and to a considerable extent based upon, the quantitative, moral, and economic ingredients of the problem. The relationship between all these factors is reciprocal: politics both affects and is affected by numbers, values, and economics. . . .

The populations of almost all countries are growing, and although the growth rate in some developed countries is higher than in some underdeveloped countries, this paper will concentrate on the political implications of population growth in the underdeveloped states of the world,[4] because growth rates by themselves do not clarify the nature of the problem. The most densely populated states are among the most highly developed and the most stable politically. The crucial element is the relation between resources (broadly defined) on the one hand and population on the other; and in the underdeveloped areas of the world this relationship is at its most critical stage. In part the problem can be described in the words of Professor Kingsley Davis, University of California demographer, who recently wrote

> Population growth will tend to be greatest where people are poorest. In this desperate situation, the less developed nations will hardly be squeamish about the means they adopt to further their national goals. Caught in the predicament of having an ever larger share of the world's people and an ever smaller share of the world's resources, they will be driven to adopt revolutionary policies.[5]

For purposes of analysis, the subject will be divided into the domestic and the international political implications of population growth. One must be aware, however, that these two facets cannot be neatly separated, because each impinges upon the other. Domestic pressures may lead to foreign adventurism of various kinds, and foreign influences may affect the domestic situation and the way in which it is perceived and handled.

II

Any political system must perform certain minimum functions to justify itself. Traditionally these functions have been defined in terms of providing external security and internal order. The Preamble to the American Constitution is a good traditional definition of a government's purpose. Recently the task of assuring the well-being of the members of society has been added to the functions of government and interpreted in broader terms than the vague reference to the general welfare which we find in our own Constitution. The Welfare State is not just an American phenomenon; in various forms and based upon various definitions it is found around the world. Peoples everywhere, and most especially those in the less developed countries, are anxious to achieve higher living standards, with all that such standards imply—and demand.

---

[4] No attempt will be made to define the term "underdeveloped states" in detail. Broadly, the category includes all of Africa except the Union of South Africa, the bulk of Central and South America, mainland Asia except Siberia, and the islands of the Pacific except Japan, Australia, and New Zealand.

[5] *Op. cit.*, p. 108.

This quest for higher standards is given particular urgency by the fact that many of these countries have recently attained political independence. A "revolution of rising expectations," to use Adlai Stevenson's phrase, has thus been superimposed upon a nationalistic revolution in vast areas of the world.

Until recently it has always been possible to blame the manifestly unsatisfactory living standards in these countries on the colonial powers, and to charge them (often unjustifiably) with deliberately maintaining a situation of need and deprivation in the colonies for the greater glory and profit of the home countries. Now, however, this argument has reached the point of diminishing returns, and the new, frequently inexperienced governments must deliver on their own. . . . [I]t is extraordinarily difficult for an underdeveloped society to reach a point at which there is a sufficient increase in savings and productivity to make a raised standard of living possible.[6] In fact, these new governments—many without a trained administrative corps, without capital, without experience—are expected to perform feats which even long-established systems would find difficult. . . .

The very fact of vast population increases accounts for many specific demands upon governments, demands extraordinarily difficult to satisfy. They include:

demands for development of industry and modernization of agriculture, with the trained manpower for both occupations;
demands for greatly expanded educational facilities;[7]
demands for increased opportunities for productive employment;
demands for adequate housing;
demands for social welfare policies in such fields as food, health, and sanitation;
demands for support of the very young and the very old sectors of the population, which increase disproportionately (because of advances in medical care) in an expanding population.

Since it is difficult for highly developed societies such as our own to meet some of these demands, we can imagine the magnitude of the problems confronting governments of underdeveloped states. But simple comparisons are misleading, because none of the underlying strengths in education, values, history and tradition, capital accumulation, and governmental experience which characterize American society and form the underpinning for our efforts to cope with domestic problems are found in the countries under discussion.

For this very reason, observers must consider what kinds of political organizations are likely to result from the pressures upon governments to perform their increased functions. The crux of the problem is that the demands can be met only after a long series of extremely hard steps that are necessary to bring about the rapid economic development of a society. The decisions which will have to be made are extraordinarily difficult, because they deal with such things as delayed satisfactions and enforced savings for capital accumulation and investment. The question is whether the peoples of the underdeveloped

[6] Industrialization might help reduce the problem, but it is itself complicated by the existence of the problem. Ashish Bose, "The Population Puzzle in India," *Economic Development and Cultural Change,* VII (April 1959), 230–248.

[7] For detailed discussion of just this one phase of development, see Harold L. Geisert, *World Population Pressures* (Washington, 1958), p. 39.

countries will make such decisions voluntarily, or whether the decisions will have to be made (and enforced) by an elite which understands the nature of the problem and is willing and able to take the actions which it requires.

We are, in effect, dealing with the question of whether a democratic society is capable of making the necessary decisions. All we can say is that we do not know the answer to it. In extreme situations of short duration people who understand the crisis are often capable of making tough, self-sacrificing decisions. But the crisis with which we deal here, while extreme, is long-range rather than immediate; each day—indeed, each hour—makes it a little greater, but the increments are neither dramatic nor easily perceived. In such a situation, will the inexperienced governments of the new countries be able to (and, equally important, will they want to) impress their uneducated publics with the seriousness of the national, rather than the individual, problem?[8] They probably will not; and if this proves to be the case, then the outlook for democratic government in the underdeveloped countries is dim.

The assumptions made so far are 1. that increased populations press increased demands on their governments; 2. that, paradoxically, governments are able to put themselves in a position eventually to meet such demands only by immediately demanding serious deprivations of their publics; and 3. that governments are unlikely to take this unpopular position, and publics are unlikely to accede voluntarily to the demands which such a position would entail.

If these assumptions are even approximately valid, then it would seem to follow logically that the governmental system most appropriate to such a situation is an authoritarian rather than a democratic one; one that is based upon the enforced decisions of relatively few rather than upon the policies agreed upon by the relatively many. The international implications of this conclusion will be considered in the following section. For the United States it means that our society might consider providing a somewhat clearer example of making voluntary sacrifices for the national welfare, and that we must learn to deal with regimes which differ from our own political and ideological preferences. Hamilton Fish Armstrong recently commented on this problem in the following terms,

> Democracy is a relative term everywhere, but as Mr. Dooley might have said, it is more relative in Asia. Let us not be too disturbed by this. In countries where perhaps nine-tenths of the people cannot read; where any experience they have had with self-government has usually been within the family, the village, or the tribe; where villages live in isolation, separated by jungles, deserts, mountains or seas; where the average income of a family is something like $100 a year and that mostly in kind, not money; where the population grows by over 2% per year; where most countries have no trained civil service; where the social services of the state, itself new and inefficient, are rudimentary or non-existent—

[8] A pessimistic view is presented by Professor Davis, in these terms: "A leader who rests his political career on the whims of . . . swollen cadres of youth is usually incapable of making solid economic improvements. He is driven to embrace the safest and most inflammatory of all issues—nationalism. He can persecute and expropriate the foreigners, the Jews, or the Christians. He can threaten war on neighboring states. He can play the Communists against the free world to get emergency funds for staving off calamity or for buying weapons. He is the unstable political offspring produced by the monstrous marriage between rapid population growth and national destitution." "Analysis of the Population Explosion," *New York Times Magazine*, September 22, 1957, p. 78.

in these conditions what we call democracy can develop only by slow stages. Even when the governing clique in the capital and the little knot of articulate intellectuals there are sincere in their admiration for representative government (and often they are) they must begin by creating rudimentary organs and build upwards cautiously, layer by layer.[9]

III

Two aspects of the international consequences of rapidly rising populations in underdeveloped countries will be discussed here: 1. what countries experiencing population pressures do to other countries, and 2. what other countries do to countries which experience rapid population growth.

In doing so, we may start with the observation that countries have traditionally felt that a large population enhances a country's position among the other states of the world, because a larger population means a greater reservoir of productive manpower, larger markets which facilitate more efficient and economical production and distribution of goods, greater chances of producing inventors, scientists, and other men of great ability,[10] and a greater population base with which to fight a conventional war. For all these reasons, countries have almost invariably interpreted a population increase as a strengthening of their position vis-à-vis other powers.

In a situation in which population presses upon resources, and in which there is no short-range prospect of dramatically increasing the available resources, only two alternatives seem possible: migration or expansion. If the first of these does not take place the second is apt to. Professor Quincy Wright's statement points in this direction: "Differentials of population pressure in neighboring areas, if generally known to the inhabitants of the overpopulated area and if maintained by artificial barriers to trade and migration, tend to international violence. . . ."[11]

If this violence is to be avoided, what chance is there for migration to relieve the population pressures which will increasingly characterize the underdeveloped countries? There are four major obstacles to migration as a solution to the overpopulation problem:

1. As long as most countries consider population as a power factor, they will be reluctant to permit the emigration of large numbers of their younger and more productive citizens (who presumably would be the ones most interested in migrating).

2. Potential receiving countries, for reasons of their own (such as cultural homogeneity, fear of being overwhelmed by alien populations, fear of competition for jobs, fear of infiltration by alien doctrines, perverted racial ideas, etc.) usually do not want large numbers of immigrants, particularly from the countries suffering most

---

[9] "Thoughts Along the China Border—Will Neutrality Be Enough?" *Foreign Affairs*, **XXXVI** (January, 1960), 257–258.

[10] Except that some of the world's outstanding statesmen have come from smaller countries, which might lead one to assume that supply follows demand in the vital commodity of statesmanship. The smaller and weaker countries need capable statesmen more than those countries which have had margins of safety for their leaders' mistakes.

[11] Quincy Wright, *The Study of International Relations* (New York, 1955), p. 364. Professor Davis expresses the same view: ". . . excessive population growth seems to intensify the struggle for scarce raw materials, to build up explosive migration pressures, and to encourage *lebensraum* wars, and . . . communism is making its greatest conquests precisely in the impoverished and crowded countries." "The Other Scare: Too Many People," *New York Times Magazine*, March 15, 1959, p. 114.

from overpopulation. There are, after all, only a limited number of developed, underpopulated areas which—given present technology—lend themselves to additional settlement. These include North and parts of South America, Siberia, Australia, and possibly some parts of Africa and the Near East, although here care would be necessary to avoid merely transferring the problem of underdevelopment from one area to another by resettling vast numbers of people. In this context, the United States has little justification for pointing a finger of scorn at the immigration policies of other countries. . . .

3. Large population movements over a short time always involve great human suffering and tragedy. And in order to come close to solving the present problem, the movements would have to be enormous. According to one estimate, merely to keep the proportions of underdeveloped to developed countries at the 1950 level would require migration of over 700 million people by the year 2000 A.D.[12] There has never been a population movement of this magnitude in the history of mankind, and human migration on such a scale seems inconceivable.

4. Finally, international migrations create alien minorities within states, thus further complicating an international situation which is sufficiently tense even without this additional ingredient of conflict.

Thus, migration scarcely seems to provide an answer to the problem. Yet it is safe to predict that migratory pressures are bound to increase. The demand in underdeveloped countries for admission to industrial, highly developed areas will become very great indeed, and the more developed societies must either adjust to that demand or propose acceptable alternatives. Since migration does not seem to be an answer,[13] it seems reasonable to expect various kinds of international disequilibrium, as indicated in the other alternative, namely, expansion brought about by aggression set off by population pressure. In this context, one automatically thinks of Japan in the 1930s, but might it not be equally realistic to think of China in the 1970s? And is it any great comfort to reflect that perhaps the Russians are thinking of this possibility too, which might explain their haste to settle Siberia?

The disastrous consequences of continued population pressures in the underdeveloped countries stagger the imagination. It can be argued that these consequences can be avoided, given more rapid economic development of these countries, which would provide more adequately for the now-existing populations and could be expected, in time, to bring about a levelling-off in birth rates. But the immediate consequence of economic development has thus far always been a greatly increased rate of population growth. Thus the crucial factor in the equation is the time element. Is there time enough, and can it be used effectively enough, to bring population increases and industrialization into some kind of balance which would assure

[12] By comparison, between 1846 and 1932, 60 million people left Europe—little more than one year's addition to world population. Political and Economic Planning, *World Population and Resources* (London, 1955), p. xxxiii. For a straightfaced but nonetheless morbidly hilarious discussion of sending surplus populations into outer space, see Garrett Hardin, "Interstellar Migration and the Population Problem," *Journal of Heredity*, L (March–April, 1959), 68–70.

[13] A very comprehensive—and discouraging—analysis of migration as a possible solution to the population problem is presented in J. O. Hertzler, *The Crisis in World Population* (Lincoln, Nebr., 1956), Chapter 8.

political stability? The answer to this question lies, in part, in how well the more highly developed countries understand the nature of the population problem of the less developed countries and what they are willing (not able!) to do to help solve it.[14]

This introduces the second aspect of this discussion: what other countries do to those states suffering from overpopulation. Here one must be particularly concerned about the impact and appeal of Communism. Specifically, what is the nature of the Communist appeal to these areas?

In the first place, the Communists argue that such problems as overpopulation and underdevelopment are the fault of the former colonial powers and their present Western allies, that they are reflections of the inability of the capitalist economic system to satisfy basic human needs. Secondly, the Communists describe birth control as a capitalist device to keep Asian and African countries weak—a strong argument, since small populations are traditionally associated with national weakness, and an attractive argument since birth control is artificial and sexual relations without it easier and more natural. They argue pointedly that developed countries such as the United States are unwilling to practice comprehensive birth control schemes on their own. Hence, advocacy of such a scheme for underdeveloped countries can rather easily be pictured as a typical capitalistic trick.[15]

Such arguments are bound to evoke a strong response. Substantively more important, however, are Communist arguments based on descriptions of the rapid improvement in living standards in the "socialist" societies as compared to the slower progress in "capitalist" economies. The comparison between India and China is frequently cited, with one country attempting to raise its standards through relatively free political institutions, while the other uses totalitarian methods. The contest is still in the balance, although the signs point to a substantially greater improvement in the Chinese condition than in that of India. (There is no way, however, to check on Chinese statistics.) If present Soviet and Chinese plans come even close to succeeding, they are bound to provide formidable arguments to the peoples of underdeveloped areas to adopt at least the economics, if not the politics, of Communist States.[16] If such a view seems unduly pessimistic, it may be well to reflect that in 1937 Communism controlled 170 million people, or 8 per cent of the world's population, while 20 years later it controlled 1 billion people, or 37 per cent. What about another 20 years hence?

IV

The question arises: what, if anything, can be done? Two facts stand out: obviously, there is no single, simple answer. Obviously, too, Amer-

[14] The assumption here is obviously that much more could be done to stimulate the development of underdeveloped countries; that in large part the problem is one of policy, not of capacity.

[15] Clurman, *op. cit.*, p. 287. To some extent, to be sure, the Communists may well be serious in their refusal to consider the population problem as a critical issue. It would run counter to Marxist ideology to assume that "successful economic development may be outstripped by the material needs of multiplying populations," *World Population and Resources*, p. 308.

[16] Karl Sax, Harvard botanist, calls attention to the old Chinese proverb, "It is difficult to tell the difference between right and wrong when the stomach is empty," and to the literal translation of the Chinese word for "peace"—"food for all." *Op. cit.*, p. xi.

ica's capacity to produce a solution is limited—which does not excuse Americans from using those capacities which are available to their fullest extent.

The outlines of a many-sided approach to the problem may be briefly suggested, as follows:

1. Minimally there is need for a greatly expanded and reoriented foreign aid program. The bulk of our foreign economic aid has not gone to underdeveloped and overpopulated countries. At best, it has gone only to a few of them.

2. Americans must face the fact that they shall have to deal with countries which prefer a socialist form of economic organization. The Communists say that the United States can never learn this; that our policies are based on an overriding desire to export Capitalism.[17] At the very least, Americans must learn to distinguish between economic and political forms of organization. Not all socialist states are dictatorships; not all capitalist countries are democracies.

3. More difficult by far is our need to accept the fact that in all probability America shall have to deal increasingly with countries which prefer centralized, authoritarian governments. Such terms as "guided democracy," "dynamic democracy," and the like are all disguises for highly centralized decision-making, which is usually a euphemism for dictatorship. It will be difficult, too, to know how and when to mediate some of the harshnesses of authoritarian regimes and help direct them gradually toward more democratic institutions and practices, without in the process interfering in other countries' domestic affairs and ruffling their nationalistic sensitivities.

[17] For a devastating reply, see George F. Kennan, "Peaceful Coexistence: A Western View," *Foreign Affairs,* **XXXVIII** (January, 1960), 171–190.

4. A crash program of research in food production methods is urgently needed. It would seem that the United States, with her high standards of research and technology, might be in the forefront of such a research effort, although it is not impossible that the Soviet Union might steal a march on the West in this field, as she has in others.[18]

5. In order to encourage private capital to invest more heavily in underdeveloped countries, the United States government might consider tax reductions, government guarantees, or other benefits for private investment in selected foreign countries.

6. One of the more encouraging aspects of the current international scene is the practice of one underdeveloped country helping another, either on a bilateral basis (Israel-Ghana, for example) or through the various agencies of the United Nations. Frequently such aid is more relevant to the situation at hand than would be aid coming from highly-developed societies. The United States might find it possible to bear more of the cost of such mutual or multilateral aid programs among the underdeveloped countries.

7. Finally, the most difficult aspect of the situation is that of facing up to the problem of encouraging birth control policies and furnishing birth con-

[18] Other kinds of research, too, have been suggested: into human fertility, social and economic factors affecting reduction of birth-rates; economic and population problems of overcrowded countries; ecological consequences of economic development; sociological and psychological consequences of rapid economic development and population increases; economic implications of very rapid rates of population increase; nutritional and health aspects of rapidly increasing populations; technological possibilities of developing substitutes for raw materials likely to become scarce in the near future. *World Population and Resources,* pp. 324–326.

trol information, upon request, to the underdeveloped countries. Obviously no pressure can be employed in such a delicate matter, but this is not to say that persuasion and discussion cannot be used as means of stimulating more interest and prompting underdeveloped societies to seek more information and assistance on birth control measures. For a variety of reasons, some of which are referred to in the foregoing discussion, it would seem more appropriate to have such advice and information channeled through the United Nations rather than to have it come from a single Western power. But the American government might stimulate birth control policies merely by indicating its willingness to support an international effort in this sphere.[19]

One would like to conclude this discussion of a serious problem on a note of hope and good cheer, but this would be entirely inappropriate in the present case. It is doubtful whether the problems brought on in the wake of the world's dramatic population increase can be solved this side of catastrophe. "Population difficulties and political instabilities are so intermingled in most of the underdeveloped areas of the contemporary world that they constitute virtually insoluble problems."[20] The decade of the 1950s may yet be looked back upon as a period of deceptive ease and quiet, when the Western democracies, confronted by one of history's most implacable challenges, preferred to avoid the stern decisions which were plainly demanded of them. And as George Kennan once put it, "a nation which excuses its own failures by the sacred untouchableness of its own habits can excuse itself into complete disaster."[21]

---

[19] The Draper Commission recommended an appropriate American policy in this field in its Third Interim Report of the President's Committee to Study the United States Military Assistance Program, transmitted to the President July 13, 1959. [Editors' note: During the administrations of Presidents Kennedy and Johnson, the American government took some significant steps in the directions indicated in this article.]

[20] Irene B. Taeuber, "Population and Political Instabilities in Underdeveloped Areas," in Hauser, *op. cit.*, p. 237.

[21] George F. Kennan, *American Diplomacy 1900–1950* (Chicago, 1951), p. 73.

2

*The Demographic Transition**

Kingsley Davis

Kingsley Davis, Professor of Sociology at the University of California, Berkeley, and a recent President of the American Sociological Society, is one of America's foremost experts on population problems.

A pattern of change through which, in a general way, every country achieving the industrial revolution has gone is the "demographic transition."

* "Identification of Fundamental Internal Social Changes which Condition Inter-Nation Relations," Paper presented at International Relations Conference, Northwestern University (April, 1959). Reprinted by permission.

It is a shift from one regime of negligible population growth to another, the first being characterized by *high* birth and death rates and the second by *low* birth and death rates. During the shift there is a rapid increase in numbers due to the lag of fertility decline behind mortality decline (the so-called "demographic gap"), but fertility eventually drops faster than mortality until it approaches the level of the latter. The shift represents an enormous gain in efficiency. When it is completed, each new generation of young adults is produced with a minimum number of pregnancies, child deaths, and woman-years, and with a maximum amount of educational attention. Furthermore, owing to the rapid decline of fertility in the later stages of the cycle, the age structure is temporarily characterized by an extremely high ratio of productive to dependent persons. For these reasons the demographic transition helped to foster the very industrial revolution with which it is so intimately linked.

This pattern, however, is more precise as an abstraction than as a reality. During the depression of the 1930's the cycle looked, in the industrial nations, as though it would soon end. Since then the birth rate has risen in nearly all these countries, giving rise in them to a second wave of population growth, especially persistent in the New-World industrial regions. Also, the magnitude and duration of the demographic gap have varied from one country to another.

Fortunately, an abstraction does not have to be borne out completely to be useful. The rise in birth rates in industrial nations has not been sufficient to bring back nineteenth-century levels, and in most of these countries it has fallen again. The recent phenomenal decline of fertility in Japan suggests that the pattern applies to an oriental as much as to a western industrializing country. In short, the model of the demographic transition has great utility, not as a complete description of reality, but as a device for allowing us to see the interrelatedness of disparate facts and to raise basic empirical questions.

THE PRESENT TREND OF POPULATION GROWTH

A significant question is this: are today's underdeveloped areas repeating the demographic transition that the currently industrial countries went through? If so, we can compute the average time it took the latter to make the transition and the average number of times they increased their population in the process, and thus reach an estimate of when the present underdeveloped nations will finish and how many people they will have. But the answer to the question is, no. There are significant differences between then and now.

The most important of these differences are these: Today's underdeveloped areas are *not* showing a rate of natural increase similar to that shown earlier by the now industrial countries; they are showing a *much greater* natural increase—the fastest ever shown in human history. This speed-up derives from birth rates that remain extremely high in the face of sharper drops in the death rate than any industrial country ever experienced. The astonishing fall in mortality has come at a more primitive economic stage than did the fastest drop in the now industrial countries, where the main decline in death rates came early in the twentieth century. This speed and timing of the drop have been possible because, with international financial and technical help, the most advanced health procedures have proved effective on a mass basis even in the most backward areas. Whereas the peoples who first industrialized had gradually to invent and test the techniques now available for fighting death, the present peasant peoples are benefiting immediately from these techniques without any necessity of understanding or contributing to their scientific bases. At the same time, precisely because the imported health measures require little or no change in social organization, and because no effort of remotely equal magnitude is made to import fertility control measures, the birth rate has remained high—higher in most cases than it evidently ever was in Western Europe. As a consequence, the unprecedented population growth is not primarily a response to economic development within the agrarian countries themselves, as it was earlier in the now advanced countries, but is in spite of, and probably to the detriment of, such development. Further, it is occurring at a time when, in many of the underdeveloped regions at least, the density of population in relation to resources is far higher than was the case in northwestern Europe, and in a world that no longer has rich empty areas to fill by migration. Finally any poor country trying to industrialize now has numerous entrenched, competitively aggressive, and sometimes politically menacing industrial nations to deal with.

With the world experiencing an unprecedented and accelerating population growth, and with a disproportionate share of this increase occurring in the underdeveloped, or poor, nations, two international results can be briefly suggested. 1. The numerical increase, coupled with already excessive population density and with other formidable obstacles, is slowing down economic development in backward areas. Yet, for other reasons, the *aspirations* of the underdeveloped peoples are moving ahead rapidly. The resulting divergence between national goals and national means is causing a high degree of political instability in these countries. 2. The political instability, plus the slow and erratic character of their economic development, is weakening the underdeveloped countries vis-à-vis the developed ones. This is creating an international vacuum similar to, but in significant respects different from, the vacuum that once gave rise to the colonial system.

The Changing Age Structure

Affecting mainly the younger ages, the drastic decline of mortality has given the underdeveloped countries not only a fast-growing but also an exceptionally young population. This complicates the economic problem by increasing the burden of child-dependency, and contributes to political instability by swelling the cadres of energetic but disenchanted youth. When the waves of young people besieging the labor market each year cannot find jobs, the ebullient energy turns to agitation, revolution, and war.

The Continuing Maldistribution of People

The population of agrarian countries has a territorial distribution exactly the opposite of what is required for industrial growth. During the process of economic development, therefore, a tremendous shift must take place in the location of persons—a shift in the direction of cities. Anything that impedes this shift also impedes economic advance. One such impediment is the fact that high fertility persists most tenaciously in the rural areas and thus obstructs the alleviation of excessive population density on farms and the modernization of agriculture. So great does the required magnitude of rural-urban migration become, and so politically troublesome does urban unemployment loom as compared to rural underemployment, that the government often pursues a policy of trying to discourage urbanization by decentralizing industry, subsidizing handicraft, investing in labor-intensive agricultural improvement, requiring official passes for internal movement, etc. In so far as such measures are successful, they dampen the rate of economic development and to this extent weaken the nation.

THE IRREPRESSIBLE URBANIZATION

Policies to the contrary notwithstanding, urbanization is rapid in virtually all underdeveloped countries, in response partly to economic advance and partly to rural overcrowding. Its political significance lies mainly in the multiplied potential it gives for rapid communication and collective interstimulation. In the swelling cities crowded with uprooted villagers and tribesmen, rumor spreads like a virus, popular aspiration soars with the visibility of the rich and the talk of demagogues, and close contact intensifies religious and ethnic hatreds. Under these circumstances the reaction to deprivation or insult or "injustice" is apt to be quick, massive, unenlightened, and violent.

NEW ROLES FOR EDUCATION

It is possible to detect in another crucial sphere—education—the enlarging inequality between industrial and non-industrial nations. Consumption and national power both depend increasingly on advanced technology. Unless a people somehow acquire the innumerable skills needed to run an industrial economy, to make and apply scientific discoveries, to devise and manufacture nuclear weapons, to maintain public health, to accomplish engineering feats, it must depend on countries that do have these skills. The underdeveloped nations, as we have just seen, are unbalanced in their development. With too many untrained laborers and consumers already, they are adding to them at the expense of capital and skills. While replacement of the population is certainly required, a multiplication of people at the expense of their quality (their trained capacities) is shortsighted. Children are so numerous in some countries that, even with a large portion of the national budget devoted to education, only a fraction of them can receive even an elementary training; in others, mass education is spread so thin that, though it touches almost all, it affects very few.

Among the industrial nations, on the other hand, education is evolving rapidly in new directions. It is doing so in part as an incidental consequence of other social changes, but mainly as a result of awakening national policy. Not only are the industrial nations becoming aware that success in international competition is crucially dependent on the classroom, but they have the money to pay for the education they need.

Each nation, whether industrial or nonindustrial, is faced essentially with three different and somewhat antithetical tasks: to indoctrinate the young with the sentiments of national loyalty and ideology of the state's structure; to give the young the knowledge and lore for living in the particular society with its unique institutions and culture; and to teach the different skills required by variegated groups making up the extraordinarily complex occupational structure. Of the three tasks, the last is technically the most difficult and the most expensive, because it requires not one kind of education but hundreds of kinds. Further, it requires not only a knowledge of present needs but also an estimate of future needs, and a mechanism for altering the supply of trainees in each speciality according to the future need for it from the national standpoint. . . .

Obviously, . . . a nation . . . has to have productive skills and performance. In modern times the realization has grown that a nation's strength depends overwhelmingly on science and engineering. As a result, national efforts are being made to ensure that the schools turn out the necessarily enormously increased supply of people trained in scientific and technical fields. This movement continues, in a way, the already established vocational trend in education, but with some major differences. Whereas the older trend was individualistic and indiscriminate, emphasizing the individual's own choice of an occupation and treating one vocational subject as being just about as important as another, the new trend is for the occupational needs of the nation to be emphasized, the important ones being given high priority. The fact that the high-priority education is expensive, and that it demands great effort and self-discipline by the student over many years, is no bar to the policy, because the necessity is beyond dispute.

We find, then, that the industrial nations on the whole are exercising more control over the schools to guarantee loyalty and to supply their need for highly trained manpower. This is but another facet of their increased mobilization of resources for national purposes. The movement has of course gone farther in communist countries than in the democracies, but the latter must perforce follow suit if they are to meet the competition. It is worth noting, too, that the underdeveloped countries in the communist camp are taking firmer ideological and vocational control of education than their counterparts in the free world. . . .

CHAPTER EIGHT

Economic Capability

Edward H. Carr once wrote the following about the impact of a state's economic capability on that state's position in international affairs:

> Economic strength has always been an instrument of political power, if only through its association with the military instrument. Only the most primitive kinds of warfare are altogether independent of the economic factor. The wealthiest prince or the wealthiest city-state could hire the largest and most efficient army of mercenaries; and every government was therefore compelled to pursue a policy designed to further the acquisition of wealth. The whole progress of civilization has been so closely bound up with economic development that we are not surprised to trace, throughout modern history, an increasingly intimate association between military and economic power.[1]

This perceptive statement emphasizes the significance of the economic element for military strength. The relationship is both direct and indirect. It reflects the fact that states' international security policies assume a first-class industrial-economic base, as well as the fact that they cost a great deal of money. The necessary funds to support a modern security establishment can be obtained only from a domestic tax base, which is dependent on the economic health of a country.

In the first edition of this book, we wrote that no matter how rich a country may be, its power ultimately depends upon the effectiveness with which it utilizes its natural resources, and this in turn depends on its level of economic development and social organization. In 1914 the German armies, though heavily outnumbered by the Russians, were able to defeat them in part at least because of the superior productivity of German industry. A generation later, German armies of equally superb equipment and morale were incapable of subduing a Russia that had by then acquired modern weapons and supporting industry. In the intervening two decades, the new Soviet government had carried out the forced industrialization of backward Russia to bring it abreast of its most dangerous Western foes. To achieve this goal Stalin had concentrated upon the development of Soviet heavy industry at the expense of light industry

[1] Edward H. Carr, *The Twenty Years' Crisis 1919–1939* (London: Macmillan & Co., Ltd., 1951), p. 113.

and consumer goods. From a level of steel production less than one quarter that of Germany's in 1914, the Soviet leaders raised Russian production until it exceeded Germany's in 1940. That, plus American lend-lease, was enough to give Russia the industrial means necessary to establish mastery over Germany. The lessons implicit in the foregoing facts still appear relevant to us.

A number of other ways in which economic capability is germane to international relations must be added to the foregoing propositions. One of these relates to the quest for economic well-being that increasingly characterizes every society in the world. Virtually all societies have become "welfare states" —in actuality or as a goal for the near future. This has two implications: Peoples in all countries demand and expect services and advancing standards of well-being. If those services and standards are not forthcoming, dissatisfactions will arise which will undermine the morale and the stability of a society, thus rendering it less effective in attaining its objectives in international relations.

Shifting directly to the international realm, we recognize that for a variety of reasons, to be more fully explored below, the drive for economic development in the emerging countries is enormously complex and expensive. Much depends, therefore, on the ability of more highly developed countries to offer support to the less advantaged. Such support may, on occasion, be given as a purely humanitarian gesture, but the usual pattern is to provide it for reasons of concrete political advantage, in the same way in which states have for long periods of time furnished loans and subventions to other states. (In the pre-World War I period, it used to be said that alliances were floated on loans.) A state's capability to render such assistance is largely dependent on its own economic situation. Obviously, highly productive and wealthy countries are in a better position to carry out large-scale and long-term assistance programs than countries that have grave economic problems of their own. It may be safely suggested that the economic competition among highly developed states for influence over and support by less developed ones will assume increased importance in the years to come.

In addition to aid, a country whose economy is sound and productive is in a far better position to make favorable trade and investment arrangements with other countries needing and desiring them than is a country which is faced with its own economic problems. This again works in favor of the economically productive state.

In a sense, the factors cited add up to this: a country's capacity in international relations is the product of many things. In very large part it is based on the reputation which the country enjoys. In a world which is increasingly oriented toward economic growth and development, a reputation for economic stability, high productivity, a high rate of growth, and an equitable distribution of product and wealth is to be prized very highly.

A relevant topic to consider in this field is the controversy concerning the relevance of actual *vs.* potential economic capacity. In the past, it has usually been possible for a country to bring its *potential* capacity to bear in the event of an international conflict situation. This has been the experience of the United States in two World Wars. Whether or not, and if so to what extent, this is still the case today is the subject of serious controversy, and the selections by Professors Knorr and Schlesinger concern this very point. Professor Knorr takes the position that the concept of economic potential is still viable, while Professor Schlesinger raises some serious questions about it and stresses the concept of the "pre-attack" capacity of states instead. The resources, population, skills, and industrial base of a country together constitute what is traditionally known as economic potential for war, which Knorr defines as "the capacity to produce military forces and supplies in time of war and thus to add substantially to, and often to multiply, the amount of combat power maintained in peacetime." At the same time, however, in view of the fact that the line between war and peace has become increasingly blurred, we must begin to treat economic potential as the wherewithal to support a whole spectrum of security programs ranging from the narrowly military through defense support and economic assistance to education and scientific research. Differences in economic potential then would refer to the relative capacities of two or more powers to provide the necessary productive resources to support foreign economic aid and development programs and a high level of investment in appropriate industries as well as a military establishment.

It would be difficult to list, in detail, all the aspects of a country's economic situation which contribute to, or detract from, its capacity in international relations. Entire courses in economics are focused on such a task. It is also difficult to separate many of the economic ingredients of state capacity from other aspects of a society which are covered elsewhere in this book, such as geography, resources, population, and scientific-technological development. These are all intertwined and interdependent. Nevertheless, attempting to single out some specific economic factors, one would surely wish to consider such aspects as a country's industrial capacity, the amount of capital available for investment purposes, and the investment opportunities presented at home and abroad. One would also wish to examine closely a country's gross national product (the monetary value of the total of goods and services produced) and the "mix" of that product. Some production is entirely oriented toward national security purposes and thus directly adds to a country's capabilities in its relations with others. Other production may have an indirect relationship, and still other items in the inventory either have no relationship at all or perhaps only a most indirect one. In fact, some items may detract from the possibility of attaining maximum strength in a society's international relationships.

A student should pay close attention to the form of economic organization which exists in the country whose foreign involvements he is studying, comparing that form, in its relevant functional and dysfunctional aspects, with other forms practiced elsewhere. Included here are such considerations as the type of planning that is characteristic in the country and the way in which product and income are distributed throughout the population. Likewise one would wish to inquire into such aspects of a nation's economy as its taxation program, its labor-management relations, and the like. It has also been suggested that countries differ in their attitudes toward innovation, including in the economic sphere. If this is so, it would be a relevant variable for the student to consider. There may be religious, cultural, or ideological impediments to the full utilization of a country's economic potential. The case of India comes readily to mind, but it is by no means the only one that could be cited. Until recently, France has been cited as an example of an economy based heavily on the small family firm, emphasizing small-scale, high profit-per-unit production, and de-emphasizing risk-taking with large production for uncertain markets.[2] In short, the cultural pattern may affect the ways in which a country's economy operates.

With respect to economic organization, the ability to utilize human and material resources depends largely on the economic structure and organization of a society. In this regard, there is a range of alternatives, from complete state control (seldom fully achieved) to completely private decision-making (also seldom reached, except in the speeches of American campaign orators). Students of international relations have long studied theories on the impact of a country's economic system on its foreign policies, such as those of the Marxists on one hand and of the free enterprise advocates on the other.

The Marxist theory, simply stated, is that capitalism breeds imperialism which, in turn, breeds war; that in the quest for economic advantage, markets, resources, and investment opportunities, the governments of capitalist countries, spurred on by the needs and desires of their business communities, have no alternative but to become externally aggressive. There are variations on this theme, including certain low-level "scandal theories" which propose that wars are the result of capitalists' influences over statesmen (war profiteers, merchants of death, and the like). The trouble with this theory is that it very frequently does not stand up to historical investigation. In fact, the traditional role of business has been more often that of the appeaser than the warmonger. Numerous international conflicts, such as those in Korea and Vietnam, make almost no sense at all if one were to attempt to explain them on the basis of economic motivation.

This is not to say that businessmen have been squeamish about making profits from war or preparations for war; but as a rule they have not been belligerent. In fact, governments have often had to persuade their business communities to extend themselves into foreign areas, using various incentives to make it profitable and congenial for them to do so. One distinguished student of international affairs, Professor Quincy Wright, has argued that capitalist societies have been relatively peaceful, in large part because the central idea of capitalism is to separate government and business. In the modern period, Professor Wright holds, war has more frequently been initiated by states

[2] David S. Landes, "Observations on France: Economy, Society, and Polity," *World Politics,* **IX** (1957), 329–350.

dominated by agrarianism or by (a form of) socialism than by those dominated by capitalism.[3]

The doubts that have been voiced about simplistic explanations of international tension and conflict may equally apply to opposing theories, such as the one that free enterprise is, by definition, peaceful and also that it is, again by definition, so efficient as to eventually overcome any other form of economic organization. As to the first point, it is important to remember that war is essentially a political phenomenon, not an economic one—that it arises out of the contacts and frictions of states regardless of their form of economic organization. As to the second point, no one would argue, surely, that capitalism is inefficient. A glance at the immense wealth and productivity of the United States is sufficiently convincing testimony to the contrary. But the question must be raised whether an economy such as that of the United States is always efficient in ways germane to international relations, or whether its efficiency lies in the satisfaction of wants and desires that have only indirect relevance to the country's external power position. This question raises the related one whether for countries that are just beginning the economic development process, the capitalist model is the most appropriate.

While it certainly appears, at least to most Western observers, that in many ways a system of state planning, such as that of the Soviet Union, is less efficient than that of the United States, one cannot yet conclude that all the returns are in and that the question can definitively be put to rest. Whatever shortcomings one can identify in the Soviet economic system, it has not broken down and it has, at least in major respects, succeeded in what it attempted to do, namely, to transform the country into a first-rank industrial power. The example of the Soviet Union, and increasingly that of Communist China as well, carries a potent appeal to peoples in the underdeveloped areas, who want development, want it fast, and are sometimes not as particular about means of achieving it as people in the more highly developed Western societies might wish them to be.

For all these reasons, it would seem best to leave the question of the most appropriate form of economic organization, viewed from the point of view of state capacity in international relations, open—as we must with so many of our questions.

[3] Quincy Wright, *A Study of War* (Chicago: The University of Chicago Press, 1942), Chap. 32.

1

*The Concept of Economic Potential for War**

Klaus Knorr

KLAUS KNORR *is Professor in the Woodrow Wilson School of Public and International Affairs, Princeton University, and a frequent government consultant. He is an outstanding authority on the economics of international resources, and indeed on the economic aspects of international relations in general. He is the author of* War Potential of Nations (*1956*), *and* NATO and American Security (*1959*).

. . . Military potential . . . is the ability of a nation to divert resources to defense in both formal peace and war. Economic (including technological) capacity is, of course, one constituent of military potential in this sense. But before concentrating on this particular factor, its relation to other major constituents must be clarified. The production of military power demands an input of manpower and other productive resources which would otherwise be directed to non-military output or, marginally, remain idle. But at no time, not even when engaged in total war, can a nation allocate all resources to the production of combat power. The proportion which can and will be diverted to this purpose depends a. on the structure and productivity of these resources and b. on the nation's will to provide for military power, i.e., to pay the price for military strength. This price is to be paid not only financially but in terms of foregoing the satisfaction of a wide range of interests—consumption, leisure, comfort, safety, etc.—that conflict with the commitment of resources to the production of military power. The will to provide for military power is therefore another constituent of a nation's defense potential.

Furthermore, given any degree of willingness to pay this price (including the discipline with which the population supports government measures), the output of military power depends upon the efficiency with which the diverted resources are employed. Hence, organizational ability and especially administrative competence represent a third major constituent of military potential. To illustrate, the amount of military power maintained by the United States at any one time is not only a function of the country's productive capacity. It also depends on the size of the defense budget (which permits a proportion of this capacity to be allotted to the output of combat power, and which is contingent upon a political decision reflecting the price the American people are willing to pay for defense), and on the efficiency with which every defense dollar—and, indeed, every non-defense dollar—is spent. As will appear in the following, any realistic analysis of economic and technological potential for defense must pay heed to these interrelationships.

II

While it is useful to theorize on the general meaning of military poten-

* *World Politics,* X (1957), 49–62. Reprinted by permission.

tial and on the general ways in which this concept can be put to predictive and manipulative use, practical application calls for an immediate descent from the general to the particular. In real life, a nation has no such thing as a military potential or an economic defense potential which is the same for all possible situations calling for the use of military power in formal peace or war. At present, for example, there are countries which have a relatively high potential for fighting with non-atomic weapons on their own territory or in nearby theaters of war; but they have a very low potential for conducting war with non-atomic arms in distant theaters of operations and a still lower, or zero, potential for waging thermonuclear war. It cannot be stressed too strongly that the analysis of the war potential of any particular country or alliance must begin with specific assumptions about the kind of situation demanding the use of military power. If we are interested in military potential, we must relate our analysis to the likely situations that require, or will require, a military effort. At the present time, and using the United States as an example in the following analysis, it is reasonable to concentrate on three such situations: 1. the long-run maintenance of an adequate defense establishment (which, in fact, it is hoped will deter aggression without jeopardy to vital American interests abroad); 2. involvement in limited wars; and 3. the outbreak of unlimited war. For illustrative purposes, we may furthermore assume that the first two situations demand a diversion of resources from the civilian to the military sector of the economy amounting to from 8 to 12 per cent and from 14 to 18 per cent of the Gross National Product (GNP), respectively.

Obviously, the basic factors governing economic defense potential are the same for the two first situations, in the sense that a nation endowed with a high economic defense potential for fighting limited war usually also enjoys a high potential for maintaining a strong military posture in the absence of formal war. The main conditions that make up economic defense potential for limited war are:

(1) The volume of the GNP

The absolute volume is patently significant, since the economic effort for defense will be measured as a proportion of total capacity for producing goods and services. The volume of GNP per capita, or per head of the labor force, is a rough index of the productivity of labor and helps in estimating how much civilian consumption can be compressed in an emergency in order to release productive factors for the defense section. Clearly, it makes a difference whether the GNP per capita is the equivalent of $2,000, $800, or $100 per year.

(2) The rate of growth of the GNP

This datum will help in estimating changes in economic defense potential over time. Growth will result chiefly from increases in the labor force, from the rate of savings and investment, and from technological innovation. These three factors each have their own bearing on economic defense potential—e.g., a country with a high rate of savings and investment may be able to sustain the conduct of limited war by temporarily switching resources to the military sector entirely or largely from investment, rather than from consumption.

(3) The structure of output

The most relevant condition is the degree to which the normal product mix approaches the output mix required for waging limited war. This includes the value of industrial as against agricultural, mining, and service production; of heavy as against light industrial production; within these categories, of production of the many goods of special importance to defense such as arms, aircraft, electronics, and fuels; and the growth rate for all of these key products.

(*4*) ***The flexibility of output***

It is important to know the relative ease and speed with which output patterns can be modified and, especially, the output of key military supplies be expanded. To the extent that this depends on the flexibility of an economy rather than on government policy, the main factors are the organizational ability of management, the mobility of labor, and the state of such industries as construction, transportation, and machine tools which facilitate the conversion of plant from one output mix to another or the shift of labor from one plant or locality to another.

(*5*) ***Science and technology***

The current pace of technological innovation in weapons production is unprecedented in history and is indeed so swift that a nation's endowment in scientists and technicians, the rates and quality of their training, the distribution of this precious personnel over various research fields, and its division between pure and applied research have become major constituents of economic defense potential.

(*6*) ***Size and structure of the defense budget***

This factor will in large measure determine a country's ready capacity for producing military supplies and skills required in limited war.

(*7*) ***The size and structure of the tax burden***

Both the magnitude of tax revenues in relation to the national income and the tax pattern affect the ease with which the financial instrument can be used in an emergency for allocating additional resources to defense production.

It should be noted that the degree of national self-sufficiency, as against dependence on foreign supplies, is considered as part of the "structure of output." For industrial nations, this problem is chiefly one of foodstuffs and primary commodities. Normally, there should be no problem so far as the long-range maintenance of defense forces in time of formal peace is concerned. But as the Suez Canal crisis and the sharp rises of raw materials prices during the Korean War showed, dependence on foreign supplies may be a very serious handicap in time of limited war. Yet, since most primary materials are storable, and since participation in international trade tends to raise labor productivity and the GNP—another determinant of economic defense potential—self-sufficiency achieved by a deliberate cutback of foreign trade is distinctly less of an asset than when it is the natural outcome of comparative production advantages.

In view of the number of main conditions affecting the economic war potentials of nations, it is immediately apparent that there is no magic key to the estimation of war potential. An estimate of any one condition cannot be expected to yield more than partial results. For instance, a mere comparison of the GNP of two countries—although it offers valuable information—is not only difficult technically but also of narrowly limited value by itself.

When the conditions of economic defense potential are discussed, reference is often made to conditions that are not actually economic, but constituents of administrative capacity or of the nation's will to provide for military power. Thus, how large an input of productive resources is needed to generate a given amount of military strength depends in large measure on the administrative efficiency with which defense dollars are spent. The flexibility of the output mix depends on administrative competence, which is a considerable element in lead-times, whenever new admixtures of military end-items are urgently required.

The maintenance of a large-scale defense effort in time of formal peace must, in the long run, rest on a commensurate degree of taxation, so that there are no consumption and investment dollars in excess of what can be spent on consumption and investment goods at current prices. If the defense effort is not put on a pay-as-you-go basis whenever full employment prevails, inflationary pressures will result and, if strong and prolonged, they will have various debilitating consequences. Whether the defense effort will or will not be mounted on a pay-as-you-go basis is not, of course, an economic but a political and psychological problem (and, since public attitudes are subject to government leadership, it is an administrative problem as well). This crucial factor of the will to provide for defense is frequently slighted in American discussions of how large a defense budget the "economy" can stand. What the "economy" can stand is something quite different from, though not unrelated to, what the electorate will stand. Provided the electorate agrees to be taxed for a defense effort requiring year after year, say, 12 per cent of the GNP, the question is whether or not this tax load (in addition to taxes for the civilian purposes of government) will undermine the "soundness" of the economy. The economy might suffer if high taxes engendered a fall in the rate of savings and investment (public as well as private) and, in a private enterprise economy, weakened the incentive to work, innovate, and employ productive resources efficiently. Such ill consequences would slow down the rate of economic growth in, and reduce the flexibility of, the economy and thereby diminish economic defense potential over time.

Contrary to the assurance with which such deleterious effects are frequently predicted, we know unfortunately little about the circumstances under which they would represent a serious risk. We do know that the high tax rates levied in the United States since the outbreak of the Korean War have not prevented a very high rate of economic growth; that the effects on the incentives and the savings of high-income groups as a whole have been minor; that harmful effects of severe taxation depend on the structure of taxation as well as on its level; and that, in democratic communities, the slackening of the electorate's will to provide for defense in peacetime is likely to keep taxes from reaching the level at which these subversive risks to the economy would become serious. . . .

2
*Economic Growth and National Security**

James R. Schlesinger

JAMES R. SCHLESINGER, *associate professor of economics at Harvard, has served as a research associate of the Foreign Policy Research Institute and as a consultant to the Naval War College. A leading authority in the field of monetary and fiscal policy as it relates to national security, he has written widely for professional and scholarly journals.*

In the past year, the discussion of economic growth as an answer to the security and other problems facing the United States has suffered some eclipse as a consequence of the recession and the need to take action to prevent economic retrogression. Despite the distractions of the recession, an underlying belief persists that overall economic capacity is likely to prove determinative in the power struggle between the West and the communist world. In the United States this conviction seemingly goes unchallenged from either end of the political spectrum, largely because it draws upon a common element in the American credo—the optimistic assumption about human nature that the exertions and energy of the typical citizen will never be undermined in a society which continues either to protect individualism and incentives (right) or to provide social justice (left). On this question, the American creed appears to have taken little account of either historical experience or humanistic knowledge.

Many economists have tended to accept the proposition that security is dependent upon growth—partly, no doubt, because they are products of the American society and value-system, but more importantly, perhaps, because through professional training they have been indoctrinated with the presupposition that given a system of ends, the more resources available, the better will those ends be accomplished. Other things being equal, such would be the case with respect to the defense problem, but other things are never equal. By concentrating on aggregate resources, economists tend to overlook certain qualitative changes which growth may induce—changes which lessen a society's capacity to deal with its security problems. When such matters are taken into account—at least in the case of a society with such vast resources as the United States—the easing of the strain on resources made possible by growth may, on balance, contribute relatively little.

The first objective of this paper is to challenge the widespread supposi-

* *Orbis,* V (1962), 453–469. Reprinted by permission. This paper may be regarded as an early by-product of a broader research project on "Professionalism and Natural Security," which is being assisted by a grant from the Social Science Research Council, to which the writer would like to express his indebtedness. Remarks akin to those in some sections of the paper were made in a lecture at the Industrial College of the Armed Forces on March 17, 1961.

tion that military potential advances monotonically with increases in economic capacity. Changes within certain ranges of aggregate income are vastly more important than larger changes in other ranges. Just as in geophysical terms the freezing point of water is critical and the distinction between 31° and 33° is vastly more significant than the much larger temperature change, say from 0° to 31°, so in politico-economic terms a critical point is reached when capacity levels are attained which can provide a nation with a full-fledged nuclear striking force. Just as phenomena such as glaciation can be explained only in terms of the critical point, so the power struggle can be analyzed only in terms of the economic critical point, which clearly demarcates those nations which are world powers from those that are not. Only the United States and the Soviet Union have passed that point today, and for the present it is somewhat futile to compare other powers to them in terms of worldwide influence. In the short run the relationship between economic capacity and power is a discontinuous one. It differs from the relationship implicit in the older concept of economic potential for war, for which many Americans have an emotional penchant, in that the latter would measure all nations by the same yardstick—thereby providing a gradual transition from Andorra to the United States.

A second objective is to inquire what connection exists between American security and economic capacity and growth under present conditions and in the foreseeable future. In the abstract, additional resources should permit the expansion of military power, but historically speaking, the correspondence between the two has rarely been close. The *will* to employ resources effectively is indispensable—as is evidenced by present American strategic weaknesses despite the country's immense economic superiority. Nuclear weapons have, if anything, reduced the dependence of power on annual productive capacity, because in a nuclear war forces-in-being will be the most important determinant of the outcome. Since advance preparations are essential, impressive forces-in-being may over time be provided by a power with an industrial base relatively modest by American standards. After the initial blow had been struck, its rival would have no opportunity to convert its superior capacity to war purposes. Substantial economic capacity may still provide the flexibility which permits a speeding up of preparations when an emergency has been detected—an advantage which may have some relevance for the United States today—but it is offset by the disadvantage that a power whose reaction time is reduced in this way is likely to be more careless about early preparations and to rely on its presumed capacity for rapid adjustment.

For the United States, which already possesses so impressive a reserve capacity, growth is not the critical variable, and the continued emphasis upon it has tended to distract our attention from other, more pressing problems. The effects of growth, moreover, are complicated; in some ways growth may tend to lessen security. There is something, for example, in the public's instinctive notion that Red China would possess an awesome advantage, if (as the public assumes) it should shortly possess a nuclear striking force, for its poverty implies that it would offer fewer enticing targets in terms of urban-industrial concentrations than would a developed industrial power. Nikita Khrushchev himself has opined that the Soviet Union, more recently arrived at urban-industrial status, could more easily survive a thermonuclear war than its American rival because of the greater Soviet ability to revert temporarily to an economy not greatly removed from subsistence agriculture. There is some truth in this supposition of the increased vulnerability of an urban-industrial society (though it is surprising to have it put forward by a proponent of Marxist-Leninist philosophy). What it suggests, however, is the need for an urban-industrial civilization to make more careful advance preparations to reduce its vulnerability. Happily, such a society will have the resources to undertake these steps.

In addition to the possibility of increased vulnerability, growth has social side-effects which may reduce the capacity for defense. Those who argue that more rapid growth is essential to American security reach their conclusion by ignoring such side-effects and by extrapolating the presumed positive effect on power of additional economic capacity. It is perhaps not inappropriate to raise the question whether in America's present position the negative effects of growth do not outweigh the positive. Many people conceive of growth as a Cold War weapon. At best it is a low-confidence weapon which has little relevance under present American conditions unless it is associated with the provision of strategic capabilities.

I

The presumed connection between economic and military capabilities reflects the fact that "in modern times many different causes contribute to render the defence of the society more expensive." This statement is drawn not from one of our contemporaries but from Adam Smith. Though the latter recognized that economic power had not always been determinative and that previous history was replete with instances of the conquest of civilized by barbarous nations, he did argue that "in modern war the great expense of firearms gives an evident advantage to the nation which can best afford that expense and consequently to an opulent and civilized over a poor and barbarous nation."[1] It is but a step from this statement to the notion of the economic potential for war (EPW), the doctrine that wars are won through the conversion of economic capacity to the production of war material. With the coming of the Industrial Revolution, the dominance of economic power came increasingly to be stressed—a tendency which reached its apogee in World War II, which was in so many respects a war of production and of material attrition. Just as it is said that "the battle of Waterloo was won on the playing fields of Eton," so it can be said with substantially less exaggeration that the battles of the Rhine and the Philippines were won in the factories of Detroit (two statements which, incidentally, in their own way reflect characteristic differences in the British and American cultures).

The triumphant role of economic capacity in World War II fostered careful study of EPW and the allied concept of the mobilization base, as well as a sublime confidence in the degree of security provided for the United States by its productive power. But the world had already changed. Future wars were not likely to be wars of material attrition, but either nuclear wars, which would be fought primarily by forces-in-being and in which there would be no time for mobilization, or limited wars, wherein a nation's full power would not be committed. Deterrence, moreover, was

[1] Adam Smith, *The Wealth of Nations* (New York: Modern Library, 1937), p. 669.

believed to be a relatively simple matter. A society had only to build up a stock of A-bombs and a retaliatory striking force; this could be done with a given outlay irrespective of over-all capacity. As long as it could be assumed that power could be immobilized through a balance of terror, aggregate economic strength would count for little.

The hypothetical world of frozen power relationships which were to characterize the anticipated nuclear stalemate never came into existence. Hopes or fears of its coming were jarred by a revolution in military technology which so reduced the size of the H-bomb that it could be placed in a missile and delivered to any point on the earth's surface. An attack of enormous power and speed could thus be launched virtually without warning, thereby placing a tremendous premium on the first strike. Achieving stability in deterrence is no longer a simple matter; it is necessary to protect the nation's retaliatory capacity against an initial attack—i.e. to provide a second-strike force. A small number of exposed bases, particularly bases close to the enemy lines and susceptible to an attack of enormous weight, will no longer do. It would permit, or even entice, an enemy to destroy our nuclear power by a first strike.

This possibility has led to recognition of the need for a larger and better protected strategic striking force. Quite naturally it has increased interest in a greater number of bases, hardened and dispersed, and in increased mobility of weapons. It has also led to interest in another form of deterrence: the preparation for disaster which involves emphasis on civilian defense and recuperative capacity. For, if an enemy knows we have prepared to cope with disaster, this increases the credibility of our nuclear threat, since presumably it reduces our unwillingness to become involved in a nuclear encounter.

Changes of this sort have led to renewed interest in economic capacity as a possible determinant of the "victor" in a nuclear-age struggle. Economic capacity, it is argued, is needed to provide maximum dispersal and hardening of bases, more weapons, and civil defense preparations including protection of the economy, which may require so vast a project as the building of underground cities. Deterrence may now involve so great an expense, to use Adam Smith's phrase, that once again an evident advantage is provided to the nation which can best afford that expense.

II

How important is economic capacity? Belief in its cruciality has recently revived, and its earlier interment as a determinative force now seems premature. To be sure, the newer interpretation, unlike the older concept of EPW, places emphasis on the *pre-attack* utilization of capacity. Reserve capacity is now regarded as relevant primarily in that one power may be reluctant to make a provocative move for fear of stirring a more vigorous defense effort on the part of its rival. To be specific, America's capacity for a substantial expansion of its military establishment provides something of a restraint on aggressive Soviet actions. Due to fear of Soviet economic development, the revised version also lays greater stress on long-range economic growth. Even with such qualifications, however, the question arises whether the revival has not gone too far.

Contemporary discussion of the bearing of growth on security fails to distinguish between three different ways in which such influence may occur:

1. growth may take place in consumption-patterns or the development of industries specifically related to the defense posture of the United States
2. growth may add to taxable capacity, thus providing revenues to finance defense-related government expenditures, and
3. growth may be of the common or garden variety, associated with the creation of industrial capacity and the supplying of consumer goods and services not directly related to the nation's defense posture.

Of the three possible influences currently only (1) is of great importance. Its predominance should occasion no surprise, for it has always been true that devoting additional energies to defense-related activities will improve the defense posture of the nation taking such steps. Such use of national energies is not necessarily related to over-all capacity, which is merely permissive, but depends instead upon the will to employ resources for strategic purposes. For reasons that will become clear shortly, in the nuclear age many types of outlays serve strategic purposes—not only expenditures which enhance military capabilities, but also outlays for family shelter and food storage, public and private buildings with deep basements, plant and equipment located away from main target areas, improved transportation facilities, and the like. Unless growth spills over into such activities, it will add little to security.

Most of the commentators who emphasize the importance of growth for security are, however, thinking in terms of (3). Ordinary economic growth did have great significance when material attrition was a principal aspect of warfare and sufficient time might exist for conversion of industrial facilities. It still, for obvious reasons, possesses substantial domestic political appeal, but under present conditions it has little relevance for security. In fact, it may be argued that the increased specialization in the economy associated with higher incomes, when new facilities are concentrated in prime target areas, detracts from security by increasing vulnerability to attack.

The more sophisticated political observers recognize the irrelevance of (3) and lay the greatest stress on (2). Conditions can be hypothesized under which limited taxable capacity could undermine our defense efforts. Though this is the primary concern of many observers, the emphasis would seem to be misplaced. This is not a critical factor at the present time, and even with modest rates of growth all the revenue requirements for an effective defense program in the foreseeable future can readily be handled. Putting aside the desirability of expansion of certain security-related capacity, it would seem wise to conclude that the concern over America's (allegedly) lagging growth rate is overdone.

There may be legitimate reasons to doubt whether America's productive facilities will actually be turned in the direction of defense-related types of output. Yet, there is no reason to doubt that these facilities are more than adequate to achieve in short order the desired levels of production in these lines. In addition, potential revenue sources seem ample to satisfy anticipated demands. Even with present capacity, the American economy could readily support defense expenditures running well over $100 billion a year. In fact, under emergency conditions, by facilitating the transition through controls, the economy could probably support expenditures of more than $250 billion a year on a temporary basis without destroying the fabric of our kind of economic system. By the end of the decade, normal economic expansion would permit defense expenditures running to $175 billion annually without undue strain.

Military spending appears likely to be a fraction of such a sum. The "high" projection of defense spending for 1970 by Eisenhower's Budget Director, Maurice Stans, just before leaving office was but $47 billion.[2] This may appear to be a "low" Republican estimate. It *is*—being based on the assumptions that deterrence is a static position, that defense costs will fall as our missile strength is built up toward present targets, that there is no need for costly counterforce strategies, and that our missile force-requirements will be unaffected by Soviet defensive measures. Such assumptions appear debatable, to say the least, though it is to be noted that the Kennedy Administration, despite the vehemence of its criticism of the nation's defense posture in the campaign, during its first months in office accepted roughly the force-levels contemplated by its predecessor and left largely unaltered the budget estimates for fiscal 1962. It was only the crisis in the summer of 1961 that induced a change in attitude and brought an increase of some $6 billion in planned expenditures. It is to be noted, also, that the build-up, especially in missile forces, is by no means spectacular, and that defense spending still remains well below 10 per cent of Gross National Product. Even if the present efforts are substantially expanded, however, it seems clear that no contemplated increase in spending on the military functions of the Department of Defense would strain our capacity.

In certain respects, present-day advances in military technology are expense-saving, thereby permitting a more economical military establishment. The main barrier to be overcome is development of the nuclear weapons-systems. Once the initial developmental costs are surmounted, missiles provide a relatively cheaper form of deterrence than do bombers, not merely because of reduced manpower and maintenance outlays, but because, at least at present, one avoids the heavy costs of saturating the enemy's defenses entailed by bomber attacks. The procurement cost of missiles is low. A Titan costs $5.1 million, a Minuteman $3 million, and a Polaris $1.1 (though the pro-rated shares of the cost of the Polaris submarine, costing $105 million, make the last system a *relatively* expensive one). Staggering destructive power thus becomes available at moderate cost. One need only imagine the kind of defense posture that could be maintained in the mid-sixties with budgets running to $100 billion per year. Titan missiles by the hundreds and Minutemen even more numerous would bristle in countless hardened sites. Mobile Minutemen would be moved at random over the nation's railroad network. Fleets of Polaris submarines would cruise beneath every sea. Presumably the yield of such weapons will be increased in time. The effect would be "awesome" —to use General Eisenhower's term. Such a force could not be destroyed by a Soviet first strike. It seems most unlikely that the Soviets would launch such an attack, if the counterblow (consisting of, say, a 4,000 megaton attack) would push Russia back to

[2] *Ten-Year Projection of Federal Budget Expenditures*, Bureau of the Budget, Executive Office of the President (January, 1961), p. 26.

1929, if not to the days of the Mongols. Until a defense against missiles is uncovered, a force so constituted could almost certainly deter direct attack.

For various reasons the adequacy of fiscal capacity in meeting the requirements of military spending alone may no longer be a complete test of the sufficiency of expenditures on security or of economic growth. A principal reason for asserting that more rapid economic growth may be necessary for defense purposes is the recognition that the increased power of nuclear weapons gradually adds to the complexity and expense of providing a credible deterrent and, what for some purposes is intertwined, the possibility of a sizable part of the population surviving an attack and making good the damage in a decade or two. Such considerations have been stimulated by Herman Kahn's monumental book, *On Thermonuclear War.*[3] The general position taken therein is: (1) providing a sizable second-strike force is essential though expensive, (2) there is a possibility that war will break out and society can reduce damage and improve its post-attack position by taking defensive steps, and (3) such defensive steps will be necessary to enable the country to resist provocations and blackmail. If the Soviet were able to protect its population and we were not, this nation would face a series of Munichs. Such protective measures are expensive: Underground shelters will have to be built to permit the bulk of the population to survive. Food will have to be stocked—perhaps a two or three year supply. Careful planning and organization will be necessary to maintain morale (and order) in the post-attack period. Enough industrial capacity will have to be placed underground to permit the society to recuperate with fair rapidity.

Kahn's analysis has been objected to, sometimes hysterically, on grounds that it is immoral in rationally contemplating the possibility of a thermonuclear exchange. Nothing could be further from the truth. No doubt, in the Clausewitzian tradition his view represents the extreme extension of military logic, but it is the function of the analyst to examine all of the possibilities. Such a logical exercise is desirable, but one should be aware of possible divergences between the logic and the probabilities. One comment in particular seems appropriate. Kahn may well be overstating the possibility either of a calculated first strike on the United States or of Soviet nuclear sabre-rattling designed to wrest concessions from a frightened West. Political leaders in the past have been bolder at times than their military analysts, but they have also been less bold. These are times which are likely to inspire caution. The risks are very great. The existence of early warning, for example, means that an attacker must fear that the defender's missiles will be on their way and his bombs will fall on empty launchers. Moreover, there would appear to be a fair possibility that society would fail to survive a massive attack as an organized entity, and this possibility would seem greater for a totalitarian society in which control would be loosened in the post-attack period. For any society the problems of morale and of organization would be staggering. Historically Russian leaders, though inclined to stern threats, have been cautious in their actions. It would appear odd if such caution were to be reduced after the advent of The Bomb. Why should the Soviet leaders today rashly jeopardize communist and Soviet gains on what might be a fatal plunge?

[3] Herman Kahn, *On Thermonuclear War* (Princeton: Princeton University Press, 1960).

Nevertheless, it seems wise to conclude that a sizable program for civil defense and post-attack recuperation should be launched. First, the exchange of blows *might* occur—and it is desirable to minimize the long-run effects of such a cataclysm. Second, Kahn is correct in stating that for some types of deterrence to work, a nation must indicate that it would be willing to accept a blow, which means it must prepare for an attack. Otherwise it would be forced through a series of diplomatic retreats without its ever actually being attacked. The kinds of outlays necessary to reduce the vulnerability of the society in thermonuclear war should be made.

This brings us back to the expenditures specifically related to the defense posture of the United States discussed under (1) above, which include private or government expenditures for shelter space, the storage of food and other vital supplies, or capital equipment which would survive an attack and facilitate recuperation. Locating plants away from main target areas simultaneously increases the capacity available in a post-attack period and by reducing vulnerability weakens the inducement for attack. At present far too high a proportion of new plants is located in the standard metropolitan areas. The government might well encourage firms to locate new plants in the smaller towns well away from target areas. In addition, the possibility of distributing surplus foods for storage near consuming, rather than producing, areas is too obvious to require more than a mention. A third important step is made possible by the high rate of technical obsolescence of capital equipment in American industry. Since the productive life of such equipment need not be finished, the more valuable items—machine tools, for example—might be stored rather than scrapped and placed in industrial depositories away from the main industrial areas. A requirement to this effect might even be imposed upon firms as part of the projected investment credit program of the administration. It would provide the United States with an important advantage over the Soviet Union, where relatively little equipment is declared obsolete until its productive life is exhausted.

These are examples of quick, inexpensive steps that may be taken to improve the defense posture of the United States. Some may be essential to national survival, but clearly they are not dependent upon economic growth. These steps, including an ambitious and costly civilian defense program, should be taken. But such programs will not exhaust our fiscal capacity. Relative to overall resources, one should be aware of how small the demands of even an expensive program would be. Kahn, who is not inclined to be niggardly, presents a hypothetical budget for 1975, inclusive of nonmilitary defense, of $100 billion[4] which is within our present capabilities. This figure may represent something of a limit, though it must be remembered that Kahn is thinking in terms of the cumulative effects of budgets over a fifteen-year period on our posture, and the longer the delay in inaugurating preparations, the greater will annual expenses be. Nevertheless one finds it difficult to envisage expenditures running much in excess of $100 billion at the end of the decade. Such a figure would represent about 15 per cent of GNP—and it would not constitute an undue strain on our economic capacity.

One additional reason exists for arguing that more rapid economic growth is essential for military se-

[4] *Ibid.*, pp. 512–521.

curity. We are in the infancy of the development of modern weaponry. The power that falls behind in the technological race will probably lose. For example, the development of a reasonably effective defense against missiles by either side would bring a sizable and perhaps a decisive shift in the power balance. Consequently, it may be argued, research and development in the long run is the crucial variable, and the larger the Gross National Product, the larger can be R&D expenditures. In dollar terms, the argument approaches a truism. How significant is it in real terms? The essential ingredient in R&D is scientific personnel. Employment costs of such personnel, without any increase in their number, will automatically reflect growth of the GNP because of the increase in the per capita incomes. With larger percentages of GNP spent for R&D, more personnel can be hired. But the critical limit in terms of specific resources is brainpower; only a very limited portion of the population appears to possess the talent for *useful* scientific research. With brainpower so limited, it is a question whether a nation which spent more than, say, 5 per cent of GNP would be doing any more at the margin than misallocating resources. The limits on the economy's absorptive capacity for R&D expenditures are inherent in the society's curve of intelligence distribution.

Nevertheless, it seems unlikely that the nation will be called on to test these limits during the next decade. R&D expenditures now run about 2.5 per cent of GNP, about half of this representing spending for the defense establishment.[5] The balance, most of which is spending by industry, is undoubtedly inflated because of the loose definition of R&D, which includes expenditures for "product improvement," styling, etc. It is anticipated that during the next decade the proportion of R&D effort devoted to defense activities will fall. Even if it were to rise, however, it could perhaps triple without crossing the brainpower limit. In any event, R&D activities will not be a factor necessitating an expansion of overall economic capacity.

Thus one may conclude that economic capacity is not the critical variable determining the military security of the United States, since it already possesses sufficient capacity to take care of foreseeable strategic requirements. Without undue concern for economic growth, the United States can provide the means for protecting itself against its foe. It has been the absolute growth of the Soviet economy which permits the USSR to mount a nuclear threat that imperils us. Our own growth rate, under present conditions, is relatively unimportant. Soviet missile might would constitute a threat irrespective of the size of our GNP. To be sure, as Soviet defense expenditures grow, the United States will be required to put up "more," but this would be true irrespective of our growth rate. The United States has the capacity to increase expenditures on defense. The real problem is overcoming the traditional reluctance of democracies to divert resources to strategic purposes. That is fundamentally a political rather than an economic problem—and although growth eases the problem somewhat by lessening the need for increasing tax rates, it does not solve it. The courage and the

[5] For present and projected expenditures for research and development, see Dexter M. Keezer, "The Outlook of Expenditures on Research and Development During the Next Decade," *American Economic Review* (May, 1960), esp. pp. 357–362.

persuasiveness of leadership is essential.

It is clear that a more rapid growth rate would provide Americans with the psychological balm of feeling more secure. Aside from the emollient provided by the avoidance of higher tax rates (which we could surely stand), it is difficult to state precisely why. The reason for feeling safer and less uncertain is different from the old one of providing for massive wartime production. It represents a type of insurance against unknown risks associated with a Malthusian-like projection of defense needs. In the final analysis, even the amount of reassurance it provides may be exaggerated because of failure to take account of the negative side-effects of growth.

III

It is frequently contended that even if growth is not presently critical for defense purposes narrowly construed, it is essential for financing certain specialized activities which may be related to security. Education is the most frequently cited example, though others may be found. On close examination it appears that this contention erects a sizable superstructure of hope and alarm on a limited basis of fact. A principal reason for the misconceptions that exist is that statistics on economic growth, which are market-oriented measures, become increasingly loosely related to the growth of real output in specialized services, as economic growth takes place.

To be sure, the ability to finance education is vital. Other influences, to which it is not always good form to draw attention in a democracy, such as educational standards or the intelligence and energy of those to be educated, are perhaps of greater importance. Still financing is essential, and up to a point increases in expenditures, made possible by growth, will encourage intellectual progress. The chief influence, however, lies not in terms of absolute expenditures, but in permitting a larger *proportion* of the nation's energy to be devoted to intellectual effort. When incomes are rising, increased expenditures are necessary merely to maintain the total energy devoted to education. Consequently, economic growth which permits larger expenditures on education need not result in an improvement in the result.

Much of the expansion of GNP these days reflects changes in the evaluation of service-type returns. The assumption of the statistician must be that changes in quality are reflected in the price, but under the impact of growth it is not unlikely that quality and price (or real and nominal production) move in opposite directions. In some areas—the services of physicians, for example, where quality depends upon expanding knowledge—enormous increases in output are possible. Increase in doctors' incomes, moreover, reflects higher capacity operations, increased efficiency, improved division of labor, as well as increased knowledgeability. But what about those sectors *where quality of service depends upon devotion to professional goals, integrity, the willingness to sacrifice?* Here the economic progress of a society, in terms of the available comforts and the ease of making one's living, is quite likely to cause retrogression. The effect may be observed in groups as diverse as research workers, students or military personnel.

In science, it is a common complaint among older researchers that the younger generation, tempted by suburban homes, family life and social activities, is less dedicated to professional goals than was its predecessor. No doubt, there is a good deal of false nostalgia in such observations, but they are also suggestive of the competing claims on the scientist's energy associated with economic growth.

In education, the most important determinants of the quality of the ultimate product are the energy, the cooperation and the intelligence of the recipient. All too frequently, economic growth and the comforts it provides as alternatives, in fact the very ease of attending an educational institution, have meant a corresponding decline in the student's willingness to work hard. The problem of investment in human capital is a difficult one.[6] The chief cost is that of personal dedication and energy; money costs are a smaller part of the whole. The American assumption that money provides the key to increased capacity is probably most wide of the mark on such matters.

Similar observations may be made about military personnel. In the military establishment, one must be prepared to lay down one's life, if necessary, and to accept frequent transfers and other disruptions of family life, including lengthy separations. Economic growth and rising incomes permit men to enjoy the luxury of avoiding such discomforts. The resignation rate of officers in recent years no doubt reflects the civilization of the military establishment and the easier transferability of talents to civilian life, but it also reflects the greater ease of making a living in the civilian life, the availability of certain comforts and prestige without sacrifice, and growing pressures for the "normalization" of family life. Rising consumption standards for the populace have increased the cost that the officer must pay in terms of alternatives foregone. Since one thing needful in the officer is the willingness to make sacrifices, many of the present difficulties of the military establishment may be attributed to economic growth.

Economists, because they desire to limit themselves to measurable aggregates, have tended to take too material a view of resources, and consequently ignore the issue posed by the efficiency of the population. Implicitly, though invalidly, they assume that other things remain equal as income expands. Yet the cost and the ultimate worth of services such as education may be wholly unconnected. Whenever dedication enters, nothing is measurable in regard to services. The only thing that can be stated is that the GNP figure ought not to be taken too seriously; it is not an adequate measure of what the nation can or cannot accomplish.

Those who assume that economic growth is conducive to security fail to take account of concurrent trends. The leisure and luxuries provided by economic growth sap the energies of a population. A public grown accustomed to high living standards may be too "spoiled" to accept sacrifice. Yet if a nuclear war is unlikely, if limited war, guerrilla wars and subversion (in short, dirty warfare) constitute the likely shape of future conflict, then capacity for endurance becomes the essential element in defense. Consequently one may argue that the side-effects of growth militate against security.

Many contemporary phenomena—including educational problems, the difficulties of the armed forces, and even economic growth itself—are symptoms of a more fundamental

---

[6] Cf. Theodore W. Schultz, "Investment in Human Capital," *American Economic Review* (March, 1961). In the writer's judgment, Professor Schultz simplifies the problem by overlooking the importance of the contribution of participants, as well as expenditures, in human capital formation.

malady: the lessened energy and drive of the American public. Recognition of this underlying reality may explain the appeal of references to sacrifice in public statements. But, speeches aside, whenever the difficulties facing the nation are considered, the solution automatically proposed is—economic growth. It can solve all our problems—education, security, depressed areas, etc. Just as in the forties it was argued that "the only cure for defects of democracy is more democracy," so at present many believe that the only cure for side-effects of economic growth is more growth.

Even the popular pastime of searching for the "national purpose" reflects the deeper malady. A nation which has a national purpose does not have to establish study commissions to devote energy to uncovering the national purpose and how it can be achieved; it goes about its job. The national purpose is built into the value systems of individuals; it does not have to be propagandized or even analyzed (save by scholars). Discussion of what is the national purpose is another luxury item made possible by substantial resources and, one may observe, generally consumed in comfortable homes or over comfortable restaurant tables.

Failing energies, the refusal to face actual problems, and the assumption that solutions are to be obtained by economic means are not characteristic of the United States alone. These are ailments of Western society generally. A more dramatic illustration may be found in France, where the officer corps, unlike its American counterpart, has been isolated from the general community and has not shared in rising living standards or changes in values. Consequently a widening gap exists between the army and contemporary French society, tenuously bridged by President De Gaulle. A group bearing military values has become estranged from a society which in its view is incapable of sacrifice, service and obedience. The officers are embittered by that ease and comfort made possible by recent economic growth; they spurn the compromises that a satisfied, comfortable society is eager to make. It is a commonplace to observe that recent French history can only be understood in light of an army which has been overseas for twenty years, engaged continually in warfare, and yet in its own view has not been given the support necessary to win a war during that period because of the defects of the society from which it sprung.

Brooks Adams, who argued in his *Law of Civilization and Decay* that societies are undermined by peace permitting economic virtues to destroy military virtues, possesses contemporary relevance. Growth is a two-edged sword. The luxuries made possible by growth foster a lackadaisicalness and a heedlessness of the future reminiscent of Tennyson's *Lotos-eaters.*[7] Nothing fails like success. The high living standards which sap energy breed complacency. The general assumption among economists and laymen that the nation would be more secure if resources were greater is but a wry half-truth. To be sure, *ceteris paribus,* additional resources would permit more effective preparation for possible hostilities, but it is also true that,

---

[7] Round and round the spicy downs the yellow Lotos-dust is blown.
We have had enough of action, and of motion . . .
Let us swear an oath, and keep it with an open mind,
In the hollow Lotos-land to live and lie reclined
On the hills like Gods together, careless of mankind.

Tennyson

ceteris paribus, a populace with lower consumption standards and less demanding expectations will be in a better position to cope with external pressures. One is reminded of Sir Charles Snow's observation, "We are becoming existential societies . . . living in the same world with future-directed societies."[8] The lack of resources can be compensated for, the growth of "existential views" unfortunately cannot be. In the long run a nation's chief resource is the national character. Increased material resources are but a poor substitute where the sense of duty or sacrifice has failed and where the soothing rationalizations of politics are welcomed by the public as balm in Gilead.

[8] Sir Charles Snow, *Science and Government* (Cambridge: Harvard University Press, 1961), p. 80.

CHAPTER NINE

The Military Dimension

Anyone living in today's world must wonder if Clausewitz's famous aphorism that "war is nothing but the continuation of political relations by other means" retains its original meaning. Clausewitz wrote in an age when the concept of limited war was rooted in the temper and technology of the times. But during the past half century alone, the political interests of victor and vanquished alike have been swept away twice by the passions of total war. And now man has added nuclear weapons and intercontinental ballistic missiles to the arsenal of total war. The destructiveness of these weapons raises the most serious question whether major war can still be contemplated as a realistic measure in the pursuit of political objectives.

In fact, the difficulty of using massive nuclear weapons in the pursuit of specific political objectives may well lead to a revision of relevant capability analysis. No one has yet developed an approach which would permit countries to dispense with such weapons—they appear to be essential as deterrents and as symbols. But on the other hand, it is by no means clear what, if any, positive functions are served by their possession—how, in other words, their possession can be translated into concrete political advantage. In fact, weapons of such massive destructive capacity appear to carry with them the greatest inhibitions on their employment. The thought that "force, the most dramatic and most fearful of the ways of exercising power, is far from the most effective, for it automatically calls forth violent resistance . . . and it leaves behind a legacy of fear and hatred. . . . The prize is seldom worth the price"[1] is particularly appropriate to the kind of force that is available to some countries today, and that is bound to be available to more countries in the future.

But in spite of this, one is still compelled to examine international relations in the light of war-making capability, because of what the sociologist would call a "cultural lag"—man's inability to adjust on short notice to drastically changed circumstances. Neither human behavior, nor the state system within which men act, have changed much since Clausewitz's day. "No single weapon —however revolutionary—suffices to change human nature; political trends de-

[1] Katherine and A. F. K. Organsky, *Population and World Power* (New York: Alfred A. Knopf, Inc., 1961), p. 11.

pend on men and societies as much as on weapons. . . ."[2] It happened that nuclear weapons were developed at a moment in history when two states were overwhelmingly more powerful than all the others. For a time this reduced the anarchy of the system to a precarious bi-polar balance of nuclear terror. Since then, other powers have entered the "nuclear club" or are about to do so, and it is a pressing question how still more states can be prevented from developing their own nuclear arsenals. One of the mockeries of the modern age is that peace itself seems to rest upon the mutual fear inspired by the magnitude of nuclear destructiveness. States have arrived at such a deadlock in their search for security that peace seems to depend upon the degree to which rival states can maintain the so-called balance of terror. On the other hand, nuclear weapons in the hands of many states and their governments are bound eventually to add to the insecurity and instability of the international system. Attempts to forestall nuclear proliferation have thus forced their way onto the agenda of international relations in an increasingly urgent way.

Although in a sense apprehension of what others can do has always been a basis for restraint in international behavior, it must still be said that it is a weak basis on which to rest one's hopes for continued peace and stability. The system is highly volatile; there are no guarantees against the kinds of miscalculations, destructive impulses, or even accidents which could blow it up.

As long as war lurks in the background of international politics, the question is not whether states require military power. Instead, the relevant issue is how much and what kinds of military power are most appropriate in trying to achieve a given state's objectives. In examining this question, one must never forget the vital political issues underlying international relations, and must realize that the answers to this question involve more than calculations of relative technological or productive capacity. The psychology engendered by an arms race has an intense impact upon the total environment for international relations. An arms race, like war itself, seems to possess its own inner dynamic: military superiority seems to transform itself from a means to an end. Thus, a proposition such as that advanced by former Secretary of State Dean Acheson, that a country must negotiate from positions of strength, is unassailably correct. Yet it results too often in policies of building positions of strength with such energy and dedication that the ultimate purpose—negotiation and settlement—tends to recede further and further into the background.

The question is: Unless we are to succumb to doctrines of inevitability even in the grip of an arms race with all its diabolic potential, are there opportunities to intersect the vicious spiral with some strategic choices that lead away from war? These considerations are more compelling when one is told that "the most serious wars are fought in order to make one's own country militarily stronger, or more often, to prevent another country from becoming militarily stronger, so that there is much justification for the epigram that 'the principal cause of war is war itself.' "[3]

[2] Raymond Aron, *On War* (New York: Doubleday Anchor Books, 1959), p. 2.

[3] Edward Hallett Carr, *The Twenty-Years' Crisis 1919–1939* (London: Macmillan & Co., Ltd., 1951), p. 111.

In the mid-1950's, Louis Halle, one of the most perceptive students of international relations, offered the following criteria by which a nation might sanely and safely measure its military power: (1) to have adequate force available, and *known* to be available, for deterring or successfully meeting any threats to its vital interests; (2) to leave no doubt in the minds of others that it has the will and competence to use this force effectively; and (3) to leave no doubt in the minds of others that its force is under responsible control.[4] Such guidelines are valuable, but they only hint at the real problems of military power; problems which are far more complex and far less amenable to such rational but still ambiguous postulates. The policy-maker, confronted by an enormous range of weapons in the hands of a potential enemy, and restricted by the scarcity of resources for his own purposes, must choose among a baffling host of weapons systems which do not lend themselves to any ready *a priori* comparison with the weapons systems of others or to a determination of adequacy. Military power costs money—a great deal of money. The price of new weapons, and the rapidity of obsolescence ("if it works, it is obsolete") add up to astronomical sums. Uncertainty as to what constitutes the most effective distribution of the components of military power obliges the major powers to prepare for more than one type of war. The powers which possess nuclear weapons must still arm for conventional wars in the hope that nuclear conflicts can be avoided. They must arm for nuclear wars in the same hope. They must do precisely what the late Secretary of State John Foster Dulles tried to avoid when, in announcing the "massive retaliation" policy, he complained that it was too bothersome and too expensive to prepare for conventional and nuclear wars, for limited and unlimited wars, for wars in the tropics, in the arctic, and places in between. While one can sympathize with those who must confront such problems, the point is that countries have found that there is no substitute for a balanced weapons system, permitting a wide range of alternative uses.

But few states, unless their national survival is clearly at stake, are anxious to build up their weapons systems to such a magnitude as to require them indefinitely to forego many other values. Furthermore, no nation can afford to neglect a wide range of ancillary conditions upon which modern military power ultimately rests: education, health, basic scientific research, capital investment, strategic intelligence, foreign aid as a means of supporting alliances and overseas bases, and so on down a long list. However compelling the concept of adequate levels of military power may be, it is ultimately weighed against corresponding values in other directions.

The problem is that the sacrifices which have to be made to achieve greater security are directly experienced; the benefits are only very indirectly experienced, and mostly in terms of the absence of greater insecurity than might otherwise have obtained. In this contest between directly-felt expenditures and other sacrifices and indirectly-felt satisfactions and benefits, it takes an act of will to decide in favor of the expenditure of manpower, wealth and resources to attain nothing but, at best, a lower level of insecurity.

[4] Louis Halle, "The Role of Force in Foreign Policy," *Social Science*, **XXX** (1955), 203–208.

An important part of the measurement of military capabilities is that of mobilized versus potential military strength. Historically no nation, least of all the United States, has ever been fully mobilized in peacetime. Normally nations set the peacetime level of their military strength according to the prevailing assumptions about the amount of military power necessary to achieve these goals. The higher a nation rates goals which are attainable only through military power, or the greater a nation's sense of insecurity, "the larger will be the amounts of military strength that are preferred."[5] Large-scale mobilization of military power invariably means the sacrifice of economic, moral, and cultural values. The classic case is Sparta, but history has known many such examples. Some societies, such as the German, historically placed a high value on military virtues and military life, and as a direct consequence of this value-pattern, the costs of mobilization were readily sustained. Soviet society was in a quasi-mobilized state for decades after the October 1917 revolution. Soviet citizens were obliged to make great sacrifices in peacetime as well as in war for the attainment of national goals. Only in recent years have Soviet leaders been forced to acknowledge that the burden of all-out military preparedness cannot be sustained indefinitely in the face of a population striving for more of the values of a consumer-oriented society.

In a sense the importance of the distinction between mobilized and potential military strength has been whittled away by the need for the "great powers" to devote such an enormous share of their productive resources to military purposes even during periods of peace. But limits, though far wider than in the past, still obtain. The advent of nuclear striking power now requires that a large share of the industrial might of a state be devoted to military ends long before war becomes a reality if protection and deterrence are to be achieved. But the decisions as to the levels of military expenditure and output that have the highest priority in time of war still assume a far more ambiguous and contingent aspect in time of peace than in time of war.

The crucial problem in appraising military power is that of relating it to one's objectives. The decision to rely upon massive retaliation as our principal deterrent in the 1950's involved a choice between alternatives which had far-reaching consequences, not all of which were fully understood at the time the decision was made. Preparation for small wars or guerilla warfare requires quite a different focus from that which envisages nuclear war as the sole strategy. Partly because the United States failed to appreciate this linkage between objectives and means, it persisted for a time in regarding a large strategic air force as an efficient and sufficient answer to the danger of aggression. Instead of developing our military potential along diversified lines, we based our military strategy upon the fleeting superiority of atomic air power that, in the end, we were unwilling to employ and that, as events have shown conclusively, has not made us or our allies invulnerable to aggression. As a consequence, Ameri-

[5] Klaus Knorr, *The War Potential of Nations* (Princeton: Princeton University Press, 1956), p. 21.

can military policy has shifted emphasis towards providing diversified means with which to meet diverse contingencies.

Military power is only meaningful in relation to strategy, and strategy is only meaningful in relation to objectives. It is a course of ruination for a country to develop costly strategies which have little or no relation to the permissible or attainable goals of national policy. In his article, "Military Forces and National Objectives," Fergusson demonstrates that if a nation is uncertain about its objectives, it will squander its economic substance and engage in untenable and irresponsible strategies that show confusion at home and alienate its allies.

There is a third way in which the appraisal of military power is related to international relations: the assurance that this power is under responsible control.[6] As the magnitude of the security problem grows, and the military claims upon the lives, resources, and direction of society increase, there is the latent danger of the transformation of national life in the direction of the "garrison state." But there is an even more subtle aspect to the problem, and that is the risk that military considerations will take precedence over political considerations in the conduct of foreign policy. Many societies have suffered the consequences of letting an exclusively or predominantly military perspective dominate national strategy. Such perspectives are usually tuned to the circumstances of the last war (provided it did not result in defeat) and to interservice rivalries. "When we recall," writes Bernard Brodie, "that both sides prior to the First World War failed utterly, with incalculable resulting costs, to adjust adequately their thinking to something as evolutionary as the machine gun, and that such failures have been characteristic rather than exceptional in the history of war, we can hardly be sanguine about the adjustments likely to be made to such a change as represented by developments in nuclear weapons."[7] Time and again societies have turned the most crucial decisions affecting their destiny over to incredibly busy men, limited by training, experience, or responsibility, with little or no motivation to examine the basic issues of international politics. In 1914 European diplomats handcuffed themselves to the mobilization schedules of the general staffs; in 1939 it was the folly of the Maginot Line; in 1949 it was American surprise at the rapidity with which the Soviet Union achieved a nuclear explosion; one wonders what other errors of political strategy may be committed in national planning that is exclusively or predominantly military in style and content. This is not a stricture on military men, often extremely capable, who are frequently the first to recognize the inherent limitations of their profession and request the political leadership to specify guidelines for policy. But unless such guidelines are provided, military planners are in danger of gradually losing the awareness of the limits to their planning—limits which result not only from the curbs on their own knowledge or curiosity, but also from the protection accorded their views. Those views must always be subject to

[6] Halle, *op. cit.*, p. 205.

[7] Bernard Brodie, "Nuclear Weapons: Strategic or Tactical?" *Foreign Affairs,* **XXXII,** No. 2 (January, 1954), 219.

criticism arising outside the structure of a military hierarchy governed by habit, tradition, interest, and formal authority.

In summary, the assessment of military power must be conducted within the context of political purposes and human values, not outside it. The costs and risks involved are too great to be left to the generals and admirals. The honest realist who accepts the proposition that military power is a concomitant of the state system assumes the obligation to appraise military power according to the strictest canons of *both* political necessity *and* human values.

1

*Military Power**

E. H. Carr

EDWARD HALLETT CARR, *a distinguished British statesman, historian and scholar, is currently a Fellow of Trinity College, Cambridge. Among more than a dozen major works in the field of diplomatic history and international relations, his book* The Twenty Years' Crisis, 1919–1939 *is a landmark. He recently completed an extensive study entitled* What Is History? (*1963*).

. . . The supreme importance of the military instrument lies in the fact that the *ultima ratio* of power in international relations is war. Every act of the state, in its power aspect, is directed to war, not as a desirable weapon, but as a weapon which it may require in the last resort to use. Clausewitz' famous aphorism that "war is nothing but the continuation of political relations by other means" has been repeated with approval both by Lenin and by the Communist International; and Hitler meant much the same thing when he said that "an alliance whose object does not include the intention to fight is meaningless and useless." In the same sense, Mr. Hawtrey defines diplomacy as "potential war." These are half-truths. But the important thing is to recognize that they are half true. War lurks in the background of international politics just as revolution lurks in the background of domestic politics. There are few European countries where, at some time during the past thirty years, potential revolution has not been an important factor in politics; and the international community has in this respect the closest analogy to those states where the possibility of revolution is most frequently and most conspicuously present to the mind.

Potential war being thus a dominant factor in international politics, military strength becomes a recognized standard of political values. Every great civilization of the past has enjoyed in its day a superiority of

* *The Twenty Years' Crisis, 1919–1939* (London: Macmillan & Co., Ltd., 1951), pp. 109–111. Reprinted by permission.

military power. The Greek city-state rose to greatness when its hoplite armies proved more than a match for the Persian hordes. In the modern world, Powers (the word itself is significant enough) are graded according to the quality and the supposed efficiency of the military equipment, including manpower, at their disposal. Recognition as a Great Power is normally the reward of fighting a successful large-scale war. Germany after the Franco-Prussian War, the United States after the war with Spain, and Japan after the Russo-Japanese War are familiar recent instances. The faint doubt attaching to Italy's status as a Great Power is partly due to the fact that she has never proved her prowess in a first-class war. Any symptom of military inefficiency or unpreparedness in a Great Power is promptly reflected in its political status. . . .

These facts point the moral that foreign policy never can, or never should be divorced from strategy. The foreign policy of a country is limited not only by its aims, but also by its military strength, or, more accurately, by the ratio of its military strength to that of other countries. The most serious problem involved in the democratic control of foreign policy is that no government can afford to divulge full and frank information about its own military strength, or all the knowledge it possesses about the military strength of other countries. Public discussions of foreign policy are therefore conducted in partial or total ignorance of one of the factors which must be decisive in determining it. . . . Many contemporary books and speeches about international politics are reminiscent of those ingenious mathematical problems which the student is invited to solve by ignoring the weight of the elephant. The solutions proposed are neat and accurate on the abstract plane, but are obtained by leaving out of account the vital strategic factor. . . . If every prospective writer on international affairs in the last twenty years had taken a compulsory course in elementary strategy, reams of nonsense would have remained unwritten.

Military power, being an essential element in the life of the state, becomes not only an instrument, but an end in itself. Few of the important wars of the last one hundred years seem to have been waged for the deliberate and conscious purpose of increasing either trade or territory. The most serious wars are fought in order to make one's own country militarily stronger or, more often, to prevent another country from becoming militarily stronger, so that there is much justification for the epigram that "the principal cause of war is war itself." . . .

2

*Military Forces and National Objectives**

Charles M. Fergusson, Jr.

Charles M. Fergusson, *a West Point graduate of 1942, saw military service during the Second World War with the 6th Cavalry Squadron and 1st Cavalry Division. He was Assistant Professor of Social Sciences at West Point before being assigned to the Command and General Staff College, Fort Leavenworth, Kansas. In addition to his other academic work, he is a graduate of the Princeton University post-graduate course in Public and International Relations.*

This article is concerned with military force and its relationship to the attainment of . . . national objectives.

* * *

The purpose of this article is not to suggest the specific military force that should be committed under any given set of circumstances. The purpose is a more modest one of examining briefly some of the various capabilities of military force, some of its limitations, and of suggesting some implications for military policy based upon these capabilities and limitations.

* * *

I. Military Capabilities

The capabilities of military force in supporting national policy will be discussed under the following major headings: offensive war capability, defense capability, deterrent capability, and other capabilities.

Offensive war capability

Since time immemorial states have frequently waged offensive war against their unfortunate neighbors. States have resorted to the overt use of military force for political, economic, and other advantages that are often obscure. Particularly during the nineteenth century, the United States herself was not unwilling to employ military force in this manner as evidenced by the War of 1812, the Mexican War, the Indian wars, and, most particularly, the Spanish-American War. Incidentally, all of these were quite limited operations.

It cannot be denied that many aggressive wars have paid handsome dividends to the aggressors. Most nations, including the United States, owe their independence to the overt use of military force. Many have expanded their territory and increased their wealth through force of arms. The United States expanded to the West—and elsewhere—at the expense of the Indians, the Spanish, and the Mexicans. Thus it seems accurate to conclude that—at least under certain circumstances in the past—military force used overtly has provided an effective

* *Military Review*, **XXXV** (1955), 114–132. Reprinted by permission. The original article carried the note that the views expressed are the author's and not necessarily those of any official branch of the American government.

means of seeking state objectives. Recent history marked by World Wars I and II and the Korean conflict indicates conclusively that the day of overt use of military force is not over. It also indicates a rather consistently dismal series of failures for the aggressors. There are probably many reasons for these failures. Any overt application has tended to unify the defenders and stimulate their greatest efforts. Acts of aggression have tended also to alienate neutrals and former allies from the aggressor.

The failures of some recent aggressions do not of course prove that future acts of aggression would be equally disastrous. The aggressor has always enjoyed a great advantage in his ability to determine the time, the place, and the type of attack. Some observers feel that special purpose—chemical, biological, and radiological, as well as atomic and thermonuclear—weapons so strengthen this advantage as to make it decisive.

Any aggressor must make a number of important decisions about his attack: what objectives to seek; what weapons or forces to apply; what geographic areas to include or exclude; and whether to employ tactical warfare, strategic warfare, or both. The terms "tactical" and "strategic" are subject to considerable confusion. As used herein, tactical warfare describes an attack directed on the enemy armed forces while strategic warfare is directed on the enemy economy and home-front. The choice of weapons makes little, if any, difference. Special purpose weapons, for example, could be used tactically or strategically depending on the nature of the target.

The aggressor may choose to wage unlimited warfare: unconditional surrender of the enemy, special purpose weapons, no geographic limitations, and both tactical and strategic warfare. Or he may choose to limit his operations in one or more ways. He may choose to seek limited objectives, he may limit his choice of weapons, he may avoid certain geographic areas, or he may concentrate his attack on enemy armed forces rather than on strategic targets or vice versa.

The many possible variations of aggressor attacks seem to fall logically into four major categories: mass destruction attacks, conventional attacks of the World War II and Korean vintage, cold war penetrations as exemplified by Czechoslovakia, Indochina, Malaya, and Greece, and bona fide civil wars. In practice it is becoming almost impossible to differentiate between the latter two because any civil war almost immediately attracts the attention of one or both of the two great powers.

* * *

Defense capability

Defense against enemy attack is the military capability most consistent with the more recent American military tradition and one many Americans would consider *the* capability of military force. Since about the turn of the century until World War II and even after, the United States placed almost exclusive reliance on latent defense in time of peace. There was some logic in the strategy because of the existence of relatively strong friendly forces—particularly the British Fleet on the Atlantic—and the absence of strong nations anywhere near our borders. However, the continued reliance on latent defense got us into the difficulties of World Wars I and II—wars which might well have been averted had the United States and the other Allies wisely used even a small fraction of their great power in what we shall later discuss as the "deterrent capability."

Today an effective defense requires a larger, more diverse, better prepared force than ever before, inasmuch as an attack can come at any time, at any place, in a variety of forms, and our allies are far weaker relative to the potential enemies than ever before.

To the extent that defense forces are ready, they obviously contribute to the "deterrent capability" as well as to the defense capability. As in the case of the aggressor, the defender must arrive at certain decisions relative to weapons, objectives, strategy, and geography. Some of these decisions are literally forced upon the defender by the actions of the aggressor, some of these choices are narrowed by the actions of the aggressor, and some are relatively unaffected.

Initially the defender does have the choice of whether to defend or not, as did the United States at the outset of the Korean conflict. Once he has chosen to defend, however, he has lost the initiative to the extent that he must fight, and fight at the time and probably—although not necessarily—at the place and with the weapons chosen by the aggressor.

The defender may choose to wage unlimited warfare or he may choose to limit his operations in one or more ways. He may choose as his objective the unconditional surrender of the enemy—as the Allies did in World War II—or he may choose to limit his objective in any one of a number of respects. He may choose merely to throw the aggressor behind the line from which the aggression was launched, or he may attempt to punish the aggressor sufficiently to force an armistice, thus settling for less than unconditional surrender.

The defender has a similar choice between limited and unlimited courses of action in the geographical areas and in the choice of tactical or strategical targets. He may choose to set no geographical limits as to the theater of operations or he may for various political or military reasons exclude certain areas. He may choose to wage both tactical and strategical warfare or he may select one and not the other. If the aggressor is waging strategical warfare, however, public opinion might refuse to accept any decision not to employ strategical warfare against the enemy, however wise the decision might otherwise be.

The weapons the aggressor chooses to employ strongly influence —although they do not determine—the choice of weapons by the defender. An appropriate defense against a mass destruction attack would by no means necessarily be effective in defending against a civil war in some allied or neutral country. In the weapons area the defender has lost the initiative to the extent that his weapons must be effective in defeating the attack.

An effective defense against a mass destruction attack would seem to require all the weapons that a society could muster.

* * *

A conventional attack might or might not be countered by special purpose defensive weapons. It would certainly require a combination of air-ground-sea forces as committed in World War II and Korea. A defense against a cold war penetration or a civil war requires conventional forces coordinated with political, economic, and psychological tools and techniques. Here the special purpose weapons may be worse than useless.

It is important to point out here that the use of special purpose weapons does not necessarily imply the choice of unlimited warfare in the other areas. The United States could, for example, have chosen to employ special purpose weapons in North Korea with no objective other than that of forcing the Communists to the north of the 38th Parallel. Whether or not this course of action would have worked is another question, but it does illustrate the fact that an unlimited choice of weapons can be employed to seek limited objectives.

Although limited warfare may constitute the most logical course of action for a defender, even in a mass destruction war, it may in practice be difficult to adopt. In order to enlist the complete support of the society to the war effort, it may be necessary—or at least the leaders may feel that it is necessary—to arouse public antipathy toward the enemy to such a point that total victory alone will satisfy. Any limitation of the objective or any negotiation may be subjected to the charge of "appeasement."

* * *

There are several possible solutions to this dilemma. The leadership of a nation must be aware of the possibilities of limited application of military force. They must be careful not to overstate the results which the military operations will bring. The military commanders themselves must be ready, willing, and able to employ their forces as ordered by responsible political authority. Also, it may be helpful to point out that limiting the objectives against an enemy or conducting negotiations with him does not indicate approval of that enemy. It merely indicates that a compromise is preferable to the costs of more ambitious objectives.

* * *

Passive nature of defense

Defense against an external attack is essentially a passive application of military force. Planning for defense involves an estimate of the capabilities, intentions, or the overt acts of other nations. Military forces are established and maintained on the actions of potential aggressors rather than upon the objectives of the defender.

Some military observers argue that defense planning must be based upon the *capabilities* of other nations. This view seemingly stems from an inexact analogy between tactics and grand strategy. It may be possible for a division commander to plan against the various capabilities of the enemy force confronting him. It is entirely a different matter for a nation to plan against the various capabilities of potential enemy nations. Other observers, agreeing that defense planning cannot provide against every enemy capability, argue that the *intentions* of the potential enemies must determine the level of defense—and most particularly the defense spending—required. As a matter of fact, United States defense planning seems to have been based neither upon capabilities nor intentions but primarily upon the overt acts of other nations.

For example, in 1945 the United States had no intention of matching the capabilities of the Soviet Union. Even after diplomatic relations worsened and the expectations of postwar harmony faded into oblivion, there was still no response in United States defense spending in 1946, 1947, and into 1948. The overt *coup d'état* in Czechoslovakia in February 1948 did cause a minor ripple in military policy, but it was not until the invasion of South Korea in June 1950 that military planning and spending was materially accelerated.

Planning for defense is complicated in another way; defense can be accomplished by a combination of offensive and defensive means which are at the same time complementary and conflicting. Consider, for example, the air defense of the continental United States. In defending against an air attack, it would be useful to possess offensive strategical airpower to strike the enemy airfields and launching areas; defensive air capability in the form of warning nets, fighter planes, and antiaircraft guns to fight the enemy planes that did get through; and passive defensive measures such as dispersion, bomb shelters, and civil defense to lessen the damage caused by enemy attacks. The conflict stems in large part from budgetary considerations. How much should be spent on each of the three defense measures listed above? This widely debated question illustrates the fact that planning for defense alone has many facets and is subject to wide controversy.

* * *

Deterrent capability

To summarize, defense against external attack constitutes the major traditional use of military force by most democratic nations in recent years. Its importance remains undiminished but its realization is infinitely more difficult. It remains to be seen whether there can be anything like an effective defense in the traditional sense when each nation possesses the capability of raining unprecedented devastation on any other nation at any time. Whatever the importance of defense, it is by no means the only contribution or even the most important contribution that military force can make to the attainment of national objectives. Few would deny that deterring an attack is far preferable to the most successful defense.

It would be inaccurate to say that the deterrent capability of military force is a new concept, unique to this era. The Swiss, among others, have long recognized that a ready military force would tend to increase the costs of an aggressor attack to such an extent that it was not worth the effort. In fact, the deterrent capability is inherent to some extent in any sizable military force, past or present. It can be said, however, that the deterrent is more important than ever before in this era of special purpose weapons; that until very recently the United States had not made effective use of it, either in theory or practice; and that as a consequence much more needs to be known of the techniques of using military force as a deterrent.

A successful deterrent would seem to require:

1. That the defender possess appropriate forces designed to meet the specific type of attack the potential aggressor is capable of launching.
2. That the defender be willing actually to use that force if sufficiently provoked. (Cold war penetrations, apparently, do not provide sufficient provocation for the commitment of special purpose weapons.)
3. That the potential aggressor have a reasonably accurate estimate of the capabilities and intentions of the defender. (This presents an interesting conflict with the conventional military attempt to keep all information out of the hands of the enemy.)
4. That the defender take into account the values of the potential aggressor if they differ materially from those of the defender. (A force that would deter State A might not be equally effective in deterring State B.)
5. That the potential aggressor be rational.

Two factors merit additional attention: the kind of attacks that are to be deterred and the military forces appropriate for deterring these attacks.

The attacks may be classified once again as mass destruction, conventional, cold war penetration, and civil war. A force effective for deterring one kind of attack may or may not be effective in deterring others.

Much of the attention currently devoted to the deterrent capability concerns the possibilities of special purpose weapons in deterring attack. It is a fact that there has been no overt use of military force either of a mass destruction or conventional nature in Europe since 1945. Considering the disproportionate conventional military strength existing on each side of the Iron Curtain, this is a remarkable accomplishment for which we should be thankful. Much of the credit must be accorded to the United States Air Force with its special purpose weapons and its capabilities of delivering these weapons. The development and maintenance of mass destruction forces is an essential military requirement into the foreseeable future.

Special purpose weapons alone, however, will not suffice. They may effectively deter a potential aggressor from launching a mass destruction attack and in some instances a conventional attack. Recent history, nevertheless, provides abundant evidence that special purpose weapons have not and probably cannot deter all conventional attacks, and they provide practically no deterrent against cold war penetration and civil wars. An effective deterrent against these types of attacks requires conventional military forces coupled with other tools and techniques.

Few would deny the vital importance of deterring a mass destruction war. However, it is almost equally important to deter the other threats. These threats are well worth deterring for the costs that they would inflict alone. Even more important, mass destruction war would be more likely to develop from a conventional war or cold war situation than from a period of relative peace.

One of the difficulties inherent in the deterrent capability is the impossibility of proving the success of the mission. The greatest success of a deterrent force may be rewarded by a clamor for the reduction of the very force that has been responsible. It can hardly be overemphasized that military force may be quite productive even when it is not actively employed against an enemy. It may be at that time producing its greatest success. . . .

. . . the deterrent capability in itself provides no real solution to the basic problems besetting the world. A combination of mass destruction and conventional forces may provide the time necessary for other forces and the surge of history to provide the solutions. This provision of time would in itself constitute no small accomplishment, the possibilities of which indicate that we should devote much greater attention to perfecting the deterrent capability. . . .

* * *

Guerrilla capability

Guerrilla warfare can be used in conjunction with any degree of military force from mass destruction operations to civil wars. In World War II the Allies gained relatively little experience in antiguerrilla operations—most guerrilla action favoring the West. The Soviet guerrillas behind the German lines, the French *maquis*, the Italian partisans, the Chinese Communists—all supported the Allied cause to a greater or lesser extent. In Korea the United Nations forces did gain some valuable, if unpublicized, experience in combating guerrillas.

The fact that the West did not

have to fight guerrillas during World War II and did have to fight them in Korea is explained in large part by the fact that the Communists supported the West in World War II and opposed it in Korea. The Communists have long recognized the importance of guerrilla warfare and have by all accounts employed it successfully. Mao Tse-tung himself is probably the world's foremost authority on guerrilla warfare. His pamphlet, *Guerrilla Warfare* published in 1937 in China, advanced the doctrine that has been widely followed not only by the Chinese Communists but also by the Soviets and by Communists everywhere.

Any future war between the East and the West would almost certainly be characterized by extensive guerrilla and antiguerrilla operations. To be effective these operations must be coordinated with conventional military operations and must to a considerable extent be commanded by military officers.

Guerrilla operations might prove more effective in a mass destruction war than in the past. Guerrilla forces operate widely dispersed and offer a poor target for special purpose weapons; they are capable of providing invaluable information about atomic targets; and the dispersal of enemy ground forces due to the atomic threat should facilitate the success of the guerrillas. In fact, in a mass destruction war, guerrilla type operations might prove the most practicable method of employing ground forces.

* * *

II. Limitations

Like the other tools and techniques of statecraft, military force suffers important limitations, costs, dangers, and disadvantages. Some of these have been implicit in our discussion of military capabilities, but they merit additional, systematic consideration. First of all the overemployment of military force in the form of wars has in the past resulted in the destruction of the very values which the military force was supposedly utilized to protect. Arnold Toynbee, the British historian, offers this as one of his major conclusions in his 10-volume *Study of History:*

> In studying the breakdown of civilizations, the writer has indeed subscribed to the conclusion—no new discovery—that war has proved to have been the proximate cause of the breakdown of every civilization which is known for certain to have broken down, insofar as it has been possible to analyze the nature of these breakdowns and to account for their occurrence. There have been other sinister institutions besides war with which mankind has afflicted itself during its age of civilization . . . yet . . . war stands out among the rest as man's principal engine of social and spiritual self-defeat during a period of his history which he is now beginning to be able to see in perspective.

This is a sobering statement for soldiers and civilians alike to ponder. If older civilizations have broken down through the intemperate application of military force, there would appear to be no logical reason why ours might not follow. Furthermore, these previous breakdowns have resulted from the employment of a rather medieval military technology. The modern military technology could prove much more efficient in destroying civilization, unless of course it is used in such a manner as to prevent the disasters of the past.

* * *

Next it is extremely important to remind ourselves that increasing the military strength of a nation does not necessarily increase its security. This seeming anomaly may result in several ways: first, the increase in military power of State A relative to State B may motivate State B (and its allies) to an even greater military effort, with a consequent decrease in security to State A. Or, State A, having increased its military force, may be tempted to employ it to overcome supposedly weaker nations, only to find that these nations were not as weak as expected. The recent history of Germany, Japan, and Italy provides excellent examples. In each case there is no question that the nations increased their military forces, at least initially. However, these forces through overt commitment precipitated an unexpected increase in strength by the defenders which led to ultimate disaster for the aggressors.

It is of great significance that the German military forces possessed a high level of technical military competence. The German Army has been widely admired and imitated. Yet the employment of this technically competent German Army brought disaster on the society it was designed to protect. Much the same can be said of Napoleon, Alexander, and perhaps most of the great captains of history. Thus the development and maintenance of technically competent military forces does not alone provide security for the society concerned. These forces must be used wisely in the pursuit of feasible objectives. In other words we are suggesting the existence of two related but nevertheless quite distinct fields of endeavor: one, the development and maintenance of technically competent military force; and the other, grand strategy or the rational employment of military forces along with the other tools and techniques in pursuit of feasible objectives. Either may be present without the other. The fact that an individual possesses great competence in one does not mean that he is equally competent, or at all competent, in the other.

Another limitation of military force lies in the many surprises which war brings in its wake. Seldom if ever have wars ended the way the participants —particularly the aggressor—anticipated. If the results could have been foreseen, the losers presumably would not have chosen to participate, assuming them to be rational. Moreover, in order to win a war, nations must—or at least feel that they must—make numerous agreements and concessions, many of which they have not foreseen and many of which they later regret. Thus during World War II the United States contributed to the building up of Soviet power and prestige, a fact that was regretted later.

* * *

Another limitation of military force involves the danger of overmobilization of nations who are weak economically. As we shall see later, this danger is far less likely in the United States than in many allied nations. This conflict between economic health and mobilization provides the basic assumption underlying the extensive American military aid programs to allied nations since the end of World War II. If many nations devote too much of their production for military purposes, they may thereby further depress an already low standard of living so as to precipitate apathy, distress, or even revolt. Assuming full employment, mobilization adversely affects the economic situation in a number of ways: it lowers the standard of living, shifts manpower from productive to unproductive pursuits, diverts production from civilian to military goods with a consequent unfortunate effect on exports and on the balance of payments, creates inflationary pressures, and necessitates an increase in costly imports, further worsening an already unfavorable balance of trade.

Finally, military force alone cannot suffice in the absence of some minimum degree of political and economic viability. Or perhaps it would be more accurate to say that the costs of employing military force are not commensurate with the probable results when the requisite political and economic institutions do not exist. For example, military force could conceivably have succeeded in saving North Vietnam from the Communists. However, the lack of effective indigenous political and economic institutions would have so increased the size, costs, and duration of the military effort required and also rendered so uncertain the ultimate results, that these results were not deemed commensurate with the costs.

* * *

III. Strategic Implications

What can we conclude from examining the capabilities and limitations of military force? What guidelines for strategy and policy follow from our analysis?

1. It cannot be repeated too often that military force is a means, an instrument, and a tool for obtaining objectives—it is not an objective in and of itself. There is nothing inherently good in military force or in military operations. These are good only to the extent that they contribute to the objectives of the society which they serve. Moreover, military force is not the only means available for achieving objectives.

2. An examination of the various capabilities of military force suggests that there is no one set way in which military force must be utilized, any more than there is any one set way that the political, economic, and psychological tools must be utilized. Like the other tools and techniques, military force can be used to help your friends or potential friends and hurt your enemies or potential enemies. Like the other tools and techniques, military capabilities cover a wide spectrum of possibilities, from the mere hint of a threat on one pole to mass destruction war on the other.

. . . our organization, training, research, personnel policies, and weapons must envisage the various types of missions which are likely to develop. It would be the height of folly to base our military plans on the assumption of a mass destruction war, only to encounter a threat of a different nature. In fact, the more successful our deterrent of mass destruction war, the more likely the threat will take the form of conventional war, cold war, or civil war.

The other tools and techniques of statecraft—in the form of diplomacy, economic warfare, and psychological warfare—have played important roles in full-scale war in the past and would certainly play an important part in any future all-out war. Whatever the importance of these tools in all-out war, it seems that they are of progressively greater importance as the threat changes from mass destruction war to conventional or cold war. If our efforts to deter mass destruction war are successful—which is quite possible—we will be confronted by situations requiring an even greater coordination of military force with the other tools and techniques of statecraft.

3. Our analysis of capabilities and limitations conflicts squarely with the so-called concept of "pure war." "Pure war" has never—to the author's knowledge—been clearly spelled out by United States writers, but apparently its proponents hold that military operations should in no way be limited by

political and economic factors but should be pursued to victory—victory being defined presumably as the unconditional surrender of the enemy. While a number, although by no means a majority, of American military officers have professed adherence to this concept from time to time, a frequent and eloquent spokesman has been General Douglas MacArthur.

* * *

General MacArthur's concept seems questionable on a number of counts. The statement that limited war is a new concept in military operations simply is not true. States have fought limited wars down through the ages of history. For relatively long periods of time, wars fought for limited objectives were the rule rather than the exception. As a matter of fact, most wars have been limited in one respect or another and as indicated earlier the United States itself has often fought for quite limited objectives.

"Pure war" is also vulnerable in its failure to recognize the political and economic content of military objectives. A strong implication extends throughout the concept that somehow military victory is separate and distinct from the other aspirations of society and is a goal worth seeking for its own value rather than for any other advantages which might be brought about as its result.

We may also question the description of war as "when politics fail, and the military takes over." This seemingly overlooks or subordinates the many important short-of-war capabilities of military force, some of which were discussed earlier. It also overlooks or subordinates the contributions that diplomacy and the other tools and techniques can make during the actual conduct of military operations.

Moreover, there seems to be an interesting inconsistency between "pure war" and the traditional military philosophy frequently expressed in the United States services that military commanders will carry out any orders in a cheerful, willing manner regardless of their personal views. If one is obsessed with the idea that there is one way and only one way to employ military force, then can he really be relied upon to exercise strategical judgments when ordered to carry out missions not in accordance with his personal views? . . .

In short, "pure war" is no longer, if indeed it ever were, an adequate philosophy for the employment of military force. It has produced many unfortunate results in the past, not the least of which is the muddying of our thought processes. It is likely to prove even more disastrous in the unlikely event that it governs future strategy.

4. Our military capabilities suggest that there is no bargain basement economy possible for United States military forces. No one service alone, no one weapon alone, can possibly succeed in accomplishing the various tasks which may have to be accomplished. Into the foreseeable future the United States must continue to develop and maintain both conventional military forces and forces trained to employ special purpose weapons. The question, "Can we afford it?" naturally follows.

We are often told that military spending is likely to "wreck the American economy." Precisely how this "wrecking" is going to come about has never been explained, and it is remarkable that so many people continue to believe and repeat this allegation so frequently without subjecting it to the critical analysis to which it is so vulnerable.

If anything can be said about military spending and the American economy, it is almost exactly opposite to the above: that military spending has been instrumental in maintaining the high levels of production and employment that the United States has enjoyed since about 1941. In 1940 we should not forget the United States still had over 8 million men—14.6 percent of the civilian labor force—unemployed. Certainly without war this level of unemployment would not have decreased anywhere near as rapidly as it did under the stimulus of military spending.

Let us make it abundantly clear that this does not mean that only huge military expenditures can ensure prosperity. . . . It does mean that the United States can afford to develop and maintain the necessary military force, both conventional and otherwise, to carry out our objectives.

Certainly there is a level of military spending which would result in a lower standard of living, a decrease in capital investment, and a consequent danger to our national economy. Since the end of World War II military spending has not come anywhere near the point where it would "wreck" the economy. This conclusion has been reached by several inquiries into the matter. One objective study has concluded that the United States can sustain an annual defense program costing up to 70 to 75 billion dollars without undue strain.

* * *

What the United States cannot afford is a mass destruction war which would almost certainly be accompanied by considerable, if not catastrophic, devastation, and which would certainly decrease the standard of living here and everywhere else. It is a strange anomaly that some who emphasize the danger to the American economy from the post-Korean level of military spending, suggest a preventive war as a solution to the problem. Such a war would certainly stimulate strong inflationary pressures, decrease civilian investment, and result in devastation, all of which *would* tend to weaken the economy. Thus to solve a problem that does not in fact exist, some would choose a course of action which would be most likely to make the assumed danger a reality.

To summarize, the United States can afford to develop and maintain the military forces, both conventional and otherwise, that will reasonably contribute to the attainment of national objectives. In fact it can hardly afford not to maintain such forces as will provide reasonable security against war, because war is the one thing which the United States can least afford.

5. Finally, the capabilities of military force on the one hand and Toynbee's thesis on the other pose a great dilemma for the United States and for all other nations—not excluding the Soviet Union. The dilemma is how can we take advantage of the capabilities of military force in the pursuit of feasible objectives without precipitating that overuse of force which has proved disastrous in the past and which promises even greater disaster in the future? To be sure, this problem far transcends the responsibility of military leaders. It is instead a problem for the entire society and particularly the political leaders—both elected and politically appointed—who represent the people. . . .

CHAPTER TEN

Scientific and Technological Development

There is a close linkage between scientific and technological capability and all of the other aspects of a country's "capability inventory." The relationship between scientific-technological capability and geography lies in the fact that the former can make profound changes in the constellation and significance of the latter. The building of canals, the improvement of communications systems, the conquest of climate are but examples of the many ways in which geography can be altered through the application of modern science and technology. As for resources, scientific discoveries and technological applications affect not only their availability (for example, through devising economical means of extraction and use), but profoundly affect the needs for certain types of resources. Thus, for example, uranium was always present in the earth's crust, but did not become an important raw material until it was required in the production of atomic materials.

We have already spoken of the impact of scientific developments, primarily through medical discoveries, on population. The development of new ways to combat disease has led to a vast increase in the world's population. Similarly, scientific findings may provide avenues for solving the problem of conception-control, although it must be added that social, religious, and cultural patterns and values may complicate and perhaps even negate the possibilities that science has made or will make available.

With reference to the reciprocal relationship between scientific findings and the economic and military capacities of states, suffice it to state, categorically, that the development of the modern economic-industrial machine has been dependent on its scientific and technological underpinnings, and that military capabilities are increasingly affected by developments in science and their applications in military technology. Conversely, of course, the needs of industry and the military have spurred scientists to new efforts and have channeled those efforts into appropriate directions.

These, then, in cursory fashion, are some of the reasons why such great significance has come to be attached to a state's scientific and technological capabilities. This significance is recent. It has only been recognized and acted upon in fairly recent times, and the impact, far from diminishing, appears to be steadily growing. The implications are important not only for the highly developed countries, but perhaps even more so for the less developed areas of the world, which in many cases build their expectations on the assumption that it may be possible for them, by applying the findings of modern science, to make a "quantum jump" from backwardness to a high level of development.

As is cogently pointed out by Professor Schilling in the selection reprinted below, science and technology have affected not only the capabilities of states and the availability of certain means of pursuing and attaining goals, but they have also affected other aspects of international relations, including the very structure of the international system and the definition of purposes and objectives of states. Scientific and technological capability also has become an important element in the prestige position of countries within the international system. Prestige is an intermediate goal of policy because it can be used as a means for the achievement of other goals. Hence, no government can afford to take questions of prestige lightly. In recent decades, prestige increasingly has become associated with scientific discoveries and their applications. The Soviet launching of the first Sputnik in 1957 is an excellent example of how a country's international prestige position suddenly improved as a consequence of a scientific-technological achievement of the first magnitude. The "race to the moon" (whatever else may be said for or against it) must in part be judged not on the basis of scientific curiosity, or even of military advantage, but on the basis of the prestige the country that wins that contest will receive.

At the same time, we must caution against the tendency to make science and technology the single determining factor in capability analysis or in other international processes. For one thing, it is not really an independent variable but is closely attached to other elements. Standards of health, education, social structure, systems of rewards or risks all affect the status of scientific research and the technological applications of the findings of that research. As Professor Schilling points out, many major changes in the character of international relations have been the result of nontechnical factors. Some recent analysts of the role of science and technology in international relations have come too close to establishing a theory of scientific determinism which would be as inappropriate as theories of economic (or any other) determinism have been in the past.

There nevertheless remains a large element of significance in the scientific and technological arsenal of states. Countries are legitimately interested in ways to improve and increase this potential and to bring it into meaningful action. It is not only a matter of the fund of gross talent a given state possesses, but the proportion of this fund that can be induced to pursue a career in science and technology, the capacity to train these people, the most efficient ways of allocating them to various facets of the process (such as basic research, applied research, education, and administration); and finally, the capacity of a society to support research at given levels. One of the interesting problems that arises here relates to the impact of governmental activities on the scientific-technological function. The selection by Marshak on the status of science in the Soviet Union, in addition to providing some specific data, also indicates some of the ways in which scientists in the Soviet system have been given greater opportunities to pursue their tasks without the type of oppressive supervision which formerly characterized that system.

But problems remain in light of the continuing and growing government participation in this area. One of these problems relates to the diversion of talent into channels which are of greatest immediate usefulness, as against the allocation of resources to pure research, whose results are uncertain and may be long-range in character. To what extent does the availability of funds determine the nature and direction of research? To what extent does it add to the strength of a country to divert scientists from academic careers, or careers in private industry, to pursue careers in and for the government. Are there costs involved which may be invisible but are not therefore unimportant?

Another very serious problem relates to the diminishing role that the layman, including the political leader, can play in making important decisions, or even ultimate ones. Many aspects of a country's economy, and many more aspects of a country's military status, have become so complex and technical that such traditions as civilian supremacy appear to be undergoing great change.

> Military policies are formulated in an environment that is increasingly affected by developments in military technology and by the civilian and military elites associated with that technology. Rapid advances in science and technology cause strains on the policy process in two major respects: 1. with regard to American foreign and military policies the problem of development of military instruments that are relevant to our national policy objectives is exacerbated by rampant extensions in the range, complexity, and destructive power of modern weapons systems; 2. with respect to our domestic political system the secrecy and technical complexities inherent in the new weapons technology impose limitations on the responsiveness of military policy to traditional democratic control arrangements.[1]

In his final Presidential address, General Eisenhower warned against the growing strength of the "military-industrial" complex. The dilemma is that a scientific and technological society cannot help but develop appropriate elites for its operation. The concept of the "garrison state" is part of the intellectual arsenal of the student of modern government. The question now arises whether there is not an equal, or perhaps even greater, probability of the coming of the "laboratory state," in which important decisions are made long before they reach the point of official decision-making and before they reach the state of public consciousness.

The chance that this may happen—that, in fact, it may already be happening—firmly draws attention to the need for contemporary societies to stress scientific and technological virtuosity, but also to do more—to devote equal attention to the understanding of social processes within and between societies, and to the understanding and appreciation of the qualitative aspects of life that draw their sustenance from the humanitarian disciplines.

[1] David W. Tarr, "Military Technology and the Policy Process," *Western Political Quarterly,* **XVIII,** No. 1 (March, 1965), 135 ff.

1

Reexamining the Soviet Scientific Challenge

Robert E. Marshak

ROBERT EUGENE MARSHAK *is Chairman of the Department of Physics and Astronomy at the University of Rochester. He is an authority in theoretical and nuclear physics, and in this capacity serves as a consultant to the Rand Corporation. He is the co-author of* Our Atomic World *(1946), and other contributions in fields of scientific analysis.*

On October 4, 1957, the USSR hurled its first sputnik into outer space. Since then, the Soviet Union has orbited the first astronaut around the earth, tested nuclear weapons of novel and advanced design, and performed a significant experiment on controlled thermonuclear reactions. This was heady wine for the Russians and led them to proclaim at the Twenty-second Communist Party Congress in November 1961: "It is a point of honor for Soviet scientists to consolidate the advanced branches of knowledge and to take a leading role in world science in all the key fields." Does this mean that the USSR has already achieved a decisive scientific and technological supremacy and that we should retire gracefully from the competition with all the consequences this would entail?

To begin with, I should like to note a completely different type of statistic. Measuring time from the first sputnik—a new reference point—six sets of Nobel prizes have been awarded for distinguished research in physics, chemistry, and medicine. Of these eighteen prizes, eleven have been won either in whole or in part by Americans and two have been won by Russians. The Nobel prizes are awarded for outstanding discoveries in pure science: if these prizes are taken as a measure of scientific achievement, the United States is far in the lead. I do not personally give great weight to these numbers but I would put this evidence on a par with drawing conclusions about the total spectrum of Soviet applied science from its space successes.

Let us now pose our general question in the form of several related questions. Is the Soviet Union ahead of the United States in applied science at the present time or will it soon forge ahead? Is the United States ahead of the Soviet Union in pure science at the present time and, if so, will the USSR soon catch up? Is it possible to do an excellent job in applied science and a poor job in pure science or conversely? If so, what relationship does this have to the structure of American and Soviet societies and the ideological conflict between the two?

On the political level, the United States is an open and reasonably democratic society in contrast to the Soviet Union which is a closed and to-

Bulletin of the Atomic Scientists (April, 1963), pp. 12–17. Reprinted by permission.

talitarian society (less closed and less totalitarian than under Stalin but still in essence a dictatorship with firm controls over its citizens). On the economic level, the United States provides wide latitude for free enterprise and individual initiative, whereas in the Soviet Union all the means of production are in the hands of the government and teamwork is encouraged and rewarded. In other words, the structure of society in the United States is characterized by openness, freedom, and lack of central control, whereas constraint, coordination, and central direction are some of the qualities which describe Soviet society.

At this point we must distinguish between pure and applied science. Warren Weaver in a 1960 essay entitled "A Great Age for Science" tells us that pure science "is not technology, it is not gadgetry, it is not some mysterious cult, it is not a great mechanical monster. Science is an adventure of the human spirit; it is an essentially artistic enterprise, stimulated largely by curiosity, served largely by disciplined imagination, and based largely on faith in the reasonableness, order, and beauty of the universe of which man is a part." This characterization is a bit flowery and would smack of "bourgeois idealism" to some of my Soviet colleagues. But it correctly emphasizes that a pure scientist derives his chief satisfaction from fashioning a new piece of knowledge just as an artist derives his greatest pleasure from carving a new piece of sculpture. The pure scientist should have complete freedom both to choose the subject matter of his investigations and to draw the conclusions to which they lead, consistent with the laws of logic and nature.

The situation is different in applied science. The applied scientist has a practical goal in mind and attempts to enlarge existing scientific knowledge in rather well defined ways to achieve this specified human purpose; usually the purpose encompasses the creation of new materials, devices, systems, methods, or processes. In other words, applied science comprises the technological applications of newly discovered scientific knowledge. It is a truism that applied scientists may create new knowledge and that pure scientists, motivated solely by curiosity, may make revolutionary discoveries of the greatest possible practical application. But the point is that applying science to satisfy man's needs automatically involves the society in which this work is done and society may be expected to call the tune. It is not surprising that the conditions most conducive to pure science may differ from those most beneficial for applied science.

The emphases on private initiative which characterize the American way of life provide a very favorable climate for basic research. In the field of pure science, the freedom of the individual researcher should be maximized and conformity, in the sense of external constraint and control, should be minimized. The pure scientist should not even be expected to contribute to the attainment of well defined goals of the state. As Jerome Wiesner, the chief coordinator of science in the U.S. government has said: "My job is to keep scientific anarchy working well enough so that people will not try to change it and create a massive department of science."

But the government control and central direction which characterize the Soviet way of life can be very effective in achieving certain well defined objectives of the nation. Once the basic knowledge has been created and a practical goal established, a highly organized team undertaking in applied science becomes both feasible and most likely to succeed. Indeed, from the vantage point of the chief coordinator of science in the Soviet Union, M. D. Keldysh, president of the Soviet Academy of Sciences, there is not much room for pure science as an end in itself. According to Academician Keldysh, "It would appear to be advisable to increase the share of allocations for scientific research and experimental design in proportion to the economic effect derived from the results of this work."

We thus have an interesting contrast. On the one hand we have the "chaos" in the U.S. which is ideal for pure scientific endeavor and which must serve as the starting point for the organization and control which are necessary to achieve national objectives in applied science. On the other hand we have the central control of the Soviet system which readily handles national objectives in applied science but which must be loosened up to provide the proper conditions for pure scientific work. The questions we have raised may therefore be rephrased. We expect the Russians to do well in applied science because they can readily set national objectives and mobilize the resources to attain them. Is this true and to what extent may we expect the Russians to make outstanding contributions to pure science? Conversely, we expect Americans to excel in pure science because of their independence and traditional freedom of thought. Is this true? To what extent may we expect individual American scientists and engineers to join into teams which can be assigned well defined goals in applied science?

Soviet Strengths and Potential

Soviet space triumphs are due to an early and precise delineation of a major national goal in applied science and a most detailed and deliberate organization of the wherewithal to achieve it. When I was in Poland last July, I was told that the Russians have offered the Poles the option of taking over the manufacture of Van de Graaff accelerators for the entire eastern bloc because the institute formerly assigned this task is now heavily engaged in the manufacture of space equipment. Russian colleagues in other fields of science constantly refer to the extent to which the Soviet space program drains off funds and personnel which might otherwise have been allotted to their programs. The singlemindedness with which the Soviet government is approaching the space race is truly impressive.

Indeed we must reckon with other well-defined national goals in applied science which the Soviets have set for themselves during the next decade. Apart from constructing spaceships which will enable men to penetrate into outer space, they propose to achieve the electrification of the entire country, comprehensively mechanize and automate production, develop methods of direct conversion of thermal, nuclear, chemical, and solar energy into electrical power, and solve the problems related to the control of thermonuclear reactions—and these are only a small part of their master blueprint for applied science. It is recognized that some of these goals are short range and may actually be reached during the next decade while others are long range and may only attain preliminary design stages. Coordination of science and technology is to be expedited by official councils consisting of scientists, engineers, and industrial leaders and further encouraged by the public press, scientific and engineering societies, and prize competitions. (More than a year ago, a new and all-embracing state committee on the coordination of research and development was set up in the Soviet Union for the express purpose of developing plans for achieving state goals in applied science.)

The Soviet Union has also taken necessary steps to increase the chances of success for these ambitious plans. It is stepping up the training of engineers (which already exceeds 125,000 per year and is three times as many as in the U.S.), increasing the output of industrial technicians and aides (which is approaching the quarter-million mark per annum and is probably five times as high as in the U.S.), coordinating the theoretical and experimental aspects of scientific and engineering training, and in general raising educational standards. Moreover, the Soviet state can set enrollment quotas for each level of education and increase or decrease the flow of certain types of scientific and engineering manpower in accordance with its master plan. It is evident that the Soviet educational system is well designed to train specialists who contribute effectively in applied science. This concentration of effort on applied science constitutes a tremendous challenge and is bound to lead to additional breakthroughs in some of the areas on which the Soviet state has focused its attention.

PURSUIT OF PURE SCIENCE

At the same time, the Soviet Union is establishing more favorable conditions for the pursuit of pure science. The draft program of the Twenty-second Congress of the Soviet Communist Party recognizes that a "high level of development in mathematics, physics, chemistry, and biology is a necessary condition for the advancement and effectiveness of technical, medical, agricultural, and other sciences." The Soviet Union implements this statement of principle by providing large installations needed for such a pure science as high energy physics and by supporting such basic studies as those on the origin of life, metabolism, and heredity. Indeed, since Stalin's death, many of the conditions of scientific freedom which are indispensable for carrying on basic research have been established again to a considerable extent. It appears that the individual research person in the Soviet Union is now relatively free to choose the subject matter of his own research although the strong emphasis on practical applications to achieve state goals may sometimes interfere with this freedom. In addition, the Soviet research person in pure science can usually—but not always—draw the conclusions to which his investigations lead without subjecting them to the requirements of some nonscientific authority.

The situation in the last respect is particularly unpredictable in the biological sciences. There is always the possibility that a powerfully placed and devout Communist like Lysenko will attempt to impose an extra-scientific conformity on his scientific colleagues. This is done in two steps: first, a potential Lysenko argues that the philosophical dogma of the Soviet state—dialectical materialism—is capable of deciding what concepts and procedures should be adopted in a given science; then, when the party line has been established, those scientists who attempt to follow the ideas and methods suggested by their own experimental data are penalized for nonconformity. This is an exquisite way to kill a science because it is done so self-righteously. As we know, under Stalin, some of the biological sciences were badly damaged by overenthusiastic proponents of dialectical materialism although the physical sciences escaped relatively unscathed. During the present era, the biological sciences have returned to a more normal state of operation and the individual research person has recaptured much—but not all—of his lost scientific freedom. The qualification is necessary because it seems that even under Khrushchev, M. M. Dubinin, the foremost representative of classical genetics in the Soviet Union, was given the directorship of a new laboratory of genetics in Siberia but was replaced a year later, allegedly on direct orders from the Kremlin. The public exhortation last spring by the distinguished Soviet physicist Peter Kapitza against the intrusion of Marxist ideology into science (with specific reference to biology) is a good indication that a Lysenko-type interference with natural science is not excluded even at this late date.

The lifeblood of pure science is open communication. The individual Soviet researcher is now free to publish his results, engage freely in scientific criticism, and have a limited number of personal contacts with his colleagues from the West, although it is never certain that even the most distinguished Soviet scientist will be permitted to attend an international conference in a foreign country. But the Soviet government is slowly recognizing that the quality and sophistication of its pure science is strongly dependent on its full-fledged acceptance of the principle of open communication among scientists of all countries. Thus, while the conditions for outstanding performance in pure science are still far from ideal in the Soviet Union, they are such a vast improvement over those which prevailed during the Stalin era that important, if not spectacular, contributions to pure science are to be expected during the next decade.

Major improvements in the quality of Soviet work in pure science may even be felt by the end of this decade because of certain organizational changes which are being undertaken now by the Soviet government. They include the decentralization of scientific research in the Soviet Union to a large number of centers stretching as far east as Novosibirsk in Siberia; the initiation of a move to improve the quality of pure scientific research in the Russian universities instead of having the bulk of the research concentrated in the specialized Academy institutes; the recent modification of examination procedures for the doctoral degree which requires outside examiners (thus breaking the chain of inferior performance in some of the leading Russian universities); and the recent revision of the mandate to the Academy of Sciences of the USSR withdrawing from its jurisdiction most of the applied science institutes.

I am convinced that a great many senior Soviet scientists are well acquainted with the conditions required for highly productive work in pure science and will increase their efforts to shield the younger scientists from external state pressures. A press release last spring quoted the Nobel laureate Igor Tamm as saying: "It often happens that when the faculty recommends a student for a research post, it is claimed that the social activity is insufficient, even if the reason for this is not any lack of political consciousness but rather an absorption in scientific work." The implication is clear: the Soviet state should recognize that science, like art, is a way of life for a talented young person.

American Strength and Potential

American accomplishments in pure science since the end of World War II have been much more impressive than the Russian contributions, ranging all the way from important discoveries in high energy and solid state physics to major breakthroughs in genetics, biochemistry, and medicine. I think that it is fair to say that only Russian mathematics and theoretical physics are in any way comparable to the quality of similar American research.

The strength of the American position in pure science is due to a combination of fortunate circumstances. The emphasis on individual initiative which characterizes the American way of life provides a very favorable climate for the practice of pure science. Most pure science in the U.S. is performed in university laboratories where the conditions of intellectual freedom are strongly sustained by a healthy tradition of academic freedom, which we have received from Europe and have passed on as a matter of course to the next generation. Academic scientific centers of high standing are so widely dispersed that scientific talent almost anywhere need not languish for lack of encouragement. We have an hospitable attitude toward foreign scientists in staffing our university departments and the foreign scientists have fully justified our confidence by contributing in an essential way to the achievements of pure science in the U.S. And our federal government provides strong financial support for university research without seriously infringing on the independence and freedom of the individual scientist.

It is therefore not surprising that the recent American record in pure science is so outstanding. Furthermore, there is every reason to expect that our record will continue in the immediate future because, apart from the qualitative superiority of American compared to Soviet basic research at the present time, the quantitative output of pure scientists in both countries is approximately the same.

When we examine American performance in applied science, the picture is much more confused. Applied research is carried on largely in American industrial laboratories and to a lesser extent in government laboratories. The problem is coordinating the applied science work at the numerous industrial laboratories in order to accomplish important national objectives. During a national emergency, setting up a large government laboratory which drafts leading scientists and engineers in order to attain a well-defined national goal is both acceptable and workable. During peacetime, or even during a tense period, this is not acceptable and therefore not workable. Some more elaborate and costly mechanism must be set up to coordinate the deliberate chaos which characterizes our free enterprise system and which provides the ideal climate for pure science. One popular mechanism is the non-profit laboratory which coordinates the applied science and development work of a large number of industrial laboratories. Setting up a national missile laboratory in analogy to the Los Alamos Atomic Bomb Laboratory established during the war has only been partially successful in the form of the Goddard Space Science Center.

We are in a genuine dilemma. How can we reconcile the openness and freedom which are essential for the practice of pure research with the coordination and control which are required for success in applied science undertakings on a grand scale, such as the man on the moon program? Evidently, national planning will be required but in what form and to what extent?

It is clear that our national planning in applied science must start on various levels. We must first establish our national goals in applied science and identify those of short-range importance for the national welfare and security and those of vital importance. The determination of national goals requires the participation of scientists and engineers at the highest level of the decision-making process on a permanent basis. It has been pointed out repeatedly that a very high percentage of scientifically and technically trained persons operate at the high administrative levels where decisions are made in the Soviet Union. In the U.S. there is a severe shortage of top administrators in policymaking positions who can exercise independent scientific and technical judgment. The absence of such people in high government councils is due to the tremendous salary differential between top administrators in industry and in government. In an attempt to obtain the scientific and technical advice needed to establish our national goals in applied science, the government has been compelled to fall back upon part-time consultants who at the same time are eagerly sought and handsomely paid by the industries which seek the development and hardware contracts. The so-called scientific scandals which may be aired during the coming year are an inevitable consequence of the disparity between our normal free enterprise way of doing things and the need of our government to cope in an organized way with the scientific and technological explosion which is upon us.

Resolving the American Dilemma

I do not wish to leave the impression that nothing has been done to provide our government with top level scientific advice to help define our national goals in applied science. After the first sputnik was hurled into orbit, President Eisenhower created the Scientific Advisory Committee which has been of invaluable assistance to the executive branch of our government. In 1958, President Eisenhower set up the Federal Council for Science and Technology which consists of high-ranking officials from the federal agencies supporting major research and development programs. And more recently, President Kennedy issued an executive order creating a semi-cabinet post for his chief science advisor, Jerome Wiesner. The American Federal Council for Science and Technology is the analog of the Soviet State Committee on the Coordination of Research and Development in that both are supposed to exercise national planning and policy roles. However, there is one very important difference: the Soviet committee embraces all scientific and technical matters whereas the U.S. council is only concerned with those applied science activities carried on by the federal government. The vast private industrial sector is outside the jurisdiction of the council and somehow does not make its proper contribution to the establishment and implementation of national goals.

I know that this is a delicate question but I would suggest that perhaps an industrial council for science and technology might be set up, consisting of some of the leading scientists in industrial research laboratories, which would present its views to the federal government, let us say through Dr. Wiesner, on desirable national goals in applied science. By learning to coordinate the advice which is extended to the government, perhaps the industrial laboratories will develop mechanisms for implementing more efficiently within the framework of the free enterprise system the national goals in applied science which are finally selected. In particular, perhaps something can be done to eliminate the wasteful duplication of effort in achieving major national goals. This duplication is a natural concomitant of the free enterprise system and the competitive spirit which leads to progress on many fronts but it becomes a dangerous luxury when large commitments of scientific and technical manpower are involved. For example, some time ago, NASA announced that the man on the moon program will require several thousand more engineers. We cannot recruit them from the universities, which have a very small number of non-teaching engineers; we can only train them from the beginning or recruit them from industry or other government laboratories. We must do both, and one function which could be performed by an industrial council for science and technology would be to effect a voluntary assignment of quotas of engineers from the different industrial laboratories to NASA in accordance with a mutually agreed upon plan, so that the national man on the moon program can be achieved as quickly as possible.

Some of our national goals require long-range planning and coordination. In order to educate a sufficient number of scientists, engineers, and technicians who will do the jobs necessary to achieve our national goals in applied science and development, we must provide funds to colleges and universities for enlarging and improving scientific and engineering facilities in the form of buildings, laboratories, and equipment. It is necessary to set up a reasonable number of technical institutes which will train the many students with science aptitudes who, for one reason or another, either do not wish or are unable to undertake a four year curriculum; this additional technical manpower will release a sizable number of more highly trained scientists and engineers for responsible positions. It is necessary to figure out ways of making it possible for women to enter more seriously upon scientific and engineering careers in the United States.

Finally, it is necessary to liquidate our Civil War after one hundred years. The treatment of Negroes in the south not only deprives the nation of a substantial reservoir of scientists and engineers, but it also inhibits high intellectual attainment on the part of the white population. Last year, the General Electric Research Laboratory made a survey of the papers published during 1960 in the leading journals of chemistry and physics by all the university, government, and industrial laboratories in the country. During this entire year, the state of Mississippi, with a population of two million, had to its credit not a single paper in chemistry or in physics. This is to be compared with the moderately-sized University of Rochester which published in excess of 100 papers during the same period. Let us recall that the state of Mississippi only accepted token integration after a display of force by federal troops. I submit that a state which is still so harsh and unyielding in its socio-political structure can hardly be expected to make its proper contribution to the achievement of our national goals in applied science, let alone sustain creative contributions in pure science.

TO THE MOON TOGETHER

Despite these many problems, I believe that our undoubted leadership in pure science will continue to be nurtured by the openness, freedom, and free enterprise spirit which characterize our society. Our accomplishments in pure science will provide a vast reservoir of ideas for important achievements in applied science, and our innate good sense and goodwill will lead to a voluntary rational measure of coordination and control in those areas which are indispensable for the achievement of our national objectives in applied science. I believe that the Soviet methods of strict supervision and control will lead to numerous short-range breakthroughs in applied science but that the momentum will not be sustained unless there are also significant advances in their pure science. A great improvement in the quality of these achievements will depend upon their ability to fully establish the conditions of scientific freedom which are essential for highly creative work in pure science.

It is unlikely that the conditions of scientific freedom in the USSR will match ours unless there is a substantial opening up of their society on all fronts and this implies the reestablishment of a large measure of political freedom. If the Soviet government comes to realize—and I believe that the Russian scientists already do—that scientific and political freedom go hand in hand and that it is difficult to guarantee scientific freedom without a major liberalization of Soviet society in all its aspects, there is bound to be a great efflorescence of pure science in the Soviet Union. And if a large measure of political freedom is established in the Soviet Union, it is quite likely that we shall be sending our American astronauts together with their Russian counterparts on joint expeditions to the moon and other celestial objects beyond.

2

*Science, Technology, and Foreign Policy**

Warner R. Schilling

WARNER SCHILLING, *Associate Professor in the Department of Public Law and Government at Columbia University, is also Research Associate in the Institute of War and Peace Studies and a member of the faculty of the School of International Affairs. As an analyst of military strategy and foreign policy, he has written widely for scholarly journals.*

This paper is meant to stimulate some general ideas about how the development of scientific knowledge and its technical application will influence the future direction of American foreign policy. The first part of the paper will survey the impact that science and technology have had on world politics in the recent past. This is perhaps the best way to alert one's self to the full range over which future change may be expected to occur. The second part will list some of the constant as well as the changing characteristics of this historical relationship. Finally, in the third part, an effort will be made to indicate a few of the foreign policy problems and opportuni-

* *Journal of International Affairs,* **XIII** (1959), 7–18. Reprinted by permission.

ties posed by present and prospective scientific and technological developments.[1]

I

The dominant technological development of the past three hundred years has been the large-scale and increasing substitution of inanimate for animate energy as the motive force for man's machines. This substitution had its early beginnings in the use of wind and water, but it was only with the discovery of how to convert the heat from the burning of fossil fuels into mechanical energy and how to convert mechanical into electrical energy and back again that inanimate energy became both plentiful and transportable. It is this energy base that has made possible that whole complex of technological, economic and social developments that we associate with modern industrial civilization.[2]

Clearly, none of the key elements in the international political process has been untouched by the industrial revolution. The structure of the state system and of states themselves, the purposes and expectations moving state policy, and the means available to states for securing their purposes have all been significantly altered.

Consider the changes in the structure of the state system, that is, in the number and relative power of its members. As the industrial revolution transformed the bases for military power, the hegemony of the industrial states over the non-industrial areas of the world became virtually complete. Indeed, the Europeans had already been able to impress their rule over the better part of the globe with such rudimentary energy advantages as the sail and gunpowder, and, until the industrialization of Japan and the United States, world politics was essentially European politics.

The structure of the European state system was no less affected by the new technology. The enhanced opportunities for union, voluntary or involuntary, saw the number of states in Europe reduced from four hundred at the time of the peace of Westphalia to less than one hundred by 1815 and a mere thirty in 1878.[3] The disparity in power between large and small states was greatly increased (contrast the vulnerability of the Lowlands in 1914 and 1940 with their military exploits against Spain in the late sixteenth century), and drastic changes occurred in the distribution of power among the Great Powers themselves, most notably by the early industrialization of England and the later displacement of France by Germany as the dominant power on the Continent.

These changes in the number, relative power, and location of the states making up the system have had great consequence for both the stability of the system itself and the character of the strategies pursued by individual states within it. Two world wars testify to the instabilities introduced by the rise of German power. Similarly, the whole character of American foreign policy has been altered as the United States moved, from a position where its sheer survival was de-

[1] Recent conversations with William T. R. Fox stimulated much of the content of this paper and the arresting phrase "the endless frontier of politics" should in particular be acknowledged.

[2] For an effort to put history in an energy perspective, see Max Born, "Europe and Science," *Bulletin of the Atomic Scientists* (February, 1958). Hereafter cited as BAS.

[3] See Quincy Wright, "Modern Technology and the World Order," in W. F. Ogburn (ed.), *Technology and International Relations* (Chicago: The University of Chicago Press, 1949), p. 181, for this point and a rewarding general treatment of the subject.

pendent upon the commitment of European power and interest elsewhere than the North American continent, to a position where its military potential exceeded that of all the European powers combined.

Equally striking have been the changes in the political structures of states themselves. The development of the urban industrial nation has made possible the rise of a variety of new elites and new political relationships between elites and masses. The impact of these new modes of government on foreign policy is to be understood by virtue of the fact that the manner in which foreign policy decisions are made can affect the content of policy itself. Thus, for those states in which technical advances in transportation and communications have been followed by a wider diffusion of political power, the possibilities for unstable or inconsistent policies (or indeed no policy at all) have been significantly increased.

The impact of changing technology on the purposes of state policy has perhaps been most marked on what might be considered the "intermediate" level of the ends-means chain. Thus, while states may have been continuous in their pursuit of such general goals as "power" and "welfare," there has been considerable variation in the operational definition of these goals. Consider, for example, the changing evaluation that states have assigned to particular areas of real estate on the globe. The success of the American revolution owes much to France's decision that her power relative to England's would be better increased by depriving England of her North American colonies than by taking the opportunity that was also present to accomplish her traditional aim of conquering the Lowlands. Similarly, the present focus of interest on the Middle East is not unrelated to the increased dependence of Western Europe on that area's oil reserves. Among many of the so-called underdeveloped states in the world today, the effort to secure an industrial technology has itself become one of the major preoccupations of foreign policy. As for the contribution of technology to changes in the more "ultimate" purposes of state policy, it must be noted that just as technological change makes possible all sorts of new arrangements of things and people, it also gives people an opportunity to differ as to how these new arrangements are to be made. Thus, the present conflict between the Soviet Union and the United States owes much to the fact that they have evolved differing conceptions of the proper arrangement of things and people in an industrial society and that they seem persuaded that their conception of the good life must and should prevail elsewhere

The relation of science to foreign policy is for the most part indirect, since society usually experiences new additions to scientific knowledge in the form of the technical applications of that knowledge. This is not the case, however, with respect to man's general expectations about the course of human events. Here, new knowledge about man and the universe in which he lives can lead directly to a reorientation of such expectations. The belief of seventeenth and eighteenth century statesmen in the balance of power as the natural order of state relations was in part a reflection of their appreciation for the picture of measured order and equilibrium that science then presented of the physical world. Similarly, international politics by the turn of the nineteenth century was conditioned by a whole host of expectations concerning the "natural" struggle of states and the "inevitability" of selection against the weaker that had been stimulated by Darwin's concepts concerning the evolutionary process.[4]

The major alternatives available to states for securing their purposes (persuasion, bargaining, and coercion) remain the same, but the techniques through which states may employ these means have been greatly altered by recent technology. The history of Anglo-American relations turned on two occasions upon the slowness of trans-Atlantic communication in the day of sail, in 1778 when British concessions "raced" against the French offer of an alliance, and again in 1812 when news of the impending British repeal of the orders-in-council arrived only after the Congressional vote for war.[5] Today the words of governments can be spread almost instantaneously around the world, and their agents are only hours away from the most distant foreign capitals. There have been accompanying changes in both the content of international communications and the personnel of the communicators and the audience, and there are those who maintain that negotiation has become all but impossible when undertaken by quickly assembled major figures before the attentive publics of the world.

What technology has given with one hand, by increasing the speed of communication, it has taken with the other by decreasing the time available for decision. Not even the telegraph was able to offset the pressures placed upon diplomats in 1914 by the mobilization tables of the general staffs, whose own time bind was the result of the contribution that the railroad had made to the speed with which large armies could be assembled on enemy frontiers.

Since, in Nicholas Spykman's classic phrase, "international relations are conducted to the constant accompaniment of the drums of battle," the relationship between technology and foreign policy is nowhere more evident than in the innovations made in the instruments for coercion.[6] In fact, the changes here have been broadly reflected in all of the elements previously discussed. Note has already been taken of the changes in the structure of the state system that resulted from the near synonymity of great military power and great industrial power. The development of governmental structures capable of controlling every sphere of human activity and the conduct of diplomacy for its impact on domestic, as well as foreign, audiences likewise reflect the increased military importance of the civilian labor force. And nowhere has the reciprocal relation between ends and means been better demonstrated than by the advent of twentieth century total war. As technology increased the number and destructive scope of the weapons of war, thereby increasing the costs in blood and treasure entailed in their production and use, compensation was sought through enlarging the purposes of war, which, in turn, served to stimulate the belligerents to still greater destructive efforts. Understandably enough, the last two wars have also left their mark on some of the general expectations of mankind, most notably that prevalent in the late nineteenth century concerning the inevitable progress of Western civilization.

---

[4] Point and illustrations from Llewellyn Woodward, "Science and the Relations Between States," BAS (April, 1956).

[5] Samuel Flagg Bemis, *A Diplomatic History of the United States,* rev. ed. (New York: Appleton-Century-Crofts, 1949), pp. 31, 157–158.

[6] Nicholas J. Spykman, *America's Strategy in World Politics* (New York: Harcourt, Brace & World, Inc., 1942), p. 25.

II

The preceding discussion has endeavored to show that no element in the international political process (actors, ends, expectations, means, or field) has been untouched by the technological developments of the past two centuries.[7] Attention may now be directed to some of the general characteristics of this relationship. Seven in all will be considered, the first three of which have been constant over time and seem likely to remain so, whereas the last four appear to be trend developments.

1. The technical developments involved in political change are usually multi- rather than mono-factor. Thus, in seeking an explanation for the British decision in 1912 to cancel plans for a close blockade of Germany, attention must be directed to a multiplicity of developments (torpedoes, mines, submarines, steam engines) rather than to any single technical innovation.[8]

2. Major changes in the character of international relations have been the result of a multiplicity of nontechnical factors as well as technical. The end of the limited warfare of the eighteenth century can only be partially explained by such important technical changes as better roads, increased metal production, or the increased efficiency of firearms and artillery. Reference must also be made to critical changes in political goals (the displacement of territorial and commercial objectives by the ideological issues of the American and French Revolutions); changes in military doctrine (organizational innovations making more easy the direction of large armies, and the development of more aggressive and sustained campaign tactics, which were in turn made possible by changes in the number and social character of troops as a result of the changes in political goals); and even changes in the general cultural ethos (lessened belief in the sinful character of man with a consequent loosening of the inhibitions against weapons development, and a shift from an interest in making products of artistic beauty to a concern for low-cost and quantity production).[9]

3. The political advantages of technological change have been unequally distributed among states, both temporarily and permanently. Economic development in Asia and elsewhere is greatly complicated by the fact that its industrialization (unlike Europe's) must follow the spectacular decline in death rates made possible by medical science. Another example is afforded by the American experience with nuclear weapons. The advantages of short-lived monopoly have been followed by a revolutionary decline in the American security position. Unlike Germany, the Soviet Union has no need to conquer the Old World before it can command the resources necessary to strike a mortal blow at the United States. The destructiveness, range and cheapness of nuclear weapons systems have stripped America of her cushions of allies, time and space and have canceled out the industrial superiority that meant defeat for her enemies in the last two world wars.

4. In the early years of the industrial revolution technology developed independently of advances in basic scientific knowledge. Steam engines were built long before the basic scien-

[7] These ordering concepts are a modified version of those advanced by Gabriel Almond some years ago.

[8] See Bernard Brodie, *Sea Power in the Machine Age* (Princeton: Princeton University Press, 1941), pp. 18–19, 76–77.

[9] See John U. Nef, *War and Human Progress* (Cambridge: Harvard University Press, 1952), Chaps. 9–11, 14, 16.

tific laws governing their behavior were formulated. However, since the turn of the last century, the development of technology has been increasingly dependent upon advances in basic knowledge about the physical world. The atomic bomb was not only contingent upon basic research in nuclear physics; many of the technical applications of this new knowledge were actually carried through by the theoretical physicists themselves.

5. Both technological innovation and the growth of new scientific knowledge appear to be increasing at an exponential rate. Scientific knowledge (as crudely measured by the volume of scientific publication) is apparently doubling every ten to fifteen years. In the first three hundred years after the invention of firearms, the improvement of the original crude product was so slow that Benjamin Franklin apparently seriously considered arming the Continental Army with bows and arrows.[10] In contrast, only ninety years passed between the first successful steamship and the disappearance of sails from warships, and a bare fifty-five years will separate the flight of Orville Wright from the first rocket to the moon.

6. Both the costs of acquiring new scientific knowledge and the costs of product innovation appear to be increasing, at least in a number of key areas. One reason why university research budgets have become so dependent on federal funds is that no other source is rich enough to meet the costs of new research. The situation in some fields of nuclear physics was well expressed by the scientist who observed that "it costs a million dollars even to ask the question." Similarly, a fighter plane could be produced for 17,000 engineering hours in 1940, but 1,400,000 hours were required by 1955.[11] The point to these trends would seem to be that not only Great Powers alone can have great technology but that in the future only Great Powers will have great science.[12]

7. In World War II science was for the first time directly mobilized in support of foreign policy. Science in its purest form (the discovery of the facts of nature for knowledge's sake alone) had developed since the seventeenth century into an essential autonomous social institution. The scientific community had certain canons with regard to the conditions of their work. Science was international (the facts of nature were open to all who chose to discover them through the methods of science) and the advancement of knowledge was dependent on freedom of research, i.e., freedom of choice with respect to the research problem and freedom to communicate the results of research. But except for the general assumption that new knowledge would ultimately benefit mankind, the scientific community largely disassociated itself from whatever practical applications that might come from their discoveries.[13]

---

[10] Publication point from Ellis A. Johnson, "The Crisis in Science and Technology and its Effect on Military Development," *Operations Research* (January–February, 1958), pp. 14–15. Franklin reference from Brodie, "Implications of Nuclear Weapons in Total War," RAND Memorandum 1842, p. 2.

[11] Victor Weisskopf, as quoted in Theodore H. White, "U.S. Science: The Troubled Quest," *The Reporter* (September 23, 1954), p. 14. Engineering figures from Johnson, *op. cit.*, p. 16.

[12] Note, however, that by a pooling of their scientific effort the states, for example, of Western Europe could achieve "great science" without necessarily achieving any of the other attributes of "Great Powerhood."

[13] See Margaret Smith Stahl, "Splits and Schisms: Nuclear and Social" (Unpub-

During the great ideological wars of the early nineteenth century, scientists and their ideas were allowed to pass freely across political frontiers, both in time of peace and war. This practice is more understandable when it is realized that as late as 1900 states also permitted the free circulation of detailed plans of their major weapons and most recent weapon innovations.[14] During World War I states made some primitive efforts to apply scientists to the problems of war, but it was only with the advent of World War II that the resources of the scientific community were brought to bear on such problems in any extensive fashion. The results of this effort (radar, the proximity fuse, the A-bomb) were such as to guarantee that its value would not be forgotten with the war's end.

III

Turning now to a brief list of foreign policy problems and opportunities, the last four developments discussed above clearly give first priority to the relationship between government and science. Had the victorious coalition against Germany not so emphatically followed the historical pattern, perhaps science could have regained some semblance of its prewar autonomy. As it was, by 1955 about 50 per cent of the nation's engineers and 25 per cent of its scientists were in the employment of the government, either directly or on contract; in universities some 70 per cent of the research budget was government financed; and scientists were invited into the highest councils of government.[15] This activity simply reflects the fact that as the two Super Powers throw one weapons system after another into the effort to maintain at least a balance of terror, neither deems it prudent to fall behind in either the discovery of new scientific principles or the application of scientific knowledge to military hardware and political-military strategy.

In the present and the future world, "the science potential of nations" must take its place alongside such traditional items as the production of steel or electric energy as a meaningful index of military potential. In 1945 and 1946 the wartime experience of scientists stimulated considerable discussion of the question of whether the government could or should influence the direction of scientific development. This is now a dead issue; the government does and must. To be sure, neither the generation of brand new ideas nor the derivation of gadgets from extant ideas follows directly in proportion to the number of scientists at work or the amount of equipment at their disposal. But the supply of scientific talent is rather limited (the debate in 1949 over whether and how to undertake a "crash program" to make an H-bomb was operationally concerned with the allocation of no more than thirty and perhaps as few as five individuals), and allocation of this talent's time (and therefore to a considerable extent the character of its product) is obviously influenced by the extent and direction of the government's appeals and support.

The question of whether our

lished Doctorial Dissertation, University of Wisconsin, 1946), Chap. 4.

14 On the early political experience of scientists, see Sir Henry Dale, "Freedom of Science," BAS (May, 1949); on nineteenth century military disclosures, Brodie, "Military Demonstrations and Disclosures of New Weapons," *World Politics* (April, 1953), pp. 283–288.

15 Lee A. DuBridge, "The American Scientist: 1955," *Yale Review* (Spring, 1955), p. 13, and American Association for the Advancement of Science, "Interim Committee Report," BAS (March, 1957), p. 82.

science potential is being developed in the most desirable or efficacious manner will be a continuing issue. Here the concepts developed for the analysis of war potential may prove quite useful.[16] Applying Klaus Knorr's major categories—resources, motivation, and administrative skill—to the current scene, it is clear that the United States is quite favorably situated vis-à-vis the Soviet Union with respect to the basic resource, students. Thus, in 1954, despite the fact that only one out of five high school graduates ended up as a college graduate, the United States still had more than twice as many college graduates as the Soviet Union. While there is some cause to believe that the "state of the arts" was better in the Soviet Union, i.e., that their students received the better education, the main point is that about 50 per cent of the Soviet students majored in science and engineering, in contrast to about 15 per cent in the United States. Accordingly, our output of scientists and engineers was only 70 per cent of that of the Soviet Union.[17]

If one could be sure that we "want" more scientists and engineers than we graduate, some examination of our administrative skills would be in order. However, the major explanation for the continued greater Soviet output would seem in any case to be a matter of motivation. The complex that makes up the American "we" in this instance has simply placed a much lower value on the production of such graduates. One way in which foreign policy can serve to compensate for America's lesser motivation is by expanding the resource base to include the NATO countries. The addition of the scientists and engineers graduated in these states would produce a total nearly equal to the Soviet output. Truly effective scientific coordination with the NATO states would require at least a partial restoration of the "international community" of science that existed before World War II, and this would entail some loss in our ability to impose and maintain secrecy. But in return we would gain in knowledge, and the progress of Soviet science is such that most of our "secrets" are really not secret anyway.[18]

The variable of administrative skills is most evident in the distribution of the Russian and American effort between applied research and basic research, the discovery of new knowledge. The Soviet Union has between 20 to 30 per cent more scientists engaged in basic research than the United States. The percentage allocated to basic research in the budgets of Russian scientific academies has been estimated at 20 to 30, which is, interestingly enough, approximately the same percentage that the Russians allocate of their gross national product to gross investment. The American emphasis on applied research would pay military dividends if a war comes soon (or if this is the only way we can maintain the balance of terror), but otherwise we shall be left to face the costs of a narrower knowledge base in

---

[16] See Klaus Knorr, *The War Potential of Nations* (Princeton: Princeton University Press, 1956).

[17] Joint Committee on Atomic Energy, 84th Congress, 2nd Session, Committee Print, *Engineering and Scientific Manpower in the United States, Western Europe and Soviet Russia* (Washington, D.C.: U.S. Government Printing Office, 1956), pp. 66, 78, 81.

[18] For some specific proposals in this connection, see the account given of a report prepared in October 1957 for Senator Henry M. Jackson in *The New York Times*, October 23, 1957. For the issue of secrecy, see Edward Teller, "Alternatives for Security," *Foreign Affairs* (January, 1958), pp. 207–208.

the future. Superior administrative skills would also seem evident in the estimate that the Russians develop new weapons systems in about half the time it takes the United States.[19]

The end result of greater motivation and superior administrative skill can be read in Edward Teller's predication that in ten years scientific leadership will pass into the hands of the Soviet Union. Reconsidered "wants" and administrative changes can not now prevent this from happening, although they can affect an American endeavor to regain that leadership.[20] The Soviets appear to have duplicated in science what Germany did before World War II in military power (mobilizing a superior force from an inferior resource base) while at the same time avoiding Germany's failure to expand their productive capacity. The political consequences of Soviet leadership will not be restricted to the fact that the Russians will have a larger knowledge base from which to develop new weapons. Just as a reputation for military power yields political results above and beyond the actual forces on hand, so too may the Soviet Union be expected to reap political benefit from its "scientific prestige," especially among the undeveloped states where scientific and technological achievements stand as symbols of the good life they hope to achieve.

The discussion of the "production" of scientific knowledge should not conclude without observing that it would be unrealistic to expect scientists to be as responsive to the demands of national policy as is the output of Hoover Dam, and it would be extremely shortsighted to wish that they were. The character of modern weapons is such that additions to or innovations in our military capabilities mainly serve to keep our security from deteriorating. Unless we should decide to remedy our long-standing deficiencies for limited war, they promise little in the way of enhanced security. If we are to produce real improvements in security, it must be in the realm of the political perspectives of our enemies, their goals and expectations. In the furtherance of such an intent-oriented (as compared to capability-oriented) security policy, the image we present of ourselves to the outside world is most critical. The scientific tradition (its freedoms and its dedication to liberating the "human mind from ignorance and consequent fear"),[21] is both an attractive and long cherished part of our "self." It, too, can bring "security," and we should not forget it.

Should the greater number of Soviet scientists result in their having a significant edge in the qualitative and quantitative production of knowledge, it by no means follows that hideous ruin and combustion will overtake our foreign policy. What is certain is that

[19] Figure on scientists from the report of the National Science Foundation, October 16, 1957, as summarized in BAS (December, 1957). Figure on budgets provided by Professor M. D. Hassialis, Columbia University, and based on discussions with Russian scientists. Figure on development time from Johnson, *op. cit.*, p. 16.

At his press conference on October 30, 1957, President Eisenhower said he had been "astonished" to learn that the major concern of his Scientific Advisory Council was where American science would be in ten years and whether the government would take the initiative in securing more funds and effort for basic research. See text, *The New York Times*, October 31, 1957.

[20] Testimony of Edward Teller, Preparedness Subcommittee of Senate Committee on Armed Services, 85th Congress, 1st and 2nd Sessions, Hearings, *Inquiry Into Satellites and Missile Programs* (Washington, D.C.: U.S. Government Printing Office, 1958), Part I, pp. 42–43.

[21] Quotation from DuBridge, *op. cit.*, p. 4.

the science of all nations will continue to stimulate new technological and political developments. The structure of the state system is still in a state of flux from the advent of nuclear power; its impact has yet to be made in Western Europe, much less in the great continental areas of India and China. Nor have secrecy, security risks and the increased influence of scientific and military elites (and hence the influence of their policy perspectives) exhausted the changes that the prospect of thermonuclear ruin will bring to internal state structures. And we may confidently expect the intermediate goals of American foreign policy to be quite different now that we have moved from an era where the enemy's conquest of Europe was the *sine qua non* for even a fifty-fifty chance to invade us, to an era where such conquest will only make somewhat more cheap the cost of his "America-bomb."

Nuclear technology has compelled the Russians to revise their expectations about inevitable war, but man's expectations have yet to react fully to relativity theory or anti-matter, not to mention machines that are capable of creative thought. Nuclear weapons systems promise a whole host of new political issues, of which test fall-out and the probability of satellite "downings" may be only a harbinger. The character of these systems can also be expected to lead to considerable proliferation among the non-violent techniques for pursuing and resolving interest conflicts, including more than a few more words about surrender.

Certainly the contribution that we can make to the economic development of India and less important states can capitalize on the potentiality of medical science to develop more effective techniques for birth control. Similarly, the fact that automation can now be substituted for the deficiencies in the human nervous system, just as inanimate power was substituted for the deficiencies of the human muscle, requires us to re-examine our theories regarding the economic prospects and problems of these countries.[22] In short, there is clearly room in our foreign policy for "scientific aid" programs, although we may here find the Soviet scientists as worrisome as we have found their "surplus" engineers and conventional weapons.

The list of possibilities and problems could be multiplied were we to venture further into the scientific future and consider such prospects as weather control, psycho-chemistry, controlled thermonuclear power, or the variety of communications which can be made from satellites. But it must be remembered that man has never been the passive tool of his technology. When the idea of the A-bomb came to Washington in 1939, it found the concept of strategic bombing waiting for it, and, as such classic instances as the divergent development of French and German military doctrine before 1940 amply demonstrate, it can make considerable difference which ideas man brings to his technology.[23]

Important as the scientific discoveries and technical innovations of the past century have been, so too have been man's social and political discoveries and innovations. The history

[22] For this conception of automation, see Gerald Piel, "Science and the Next Fifty Years," BAS (January, 1954). Some economic possibilities are outlined in Richard L. Meier, "Automation Technology and Economic Development," BAS (April, 1954).

[23] For a very stimulating discussion of the contribution that political science can make in this connection, see Harold Lasswell, "The Political Science of Science," *American Political Science Review* (December, 1956).

of these years must also be written with reference, for example, to the Protestant ethic, nationalism, bureaucracy, the balance of power, collective security and Marxist-Leninist doctrine, not to mention the content of the social sciences. In brief, there is an "endless frontier" to politics, as well as science, and man's fate will be determined as much by his "adventures" along the one as the other.

Part III

Ends and Means in Foreign Policies

CHAPTER ELEVEN

Intentions, Objectives, and Policy Aims

One of the most difficult problems in the study of international relations is that of explaining why nations behave as they do. So far in this book, we have written of the problems that arise when autonomous units confront each other in an environment where there is no assured consensus on ends or means and where there are no institutions that can regulate or prescribe the course of relations that ensues as a result of this contact. We have dealt with some aspects of the capacity of states to formulate, pursue, and achieve objectives in their relations with other states, but we must now confront the even more difficult task of grappling with the definition of these objectives themselves.

In doing so, we approach the problem from the point of view of the participating units. (Cf. discussion in Sondermann, Chapter 1 on shifting levels of analysis.) This is so because, while the general international system does exercise an influence, the specific definition of states' objectives is in the final analysis performed by the separate states themselves and their leaders. In this area of the study of international relations we operate on the basis of many assumptions but little tested knowledge. It is temptingly easy to base an entire theoretical construct of international relations on assumptions about the motivations of individuals, groups, governments, and states, but it is very difficult to prove that those assumptions correspond to objective reality in an invariable and therefore predictable fashion.

To begin with, we make these assumptions: 1. that the activity of individuals is, consciously or not, goal-oriented; 2. that varying factors, internal and external to the actor, influence the definition of his goals as well as his chances for attaining those goals; and 3. that all groups involved in international relations have multiple objectives, the ingredients of which may at times be contradictory or mutually exclusive. In order to make sense of a statement of goals, therefore, one must know how terms are defined, what priorities are given to various objectives, and what specific resources are to be devoted to their attainment. Some students, in fact, go so far as to suggest that because of built-in problems and ambiguities, the definition of general policy aims is inherently less important than the day-to-day pursuit of concrete objectives.[1] While recognizing the problems that are involved, the editors of this volume proceed on the somewhat different assumption that the clarification of aims is an important precondition for evaluating the appropriateness of concrete policies. Two sociologists, Professors Thompson and McEwen, present below a general framework within which one may approach the definition of policy aims.

Most terms in common usage contain—and conceal—seriously disqualifying ambiguities; Stone in this chapter identifies many of the problems inherent in the use of big words and concepts, such as peace, justice, and so forth. Some other examples can be cited as well: "survival" or "self-preservation" of a given state is often cited as the *sine qua non* of its policy. But, one might well ask, what is the "self" that is to be preserved? For that matter, what do terms such as "preservation" or "survival" mean? Do they refer to the maintenance of a momentary *status quo,* or do they also take into account changes in the internal composition or external position of states? Another term frequently used is "independence." It has, to be sure, referents in real life. We find that especially for the newer countries, the stress on independence is very strong. This in part explains the emphasis on "neutralism" discussed in Chapter 15 below. To be wholly realistic, one is forced to the conclusion that no country, not even the most powerful one, is ever fully independent of decisions made in other countries, over which only very imperfect control can be exercised.

"Territorial integrity," another term often used to define state objectives, is no less free of ambiguity than the terms already mentioned, since it fails to specify precisely which territory is to be protected, and against what. Taking the case of the United States as an instructive example, does the term "territorial integrity" imply that this country would defend only its own territorial boundaries? If so, what does one make of the foreign bases which were established for the specific reason of protecting the national realm? Would these not also have to be defended? The difficulties underlying these concepts, especially that of "national security," are treated brilliantly in the selection by Arnold Wolfers.

Some students of international politics maintain that all human behavior is characterized by a "power drive."[2] Bertrand Russell, for example, wrote that "of the infinite desires of man, the chief are the desires for power and glory," and added that some human desires, unlike those of animals, "are essentially

1 Charles Burton Marshall, *The Limits of Foreign Policy* (New York: Holt, Rinehart & Winston, Inc., 1954).

2 Hans J. Morgenthau, *Politics Among Nations* (New York: Alfred A. Knopf, Inc.), succeeding editions.

boundless and incapable of complete satisfaction."[3] Other competent observers agree, and although some might not classify the power-drive as either unlimited or omnipresent, they feel that the concept of power provides the best organizing focus for the study of relations among individuals and groups, including the massive and complex groups whose interaction is the subject matter of the study of international relations.

Yet one should be cautious before accepting any single-motive explanation of behavior and applying it to the infinite variety of patterns found in international relations. Certainly considerations of power are important; probably they are seldom if ever completely absent from the minds of statesmen. But this is not the same as claiming for them a first priority in each and every type of situation. Much will depend upon how power is defined. If it is equated with physical force alone, one finds that many contemporary international relationships cannot be explained at all by sole reference to relative possession of physical strength. If power includes, as it must, not only physical but also psychological, economic, and even moral ingredients, then one may wonder whether the concept has not become too broad to be useful for purposes of analysis.

Among other objectives are those of aggrandizement and expansion—either physical, economic, cultural, or ideological. Again, no doubt, these are frequently important goals of states in international relations, and it might be an interesting exercise to establish categories of states according to the frequency with which they engage in actions designed to achieve one or more of these aims. Yet one should hesitate before drawing conclusions from such categorizations. It is not easy to divide the states of the world into neat categories on any single basis. Attempts to do so through the use of categories such as peace-loving *vs.* aggressive, satiated *vs.* unsatiated, "haves" *vs.* "have-nots," and so forth, almost invariably suffer from serious shortcomings. Often, virtue may simply be lack of opportunity. States behaving in certain ways in one area, at one period, or with respect to one problem may behave quite differently in other areas, at other times, and on other issues. A presently non-expansionary state, for example, may simply be one that is content with the fruits of past expansionary policies.

The problems inherent in the task of defining goals of state behavior are clear; the solution to these problems is less obvious. Given the complexity of the subject, Professor Morgenthau has suggested a solution by employing the concept of "national interest" as a guide to the analysis of a country's behavior in international relations. In alerting us to distinctions from subnational or supranational interests, the concept undoubtedly has its usefulness. The difficulty with it is that it is vague, that it differs from country to country, and within countries from period to period. Thus, even after one has said "national interest," one has really only pushed back the question of defining the motivation of state behavior. The next task must inevitably be the precise definition

[3] Bertrand Russell, *Power: A New Social Analysis* (New York: W. W. Norton & Company, Inc., 1938), pp. 9–11.

of that "national interest" in time and space. Indeed, some students of the subject reject the concept altogether.

The more adequate conceptualization and categorization of objectives thus seems to be an outstanding need for the student of international relations. This is especially true as it is difficult to distinguish between "objectives" and "policies," between "ends" and "means." Much semantic confusion ensues as a result of this difficulty. The various categories have a way of shading off into one another. Some objectives may be so immediate that they are easily confused with specific policies. Some policies may be so long-range in nature as to be tantamount to objectives of states.

One possible way out of this problem may be to distinguish between objectives and policies in terms of time. This would involve the distinction between immediate objectives, corresponding to short-term policies; intermediate objectives, corresponding to longer, but still limited-term policies; and long-range objectives, corresponding to permanent policies. Another tool of analysis that may be useful in the interpretation of state objectives would be to distinguish a given country's aspirations from the point of view of their object. Thus, a country's objectives for itself would certainly differ from those it holds for its close allies. These in turn would differ from those for potential allies, neutral states, and potential or actual adversaries. Note, however, the ambiguity of such terms as "potential," "allies," and "adversaries." One's allies at one time may become one's adversaries at other times, and vice versa; one's potential adversaries are, conversely, also one's potential allies.

Relatively few professional students of world politics have grappled with this complex topic. The selections reprinted in this chapter constitute some of the most fruitful thinking on the subject to date. But much more work clearly remains to be done before either theorists or practitioners of international relations can begin to be satisfied with their knowledge concerning the key question of state objectives.

1

*Quest for Survival**

Julius Stone

JULIUS STONE, *a distinguished scholar in the field of international law and human rights, has served as Challis Professor of International Law and Jurisprudence at Harvard since 1942. His many books include* The International Court and the World Crisis *(1962), and* Social Dimensions of Law and Justice *(1965).*

. . . It is easy enough of course to formulate common objectives which all people share. But you will usually find when you look closely at these so-called common objectives that, somehow, the conflicts between nations manage to go on behind them. Behind the common objective, peace, lie the gravest conflicts as to what each side requires in order to assure it of peace. Almost everybody wants peace; the problems arise because peoples also want other things which they may not be able to get without war. Behind the objective of justice for all, lie conflicting national versions of what justice means. Behind the objectives of human welfare lurk the conflicts arising from the uneven economic development of peoples, and the tensions deriving from demands for a more equitable redistribution of the goods of the world. Behind the common objectives of disarmament lie conflicts as to the means for bringing it about. Behind the objective of a free united Germany are the intractable questions. What kind of a Germany and on what terms? The hard problems, indeed, of international politics, are not so much problems of ultimate objectives, as problems of what should be the next steps towards the objectives, and what sacrifices each nation should be willing to make in order to render them achievable. . . .

* *Quest for Survival* (Cambridge: Harvard University Press, 1961), pp. 74ff. Reprinted by permission.

2

*Organizational Goals and Environment: Goal-Setting as an Interaction Process**

James D. Thompson **William J. McEwen**

JAMES D. THOMPSON *is Professor of Sociology and Director of the Administrative Science Center at the University of Pittsburgh. As a scholar in the field of processes in complex human organizations and organizational ecology, he writes frequently for professional and scholarly journals.*

WILLIAM J. MCEWEN, *a social anthropologist, is Professor of Environmental Medicine at State University of New York Downstate Medical Center. He has carried out extensive research in Latin America and the Caribbean.*

In the analysis of complex organizations the definition of organizational goals is commonly utilized as a standard for appraising organizational performance. In many such analyses the goals of the organization are often viewed as a constant. Thus a wide variety of data, such as official documents, work activity records, organizational output, or statements by organizational spokesmen, may provide the basis for the definition of goals. Once this definition has been accomplished, interest in goals as a dynamic aspect or organizational activity frequently ends.

It is possible, however, to view the setting of goals (i.e., major organizational purposes) not as a static element but as a necessary and recurring problem facing any organization, whether it is governmental, military, business, educational, medical, religious, or other type.

This perspective appears appropriate in developing the two major lines of the present analysis. The first of these is to emphasize the interdependence of complex organizations within the larger society and the consequences this has for organizational goal-setting. The second is to emphasize the similarities of goal-setting *processes* in organizations with manifestly different goals. The present analysis is offered to supplement recent studies of organizational operations.[1]

It is postulated that goal-setting behavior is *purposive* but not necessarily *rational;* we assume that goals may be determined by accident, i.e., by blundering of members of the organization and, contrariwise, that the most calculated and careful determi-

[1] Among recent materials that treat organizational goal-setting are Kenneth E. Boulding, *The Organizational Revolution* (New York: Harper & Row, Publishers, 1953); Robert A. Dahl and Charles E. Lindblom, *Politics, Economics, and Welfare* (New York: Harper & Row, Publishers, 1953); and John K. Galbraith, *American Capitalism: The Concept of Countervailing Power* (Boston: Houghton Mifflin Company, 1952).

* *American Sociological Review,* **XXIII** (1958), 23–31. Reprinted by permission.

nation of goals may be negated by developments outside the control of organization members. The goal-setting problem as discussed here is essentially determining a relationship of the organization to the larger society, which in turn becomes a question of what the society (or elements within it) wants done or can be persuaded to support.

GOALS AS DYNAMIC VARIABLES

Because the setting of goals is essentially a problem of defining desired relationships between an organization and its environment, change in either requires review and perhaps alteration of goals. Even where the most abstract statement of goals remains constant, application requires redefinition or interpretation as changes occur in the organization, the environment, or both.

The corporation, for example, faces changing markets and develops staff specialists with responsibility for continuous study and projection of market changes and product appeal. The governmental agency, its legislative mandate notwithstanding, has need to reformulate or reinterpret its goals as other agencies are created and dissolved, as the population changes, or as non-governmental organizations appear to do the same job or to compete. The school and the university may have unchanging abstract goals but the clientele, the needs of pupils or students, and the techniques of teaching change and bring with them redefinition and reinterpretation of those objectives. The hospital has been faced with problems requiring an expansion of goals to include consideration of preventive medicine, public health practices, and the degree to which the hospital should extend its activities out into the community. The mental hospital and the prison are changing their objectives from primary emphasis on custody to a stress on therapy. Even the church alters its pragmatic objectives as changes in the society call for new forms of social ethics, and as government and organized philanthropy take over some of the activities formerly left to organized religion.[2]

Reappraisal of goals thus appears to be a recurrent problem for large organization, albeit a more constant problem in an unstable environment than in a stable one. Reappraisal of goals likewise appears to be more difficult as the "product" of the enterprise becomes less tangible and more difficult to measure objectively. The manufacturing firm has a relatively ready index of the acceptability of its product in sales figures; while poor sales may indicate inferior quality rather than public distaste for the commodity itself, sales totals frequently are supplemented by trade association statistics indicating the firm's "share of the market." Thus within a matter of weeks, a manufacturing firm may be able to reappraise its decision to enter the "widget" market and may there-

[2] For pertinent studies of various organizational types see Burton R. Clark, *Adult Education in Transition* (Berkeley and Los Angeles: University of California Press, 1956); Temple Burling, Edith M. Lentz, and Robert N. Wilson, *The Give and Take in Hospitals* (New York: G. P. Putnam's Sons, 1956), especially pp. 3–10; Lloyd E. Ohlin, *Sociology and the Field of Corrections* (New York: Russell Sage Foundation, 1956), pp. 13–18; Liston Pope, *Millhands and Preachers* (New Haven: Yale University Press, 1942); Charles Y. Glock and Benjamin B. Ringer, "Church Policy and the Attitudes of Ministers and Parishioners on Social Issues," *American Sociological Review*, **XXI** (April, 1956), 148–156. For a similar analysis in the field of philanthropy, see J. R. Seeley, B. H. Junker, R. W. Jones, Jr., and others, *Community Chest: A Case Study in Philanthropy* (Toronto: University of Toronto Press, 1957), especially Chaps. 2 and 5.

fore begin deciding how it can get out of that market with the least cost.

The governmental enterprise may have similar indicators of the acceptability of its goals if it is involved in producing an item such as electricity, but where its activity is oriented to a less tangible purpose such as maintaining favorable relations with foreign nations, the indices of effective operation are likely to be less precise and the vagaries more numerous. The degree to which a government satisfies its clientele may be reflected periodically in elections, but despite the claims of party officials, it seldom is clear just what the mandate of the people is with reference to any particular governmental enterprise. In addition, the public is not always steadfast in its mandate.

The university perhaps has even greater difficulties in evaluating its environmental situation through response to its output. Its range of "products" is enormous, extending from astronomers to zoologists. The test of a competent specialist is not always standardized and may be changing, and the university's success in turning out "educated" people is judged by many and often conflicting standards. The university's product is in process for four or more years and when it is placed on the "market" it can be only imperfectly judged. Vocational placement statistics may give some indication of the university's success in its objectives, but initial placement is no guarantee of performance at a later date. Furthermore, performance in an occupation is only one of several abilities that the university is supposed to produce in its students. Finally, any particular department of the university may find that its reputation lags far behind its performance. A "good" department may work for years before its reputation becomes "good" and a downhill department may coast for several years before the fact is realized by the professional world.

In sum, the goals of an organization, which determine the kinds of goods or services it produces and offers to the environment, often are subject to peculiar difficulties of reappraisal. Where the purpose calls for an easily identified, readily measured product, reappraisal and readjustment of goals may be accomplished rapidly. But as goals call for increasingly intangible, difficult-to-measure products, society finds it more difficult to determine and reflect its acceptability of that product, and the signals that indicate unacceptable goals are less effective and perhaps longer in coming.

Environmental Controls Over Goals

A continuing situation of necessary interaction between an organization and its environment introduces an element of environmental control into the organization. While the motives of personnel, including goal-setting officers, may be profits, prestige, votes, or the salvation of souls, their efforts must produce something useful or acceptable to at least a part of the organizational environment to win continued support.[3]

In the simpler society social control over productive activities may be exercised rather informally and directly through such means as gossip and ridicule. As a society becomes more complex and its productive activities more deliberately organized, social controls are increasingly exer-

[3] This statement would seem to exclude antisocial organizations, such as crime syndicates. A detailed analysis of such organizations would be useful for many purposes; meanwhile it would appear necessary for them to acquire a clientele, suppliers, and others, in spite of the fact that their methods at times may be somewhat unique.

cised through such formal devices as contracts, legal codes, and governmental regulations. The stability of expectations provided by these devices is arrived at through interaction, and often through the exercise of power in interaction.

It is possible to conceive of a continuum of organizational power in environmental relations, ranging from the organization that dominates its environmental relations to one completely dominated by its environment. Few organizations approach either extreme. Certain gigantic industrial enterprises, such as the *Zaibatsu* in Japan or the old Standard Oil Trust in America, have approached the dominance-over-environment position at one time, but this position eventually brought about "countervailing powers."[4] Perhaps the nearest approximation to the completely powerless organization is the commuter transit system, which may be unable to cover its costs but nevertheless is regarded as a necessary utility and cannot get permission to quit business. Most complex organizations, falling somewhere between the extremes of the power continuum, must adopt strategies for coming to terms with their environments. This is not to imply that such strategies are necessarily chosen by rational or deliberate processes. An organization can survive so long as it adjusts to its situation; whether the process of adjustment is awkward or nimble becomes important in determining the organization's degree of prosperity.

However arrived at, strategies for dealing with the organizational environment may be broadly classified as either *competitive* or *co-operative*. Both appear to be important in a complex society—of the "free enterprise" type or other.[5] Both provide a measure of environmental control over organizations by providing for "outsiders" to enter into or limit organizational decision process.

The decision process may be viewed as a series of activities, conscious or not, culminating in a choice among alternatives. For purposes of this paper we view the decision-making process as consisting of the following activities:

1. Recognizing an occasion for decision, i.e., a need or an opportunity.
2. Analysis of the existing situation.
3. Identification of alternative courses of action.
4. Assessment of the probable consequences of each alternative.
5. Choice from among alternatives.[6]

The following discussion suggests that the potential power of an outsider increases the earlier he enters into the decision process,[7] and that competi-

[4] For the *Zaibatsu* case see Japan Council, *The Control of Industry in Japan* (Tokyo: Institute of Political and Economic Research, 1953); and Edwin O. Reischauer, *The United States and Japan* (Cambridge: Harvard University Press, 1954), pp. 87–97.

[5] For evidence on Russia see David Granick, *Management of the Industrial Firm in the U.S.S.R.* (New York: Columbia University Press, 1954); and Joseph S. Berliner, "Informal Organization of the Soviet Firm," *Quarterly Journal of Economics,* **LXVI** (August, 1952), 353–365.

[6] This particular breakdown is taken from Edward H. Litchfield, "Notes on a General Theory of Administration," *Administrative Science Quarterly,* **I** (June, 1956), 3–29. We are also indebted to Robert Tannenbaum and Fred Massarik who, by breaking the decision-making process into three steps, show that subordinates can take part in the "manager's decision" even when the manager makes the final choice. See "Participation by Subordinates in the Managerial Decision-Making Process," *Canadian Journal of Economics and Political Science,* **XVI** (August, 1949), 410–418.

[7] Robert K. Merton makes a similar point regarding the role of the intellectual in public bureaucracy. See his *Social Theory*

tion and three sub-types of co-operative strategy—*bargaining, co-optation,* and *coalition*—differ in this respect. It is therefore possible to order these forms of interaction in terms of the degree to which they provide for environmental control over organizational goal-setting decisions.

Competition

The term competition implies an element of rivalry. For present purposes competition refers to that form of rivalry between two or more organizations which is mediated by a third party. In the case of the manufacturing firm the third party may be the customer, the supplier, the potential or present member of the labor force, or others. In the case of the governmental bureau, the third party through whom competition takes place may be the legislative committee, the budget bureau, or the chief executive, as well as potential clientele and potential members of the bureau.

The complexity of competition in a heterogeneous society is much greater than customary usage (with economic overtones) often suggests. Society judges the enterprise not only by the finished product but also in terms of the desirability of applying resources to that purpose. Even the organization that enjoys a product monopoly must compete for society's support. From the society it must obtain resources—personnel, finances, and materials—as well as customers or clientele. In the business sphere of a "free enterprise" economy this competition for resources and customers usually takes place in the market, but in times of crisis the society may exercise more direct controls, such as rationing or the establishment of priorities during a war. The monopoly competes with enterprises having different purposes or goals but using similar raw materials; it competes with many other enterprises for human skills and loyalties, and it competes with many other activities for support in the money markets.

The university, customarily a non-profit organization, competes as eagerly as any business firm, although perhaps more subtly.[8] Virtually every university seeks, if not more students, better-qualified students. Publicly supported universities compete at annual budget sessions with other governmental enterprises for shares in tax revenues. Endowed universities must compete for gifts and bequests, not only with other universities but also with museums, charities, zoos, and similar non-profit enterprises. The American university is only one of many organizations competing for foundation support, and it competes with other universities and with other types of organizations for faculty.

The public school system, perhaps one of our most pervasive forms of near-monopoly, not only competes with other governmental units for funds and with different types of organizations for teachers, but current programs espoused by professional educators often compete in a very real way with a public conception of the nature of education, e.g., as the three R's, devoid of "frills."

The hospital may compete with the mid-wife, the faith-healer, the "quack," and the patent-medicine manufacturer, as well as with neighboring hospitals, despite the fact that general hospitals do not "advertise" and are

and Social Structure (Glencoe: Free Press of Glencoe, Inc., 1949), Chap. 6.

[8] See Logan Wilson, *The Academic Man* (New York: Oxford University Press, 1942), especially Chap. IX. Also see Warren G. Bennis, "The Effect on Academic Goods of Their Market," *American Journal of Sociology,* **LXII** (July, 1956), 28–33.

not usually recognized as competitive.

Competition is thus a complicated network of relationships. It includes scrambling for resources as well as for customers or clients, and in a complex society it includes rivalry for potential members and their loyalties. In each case a third party makes a choice among alternatives, two or more organizations attempt to influence that choice through some type of "appeal" or offering, and choice by the third party is a "vote" of support for one of the competing organizations and a denial of support to the others involved.

Competition, then, is one process whereby the organization's choice of goals is partially controlled by the environment. It tends to prevent unilateral or arbitrary choice of organizational goals, or to correct such a choice if one is made. Competition for society's support is an important means of eliminating not only inefficient organizations but also those that seek to provide goods or services the environment is not willing to accept.

Bargaining

The term bargaining, as used here, refers to the negotiation of an agreement for the exchange of goods or services between two or more organizations. Even where fairly stable and dependable expectations have been built up with important elements of the organizational environment—with suppliers, distributors, legislators, workers and so on—the organization cannot assume that these relationships will continue. Periodic review of these relationships must be accomplished, and an important means for this is bargaining, whereby each organization, through negotiation, arrives at a decision about future behavior satisfactory to the others involved.

The need for periodic adjustment of relationships is demonstrated most dramatically in collective bargaining between labor and industrial management, in which the bases for continued support by organization members are reviewed.[9] But bargaining occurs in other important, if less dramatic, areas of organizational endeavor. The business firm must bargain with its agents or distributors, and while this may appear at times to be one-sided and hence not much of a bargain, still even a long-standing agency agreement may be severed by competitive offers unless the agent's level of satisfaction is maintained through periodic review.[10] Where suppliers are required to install new equipment to handle the peculiar demands of an organization, bargaining between the two is not unusual.

The university likewise must bargain.[11] It may compete for free or unrestricted funds, but often it must compromise that ideal by bargaining away the name of a building or of a library collection, or by the conferring of an honorary degree. Graduate students and faculty members may be given financial or other concessions through bargaining, in order to prevent their loss to other institutions.

The governmental organization may also find bargaining expedient.[12] The police department, for example, may overlook certain violations of statutes in order to gain the support of minor violators who have channels of information not otherwise open to de-

[9] For an account of this on a daily basis see Melville Dalton, "Unofficial Union-Management Relations," *American Sociological Review*, XV (October, 1950), 611–619.

[10] See Valentine F. Ridgway, "Administration of Manufacturer-Dealer Systems," *Administrative Science Quarterly*, **I** (March, 1957), 464–483.

[11] Wilson, *op. cit.*, Chaps. 7 and 8.

[12] For an interesting study of governmental bargaining see William J. Gore, "Administrative Decision-Making in Federal Field Offices," *Public Administration Review*, **XVI** (Autumn, 1956), 281–291.

partment members. Concessions to those who "turn state's evidence" are not unusual. Similarly a department of state may forego or postpone recognition of a foreign power in order to gain support for other aspects of its policy, and a governmental agency may relinquish certain activities in order to gain budget bureau approval of more important goals.

While bargaining may focus on resources rather than explicitly on goals, the fact remains that it is improbable that a goal can be effective unless it is at least partially implemented. To the extent that bargaining sets limits on the amount of resources available or the ways they may be employed, it effectively sets limits on choice of goals. Hence bargaining, like competition, results in environmental control over organization goals and reduces the probability of arbitrary, unilateral goal-setting.

Unlike competition, however, bargaining involves direct interaction with other organizations in the environment, rather than with a third party. Bargaining appears, therefore, to invade the actual decision process. To the extent that the second party's support is necessary he is in a position to exercise a veto over final choice of alternative goals, and hence takes part in the decision.

Co-optation

Co-optation has been defined as the process of absorbing new elements into the leadership or policy-determining structure of an organization as a means of averting threats to its stability or existence.[13] Co-optation makes still further inroads on the process of deciding goals; not only must the final choice be acceptable to the co-opted party or organization, but to the extent that co-optation is effective it places the representative of an "outsider" in a position to determine the occasion for a good decision, to participate in analyzing the existing situation, to suggest alternatives, and to take part in the deliberation of consequences.

The term co-optation has only recently been given currency in this country, but the phenomenon it describes is neither new nor unimportant. The acceptance on a corporation's board of directors of representatives of banks or other financial institutions is a time-honored custom among firms that have large financial obligations or that may in the future want access to financial resources. The state university may find it expedient (if not mandatory) to place legislators on its board of trustees, and the endowed college may find that whereas the honorary degree brings forth a token gift, membership on the board may result in a more substantial bequest. The local medical society often plays a decisive role in hospital goal-setting, since the support of professional medical practitioners is urgently necessary for the hospital.

From the standpoint of society, however, co-optation is more than an expediency. By giving a potential supporter a position of power and often of responsibility in the organization, the organization gains his awareness and understanding of the problems it faces. A business advisory council may be an effective educational device for a government, and a White House conference on education may mobilize "grass roots" support in a thousand localities, both by focussing attention on the problem area and by giving key people a sense of participation in goal deliberation.

Moreover, by providing overlap-

[13] Philip Selznick, *TVA and the Grass Roots* (Berkeley and Los Angeles: University of California Press, 1949).

ping memberships, co-optation is an important social device for increasing the likelihood that organizations related to one another in complicated ways will in fact find compatible goals. By thus reducing the possibilities of antithetical actions by two or more organizations, co-optation aids in the integration of the heterogeneous parts of a complex society. By the same token, co-optation further limits the opportunity for one organization to choose its goals arbitrarily or unilaterally.

Coalition

As used here, the term coalition refers to a combination of two or more organizations for a common purpose. Coalition appears to be the ultimate or extreme form of environmental conditioning of organizational goals.[14] A coalition may be unstable, but to the extent that it is operative, two or more organizations act as one with respect to certain goals. Coalition is a means widely used when two or more enterprises wish to pursue a goal calling for more support, especially for more resources, than any one of them is able to marshall unaided. American business firms frequently resort to coalition for purposes of research or product promotion and for the construction of such gigantic facilities as dams or atomic reactors.[15]

Coalition is not uncommon among educational organizations. Universities have established joint operations in such areas as nuclear research, archaeological research, and even social science research. Many smaller colleges have banded together for fund-raising purposes. The consolidation of public school districts is another form of coalition (if not merger), and the fact that it does represent a sharing or "invasion" of goal-setting power is reflected in some of the bitter resistance to consolidation in tradition-oriented localities.

Coalition requires a commitment for joint decision of future activities and thus places limits on unilateral or arbitrary decisions. Furthermore, inability of an organization to find partners in a coalition venture automatically prevents pursuit of that objective, and is therefore also a form of social control. If the collective judgment is that a proposal is unworkable, a possible disaster may be escaped and unproductive allocation of resources avoided.

DEVELOPMENT OF ENVIRONMENTAL SUPPORT

Environmental control is not a one-way process limited to consequences for the organization of action in its environment. Those subject to control are also part of the larger society and hence are also agents of social control. The enterprise that competes is not only influenced in its goal-setting by what the competitor and the third party may do, but also exerts influence over both. Bargaining likewise is a form of mutual, two-way influence; co-optation affects the coopted as well as the co-opting party;

[14] Coalition may involve joint action toward only limited aspects of the goals of each member. It may involve the complete commitment of each member for a specific period of time or indefinitely. In either case the ultimate power to withdraw is retained by the members. We thus distinguish coalition from merger, in which two or more organizations are fused permanently. In merger one or all of the original parts may lose their identity. Goal-setting in such a situation, of course, is no longer subject to inter-organizational constraints among the components.

[15] See "The Joint Venture Is an Effective Approach to Major Engineering Projects," *New York Times,* July 14, 1957, Section 3, p. 1 F.

and coalition clearly sets limits on both parties.

Goals appear to grow out of interaction, both within the organization and between the organization and its environment. While every enterprise must find sufficient support for its goals, it may wield initiative in this. The difference between effective and ineffective organizations may well lie in the initiative exercised by those in the organization who are responsible for goal-setting.

The ability of an administrator to win support for an objective may be as vital as his ability to foresee the utility of a new idea. And his role as a "seller" of ideas may be as important to society as to his organization, for as society becomes increasingly specialized and heterogeneous, the importance of new objectives may be more readily seen by specialized segments than by the general society. It was not public clamor that originated revisions in public school curricula and training methods; the impetus came largely from professional specialists in or on the periphery of education.[16] The shift in focus from custody to therapy in mental hospitals derives largely from the urgings of professionals, and the same can be said of our prisons.[17] In both cases the public anger, aroused by crusaders and muck-rakers, might have been soothed by more humane methods of custody. Current attempts to revitalize the liberal arts curricula of our colleges, universities, and technical institutes have developed more in response to the activities of professional specialists than from public urging.[18] Commercial aviation, likewise, was "sold" the hard way, with support being based on subsidy for a considerable period before the importance of such transportation was apparent to the larger public.[19]

In each of these examples the goal-setters saw their ideas become widely accepted only after strenuous efforts to win support through education of important elements of the environment. Present currents in some medical quarters to shift emphasis from treatment of the sick to maintenance of health through preventive medicine and public health programs likewise have to be "sold" to a society schooled in an older concept.[20]

The activities involved in winning support for organizational goals thus are not confined to communication within the organization, however important this is. The need to justify organization goals, to explain the social functions of the organization, is seen daily in all types of "public relations" activities, ranging from luncheon club speeches to house organs. It is part of an educational requirement in a complicated society where devious interdependence hides many of the functions of organized, specialized activities.

---

[16] See Robert S. and Helen Merrell Lynd, *Middletown in Transition* (New York: Harcourt Brace & World, Inc., 1937), Chap. 6.

[17] Milton Greenblatt, Richard H. York, and Esther Lucille Brown, *From Custodial to Therapeutic Patient Care in Mental Hospitals* (New York: Russell Sage Foundation, 1955), Chap. 1, and Ohlin, *loc. cit.*

[18] For one example, see the Report of the Harvard Committee, *General Education in a Free Society* (Cambridge: Harvard University Press, 1945).

[19] America's civil air transport industry began in 1926 and eight years later carried 500,000 passengers. Yet it was testified in 1934 that half of the $120 million invested in airlines had been lost in spite of subsidies. See Jerome C. Hunsaker, *Aeronautics at the Mid-Century* (New Haven: Yale University Press, 1952), pp. 37–38. The case of Billy Mitchell was, of course, the landmark in the selling of military aviation.

[20] Ray E. Trussell, *Hunterdon Medical Center* (Cambridge: Harvard University Press [for the Commonwealth Fund], 1956), Chap. 3.

GOAL-SETTING AND STRATEGY

We have suggested that it is improbable that an organization can continue indefinitely if its goals are formulated arbitrarily, without cognizance of its relations to the environment. One of the requirements for survival appears to be ability to learn about the environment accurately enough and quickly enough to permit organizational adjustments in time to avoid extinction. In a more positive vein, it becomes important for an organization to judge the amount and sources of support that can be mobilized for a goal, and to arrive at a strategy for their mobilization.

Competition, bargaining, co-optation, and coalition constitute procedures for gaining support from the organizational environment; the selection of one or more of these is a strategic problem. It is here that the element of rationality appears to become exceedingly important, for in the order treated above, these relational processes represent increasingly "costly" methods of gaining support in terms of decision-making power. The organization that adopts a strategy of competition when co-optation is called for may lose all opportunity to realize its goals, or may finally turn to co-optation or coalition at a higher "cost" than would have been necessary originally. On the other hand, an organization may lose part of its integrity, and therefore some of its potentiality, if it unnecessarily shares power in exchange for support. Hence the establishment *in the appropriate form* of interaction with the many relevant parts of its environment can be a major organizational consideration in a complex society.

This means, in effect, that the organization must be able to estimate the position of other relevant organizations and their willingness to enter into or alter relationships. Often, too, these matters must be determined or estimated without revealing one's own weaknesses, or even one's ultimate strength. It is necessary or advantageous, in other words, to have the consent or acquiescence of the other party, if a new relationship is to be established or an existing relationship altered. For this purpose organizational administrators often engage in what might be termed a *sounding out process*.[21]

The sounding out process can be illustrated by the problem of the boss with amorous designs on his secretary in an organization that taboos such relations. He must find some means of determining her willingness to alter the relationship, but he must do so without risking rebuff, for a showdown might come at the cost of his dignity or his office reputation, at the cost of losing her secretarial services, or in the extreme case at the cost of losing his own position. The "sophisticated" procedure is to create an ambiguous situation in which the secretary is forced to respond in one of two ways: 1. to ignore or tactfully counter, thereby clearly channeling the relationship back into an already existing pattern, or 2. to respond in a similarly ambiguous vein (if not in a positive one) indicating a receptiveness to further advances. It is important in the sounding out process that the situation be ambiguous for two reasons: 1. the secretary must not be able to "pin down" the boss with evidence if she rejects the idea, and 2. the situation must be

[21] This section on the sounding out process is a modified version of a paper by James D. Thompson, William J. McEwen, and Frederick L. Bates, "Sounding Out as a Relating Process," read at the annual meeting of the Eastern Sociological Society, April, 1957.

far enough removed from normal to be noticeable to the secretary. The ambiguity of sounding out has the further advantage to the participants that neither party alone is clearly responsible for initiating the change.

The situation described above illustrates a process that seems to explain many organizational as well as personal inter-action situations. In moving from one relationship to another between two or more organizations it is often necessary to leave a well defined situation and proceed through a period of deliberate ambiguity, to arrive at a new clear-cut relationship. In interaction over goal-setting problems, sounding out sometimes is done through a form of double-talk, wherein the parties refer to "hypothetical" enterprises and "hypothetical" situations, or in "diplomatic" language, which often serves the same purpose. In other cases, and perhaps more frequently, sounding out is done through the good offices of a third party. This occurs, appparently, where there has been no relationship in the past, or at the stage of negotiations where the parties have indicated intentions but are not willing to state their positions frankly. Here it becomes useful at times to find a discrete go-between who can be trusted with full information and who will seek an arrangement suitable to both parties.

Conclusion

In the complex modern society desired goals often require complex organizations. At the same time the desirability of goals and the appropriate division of labor among large organizations is less self-evident than in simpler, more homogeneous society. Purpose becomes a question to be decided rather than an obvious matter.

To the extent that behavior of organization members is oriented to questions of goals or purposes, a science of organization must attempt to understand and explain that behavior. We have suggested one classification scheme, based on decision-making, as potentially useful in analyzing organizational-environmental interaction with respect to goal-setting and we have attempted to illustrate some aspects of its utility. It is hoped that the suggested scheme encompasses questions of rationality or irrationality without presuming either.

Argument by example, however, is at best only a starting point for scientific understanding and for the collection of evidence. Two factors make organizational goal-setting in a complex society a "big" research topic: the multiplicity of large organizations of diverse type and the necessity of studying them in diachronic perspective. We hope that our discussion will encourage critical thinking and the sharing of observations about the subject.

3

*Another "Great Debate": The National Interest of the United States**

Hans J. Morgenthau

HANS J. MORGENTHAU *is Albert A. Michelson Distinguished Service Professor and Director of the Center for the Study of American Foreign Policy at the University of Chicago. A frequent consultant to the U.S. Department of State and the Defense Department, he is the author, among other books, of* Politics Among Nations *(1948);* Dilemmas of Politics *(1958); and* Purpose of American Politics *(1960).*

II

* * *

. . . what is the national interest? How can we define it and give it the content which will make it a guide for action?

* * *

It has been frequently argued against the realist conception of foreign policy that its key concept, the national interest, does not provide an acceptable standard for political action. This argument is in the main based upon two grounds: the elusiveness of the concept and its susceptibility to interpretations, such as limitless imperialism and narrow nationalism, which are not in keeping with the American tradition in foreign policy. The argument has substance as far as it goes, but it does not invalidate the usefulness of the concept.

The concept of the national interest is similar in two respects to the "great generalities" of the Constitution, such as the general welfare and due process. It contains a residual meaning which is inherent in the concept itself, but beyond these minimum requirements its content can run the whole gamut of meanings which are logically compatible with it. That content is determined by the political traditions and the total cultural context within which a nation formulates its foreign policy. The concept of the national interest, then, contains two elements, one that is logically required and in that sense necessary, and one that is variable and determined by circumstances.

Any foreign policy which operates under the standard of the national interest must obviously have some reference to the physical, political, and cultural entity which we call a nation. In a world where a number of sovereign nations compete with and oppose each other for power, the foreign policies of all nations must necessarily refer to their survival as their minimum requirements. Thus all nations do what they cannot help but do: protect their physical, political, and cultural identity against encroachments by other nations.

It has been suggested that this reasoning erects the national state into the last word in politics and the na-

* *American Political Science Review,* **XLVI** (1952), 971–978. Reprinted by permission.

tional interest into an absolute standard for political action. This, however, is not quite the case. The idea of interest is indeed of the essence of politics and, as such, unaffected by the circumstances of time and place. Thucydides' statement, born of the experiences of ancient Greece, that "identity of interest is the surest of bonds whether between states or individuals" was taken up in the nineteenth century by Lord Salisbury's remark that "the only bond of union that endures" among nations is "the absence of all clashing interests." The perennial issue between the realist and utopian schools of thought over the nature of politics . . . might well be formulated in terms of concrete interests *vs.* abstract principles. Yet while the concern of politics with interest is perennial, the connection between interest and the national state is a product of history.

The national state itself is obviously a product of history and as such destined to yield in time to different modes of political organization. As long as the world is politically organized into nations, the national interest is indeed the last word in world politics. When the national state will have been replaced by another mode of organization, foreign policy must then protect the interest in survival of that new organization. For the benefit of those who insist upon discarding the national state and constructing supranational organizations by constitutional fiat, it must be pointed out that these new organizational forms will either come into being through conquest or else through consent based upon the mutual recognition of the national interests of the nations concerned; for no nation will forego its freedom of action if it has no reason to expect proportionate benefits in compensation for that loss. This is true of treaties concerning commerce or fisheries as it is true of the great compacts, such as the European Coal and Steel Community, through which nations try to create supranational forms of organization. Thus, by an apparent paradox, what is historically relative in the idea of the national interest can be overcome only through the promotion in concert of the national interest of a number of nations.

The survival of a political unit, such as a nation, in its identity is the irreducible minimum, the necessary element of its interests vis-à-vis other units. Taken in isolation, the determination of its content in a concrete situation is relatively simple; for it encompasses the integrity of the nation's territory, of its political institutions, and of its culture. Thus bipartisanship in foreign policy, especially in times of war, has been most easily achieved in the promotion of these minimum requirements of the national interest. The situation is different with respect to the variable elements of the national interest. All the cross currents of personalities, public opinion, sectional interests, partisan politics, and political and moral folkways are brought to bear upon their determination. In consequence, the contribution which science can make to this field, as to all fields of policy formation, is limited. It can identify the different agencies of the government which contribute to the determination of the variable elements of the national interest and assess their relative weight. It can separate the long-range objectives of foreign policy from the short-term ones which are the means for the achievement of the former and can tentatively establish their rational relations. Finally, it can analyze the variable elements of the national interest in terms of their legitimacy and their compatibility with other national values and with the national interest of other nations. We shall address ourselves briefly to the typical problems with which this analysis must deal.

The legitimacy of the national interest must be determined in the face of possible usurpation by subnational, other-national, and supranational interests. On the subnational level we find group interests, represented particularly by ethnic and economic groups, who tend to identify themselves with the national interest. Charles A. Beard has emphasized, however one-sidedly, the extent to which the economic interests of certain groups have been presented as those of the United States.[1] Group interests exert, of course, constant pressure upon the conduct of our foreign policy, claiming their identity with the national interest. It is, however, doubtful that, with the exception of a few spectacular cases, they have been successful in determining the course of American foreign policy. It is much more likely, given the nature of American domestic politics, that American foreign policy, insofar as it is the object of pressures by sectional interests, will normally be a compromise between divergent sectional interests. The concept of the national interest, as it emerges from this contest as the actual guide for foreign policy, may well fall short of what would be rationally required by the over-all interests of the United States. Yet the concept of the national interest which emerges from this contest of conflicting sectional interests is also more than any particular sectional interest or their sum total. It is, as it were, the lowest common denominator where sectional interests and the national interest meet in an uneasy compromise which may leave much to be desired in view of all the interests concerned.

The national interest can be usurped by other-national interests in two typical ways. The case of treason by individuals, either out of conviction or for pay, needs only to be mentioned here; for insofar as treason is committed on behalf of a foreign government rather than a supranational principle, it is significant for psychology, sociology, and criminology, but not for the theory of politics. The other case, however, is important not only for the theory of politics but also for its practice, especially in the United States.

National minorities in European countries, ethnic groups in the United States, ideological minorities anywhere may identify themselves, either spontaneously or under the direction of the agents of a foreign government, with the interests of that foreign government and may promote these interests under the guise of the national interest of the country whose citizens they happen to be.

* * *

The usurpation of the national interest by supranational interests can derive in our time from two sources: religious bodies and international organizations. The competition between church and state for determination of certain interests and policies, domestic and international, has been an intermittent issue throughout the history of the national state. Here, too, the legitimate defense of the national interest against usurpation has frequently, especially in the United States, degenerated into the demagogic stigmatization of dissenting views as being inspired by Rome and, hence, being incompatible with the national interest. Yet here, too, the misuse of the issue for demagogic purposes must be considered apart from the legitimacy of the issue itself.

---

[1] *The Idea of National Interest: An Analytical Study in American Foreign Policy* (New York: The Macmillan Company, 1934).

The more acute problem arises at the present time from the importance which the public and government officials, at least in their public utterances, attribute to the values represented and the policies pursued by international organizations either as alternatives or supplements to the values and policies for which the national government stands. It is frequently asserted that the foreign policy of the United States pursues no objectives apart from those of the United Nations, that, in other words, the foreign policy of the United States is actually identical with the policy of the United Nations. This assertion cannot refer to anything real in actual politics to support it. For the constitutional structure of international organizations, such as the United Nations, and their procedural practices make it impossible for them to pursue interests apart from those of the member-states which dominate their policy-forming bodies. The identity between the interests of the United Nations and the United States can only refer to the successful policies of the United States within the United Nations through which the support of the United Nations is being secured for the policies of the United States.[2] The assertion, then, is mere polemic, different from the one discussed previously in that the identification of a certain policy with a supranational interest does not seek to reflect discredit upon the former, but to bestow upon it a dignity which the national interest pure and simple is supposed to lack.

The real issue in view of the problem that concerns us here is not whether the so-called interests of the United Nations, which do not exist apart from the interests of its most influential members, have superseded the national interest of the United States, but for what kind of interests the United States has secured United Nations support. While these interests cannot be United Nations interests, they do not need to be national interests either. Here we are in the presence of that modern phenomenon which has been variously described as "utopianism," "sentimentalism," "moralism," the "legalistic-moralistic approach." The common denominator of all these tendencies in modern political thought is the substitution for the national interests of a supranational standard of action which is generally identified with an international organization, such as the United Nations. The national interest is here not being usurped by sub- or supranational interests which, however inferior in worth to the national interest, are nevertheless real and worthy of consideration within their proper sphere. What challenges the national interest here is a mere figment of the imagination, a product of wishful thinking, which is postulated as a valid norm for international conduct, without being valid either there or anywhere else. At this point we touch the core of the present controversy between utopianism and realism in international affairs. . . .

The national interest as such must be defended against usurpation by nonnational interests. Yet once that task is accomplished, a rational order must be established among the values which make up the national interest and among the resources to be committed to them. While the interests which a nation may pursue in its relation with other nations are of infinite variety and magnitude, the resources

[2] See, on this point, Hans J. Morgenthau, "International Organizations and Foreign Policy," in *Foundations of World Organization: A Political and Cultural Appraisal,* Eleventh Symposium of the Conference on Science, Philosophy and Religion, edited by Lyman Bryson, Louis Finkelstein, Harold D. Lasswell, R. M. MacIver (New York, 1952), pp. 377–383.

which are available for the pursuit of such interests are necessarily limited in quantity and kind. No nation has the resources to promote all desirable objectives with equal vigor; all nations must therefore allocate their scarce resources as rationally as possible. The indispensable precondition of such rational allocation is a clear understanding of the distinction between the necessary and variable elements of the national interest. Given the contentious manner in which in democracies the variable elements of the national interest are generally determined, the advocates of an extensive conception of the national interest will inevitably present certain variable elements of the national interest as though their attainment were necessary for the nation's survival. In other words, the necessary elements of the national interest have a tendency to swallow up the variable elements so that in the end all kinds of objectives, actual or potential, are justified in terms of national survival. Such arguments have been advanced, for instance, in support of the rearmament of Western Germany and of the defense of Formosa. They must be subjected to rational scrutiny which will determine, however tentatively, their approximate place in the scale of national values.

The same problem presents itself in its extreme form when a nation pursues, or is asked to pursue, objectives which are not only unnecessary for its survival but tend to jeopardize it. Second-rate nations which dream of playing the role of great powers, such as Italy and Poland in the interwar period, illustrate this point. So do great powers which dream of remaking the world in their own image and embark upon world-wide crusades, thus straining their resources to exhaustion. Here scientific analysis has the urgent task of pruning down national objectives to the measure of available resources in order to make their pursuit compatible with national survival.

Finally, the national interest of a nation which is conscious not only of its own interests but also of that of other nations must be defined in terms compatible with the latter. In a multinational world this is a requirement of political morality; in an age of total war it is also one of the conditions for survival.

4

*National Security as an Ambiguous Symbol**

Arnold Wolfers

ARNOLD WOLFERS, *who was for many years Sterling Professor of International Relations at Yale University, was Director of the Washington Center for Foreign Policy Research until his retirement last year. As an analyst of strategy and foreign policy, he is the author of* Britain and France Between Two Wars *(1940), and co-author of* The Anglo-American Tradition in Foreign Affairs *(1956).*

Statesmen, publicists and scholars who wish to be considered realists, as many do today, are inclined to insist that the foreign policy they advocate is dictated by the national interest, more specifically by the national security interest. It is not surprising that this should be so. Today any reference to the pursuit of security is likely to ring a sympathetic chord.

However, when political formulas such as "national interest" or "national security" gain popularity they need to be scrutinized with particular care. They may not mean the same thing to different people. They may not have any precise meaning at all. Thus, while appearing to offer guidance and a basis for broad consensus they may be permitting everyone to label whatever policy he favors with an attractive and possibly deceptive name.

In a very vague and general way "national interest" does suggest a direction of policy which can be distinguished from several others which may present themselves as alternatives. It indicates that the policy is designed to promote demands which are ascribed to the nation rather than to individuals, sub-national groups or mankind as a whole. It emphasizes that the policy subordinates other interests to those of the nation. But beyond this, it has very little meaning.

When Charles Beard's study of *The Idea of National Interest* was published in the early years of the New Deal and under the impact of the Great Depression, the lines were drawn differently than they are today. The question at that time was whether American foreign policy, then largely economic in scope and motivation, was aimed not at promoting the welfare interests of the nation as a whole but instead at satisfying the material interests of powerful sub-national interest or pressure groups. While it was found hard to define what was in the interest of national welfare or to discover standards by which to measure it, there could be no doubt as to what people had in mind: they desired to see national policy makers rise above the narrow and special economic interests of parts of the nation to focus their attention on the more inclusive interests of the whole.

Today, the alternative to a policy of the national interest to which people refer is of a different character.

* Reprinted with permission from *Political Science Quarterly*, **LXVII** (1952), 481–502.

They fear policy makers may be unduly concerned with the "interests of all of mankind." They see them sacrificing the less inclusive national community to the wider but in their opinion chimeric world community. The issue, then, is not one of transcending narrow group selfishness, as it was at the time of Beard's discussion, but rather one of according more exclusive devotion to the narrower cause of the national self.

There is another difference between the current and the earlier debate. While it would be wrong to say that the economic interest has ceased to attract attention, it is overshadowed today by the national security interest. Even in the recent debates on the St. Lawrence Seaway, clearly in the first instance an economic enterprise, the defenders of the project, when seeking to impress their listeners with the "national interest" involved, spoke mainly of the value of the Seaway for military defense in wartime while some opponents stressed its vulnerability to attack.

The change from a welfare to a security interpretation of the symbol "national interest" is understandable. Today we are living under the impact of cold war and threats of external aggression rather than of depression and social reform. As a result, the formula of the national interest has come to be practically synonymous with the formula of national security. Unless explicitly denied, spokesmen for a policy which would take the national interest as its guide can be assumed to mean that priority shall be given to measures of security, a term to be analyzed.[1] The question is raised, therefore, whether this seemingly more precise formula of national security offers statesmen a meaningful guide for action. Can they be expected to know what it means? Can policies be distinguished and judged on the ground that they do or do not serve this interest?

The term national security, like national interest, is well enough established in the political discourse of international relations to designate an objective of policy distinguishable from others. We know roughly what people have in mind if they complain that their government is neglecting national security or demanding excessive sacrifices for the sake of enhancing it. Usually those who raise the cry for a policy oriented exclusively toward this interest are afraid their country underestimates the external dangers facing it or is being diverted into idealistic channels unmindful of these dangers. Moreover, the symbol suggests protection through power and therefore figures more frequently in the speech of those who believe in reliance on national power than of those who place their confidence in model behavior, international cooperation, or the United Nations to carry their country safely through the tempests of international conflict. For these reasons it would be an exaggeration to claim that the sym-

[1] Hans Morgenthau's *In Defense of the National Interest* (New York: Alfred A. Knopf, Inc., 1951), is the most explicit and impassioned recent plea for an American foreign policy which shall follow "but one guiding star—the National Interest." While Morgenthau is not equally explicit in regard to the meaning he attaches to the symbol "national interest," it becomes clear in the few pages devoted to an exposition of this "perennial" interest that the author is thinking in terms of the national security interest, and specifically of security based on power. The United States, he says, is interested in three things: a unique position as a predominant Power without rival in the Western Hemisphere and the maintenance of the balance of power in Europe as well as in Asia, demands which make sense only in the context of a quest for security through power.

bol of national security is nothing but a stimulus to semantic confusion, though closer analysis will show that if used without specifications it leaves room for more confusion than sound political counsel or scientific usage can afford.

* * *

. . . attention should be drawn to an assertion of fact which is implicit if not explicit in most appeals for a policy guided by national security. Such appeals usually assume that nations in fact have made security their goal except when idealism or utopianism of their leaders has led them to stray from the traditional path. If such conformity of behavior actually existed, it would be proper to infer that a country deviating from the established pattern of conduct would risk being penalized. This would greatly strengthen the normative arguments. The trouble with the contention of fact, however, is that the term "security" covers a range of goals so wide that highly divergent policies can be interpreted as policies of security.

Security points to some degree of protection of values previously acquired. In Walter Lippmann's words, a nation is secure to the extent to which it is not in danger of having to sacrifice core values, if it wishes to avoid war, and is able, if challenged, to maintain them by victory in such a war.[2] What this definition implies is that security rises and falls with the ability of a nation to deter an attack, or to defeat it. This is in accord with common usage of the term.

Security is a value, then, of which a nation can have more or less and which it can aspire to have in greater or lesser measure.[3] It has much in common, in this respect, with power or wealth, two other values of great importance in international affairs. But while wealth measures the amount of a nation's material possessions, and power its ability to control the actions of others, security, in an objective sense, measures the absence of threats to acquired values, in a subjective sense, the absence of fear that such values will be attacked. In both respects a nation's security can run a wide gamut from almost complete insecurity or sense of insecurity at one pole, to almost complete security or absence of fear at the other.[4]

---

2 Walter Lippmann, *U.S. Foreign Policy* (Boston, 1943), p. 51.

3 This explains why some nations which would seem to fall into the category of *status quo* Power *par excellence* may nevertheless be dissatisfied and act very much like "imperialist" Powers, as Morgenthau calls nations with acquisitive goals. They are dissatisfied with the degree of security which they enjoy under the *status quo* and are out to enhance it. France's occupation of the Ruhr in 1923 illustrates this type of behavior. Because the demand for more security may induce a *status quo* Power even to resort to the use of violence as a means of attaining more security, there is reason to beware of the easy and often self-righteous assumption that nations which desire to preserve the *status quo* are necessarily *"peace-loving."*

4 Security and power would be synonymous terms if security could be attained only through the accumulation of power, which will be shown not to be the case. The fear of attack—security in the subjective sense—is also not proportionate to the relative power position of a nation. Why, otherwise, would some weak and exposed nations consider themselves more secure today than does the United States?

Harold D. Lasswell and Abraham Kaplan, *Power and Society* (New Haven: Yale University Press, 1950), defining security as "high value expectancy" stress the subjective and speculative character of security by using the term "expectancy"; the use of the term "high," while indicating no definite level, would seem to imply that the security-seeker aims at a position in which the events he expects—here the continued unmolested enjoyment of his possessions—have considerably more than an even chance of materializing.

The possible discrepancy between the objective and subjective connotation of the term is significant in international relations despite the fact that the chance of future attack never can be measured "objectively"; it must always remain a matter of subjective evaluation and speculation. However, when the French after World War I insisted that they were entitled to additional guarantees of security because of the exceptionally dangerous situation which France was said to be facing, other Powers in the League expressed the view that rather than to submit to what might be French hysterical apprehension the relative security of France should be objectively evaluated. It is a well-known fact that nations, and groups within nations, differ widely in their reaction to one and the same external situation. Some tend to exaggerate the danger while others underestimate it. With hindsight it is sometimes possible to tell exactly how far they deviated from a rational reaction to the actual or objective state of danger existing at the time. Even if for no other reasons, this difference in the reaction to similar threats suffices to make it probable that nations will differ in their efforts to obtain more security. Some may find the danger to which they are exposed entirely normal and in line with their modest security expectations while others consider it unbearable to live with these same dangers. Although this is not the place to set up hypotheses on the factors which account for one or the other attitude, investigation might confirm the hunch that those nations tend to be most sensitive to threats which have either experienced attacks in the recent past or, having passed through a prolonged period of an exceptionally high degree of security, suddenly find themselves thrust into a situation of danger. Probably national efforts to achieve greater security would also prove, in part at least, to be a function of the power and opportunity which nations possess of reducing danger by their own efforts.

Another and even stronger reason why nations must be expected not to act uniformly is that they are not all or constantly faced with the same degree of danger. For purposes of a working hypothesis, theorists may find it useful at times to postulate conditions wherein all states are enemies—provided they are not allied against others—and wherein all, therefore, are equally in danger of attack.[5] But, while it may be true in the living world, too, that no sovereign nation can be absolutely safe from future attack, nobody can reasonably contend that Canada, for example, is threatened today to the same extent as countries like Iran or Yugoslavia, or that the British had as much reason to be concerned about the French air force in the twenties as about Hitler's *Luftwaffe* in the thirties.

This point, however, should not be overstressed. There can be no quarrel with the generalization that most nations, most of the time—the great Powers particularly—have shown, and had reason to show, an active concern about some lack of security and have been prepared to make sacrifices for its enhancement. Danger and the awareness of it have been, and continue to be, sufficiently widespread to guarantee some uniformity in this respect. But a generalization which leaves room both for the frantic kind of struggle for more security which characterized French policy at times and for the neg-

[5] For a discussion of this working hypothesis—as part of the "pure power" hypothesis—see my article on "The Pole of Power and the Pole of Indifference" in *World Politics*, IV, No. 1 (October, 1951). [Reprinted, in part, in Chap. 3, above.]

lect of security apparent in American foreign policy after the close of both World Wars throws little light on the behavior of nations. The demand for conformity would have meaning only if it could be said—as it could under the conditions postulated in the working hypothesis of pure power politics—that nations normally subordinate all other values to the maximization of their security, which, however, is obviously not the case.

There have been many instances of struggles for more security taking the form of an unrestrained race for armaments, alliances, strategic boundaries and the like; but one need only recall the many heated parliamentary debates on arms appropriations to realize how uncertain has been the extent to which people will consent to sacrifice for additional increments of security. Even when there has been no question that armaments would mean more security, the cost in taxes, the reduction in social benefits or the sheer discomfort involved has militated effectively against further effort. It may be worth noting in this connection that there seems to be no case in history in which a country started a preventive war on the grounds of security—unless Hitler's wanton attack on his neighbors be allowed to qualify as such—although there must have been circumstances where additional security could have been obtained by war and although so many wars have been launched for the enhancement of other values. Of course, where security serves only as a cloak for other more enticing demands, nations or ambitious leaders may consider no price for it too high. This is one of the reasons why very high security aspirations tend to make a nation suspect of hiding more aggressive aims.

Instead of expecting a uniform drive for enhanced or maximum security, a different hypothesis may offer a more promising lead. Efforts for security are bound to be experienced as a burden; security after all is nothing but the absence of the evil of insecurity, a negative value so to speak. As a consequence, nations will be inclined to minimize these efforts, keeping them at the lowest level which will provide them with what they consider adequate protection. This level will often be lower than what statesmen, military leaders or other particularly security-minded participants in the decision-making process believe it should be. In any case, together with the extent of the external threats, numerous domestic factors such as national character, tradition, preferences and prejudices will influence the level of security which a nation chooses to make its target.

It might be objected that in the long run nations are not so free to choose the amount of effort they will put into security. Are they not under a kind of compulsion to spare no effort provided they wish to survive? This objection again would make sense only if the hypothesis of pure power politics were a realistic image of actual world affairs. In fact, however, a glance at history will suffice to show that survival has only exceptionally been at stake, particularly for the major Powers. If nations were not concerned with the protection of values other than their survival as independent states, most of them, most of the time, would not have had to be seriously worried about their security, despite what manipulators of public opinion engaged in mustering greater security efforts may have said to the contrary. What "compulsion" there is, then, is a function not merely of the will of others, real or imagined, to destroy the nation's independence but of national desires and ambitions to retain a wealth of other values such as rank, respect, material possessions and special privileges. It would seem to be a fair guess that the efforts for security by a particular nation will tend to vary, other things being equal, with the range of values for which protection is being sought.

In respect to this range there may seem to exist a considerable degree of uniformity. All over the world today peoples are making sacrifices to protect and preserve what to them appear as the minimum national core values, national independence and territorial integrity. But there is deviation in two directions. Some nations seek protection for more marginal values as well. There was a time when United States policy could afford to be concerned mainly with the protection of the foreign investments or markets of its nationals, its "core values" being out of danger, or when Britain was extending its national self to include large and only vaguely circumscribed "regions of special interest." It is a well-known and portentous phenomenon that bases, security zones and the like may be demanded and acquired for the purpose of protecting values acquired earlier; and they then become new national values requiring protection themselves. Pushed to its logical conclusion, such spatial extension of the range of values does not stop short of world domination.

A deviation in the opposite direction of a compression of the range of core values is hardly exceptional in our days either. There is little indication that Britain is bolstering the security of Hong Kong although colonies were once considered part of the national territory. The Czechs lifted no finger to protect their independence against the Soviet Union and many West Europeans are arguing today that rearmament has become too destructive of values they cherish to be justified even when national independence is obviously at stake.

The lack of uniformity does not end here. A policy is not characterized by its goal, in this case security, alone. In order to become imitable, the means by which the goal is pursued must be taken into account as well. Thus, if two nations were both endeavoring to maximize their security but one were placing all its reliance on armaments and alliances, the other on meticulous neutrality, a policy maker seeking to emulate their behavior would be at a loss where to turn. Those who call for a policy guided by national security are not likely to be unaware of this fact, but they take for granted that they will be understood to mean a security policy based on power, and on military power at that. Were it not so, they would be hard put to prove that their government was not already doing its best for security, though it was seeking to enhance it by such means as international cooperation or by the negotiation of compromise agreements—means which in one instance may be totally ineffective or utopian but which in others may have considerable protective value.

It is understandable why it should so readily be assumed that a quest for security must necessarily translate itself into a quest for coercive power. In view of the fact that security is being sought against external violence—coupled perhaps with internal subversive violence—it seems plausible at first sight that the response should consist in an accumulation of the same kind of force for the purpose of resisting an attack or of deterring a would-be attacker. The most casual reading of history and of contemporary experience, moreover, suffices to confirm the view that such resort to "power of resistance" has been the rule with nations grappling with serious threats to their security, however much the specific form of this power and its extent may differ. Why otherwise would so many nations which have no acquisitive designs maintain costly armaments? Why did Denmark with her state of complete disarmament remain an exception even among the small Powers?

But again, the generalization that nations seeking security usually place great reliance on coercive power does not carry one far. The issue is not whether there is regularly some such reliance but whether there are no significant differences between nations concerning their over-all choice of the means upon which they place their trust. The controversies concerning the best road to future security that are so typical of coalition partners at the close of victorious wars throw light on this question. France in 1919 and all the Allies in 1945 believed that protection against another German attack could be gained only by means of continued military superiority based on German military impotence. President Wilson in 1919 and many observers in 1945 were equally convinced, however, that more hope for security lay in a conciliatory and fair treatment of the defeated enemy, which would rob him of future incentives to renew his attack. While this is not the place to decide which side was right, one cannot help drawing the conclusion that, in the matter of means, the roads which are open may lead in diametrically opposed directions. The choice in every instance will depend on a multitude of variables, including ideological and moral convictions, expectations concerning the psychological and political developments in the camp of the opponent, and inclinations of individual policy makers.

After all that has been said little is left of the sweeping generalization that in actual practice nations, guided by their national security interest, tend to pursue a uniform and therefore imitable policy of security. Instead, there are numerous reasons why they should differ widely in this respect, with some standing close to the pole of complete indifference to security or complete reliance on nonmilitary means, others close to the pole of insistence on absolute security or of complete reliance on coercive power. It should be added that there exists still another category of nations which cannot be placed within the continuum connecting these poles because they regard security of any degree as an insufficient goal; instead they seek to acquire new values even at the price of greater insecurity. In this category must be placed not only the "mad Caesars," who are out for conquest and glory at any price, but also idealistic statesmen who would plunge their country into war for the sake of spreading the benefits of their ideology, for example, of liberating enslaved peoples.

* * *

CHAPTER TWELVE

The Art of Diplomacy

Diplomacy is, as Livingston Merchant has observed, "as old as the hills."[1] In its most obvious form it is that kind of contact between nations that takes place through the permanent representatives of each state in the capital city of each other state; it is, in other words, what diplomats do. Webster describes it as representing "the management of international relations by negotiation; the method by which these relations are adjusted and managed by ambassadors and envoys," just as the great and authoritative British diplomatist, Sir Ernest Satow, also defined the concept in terms of its *method* when he described diplomacy as the application of intelligence and tact to the conduct of official relations between governments. A recent college text points to the *substance* of diplomacy by describing it as "the accumulative political, economic, and military pressures upon each side, formalized in the exchange of demands and concessions between negotiators."[2] In a definition based on *function,* a seasoned American diplomat employs a useful physical analogy when he describes diplomacy "as a complex and delicate instrument that measures forces working at the epicenters of international relations, [but] unlike the physicist's seismographs—which can only record disturbances—the subtle machinery of diplomacy can be used to arrest, ameliorate, or reduce the discord, misunderstandings, and disagreements which precipitate international crises."[3]

Traditionally, the professional diplomat has been considered to have a twofold function. He presents the views and advances the interests of his government toward the government of the state to which he is accredited; and he interprets the latter's policies, capabilities, and ambitions to his own government. These essentially representational tasks can be extraordinarily difficult, requiring the utmost in skill and craftsmanship. A nineteenth century Austrian diplomat put the needed qualifications in the following terms:

> What a hard trade is the diplomatist's! I know of none which demands so much abnegation, so much readiness to sacrifice one's interests for the sake

[1] "New Techniques in Diplomacy," in *The Dimensions of Diplomacy,* ed. by E. A. J. Johnson (Baltimore: The Johns Hopkins Press, 1964), p. 117.

[2] Ernst B. Haas and Allen S. Whiting, *Dynamics of International Relations* (New York: McGraw-Hill Book Company, 1956), p. 135.

[3] E. A. J. Johnson, *The Dimensions of Diplomacy,* p. xi.

> of duty, so much courage. The ambassador who properly discharges his obligations, never betrays fatigue, boredom, disgust. He disguises the emotions which he feels, the temptations to succumb which assail him. He knows how to pass over in silence the bitter deceptions which are dealt to him, as well as the unexpected satisfactions with which his fortune, though rarely, rewards him. Jealous of his dignity, he never ceases to be cautious, takes care to quarrel with nobody, never loses his serenity, and in all the great crises, when the question of war arises, shows himself calm, impassive, and sure of success.[4]

A twentieth century American statesman, without subtracting any of these traditional qualifications from those required under contemporary conditions, adds these special newer demands:

> To the diplomatist immersed in the infinite complexity of daily detail, the most exasperating of questions is one of the commonest. It comes to him from the inquiring reporter, the Olympian editor, the ironical legislator, the harassed citizen. What is *the* foreign policy of the United States? If only they would make it plural, he sighs, how much more understanding the question would be. He resents, as does every tactician, questions about strategy; and, as does every strategist, questions about the object of strategy. Yet, whatever the motive of the question, it is a good one. It requires him to face his problems, to epitomize and declare his line of action.[5]

These represent a third dimension of the diplomat's responsibility, brought on by the increased awareness of and concern with international developments outside the narrow confines of the chancellories, broadening the perimeters to include not only the legislative branch of government, but the press and public opinion as well. Some of the philosophical implications of this increased public role are set forth below by Olson in contrasting the viewpoints of the proponents and opponents of "democratic diplomacy."

The practice of diplomacy has undergone a number of changes during the present century, notably greater publicity for diplomatic negotiations, less freedom of action for the professional diplomat, and more direct negotiations between foreign ministers and heads of state. In the case most notably of the United States, there has also occurred a proliferation of professional and administrative staff in embassies abroad, growing out of extraordinary increase in functions based upon tasks assigned to or assumed by cabinet departments at home other than the Department of State. Hence, an important embassy such as that in Rome may have in addition to conventional Foreign Service officers and military, naval and air attachés, intelligence agents, labor attachés, foreign aid officials, cultural attachés, information officers, agricultural attachés, press attachés and treasury officials.

Not all observers are convinced that all these changes are necessary or desirable, and some argue forcefully that we should revert to some extent to ear-

[4] Quoted in R. B. Mowat, *Diplomacy and Peace* (New York: McBride & Co., 1936), pp. 56–57.

[5] Dean Acheson. *Power and Diplomacy* (New York: Atheneum Publishers, 1962), p. 1.

lier diplomatic methods.[6] But to liberal internationalists whose spokesman was Woodrow Wilson, there was one great evil in earlier methods—the secrecy which attended negotiations and even the agreements resulting from such closed-door parleys. Secrecy contributed to the general tension and uneasiness, because no state could ever be sure that it might not be the victim of some arrangement of which it knew nothing—or, in any event, of which it did not know enough to set up counteracting secret arrangements of its own. Most students of the subject would agree that (except possibly in wartime) little can be said for secret agreements, especially of the type whose carefully-timed revelation tended to poison the international atmosphere and to contribute to suspicion and misunderstanding. But as in everything else, the pendulum of opinion on this issue swings back and forth; it is increasingly argued that there is, after all, a great deal to be said for negotiations which are kept confidential until a final agreement is reached and made public. Obviously rooms in which such negotiations occur cannot be hermetically sealed off, nor would it necessarily be in the interests of the democratic representatives if they were. As an American Assistant Secretary of State has recently observed:

> A democratic government can—for a little while at least—cloak its tactics in official secrecy. But it does well to assume that its ultimate intentions are bound to show. Many people are looking on; many are asking questions; there is too much tradition and habit and impulse toward openness for a democracy to keep a very big secret for very long. And while this adds to the frustration of doing business in world affairs, it is, in the end, not a price but a blessing of the system.[7]

Accompanying the Cold War has been another innovation in diplomatic practice that has found less than universal acclaim, and that is the procedure whereby foreign ministers, and even *heads* of states, participate personally and frequently in direct negotiations with one another. Certainly there are advantages to the so-called summit-meeting. Top decision-makers may benefit by getting to know one another personally, not because acquaintance necessarily leads to cordiality, but because it provides the opportunity to size up one's counterpart in another government. When differences in position have been narrowed down to manageable proportions by lower-level negotiators, the ultimate decision that will have to be made can be made only by top personnel. Under such circumstances, a personal meeting may play a positive function in settling specific international problems.

There are, however, certain disadvantages to "diplomacy at the top." If negotiations take place at a very high level, it is impossible to conduct them in complete confidence, save under war-time conditions. There are bound to be information leaks. There are official briefings of the press. The negotiators, hav-

[6] See especially Ellis Briggs, *Farewell to Foggy Bottom: the Recollections of a Career Diplomat* (New York: David McKay Co., Inc., 1964) and Harold Nicolson, *Evolution of Diplomatic Method* (London: Constable and Co., Ltd., 1954).

[7] Harlan Cleveland, "Crisis Diplomacy," *Foreign Affairs,* **XLI** (1963), 642.

ing had to state their positions publicly, will tend to do so in maximum terms, backed by moralistic or legalistic appeals. Then they find themselves unable to back down, for public opinion has been aroused and expectations have been raised. Since the essence of negotiation is compromise, the effects of this publicity are obviously destructive. One might go so far as to say that public negotiations are not negotiations at all. Further, a summit-negotiation is in its very nature a race against time, because senior decision-makers are seldom able to take the requisite weeks or even months from their demanding tasks. Pressures of time lead to pressure for results, and the imprecision in the resulting documents can lead to misinterpretation and possibly even to a resumption of the very tension that the summit conference was convened to ameliorate in the first place.

Sir Harold Nicolson has placed much of the blame for misuses of diplomatic method since the First World War on the philosophies and practices of spokesmen of the United States (although it perhaps also should be noted that he does not deem some Soviet methods to be worthy of the term "diplomacy" at all). In Professor Craig's essay below, the characteristics of Soviet diplomacy are delineated and clarified. Western and Soviet diplomats work under different conditions, with different objectives and assumptions, and in an international environment characterized by the absence of the kind of consensus of value and procedure which marked the old diplomacy. It goes without saying that all this leads to frequent misunderstanding and contradictions in interpretation, both of intention and of method. Even if it does promote "understanding" of one another, the chances for resolving conflict are not thereby automatically enhanced. One might even go so far as a recent editorial which states:

> The old diplomacy of persuasion, compromise, and patient conciliation has come to a dead end, even if diplomats must pretend to the contrary. When the differences between two parties are as profound as they are between the West and the Soviet world—when the political assumptions, economic beliefs, and the very modes of individual existence are so far removed as to be incomparable, then the very basis of this old diplomacy is abolished. It can only operate now within the alliances; between the two blocs, it falls freely in a vacuum.[8]

It is easy to underestimate the distinct potentialities of diplomacy in performing a number of important tasks in international relations. Diplomats provide essential channels for collecting information concerning the views and policies of other countries and for communicating their own countries' views and policies to other governments—with politeness and restraint, but with accuracy and precision. The diplomatic method can, if the policy-makers so desire, provide a convenient and easily accessible way to solve specific international problems. Diplomats can teach the rest of us how to live patiently and in good humor with unresolved problems. Referring to "the old virtues of the diplomat," a famous foreign correspondent has cited his

[8] *The Reporter,* August 20, 1959, p. 2.

rejection of personal prejudices, his aloofness from political parties, his suavity, his resolve not to create unnecessary incidents or to provoke needless crises, his horror of vehemence, his unsusceptibility to considerations of *amour-propre,* and his ability to carry on conversations as long as necessary to arrive at a compromise, without interrupting them to hold up the half-achieved results prematurely to the public for mass approbation or disapprobation.[9]

Despite its critical tone, the selection from Nicolson provides certain criteria for a revival of effective diplomacy. He advocates greater attention to building a competent and respected diplomatic service. He argues for honesty and probity on the part of diplomats in their relations with one another. He stresses the need for continuous and confidential negotiations and for precision in thought, terms, and actions. If these suggestions could be implemented, one might look forward to the emergence, or reemergence, of a method of conducting international relations which would be more effective than diplomacy has been permitted to be in recent decades.

In his provocative text, *Politics Among Nations,* Professor Morgenthau has advanced as fundamental rules for a successful diplomacy these propositions: first, that diplomacy must be divested of the crusading spirit; second, that it must look at the political scene from the point of view of other nations; and third, that nations must learn to compromise on all nonvital issues.[10] Winston Churchill, speaking in 1948, expressed the view that

> With all consideration of the facts, I believe it right to say today that the best chance of avoiding war is, in accord with the other Western democracies, to bring matters to a head with the Soviet Government, and by formal diplomatic processes, with all their privacy and gravity, to arrive at a lasting settlement. There is certainly enough for the interests of all if such a settlement could be reached. Even this method, I must say, however, would not guarantee that war would not come. But I believe it would give the best chance of coming out of it alive.[11]

It is no accident that in everyday parlance, the very word "diplomacy" is linked with tact, consideration, and understanding. In the clash of gears in the machinery of power politics, it is the diplomatic method that may provide the lubricating influence so essential to the smooth running of foreign affairs. It is no longer merely a nicety of world political relations; it is a necessity.

[9] Sidney Huddleston, *Popular Diplomacy and War* (London: Holborn Publishing Company, 1958), p. 271.

[10] Pp. 439–441.

[11] *Parliamentary Debates* (Hansard), House of Commons, **CDXLVI,** No. 48, 562–563.

1

*Diplomacy Then and Now**

Harold Nicolson

SIR HAROLD NICOLSON *was educated at Oxford University and served in the British Foreign Service from 1909 to 1929, both at the Foreign Office in London and at various posts abroad (Constantinople, Madrid, Teheran, Berlin). He was a member of the British delegation to the Peace Conference of 1919 and a member of the League of Nations Secretariat 1919–1920. Among his numerous works are* Peacemaking 1919 (*1933*); Curzon; The Last Phase (*1934*); Diplomacy (*1939*); The Evolution of Diplomatic Method (*1954*); The Age of Reason (*1960*); *and* Monarchy (*1962*).

Since 1914 the structure of the world has changed. Compared to the present struggle between West and East, the rivalries of the eighteenth and nineteenth centuries sink into insignificance. Today we are faced, not with a clash of interests, but with a fight between ideologies, between the desire on the one hand to defend individual liberties and the resolve on the other hand to impose a mass religion. In the process the old standards, conventions and methods of international negotiation have been discredited. Had it not been for the invention of the atomic bomb, we should already have been subjected to a third world war.

Members of the Communist bloc today are convinced that sooner or later they will acquire world dominion and will succeed in imposing their faith and their authority over the whole earth. They strain towards this objective with religious intensity and are prepared to devote to its achievement their lives, their comfort and their prospects of happiness. Anything that furthers their purpose is "right"; anything that obstructs it is "wrong"; conventional morality, even the creation of confidence, has no part in this scheme of things. Truth itself has lost its significance. Compared to the shining truth of their gospel, all minor forms of veracity are merely bourgeois inhibitions. The old diplomacy was based upon the creation of confidence, the acquisition of credit. The modern diplomatist must realize that he can no longer rely on the old system of trust; he must accept the fact that his antagonists will not hesitate to falsify facts and that they feel no shame if their duplicity be exposed. The old currency has been withdrawn from circulation; we are dealing in a new coinage.

This transformation of values has been aided by a new or "democratic" conception of international relations. In the old days the conduct of foreign affairs was entrusted to a small international élite who shared the same sort of background and who desired to preserve the same sort of world. To-

* *Foreign Affairs,* **XL** (1961), 39–49. Copyrighted by the Council on Foreign Relations, Inc., New York. Reprinted by permission.

day the masses are expected to take an interest in foreign affairs, to know the details of current controversies, to come to their own conclusions, and to render these conclusions effective through press and parliament. At the same time, however, current issues have been rendered complex and interconnected; it is not possible to state issues, such as the Common Market, in short and simple terms. Thus, whereas the man in the street is expected to have an opinion on international problems, the very complexity of these problems has rendered it difficult to provide him with the information on which to base his judgment.

A further difficulty arises over the contrast between "secret" and "open" diplomacy. This stems from the misuse of the word "diplomacy" to signify both foreign policy and negotiation. Foreign policy should never be secret, in the sense that the citizen should on no account be committed by his government to treaties or engagements of which he has not been given full previous knowledge. But negotiation must always be confidential. Very often, these days, negotiations are hampered or even frustrated by leakages to the press. Breaches of confidence are always news.

A further democratic myth is that of egalitarianism. Every country, however small its power, however restricted its resources, is regarded as the "equal" of every other country. Important decisions are taken, not owing to the strength of those who support those decisions, but according to the voices of the weak.

The Soviet Union, moreover, while itself destroying the freedom of several formerly independent countries, has managed to create the myth that it is the champion of the oppressed in their struggle against "colonialism." Preferring as it does ideal to actual truth, it manages to persuade the once subject races of the world that Communism is bound to become the universal religion of the future and that under Communism they will be able to divest themselves of their former inferior status and become the rulers of their section of the world. Thus, for the present at least, Communism is identified with nationalism, and nationalism with ambition. The wind of change howls like a hurricane across Asia and Africa. Everything associated with the past is represented as iniquitous, everything that looks to the future is colored with glamor and glory. The West is associated with the past; the East with the future. It might be said, therefore, and has often been said, that the West is fighting a losing battle. This is a fallacious proposition. If we can avoid committing arrant mistakes—such as the mistake of Suez and the mistake of Cuba [Editors' note: The reference here to "Cuba" has to do with the Bay of Pigs fiasco in 1961.]—we can maintain a defensive position for the next fifty years. Meanwhile the massive front of the Communist world may have started to disintegrate. The Marxist view of society and of the inevitability of history assumes that the masses can be conditioned to believe eternally in the same creed. That is a misconception of human nature; always there will be heretics and the more they are repressed the more ardent and convinced they become. The West in the end will be rescued by the heretics of the East.

II

I was reading recently an interesting book called "The Ugly American" in which the failure of the West to stem Communist infiltration into Southeast Asia is ascribed to the old-fashioned conception of diplomacy which prevails in Washington. Whereas the Soviet authorities concentrate on winning the support of the masses, the Americans are said to be concerned mainly with winning the support of the governing classes. A symptom of this difference of approach is that, whereas American diplomatists seldom can speak any language other than their own, Soviet diplomatists are chosen because of their familiarity with the language and dialects of the countries to which they are sent.

This is a specious contention. Governments, even in new or backward countries, are composed of the more educated people who, in Southeast Asia, are usually able to speak English or French. Such people take pride in their linguistic attainments and would be hurt if addressed in their native language by foreign diplomatists. . . . In theory, of course, it appears illogical that the American ambassador at Oslo should be unable to speak or even read Norwegian. Yet in practice those with whom he negotiates can all speak English and he has on his staff translators who provide him daily with an accurate summary of the Norwegian newspapers.

A diplomatist, moreover, should not concentrate solely on conditions in the country to which he is accredited. He must at the same time be aware of conditions and opinions in his own country. Really to know the language, traditions, prejudices and inhibitions of a country such as Laos, for example, entails years of study and long residence. A man by such methods may learn a great deal about Laotian opinion but in the process he gets out of touch with opinion in his own home country. He is apt to "go native" and his judgment may be warped by purely local sentiments. It may be that the Russians, with their uniform policy of destroying the influence of capitalism everywhere and by any means, can afford to send agents into every Laotian village to persuade the headmen of the philanthropy of the Soviet creed. It may be that by the "cell" method they are able to create disturbances, organize riots and demonstrations, and even overturn governments. Yet in the end their methods may land them in an illogical situation. They may find that in preaching self-government they lose control of the governments they have themselves created. An ambitious politician may be glad to have been brought to power by a students' demonstration; but he will see to it that no students' demonstrations recur.

Although policy should be directed and controlled by the ambassador himself, and although it does not matter much if the ambassador cannot himself speak a difficult local language, it is essential that he be aided and advised by a staff of permanent officials who have lived for long in the country, have studied the local traditions and character, and are acquainted with the background and temperament of those having local influence. Such a staff of experts exists in all well-founded embassies. In the British Foreign Service there existed in the old days the Levant Consular Service and the Chinese Consular Service, which provided the embassies with a pool of experts from which they could draw their advisers. These men were honest patriots; there is no need to suppose, as the authors of "The Ugly American" imply, that they had all gone so native as to become spies. On the other hand, to know everything about a foreign country requires at the very least a lifetime of experience. And if a man spends his whole life in any given community he is bound to develop affections and prejudices which distort his evidence. It is difficult to conceive of a person so circumstanced who would be so objective as to be immune to all subjective impulses. My own experience of such local experts is that they become either so gullible as to believe whatever they are told, or so suspicious as to doubt the veracity of even the most honest. If ambassadors were required to become experts, then surely great confusion would arise.

So strongly is this danger anticipated by the British Foreign Office that it is their habit, when a man has been too long in the Far East, to appoint him somewhere in Latin America. Such mutations are often resented by the official himself and cause surprise to the public. "How odd," people exclaim, "to send to Montevideo a man who has lived for years in Indonesia! How like the Foreign Office!" It is not so odd or irrational as all that. The business of a diplomatist is to represent his own government in a foreign country; if he lives too long in a foreign country, he may lose touch with his own home opinion and his representative value will be diminished. Expert knowledge is essential to judgment; but such knowledge can be obtained from experts whose business it is to advise and inform, not to judge or decide.

III

A second aspect of American diplomacy as criticized, and indeed ridiculed, in "The Ugly American" is the social aspect. The authors of this engaging book imply that American officials abroad are not democratic enough.

I admit that all Foreign Services possess their cocktail side. In the days of the old diplomacy, when foreign affairs were a class specialty, the social element was assuredly important. In Tsarist Russia, for instance, or in Vienna, where the top ranks of society did in fact exercise a great influence over ministers and cabinets, it was highly important for an ambassador and his staff to be socially acceptable. The French Embassy, for instance, some of whose members were deficient in social polish, found itself at a disadvantage in snobbish posts such as St. Petersburg or Vienna when in contact with the local society. The leaders of these societies regarded themselves as the cream of European aristocracy and did not enjoy mingling with people whom they regarded as bourgeois in their origins and manners. Stupid though they may have been, they yet were people of influence in governmental circles and thus it was essential that they should be entertained and consoled. Now that these aristocracies have either been eliminated or have lost all political influence, this necessity no longer exists. Why, if this be not so, should ambassadors be provided with large houses and an entertainment account? Yet whom are they supposed to entertain?

These questions are more pertinent than they seem. In totalitarian countries the names of those who visit foreign embassies are reported to the police. Those whose ambitions or livelihood are dependent on the favor of their superiors do not wish to fall into disfavor by frequenting foreign embassies. Therefore the operative people hesitate to attend embassy parties, or if they do so, arrive in a gang, so that they can all watch each other. Conversely, the ambassador, being anxious to cultivate the good will of those in power, is afraid of seeing too much of the Opposition. In Tsarist Russia, for instance, an ambassador could not ask the liberal leaders to dinner without risking the displeasure of the Court. In free countries this danger does not occur and the members of the government neither know nor care who dines or lunches at the French, Russian or German Embassies. It may arise, however, especially in totalitarian countries, that only unimportant people go to the embassy parties and that these parties tend to degenerate into stagnant pools in which the same old carp circle round and round gazing at each other with lacklustre eyes. Yet the theory persists that a great country should possess a great embassy; that the greatness of that embassy can be assessed by the size of its entertainment; and thus the dreary old round continues to persist, whether those who are entertained are influential or not. Diplomatic parties are invariably dull parties, since they lack spontaneity. Ambassadors, I suggest, would be well advised to invite important people to small parties of five or six, and to satisfy the multitude by large occasional receptions to which numbers of people can boast of having been asked.

Should the junior members of the staff confine themselves to the accepted circle of embassy guests or should they go out into the wilds? It may require deep devotion to his profession, or a passionate interest in the works of Ibsen, to persuade a young man at an embassy in Oslo to mix with Norwegian society. My own advice to the junior diplomatist is not to confine himself lazily to the easy circle of his own embassy but to cultivate the society of journalists both foreign and native. It is from them that he will derive useful advice and commentary. When I look back on the years before Hitler that I spent in the British Embassy at Berlin, I am grateful for the hours I devoted to talking to journalists in the Adlon Bar. I learned more from them than I did from any other form of social relations. Had I spent an equal amount of time discussing the future with trade-union leaders or factory workers, I should have derived false impressions. Nobody could then have foreseen that the trade-union movement with its elaborate organization could have been swept aside by Hitler's rhetoric in the course of a few days. It was the journalists of the Adlon Bar who first warned me of the coming of the Nazi movement. Diplomatic field work often misleads.

While I contend, therefore, that an ambassador and his senior officials need not, and indeed ought not, to be too closely identified with the country to which they are accredited, and while I agree that the social or representative aspect of diplomacy needs to be reexamined and possibly revalued, I assert that the old principle that the art of negotiation depends on reliability and confidence is an eternal principle, however much one's antagonists may profit by temporary tricks. I have frequently written that good diplomacy is akin to sound banking and depends on credit. Even if your opponent scores a trick or two by sharp practice, you should yourself abide by the rules of the game. I remember once, when appointed to the Middle East, asking my father, who had had great experience of the problem, by what means one could ascertain what went on at the back of the oriental mind. "Never worry about that," he answered. "There may be nothing at the back of his mind. Concentrate on making quite sure that he is left in no doubt as to what is at the back of *your* mind." That was good advice. The twists and turning of an oriental mentality constitute a labyrinth which it is useless to penetrate or explore; let the straight and simple lines remain on your side of the argument; however much you may try, you will never be able to weave a pattern as intricate as theirs. There will always be an area of deception into which the Westerner will hesitate to enter; it would be like playing poker with a man a hundred times richer than oneself; it is advisable therefore for the Westerner to stick always to truth, in the expenditure of which he possesses ample reserves. His actions will in any case be misrepresented; if they be based on demonstrable truth, then the misrepresentation will be apparent even to the least educated.

IV

It is often said, again, that with the development of communications the role and function of an ambassador have been much diminished and that the diplomatist today has been reduced to the status of a clerk at the end of the telephone line. In the first place, the telephone is a dangerous little instrument through which to convey information or to transmit instructions. One of the most important assets of sound diplomacy is precision; the telephone (as was demonstrated by the U-2 incident) is an imprecise instrument, and liable to create misunderstanding.

Moreover, a moment's reflection should convince people that the gibe about "a clerk at the end of the telephone" is an empty gibe. It may be true that it is no longer possible for an ambassador at some distant post to create situations that may lead either to his repudiation or recall, or else to war. That is a great gain. It may be true that the independence of his action may be curtailed, and rightly curtailed, by the fact that his own chief in London or Washington can reach him on the telephone or, if the worst comes to the worst, can descend upon him in an airplane. But the fact remains, and will always remain, that the man on the spot is in a key position and that no action should be taken at headquarters without his advice being sought. No large business undertaking, no newspaper, would be represented in a foreign capital by a man whose stature was no higher than that of a clerk at the end of a telephone. It is the business of a representative abroad to study local conditions; to assess the areas of local susceptibility; to cultivate the acquaintance of local politicians, and thus to be in a position to advise his own minister how far he can go and how far he can trust those with whom he is negotiating. In offering such advice he will rely on the information furnished him by his own experts, upon his personal contacts with local politicians, upon a careful study of the local press, and upon exchanges of views and information with his diplomatic colleagues and resident press correspondents. Again and again have I heard the slogan that ambassadors today have ceased to count. I do not hear a similar statement applied to the local representatives of large firms or newspapers. Yet the position is identical. You do not send abroad a clerk to represent you; you send a man in whose intelligence, initiative and integrity you place full confidence. The only difference today is that things move with great celerity. There is less time for reflection.

Another element of change is the use made today in international negotiation of the weapon of propaganda. In the old days when foreign affairs were recognized to be a specialized study and when their conduct was left to the experts, the element of propaganda scarcely entered into consideration. Today it is sometimes preponderant. It is a dangerous weapon, being all too apt to backfire or recoil. It is one which our antagonists, by concentrating on the shadows of the past and by indicating the sunshine of a Communist future, can employ with great effect. There is, moreover, always an element in propaganda which is exaggerated and untrue; the West finds such assaults more difficult than does the East. Yet here again truth will prevail in the end. Our attitude toward propaganda must always remain a defensive attitude; we must content ourselves with being scrupulously careful not to present our antagonists with propaganda weapons against us. It is admittedly unfortunate that in the propaganda war the East appears to win all the battles all the time. Owing to a series of small successes, of accidental triumphs, they build up an aggregate impression of invincibility and inevitability. This is the impression which they desire to convey and we desire to avoid. It is a difficult task but not one that can be accomplished by telling untruths. The Communists are convinced that there is a "glorious lie," or a "mass untruth," which "becomes true" since it serves the cause of Communism. Yet the saying of Abraham Lincoln remains true: you can't fool all the people all of the time. The misfortune is that one can fool a large number of people for sufficient time for great damage to be done. I admit that the introduction of the propaganda element has greatly complicated the task of Western diplomacy. It is easy enough to convince uneducated people that they are being exploited or suffering humiliations and oppression. It is more difficult to preach to them the rewards of freedom. People who have been convinced that their rights have been disregarded will be glad to throw stones at windows or to overturn motorcars; the doctrine of individual liberty inspires no such acts of passion. We are at a disadvantage when it comes to applying propaganda to the have-nots. Dollars are not always enough; and the fact that our doctrine appeals more to the privileged classes is a fact which cannot be exploited or even avowed.

The principle of egalitarianism has altered the balance of diplomatic power. Even within my own lifetime the affairs of the world were dominated by the eight great powers, whose strength, when it came to a conflict, was overwhelming. The British Government, for instance, could change the whole balance of the Eastern Question by dispatching three frigates to Besika Bay. Today action on the part of the great powers could, even if they were united, be blocked by the votes of the small powers. The Security Council of the United Nations was intended to be a sort of cabinet of action. Its decisions are negatived, however, by the veto of the Soviet Union, a veto which to date has been exercised ninety-five times. Thus the power of decision has been to all intents and purposes transferred to the Assembly, in which a majority of the ninety-nine nations represented can block all action. This majority, while not invariably adhering to the Russian line, is at least united in hostility to anything that savors of the old colonialism. Thus power has been transferred into the hands of those who lack strength, and a situation has been created which is dominated by uncertainty. Uncertainty and the unpredictable are dangerous elements in any international situation. It is impossible to conduct sound banking when there exists no stability of exchange.

2

*Totalitarian Approaches to Diplomatic Negotiation**

Gordon A. Craig

GORDON A. CRAIG, *Professor of European and Diplomatic History at Stanford University, is a frequent contributor to scholarly journals. His works include* From Bismarck to Adenauer: Aspects of German Statecraft *(1958) and* Europe Since 1915 *(1961).*

In a treatise that is justly admired by students of diplomacy, François de Callières wrote in 1716: "The art of negotiation . . . is so important that the fate of the greatest states often depends upon the good and bad conduct of negotiations and upon the degree of capacity in the negotiators employed. . . . It is not necessary to turn far back into the past to understand what can be achieved by negotiation. We see daily around us its definite effects in sudden revolutions favorable to this great design of state or that, in the use of sedition in fermenting the hatreds between nations, in causing jealous rivals to arm against each other so that the *tertius gaudens* may profit, in the formation of leagues and other treaties of various kinds between monarchs whose interests might otherwise clash, in the dissolution by crafty means of the closest unions between states: in a word, one may say that the art of negotiation, according as its conduct is good or evil, gives form to great affairs and may turn a host of lesser events into a useful influence upon the course of the greater."[1]

Since these words were written, changes in the methods of communication, in the nature of international society, and in the distribution of political power within the states that comprise it have profoundly affected the forms and the techniques of diplomatic negotiation; but its importance as an instrument of national power has in no way been diminished. There is no easier way to demonstrate this than to consider the role of negotiation in the history of the totalitarian states of the first half of the twentieth century. The failure of the Fascist and National Socialist governments to understand or take advantage of the uses of negotiation was not the least important cause of the difficulties that in the end overwhelmed Italy and Germany; whereas the Soviet regime's ability to devise new techniques of negotiation and to adapt traditional ones to its own purposes carried it through the hazards of the inter-war period and, after the Second World War, consolidated and expanded the position won by Soviet arms.

[1] *The Practice of Diplomacy,* being an English rendering of François de Callières' "De la manière de négocier avec les souverains," presented with an introduction by A. F. Whyte (London, 1919), pp. 7, 16.

* In A. O. Sarkissian, ed., *Studies in Diplomatic History and Historiography* (London: Longmans, Green & Company Ltd., 1961), pp. 107–125. Reprinted by permission of the editor and of the author.

I

The deficiencies of Fascist diplomacy and the amateurishness of its leaders' ventures into negotiation may be explained, in part at least, by the fact that the first years of Mussolini's political life were spent as a journalist. The talents that are required to make a man a good newspaperman are different from those that one expects to find in a competent diplomat. Cavour is one of the rare individuals who have possessed both kinds, and Mussolini, in this and other respects, was no Cavour. The Duce's newspaper experience left him with a tendency to be preoccupied with style rather than with substance, with a hankering after sensational strokes and dramatic coups that would look good in headlines, and —although this hardly accords with that cynicism that newspapermen are traditionally supposed to possess—with an excessive regard for newspaper opinion and a dangerous sensitiveness to newspaper criticism.

Mussolini's fundamental attitude toward diplomacy, and the attention he paid to its purely verbal aspects, were bound up, in a curious way, with his editorial policy for *Il Popolo d'Italia*. He once explained how he had impressed upon that journal, "in thousands of articles, headlines, drawings and sketches inspired by me, a polemical and aggressive character, one of continual battle";[2] and, after he became chief of state, he seemed to feel that it was only fitting that this should become the characteristic mark of every aspect of Fascist policy, including foreign policy. He was forever talking about "the Fascist style" which he equated with courage, resolution, action, forcefulness, dynamism. "Note that I do not love the hesitant and conventional form," he said in December 1925. "I affirm."[3]

This dislike of the hesitant and the conventional extended to those forms of diplomacy which sought, with a minimum of public display and a maximum of deliberation and reflection, to solve European problems in the first postwar decade, as well as to the frequent attempts made, at Geneva and elsewhere, to reach collective agreements by means of multilateral negotiation. All of these were, in a phrase frequently used by the Duce's son-in-law, "contrary to our diplomatic style."[4] Mussolini's prejudice against multilateral negotiation can probably be traced back to the chastening experience of his first diplomatic venture, when, at the Lausanne Conference of November 1922, his *gaucheries* were received by the other delegates with an amusement that bordered on scorn.[5] But there can be little doubt that it was rooted also in his belief that the satisfactions to be gained from collaborative diplomacy in the interest of general appeasement were not worthy of Fascist Italy, which must dazzle the world with spectacular triumphs of its own.

During the first decade of his regime, however, Mussolini could not afford, and did not attempt, to base his policy upon these prejudices. The defiant, and only partly successful, stroke at Corfu in August 1923[6] was not imitated in the years that followed; and, if Mussolini was prone to ringing declarations of imminent action, he generally allowed the word to stand for

---

[2] Herman Ellwanger, *Sulla lingua di Mussolini* (Verona, 1941), p. 22.

[3] Benito Mussolini, *Scritti e discorsi* (Milano, 1934–9), V, 321 ff.

[4] Galeazzo Ciano, *L'Europa verso la catastrofe* (Verona, 1948), p. 338.

[5] See Harold Nicolson, *Curzon: The Last Phase* (London, 1934), pp. 288 ff.

[6] See Gaetano Salvemini, *Prelude to World War II* (New York, 1954), pp. 44 ff.

the deed. Thus, in February 1926, when he electrified Europe by a clear threat of military action north of the Brenner unless an end was made to criticism of his policy in the South Tyrol by the Austrian and German parliaments, he backed down quickly when the Austrians proposed to bring the matter before the League of Nations, delivering a second speech in which, behind "a characteristic parade of truculence," he converted his earlier menaces into "an inoffensive intimation that he would defend himself if attacked by others."[7]

Throughout these early years, the exigencies of domestic policy reduced Mussolini's dynamism to what has been called a "random and uncoordinated striking-out in all directions in the hope of scoring points on the cheap."[8] The best that can be said of it is that it did no real harm to Italy's basic interests, since Mussolini was content to leave the bulk of the diplomatic business of the state, which was, as elsewhere, carried on by the continuous negotiations that go on in embassies and foreign offices, in the hands of the professional foreign service and the permanent officials in the Palazzo Chigi. By making concessions to their leader's vanity, these officials were able to moderate his outbursts and control his ambitions, while cementing relations with those Powers, like Great Britain, who were willing to respect Italy's traditional interests and even to assent to modest increases in her influence in Africa and eastern Europe.[9]

All of this changed when the deterioration of economic conditions in the early 1930s, and the consequent disruption of European power relationships, opened new vistas to Mussolini's eyes and made him impatient with old restraints. The dismissal of Grandi as Foreign Minister in July 1932 marked the inauguration of a new policy of all-out revisionism and, simultaneously, the beginning of that decline of the influence of the professionals in Italian diplomacy that was to reach its nadir in the Foreign Ministry of Galeazzo Ciano.[10] As their role diminished, negotiation became almost a forgotten art in the Italian service, a tendency encouraged by the belief that the goals Italy now sought must be attained not by diplomacy but by heroism.

Even the atmosphere of conventional courtesy that customarily reigns in the diplomatic corps and is conducive to the useful exchange of views was dispelled by Ciano. Once he had become Foreign Minister, he seems to have determined to realize his father-in-law's stylistic ideals and insisted that Italian diplomats must henceforth make their behaviour reflect the approved *tono fascista*.[11] The meaning of this phrase is elusive; it seems to have meant a proud and militant bearing that would impress the foreigner with the dignity and strength of the new Italy. Its practical effect was to make ambassadors dispense with traditional forms and usages of polite intercourse (Ciano insisted on the deletion of even the most conventional expressions of good will from ambassadorial declarations),[12] to be constantly on the alert for slights to Italy's honour, to adopt a hectoring tone in delivering communi-

---

[7] A. J. Toynbee, *Survey of International Affairs*, 1927 (Oxford, 1929), p. 199.

[8] H. Stuart Hughes, "The Early Diplomacy of Italian Fascism," in *The Diplomats, 1919–1939*, edited by Gordon A. Craig and Felix Gilbert (Princeton, 1953), pp. 224 ff.

[9] *Ibid.*, pp. 216 ff.

[10] See especially Felix Gilbert, "Ciano and His Ambassadors," in *The Diplomats*, pp. 512 ff.

[11] Raffaele Guariglia, *Ricordi, 1922–1946* (Napoli, 1950), p. 193.

[12] *Ibid.*, pp. 255 ff.

cations and complaints to the governments to which they were accredited, and, in general, to conduct themselves, especially in countries that were not bound by ideological or more formal ties to Italy, as if they were in an enemy camp.

This made it virtually impossible for envoys abroad to perform effectively their duties of representation, reporting and negotiation. Representing Italian interests seemed now to consist for the most part of continual protestation against criticisms of Fascism, even when they were made by private citizens; and this, as one Italian diplomat noted, was ludicrous, when one remembered that Fascist Italy was "all too prone to criticize, injure, jeer at, and menace all the peoples of the world, and not in private conversations, but in manifestations of an official character and in articles in a press which the whole world knew was rigidly controlled by the government."[13] Ambassadorial reporting degenerated into demonstrations of conformity to Fascist style; and the reports from posts like Belgrade, Sofia, and Bucharest in the last years of the peace contained little of interest except descriptions of the ambassadors' success in bullying their hosts.[14] Finally, the possibilities of ambassadorial negotiation of any kind were handicapped, not only by this new cult of bad manners, but also by the apparent belief in the Palazzo Chigi that, in certain capitals—Paris, for example—an attitude of disdainful reserve was all that should be expected of a Fascist diplomat. "What ought I try to accomplish in Paris?" asked Guariglia as he left for his post in November 1938. "Nothing," answered Ciano. "It will be difficult," the ambassador replied, "but I will do my best."[15]

The subordination of diplomacy to the *tono fascista* was even more patent in the negotiations that Ciano carried on personally at Mussolini's orders. In these he appears to have been more interested in the speed with which an agreement could be reached and the publicity that could be garnered from it than in anything else. In general, his negotiations were amateurish in technique and dangerous in result.

The best illustration of these failings is to be seen in the negotiations for the Pact of Steel of May 1939, "this fatal error," as Guariglia calls it, "of inauspicious memory."[16] The reasons for seeking a military alliance with Germany were in themselves hardly compelling. There is strong reason to believe that Mussolini was goaded into abandoning his earlier reserve by scornful articles in the French press about Italo-German friction,[17] although he may have been moved also, as Italian and British diplomats have argued, by a desire to replace the loose Axis tie, which gave Italy no control over her German associate and no right to be consulted by her, by a formal treaty which gave her both these things.[18] However that may be, the way in which the pact was negotiated on the Italian side was nothing short

---

13 Emanuele Grazzi, *Il principio della fine* (Roma, 1945), p. 13.

14 Ministro degli Affari Esteri, *I documenti diplomatici italiani* (Roma, 1952 et seq.), 8th series, Vol. XII, Nos. 100, 177, 672, 819.

15 Guariglia, *op. cit.*, p. 357.

16 *Ibid.*, p. 395.

17 Mario Toscano, *Le origini del Patto d'Acciaio* (2nd ed., Firenze, 1956), p. 308.

18 Massimo Magistrati, *L'Italia a Berlino, 1937–1939* (Verona, 1956), pp. 348 ff.; *Documents on British Foreign Policy, 1919–1939*, edited by E. L. Woodward and Rohan Butler (London, 1949 et seq.), 3rd series, Vol. V. No. 598. ("Mussolini has bought the right to be consulted by Hitler, and the price is the pact." Sir Percy Loraine.)

of slipshod. Mario Toscano has pointed out that the most inexcusable aspects of Ciano's conduct were his willingness to leave the actual drafting of the treaty of alliance entirely to the Germans, and his failure, during the talks with Ribbentrop in Milan, "to discuss or even to set limits on the general nature of its contents."[19] As for Mussolini, while his Foreign Minister was placing this dangerous degree of trust in German intentions, his sole interest was apparently to have the pact proclaimed in the press even before its terms were worked out, presumably to put an end to the gibes in Paris.

Some time later, when he handed the draft treaty to Ambassador Attolico in Berlin, the Director of the Legal Department of the German Foreign Ministry told him that "the Foreign Minister [Ribbentrop] considered that the draft corresponded completely with what he and Count Ciano had recently agreed and that, therefore, it presumably did not require any more negotiations on the final version."[20] Since there was no clear definition, in either the Italian or the German record of the Milan talks, of what had been agreed upon there, it was difficult to contest this;[21] and, in any case, the Italian government seemed too eager for ratification to haggle over amendments. When Ciano and General Pariani came to Berlin at the end of May, some minor changes, based on suggestions of Attolico, were made;[22] but the final document was nevertheless dangerously imprecise.[23]

Unlike most treaties of military alliance, the Pact of Steel included no definition of the *casus foederis,* no escape clauses, no stipulation of necessary consultation. There was not even a secret protocol defining German intentions; and the promise that no war was contemplated for three years, which had been requested by the Italians, was purely verbal and was not intended to be kept, as Ciano was to discover in his talks with Hitler and Ribbentrop at Salzburg in August 1939. On the other hand, the treaty so precipitately negotiated by Ciano was, as far as Italy's obligations were concerned, rigid and unconditional; and, unless Mussolini was prepared to repudiate his pledge, in case of German action of which he disapproved, Italy was bound to fight at a time of Germany's choosing. Moreover, the Germans were protected against any real possibility of Italian withdrawal by Mussolini's concern over what the newspapers wrote about him. Events were to show that, even when Hitler agreed in August 1939 to Italy's abstention from immediate hostilities—an agreement won in part by the skilful way in which Attolico presented Italy's deficiencies in materials and weapons[24]—the Duce was not content. Smarting under charges that he had broken his word, he led his country into a war for which she was neither

[19] Toscano, *op. cit.,* pp. 318 ff.

[20] *Documents on German Foreign Policy 1918–1945: From the Archives of the German Foreign Ministry* (Washington, 1949 et seq.), series D, vol. VI, no. 371. Hereafter cited as *German Documents.*

[21] Toscano, *op. cit.,* p. 339.

[22] Magistrati, *op. cit.,* pp. 344 ff.

[23] See the text in *German Documents,* series D, IV, no. 426. Ferdinand Siebert has written: "Seldom indeed in history has an alliance been concluded which, despite all its fine talk about cohesion, ideological kinship, and solidarity was based—thanks to the levity of one partner and the disingenuousness of the other—on so many ambiguities and imprecisions as the German-Italian Pact of Friendship and Alliance of May 1939." "Das deutsch-italienische Stahlpact," *Vierteljahrshefte für Zeitgeschichte,* 1959, p. 390.

[24] *Documenti diplomatici italiani,* 8th series, XIII, nos. 293, 298, 304, 307; Magistrati, *op. cit.,* pp. 432 ff.; Galeazzo Ciano, *Diario* (Roma, 1946), I, 150; *German Documents,* series D, VII, Nos. 307, 308, 317.

materially nor psychologically prepared.

Given Mussolini's temperament, this might have been impossible to prevent in any case; but it was facilitated by the nature of, and the obligations imposed by, the Pact of Steel. All in all, it can hardly be denied that the neglect and misuse of negotiation deprived those Italians who desired peace in 1939 and 1940 of weapons with which to combat the vanity and impulsiveness of their leaders.

II

In retrospect it would seem that the weakness of Italian diplomacy arose from the essential frivolity of the officials charged with the task of conducting it; and, behind Ciano's shocked protest, upon learning in August 1939 of Hitler's intention of going to war, that "no indication had been given by Germany, either in the conversations at Milan, or in the talks during his visit to Berlin, that the situation in respect of Poland was so grave,"[25] lies a pathetic admission that he had not mastered the art of negotiating even with his own allies.

Adolf Hitler can hardly be accused of Ciano's kind of *leggerezza.* He both understood what could be gained by negotiation and, at various times in his career, demonstrated his ability to use it, in ways of which Callières would have approved, "in the dissolution . . . of the closest unions between states" and "in the formation of leagues . . . between monarchs whose interests might otherwise clash." His faults as a statesman are, therefore, of a different order from Mussolini's. He is to be criticized, not for lack of diplomatic proficiency, but rather for the fact that he refused to be content with the great gains that negotiation could bring to his country, but sought greater ones in war.

Despite the suspicion with which he was viewed by professional diplomats when he came to power, Hitler showed considerable facility in the use of diplomatic means during his first years. In the unfolding of his policy, there was, for one thing, little of the incoherence that had characterized Italian policy in the 1920s. Hitler was aware that the revisionism and expansion upon which his heart was set could be pursued only after the home front had been stabilized and Germany's armed forces built up. While the *Gleichschaltung* was being carried out, therefore, and the Versailles Treaty undermined, the Führer encouraged foreign states to believe that his government would effect no radical break with the policy of the past. This he did, in the first place, by retaining the existing Foreign Ministry staff and by relying on diplomats who were known abroad and whose continued employment would have a reassuring effect.[26]

In the second place, unlike Mussolini, Hitler was not given to complicating the work of his diplomats in the field (whose task, essentially, was to explain away the brutalities of his domestic programme and to portray him as a force for European order) by inveighing against the international *status quo.* His public pronouncements at this stage were pacific, disarming, even ingratiating, designed to divert foreign attention from his real intentions and to blunt criticism of, or split possible opposition to, his policies, by promising concessions or hinting at

[25] *German Documents,* series D, VI, No. 43.

[26] Karl Dietrich Bracher, "Das Anfangsstadium der Hitlerischen Aussenpolitik," *Vierteljahrshefte für Zeitgeschichte,* 1957, pp. 69–70.

willingness to make agreements desired abroad.[27] Hitler realized that the public statements of heads of government were not the least important of modern channels of negotiation, and he showed great skill in using this means of advancing his purposes and supporting the efforts of his envoys at Geneva and foreign posts. It was by this means that he was able, after his withdrawal from the Disarmament Conference and the League of Nations in October 1933, to mislead the other Powers by his professed willingness to consider any schemes of arms limitation that they might propose; and this channel was also used with effect in persuading states which criticized his withdrawal from the collective security system to enter bilateral negotiations with him.

In the last-mentioned area of negotiation, Hitler's first years were marked by two successes that were admirably designed to protect him from collective counteraction as his policy evolved. These were the pact with Poland, which drove a wedge into France's eastern alliance system,[28] and the Anglo-German naval agreement of June 1935, which split the Stresa Front and destroyed the last possibility of reprisals for Hitler's violations of the arms clauses of the Versailles Treaty.[29] The notable feature of these examples of "dynamic" diplomacy is that there was nothing impulsive about them. The possibility of a treaty with Poland seems to have been in Hitler's mind as early as April 1933;[30] in September he instructed his Foreign Minister to talk with his Polish opposite number about "the best means of creating a better atmosphere in the relations between the two states"; and in November he authorized the formal negotiations that eventuated in the treaty of 26 January 1934.[31] The idea of a pact with Britain had interested Hitler for an even longer period, stretching back before his coming to power; and, after he became Chancellor, he took it up and played an important role in pushing the naval negotiations to a successful issue. His private talks with Lord Allen of Hurtwood in January 1935, with the British Ambassador in February, and with Sir John Simon in March, and his public address of 21 May 1935 certainly made a more important contribution to the pact's conclusion than the tactics used by Ribbentrop when he led the German delegation to London in June.[32]

After the middle of 1935, when Germany's growing military might supplied an authoritative backing for her diplomacy, Hitler was never again as dependent upon negotiation as he was in his first years; and, after 1936, when he was given his first proofs of the weakness and indecision of the

[27] A good example is Hitler's speech of 17 May 1933 concerning Germany's stand on disarmament. See *The Speeches of Adolf Hitler,* edited by Norman H. Baynes (Oxford, 1942), II, 1041–1058.

[28] Richard Breyer, *Das Deutsche Reich und Polen, 1932–1937* (Würzburg, 1955), pp. 106 ff., and 113.

[29] See, for instance, the speech of 21 May 1935 in *The Speeches of Adolf Hitler,* II, pp. 1218–1246.

[30] Herbert von Dirksen, *Moskau, Tokio, London: Erinnerungen und Betrachtungen zu 20 Jahren deutscher Aussenpolitik, 1919–39* (Stuttgart, 1950), p. 123.

[31] Republic of Poland: Ministry for Foreign Affairs, *Official Documents concerning Polish-German and Polish-Soviet Relations, 1933–39* (London, 1940), pp. 11–24; *German Documents,* series C, II, Nos. 84, 87, 88, 217, 218, 219.

[32] See W. Malanowski, "Das deutsch-englische Flottenabkommen vom 18. Juni 1935 als Ausgangspunkt für Hitlers doktrinäre Bündnispolitik," *Wehrwissenschaftliche Rundschau,* 1955, p. 416; D. C. Watt, "The Anglo-German Naval Agreement of 1935; an Interim Report." *Journal of Modern History,* 1956, pp. 157, 159ff.

western democracies, his tendency was to rely more upon military pressure than upon negotiating skill and persuasiveness. The tone of German diplomacy now began to change; Hitler's public statements on foreign policy became menacing; and, especially after Ribbentrop became Foreign Minister in February 1938, the style of Foreign Ministry communications became peremptory and sometimes arrogant.[33] Ribbentrop himself had such an exalted conception of his role that he was led to indulge in astonishing displays of bad manners when he felt that his dignity had been hurt.[34] Aside from this, he had no real sympathy for genuine negotiation. As Attolico once said, he could see nothing but his own version of the facts;[35] he had no patience with lengthy deliberations, being desirous of headlong decisions;[36] and he was interested, not in agreements of mutual advantage, but only in settlements that were imposed upon his *vis-à-vis,* or treaties of alliance that were directed against third powers.

These traits were not considered as weaknesses by Ribbentrop's master who had now lost his own interest in negotiation and the benefits it might bring. By the end of 1937, as the minutes of his conference with his generals on 5 November reveal,[37] he was thinking of triumphs that could be won only by the sword; and negotiation had become the handmaiden to war. The change of attitude is clearly seen in the instructions given to Konrad Henlein, the leader of the Sudeten German party, who was ordered, as he pursued his negotiations with the Czech government, to set his claims so high that the Czechs would rather fight than accept them.[38] The same point of view determined Hitler's own tactics as the Polish dispute came to a head a year later. The Führer seems to have been genuinely concerned lest the Poles decide to accept the terms that they had rejected in March 1939 or lest they, or someone else, submit counter-proposals that might compel him to accept a compromise short of war. To prevent this, he not only declined the good offices of third powers,[39] but refused to allow his ambassadors to Poland and Great Britain, who were on leave in Germany, to return to their posts.[40] On 22 August 1939, Hitler openly admitted his preference for violent solutions by saying to his generals: "Now Poland is in the position in which I wanted her . . . I am only afraid that at the last moment some swine or other will yet submit to me a plan for mediation."[41]

The irrationality that prompted this insistent refusal of present advantage and this fateful trust in the uncertain promises of war was to recur in June 1941, when Hitler declared war upon the Soviet Union. The declara-

[33] This change was apparent even in the language of professionals like Ernst von Weizsäcker, the Under Secretary. See the language in which he "categorically refused" to accept a French protest after the Prague coup of March 1939. *German Documents,* series D, VI, No. 20.

[34] See Paul Schmidt, *Statist auf diplomatischer Bühne, 1923–1945* (Bonn, 1949), pp. 457 ff.

[35] *Documenti diplomatici italiani,* 8th series, XII, No. 503.

[36] Ernst L. Presseisen, *Germany and Japan: A Study in Totalitarian Diplomacy 1933–1941* (The Hague, 1958), pp. 198, 208.

[37] *German Documents,* series D, I, No. 19.

[38] *Ibid.,* series D, II, No. 107.

[39] *Survey of International Affairs, 1939–1946: The Eve of War 1939,* edited by Arnold Toynbee and Veronica M. Toynbee (London, 1958), pp. 342 ff. and 377.

[40] *German Documents,* series D, VI, no. 674; VII, Nos. 2, 32, 82; Carl W. Schorske, "Two German Ambassadors," in *The Diplomats,* pp. 509–510.

[41] *German Documents,* series D, VII, No. 192.

tion followed a period of twenty-two months in which the Nazis had won tremendous concessions from Moscow by a combination of negotiation and subtle menace, and during which the Soviet Union had yielded on every contested point of the partition of eastern Europe that had been stipulated in Hitler's most spectacular diplomatic stroke, the agreement with the Soviets in August 1939. It has been said that in those twenty-two months "the Soviet Union had gone to greater lengths in appeasing Germany than the British and French governments had gone during the period between Hitler's advent to power and 15 March 1939";[42] and it was not certain that the limits of that appeasement had yet been reached.[43] Yet Hitler the warrior had superseded Hitler the negotiator; and even the knowledge that Great Britain was still unsubdued did not dissuade him now from transforming the conflict in which he was already engaged into a two-front struggle that would in the end destroy his country.

III

In sharp contrast to Hitler's approach to negotiation is that of the Soviet Union. Far from preferring the arbitrament of war to decisions made at the council table, the Soviets have generally valued diplomacy for its ability to win great triumphs at small risk and have shown virtuosity, not only in mastering its procedures and forms, but also in devising formidable negotiating techniques of their own.

In the first stages of the Soviet experiment, there was, it is true, some tendency to regard diplomacy as an outworn bourgeois institution, and Leon Trotsky actually spoke of shutting up the Foreign Office completely.[44] This mood soon passed, and, from the days when G. V. Chicherin led a top-hatted and striped-trousered delegation to the Genoa conference of 1922, the Soviet Union has made full use of all the possible channels of diplomatic negotiation and shown complete command of the time-tested methods of the profession.[45] The official Soviet history of diplomacy says proudly: "Soviet diplomacy is master of its technique. In its relations with Foreign Powers, it defends the interests of its country in the most worthy manner; and, with an incontestable authority and with impeccable special skills, it conducts negotiations and concludes agreements advantageous to its country."[46]

One need only think of some of the diplomatic successes won at moments when the Soviet Union was vulnerable to outside pressure, or threatened by outside attack, to admit the justice of this. In the first ten years after the Bolshevist revolution, the Soviet Union often faced the possibility of complete diplomatic isolation. It escaped this by its success in persuading England and other countries to enter negotiations for trade agreements, by the subsequent treaties of recognition

[42] *Survey of International Affairs, 1939–1946: The Initial Triumph of the Axis,* edited by Arnold Toynbee and Veronica M. Toynbee (London, 1958), p. 365.

[43] As late as 28 April 1941 the German Ambassador in Moscow was sure that the Soviet government was "prepared to make even further concessions." *Nazi-Soviet Relations, 1939–1941,* edited by R. J. Sontag and James S. Beddie (Washington, 1941), p. 332.

[44] Theodore H. von Laue, "Soviet Diplomacy: G. V. Chicherin, Peoples Commissar for Foreign Affairs," in *The Diplomats,* p. 235.

[45] A number of western studies of diplomacy, including Sir Ernest Satow's *Guide to Diplomatic Practice,* and Jules Cambon's *Le Diplomate,* were translated into Russian in the interwar years and used in training courses.

[46] V. P. Potemkin *et al., Histoire de la diplomatie* (Paris, 1946–47), III, 787.

concluded with the major Powers, by continuous negotiation in areas like Afghanistan, the Middle East and Poland for protective or diversionary purposes, and by the masterful cultivation of the association with Germany that was inaugurated so sensationally at Rapallo in 1922 and confirmed by the Treaty of Berlin in 1926.[47] These successes were won for the most part by patient negotiation and the skilful use of the techniques of classical diplomacy, especially the art of playing upon the differences of other powers or appealing to their greed or their apprehensions. In the use of the traditional arts of bargaining, Soviet negotiators, in these early days and later, showed themselves the equals of their adversaries, sometimes to the surprise of the latter;[48] and in preparing their case before the opening of negotiations, in mastering the agenda and the technical aspects of items included on it, and in tactical adroitness in exploiting the legal aspects of existing agreements which bore on current negotiations, they sometimes showed an embarrassing superiority of performance, as the first post-Second World War meetings of the Foreign Ministers showed all too clearly.[49]

Despite the excellence of their training in the external forms of diplomacy, and their skill in using it, Soviet negotiators have always had a fundamentally different approach toward diplomacy from that of their western colleagues. To them diplomacy is more than an instrument for protecting and advancing national interest; it is a weapon in the unremitting war against capitalist society. Diplomatic negotiations, therefore, cannot aim at real understanding and agreement; and this has profound effects upon their nature and techniques.[50]

For one thing, it means that not all of the negotiations entered into by the Soviet government are intended to eventuate in settlements, a fact that irritates or baffles some western diplomats and seems to represent a complete denial of the purpose of diplomacy.[51] Negotiations may be begun, or agreed to, by the Soviets, not as a

[47] The latter treaty in particular played a part in the initiation of the negotiations that led to the Nazi-Soviet pact in August 1939. See *German Documents,* series D, VI, Nos. 406, 490, 579, 607.

[48] Thus, during the negotiations for American recognition of the Soviet Union in November 1933, the British Ambassador in Washington could write: "M. Litvinov has proved somewhat of a surprise to the State Department. I learn on good authority that he has been showing himself the toughest of negotiators. He has evinced no trace of any ambition to achieve a personal success. He has had the blandest, but firmest, of retorts ready for any question, and has appeared quite ready to depart empty-handed at any moment." *British Documents,* 2nd series, VII, no. 542. Speaking of Molotov's conversations in Berlin in November 1940, Paul Schmidt wrote: "Molotov had a certain mathematical precision and unerring logic in his way of speaking and presenting arguments. In his precise diplomacy he dispensed with flowery phrases and, as though he were teaching a class, gently rebuked the sweeping vague generalities of Ribbentrop and, later, even of Hitler." *Statist auf diplomatischer Bühne,* p. 516.

[49] Newspaper reports of the meeting of Foreign Ministers in London in 1945 would seem to bear this out. See, more recently, "Topics of the Times," *New York Times,* July 26, 1959; and John Foster Dulles, *War and Peace* (New York, 1950), pp. 27 ff.

[50] See Stephen D. Kertesz, "Diplomacy in the Atomic Age," *Review of Politics,* 1959, pp. 132 and 193; and "American and Soviet Negotiating Behavior" in *Diplomacy in a Changing World,* edited by Stephen D. Kertesz and M. A. Fitzsimons (Notre Dame, 1959), pp. 144 ff.

[51] "I have 'done' many conferences in my life but never went into one without some hope of a fairly quick result. No one could say the same today. Results are often not expected, and often not even desirable. . . ." Lord Vansittart, "The Decline of Diplomacy," *Foreign Affairs,* 1950, p. 184.

means of promoting agreement on an issue, but of delaying it, pending the clarification of problems in other areas or the successful completion of other talks. They may be started out of mere speculation, as a means of eliciting the views, defining the interests, or testing the tenacity of the parties on the other side. They may be designed for purely propaganda purposes, as "elaborate stage plays" to edify and win the sympathy of the uncommitted part of the world.[52] Because of this, as Philip Mosely has written, the first task of the diplomats who engage in talks with Soviet negotiators is to try to discover whether the latter have instructions to negotiate seriously or, indeed, have any instructions at all, beyond a general directive to make propaganda for the Communist cause.[53] If they do not, the result is apt to be what a British Foreign Secretary has described, in a moment of exasperation, as "negotiation by equivocation."[54]

Even when Soviet diplomats have been instructed to seek a settlement, the subsequent negotiations are apt to diverge in marked respects from the rules that have traditionally guided diplomatic intercourse in the western world. Soviet diplomats do not subscribe to Callières's belief that there exists between negotiators a *commerce d'avis réciproque*.[55] Bound themselves by rigid directives that allow little flexibility they cannot understand the freedom of manoeuvre permitted to western diplomats. Moreover, since they regard their opposite numbers as ideological enemies, they are bound to view all their moves, however trivial, with suspicion[56] and to regard any means that promise to win advantage over them as legitimate.

These things being so, negotiations with the Soviets have generally been marked by an almost automatic Soviet opposition at the outset to all proposals from the other side of the table, followed by persistent and uncompromising advocacy of the Soviet point of view. The tactic of initial rejection extends to the most innocuous suggestions made by the partner in negotiation, since the Soviets apparently believe that "the trivial is the first line of defence on which to meet the enemy assaults that always aim at the crucial."[57] In September 1929, when Arthur Henderson presented M. Dovgalevsky with a list of questions that he felt should be discussed and settled before the resumption of diplomatic relations between their two countries, the Soviet representative came to the second meeting with a list of his own, with the questions in quite a different order, and proceeded to fight, with a zeal out of all proportion to its object, for his arrangement.[58] This sort of thing has been normal practice and has come to be expected by western negotiators.

The stoutness with which the So-

[52] Henry A. Kissinger, "Reflections on American Diplomacy," *Foreign Affairs,* 1956, p. 46.

[53] Philip E. Mosely, "Some Soviet Techniques of Negotiation," in *Negotiating with the Russians,* edited by Raymond Dennett and Joseph E. Johnson (New York, 1951), p. 274.

[54] Selwyn Lloyd, describing Gromyko's tactics during the London talks of July 1959. *New York Times,* July 22, 1959.

[55] *The Practice of Diplomacy,* pp. 20–21.

[56] Writing of Molotov's behavior at the London meeting of the Foreign Ministers in 1947, Herbert L. Matthews said: "He is innately suspicious. He seeks for hidden meanings and tricks where there are none. He takes it for granted that his opponents are trying to trick him and put over something nefarious." *New York Times,* December 7, 1947.

[57] Nathan Leites, *A Study of Bolshevism* (Glencoe, Ill., 1953), pp. 55 ff.

[58] *British Documents,* 2nd series, VII, No. 20.

viets hold to their own proposals has become proverbial. "Anyone accustomed to dealing with M. Litvinov," Sir Esmond Ovey wrote from Moscow in December 1929, "will remember how he frequently appears to be on the point of agreeing to suggestions made to him, but in practice, when pressed for any definite statement, he invariably reverts to his original point of view."[59] Similar statements have been made in more recent times about the persistence of Molotov and Gromyko.[60] Nor has this inflexibility in negotiation been easily shaken by non-diplomatic means. It is true that, in the years 1940 and 1941, during the almost continual Soviet-German negotiations about the disposition of eastern Europe, the Soviet Union was forced repeatedly to yield to German gains, in face of *faits accomplis* backed by the threat of force.[61] But in the inter-war years and in the period since 1945, other cases of this are hard to find; and attempts to bring non-diplomatic pressure to bear on the Soviets, far from succeeding, have sometimes merely given them an opportunity to claim loudly and publicly that they were being threatened by imperialist Powers. When the British government sought in 1933 to intimate in private negotiations that they would break off economic relations unless the Soviets released British engineers who were accused of wrecking and espionage, the Soviet government replied with press releases claiming "gross external pressure" and persisted in their course.[62]

The granting of concessions in the hope of eliciting concessions in return has had no more effect in persuading Soviet negotiators to modify their positions. In the fruitless Anglo-French negotiations with the Soviet Union in the summer of 1939, the western governments repeatedly conceded points described by the Soviet negotiators as being of fundamental importance, hoping that this would facilitate agreement, only to discover, once they had done so, that new points were now of fundamental importance to the Russians, whose intransigence was in no wise diminished. This led Lord Halifax to question the genuineness of the Russian desire for a treaty and to complain to the Soviet Ambassador that "the Soviet Government had not budged a single inch, and we had made all the advances and concessions. Saying 'No' to everything was not my idea of negotiation."[63] In the years since 1939 other diplomats have learned, as the British did then, that yielding points, or even changing one's original position for reasons other than the presentation of new evidence, merely encourages the Soviets to hold fast.[64]

Soviet inflexibility is generally combined with the skilful use of tactics designed to wear out the patience or weaken the judgment of their adversaries. Among these tactics is the use of bad manners, not out of personal or ideological vanity, which was responsible for the discourtesies of Ribbentrop and Ciano, but with the calculated intention of disconcerting their partners in negotiation, throwing them off balance, and thus betraying them into ill-advised decisions. It was a convention of the old diplomacy that one

---

59 *British Documents,* 2nd series, VII, No. 43.

60 See Sidney Gruson's remarks on Gromyko's negotiating style, in *New York Times,* July 26, 1959.

61 See *The Initial Triumph of the Axis,* pp. 319 ff., 364 ff.

62 *British Documents,* 2nd series, VII, No. 306.

63 *Ibid.,* 3rd series, VI, No. 135; *The Eve of the War 1939,* p. 454.

64 John N. Hazard in *Negotiating with the Russians,* p. 46.

pretended not to notice the artifices employed by one's adversary and accepted the verbal formulas with which he covered them.[65] The Soviets have no patience with this kind of tolerance. "I may be mistaken," said Sir Anthony Eden at the Moscow conference of Foreign Ministers in 1943, "but . . ." "You *are* mistaken," Molotov interrupted harshly, breaking the thread of Eden's argument and destroying its effect.[66] By this kind of crude attack upon the rules of elementary courtesy and by false accusations, name-calling and the imputation of the worst possible motives to their adversaries, Soviet negotiators have been able on occasion to obscure the real issues at stake, to divert the course of discussion to subsidiary points, and even to bully a conference into accepting their point of view. Deliberate assault upon the values and forms of the old diplomacy is a means by which the Soviets seek to impose their views and their standards on the rest of the world, and they have not been entirely unsuccessful.[67]

The most successful Soviet tactic is their use of time. Kurt Schumacher once said to an American diplomat, "The day you Americans are as patient as the Russians, you will stop losing the cold war."[68] American negotiators, and western diplomats in general, have found it difficult to learn this lesson and have sometimes, in their anxiety for a happy conclusion to talks, seized upon illusory concessions or grasped at dangerous "agreements in principle" in order to be able to claim a success.[69] This weakness is something the Soviets are constantly watching for; and, because they are free from parliamentary or public pressure, they are usually able to hold their ground calmly, while insinuating into the foreign press charges that their adversaries are needlessly protracting negotiations. Since they have often been dealing with democratic countries in which there are parties or pressure groups sympathetic to the Soviet Union, these tactics have frequently been effective.

The practice of prolonging negotiations for months and even years, coupled as it sometimes is with a shifting of the centre of negotiation from the ambassadorial to the ministerial level and from there to the levels of heads of state, often has the effect of blurring the outlines of the issues at stake and making less precise the original points of difference. The Soviets make the most of this by issuing press communiqués which are designed to confuse the general public and which often impute to their opponents views that weaken their position while strengthening the Soviet case. This kind of tactics was used with effect in the repeated and protracted negotiations in the 1920s over the question of the Russian debts and enabled the Soviet Union to avoid payment without penalty. A more recent example of their use was afforded when, at the end of his visit to the United States in 1959 and his talks with the President about

[65] See François Walder, *Saint-Germain ou la negoçiation* (Paris, 1958), p. 110.

[66] Philip E. Mosely in *Negotiating with the Russians*, pp. 283 ff.

[67] See Lord Strang, *Home and Abroad* (London, 1956), p. 206.

[68] Charles W. Thayer, *Diplomat* (New York, 1959), p. 96.

[69] A good example is afforded by the attitude of the Labour Party during the Anglo-Soviet trade negotiations in 1924, when they were so eager for agreement that they forced the Foreign Office to accept an unworkable formula. See Philip Viscount Snowden, *An Autobiography* (London, 1934), II, 680–6. See also remarks of John Foster Dulles before the National Press Club in January 1958. *Department of State Bulletin*, February 3, 1958.

the Berlin problem, Premier Khrushchev informed the press that he was satisfied that the President recognized that the existing situation in Berlin was "abnormal."[70] The President may indeed have used this term, for the Western Powers have never denied the abnormality of the Berlin situation, while attributing it to the failure to unite Germany. He did not, however, mean to suggest that this abnormality could be corrected by withdrawing Western troops from the city or altering its status to the advantage of the East German regime, although this was what Khrushchev implied. But so many talks had been held on the subject since the original Berlin note, and in so many different places and with so much publicity, that it was not easy for newspapermen to detect the distortion immediately; and, once it had been printed, it could be cited, and has since been cited, as a significant American admission of the fundamental weakness of the western position in Berlin. One of the main tasks of those engaged in negotiations with the Soviet Union consists in keeping the record straight, so that it can be revealed to the public at any time without tactical disadvantage to them,[71] and so that their position will not be eroded by unwitting concessions imposed on them by imputation.

These techniques of negotiation helped protect the Soviet Union in its most vulnerable years, defended its interests in the period before the outbreak of the Second World War, and won from its Allies more than adequate compensation for the losses it suffered in that war. But these have not been the only effective weapons in the Soviet diplomatic armoury; and, in a more thorough analysis of Soviet negotiating behaviour, attention would have to be paid to other methods that have helped consolidate the war-time gains and now threaten to expand them. These would include the new methods of economic diplomacy, which have been used with undeniable success by Soviet negotiators of agreements for technical assistance and aid to underdeveloped countries,[72] and the various techniques of public negotiation, with particular reference to their use in the United Nations.[73] Even in a brief account it can be noted that the Soviet Union has effectively emulated Hitler's use of the public statement as a means of negotiation and has employed the exchange of letters between heads of state for the same purpose. Indeed, it might almost be said that by these means the Soviet Union has been able to be a party to negotiations to which she has not been invited, for, by timely use of threats against NATO members,[74] of proposals for disengagement of Soviet and Allied troops from central Europe,[75] or of invitations to summit conferences,[76] she has forced the periodic meetings of the NATO Council to discuss *her* views, *her* policies, *her* proposals rather than their own, and to spend time and energy combating the divisiveness promoted within the alliance by her tactics.

---

[70] Max Frankel in *New York Times*, September 30, 1959.

[71] On this, see Thayer, *op. cit.*, p. 98.

[72] Klaus Knorr, "Ruble Diplomacy," *Memoranda of the Center of International Studies* (Princeton, 1956).

[73] See Kertesz in *Review of Politics*, 1959, p. 376.

[74] Editorial, "Soviet Atomic Diplomacy," *New York Times*, March 28, 1957; editorial, "Soviet Campaign," *ibid.*, December 13, 1958.

[75] See Gordon A. Craig, "Germany and NATO," in *NATO and American Security*, edited by Klaus Knorr (Princeton, 1959), pp. 254 ff.

[76] *Department of State Bulletin*, June 2, 1958, pp. 906 ff.

IV

Some years ago, when Sir Harold Nicolson delivered his Chichele Lectures on the evolution of diplomatic method, he said: "I have not observed that . . . the Soviet diplomatists and commissars have evolved any system of negotiation that might be called a diplomatic system. Their activity in foreign countries or at international conferences is formidable, disturbing, compulsive. I do not for one moment underestimate its potency or its danger. But it is not diplomacy: it is something else."[77]

There are doubtless many who would agree with Nicolson in lamenting the decline of the older diplomacy and in refusing to consider the Soviet Union's way of conducting international relations as diplomacy at all;[78] but the question of nomenclature need not be debated here. What is clear is that the Soviet approach to negotiation has been less impulsive, more systematic and more effective in its results than that of either Italian Fascism or German National Socialism. In an age when war is no longer acceptable as a continuation of policy by other means, and when the importance of reaching settlements short of war is undeniable, the Soviet methods of negotiation would appear to deserve as much study by western diplomats as their own diplomatic tradition has received from their professional colleagues within the Soviet Union.

[77] Harold Nicolson, *The Evolution of Diplomatic Method* (London, 1954), p. 90.

[78] "Diplomacy could flourish only so long as there was a loose, tacit and general agreement to behave *more or less* like gentlemen." Vansittart in *Foreign Affairs,* 1950, p. 185. It is interesting to note that Adolf Hitler, at least before he came to power, felt a fundamental incompatibility between Soviet and Western diplomacy. In 1932 he wrote: "I look upon . . . Soviet diplomacy not only as being unreliable but, above all, as being incapable of being considered of the same nature as the foreign political activity of other nations, and, in consequence, as being something with which one cannot negotiate or conclude treaties." Thilo Vogelsang, ed., "Hitlers Brief an Reichenau vom 4. Dezember 1932," *Vierteljahrshefte für Zeitgeschichte,* 1959, p. 434.

3

*Democratic Approaches to Diplomacy**

William C. Olson

As the range of alternatives open to a democracy narrows with its awareness of great peril, the competence of the ordinary citizen in the making of great decisions tends to come more and more into question. At the same time, as the Cold War settles down to a war of ideology in which the concept of the sovereignty of the people finds itself pitted against the concept of an elite vanguard of the proletariat, the necessity for nurturing viable democratic institutions of survival becomes ever more apparent. Noted con-

* Excerpts from "The Public Ingredient in Statecraft," *World Politics,* X (1958), 318–326. Reprinted by permission.

tributors to the subject of open discussion of foreign affairs have recently advanced some of their most telling arguments on this question of the role of the people in foreign affairs.

The very familiarity of Lippmann's [views] renders unnecessary any but a brief recapitulation of his thesis with reference to foreign policy. The malady of the democracies is the devitalization of the governing power caused by the unwarranted intrusion of the public into the policy-making processes of the great powers of the West. Because its opinion about events moves more slowly than the events themselves, the public is invariably concerned (when it is concerned at all) about situations which no longer exist. Emotional involvement further complicates matters, negatively through the propensity of leaders to portray wicked national enemies as deserving of passionate hatred, positively by the penchant for utopian dreams of a new Golden Age after the current war to end wars makes the world safe for democracy. Drugged by propaganda, the public never learns from experience, so that the deadly cycle of unreadiness—frantic preparation—demobilization goes on and on. Intimidated and insecure, politicians advance "only as they placate, appease, bribe, seduce, bamboozle, or otherwise manage to manipulate the demanding and threatening elements in their constituencies." Their decisions rest upon what is popular, not what is good or right. Combined pressures of unknowing mass opinions and of "boss-ridden oligarchies" (Lippmannese for representative assemblies) enfeeble the executive leadership of most democratic states, which have fallen victim to an internal revolution reversing the proper relationship of the rulers and the ruled. Democratic foreign policy fails *because* it is democratic.

[Sir Harold] Nicolson also regrets the passing of the *ancien régime*, particularly the "old diplomacy" in which he himself was schooled, and the emergence of what he terms the "Wilsonian" or the "American" method of diplomacy. This unfortunate transformation came about through the internalization of foreign policy, "the belief that it was possible to apply to the conduct of *external* affairs, the ideas and practices which, in the conduct of *internal* affairs, had for generations been regarded as the essentials of liberal democracy." By the end of World War I, the now-dominant Americans added their distrust of diplomacy (especially of the secret variety) and their missionary zeal for egalitarianism to the prevailing sentiment against war. The idealistic and "dangerous" Wilson preached that covenants should not only be open, but be openly arrived at, and that diplomacy should be conducted in full view of the public. This, perhaps the "most confusing of all the fallacies that we owe to President Wilson," continues to corrode the international effectiveness of the Western powers. At Paris he may quickly have perceived that negotiation and policy were two different things, but the public never has grasped the distinction. Furthermore, the stability characteristic of the old diplomacy has given way to "utmost instability." In televised negotiation, rational discussion is suspended in favor of endless propaganda harangues addressed not to the other delegates but to the public back home. Assailing the view that the people are always right and that their misfortunes are due to professionals, the British writer revises Lincoln's phrase to read, "although it may be difficult to fool all the people all the time, it is easy to fool them for a sufficient period of time to compass their destruction." Here Nicolson comes very close to Lippmann's conviction that the public intrusion into foreign affairs has brought on "something which can be called an historic catastrophe."

George Kennan, . . . former Director of the Policy Planning Staff of the State Department, asserted in 1951 that much of our "trouble" stems from the degree to which executive leadership in Washington feels itself beholden to short-term tides of popular judgment. Public opinion (or what passes for it in official circles) "can be easily led astray into areas of emotionalism and subjectivity which make it a poor and inadequate guide for national action."[1] Later, he candidly argued in favor of a freer hand for "the ruling group,"[2] stating that America "must take a tighter control of its own life and evolve a greater sense of purpose with regard to the shaping of its own development."[3]

Turning more directly to foreign affairs, Kennan notes how many dislike the fact that governments, not peoples, engage in foreign affairs, and yearn for more direct people-to-people relations, unmarred by meddling interference from government. Because of the inevitable association of power with responsibility, Kennan argues that only governments can speak responsibly in foreign affairs. Yet, because a government represents the dominant political faction as well as the nation as a whole, its pronouncements and programs abroad reflect not only the nation but competing political forces within it. To follow a constructive course in international relations often runs counter to the dictates of the internal political struggle. The more democratic a country is, the more this tends to be so. A regime which is "strong and authoritative" (Kennan does not say "authoritarian") may more easily undertake an intelligent course than one caught in the throes of domestic politics.[4]

Despite certain differences in emphasis (e.g., Nicolson devotes a great deal of attention to historical aspects of diplomacy), there is no mistaking the essential oneness in the viewpoint of these critics of public interference in statecraft. The criticism has aroused Henry Wriston to a vigorous defense of what he proudly calls "democratic diplomacy." Where Lippmann "brooded upon the events" which have precipitated the decline of the West, Wriston praises the "adaptability, resourcefulness, imagination, and skill that made it possible for a people civilian in thought and habit to mobilize their energies to win victories in two successive wars over nations steeped in militarism." Public opinion, far from being the source of a disastrous collapse of Western civilization, lies at the very foundation of a successful American system. Scholars, professionals, and "tired commentators" who propose schemes for the elimination of politics in diplomacy in favor of their own particular brand of *expertise* overlook the facts of life; "it is absurd to find men arguing for such a utopian program while pretending to deal realistically with world problems." The professional diplomat, like the professional soldier, must subordinate his will to that of the people. As Wriston sees its function, public opinion "is not expected to deal in nuances, in procedures, in techniques. Actually it

---

[1] *American Diplomacy, 1900–1950,* Chicago, 1951, p. 93; reviewed by Grayson Kirk in *World Politics,* V, No. 1 (October, 1952), 110–115.

[2] *Realities of American Foreign Policy,* Princeton, 1954, p. 44; reviewed by William G. Carleton in *World Politics,* VII, No. 4. (July, 1955), 627–639.

[3] *Realities of American Foreign Policy,* p. 110.

[4] *Ibid.,* p. 44.

needs only to respond to situations in clear and simple terms. For example, public opinion must decide that the United States is to go it alone or have a 'career in the world'; it must determine to let the devil take the hindmost or temper competition with cooperation; it must agree or refuse to pay the bill for deterrent armaments; it must weary of the stridency of the chauvinist, the exploiter of issues—and show its disapproval; . . . it must bring the moral simplicity of the golden rule to bear upon international issues."

II

Morality, in one form or another, plays an important role in each of these interpretations. In a phrase that has often been quoted, Kennan characterized the most serious fault in past policy formulation as being the legalistic-moralistic approach to international problems, involving "the carrying-over into the affairs of states of the concepts of right and wrong, the assumption that state behavior is a fit subject for moral judgment."[5] Explicitly rejecting this criticism, Wriston cites as both genuine and significant the "profound moral commitment" of the Marshall Plan, the winning of the Battle of Britain "by heart, by courage, by faith," the "soul force" of Gandhi which defeated every other kind of power, and the "faith in the reality and vitality of spiritual forces" exemplified by Eisenhower at Geneva. Kennan denies that he ever meant to suggest that the United States neglect certain fundamental moral concepts characterizing the very spirit of our way of life in promulgating its foreign policy, but does oppose the assumption that our particular set of moral values, growing out of our own traditions and religious groupings, are necessarily valid for people everywhere.[6] Nor would such an assumption be made by Wriston, who asks that policy be based upon moral considerations as well as the more tangible factors of power, arguing that the "human spirit cannot be entered upon a balance sheet, nor weighed, nor measured, nor counted." He is highly critical of analysts of foreign affairs who, in listing factors of national power, appear to neglect the moral element. Unlike the other authors, Wriston identifies morality with public opinion: "Democracy itself finds its roots in the equality of men, which is explicable upon no basis except religious grounds. Public opinion provides the strongest foundation for diplomacy when spiritual strength is given its rightful position of priority among all the factors that shape policy." Contrast this with Sir Harold, who is weary of the "egalitarian illusions" of Americans. To the venerable British diplomatist there is a moral element involved, but it lies more subtly in a belief that "Americans possess more virtue than any giant Power has yet possessed." In an earlier book on diplomacy, Nicolson argued that it "is not a system of moral philosophy. . . . The worst kind of diplomatists are missionaries, fanatics and lawyers. . . . Thus it is not religion which has been the main formative influence in diplomatic theory; it is common sense."[7] Lippmann, in using the moral argument *against* democracy in the conduct of foreign affairs and associating virtue only with an elite imbued with the "public philosophy," finds in contemporary public influence on foreign policy the very antithesis of morality in politics.

This is the heart of the matter. One's moral philosophy applies to is-

[5] *American Diplomacy, 1900–1950,* p. 100.

[6] *Realities of American Foreign Policy,* p. 47.

[7] *Diplomacy* (London, 1939), p. 50.

sues involving the governing of men by men. Diplomacy may not itself be a system of moral philosophy, but the goals and objectives of diplomacy necessarily reflect the moral predispositions and judgments of the nation and its political leaders. Democracy is a normative concept. Either people have a right to govern themselves, taking the consequences of their decisions, or they do not, in which case a paternalistic elite could better perceive and pursue the national interest. Few national problems fail to derive, in some way, from international relations; to eliminate foreign policy from the area of legitimate concern of the people is to eliminate the democratic principle itself. If the guiding ideal is to be government *by* the people, then foreign policy must be their concern; if it is to be merely government *for* the people, then the executive should be supreme, in diplomacy as in other aspects of statecraft. But in the latter case, the elitists would have to make a case for efficiency as well as for morality, for the elite systems of this century have hardly distinguished themselves by their finesse and permanence in foreign affairs, to say nothing of their moral rectitude. As Churchill is said to have observed, democracy is the worst form of government ever devised, except for every other form.

Despite philosophical differences, the authors reach essentially the same conclusion on one point: the necessity for the enhancement of professional diplomacy if the United States is to maintain (in Wriston's view) or to regain (in Lippmann's) its leadership of the West and the world. Nicolson venerates the old French method of diplomacy which, as it was developed by Richelieu and Callières, combined a centralized authority for policy formulation with a professional service for its implementation. Dignified, gradual, sensitive to the realities of power, it attached importance to experience and knowledge, but did not assign any role or responsibility to the people. Kennan, though apparently resigned to some degree of amateurism in American foreign affairs, nevertheless pleads for the "principle of professionalism" in order to produce a corps of officers of unparalleled quality. By deploring the eclipse of executive power which has undermined the authority of leaders to speak and act for the nation, Lippmann clearly indicates the necessity for a return to executive leadership and responsibility, which obviously implies more professionalism and responsibility in the handling of foreign affairs. By devoting one half of his book to the professional diplomat, Wriston confirms the trend, exemplified in his own special assignment in 1954 as chairman of the Public Committee on Personnel for the State Department, toward establishing professional diplomacy as a permanent feature of the American process.

III

None of the authors deals with one crucial aspect of this concept of professionalism in a democracy. Does not this concept encompass sensitivity to, and systematic analysis of, public opinion in both the country to which the diplomat is accredited and, perhaps even more importantly, the country which he represents? One of the alleged abuses of American diplomatic practice which led to the "Wristonization" of the Foreign Service was a tendency of officers long away from home to represent the outside world to America more than the other way around. Now, to the discomfiture of some of them, FSO's are required to serve terms at Washington desks, the better, presumably, to sense the changing moods and patterns of American life and the better, presumably, to represent their homeland when they once again take assignments in the field. Yet, if the process is nothing more than one of political and sociological osmosis, whereby the specialist is supposed somehow to "sense" the political milieu of his own country, it is scarcely likely to produce the kind of result envisioned by those who brought him home. Public opinion analysis, though hardly yet a science, has advanced far enough to provide something better than that.

If part of the diplomat's initial training and continuing responsibility were to include careful attention to the stresses and the harmonies among the many different strands that make up the fabric of public opinion, he would be better able to interpret his country to foreigners and to analyze the directions into which public pressures may be forcing the policies of the government he represents. Very little is accomplished simply by deploring the fact of democratic control, for it is a fact. Rather, a useful and essential task, along with raising the level of public understanding of foreign affairs, is heightening the degree of comprehension of the public mind on the part of the professional. This should be part of the meaning of professionalism in democratic diplomacy. Even if the professional is to be given more leeway, as Kennan and Nicolson advocate, he must know the range and limitations of his support, so that "leeway" or "freedom of action" are not taken to be a kind of exclusive authority appropriate only to an aristocracy. And, as C. J. Friedrich has pointed out with reference to Sir Eyre Crowe's disparagement of its role in diplomacy, public opinion has long had an influence on policy, whether the professional diplomatist has been willing to admit it or not.[8]

Analysis of national opinion abroad, or at least relevant segments of it, has for some time been an accepted responsibility of legations and embassies, and was a well-used technique in HICOG. Much less attention seems to have been paid to the analysis of opinion at home.[9] Does the evidence, unfortunately all too abundant, that the American people are emotional, shortsighted, and subject to manipulation by irresponsible politicians merely serve to confirm existing elitist predispositions among some diplomats, who soberly believe that only men like themselves are capable of comprehending and serving the national interest? Yet Kennan himself, while rejecting as unreliable the short-term judgments of the public, seems to concede that in the long run the public judgment is sound.[10] It is difficult to see just how an analytically valid distinction can be made in these terms, since the polls have largely been confined to essentially short-run situations. To be sure, the public may be characterized as possessing certain rather basic predispositions toward the

[8] C. J. Friedrich, *Constitutional Government and Democracy* (Boston, 1946), pp. 589–590.

[9] During the foreign aid hearings in the spring of 1957, it was revealed that the Secretary of State's confidential emergency funds had been used to take a sample of public opinion purporting to reveal overwhelming support for continued foreign aid. The House Government Operations Committee later issued a statement reporting that, since 1943, the Department of State had "illegally" spent more than one-half million dollars on polls on various foreign-policy issues, and severely criticized the Bureau of the Budget for failing to prevent this practice. *House Report 1166*, August 14, 1957; *Congressional Quarterly*, **XV**, No. 33 (week ending August 16, 1957), 976.

[10] *American Diplomacy, 1900–1950*, p. 93.

outside world and, at the same time, as developing new attitudes with reference to immediate issues, such as the Girard case. The combination of these, as they impinge upon one another, make up the national will. Only by developing sensitivity to the several kinds of manifestation of public opinion can the diplomat (or anyone else, for that matter) know the range of public acceptance within which foreign policy must operate. And if he either misunderstands or rejects the very nature of democratic society, a nation which cherishes democratic values and procedures can ill afford to entrust its representation to him.

From this it follows that to the degree to which the diplomat is called upon to heed public opinion, the national interest dictates that the level of public sophistication be continually elevated. No doubt this carries with it the danger of a kind of "hidden persuasion" by the social engineer skilled at manipulating the mass mind for his own purposes. Yet it can also be the kind of adult education represented by world affairs study and discussion groups like those encouraged by the Foreign Policy Association, for example, which are increasingly active from one end of the country to the other. In resting his case Wriston cites, as the key to the improvement of American foreign policy, public enlightenment through voluntary associations, pressure groups, the now world-conscious daily press, and through what de Tocqueville long ago observed as the American tendency to treat every conversation as a town meeting.[11]

There is still another dimension which must be developed if democratic diplomacy is to be cultivated. This involves public acceptance of the legitimate role, the intelligence, the loyalty, and the integrity of the professional. In this respect we may be better off now than we were several years ago, at a time when Lippmann, writing his book, could observe the clever nurturing of public distrust of the diplomat for purposes of political advantage. To respect the professional's sphere of competence is quite a different matter from turning the affairs of state over to him completely, giving him an unfettered hand to control the national destiny. If the diplomat continues to be the whipping boy of American politics he can neither respect nor represent the American people. They have an obligation to him, just as he has his obligation to them.

IV

Taken together, these divergent commentators on the crisis in Western diplomacy provide a welcome antidote for those zealots who, caught up in the ebullience of the Cold War, would either endanger America to save democracy or sacrifice democracy to save America. The value of the public philosophy as expressed by Walter Lippmann lies in its reminder that the privilege of democracy can be ruinous unless tempered by responsibility. The value of democratic diplomacy as elaborated by Henry Wriston lies in its promise that, in the ideological struggle in which the West is locked, the noble concept that government by the people shall not perish from the earth may yet prevail. Thus, in a deeper sense, both schools of thought are "right" as analyses of a critical problem in foreign policy. The solution of the problem lies not in the creation of a superdiplomat, or even a super-Secretary of State who carries the foreign policy of the country under

[11] Wriston's more recent article, "Education and the National Interest," *Foreign Affairs*, **XXXV**, No. 4 (July 1957), 564–580.

his homburg, where it is unresponsive to the political process. It lies rather in the continual development of a more enlightened and more sensitive public, and an educational system capable of producing both responsible laymen with a basic understanding of international relations and also highly trained and highly motivated specialists capable of practicing the difficult art of democratic diplomacy.

CHAPTER THIRTEEN

Psychological Methods in Policy Implementation

With the diminishing usefulness of methods of outright physical coercion, countries have turned to other means of trying to achieve their goals in international relations. One of these alternatives involves the employment of psychological methods.

The term "psychological methods" refers to a variety of activities. Perhaps, as Davison suggests below, the term "political communication" would be more appropriate. The first of the activities involved is propaganda, defined as the manipulation of facts and symbols to attain desired results in the minds of an audience. The dividing line between propaganda and psychological warfare is shadowy, although the element of hostility is more marked in the latter than the former. Still another related method is that of subversion. While subversion may take overt physical forms, its relevance to the present discussion is that it represents an attempt to enlist individuals and groups within some countries to work for the advantage and interests of other countries.

Psychological methods are directed both toward domestic and foreign targets, and are designed to serve two purposes. Domestically, governments use propaganda to rally the people of a country in support of government policies, because policies will be more effective internationally if it is known by others that they have the support of important publics at home. For example, Woodrow Wilson's position at the Paris Peace Conference was weakened by the results of the Congressional elections of 1918 and the clear indications from opposing Senators that they would not support the results of the negotiations in which he was engaged.

Internationally, such policies are designed to achieve certain results in other states. These desired consequences may be of two types: in cases where another government is hostile to the purposes of the government employing the psychological methods, such methods are designed to create internal opposition and dissension, thus weakening the support which those policies enjoy domestically. Similarly, psychological methods may be used to encourage and promote policies which are advantageous to the state that utilizes and applies these methods. For example, it is not at all unusual for one government to help cement the prestige and reputation of a friendly government in another country, through such means as appropriately-timed state visits, declarations, and popular policy-moves. As is obvious from this discussion, the use of psychological methods is both defensive and affirmative. A given government will use them not only to create positive support for its policies, but also to ward off the negative effects that the use of similar policies by other states might have in the absence of countervailing efforts.

The use of psychological methods is not an entirely new development in international relations. Bismarck, for example, used the press in order to bring about a certain state of affairs between Prussia and France. During the First World War, stories of atrocities, reports of starvation due to blockade, and even President Wilson's Fourteen Points were designed, in whole or in part, to bring about changes in the opinion of important publics and therefore in the policies of important countries. The Second World War saw an extension and refinement of such methods, and in the contemporary period of chronic tension its use has proliferated.

Yet there are certain new and arresting developments in this field. One student of the subject has suggested that the real innovation may be "the frank recognition of propaganda as a regular branch of government alongside economic and military departments."[1] Among the new elements is first of all the availability of new and vastly improved means of communication, permitting a far greater scope for the application of psychological methods. Secondly, inquiries by psychologists have yielded more—and more reliable—information about how men's minds can be influenced (though, as the selections in the present chapter will show, it is not clear that governments and other agencies involved in the application of psychological methods always act on the basis of the new findings). Finally, the conduct of foreign relations in many countries has become democratized, in the sense that larger publics are involved. They may not participate actively in the decision-making process, but they are increasingly influential in setting general directions and limits within which policy-makers must operate. This being the case, it has become more profitable to attempt to influence the beliefs and actions of larger groups across national boundaries.

The key question to be asked of any operation, of course, is that of effectiveness. Whether a given method is effective or not depends on a number of things. It depends on the validity of the assumptions which underlie its use. In this connection, the article by Davison is most valuable and instructive, because the author not only outlines the false assumptions on which much of political communication has been based, but also presents some important findings from recent social science research that indicate more appropriate policies in terms of content and audience. These are necessary and useful cautions against the

[1] John B. Whitton, "Propaganda in Cold Wars," *Public Opinion Quarterly*, XV (1951), 142–144.

indiscriminate use of propaganda, or too great reliance on it.[2] Additionally, it may be argued that democratic societies find themselves at a disadvantage in psychological contests with non-democratic adversaries. For one thing, they lack the clearly defined ideological base. One of the main ingredients of liberal democracy is the willingness to tolerate, in fact to encourage, diversity of belief. In addition, the report of a special committee appointed by President Eisenhower early in his term is instructive. That committee argued that the pursuit of effective psychological warfare was based on certain preconditions, including fanaticism, utmost flexibility and maneuverability, and a great deal of money. Included also was the willingness to proceed "with no holds barred and no questions asked." An inspection of this list will reveal that autocratic regimes are more likely to satisfy all of these requirements, with the possible exception of money, then are democracies. Furthermore, there are no democratic equivalents to the disciplined Communist parties found in most countries of the world.[3]

To use psychological methods in international relations is essentially to engage in an exercise in communications. The crucial ingredients in this process can be summarized in the following questions:

1. *Who* does the communicating? Is it best for cross-national communications to be performed by governments or by private agencies? In the same context, the question arises: who controls the in-flow of communication into a given country and the circulation of information within the country? Who, to use a phrase employed by students of the communications process, are the "gatekeepers," and how do they behave?

2. *What* is to be communicated? Here, of course, the clear rule is that the content of communication must depend on a large number of factors in the total process. Most notably, it must depend on the audience to which the communication is to be directed.

3. *To whom* is the communication addressed? Is it geared to mass audiences or to specific audiences, at home or in other countries. If the object is to influence specific publics, how are they to be singled out? What are the relevant characteristics of the audiences, and how can the message be most appropriately geared to appeal to them? Should the major efforts be directed to audiences in countries which are hostile to one's purposes, countries which are friendly, or countries which do not fall into either of these categories?

4. *What media* are to be employed in communicating the message. The answer to this question depends, in part, on the content and the audience of a message.

5. What are the *results* which a given act of communication achieves? One must assess these results both in terms of the intended and the unintended con-

[2] *E.g.*, Ralph K. White, in "The New Resistance to International Propaganda," *Public Opinion Quarterly*, **XVI** (1952), 539–551.

[3] Arthur Krock, "Why We Are Losing the Psychological War," *New York Times Magazine*, August 8, 1957, pp. 12 ff.

sequences. On the basis of this kind of assessment, future strategies must be evolved.

Psychological methods, by themselves, are unlikely to replace other methods of projecting policy in international relations. The political-diplomatic instrument, the use of economic means, and even the employment—actual or potential—of force will always play a significant role in international relations. Psychological approaches can facilitate or hinder the achievement of results, but they cannot substitute for other ways of attempting to gain one's ends. It is perhaps best to speak of psychological methods as supplementary to other policies rather than as substitutes for them. They can help attain given ends if their employment is skillfully combined with the use of other methods of policy referred to elsewhere.

1

*National Power and International Responsiveness**

Dean G. Pruitt

DEAN G. PRUITT *is Assistant Professor of Psychology and Assistant Research Professor at the Center for Research on Social Behavior at the University of Delaware. His studies on human decision making and articles on international relations theory from a social psychologist's viewpoint have appeared in numerous scholarly journals.*

Recent years have witnessed a great ferment in the field of political science over the need for more theory in international relations. Almost everyone seems to recognize that there is such a need but few people seem to be successful in filling it. The result is a tradition of inspirational writing which Chadwick Alger has called the "Toward Literature": "Toward greater order in the study of international politics," "Toward an equilibrium theory of international relations and institutions," "Decision making as an approach to the study of international politics." The present paper, which is an addition to this Toward Literature, might be subtitled "Toward a reexamination of the concept of national power from the viewpoint of a social psychologist."

It may seem inappropriate for a student of psychology to be writing a paper on the theory of international relations. The General Assembly may look a bit too big to be crammed into a light-proof isolation booth; De Gaulle, a bit too busy to answer a questionnaire on the authoritarian personality. The odor of cocktails and the odor of albino rats may seem more distinct than alike. Yet there is a basic similarity between the two fields: *both are concerned with the behavior of organisms.* And because of this similarity, I believe that the approaches and prin-

* *Background,* **VII** (1964), 165–178.

ciples developed in each field are potentially useful to the other.

Having said this, I must hasten to add that here is a danger of generalizing too freely from any field of knowledge to another. At one time many psychologists believed that wars are primarily the displaced expression of those unconscious wishes to murder one's friends and relatives which arise from the frustrations of everyday life. Such an approach is naive because it ignores the role of government and the role of rational thinking in international affairs. The lesson provided by this example is that the specialist in one field must learn something about the other field before he can contribute to it. (Just how much he must learn remains an open question.) Knowing something of the other field, he can then sometimes draw on his own distinctive viewpoint to find and fill gaps in the other field.

THE CONCEPT OF NATIONAL POWER

1. Usage of the term

Writers of textbooks on international relations differ in their definitions of "national power." Yet there seems to be a common core of meaning, perhaps best expressed as "the ability to influence the behavior of another nation in accordance with the goals of one's own nation." Having defined power, most textbooks turn to a discussion of the determinants of power, which usually turns out to be a list of those possessions or *resources* of a nation which contribute to its ability to influence other nations or resist influence; for example, geographical position, possession of raw materials, size of population, per capita income, level of industrialization, governmental stability and efficiency, strength of the military establishment, national morale, strength of allied nations.

Finally, in most textbooks, there are several chapters on the impact of national power on international politics. Two rather different kinds of models are used in these chapters on impact. I call them Type I and Type II Models.

2. Type I models

Underlying models of the first type is an assumption that every nation has a single, characteristic *level* of power. One author, Organski (1958), has gone so far as to suggest a rough index for measuring this level, namely size of population multiplied by per capita income, i.e., national income. Though other theorists may differ with Organski about the value of his particular index, most textbook writers seem to imply that such an index can be constructed on the basis of some combination of the resources of nations which I have just enumerated.

If we have a rough idea of the level of power possessed by each nation, it is possible by addition to compute a rough index of the level of power possessed by an alliance of nations. This lays the groundwork for the much-discussed "Balance of Power" model which, in the clearest formulation I can find, namely that of Organski (1958), asserts something like the following: Every nation strives to maintain and increase its level of power, using among other tactics alliance with other nations. In an effort to maintain their own power, nations generally "ally themselves in such combinations that no nation or group of allies will be allowed to achieve a preponderance of power." The result is usually two or more loose blocs roughly equal to one another in level of power. This state of affairs is called a "balance of power." And as long as such a balance can be maintained, "the independence of small nations is safe and there will be world peace." Organski goes on to criticize the Balance of Power model and to propose his own "Power Transition" model. But the latter need not concern us here. Suffice it to say that both models use the notion of level of power to predict and explain the composition of international alliances and the outbreak of wars. Clearly these Type I models attempt to explain some lofty phenomena.

Assuming that every nation has a characteristic level of power, it is also possible to construct a hierarchy of nations ranging from the most to the least powerful. This helps predict the outcome of knock-down, drag-out conflicts. When two nations have a showdown over some issue, we predict that the one which is higher in the power hierarchy is more likely to win. The power hierarchy is also useful for predicting which nations will be consulted when big decisions are made on the international scene. A conference for settling the problems of the world which did not include the United States, Russia, England, and France would be a mockery. Again, a Type I model helps understand some very important issues.

Nevertheless, Type I models have definite limitations in their explanatory power. We can only go so far with the assumption that every nation has a single level of power. Beyond a certain point this concept falls flat on its face. In particular, the notion of a power hierarchy provides little if any insight into the influence which small nations often have over large ones.

In a book entitled "The Power of Small States," Annette Baker Fox (1959) describes such a case. On any scale of relative power Germany was more powerful than Turkey in 1941. Yet the Turks were able to extract from the Germans a number of important and costly concessions, including contributions to a Turkish war machine the only conceivable use for which was defense against Germany herself. In such cases, of course, the pattern of influence is usually *mutual*. During the same period, Turkey made a number of concessions to Germany, primarily pledging neutrality and the shipment of chrome.

We are dealing here with relatively minor issues: how many guns are sent to Turkey, how much chrome is shipped in return, whether a prisoner is returned from Israel to the United States, whether and when Castro nationalizes American factories. These are not the great issues which Type I models help explain . . . but they have some importance. And if we want to understand how *they* work we need concepts other than level of power and hierarchical order.

3. Type II models

When the notions of level of power hierarchy fail to explain things, the theorists seem to shift subtly into another framework in which *power differs from issue to issue.* On the issue of arms shipments, Turkey had power over Germany. On the issue of Turkish neutrality, Germany had power over Turkey.

This second conception of power is most often found in *explanations* of concrete events, such as relations between Turkey and Germany during the war. Occasionally one also finds isolated *generalizations* within this framework, and these are what I call "Type II models." They usually relate certain kinds of national resources to certain kinds of influence . . . e.g., the existence of natural barriers between a nation and its neighbors adds to that nation's power to defend itself from attack but detracts from its power to enforce its will on neighboring nations by means of arms. But there seems to be no systematic Type II theory relating specific kinds of resource to specific kinds of influence. Most authors simply give the reader a list of resources and some interesting examples of influence and tell him, "Here, you figure it out."

4. *Why Type II models are fragmentary*

How can the existence of these deficiencies be explained? Why has theorizing of the first type forged ahead while theorizing of the second type lagged behind? I believe that the answer lies primarily in the overriding emphasis which theorists have placed on the resources of nations as the basis of their power. Differences in resources are certainly the major source of influence in international affairs. Because of this, Type I models have been useful for understanding and predicting many of the major trends in international politics. But when we try to understand individual cases of influence such as the German shipments of arms to Turkey, we usually need more variables. Knowledge of resources is not enough. Yet that is all the theories provide.

Why have the theorists failed to go further? Such questions are always hard to answer. But I think the reason may lie primarily in the way we formulate the notion of power in words. The General Semanticists have suggested that words often determine our thoughts. And I think this may be the case here. I am thinking of the verbal formulation "X has power over Y" . . . "Russia has power over Czechoslovakia." According to the words we use, power is something a nation *has* . . . and this implies that we should look for it among a nation's possessions . . . that is, a nation's *resources.* Thus the formulation of power as something a nation "has" leads to a search for its origin among a nation's resources.

To overcome this mental set, I suggest that we need a thorough description of the process, i.e., the steps, through which one nation influences another. We need to follow the causal chain from action on one end to reaction on the other and become acquainted with the forces which impinge on every major link of this chain. When this is done we will know a great deal more about the variables which determine international influence and, *ipso facto,* the sources of power.

Among other things, this implies a careful study of what happens within a nation when it complies with the wishes of another nation . . . in other words a study of the process of *compliance,* and also a study of the process of *defiance.* Essentially I am agreeing here with Richard Snyder (Snyder, Bruck and Sapin, 1954) who urges a study of national decision making as a prelude to the discovery of general laws about national behavior on the international scene.

AN INTERVIEW STUDY IN THE DEPARTMENT OF STATE

I have been aided in my thinking about international compliance by an interview study I conducted in 1960 in one section of the State Department.[1] In this study, I interviewed 14 of the 16 members of what I call, to preserve anonymity, the "XYZ" Office, This is a branch of one of the geographical bureaus of the Department of State, which handles United States relations with a group of *friendly* nations. Each officer was asked to list the last four

[1] This study was conducted under the auspices of the Graduate Program of Training and Research in International Relations at Northwestern University.

problems on which he had been working. From this list I picked the two which were nearest to being completed and about which the informant seemed to have the most information, and then asked a standardized series of questions on each case lasting about half an hour. The questions dealt mainly with the *organization* of problem solving . . . who was contacted and for what reason. But in many cases, the answers also contained information on the content of the problems and related policies. My analysis consisted of a detailed comparison of the twenty-eight cases and a search for trends. Part of the results have already been published (Pruitt, 1962).

My most interesting findings concerned the role which the men in this office seem to have as "brokers" in the business of international influence. They seemed to have one foot in each camp. On the one hand they would devote much time to attempting to persuade representatives of other countries to agree to policies favorable to American interests. On the other hand, they also spent a lot of time trying to persuade the American government to accept policies favorable to the needs of other countries. The latter feature of their role took two forms. Sometimes a representative of a foreign government which comes under the jurisdiction of the XYZ Office would request some sort of action by the United States government. An XYZ officer would then bring the request to the attention of appropriate officers in other parts of the government and often, though not always, *urge agreement* to the request. At other times, an XYZ officer would learn that another agency was considering a policy which might affect a nation under the jurisdiction of his office. If he felt that the policy could antagonize the nation in question, he would *often urge that it not be adopted.* There was conscious recognition of the latter part of this role. As a matter of fact, one of the co-directors of the office made the following blunt statement to me: "One of the basic policies of the XYZ Office is to prevent other agencies from irritating too much the countries under our wing, as for instance to stop the Agriculture Department from undercutting a commodity market in ____________."

Naturally with such an orientation, the XYZ Office was often in conflict with other agencies which represented more purely national interests. Out of the twenty-five cases in which a question was asked about conflict, fourteen involved some sort of disagreement between XYZ officers and representatives of one or more other agencies. Of the eleven cases in which I learned something about the nature of the conflict, nine involved disagreements over the extent to which the government should make concessions to the other country . . . *with the XYZ Office always favoring more concessions.* Such conflicts were usually resolved in meetings of ad hoc interagency committees. Sometimes the opposing agencies won, but often the viewpoint of the XYZ Office prevailed.

But why should XYZ officers favor concessions to other countries? In the course of the interviews, a number of reasons were given. In general, these boiled down to a fear that the other nation would become less cooperative if concessions were not made to it. Various reasons were given for *needing* the future cooperation of other nations, for example, the presence of American military bases in another country. As one officer put it, "If the relations with (that nation) were to deteriorate, we might have to withdraw from our bases there." In another example, concessions to a nation were justified by the fact that many other negotiations were going on at the same time with that nation and might be prejudiced by a failure to make concessions in a given case. The likelihood that the other nation would stop cooperating also seemed important. In one case concessions were justified on the basis of the unstable political situation in a nation. The officers involved were almost certain that if concessions were not made, the public in that nation would elect a communist-oriented government which might eject American interests from the country.

IMPLICATIONS OF THE STATE DEPARTMENT DATA FOR A THEORY OF COMPLIANCE

I feel that these findings, fragmentary as they are, provide a partial basis for building a *theory of compliance* . . . that is, of the factors which cause one nation to comply with the wishes of another. The study suggests four types of variables that determine the degree of compliance.

1. Resources

The resources which nations possess certainly play a big part in determining their influence; but my study suggests the need to broaden our notion of resources. The possession of *anything which another nation needs or fears* is a potential source of influence over the other nation. Thus a nation's resources vis-à-vis the United States may include such peculiar things as the ability to give or withdraw the right to establish an American base on the nation's soil or the prospect of being able to say "no" to the United States in future negotiations where the United States is trying to get cooperation.

2. Needs

This brings us immediately to the subject of needs. The possession of a resource can only produce influence if the other nation has a complementary need. The capacity to say "no" to a military base is only a source of influence over the United States if the United States needs the base. If the Communist threat should diminish tomorrow, American need for bases would also diminish, and many of the world's nations would find that they have less influence over us. Or take the case of Turkey and Germany in the last war. Turkey had influence over Germany primarily because Germany desperately needed Turkish chrome. Had Turkey wanted to influence Liberia, the possession of chrome would have been substantially less valuable because of the small need for this mineral in the Liberian economy. Need must be part of a theory of compliance.

3. Credibility

For threats and promises to be effective in interpersonal relations, the person they are supposed to influence must believe that the reward promised or the punishment threatened is truly contingent on his willingness to cooperate. The more likely it seems to a child that he will be spanked if he misbehaves, and only if he misbehaves, the more cooperation we get from him. The more likely it seems that he will get a piece of candy if he behaves, and only if he behaves, the better will be his behavior. The term "credibility" refers to the extent to which the person to be influenced believes that rewards or punishments are contingent on his actions. Threats and promises are more or less "credible."

The same kind of consideration probably applies to international relations. A nation is more likely to comply with the wishes of another, the more credible the other's threats and promises. Evidence of this was found in my study. The officers I talked to did not mention having received *formal* threats or promises from other nations. But they *acted as if* such threats and promises, especially threats, were *implicit* in the relationships with other nations. The more credible these implicit threats, the more effort seemed to be made to please the nation in question. A case in point is the nation which always seemed on the brink of electing a communist government. The danger of such a move seemed imminent and believable. As a result, this nation, despite its small size, received large amounts of aid and other favors from the United States. A comparable nation was usually turned down when it asked for aid. The officer who handles relations with that nation told me that when they are turned down, they are "always understanding." Perhaps if that nation were less "understanding," it could mount a more credible threat of defection from the Western World and thereby command more aid.

4. *Good will*

If we look at the interviews in another light, it seems clear that the XYZ officers were attempting to elicit future cooperation from other nations by cooperating with these nations in the present. In other words they were trying to build or protect something in the other nation upon which to draw, as a resource, in the future. In some cases they were trying to develop favorable public opinion in the other country. At other times they seemed to be striving to prevent decision makers abroad from feeling the necessity to punish the United States. For want of a better term, I have called this "something" they were trying to build or protect "good will." It seems to have a place in a theory of compliance . . . the more good will toward another nation, the more compliance to the needs and wishes of that nation. I did not find any direct evidence that good will affects *American* compliance, but the eagerness with which it was sought by the XYZ officers suggests that they believe it to be an important source of compliance in other nations, and this leads me to suspect that it belongs in the model.

5. *The nature of compliance*

Four variables which seem to influence the extent of compliance have just been named, but little has been said about the nature of compliance, itself. The State Department Study revealed two facets of compliance: 1. doing things which another party asks you to do and 2. *not* doing things which are likely to antagonize the other party. Only the first of these facets involves an *influence attempt* from the other party . . . when we fail to antagonize another person or nation, he usually knows nothing about it. Accordingly, only the first facet of compliance can be said to involve "influence." Yet both facets seem to coexist: A nation which will do favors for another on request, will usually also try to avoid antagonizing the other nation. Hence, in this context, influence is only one aspect of a broader phenomenon "compliance" and should not be studied as a separate entity.

Proposals for a Theory of Compliance

I have argued so far that compliance is a unitary phenomenon and have mentioned four types of variables which affect it. But how can all of this be put together? I wish to sketch now the beginnings of a theory of compliance which I have been developing recently. I have based this work in part on what I am sure many will feel to be an overinterpretation of my State

Department data and in part on analyses of interpersonal relations. The resulting theoretical sketch is applicable to relations between actors *at any level:* international, intergroup or interpersonal.

1. Basic model

First of all a framework is needed, and I find the *psychological decision making framework* most compatible, with its assumption that people consider various alternative courses of action and choose the one which is most attractive. A similar framework is employed by Cartwright (1959) in his analysis of power.

Use of the decision making framework has important implications for the theory. It forces us to link the variables determining compliance not to the act of compliance itself but to the *evaluation of an alternative* which involves compliance. Whether that alternative is actually chosen depends both on its attractiveness *and on the attractiveness of the other alternatives which are under consideration.* This last point is critical, because whether a person or nation complies or not may be determined almost completely by the attractiveness of other alternatives.

An illustration from everyday life may help clarify this point. Suppose a girl is asked to go on a date by a man she finds mildly enjoyable. Her alternatives are to comply with his request or to stay at home. The alternative of compliance seems more attractive and she goes out with the boy. Now suppose that on a later weekend he asks her out again but this time she has a third alternative of visiting her sister and playing with her nephews. Though the alternative of going on the date may be just as attractive as before, she may find the visit to her sister even more attractive and decide to do that instead. To put it in other words, her tendency to comply remains the same as before; the boy has just as much influence over her. Yet now she does not comply because her tendency to do something else is stronger.

Parallel examples can be found in international affairs. A nation is less likely to comply with the wishes of another, the more attractive alternative courses of action seem to be. Compare, for example, American compliance with French wishes in the diplomatic isolation of Guinea and American defiance of French wishes during the invasion of Suez. The arguments for compliance may well have been just as strong in both cases, but the value of alternative courses of action differed considerably. Catering to Guinea did not seem particularly worth while at the time, so the alternative of compliance was chosen. On the other hand, in the Suez crisis, considerations of global peace made the alternative of intervening against the French extremely compelling to the President of the United States.

2. Evaluation of the alternative of compliance

I have talked about the value placed on alternative *to* compliance, but what about the value of compliance, itself, in various situations? What determines that?

The attractiveness of compliance seems to depend in part on lasting orientations toward the other person or nation and in part on factors specific to the particular issue under consideration. I will consider the latter first.

Compliance may look attractive because of the intrinsic merits of the action involved. A girl may agree to go to a movie with a boy not because of the boy but because of the movie. Influence can hardly be said to have taken place, yet there is compliance with the boy's suggestion. Or the

United States may decide to give aid to Thailand not because the Thais have requested it, but because it will be used to fight Communism. Again there is compliance but no influence. The *perceived cost* of compliance is also important. If the Guatemalan government should ask the United States to station troops on its soil to prevent a revolution, the United States might want very much to comply but be deterred by fears of adverse world public opinion. The urge to comply would be great, but the cost of compliance greater.

At other times compliance becomes attractive because the other party has used certain compelling arguments or issued specific threats and promises. The more intimately such threats and promises intersect with needs and fears of the first party and the more credible the first party finds them, the more likely he is to comply. In such cases, the other party can be said to have exerted influence, but the tendency to comply does not outlive the specific issue involved.

Factors specific to the issue have their place, but I find more intriguing the role of *continuing orientations* toward other people and nations. Let me illustrate this first in interpersonal affairs.

I believe that all of us have a continuing orientation toward almost everyone we know, which leads us to put more or less value on alternatives that involve compliance with his wishes. I call such an orientation "responsiveness," borrowing the term from Karl Deutsch (1957). For example, I am highly responsive toward my wife . . . which means that I find compliance with her wishes an attractive alternative most of the time. I don't always comply, of course. Sometimes compliance is too costly and sometimes other alternatives are more attractive. But I comply a good deal of the time. I am less responsive toward my students and, therefore, find the alternative of helping them somewhat less appealing . . . though usually appealing, of course. Toward strangers I am even less responsive and, correspondingly, less willing to be helpful.

Interpersonal responsiveness has a very interesting feature. When you are at all responsive toward another person, you tend to be more willing to comply with his wishes the more important they are *to him*. The stronger my wife feels about something, the more highly I evaluate compliance with her wishes. And yet, if my wife wanted me to stay home and a student wanted to meet me in my office in the evening, I might comply with the wishes of my student if he felt very strongly about the need for help at that hour and my wife was less strongly opposed to my going.

Now let us turn to international relations. I submit that similar considerations hold at this level . . . that nations have more or less responsive orientations toward one another . . . which endure over a period of time and change in an orderly way. For example, I would say that the United States is very responsive to Great Britain and places high value on complying with all of her wishes . . . though of course other considerations may force us not to comply in specific situations. The relationship of responsiveness is not transitive: Great Britain is also highly responsive to the United States. The United States is only moderately responsive to the needs of Burma . . . and seems to be completely unresponsive to the needs of Communist China . . . perhaps even "negatively responsive" if we can use such a term.

In the United States government, orientations of responsiveness appear to be located primarily in policies of the geographical offices of the Department of State . . . such as the XYZ Office, which has the conscious policy in the case of one country of "Keeping the people happy in ___________." The proposals generated by such offices reflect these orientations. These proposals vie, in interagency committee meetings, with the proposals from other agencies . . . in the same way that more or less compliant alternatives often compete in the thinking of a single individual. (According to my findings, the agency which feels the strongest about its proposal will often win out in the end . . . though this, of course, is only one principle by which such interagency conflicts are resolved.)

As I suggested earlier, in interpersonal relations we tend to evaluate an alternative more highly the more benefit it holds for a person toward whom we are responsive. I believe that the same holds true for international politics . . . that is, that nations place a greater premium on compliance with the wishes of most other nations, the more this compliance will benefit the other nation. The stronger the Canadians, or almost any other government, feel about an issue, the more likely the United States is to comply with their wishes. Partial support for this conclusion can be found in a quote from my notes on one of the interviews. The respondent was explaining what they do with requests from other nations: "When another country makes a proposal, we consider whether it's reasonable. If we decide that it is reasonable, we present it to the other agencies involved. In addition, *we try to evaluate the strength of feeling of the other nation* and what effect honoring their note will have on our general goals. If we feel that it is unreasonable or unwise or that *the country is not really terribly interested in it,* we will pass it on with just a comment that the (officials of blank) have asked us to send this over. But if it seems like a good thing to support, XYZ may push it strongly with the other agencies" (italics added). There is a lot of material in this quotation, but partially hidden in it are a number of references to the importance of an issue to the other nation and the relevance which this has for the vigor with which XYZ officers will argue for compliance in an interagency committee meeting. This is not the best evidence, but I believe it contains some support for my conclusion.

3. *Sources of responsiveness*

To review partially what has already been said, responsiveness can be thought of as a continuing orientation toward another party which determines, in part, the value of complying with the wishes of that party. The higher the level of responsiveness, the more attractive compliance seems to be. Now we must explore the determinants of the *level* of responsiveness.

I divide the determinants of responsiveness into two main categories: a. expectations about reward and punishment, and b. good will.

The first source is intimately related to the notion of *resources* in traditional theories of power. When the other party has resources which are needed or feared, his cooperation becomes more important, and it often seems wise to try to curry favor and avoid friction with him. The result is increased responsiveness . . . to honor his requests and avoid hurting him gain in attractiveness. We see such a process often in business organizations. As a man rises and gains more control over the fate of others, his requests are more often honored and a greater effort is made to avoid antagonizing him. Interestingly enough, a man who has risen in business will sometimes become more responsive to those below him who once were his coequals. Now he needs their support, while previously they were competitors.

The same seems to be true in international relations. The more resources a nation has and the more needed or feared these resources are by other nations, the greater the responsiveness of other nations . . . provided one thing . . . provided that credibility also exists. A nation's resources can command responsiveness only to the extent that other nations believe that its use of these resources is contingent on their good behavior. The more contingency they see, the more credibility we say exists.

I am not talking here about *overt* threats and promises. My data suggest that the importance of such things has been overemphasized . . . at least in describing relations between friendly nations. I am suggesting that in most cases a nation does not need to verbalize threats and promises to mobilize the cooperation of its neighbors. It only needs to *display* its resources and, of course, to mete out rewards and punishments as they are earned to keep up the credibility of its position. Other nations seem to catch on and act as if threats and punishments existed, even though these are only implicit.

The other source of responsiveness, good will, is more elusive. In *interpersonal* relations there are three kinds of good will, all of which determine a person's level of responsiveness: a. *Sentimental* good will, deriving from gratitude, love or anger toward the other person; b. *Judgmental* good will, deriving from labeling of the other person as a "good guy" or a "bad guy" or some sort of guy in between; and c. *Tactical* good will, which derives from the desire to maintain credibility and leads to repayment in kind of favors and disservices. All three types are affected by the behavior of the other person. They cause us to become more responsive when the other person has been helpful and less responsive when the other person has hurt our interests. They are influenced by other things, as well.

The respondents to my interviews acted as though the good will of other nations makes a big difference in how responsive these nations will be toward the United States. Sometimes the officers seemed to be afraid of a decline in *emotional* or *judgmental* good will . . . that is, that the populations of other countries would become angry with the United States or perhaps label America as "bad," and force their governments to become less responsive toward us. At other times they seemed to fear that national leaders abroad would find it tactically advisable to punish America for some sort of misdeed and, thereby, become less responsive to American interests. These data suggest that all three forms of good will have an effect on international responsiveness and hence on international affairs. The alternative to believing this is to believe that the XYZ officers are fencing with windmills; that their concern with the various forms of good will abroad is a product of erroneous thinking about international affairs. Perhaps they are in error, but it seems unlikely. Some forms of good will may be less important in international affairs than in interpersonal affairs. For example, gratitude, love, anger and labels of "friend" and "enemy." But it seems to me that they all play some part.

Summary

In summary, I have criticized some aspects of the traditional theory of power and suggested the need for an analysis of compliance as a step toward a more vigorous tradition of theorizing. I have presented some exploratory data on compliant behavior in an office of the State Department that deals with friendly nations, and have interpreted these data to find support for a theoretical sketch which stresses the importance of enduring orientations of "responsiveness" toward other nations.

2

*Political Communication as an Instrument of Foreign Policy**

W. Phillips Davison

W. PHILLIPS DAVISON *is a Senior Research Fellow of the Council on Foreign Relations in New York.*

Heavily affecting the conduct of United States propaganda activities from the time of Tom Paine to the present have been certain conceptions about what information can do, how it affects behavior, and how it should be used. First, it is clear that Paine's view of the press (now including radio, television, and motion pictures) as a power that governs the sentiments of mankind has been and continues to be widespread. According to this mode of thought, propaganda is an effective instrument for influencing opinion. True information will correct misconceptions regarding the United States and United States policy. Communist propaganda will be counteracted if its falsity can be demonstrated. If hostile propaganda is not countered, according to this view, it can exert a dangerous influence on impressionable minds.

A second common conception about propaganda activities is that they should be aimed at a mass audience. If enough people can be persuaded to adopt a given opinion, then the policy of their government will be affected, at least in a democracy. Mass attitudes are thus seen as the primary target of propaganda.

A third popular idea is that propaganda should be directed primarily to audiences who hold opinions different from those of the propagandist. These are the people who need to be won over. Tom Paine proposed to convert the British to the American point of view. The Committee on Public Information in World War I sought to undermine enemy morale. The expression "psychological warfare," widely used in World War II, carried with it the implication that the audience was composed largely of hostile elements. Propaganda leaflets were sometimes referred to as "paper bullets." More recently, the arsenal of American propagandists has been said to contain "truth bombs."

It should be emphasized that these views about propaganda, while widely held in the United States and in some other countries, are not entertained by all professional practitioners of the art. Many personnel in the U.S. Informa-

* *Public Opinion Quarterly,* **XXVII** (1963), 28 ff. Reprinted by special permission of Public Opinion Quarterly, Princeton, New Jersey.

tion Agency would not subscribe to them, or would endorse them only in part. The Soviets have shown that they look at propaganda very differently. Nevertheless, as far as democratic countries are concerned, these conceptions are so generally accepted among the public that they heavily influence the conduct of foreign information programs. . . .

During the past few decades social science research has increasingly led to questions about the validity of these popular conceptions. Some appear to be misleading, others to require considerable refinement. More and more evidence has piled up to indicate that the mass media are effective instruments of persuasion only under rather special circumstances, and that the primary capabilities of propaganda lie in a very different direction.

First, it is now widely accepted by social scientists that information by itself is not usually able to reverse established attitudes.[1] If an attitude is useful to a person, if it helps him maintain his personal integrity or a satisfactory social adjustment, even very skillful and sustained propaganda will ordinarily be unable to shake it. People defend themselves resourcefully against information with which they disagree. They do this in part by refusing to expose themselves to unwelcome communications, by forgetting them, by distorting them, or by finding counterarguments. The editorial preference of a large majority of American newspapers for Republican candidates ever since 1932 has not succeeded in preventing the election of Democratic presidents in all but two national contests since then. Almost a generation of sustained Communist propaganda does not seem to have been successful in making convinced Communists out of most people in Eastern Europe.

On the other hand, it has become clear that information can have a very significant effect in strengthening and nourishing attitudes that already exist. People look for communications that reinforce their predispositions, and welcome information that proves them right and helps them to take actions they are inclined to take anyway. Voting studies have been particularly important in showing that individuals expose themselves to propaganda with which they agree, and that this propaganda strengthens them in their convictions and helps to get them to the polls.[2]

Information can also play an important part in establishing new attitudes on new subjects, and can sometimes change lightly held attitudes. People who know nothing or very little about an issue can often be swayed *if*, and it is a big if, a communicator is able to gain their attention. This is one reason why American films have been so important in shaping attitudes toward the United States. Many of the people in foreign countries who see these films do not give their attention to very much other information about this country. The importance of information in establishing new attitudes is also one reason why the emerging countries will be such an important

---

[1] Much of the experimental research on mass communications has been summarized by Joseph T. Klapper in *The Effects of Mass Communication* (New York: Free Press of Glencoe, Inc., 1960). Because of the volume and diffuse character of research in this field, individual studies will not be cited here, except by way of example.

[2] The familiar pioneering study that inspired much of the research in this area was conducted in Erie County, Ohio, in the 1940 election. Cf. Paul F. Lazarsfeld, Bernard Berelson, and Hazel Gaudet, *The People's Choice* (New York: Columbia University Press, 1948).

arena for propagandists in the coming years. In these countries, opinions on world issues are just beginning to be formed.

At the same time that research has shown that well-grounded attitudes rarely change as a result of propaganda alone, it has also indicated ways that attitudes can and do change. Attitudinal shifts usually occur when the situation in which a person finds himself changes, when his old attitudes are no longer useful to him, and when new attitudes are likely to bring him into better adjustment with his environment. Thus, combat replacements who were assigned to established units in World War II gradually altered their attitudes in the direction of those held by the men in the established units to which they were assigned.[3] People whose economic situation changes often adopt new political attitudes that serve their new interests better. Research on the opinions that people in different nations have of each other suggests that positive or negative attitudes frequently reflect good or bad relations between the governments involved. Friction between governments can lead to a hostility between peoples, and good intergovernmental relations often lead peoples in the states involved to have more favorable images of each other.[4] Basic attitude changes are thus usually brought about by changes in the social, political, or economic environment—*not* by propaganda.

These observations, which will have a very familiar ring to those acquainted with the social scientific literature, suggest the need for radical revision in some of the popular conceptions about propaganda that were described above. The most rewarding target for propaganda is ordinarily not the individual with differing opinions, but rather the person who shares at least partly the views of the propagandist or whose attitudes have not yet become firmly established.

Does this mean that communications are of little value as an instrument in foreign policy? One might conclude that little is to be gained by preaching to the converted and to the indifferent. On the other hand, it can also be argued that one gains a great deal. By reinforcing the convictions of those who are already favorably disposed, by providing them with evidence that their beliefs are correct, and by giving them information about what they might do to achieve their goals, the propagandist can often stimulate action on the part of people who are in basic agreement with him. This action tends to change the social environment and thus may affect hostile elements within that environment also, since some of those who were previously opposed to the propagandist are likely to change their attitudes to conform to the new situation. To take an example from election campaigns, a Democrat who is surrounded by enthusiastic, well-organized, and vocal Republicans is more likely to change his voting intention than if his associates do not feel strongly about their political opinions or keep these opinions to themselves. The propagandist can play an important part in stimulating both enthusiasm and organization.

ORGANIZATIONS AS USERS OF INFORMATION

The fact that propaganda can help to promote organization is perhaps

[3] M. Brewster Smith, "The Combat Replacement," in Samuel A. Stouffer *et al.*, *The American Soldier* (Princeton, N.J.: Princeton University Press, 1949), **II**, 243–272.

[4] William Buchanan and Hadley Cantril, *How Nations See Each Other* (Urbana, Ill.: University of Illinois Press, 1953).

more significant in the foreign policy context than the fact that it can affect individuals. This is because unorganized individuals rarely have political significance; only if they work together, talk together, or vote together are they likely to have an effect on the political scene. Organizations are much more important, and they are large users of communications. As the literature of industrial sociology and public administration emphasizes, upward, downward, and lateral communication within an organization is vital to its successful functioning. Furthermore, organizations require an enormous amount of information originating outside themselves if their members are to do their jobs properly. Many organizations make use of communications from abroad. Industrial and scientific groups try to obtain the information that will be most useful to their work, regardless of where it originates. Governments are particularly large consumers of political information from abroad, as is testified by the volume of diplomatic reporting and the voracious appetite of all foreign offices for media that contain news about foreign areas. Private organizations concerned with foreign policy likewise require large quantities of international news.[5]

If propagandists can provide information that is useful to existing organizations, or if they can help new organizations to form, they are much more likely to have a significant political impact than if they focus their attention on influencing individuals. The world-wide Communist propaganda apparatus is an outstanding example of this. It works in close conjunction with existing Communist organizations by providing them with information about the party line, by helping to train and indoctrinate those already recruited, and by assisting in the attraction of new members.

The United States information services also devote substantial attention to serving foreign organizations. They furnish political groups in new countries with material about the workings of democracy. They help to supply the leaders of friendly nations with information they require to make daily decisions. They assist in training new personnel for a wide variety of organizations.[6] Their work in providing information that helps emerging countries to develop new institutions of industry and commerce, and to expand old ones, has great long-term political significance.

A dramatic instance of the organizational importance of communications is afforded by the work of the British Broadcasting Corporation and certain other Allied agencies during World War II. One of the chief tasks of these agencies was to encourage resistance movements in German-occupied Europe. The BBC initially promoted the formation of resistance movements by letting individuals on the continent know that they were not alone—that there were others who shared their opinions. It urged all those who were resistance-minded to get together and form groups. It then attempted to provide political and technical information that would be useful

[5] Much of the research on the interest of American organizations in information from abroad is contained in the five volumes edited by Alfred O. Hero, *Americans in World Affairs Communications* (Boston: World Peace Foundation, 1959 and 1960).

[6] The most recent general treatment of the U.S. Information Agency is that of Wilson P. Dizard, *The Strategy of Truth* (Washington, D.C.: Public Affairs Press, 1961). Important parts of the United States foreign information program are also conducted by the Department of State, the Department of Defense, and the Agency for International Development.

to these groups. It gave them news that was relevant to their activities and that was likely to support their morale. It also let them know about techniques that had been used successfully to interfere with Nazi military operations. In this case, a foreign source provided not only *external* communications to a group of organizations but in some cases provided *internal* communications as well. That is, it enabled members of groups that had no reliable internal channels to keep in touch with each other.

A Summing Up

Social science research thus suggests that the principal target of propaganda should not be a mass of individuals whose attitudes are to be changed, but much more a set of groups and organizations that are to be assisted. This is not to say that the propagandist should be unconcerned with individual psychology. The opposite is the case. But he should think of individuals primarily as members or potential members of politically significant bodies. His task is to identify organizations that require certain types of information and then supply this to them. The information in question may not be political at all—it may be about disease prevention or farming techniques—but its effects are likely to be political. He may be considered a persuader, in that he may ultimately affect attitudes, but it is more useful operationally to think of him as a purveyor of information that can be used to achieve both his goals and those of his audience.

It is not enough that this approach, if indeed it is correct, should be understood by those who are engaged in using political communication as an instrument of foreign policy. Many officials in the U.S. Information Agency and other organizations carrying on foreign information programs already appear to look at their tasks substantially in the way suggested here. If these people are to do their jobs efficiently, however, a working philosophy such as this will have to be more generally accepted by Congress and by the public. As long as American propagandists are expected to convince Communists that they should turn into democrats, to persuade street mobs in foreign nations that they should stop anti-American demonstrations, or to explain away racial discrimination in the United States, they will have a more difficult time getting on with their less spectacular but ultimately more important functions.

Finally, it should be apparent from the way the words "propaganda" and "propagandist" have been used in the foregoing that they are not intended to carry a pejorative connotation. The expression "propagandist" has been employed in this paper to refer to anyone who uses an information program to help achieve his goals. Thus, the most objective news file can be considered propaganda under certain conditions, for instance, if it is provided to assist a friendly foreign government in making wiser decisions.

The low esteem in which propaganda is held by the public in this country is itself a block to the more efficient utilization of political communication as an instrument of foreign policy. But that is another story. At this point it is sufficient to observe that propaganda has not always occupied a low estate in the United States. The Committee of Foreign Affairs, of which Tom Paine was Secretary, grew out of the Committee of Secret Correspondence of the Continental Congress. Thus, in this country, propaganda might be considered the senior foreign service.

CHAPTER FOURTEEN

Economic Aspects of Foreign Policy

Now that weapons of physical destruction have become so potentially devastating, violent resolutions of conflict becomes less and less rational. Political leaders are required to turn their attention to other means by which international relations can be conducted. Alternative processes by which international conflicts can be carried on or resolved must be discovered. Elsewhere we have discussed aspects of diplomacy, political settlement, and psychological methods. In the present chapter we are concerned with some of the economic methods that countries utilize in their relations with one another.

Economic policies are employed in various ways and for various purposes. It is important to distinguish between economic policies pursued for purely economic reasons, economic policies pursued for political or strategic reasons, or economic policies pursued for some combination of reasons. It would be a mistake to regard economics merely as a handmaiden for politics and to assume political motivations for all economic actions. It would likewise be an error, however, to disregard the close relationship between economic policies and political considerations.

In Part III of this book, which dealt with elements of state capacity to achieve given goals, we warned against the temptation to engage in "single-factor" analysis. Likewise, it seems appropriate now to avoid the temptation to consider single lines of policy—be they diplomatic, economic, psychological—as being most common or most fruitful. The usual process by which policy is projected into the international sphere is multidimensional, and economic methods in international relations are apt to be most effective when they are combined with other methods of policy.

In many past discussions of international relations, most relationships tended to be explained primarily or exclusively in terms of economic considerations. Imperialism, particularly, was considered to be an economic phenomenon. According to the Marxist-Leninist interpretation, an overly productive capitalist economic system searched for safe places to invest surplus capital, to obtain needed raw material resources to feed its insatiable industrial needs, and to find guaranteed and profitable markets for its finished products. Hence, it was held, governments—reflecting the dominant economic interests of the country—engaged in aggressive imperialism to acquire and dominate areas which could provide these opportunities. The theory suffered a blow when historians discovered that, in a number of cases, the emphasis had been the other way around: that governments, in pursuit of political and strategic advantages, had pressed economic interests to penetrate into other areas, so that the governments would then have a pretext for becoming politically involved in those areas.[1]

The concentration on the economic aspects of international politics lasted until fairly recently. It was responsible for the fact that between the two World Wars, great emphasis was placed on economic methods to preserve the peace. The League of Nations system of economic sanctions was designed to discourage potential aggressors. It was tried only once, in the sanctions imposed against Italy during the Ethiopian War, and—for political reasons—it was used imperfectly. As a result, it was unsuccessful and did not stop, or even greatly hinder, Italy's conquest in East Africa. In fact, it achieved the unintended result of driving Italy into the arms of Germany. Preoccupation with economic aspects of international relations also accounted in the interwar period for the prevalent American interpretation that this country had entered the First World War for economic reasons. This led to an attempt to close this avenue of future involvement through the ill-fated neutrality legislation of the 1930's. As in the case of the sanctions against Italy, these laws did not work. In fact, they must bear at least some of the blame for the deterioration of European political relations in the 1930's and the eventual outbreak of the Second World War, since they seemed to signal Nazi aggressors that they could proceed with impunity and without fear of American involvement on the side of their victims.

These rather poor experiences in the analyses of the economic ingredient of international politics, and the disastrous policy effects that the analyses yielded, led to a widely shared feeling that the economic aspects of international relations could be disregarded. The conclusion was wrongly drawn that previous analyses had not been faulty, but rather that they had been addressed to the wrong feature of the international system, and that the political-strategic sphere was all that mattered. But this extreme swing of the pendulum could not be sustained in light of the obvious fact that economic considerations *do* play a significant part in the relations between states. If they are disregarded, the observer, analyst, or practitioner of international relations will not achieve a rounded picture of the processes involved in these relations.

In the postwar decades, economic policies have attained new significance, and the close relationship between international economics and international politics is being increasingly recognized. One reason for the linkage is that many states have become "welfare states," whose governments are deeply concerned with assuring the economic and social well-being of their peoples. Every country is, to a greater or lesser extent, dependent on other countries for imports of important goods and services and for export markets. Foreign trade has

[1] Eugene Staley, *War and the Private Investor* (Chicago: University of Chicago Press, 1935).

a "multiplier" effect, and the need for imports and exports is diffused throughout the entire modern production and distribution process. While in the case of some countries, the total figures of foreign trade may not seem overly impressive, the role of import and export totals may be likened to the function of spark plugs in cars, which constitute less than one per cent of the total cost of an automobile, yet are indispensable to its proper operation.

We have spoken previously about the connections between economic and political considerations. Very often the two go hand in hand. But there may be times when they are in tension, contradiction, or are incompatible. While one cannot make sweeping statements as to which of the two considerations always prevails, it does seem appropriate to say that in recent years the political (including the military and strategic) consideration has most often been given priority. Yet, obviously, foreign policy must serve not only a country's political and strategic interests, but its economic interests as well.

This being so, it is sometimes difficult for a government to make effective use of economic pressures. There will always be some internal opposition in one's own country, from economic groups that will be adversely affected by the employment of one or another method of economic pressure. Although a given policy may be to the benefit of the economy as a whole, there will always be sections of the economy that are hurt. Needless to say, opposition will be more effective within a democratic rather than an authoritarian society, though it is not completely precluded in the latter. It has been suggested that perhaps it is good for economic methods to be difficult to employ, because otherwise countries might be far more tempted to utilize them often. The risk in this would be that the real problems would be concealed. If a country uses economic pressures in the expectation that these pressures *alone* will yield the desired results, it will frequently find that this is not so, and that economic methods have to be combined with other measures of policy to be effective.

There are many types of pressures that may be used. We will list some of them briefly.[2] They include 1. financial manipulations to diminish the value of an opponent's currency and enhance that of one's own country; 2. economic penetration of weaker countries on the part of more powerful ones, with the eventual objective of exerting pressure on the government of the penetrated society; 3. exploitation of a strategic economic position, through such policies as price-fixing, dumping, the imposition of quotas, exchange controls, and so forth; 4. the boycott—a refusal to buy from another country; 5. the embargo—a refusal to sell to another country; 6. the use of economic subsidies, about which more will be said below; 7. preemptive buying of goods produced in other countries, in order to withhold them from other purchasers; and 8. stockpiling of important goods.

By far the most common method of economic pressure has been the imposition of tariffs on the importation of specified goods from other coun-

[2] Charles C. Abbott, "Economic Penetration and Power Politics," *Harvard Business Review,* **XXVI** (1948), 410–424.

tries. Most economists are agreed that, from the over-all point of view, free trade would be of the greatest advantage to the greatest number of countries. But in spite of this judgment, tariffs have traditionally been used to serve a number of domestic or foreign policy ends for the country that imposes them. Tariffs may be imposed as revenue-raising procedures; they may be enacted to protect national industries for economic, political, or strategic reasons; and they may be designed to injure (or threaten to injure) the economies of other countries, in order to achieve some economic or political concessions.

At the present time, groups of countries are combining their economic spheres in order to gain the advantages of larger trading areas and to overcome the problems of tariff and other economic barriers. The most impressive achievement in this regard has been the European Economic Community ("Common Market"), but groupings in other areas also exist. The question is whether, once large free-trade areas have been established, it will be possible to reduce impediments to the free trade between such areas, or whether regional arrangements will be used to create such impediments against trade with countries outside the group. Efforts at over-all reductions of tariffs, such as the Organization for Economic Cooperation and Development, that attempts to link the economies of several trade areas, and operations under the General Agreement on Tariffs and Trade, which are designed to have world-wide favorable results, attempt to counteract the tendency to divide the world onto separate free-trade areas.

Nothing is ever entirely "new" in a field such as that of international relations, and programs of aid to other countries have historical antecedents. Nevertheless, the scope of such programs, and the consciousness with which they are being enacted and operated, is one of the new elements in the relations between countries, and it certainly is the most significant aspect of the use of economic methods in international politics. A large number of countries, having within their borders more than sixty per cent of the world's population, find themselves economically underdeveloped. Their "traditional" societies, to use a phrase by W. W. Rostow, have been centered primarily on the production of agricultural goods and the extraction of raw materials for export. Their value systems held little expectation for progress. Consumption approached production levels, thus leaving insufficient surplus capital for investment that could promote economic growth.

A concomitant of the rising nationalism, which resulted in the creation of many of these units as separate states, has been the pressing desire for improvement in the economic and social spheres. Improved communications channels have brought to the peoples of these countries the knowledge that the way in which they have lived traditionally is not the only way possible to live; that other societies enjoy many more of the material benefits that contemporary civilization can bestow. The quest, therefore, has been for improvement, on a large scale, and in a short time.

For a very great number of reasons, the process by which a society can raise its standards of productivity and of living is very complex and long. It requires strenuous exertions on the part of the country itself, and it requires large-scale assistance from other countries. As policy-makers and scholars, Rostow and Galbraith are both unusually well-qualified to discuss some of the ensuing problems and policy-choices.

Efforts have been afoot since the end of the second World War to improve conditions in the underdeveloped areas of the world, to permit them, in Rostow's phrase, to reach the "take-off" phase of economic development and growth.[3] The United States and other Western countries have aid and development programs which provide various forms of assistance to these states, albeit on too small a scale to bring about rapid transformations of their economies and societies. The Soviet Union has developed a highly concentrated and selective foreign aid program. Numerous programs under the auspices of the United Nations, its specialized agencies (such as the World Health Organization, the Food and Agriculture Organization, and UNESCO) are likewise designed to contribute toward an alleviation and eventual solution of the problem.

Nevertheless, none of these programs, either by themselves or combined, can suffice to bring about needed improvements as rapidly as the peoples living in these areas desire. The world is confronted with what has been termed a "revolution of rising expectations"—a set of demands by the peoples of the underdeveloped areas, composing a majority of the world's population and growing at a rapid pace, who want improvement in their conditions. They want it quickly, and they are not always choosy on the question of how the development is to occur. Yet long-term rapid improvement in living standards is extraordinarily hard to bring about. As Rostow has pointed out, such improvement requires not only external assistance, but a shifting of internal values and patterns. Furthermore, the medical revolution of our age has made it easy to fight disease and thereby to decrease death rates dramatically. This decrease is reflected in sharply rising population figures, with particularly impressive growth curves among the young and the old. This, in turn, means that education, health care, provisions for old age, and so forth, absorb a growing proportion of the resources of the countries involved. The population growth means that the rate of increase in economic productivity must outpace the rate of population increase. To bring about greatly increased productivity requires vast capital investments—many of them in activities that will not immediately yield direct returns (roads, harbors, efficient administrative systems, and the like). The societies do not contain surplus capital in amounts sufficient for such investment. Private investors are reluctant to invest money where there is political and social unrest (particularly when investment opportunities in more highly developed countries are good). Thus the only feasible alternative is aid from other governments, on a scale vastly larger than that experienced thus far.

Relations between the underdeveloped and the more highly developed areas of the world constitute one of the most serious contemporary and future

[3] W. W. Rostow, *The Stages of Economic Growth* (Cambridge: Cambridge University Press, 1960), *passim.*

problem areas in international relations. In fact, some astute observers suggest that, just as the East-West conflict was characteristic of the first two postwar decades, so a North-South conflict (between the more and the less developed countries) will mark much of the remainder of the century. The tensions between the more and the less developed countries would exist irrespective of the East-West confrontation, but at the moment—disregarding the more long-range prediction just advanced—the fact that the more highly developed states of the world *are* antagonistic contributes to the tension. This is so because the United States, the Soviet Union, Communist China, and the allies of these countries compete for influence in and over the less developed states. All sides assiduously attempt to win the approval and support of these countries. It has been suggested that the outcome of the "cold war" between the contending blocs may well be decided in the presently underdeveloped countries.

1

*A Non-Communist Manifesto**

Walt Whitman Rostow

WALT WHITMAN ROSTOW *was educated at Yale University and later became a Rhodes Scholar. He served as special assistant to President John F. Kennedy in the field of national security affairs in 1961, and later as the Chairman of the Policy Planning Council of the Department of State. As an economist and historian his works include* The U.S. in the World Arena *(1960), and* The Stages of Economic Growth *(1960), among numerous other contributions. He is presently on the White House staff as a foreign policy adviser to the President.*

I. FIVE STAGES OF NATIONS

What follows is an economic historian's way of envisaging the sweep of modern history as a set of "stages of growth." It is both a theory of economic growth and a partial theory about modern history. It grapples with many issues. How, and under what impulses, did traditional, agricultural societies begin moving towards modernisation? When and how did regular growth come to be a built-in feature of each society? What forces drove this growth along and determined its contours? What relation did the relative sequence of growth bear to outbreaks of war? Finally, where is compound interest taking us? To communism, to the affluent suburbs, to destruction, to the moon?

This theory of growth is in a sense an alternative to the Marxist interpretation of modern history. But it in no sense implies that the worlds of politics, social organisation and culture are a mere superstructure deriving from the economy. One should never forget Keynes's dictum:

* *The Economist,* August 15, 1959, pp. 409–416. Reprinted by permission.

If human nature felt no temptation to take a chance, no satisfaction (profit apart) in constructing a factory, a railway, a mine or a farm, there might not be much investment merely as a result of cold calculation.

To begin with a brief impressionistic definition of the stages of growth. It is possible to place all societies within one of five economic categories. There are:

the traditional society;
the transitional society, in which the foundations of change are being laid;
the society in the crucial process of "take-off";
the maturing society, in which new methods and outlooks are spreading through the whole economy;
and finally the society which has reached the age of high mass consumption.

For each country, it is possible to identify the leading sectors whose momentum dominated the take-off, the sectors whose high rate of expansion brought the economy to maturity, and the particular ways in which each society reaching the high mass consumption stage has chosen to dispose of its income. In short, the "stages" are not a disembodied response to an abstract set of Hegelian ideas; they are a matter of factual history seen in the light of economics.

Economics in the conventional market sense is not, however, sufficient here. The demand which, together with technology and the quality of entrepreneurship, determines the pattern of investment, and which responds to the resulting changes in price or in income, is not only the expression of private tastes and choices; it springs also from social decisions and from the policies of governments.

Private and public choices

How, for example, should the traditional society react to the intrusion of a more advanced power? With cohesion, promptness and vigour, like the Japanese? By making a virtue of fecklessness, like the oppressed Irish of the eighteenth century? By slowly and reluctantly altering its traditional characteristics, like the Chinese?

When independent modern nationhood is achieved, how should the national energies be used? In external aggression, to right old wrongs or to exploit new possibilities for enlarged national power? In completing the political victory of the new national government over regional interests? Or in modernising the economy?

Once the take-off is successfully achieved and growth is under way, how far should the aim of diffusing technology and maximising the rate of growth be modified by the desire to increase consumption per head and welfare?

When technological maturity is reached, and the nation has at its command a modernised industrial machine, to what ends should it be put, and in what proportions? To increase social security, through the welfare state? To expand mass consumption into the range of durable consumer goods and of services? To gain stature and power on the world scene? To increase leisure?

In surveying now the broad contours of each stage of growth, we are examining, then, not merely the sectoral structure of *economies* transforming themselves: but a succession of strategic choices made by whole *societies.*

The central economic fact about traditional societies is the existence of a ceiling on productivity. In this class can be grouped the whole pre-Newtonian world (Newton being here used as a symbol for that watershed in history when men came to believe that the external world was subject to knowable laws and capable of productive manipulation)—the dynasties in China; the civilisations of the Middle East and the Mediterranean; the world of medieval Europe—and the post-Newtonian societies which, for a time, remained unmoved by man's new ability.

Traditional societies

The traditional societies are not static. Their story has been one of endless change. Trade within and between them fluctuated with the degrees of political and social turbulence, the efficiency of central government, the upkeep of the roads. Varying degrees of manufacture developed and underwent sporadic improvement; productivity in agriculture could rise with the improvement of irrigation or the discovery of a new crop. But the level of productivity was limited by the inaccessibility of modern science.

It followed that food production typically absorbed 75 per cent or more of the working force; and from this primacy of agriculture there followed in turn a hierarchical social structure with little scope for vertical mobility—with wealth and power concentrated in the hands of those who controlled land rents. Social values were geared to the limited horizons which men could perceive. Income above minimum consumption levels was largely spent in non-productive or low-productivity outlays—religious feasts and ceremonies, monuments, wars, high living for the land-owning minority. Family and clan connections played a large role. Political power tended to lie in the various regions rather than in the capital; the landowners in any case usually maintained great influence over such central political power as existed.

Change must be many-sided

Implicit in these characteristics is the need for a many-sided transformation before growth can be established and lead on to maturity. A predominantly agricultural society must be transformed into one predominantly occupied in industry, communications, trade and services. A society built around mainly self-sufficient regions must orient its commerce and thought to the nation and to a still larger international setting. Attitudes towards the having of children—initially the residual blessing and affirmation of immortality in a hard life bounded by narrow personal horizons—must change so as ultimately to provide a decline in the birth-rate, as the possibility of individual progress and the decline in the need for unskilled farm labour produces a new calculus.

Income above minimum levels of consumption must be shifted into the hands of people who will spend it on roads and railways, schools and factories, rather than on country houses and servants, personal ornaments and temples. Men must come to be valued not for their connection with a clan, a class, or even a guild, but for their individual ability to perform increasingly specialised functions. Above all, man must come to regard his physical environment not as virtually a factor given by nature and providence, but as an ordered world that can be manipulated in ways which yield productive change.

All of this—and more—is involved in the passage from a traditional to a modern growing society. These changes do not occur either simultaneously or in a random sequence. Some of them must be well advanced before growth can set in at all.

II. The Transitional Society

Most societies have made the transition to sustained growth under the impact of an external challenge. The small group of which this is not true includes the United States and the older British Dominions. These were, in Louis Hartz' phrase, "born free," created out of a Britain already far along in the transitional process. The creation of the preconditions for take-off was, for them, mainly an economic and technical matter, comprising the building of social overhead capital (railways, ports, roads) and the finding of an economic setting in which a shift to industry was profitable. For the rest of the world, however, change had to be more basic.

The purely economic explanation is simple. For growth to become self-sustained, all that is necessary is a rise in the rate of investment and the stock of capital per head. The economic difference between a traditional and a modern society is merely a question of whether its rate of investment is low relative to its rate of population increase—say, under 5 per cent of national income—or whether it has risen to 10 per cent or over. With a capital-output ratio of about 3 to 1, a society that invests more than 10 per cent of its national income will outstrip any likely population growth; and a regular increase in output per head can then be assumed.

This is the formula. But in order to get the rate of investment up, some men in the society must be able to manipulate and apply modern science and useful cost-reducing inventions. Some others must be ready to undergo the strains and risks of leadership in bringing the flow of available inventions productively into the capital stock. Others, again, must be prepared to lend their money on long term, at high risk, to back the innovating entrepreneur—not in money lending, foreign trade or real estate, but in modern industry. And the population at large must learn to operate an economic system whose methods are constantly changing, and which increasingly confines the individual in large and disciplined organisations, allocating to him narrowly specialised, recurrent tasks.

Capital formation is not merely a matter of maximising profit; it is a matter of a society's effective attitudes towards science, applied science, and risk-taking as well as the adaptability of the working force. Nor, even from the purely economic angle, can it be usefully regarded as a single, undifferentiated, aggregate process. Of especial importance here is the problem of increased productivity in agriculture and the extractive industries, and the problem of social overhead capital.

Food and funds

First, agriculture and the extractive industries (mining, etc.). These constitute accessible natural resources which offer a quick yield of increased productivity to new techniques. Modernisation takes a lot of working capital, and much of this must come from rapid increases in output; capital imports can help, of course, but generally speaking, loans must be serviced, and the easiest way of servicing them is to bring the hitherto unexploited backlog of innovations to bear on the society's land and other natural resources. More specifically, agriculture must supply more food to meet the likely rise in population and the proportionately greater increase in the number of town-dwellers. It must supply expanded markets for the potential leading industrial sectors. It must provide, as farmers' real income rises, a source of taxation from which the government's functions in the transition may be financed. It must also provide an expanded supply of loanable funds to the modern sector, thus transferring surplus income from those who would waste it in prodigal living to those who will invest it and then regularly plough back their profits.

Social overhead capital also has a crucial role. A very high proportion of total investment must go into transport and other social overhead outlays. These outlays have three distinctive characteristics. First, their periods of gestation and pay-off are usually long. Unlike double cropping or the application of chemical fertilisers, a railway system is unlikely to yield its results in a year or two from the time its construction is undertaken. Secondly, social overhead capital is generally "lumpy"; other forms of investment can proceed usefully by small increments, but you either build the line from, say, Chicago to San Francisco or you don't. Thirdly, its profits often return to the community as a whole, indirectly, rather than directly to the initiating entrepreneurs. These three characteristics decree that governments must usually play an extremely important role in the process of building overhead capital—and thus in the "preconditions period" in general.

Nationalism above profit

Turning to the non-economic side of the preconditions for take-off: the broad lines of necessary social change are becoming familiar enough. A new leading élite must emerge and be given scope to begin the building of a modern industrial society. This élite must to a degree supersede in authority the old land-based élite, whose grasp on income above minimum levels of consumption must be loosened or broken if they do not themselves divert this surplus into the modern sectors. Generally, the horizon of expectation must lift; and men must accept a life of change and specialised function.

As a matter of historical fact, xenophobic nationalism has been the most important motive force in the transition from traditional to modern societies—vastly more important than the profit motive. Men have been willing to uproot traditional societies primarily not to make more money, but because the traditional society failed, or threatened to fail, to protect them from humiliation by foreigners.

In Germany it was certainly a nationalism based on past humiliation and future hope—the Junkers and the men of the East, more than the men of trade and the liberals of the West—that did the job. In Russia a series of military intrusions and defeats was the great engine of change: Napoleon, the Crimea, the Russo-Japanese War, the First World War. In Japan it was the "demonstration effect" not of high profits or manufactured consumers' goods, but of the Opium War in China in the early 1840s, and Admiral Perry's seven black ships a decade later, that cast the die.

What happens in colonies

In the colonial world, a dual "demonstration effect" has operated. The imperial powers brought about transformations in thought, knowledge, institutions, and the supply of social overhead capital, which moved the colonial society along the transitional path. Ports, docks, roads, and later railways were built; a centralised tax system was imposed; some colonials were drawn into modern trading and production activities; some modern goods and services were diffused sufficiently to alter the conception of attainable consumption standards; and the opportunity for a western education was opened to a few at least.

The reality of the effective power that went with an ability to wield modern technology was demonstrated; and the more thoughtful local people drew appropriate conclusions. A concept of nationalism inevitably crystallised around an accumulating resentment of colonial rule. In the end local coalitions emerged which generated political and, in some cases, military pressure capable of forcing withdrawal —coalitions created by both the positive and negative types of "demonstration."

Xenophobic nationalism has not, of course, been the only force at work. The merchant has seen in modernisation the prospect not only of profits, but also of the high status denied him in the traditional society. There have almost always been intellectuals who saw in modernisation ways of increasing the dignity and value of human life, for individuals and for the nation as a whole. And the soldier—an absolutely crucial figure of the transition—often brought much more to the job than resentment of foreign domination or dreams of future national glory in battle. Thus, out of mixed interests and motives, coalitions were formed in these traditional societies which aimed to make a strong national government; they fought, and eventually overcame, the main enemies of this objective—the political and social groups rooted in regionally based agriculture, joined in some cases by colonial or quasi-colonial powers.

These transitional coalitions (e.g. in Germany the coalition of Junkers and the western men of commerce and industry; in Japan, the Samurai and the grain merchants; in post-1861 Russia, the commercial middle class and the more enterprising civil servants and soldiers) have often shared only one solid common conviction: namely, that they had a stake in the creation of an independent modern state. Once modern nationhood is established, the different elements in the coalition press to mobilise the newly triumphant nationalist political sentiment in different directions; the soldiers (say) aggressively abroad; the professional politicians, to drive home the triumph of the centre over the regions; the merchants, to economic development; the intellectuals, to social, political and legal reform.

The state's key role

The cast of policy, at home and abroad, of newly created or newly modernised states depends greatly, then, on the balance of power within the coalition that emerges. The length of time and the vicissitudes of transition from traditional to modern status depend substantially on the degree to which local talent, energy and resources are channelled into the domestic tasks of modernisation as opposed to alternative possible objectives of nationalism; and this channelling must be largely a function of political leadership.

This is because the central government, in the period of preconditions, must be capable of organising the nation so that unified commercial markets develop. It must create and maintain a tax and fiscal system which diverts resources into modern uses. In particular, as emphasised earlier, the state has an inescapable responsibility for ensuring that the stock of social capital required for take-off is built; and it is also likely that only vigorous central leadership can bring about those radical changes in productivity in agriculture and extractive industry whose quick achievement may also constitute a precondition for take-off.

In short, the technical nature of the economic tasks to be performed in the transition implies that the most important precondition for take-off is often political: that is, the establishment of an effective modern government.

III. THE TAKE-OFF

The "take-off" is a convenient name for that short stage of development, concentrated within two or three decades, in which the economy and the society of which it is part transform themselves so that economic growth becomes more or less automatic. This period can be approximately identified for Great Britain as falling between 1783 and 1802; for France, from 1830 to 1860; for the United States, from 1843 to 1860; for Germany, from 1850 to 1873; for Sweden, from 1868 to 1890: for Japan, from 1878 to 1900; for Russia, from 1890 to 1914. Argentina, Turkey, India, and China may be regarded as passing through the take-off period now.

The period is marked in general terms by a decisive shift—made possible by the full establishment of the preconditions discussed earlier—in the rate of investment, from about 5 per cent of the net national product to 10 per cent or more; with the historically typical population increase of between 1 and 1½ per cent per annum, an investment rate of about 10 per cent is necessary to ensure a sustained increase in capital per head. A take-off period also requires the development of one or more substantial manufacturing sectors, with a high rate of growth. Finally it requires that the political, social and institutional framework shall have so developed as to keep up a forward impetus of growth. This third condition includes a considerable capacity to mobilise capital from domestic sources—whether capital imports are also available or not.

The impetus and process of take-off have assumed many forms. The rate and productivity of investment can rise, and the process of growth become self-reinforcing, by many different technical and economic routes, in many different political, social and cultural settings, driven along by a wide variety of human motivations.

Land reforms and ploughing back

The internal supply of finance for the take-off has usually come from two types of sources: from shifts in the control over flows of income, and from the ploughing back of profits in particular rapidly expanding sectors. In Meiji Japan and Tsarist Russia the substitution of government bonds for the great landholders' claim on the flow of rent payments redistributed income into the hands of men more inclined to seek material advance and to accept innovations. Two positive impulses arose from land reform: the state itself used the flow of payments from peasants, now diverted from landlords' hands, for activity which encouraged economic development; and some of the more enterprising former landlords invested in commerce and industry.

In both cases, the real value of the government bonds exchanged for land depreciated; and in general the feudal landlords suffered a certain confiscation effect. Contemporary India is relying on income transfer by this route to a very limited extent; but Communist China has systematically transferred all non-governmental pools of capital into the hands of the state—and it is drawing heavily for capital resources on the mass of peasants.

How inflation helped

Inflation has also been important to several take-offs. In Britain of the late 1790s, the United States of the

1850s, and Japan of the 1870s, capital formation was aided by price inflation, which shifted resources from consumption to profits. The shift of incomes into more productive hands has, of course, been aided also by banks and capital markets. Virtually all take-off periods have been marked by the extension of both these sorts of institution.

A further necessary condition has been the existence of one or more rapidly growing sectors whose entrepreneurs, private or public, ploughed back a very high proportion of profits into new capacity. There are periods in economic history when quite substantial improvements in the machinery of capital supply do not, in themselves, initiate a take-off; e.g., banking developments in Britain in the century before 1783, in Russia before 1890. In other words, the demand side of the investment process, rather than the supply of loanable funds, may be the decisive element in the take-off.

One extremely important source of ploughed-back profits is foreign trade. Developing economies have created major export industries from their natural resources; and the expanded yield of these has financed the import of capital equipment during the take-off. United States, Russian, and Canadian grain, Swedish timber and pulp, and Japanese silk, all fulfilled this function during their countries' take-off periods. Chinese exports to the communist block, wrung at great administrative and human cost from the agricultural sector, now play the same role.

The development of export sectors does not itself, however, guarantee accelerated capital formation. Their proceeds can be used to finance hoards (as in the famous case of Indian bullion imports) or Cadillacs (as, occasionally, these days). Finally, foreign capital flows have, as in the United States, Russia, Sweden, and Canada, proved extremely important to the take-off, notably when lumpy overhead capital construction of long gestation period was required; but take-offs have also occurred (i.e., Britain and Japan) based almost wholly on domestic sources of finance.

Leading sectors

There is also much variety in the sectors which have played the key role in the take-off process. The original sector of primary growth in Britain was cotton textiles. This is not a representative case; the development of modern cotton textile industries in substitution for imports has more typically marked the pre-take-off period (e.g. in India, China, Mexico). The difference lies partly in the fact that by the late 18th century, the period of maximum growth in cotton, the preconditions for take-off in Britain were very fully developed. Progress in a number of industries had been considerable throughout the 18th century, and the social and institutional environment was propitious. But two further technical elements were important. First, the industry was large in relation to the whole economy; a high proportion of its output was exported; and its evolution was consequently a more massive fact, with wider secondary repercussions, than if it had been scaled to the domestic market alone. Industrial enterprise on this scale had secondary reactions on the development of urban areas, on the demand for coal, iron and machinery, for capital and ultimately for transport.

Secondly, technological developments in British cotton brought a sharp reduction in real costs and prices, and so tapped a source of effective demand for rapid expansion. This advantage was not enjoyed by later established cotton industries, for they merely substituted domestic for foreign-manufactured cotton textiles; there was no sharp fall in the real cost of acquiring cotton textiles, and no equivalent increase in real income.

The introduction of railways has been the most powerful single initiator of take-offs. It has had three major kinds of impact on growth during the take-off period. First, it has lowered internal transport costs and brought new areas and products into commerce. Secondly, it has often been a prerequisite to the development of a major new and rapidly enlarging export sector which in turn has generated capital for internal development. Thirdly, and perhaps most important for the take-off itself, its requirements have led to the development of modern coal, iron and engineering industries. In the absence of the general preconditions, however, very substantial railway building has failed to initiate a take-off, as for example in India, China, pre-1895 Canada, pre-1914 Argentina.

The role of armies

The enlargement and modernisation of armed forces can constitute a leading sector, as in the Russian, Japanese, and German take-offs, and in current Chinese communist plans. Historically, however, its role has been ancillary.

Raw materials and foodstuffs can play the role of leading sectors if they involve the application of modern processing techniques. The timber industry, built on the steam saw, fulfilled this function in Sweden; the shift of Denmark to meat and dairy products, after 1873, appears to have reinforced the development of a manufacturing sector in the economy; even the export of Japanese silk thread had important secondary effects, because of the export market's requirement for uniform high grade yarn, in developing modern production techniques. The role of leading sector has been assumed, finally, by a wide range of consumption goods produced in substitution for imports, as in Australia, Argentina, and perhaps contemporary Turkey.

There is, clearly, no one pattern or sequence for the take-off. There is no need for a growing society to recapitulate the course of events in Britain, the United States or Russia.

IV. THE DRIVE TO MATURITY

The road to maturity has everywhere been greatly influenced by the nature of the take-off. For one major group of nations the path lay in a complex of industries whose possibilities were, in part, unfolded from the railways. The requirements of railway maintenance placed a high premium on the production of cheap and good steel, because steel rails last longer than iron rails; in a sense the steel industry flowed from the railways, as in Britain, the railways had flowed from the requirements of cotton. But once good cheap steel was available, many further uses for it unfolded. The history of the engineering profession tells the story in compressed form. From railway engineering it fanned out into mechanical, chemical and electrical specialities, naval construction and civil engineering. It was in the technical experience of building and operating the railways that a good part of the foundations were laid for the march of the western world into maturity. The rise of steel is the central symbol of the post-railway movement to maturity in continental Europe and the United States.

Britain arrived at maturity first. But somewhere between the Crystal Palace exhibition of 1851 and the European slump of 1873—in the golden age, that is, of Victorian industrial prosperity—the relative position of the industrial powers shifted, in such a way that the United States, Germany, France and Britain entered the post-railway-building Age of Steel roughly together. Several factors combined to slow down the relative rate of Britain's development; but one is especially significant. It is one thing to be a mature economy, out at the margin of technology, having available each year only a rough approximation to the new technology created in, say, the previous year; it is a quite different thing to be a latecomer with a big unapplied backlog of technology available.

Once the United States and continental western Europe had completed their take-off, much of the British lead was gone; for they could bring the backlog of technology to bear more rapidly than it had been created. The story is being repeated now as Russia closes the technological gap on the West; China, India, Brazil and others promise to repeat the trick again on the older mature powers, including Russia, in the next half century or so.

Sweden accepts a challenge

For Sweden, the turning point into maturity came in the early 1890s, in the form of a challenge—a depression marked by a sagging away of the export markets on which most of the Swedish take-off had been built. (This is a normal occurrence. The take-off

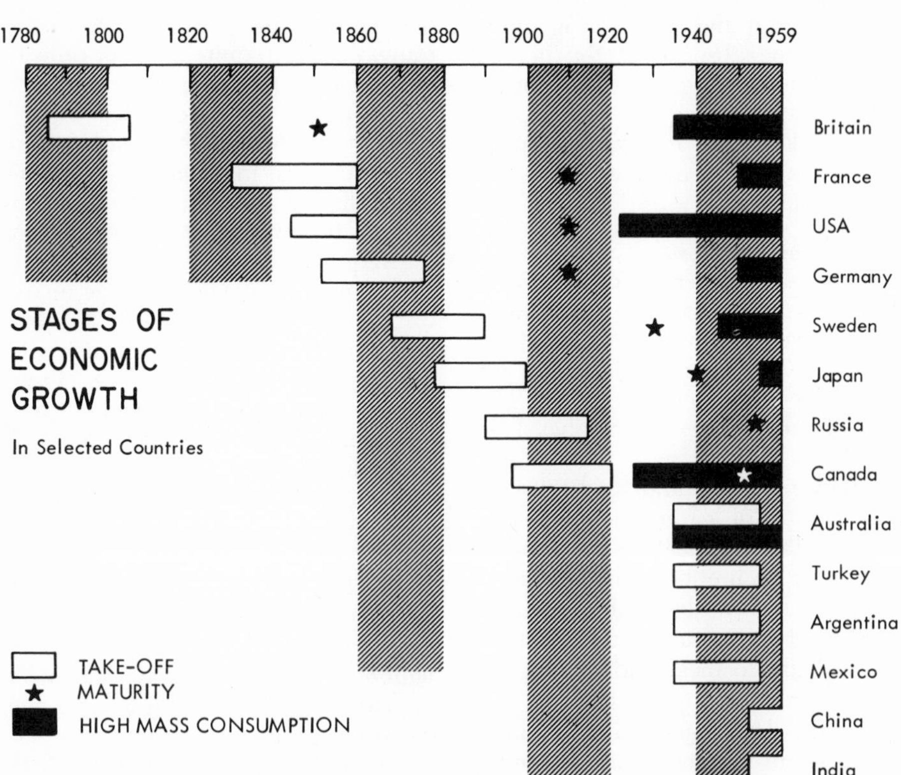

Note that Canada and Australia have entered the stage of high mass consumption before reaching maturity

is, structurally, a surge in output in a relatively few sectors. It is of the nature of investment that these sectoral surges should be overdone; indeed, this is the essence of the trade cycle. It then becomes necessary for the economy to re-group, reallocate its resources, and resume growth in new leading sectors. In fact, one measure of whether take-off has been achieved is a society's ability to redeploy in this way.)

In Sweden, there was a positive response; a shift from timber into woodpulp, from the export of unplaned to planed board and to matches. The Norrland ores began to be systematically exploited by modern methods; from pig iron there was a surge into highly refined steel and engineering industries; hydro-electric power was exploited, laying the basis for a highly skilled electrical industry which was later to help the railways to convert to electricity from coal. Sweden began to produce at home many manufactures hitherto imported. The 1890s marked, in Lindahl's phrase, the beginning of a phase of "differentiation of production." By the end of the 1920s Sweden had become a fully mature society, ready for the welfare state and the age of durable consumer goods.

Japan's narrow range

The story of Japan, in broad outline, bears a family resemblance to that of Sweden, despite its greater poverty of resources per head and a cultural and political setting that could hardly be less similar. The resemblance lies in the remarkably purposeful forward surge to maturity from, say, 1880 to 1940, in which a relatively narrow array of natural resources was harnessed by a diligent population to the best that modern technology could offer.

Japan offers a classic case of the role of agriculture in the transitional period; but agricultural dynamism alone could not have lifted Japan into take-off. In the 1880s and 1890s a whole series of new industries took hold, initially sparked by government initiative, but turned over to private enterprise as new men emerged ready to carry responsibilities and risks. Japan's take-off—say between 1880 and 1900—was built on railways, on shipbuilding, on cotton, on silk cultivation and manufacture, on coal and pig iron, and finally on a surge of military outlays helping to build up the engineering industry.

In 1900, Japan was still a society whose modern industrial sector was small and largely dominated by textiles. It was between 1900 and 1920—notably stimulated by the first world war—that this sector began to fan out into chemical fertilisers, steel, and electrical equipment. In the 1930s the engineering industries came into their own, under the stimulus of Manchuria and of war outlays and preparations; and the value of output in metals, machinery and chemicals at last came to outrank textiles. Thus, starting its take-off about thirty years after Germany and ten years after Sweden, Japan also reached maturity about the same period after them, just about in phase.

Russia, after a particularly long transition period—until 1861 the traditional society gave way only very slowly—began its take-off about 1890. This, like the concurrent Canadian take-off, was aided by the world rise in grain prices which occurred in the mid-90s; for this rise made attractive, in both countries, the laying of vast railway nets. It was the railway, with its multiple impact on growth, that took Russia through its take-off by the outbreak of the first world war. Coal, iron and engineering surged ahead, as did a modern cotton industry to meet the expanded home demand. The Baku petroleum field expanded to its natural limit; the Ukrainian coal-iron complex was brought to life, as the Ruhr and the Pennsylvania and Mid-Western complexes had been half a century earlier.

Tsarist take-off

It is often forgotten nowadays that for two decades before 1914 Russia's industrial output as a whole had been increasing on the average about 8 per cent per annum. The communists inherited an economy which had taken off; the five year plans are to be understood not as a take-off but as a drive to maturity—the process of industrial differentiation, the advance on a wide front. With certain specific differences stemming from the objectives of the communist leadership, the broad pattern of Soviet economic growth between 1929 and, say, Stalin's death is like that of western Europe and the United States of the pre-1914 decades; this was the post-railway age in Russia, the age of steel, machine tools, chemicals and electricity.

There were essentially three differences. First, the Soviet government damped the rise in consumption and concentrated on capital formation and military items, giving a disproportionate emphasis to the metal using industries as opposed to, say, housing, textiles or transport. Secondly, despite large capital outlays in agriculture, collectivisation damped productivity and decreed that a quite abnormal proportion of the labour force should remain on the land. Thirdly, the Russian surge to maturity came when the backlog of accumulated technological possibilities included developments (notably in aeronautics, electronics, atomic energy) which were not available to earlier developing societies, so that when Russia drew technologically abreast it did so at a different level from that of the powers that had reached maturity by 1914. In its broad shape and timing, then, there is nothing about the Russian sequence that does not fall within the general pattern—though, like all other national stories, it has unique features.

Doing without a Ruhr

These case studies carry important implications for today. The variety of sectoral patterns in the drive to maturity needs emphasis in a world where so many nations are seeking take-off. The minds of the leaders of the undeveloped countries are likely to be filled with visions of, say, the American, German, and Russian patterns—as they understand them—rather than the probably more relevant Swedish and Japanese patterns. But few nations have been endowed with a Pennsylvania, a Ruhr, a Black Country or a Ukraine. Most have some narrower range of natural resources whose vigorous exploitation, in a world market, can do the trick. And some must rely almost wholly on the skill, motivation and energy of their peoples like Switzerland, Israel, and Hongkong, which have performed a kind of economic rope trick, climbing into industrialisation with virtually no visible means of support.

So far, maturity has been discussed from the side of changes in technology and the composition of the working force—that is, the side of supply. What about demand and real income per head? Can we associate the end of take-off with some clear-cut figure for gross national product per head, maturity with another, the age of high mass consumption and durable consumer goods with a third? In an exploratory mood it may be surmised that for each stage there will be found not a single, typical figure but a band. By the end of take-off real annual income may lie, in current American dollars, anywhere from, let us say, $150 per head to $300; by the end of the drive to maturity anywhere from $400 to $600.

Just as traditional societies may, according to the pressure of population upon resources, trading patterns, etc., have annual incomes per head varying considerably up from a (say) $40 per head minimum, so such differentials may persist through the whole sweep of the growth process into maturity. It is important not to confuse being technologically mature with being rich; for example, military potential must not be confused with national income per head or consumption per head.

From confidence . . .

The development of the maturing society has important non-economic aspects. At the end of take-off, the new modern elements are in full and confident power, with their opponents in retreat or disarray. Post-1815 Britain, post-Civil War America, Bismarck's Germany after 1870, Stalin's Russia of the five year plans—these were all societies run by men who knew where they were going. By and large these were confident periods, with big palpable tasks whose results could quickly be seen; and the society, reluctantly or otherwise, gave its industrial leaders their head. The fortunes of the urban and agricultural workers varied, during the drive to maturity, from comfortable Sweden to Stalin's forced labour society; but generally the power of those who controlled capital and technology was not seriously opposed.

Nevertheless, the process had within it the seeds of its own modification. First, it involved a change in the working force. Advancing maturity brings not only a growth of urban population but an increase in the proportion of white collar workers, highly trained technicians and professionals—the increasingly knowledgeable children of the city and the world of technology. Their real wages are likely to be rising; and, more important, they perceive that by organising and making their presence felt they can achieve higher real wages and greater security. Thus the very process of moving towards maturity generates the kind of social pressures which in turn enforce humane modifications to that process —from the British factory legislation of the 1840s through Bismarck's concessions, Lloyd George's reforms, the American Progressive era, and perhaps the concessions made to the Russian consumer and technician since 1953.

Secondly, the character of the leadership changes, from the buccaneering cotton, railway, steel and oil baron to the efficient professional manager of a highly bureaucratised and differentiated machine.

. . . to doubt

Thirdly, the society as a whole becomes a bit bored with the miracle of industrialisation, developing second thoughts about its merits as a unique and overriding objective. The Fabians and the muck-rakers, Ibsen and Shaw and Dreiser, express these second thoughts; and Marx fits into the same framework of protest against the human costs of the drive to maturity.

These changes in the structure, ambitions and outlook of the society lead up to a set of searching choices concerned with future objectives. How shall the mature industrial machine, with compound interest built into it, be used? To offer increased security, welfare, and perhaps leisure for all? To offer enlarged real incomes, including manufactured consumer gadgets, to those who can earn them? To assert the stature of the new mature society on the world scene by military adventures? Maturity, like middle age, is a time of dangerous as well as promising choices.

V. The Age of High Consumption

When the values of the market place and the imperatives of diffusing the new technology lose their monopolistic control over men's minds, what happens next? Each society which has attained maturity has struck a different balance, determined by geography, resources, values, and the dominant political leadership, between four broad objectives. These are:

> The national pursuit of external power and influence, about which more will be said later;
>
> the welfare state, in which increases in output and incentives in the private sector are given a lower priority in relation to the cushioning of hardships arising from the trade cycle, the increase of social security, the redistribution of income, and a general mitigation of harshness;
>
> the expansion of mass consumption levels, beyond basic food, shelter and clothing, not only into better food, shelter and clothing but into durable consumer goods and services;
>
> and, finally, leisure—the reduction of the working week and the easing of the intensity of labour.

This balance has varied over time as well as between countries.

In America, the "Progressive Era" from 1901 to 1916 brought a shift of social objectives rather than a drastic reallocation of resources. By 1916 the United States had accepted the most revolutionary of all forms of economic policy, the progressive income tax; it had created a climate in which big business curbed itself or was, to a degree, curbed; the trade unions were explicitly given the right to organise; a federal reserve banking system had been created, partly to exercise a degree of control over the trade cycle. The public interest also won new recognition in the policy of conservation, national parks and reservations.

Suburbs and gadgetry

The same period saw Americans make another significant decision about the direction of national affairs. In the 1890s a wide-spread mood was generating that it was time for the United States to play a major role in the world scene; to move out from behind the protective barrier represented by the Monroe Doctrine. But the so-called Large View symbolised by Theodore Roosevelt failed to take hold. The Philippines were kept; but Americans in the end turned their backs on the acquisition of empire, opting in foreign policy for a version of the British Liberal rather than the British Conservative tradition.

It was into the third post-maturity alternative—new dimensions of consumption—that American resources increasingly flowed; the trend was damped by the rise in urban living costs down to 1920, but became palpable in the boom of the ensuing decade. The 1920s were marked, first, by the rise of a new middle class; the era of the professional technician and the white and blue collar workers had come. They were marked by a flow not only to the cities but also, and more strongly, to the suburbs. They were marked above all by the rise of the automobile; the United States took to wheels—and began a vast inner immigration into new single-family houses in the suburbs, filled increasingly with radios, refrigerators, and the other gadgetry of a society whose social mobility and productivity had all but wiped out personal service. Americans shifted their food consumption to high grade foods, increasingly purchased in cans, or later, frozen.

Then came, of course, a decade's severe and protracted depression. In its onset, this was a perfectly normal cyclical downturn; it went abnormally deep because of the breakdown of institutions of credit at home and abroad. Its length, however, was related directly to the stage of growth that the United States had entered. When investment comes to be centred on industries and services based not on cost-reducing industrial processes—as, for instance, in the railway age—but on expanding consumption, full employment is needed, in a sense, to support full employment. Unless consumption levels press outward, capacity in consumers' goods industries and those supplying them will be under-used, and the impulse to invest will be weak. American industry appeared almost to have stabilised at a lower level, when World War II, like a sort of *deus ex machina,* restored full employment.

During the 1930s American society did more, of course than merely experience depression. It threw its weight hard towards another post-maturity alternative, that is, social welfare; and the contours of the welfare state were rounded out, under Franklin Roosevelt, to remain an accepted part of the American scene.

The fourth phase, the great post-war boom of 1946–56, can be regarded as a resumption of the boom of the 1920's, with a resumed march to the outer suburbs, and a resumed extension of ownership for cars, refrigerators, and gadgets generally. This extension has reached the point where it is clear that American growth can no longer continue to be based so heavily on the diffusion, to a higher and higher proportion of the community, of standard consumer durables. In all sectors growth curves are subject to long run deceleration; as the automobile industry has found.

The baby boom

What, then, does the future hold? Are Americans, having fashioned this suburban, mobile civilisation, going to settle down to tidy it up a little and enjoy the benefits of affluence with a four day working week? The prospect is altered by the extraordinary and unexpected decision of Americans to have more babies. The wartime rise in the birth rate from 18 per 1,000 to about 22 was to a large extent a phenomenon of resumed full employment and early wartime marriages. But in the postwar years the birth rate moved further up and stayed at about 25 per 1,000, yielding a population rise of 1.5 per cent per annum; the consequent changes in the age structure of the population and in the rate of family formation are of major economic significance.

Combined with other circumstances—notably the cumulative deficit in social capital and the cost of the arms race—the increase in the ratio of dependants to producers is likely to make the next decade of American history one of vigorous expansion of output with a degree of austerity at the level of private consumption. By its own choice, American society in 1959 is less affluent than it looks.

Britain's lag and new surge

Why, after 1851, did Britain not move faster from technical maturity into the age of high consumption? First, maturity is a matter of virtuosity and the spread of technique on the supply side. In the 19th century British real income per head certainly rose, but in the form of more and better food and clothing, better housing, public utilities and transport. The age of consumer durables began modestly in the 1890s with the bicycle boom; it gripped Britain solidly only in the later 1930s, to be then interrupted by war. The surge of high mass consumption was properly resumed only in the 1950s; it is now well under way.

Secondly, nineteenth-century Britain was a major industrial region in a world economy—just as New England was a major industrial region in the American continental economy. Capital and manpower, being then mobile, were drawn to the points of expected higher private yield and real wages. Britain, in sending capital abroad to open up farming territories or build railways, was indeed obtaining invisible imports in the short run and cheaper supplies of food and raw materials in the long run. But it was doing more. British emigration and capital exports benefited the whole world trading area. The relatively slow rise in real income—and in population—in advanced areas like Britain and New England is partly to be explained by a policy which permitted men and capital to seek points of highest expected real wages and private profitability.

Thirdly, the timing of the stages of growth was affected, in Britain as elsewhere, by intervals when resources were devoted to war, wasted in gold mining, or wasted—as in the inter-war years—because public policy failed promptly to create the conditions for a regular movement forward. Nothing in the stages of growth analysis guarantees that real income per head will move steadily forward at the same pace everywhere. Nothing makes the stages independent of wastage of capital in war or in attractive but unproductive pursuits, or of the course of public policy.

European choices

Western Europe as a whole made a different sequence of choices from America's among the post-maturity alternatives. Before 1914 its societies moved more sharply towards the welfare state than did America. Basically, this was probably because they were less agrarian in their political balance; but other elements counted, notably the greater weight of socialist doctrines and ideals within the industrial working force and among intellectual leaders.

In the 1920s western Europe faced more severe problems of reconstruction and readjustment than the United States, and it did not proceed straight away into the age of consumer durables. In general there was, for most of Europe, only about four years of normal prosperity, 1925–1929, which approximately restored, or slightly improved on, 1913 levels of output. In consequence western Europe fell relatively behind America. This failure to expand corresponds, in terms of the analysis of the stages of growth, to a failure to make the logical move into the normal stage of growth beyond maturity.

In the 1930s, when the policies of European governments began to create an environment of greater prosperity, income elasticities of demand expressed themselves in a disproportionate rise in demand for consumer durables and services. In 1929, for instance, the motor vehicle production of the four major European nations was only 13 per cent of that of America; by 1938 the corresponding figure was 44 per cent.

The worker's awakening

The lag in Europe's shift to the roads can be partly accounted for by lack of capital for road building; by the monopolistic power of the railways and the governments behind them; by the earlier American start with the concept of the mass produced car for the mass market; by the greater distances in the United States and the greater availability of cheap suburban housing sites. But it is also true that American society with its egalitarian bias and its traditional high wages took more easily to the concept of high mass consumption. The European worker took only slowly to the idea that the gadgets, travel, and other services a mature economy can afford, were really for him.

But of course another factor determined the outcome. In almost every mature society the Great Depression broke the hold of a generation of political leaders whose desire had been to re-create a pre-1914 "normalcy." In the United States it brought to power leaders who installed a version of the welfare state; in Britain, governments that built prosperity of a sort on housing, the devaluation of 1931 and Empire Preference; in France, a Popular Front government. But in Germany and Japan the breakdown—economic, diplomatic and military—of the system implicit in the Versailles settlement brought regimes which opted for a quite different use of the potentialities of mature economies: military expansion. The rise of these regimes imposed in turn a quite different set of imperatives on all other societies. In the short run, rearmament became a factor in European recovery; in the not-so-long run there was a major war.

Un-American activity

In the postwar years, an interval of reconstruction followed. But this time western Europe, and to a degree Japan, broke out into the phase of durable consumers' goods and services. Between 1950 and 1955 the gap between American and western European outlays on consumer durables began to narrow, and reached a point where it can almost wholly be explained in terms of relative incomes and prices. All the postwar mature societies of the West and Japan are behaving in a remarkably "American" manner; the only major exceptions are the Americans themselves, with their curious new obsession with family life, privacy, do-it-yourself, getting away in caravans and motor boats, and writing impiously about the Organisation Man.

It must be emphasised again that western Europe's consumer boom is not a strictly postwar development. The Great West Road, Coventry, the Morris works, are earlier phenomena; and the Volkswagen—as a conception—is a product of pressures for a kind of consumption to which Hitler's government felt a need to respond, if only by gesture. But it is only in the postwar years that the obstacles—technical, political, and sociological—were cleared away. The momentum of western Europe, which compares favourably with those both of the pre-1914 years and of the postwar United States, can be largely attributed to the acceptance of the age of high mass consumption.

What lies beyond?

The era of high consumption has by no means come to an end even in the United States; and it is still gathering momentum in western Europe and in Japan. There is bound to be variety in the patterns of consumption that will emerge as compound interest grinds on and as the income elasticities of demand, in their widest sense, reveal themselves in different societies. For example, other societies need not invest as much as the United States in the automobile, or set up the suburbs so far away from the centres of cities. There are grave geographical and physical limits to the repetition of this pattern, except perhaps in Russia. To the degree that consumer sovereignty is respected and real incomes increase it is likely, however, that similar though not identical patterns of structural evolution will emerge in different societies passing through the high consumption phase.

Leaving aside the arms race and the threat of war; what lies beyond? The life of most human beings since the beginning of time has been mainly taken up with gaining food, shelter and clothing. What will happen when diminishing relative marginal utility sets in, on a mass basis, for real income itself? Are poverty and civil strife a necessary condition for a lively human existence?

Present generations are unlikely to have to face this problem; others more urgent stand in the way. There are the modern weapons of mass destruction which, if not tamed and controlled, could solve this and all other human problems once and for all. There is also the fact that the whole southern half of the globe plus China is caught up in the stage of preconditions for take-off or in the take-off itself. Shall we see, in a little while, a new sequence of political leaders enticed to aggression by their new found technical maturity; or a global reconciliation of the human race?

2

*Economic Development: Rival Systems and Comparative Advantage**

John Kenneth Galbraith

J. Kenneth Galbraith, *Professor of Economics at Harvard, has had a distinguished record of public service since 1940. He was economic advisor to the National Defense Advisory Commission, director of the Office of Economic Security Policy of the State Department and served as United States Ambassador to India under President John F. Kennedy. His books include* The Affluent Society *(1958) and* The Liberal Hour *(1960).*

One of the well-observed features of economic development in the 20th century is the need to choose between two broad political and economic designs. This choice, one from which developing nations of the 18th and 19th centuries were conveniently exempt, is between Western constitutional organization on the one hand and Marxian and neo-Marxian polity and economic organization on the other.

These are not, as everyone knows, homogeneous alternatives. Wide differences separate a state such as Poland, where the agriculture, and hence close to half the economy, remains in private hands and subject to market influences, from the far more com-

* *Department of State Bulletin,* **XLVII** (1962), 13–17.

pletely socialized economy of the Chinese mainland. There are similar distinctions between the non-Marxian economies, which, in this case, are enlarged by terminological preference and political semantics. In Scandinavia, the United Kingdom and modern India the word "socialism" is politically evocative. As a result politicians try to find as much of it as possible. In the United States, steps that would elsewhere be identified with socialist enlightenment—social security, agricultural price guarantees, even the public development of public power sites—are firmly for the purpose of making private enterprise function better.

Also one must be cautious in speaking of a "choice" between the two designs. Geography and the proximity of military power have had much to do with the decision. Had Poland, to select a country not unaccustomed to movement, been radically relocated after World War II to approximately the position of Paraguay, her subsequent economic and political history would have been rather different. Individuals do commit themselves as a matter of free choice to a Marxian political and economic design. But nations have rarely done so in the normal course of unmanaged elections—a reluctance, incidentally, which was foreseen by both Marx and Lenin.

Nevertheless these broad alternatives exist. My purpose is to weigh their advantages and disadvantages from the standpoint of the developing country. I am aware that an American ambassador will not be considered by everyone a wholly impartial judge. And even in this liberal and sophisticated gathering there would doubtless be eyebrow-lifting if my evidence were to lead me to the wrong conclusion.

But the choice merits serious assessment. Much of the present literature consists of declarations of superiority by one side or the other. We share with the Communists a strong faith in the value of robust assertion. Were the advantage all on our side, we would have little reason to worry. But we do worry, and it might be well, accordingly, for us to have a moderately unemotional appraisal of what we have to offer the developing nations as compared with the Communists.

THE GOAL OF DEVELOPING COUNTRIES

The goal of the developing country can be quickly stated: It is to bring itself as rapidly as possible into the 20th century and with the apparatus of individual and group well-being—food, clothing, education, health services, housing, entertainment, and automobiles—which is associated in every mind, urban and rural, bourgeois and Bolshevist, with 20th-century existence. Here and there are some that demur. But in my observation the most monastic Christian, the most contemplative Buddhist, and the most devout Gandhian cannot be considered completely secure against the charms of the bicycle, motor scooter, or transistor radio.

The things associated with modern civilization are now denied by backwardness and poverty. The task of the two systems is to overcome this poverty. The causes of poverty, in turn, are not simple—although the problem has suffered prodigiously from oversimplification. One cause, clearly, is an oppressive social structure which channels return from the many to the few and which denies the individual the natural reward of his efforts at self-improvement. Another is a feeble, nonexistent, or corrupt apparatus of public administration which denies to the country the things—law and order, education, investment in roads, power, manufacturing—which are possible only where there is effective public authority. Or poverty may be itself a cause of poverty; it denies the country capital for investment, revenues for education, or purchasing power for consumer products which, in turn, are an incentive to effort. Thus property perpetuates itself. Such are the fundamentals that both systems must attack. It is unlikely that the same causes operate in the same form and with the same intensity in any two cases. An effective attack, therefore, requires not only efficient remedies but effective diagnosis of the condition to be cured.

Both systems agree on a number of important points. It is common ground that a shortage of capital is a likely cause of stagnation. Both agree on the need for a massive volume of investment to initiate and stimulate not only economic but social advance. There is agreement also that this investment should be in accordance with a carefully conceived plan. (Here we have paid the Soviets the compliment of appropriating an important idea.) There is increasing agreement that a principal object of this investment must be in the educational and cultural improvement of people themselves. The visitor to the more remote parts of Soviet Asia is immediately impressed by the volume of resources going into schools, colleges, adult education programs, and other forms of cultural extension as part of the attack on the traditional backwardness of these areas. If, in the years following World War II, we thought too much of investment in terms of physical capital and too little of the importance of a literate and educated populace, this is an error we are now correcting.

There are, however—and this will doubtless come as a relief—important differences between the two approaches, and these are vital. The first lies in the diagnosis of the causes of poverty and the related remedy. The second difference is in the way development is organized. The third is in the political and constitutional environment of development. Let me take up each of these differences in turn.

Diagnosing the Causes of Poverty

In the Marxian view poverty is principally caused by institutions which chain the country to its past—which hold it in colonial subjection, which exploit and subjugate the masses and deny them the reward of their labor, which make government not the efficient servant of the many but the corrupt handmaiden of the few.

In the predominant Western view the poor are the victims of their poverty. All societies have capacity for growth; the poor society lacks the resources to invest in growth. Having less than enough for its current needs for food, clothing, and shelter, it has nothing for investment in education, improved agriculture, transportation, public utilities, or industrial enterprise.

Each of these views leads naturally to a prescription. If institutions hold a country to its past, the answer is the elimination of these institutions. If the problem is the self-perpetuating character of privation, the answer is to provide the catalyzing resources—specifically, economic aid and assistance in its use—which the country cannot supply to itself.

This is the first difference. The Marxian emphasis is on the institutions that inhibit progress and the need to eliminate them. Our emphasis is on the self-perpetuating character of poverty and the catalyzing role of aid. It will be noted that each system has a cause and remedy that is not without convenience to itself. The Soviets, at least until recently, were short of capital. They had a revolution which could be exported at moderate expense. Accordingly it was convenient to associate backwardness with colonialism, feudalism, and repressive capitalism, all of which could be eliminated by revolution. By contrast, we had capital. This we could export with greater ease than comprehensive social change.

The second difference is in the way development is organized. Although there is room for some national preference, and heresy cannot be entirely eliminated, the Marxian commitment is still to state ownership of the means of production—of land, capital plant, and natural resources. Private ownership of productive resources and their use for private gain is one of the retarding institutions. Its elimination leaves the state in possession and this continues. Incentives to individual and group effort are strongly supported. But incentives which use the device of property ownership to combine reward for individual effort with reward for management of property are excluded in principle and in large measure in practice.

The non-Marxian design for organizing development is not so easily characterized. In the past many countries—Japan, Germany, Canada, and to a remarkable degree also the United States—have made state ownership of canals, turnpikes, railroads, electric power and other utilities, and even steel mills the fulcrum of development policy. India, Egypt, and some South American countries are taking the same course today. However, the main and indeed overwhelming reliance in non-Marxian development, both in agriculture and industry, is on private ownership of productive plant. This is true of countries, such as India, which choose to describe themselves as socialist.

Western Advantage in Providing Capital

The foregoing differences are sufficiently sharp so that we can relate them to results. And in Eastern Europe and China, not to mention the much older case of the Soviet Union, there is now an ample experience of Marxian development on which to draw.

Two major advantages lie with the Western or non-Marxian alternatives. There is, we have anciently been advised, a certain physical difficulty in extracting blood from a stone. This, however, is comparatively easy as compared with getting savings out of a poor society. When people do not have enough to eat, they are loathe to forego any part of their meal in order to eat better in the future. Pleas on behalf of children and grandchildren leave the man of simple, uncomplicated intelligence unmoved; he reflects that starvation will prevent his having children and, *pro tanto,* grandchildren as well. But Marxian no less than non-Marxian societies must have savings; without them there can be no growth. Accordingly, the Western pattern of development, with its prospect of assistance from outside the country, eases one of the most painful problems of development. This is why economic aid has become such an important feature of Western foreign policy. It is the process by which savings are transferred from countries where saving is comparatively unpainful to those where it is very painful. It exploits one of the major advantages of our system.

The Communist countries are not without resources in this respect. The Soviet Union, though its capacity has been far less than ours, has spared some savings for other countries. Communist economic and political organization deals more effectively—or ruthlessly—with unproductive and excessively luxurious consumption, of which there is always some and may be much in the poor country. And Communist organization can, within limits, squeeze blood from its turnip. The penalty is the pain, and this cannot be avoided. The rioting in Poland in 1956 which brought Mr. Gomulka to power was occasioned in large measure by the enforcement of a rate of saving that was too grim for the people to bear. These last years on the Chinese mainland have evidently been ones of serious trouble and tension. Part of the problem is inherent in socialist organization of agriculture to which I will advert in a moment. But some has certainly been the consequence of squeezing a large volume of savings out of a very poor population.

The larger consequence is that Marxian development risks the alienation of the people as non-Marxian development does not. It seems doubtful if a majority of the Chinese people are very pleased with their government and would vote for it in an uninhibited poll. By contrast, in India, after a decade of development, there has been an overwhelming vote for the government that led the task. If the Indian Government had to subtract the $7.3 billions it has received from the West in overseas loans and grants since independence from the meager incomes —an average of about $70 per year—of its own people, its popularity might well have suffered. We see in India, in remarkably clear relief, the advantages of the Western design in providing capital.

Western Advantage in Agriculture

The second and equally substantial advantage of Western development is in the matter of agriculture. Industry, on the record at least, is fairly tolerant as to forms of organization. American industry works well under private ownership. Even the most reluctant among us must agree that the Soviets have made considerable progress with socialism. So no decisive contrast can be registered here. But the undeveloped country is, by definition, a pastoral or agrarian community. The agricultural policy is, accordingly, vital. And it is far from clear, as a practical matter, whether it is possible to socialize a small-scale, densely populated, peasant agriculture. Even in the Soviet Union the agricultural problem has not been wholly solved. And here, at least, there is no serious talk of catching up. Each year we insouciantly extend our advantage in manhour productivity without effort and somewhat to our regret. Outside the Soviet Union, agriculture has been even more of a problem. Poland and Yugoslavia have had to revert to private ownership. In China, by all external evidence, the effort to socialize agriculture has brought a serious crisis. Certainly it has forced her to turn to the West for the largest food imports in history.

There are good reasons for this failure. Farmers, when they are small and numerous, cannot be brought unwillingly into a state-run system of agriculture for they can defeat any system that is available for their control. The employees of a factory, like the men of an army, are subject to external discipline. Failure in performance can be detected, judged, and penalized. (The same rule holds for certain types of plantation agriculture.) A scattered peasantry, carrying on the diverse tasks of crop and especially of livestock husbandry cannot be so regimented. As a consequence, productivity falls off. Working for others, the farmer works at the minimum rather than the maximum, and the difference between the two is enormous. He can be made to work at the maximum by giving him land to work and rewarding him with the fruits of his labor or some substantial share to consume or exchange as he wishes. But this is to restore individual proprietorship—private capitalism—which its doctrine excludes.

One day the Marxian economies may succeed in socializing agriculture—no effort is being spared. And the ability of the small man in agriculture to sabotage a system he dislikes or which treats him badly is not confined to communism. It is the reason for the low productivity and backwardness of the latifundia of Latin America and the feudal domains of the Middle East. But the fact that it accepts independent agricultural proprietorship is the second clear advantage of Western development.

Eliminating Retarding Institutions

I come now to a disadvantage of Western development. The Marxian alternative, I have noted, emphasizes the destruction of the bonds that tie the economy to the past. Our emphasis is on capital, education, technical assistance, and the other instruments that allow of change. Until recently, at least, we have been tempted to suppose that any society is a platform on which, given these missing elements, development can be built.

In fact, institutions do chain economies to the past, and the breaking of these chains is essential for progress. The promise that this will be done is a valid and an appealing part of the Marxian case. There is no chance of agricultural development in the underdeveloped and hence agricultural country under systems of absentee landlordism, with the workers or sharecroppers confined by law and tradition to a minor share of a meager product. And feudal systems of farming extend their corrupting influence to government, to the provision of public sinecures to those who lack a claim on the land, to the milking of middle-class and industrial enterprise, and to the destruction of incentives, and the morale of the society itself. "In our country," a South American guide once told me, "those who do the least get the most. I hear that in the United States it is the other way around. It's a better system." Progress does require the radical elimination of retarding institutions. If elimination can be had from no other source, the Marxian alternative will sooner or later be tried. The revolution they offer here, we should remind ourselves, is less the Russian Revolution than the French Revolution.

Political Environment

I come now to the final point of comparison—one, unfortunately, which has been much damaged by bad rhetoric. From the earliest days of their development, personal liberty, equal justice under law, and constitutional government have been important to Englishmen and to Americans. They haven't been the concern of everyone, but we have never supposed they were the fad of the esoteric and privileged minority.

And so it is in the undeveloped country today. The Andean Indian and the landless worker in the Indian village do have a preoccupying concern with keeping themselves fed. But the general yearning for the dignity of democratic and constitutional government is very great. No people who live under a dictatorship ever feel themselves to be first-class citizens.

There can be little question that most people believe that liberty and constitutional process are safer with the Western than with the Marxian alternative. We haven't, in my view, made as much of this advantage as we might. But the Communists are under the considerable handicap that their alternative involves a step into the dark. And while the details are obscure, most people know that it does not involve free selection of rulers by the governed, *habeas corpus,* equal justice under law, and a voluntary return to other economic arrangements should the experiment prove unpalatable.

Making Use of the Advantages

On first assessment, then, the advantage of the non-Marxian alternative for the developing country is considerable. It promises at least a partial avoidance of the pain that for the poor country is inherent in finding savings for investment and growth. It promises an acceptable and viable system of agriculture rather than a certain unpalatable and possibly unworkable one. And it offers personal liberty and constitutional process. Against this the Marxian alternative promises a more rigorous attack on the institutions—the unproductive claims on revenue and especially the feudal control of land—which exclude change.

But this is not a game where one can count the cards and decide the winner. Some cards count for more than others, and there is the unfortunate possibility that some good cards will not get played.

The Marxian promise can be decisive. That is because the things we offer are only effective and attractive after the retarding institutions are eliminated. In a country where land and other resources are held by and operated for the benefit of a slight minority and where the apparatus of government serves principally to reinforce such privilege, aid is not of much use. It will also benefit not the many but the few. Our promise of independent proprietorship is obviously nullified so long as land remains in the hands of the few. And personal liberty and constitutional government have little meaning in countries where government is of the privileged for the rich.

We must, in short, meet the Marxian promise of reform of retarding institutions. We cannot organize revolution. We can place our influence solidly on the side of reform. Having done this, our cards give us a clear advantage. To be sure, we must play them. We must make good with aid on our promise of a less painful savings and investment process. We must give firm support to the small farmer. We must be clear in our commitment to constitutional process and personal liberty. We cannot suppose that these are wanted only by people of Anglo-Saxon origin of good income. And we must not excuse dictatorship on grounds of anticommunism or convenience in the absence of visible alternatives. The price of doing so, as we have so painfully learned, is disaster magnified by postponement.

These are highly practical matters. If there are no advantages in our alternative, it won't be chosen. The first resort to the Marxian alternative in this hemisphere was in a country where the concentration of wealth and land ownership was extreme, where these had extended a corrupting influence to other economic life and to government, and where dictatorship had been endemic. This being the experience with the Western alternative, it was not remarkable that so many were so little perturbed by the alternative. India, in face of formidable difficulties, is firmly committed to development on the Western model. That is because already in British India and over the whole country at the time of independence there was a strong attack on retarding institutions —especially on the feudal claims of princes, zamindars and great landlords, and government which was an extension of this landed power; because a substantial measure of peasant ownership had replaced the old system; because aid from outside eased the problem of supply capital; and because people felt secure in the protection of constitutional guarantees and representative government.

The lesson is clear. The advantages are with us. We must, however, have confidence in them and exploit them to the full.

CHAPTER FIFTEEN

Policies of Non-Commitment

If one compares a map of the world in 1939 or 1945 with one in the mid-1960's, the most significant change in the structure of the international environment relates to the growth in the number of countries which constitute the system of states that one studies in international relations. Almost without exception, these new states are former colonial territories and have since the war changed that status to the new status of national independence. This development, of unprecedented scope and rapidity, is one of the most important and far-reaching changes in the history of the international system.

Most of the new states lie in Asia and Africa. No two of them are completely alike, of course, but the newly independent countries do show certain similarities which permit us to make some general statements about them. All of these areas have a history of Western domination of varying lengths and varying degrees of severity and/or benefit. All of them fall into the category usually referred to as "underdeveloped."[1] This means that these countries tend to be characterized by a precarious economic and social base, low productivity, and low standards of living. Their economies have traditionally been almost completely dependent on the production of agricultural commodities and the extraction of raw materials, with little industrial development. Their inhabitants lack most of the necessities and amenities of life that citizens in the more highly developed states have long since come to take for granted. In Leonard Kenworthy's pithy, if tragic, phrase, two-thirds of the world's population are "ill-fed, ill-clothed, ill-housed, illiterate, and ill."[2] And although, as we indicated earlier, attempts are being made to alleviate these deplorable situations, progress is slow and the absolute gap between the more and the less developed countries is widening rather than narrowing.

The social and economic problems faced by these new states have to some extent been covered in the preceding chapter. We now turn to the political

[1] The term "underdeveloped," although preferable to the term "backward" which was used in the 1940's, is not without ambiguities. In a sense, every country is "underdeveloped" if present conditions are viewed in relation to future potential. For a clear discussion of this ever-changing semantic phenomenon, see Arthur C. Turner, in *Tension Areas in World Affairs* (Belmont, California: Wadsworth Publishing Co., Inc., 1964), p. 9 n.

[2] The phrase was used some years ago at a Quaker Meeting in Philadelphia.

and, to some extent, the military problems confronting these societies. Although once again one must make allowance for individual deviations from the pattern, the general policy line which most of these countries have pursued has been one of reluctance or outright refusal to align themselves with either of the major power centers, and of insistence upon pursuing policies independent from those of the major powers. The generic term commonly attached to this policy line is that of "neutralism." There has, understandably, been concern, puzzlement, and more than a little irritation on the part of the Western powers toward neutralism; Professor Kissinger's comments, printed below, give some evidence of this. American politicians and statesmen have taken issue not only with the policy of non-commitment or neutralism itself, but also with the tone of superior morality which is often attached to it—this in spite of the fact that one should have thought certain of them would not avail themselves of the opportunity to object to expressions of high morality of which so many of them seem extraordinarily fond themselves. Our task here, however, is not to take issue, not to object, not to try to reform, but rather to understand what has prompted most of the countries under discussion to adopt the positions which characterize their policies.

The options before new states in today's world environment are not different from those before older and more established societies. They can align themselves with the Western coalition, whose professed purpose is to oppose the expansion of Communism and to protect and safeguard areas in which free institutions have an opportunity to be built and to flourish. Secondly, they can align themselves with either of the major Communist powers, the Soviet Union or China, in their efforts to expand the area in which the principles and practices of Marxism, as currently interpreted and applied, hold sway in economic, social, and political relations. Thirdly, they can make efforts to join with other states which belong to neither camp led by the major powers. Finally, they have the option to adopt a stance of complete independence of action.

In practice, the policies of the new states have tended to shift between the third and the fourth of these alternatives. There have been, and continue to be, attempts to form blocs designed to enhance the power of individual states through common action. Very frequently such common action takes place in the halls of international organizations. One can argue that, on the whole, the very number of new countries represented at the United Nations tends to control the policies of that organization, if only negatively by preventing certain stands from being taken and certain courses of action from being pursued. It is not as easy to see how the so-called Afro-Asian bloc can positively influence the policies of the organization, because while it has numbers, it lacks financial, economic, and military capacity to implement affirmative courses of action. To the extent that numbers of countries can agree to pursue common policies, both within and outside the United Nations, these policies do appear to command more respectful attention on the part of other powers than would the separately-expressed preferences of single countries.

Yet since it has in practice proved difficult for the new states to group themselves on a continuing basis in the pursuit of important policies, the fourth option—that of independence of action—has likewise been pursued over a period of time by a large number of these societies.

None of the new states, and very few of the older ones, have aligned their interests primarily with those of the Soviet Union or Communist China. One must except from this statement the governments of North Vietnam and North Korea, which are of course in a different category; certain other Asian and a few African states also seem close to one or the other of the Communist systems, but their relations still fall short of an integrated pursuit of common policies. In some ways one might have thought that more of these states would adopt this option; rapid Soviet and Chinese economic progress has furnished a tempting example for societies who make economic advancement the most immediate of their social goals. For most of these states, too, hopes for economic improvement would seem to depend on strict control of the economy—in brief, on a pattern that resembles the socialist rather than the capitalist form of economic organization; and one that more closely approaches authoritarian than democratic forms of political organization. Nonetheless, the fact is that while the countries involved have (with variations) adopted many aspects of economic and political organization from Communist countries, most of them have not let themselves be drawn into the Communist political orbit.

The question arises, from the American point of view, why so few of the new states have chosen the first alternative—that of joining one of the alliance systems in which the United States is the leading partner. The Western approach would seem to bolster freedom, would encourage diversity, would promote economic advancement, and would safeguard security. This argument, however, has not recommended itself to many new states, and a variety of reasons can be adduced for their failure to enter into closer relations with the United States and other Western countries.

Historically, these new states all have a very recent past of colonial domination. While colonialism was not all bad, it was certainly not all advantageous either. The important point, however, is that it is remembered as having been bad, and that present interpretations of it, in the countries concerned, picture it as an unmitigated evil. Hence, in the first place, there is a very strong feeling in these countries that under no circumstances must they permit themselves to fall again under the domination, in whatever form or for whatever purpose, of an outside power. In the words of one African leader:

> Having struggled most of my life against the colonial régime, having freed my country of its after-effects, I need not take lessons from anyone about colonialism. I do not tolerate that anyone, under the pretext of serving some special kind of revolution, shall meddle in the affairs of [my country].[3]

The fact that, in these countries, the United States is generally identified with Western colonialism may seem monstrously unfair to Americans, who recall that theirs was the first anti-colonial revolution, and who remember their

[3] Habib Bourguiba, "The Tunisian Way," *Foreign Affairs,* 44 (1966), 486.

government's strong anti-colonial stand during and immediately after World War II, when American efforts were instrumental in persuading the British and the Dutch to relinquish large parts of their former colonial empires. On the other hand, American policy on the issue of colonialism since the late 1940's has been influenced by the fact that among our strongest allies, in NATO, are the principal former colonial powers whose rule has been replaced by the elites now governing the new states. For a political leader of one of the newer countries to be charged with being "pro-Western" is tantamount to being "pro-Communist" in the United States, or "bourgeois" (or "Khrushchevist") in Communist China. The nationalism of the new societies expresses itself in terms of opposition to former colonial powers, distrust of any states allied with them, and an extraordinary sensitivity to any real or fancied attempts on the part of these states to influence their behavior.

Another probable reason for the failure of these states to align with the West is the view of many of them that a coalition with the United States would be a) dangerous; b) too demanding; c) too uncertain; and d) unnecessary in any event. The danger is perceived in terms of being drawn into conflicts involving the major partner but in which the newer, weaker partner would have but a minor interest. Likewise, it is argued, if the world situation should deteriorate into war between the major contestants, their allies might well become battlefields—a fate from which any country would wish to protect itself. A coalition with the West is perceived as being too demanding in the sense that these societies prefer to concentrate their attention and their resources on internal improvements, political stability, and economic viability—all of which are desperately needed. Uncertainty arises from the consideration that in a world system in which both major contestants control nuclear arsenals, both will be deterred from using these forces in any situation short of an ultimate threat to their core values. If President de Gaulle of France can conclude that the American pledge to defend Western Europe cannot be counted on, it is perhaps understandable that African and Asian political leaders will draw similar conclusions with respect to their own countries.

Finally, it may well be that formal alignments with the West are regarded as unnecessary because of the presumption that in periods of threat and danger (emanating from non-nuclear powers) the United States—and, quite possibly, the Soviet Union as well—will come to the aid of the threatened countries anyway. It is particularly instructive to note, for example, American (*and* Soviet) aid to India during her border conflicts with China; it is likewise instructive to recall the estrangement between the United States and Pakistan, one of the few formal allies of America on the Asian mainland; the apparent lessons are apt to be quite well understood by the leaders of other neutral countries. We may indeed be in a period in which, according to Henry Kissinger, "neutrals enjoy most of the protection of allies and allies aspire to have the same freedom of action as do neutrals."[4]

It should be said that the neutralist states themselves might well reject the

[4] Henry Kissinger, "Coalition Diplomacy in a Nuclear Age," *Foreign Affairs,* **42** (July, 1964), 530.

rather negative, reactive interpretation which is attached to their policies in the preceding paragraphs. They would argue that, far from constituting lack of concern or responsibility, their policies are uniquely designed to make a positive, constructive contribution to the international system. They might base their argument on the proposition that a world which is neatly divided between only two contesting camps is brittle and dangerous; that a multiplicity of power centers is in the general interest of the flexibility and stability of the system (Cf. Chapter 4). More concretely they would surely argue that their unaligned status places them in a position where they can render concrete services in mediating, negotiating, or staffing peace-keeping functions involving disputes between the major camps. This is in line with what Robert Scalapino has called the "tolerant component" of the modern Far East, which he has described in terms of the "quest for the greater harmony, for the complete synthesis of conflicting ideas. . . ."[5]

Finally, and more practically, neutralist statesmen might well argue that their independent stance not only makes it possible for them to render services *to* both sides, but for them to gain advantages *from* both sides, on behalf of the peoples and societies they lead. In the contest for friendship, for support, if not for formal affiliation, none of the major powers can afford to antagonize the new states. Thus they find themselves in a happy situation in which they have much to gain. Not unlike the United States in the early decades of its history when, as Samuel Flagg Bemis has frequently pointed out, *it* was the beneficiary of the European balance of power, these new states of the 20th century find themselves the beneficiaries of the contemporary world-wide power constellation.

Non-commitment and neutralism are no more static than commitment and alignment have been. Old patterns change and new patterns emerge. France endeavors to alter the NATO structure. India becomes far more directly involved in major-power politics than she had before. Pakistan concludes that her interests and those of China coincide sufficiently to contemplate a rapprochement. The internal political structures of Ghana and of Indonesia undergo basic changes which profoundly affect their places in international politics.

A flexible response to non-commitment, based on appreciation of the fact that other countries have their own problems, outlooks, and goals no less than one's own country does, seems the most appropriate response to the trend that shows no sign of diminishing. As Charles Burton Marshall has so cogently observed in an essay entitled "Understanding the Unaligned," the "problem seems to be not quantitative but qualitative; the question is not whether to meet each other halfway, but how to approach each other on intersecting tangents."[6]

[5] Robert Scalapino, "Neutralism in Asia," *American Political Science-Review*, **XLVIII** (1954), 49–62. Portions of this excellent article were reprinted in the first edition of this book.

[6] In *Neutralism and Nonalignment: The New States in World Affairs*, ed. Laurence W. Martin (New York: Frederick A. Praeger, Inc., 1962), p. 29.

1

*The Diplomacy of New Nations**

Gordon A. Craig

. . . [O]ne of the aspects of the Diplomatic Revolution of Our Times has been the remarkable expansion of the membership of the international diplomatic community during the last fifty years. . . . before 1914 only about twenty states in the whole world had any serious and continuous interest in foreign affairs and . . . all but two or three of those were European powers. In the period after the first World War, this picture began to change, partly because of the existence and the influence of the League of Nations. But the expansion of the international community that took place between 1919 and 1939 seems almost negligible in comparison with what has been happening since 1945. The second World War smashed what was left of European dominance in world affairs and simultaneously destroyed the ability of the former colonial powers to resist the demands of their subject peoples for independence; and the result of this has been the creation of over forty new states since 1945, most of them in Africa and Asia. When the United Nations was founded in 1945, it had fifty-one members. At the end of 1960 there were ninety-nine member states, forty-six of which were members of the so-called Afro-Asian bloc. These new states are proud of their independence and insistent upon demonstrating this in their foreign policy, and their diplomatic behavior has become a matter of great importance and constant concern to the more established powers, and to the leaders of the western and totalitarian blocs in the great power competition being waged today.

I

It is safe to say that we have all at one time or another found ourselves being profoundly irritated by some aspect of the foreign policy or diplomatic behavior of these states. This is perhaps only natural. We are ourselves citizens of a powerful and established nation, and most of these new states are neither powerful nor established, and their conduct strikes us at times as being pretentious. When we feel this way we are, of course, reflecting what may almost be described as the traditional attitude of Great Powers toward lesser ones. In 1878, during the meetings of the Congress of Berlin, the British Foreign Secretary Lord Salisbury was given residential quarters in Potsdam; and, after he had been there a day or so, someone asked him how he liked them. Salisbury looked gloomily past his interrogator at a group of representatives from the Balkan states and said: "At Potsdam we have mosquitoes. Here we have minor powers. I don't know which is worse." The standard attitude of Great Power statesmen in the nineteenth century was that the small states, like the

* *University*, No. 9 (Summer, 1961), 3–8. Reprinted by permission.

mosquito, were apt to be both irritating and irresponsible. After the first World War, when an organization was founded that gave the lesser states an assembly in which they were considered the equals of the Great Powers and where they could actually discuss and criticize the policies of their stronger neighbors, this resentment grew and was sometimes imperfectly concealed. When Sir Austen Chamberlain was Foreign Secretary of Great Britain, one of his critics said that, whenever he appeared at the League of Nations, his face betrayed his displeasure, and he always seemed to be saying, "We are perfect. We are British. And yet you, you dagoes, dare to come here and criticize US!" Some of this irritation has carried over to our own times and is all too often expressed in speeches in our representative chambers and in articles in our newspapers, which are always complaining because states which they claim are smaller than Texas have votes equal to that of the United States in the UN Assembly.

This sense of irritation has been enhanced by some special circumstances. Since 1948, we have been engaged in a great contest with the totalitarian bloc; and we have regarded this struggle as a war of ideas, a struggle between freedom and slavery, between good and evil, in which no right-thinking person should have any hesitation about declaring himself on our side. But the new nations have for the most part refused to declare themselves to be on our side and have clung to the concept of neutrality. Neutrals have never been popular with belligerents, least of all in conflicts which appeared to the belligerents to be religious wars. In April 1630, at the height of the Thirty Years War, the Swedish King Gustavus Adolphus sought to induce the Kurfürst of Brandenburg to join him in the war against the Catholic powers. The Brandenburg representatives indicated delicately that their prince preferred to remain uninvolved. At this the choleric King exploded. "For God's sake," he said, "think things over a bit and fasten upon *mascula consilia*. . . . I don't want to know or hear anything about any neutrality. His Highness must be either friend or foe. When I come to the border, he is going to have to blow hot or cold. God and the Devil are fighting here. If His Highness wants to fight on God's side, good! Then let him join me. If he prefers to stand by the devil, then in truth he is going to have to fight with me. There is no third position. . . . *Was ist doch das für ein Ding: Neutralität?* I don't understand it!" Back in 1956, Mr. Dulles and Mr. Nixon made a couple of speeches that echoed the great Swedish king's sentiment, if not his tumultuous style; and we have all, I dare say, had moments in which we felt the same way.

Many of us will have done so, for instance on those not infrequent occasions when the neutrality of the new states has turned out to be a rather inconsistent neutrality. It has sometimes seemed in debates in the Assembly of the UN, for instance, that the new states have a special kind of neutrality which is reflected in abstention from all projects that might hurt the Soviet bloc and all projects that might help the position of the Western Powers—a kind of "heads they're right, tails you're wrong" neutrality. Thus, in the late fall of 1956, the Afro-Asian bloc showed unanimity in condemning the action taken by Great Britain and France at Suez, but showed no similar agreement when it was suggested that the Soviet action in Hungary merited the same kind of criticism. Nor was this the only occasion on which what appeared to be a double standard was used; and this has caused understandable irritation.

NOBLESSE OBLIGE?

Finally, the diplomatic behavior of some of the new states has been accompanied by a tendency to moralize that is all the more irritating because it seems unjustified. During his labored explanations to the Indian parliament of his behavior in the Hungarian crisis of 1956, Mr. Nehru so frequently disclaimed the idea that "we are nobler or higher or purer than other countries" that Western observers could not help but feel that so much protestation indicated a belief that India really was superior morally; and this impression has been strengthened by the lectures which Mr. Nehru and Mr. Menon have on occasion given other nations for their failure to do things which an examination of the record shows India also fails to do. India's unwillingness to submit the Kashmir dispute to arbitration would seem good reason for its government not to criticize other nations for failing to avail themselves of the instruments of judicial settlement.

II

To be irritated at these characteristics of the diplomatic behavior of the new states is understandable, but a tendency to irritation is not in itself a very positive or productive quality. If our relations with these states are to be effective, we shall have to master our own feelings and see matters a bit more from their point of view than we are always ready to do.

In the first place, we should remember what is the most obvious thing about them—that most of them are new members of the international community—and we should remember the natural consequences of this. They lack the experience; they lack the assurance; in some cases they lack even the trained public servants which a state needs if it is to conduct foreign relations. Their diplomats at the UN have sometimes arrived with only the most rudimentary knowledge of what their function is and how it is to be discharged. Like late comers to any established society, they have an inferiority complex that is apt to express itself in assertiveness and even arrogance. They are suspicious of slights and are constantly expecting condescension. Their individual and collective feelings are over-sensitive and betray them into gestures that are excessive and even unwise. Their attitude is apt always to be on the verge of belligerence. The spirit with which they approach their task was perhaps most clearly and succinctly expressed by Jawaharlal Nehru in the first meeting of the Asian nations at Delhi in 1947, when he said, with no provocation:

> Far too long have we of Asia been petitioners in Western courts and chancellories. That story must now belong to the past. We propose to stand on our own feet. . . . We do not intend to be the playthings of others.

This kind of shrill protestation typified the general attitude of the new states when they first entered the diplomatic community.

In the second place, because they have recently won freedom, in some cases after long years of struggle, their chief objective in foreign affairs is to assert, to preserve and to enhance their independence, which they see subject to a variety of threats: territorial, economic, ethnic, and cultural. Their desire to establish their independence sometimes takes relatively innocuous forms. In its first vote in the UN Assembly, for example, the new state of Nigeria voted to admit the question of Red China's membership in the world organization to the Assembly's agenda. This gesture led one Western diplomat to speak of "Nigeria whose name should be Unpredictability," and it was interpreted by others as a vote against the very Powers who had supported Nigeria's preparation for statehood. It would have been more accurate to regard it merely as a demonstration by Nigeria that, now it was independent, it was determined to be truly so and that the Western powers would be well advised not to take its support for granted on all questions.

To Remain Free

In the case of the Afro-Asian states in general, it is safe to say that their burning desire to preserve their independence has in large part determined their adoption of a neutral position in the Cold War. The wisest of their statesmen doubtless feel that a complete bi-polarization of global politics would be the surest way, first, of restricting their freedom (by making them members of a political bloc whose leaders were Great Powers) and, second, of destroying their freedom in the war that such a complete bi-polarization would in their opinion inevitably cause. In their neutrality, they see both a chance to remain free and an opportunity, by joint action with other states like themselves, to use their influence to prevent the coming of war. Other statesmen of new nations have resented what appears to be the attempt of the big powers to form them into leagues without having the courtesy even to consult them. Thus, at the time of the announcement of the plan to form the South East Asia Treaty Organization (SEATO), the newspaper *Times* of Ceylon wrote:

> Mr. Dulles does not trouble to find out how Asia's repugnance to communism might be utilized in the cause of world democracy, *with Asia's consent.* He is in a hurry and, with bland arrogance, imagines that because Free Asia abhors communism, it will automatically embrace any Made-in-Washington scheme for liberating the Asians in spite of the Asians. . . .

The West's perhaps over-anxious desire to have an unambiguous declaration of friendship in the form of membership in SEATO or in the abortive Middle East Defense Command or in the Baghdad Pact has stimulated neutralism simply because it has appeared to be a desire to impose shackles upon states that have recently won their freedom.

That the neutrality of the new states would tend, at least for a time, to be somewhat inconsistent should not have been surprising. These were all states which were not only newly independent but were states with a long colonial past. They could not help but be more suspicious of their old masters than they were of other powers, and to be susceptible to slogans that echoed their own sentiments even when those slogans were used by powers whom they had good reason to distrust. Thus, at the Bandung Conference of 1955, when twenty-nine African and Asian states gathered together, Mr. Soekarno's key-note speech stressed their common opposition to colonialism, poverty and involvement in international wars, and, when Chou En-lai, who was making his first international appearance, echoed those sentiments in a skillful and conciliatory address, there was general satisfaction. But when Sir John Kotewala of Ceylon said that, as long as they were all against colonialism, they ought to note the new colonialism of the Soviet Union in eastern Europe and ought "to declare openly [their] opposition to Soviet colonialism as much as to Western colonialism," he was upbraided by Nehru and criticized by several of the other members of the meeting, whose emotions proved to be stronger than their logic. A year later, when Britain and France attacked Egypt, the critics of Sir John Kotewala found confirmation for their worst suspicions of the imperialist powers; and their feelings were so inflamed that many of them quite sincerely felt that the Hungarian blood-bath was a matter of an entirely different order.

MORALITY . . .

In the third place, with respect to the tendency of these states to adopt a high-flown moral tone, it should be noted that this too, while irritating, is understandable. It is the result, in part at least, of an efflorescence of cultural nationalism which leads them to seek to assert the uniqueness and superiority of their approach, not only to matters of the spirit, but to political matters as well. At one time many of these nations had distinctive traditions of life and thought, which died out during the subsequent period of European supremacy and were replaced with Western ideas and institutions. When the new nations emerged as independent entities, they often sought to rid themselves of Western forms and ideas and, by searching their own past, to find cultural values they could call their own. The years in which India, for instance, was fighting her long fight for freedom from British rule, were also years in which every step forward was accompanied by warnings from her own greatest political thinkers that freedom would mean nothing if it merely led to a subordination to western ideas. Thus, at the turn of the century, Vivekananda was writing:

New India is saying, 'If we only adopt Western ideas, Western food, Western dress, and Western manners, we shall be as strong and powerful as the Western nations.' On the other, Old India is saying: 'Fools! By imitation, others' ideas never become one's own—nothing unless earned is your own.' . . . Oh India! This is your terrible danger. The spell of imitating the West is getting such a strong hold on you that what is good and what is bad is no longer decided by reference to the Shastras.

A little later, Rabindranath Tagore echoed this thought:

Europe has her past. Europe's strength lies in her history. We in India must make up our minds that we cannot borrow other peoples' history and that, if we stifle our own, we are committing suicide. . . . It does India no good to compete with Western civilization in its own field.

This insistence upon remaining true to one's own past and following ideas that are unique to one's own culture is felt to some extent by all of the new nations which have anything resembling a real history or political past; and their leaders today pay obeisance to this idea. And they are not disinclined, in cases where a return to the past is impossible, and this of course is sometimes true, to claim a special virtue for their ideas anyway and to assert that they are unique to their own culture and superior to western ideas.

To give one example of this, much has been made since the Bandung Conference of 1955 of what has been called a characteristically Asian and morally superior set of principles for the governance of foreign relations. This was the so-called *panca-sila*—a set of five principles signed by Nehru and Chou En-lai at Bandung and since subscribed to by other Eastern states. Supposedly based on the Buddhist code of ethics, the five principles of the *panca-sila* are: 1. mutual respect for each other's territorial integrity and sovereignty; 2. non-aggression; 3. non-interference in each other's internal affairs; 4. equality and mutual benefit in all dealings; and 5. peaceful coexistence and economic cooperation. This code has been so highly vaunted by eastern writers that it does little good to point out—as Adda Bozeman has pointed out—that, in the first place, Buddhism has long ceased to be a frame of reference for individual conduct in India and China and that neither Nehru nor Chou En-lai is much influenced by Buddhism in his thinking; or that, in the second place, the Buddhist origin of the five principles is spurious in any case. As principles of international action, these five ideas are the end result rather of the modern history of international organization as developed in the Western world; and they are more honored in the West today than they are by Chou En-lai. But it would be idle to attempt to impress this upon ardent followers of Mr. Nehru; and in general it must be admitted that the force of cultural nationalism is so great that this kind of moral posturing is, for a time at least, inevitable.

Moreover, I think we would be well advised, in tolerating this and the other characteristics of new-state diplomacy, to remember that we ourselves were once a new and inexperienced nation and that throughout the whole of our early experience, we shared the very traits that we find objectionable in these newer ones. We would do well to remember, for instance, a passage by Alexis de Tocqueville which sounds as if it might be about a newcomer to an Assembly meeting in New York, but is really about us in our youth.

> An American leaves his country with a heart swollen with pride; on arriving in Europe, he at once finds that we are not so engrossed by the United States and the great people who inhabit it as he had supposed, and this begins to annoy him. . . . [He is also ignorant of the place he occupies in European society.] He is afraid of ranking himself too high; still more is he afraid of being ranked too low. This two-fold peril keeps his mind constantly on the stretch and embarrasses all he says or does. . . . He is like a man surrounded by traps; society is not a recreation for him but a serious toil; he weighs your least actions, interrogates your looks, and scrutinizes all you say lest there should be some hidden allusion to affront him. . . . He is full of scruples and at the same time of pretensions; he wishes to do enough, but fears to do too much, and as he does not very well know the limits of the one or of the other, he keeps up a haughty and embarrassed air of reserve.

Lo, the poor Indonesian or Nigerian! But so once were we.

Neutrality . . .

Nor should we forget, when we are complaining about neutrals, that we were once the greatest and the noisiest of all neutrals, that by our efforts in the nineteenth century we promoted the general recognition of neutral rights, and that, in the opinion of a great international lawyer, J. L. Brierly, it was we who spread the notion, so prevalent in the nineteenth century (but now conveniently forgotten by us), that neutrals were rather more virtuous than other people.

I need hardly add that we have no right to forget our own fulminations about colonialism (and the way in which we permitted them to influence our attitudes in foreign affairs in earlier days) and our habit of moralizing on every possible occasion. Mr. Charles Dickens was so affronted by our claims of superiority of culture, manner, dress, and thought that he devoted long stretches of *Martin Chuzzlewit* to this congenital weakness of ours. It is in *Chuzzlewit* that he introduces us to General Choke who asks:

> What are the Great United States for, sir, if not for the regeneration of man? But it is nat'ral in you to make such an enquerry, for you come from England and you do not know my country.

Nor have we even today brought this tendency to attribute superiority to ourselves under control. I seem to remember an article of Mr. Walter Lippmann not so long ago, arguing that we would make more friends in the world if we did not always seem to claim that we were not only the strongest and richest nation in the world but the best too. And I know I have seen recently a cartoon in the *New Yorker* purporting to show a worried conference on the world situation in what appears to be the National Security Council with one brash young man saying: "I don't know what we're so worried about. I mean, we're the good guys and they're the bad guys and the good guys always win, don't they?"

III

If we remember these things, we can perhaps, by a process of identification, get a little closer to the position of these new nations; and, if we do that, we can prevent ourselves from being annoyed by characteristics that were until recently our own. This does not mean that we have no reason to be concerned about the course that has been followed by these nations. It means only that we can turn our minds away from such superficial things as manners of speech and attitude and concentrate upon sources of more legitimate concern. And of these there are several.

. . . [N]ineteenth-century statesmen always put a high valuation upon *objectivity* (which I equated with freedom from illusions and the ability to assess a situation realistically), *patience* (the ability to wait upon events), and *proportion* and *restraint* (which I defined as the ability to see one's own limitations). I don't think it can be denied that all too often the new states have shown a conspicuous lack of these qualities and, because of this, have opened themselves to grave risks. This is true even of the strongest of them. In March 1956 Mr. Nehru in an interview printed in the *New York Times* said, "Geography made India in her long past almost a closed country. Surrounded by the seas and the mighty Himalayas, it was not easy of entry." Even as history, this is inaccurate, in view of the number of times India has been invaded since antiquity; and, as a basis for a foreign policy in our own day, it is wholly inadequate. Yet in some ways Nehru's policy has been based precisely upon this illusion of inaccessibility (this perhaps explains his curiously quiescent attitude in the Laos situation), and to the extent that this has opened his country to risks, this is a matter that must affect us all. The degree of self-delusion in the foreign policy of Prime Minister Nasser of Egypt need hardly be commented on. His dream of a North African Empire is perhaps rooted in the memory of the great medieval Muslim Empire which once ruled the Mediterranean world; and the reestablishment of that empire would, in almost any conceivable circumstances, be unrealistic. But Nasser has also demonstrated, on at least one occasion, that he is incapable even of estimating his own military capabilities; and it is this combination of grandiose ambition and illusion that could well, unless it is checked by his own friends and allies, touch off troubles in the Middle East from which the world might not recover. Of all the leading statesmen of the new states, it is Nasser who comes closest to sharing some of the most dangerous characteristics of Mussolini, on the frailties of whose diplomacy I touched [upon earlier].

Irrationality . . .

Lack of objectivity and proportion and lack of patience have also led, in the case of some of the new nations, to a high degree of vulnerability to Soviet economic and cultural diplomacy, and, unless corrected by caution, this could well lead to the very thing which these nations fear most of all: the loss of their freedom. In trade and aid negotiations with the Western powers, the new nations as a class have revealed a high degree of irritability and have given every evidence of resentment when conditions were placed upon loans to them or attempts were made to elicit assurances concerning the uses to which the loans would be put. The fact that Western queries have for the most part been prompted by a sincere desire to see that the economy of the borrower would receive maximum benefit has done nothing to appease their feelings; and they have sometimes seemed to derive malicious pleasure from comparisons between our conditional approach to foreign aid and the freehanded way in which the Soviets have given them economic and technical assistance. Yet they have not seen fit to remember or to ponder a statement made by Premier Khrushchev to a group of visiting U.S. Congressmen in 1955 when he said, "We value trade least for economic reasons and most for political purposes." Behind every generous agreement with the Soviet bloc lies the cold purpose of the Soviets to use economic entanglement as the first step toward domination; and the states who have gone blithely into these agreements are assuming grave risks.

The new nations are similarly vulnerable to Soviet cultural diplomacy, and one cannot pick up a newspaper these days without finding a disturbing item like the one in Friday's *Los Angeles Times:*

> Addis Ababa, Ethiopia (AP). The Soviet Union and Ethiopia have signed a cultural agreement described here as one of the most comprehensive Moscow has concluded with an African country. The Russians offered scholarships in agriculture, scientific training, and languages. Ethiopia agreed to accept Russian education officers for the study of African problems.

The desire for economic progress and technical education is characteristic of all of the new states. They are convinced that true equality in the international community will be theirs only when they are industrialized; and for that they need lots of help. They are not willing to wait or to weigh offers, to consider all the risks involved or, indeed, to probe the motives of the donors. And this impatience, combined with the lack of objectivity and proportion that comes from ambition and from old resentments, represents a grave threat to the new nations and, by extension, to the free world, which cannot help but be threatened by continued vulnerability to communism on the part of these nations.

One must hastily add, on the other side, that there are signs of growing sophistication on their part and some evidence that they are not so prone to taking Soviet bloc assurances at their face value as they formerly were.

Mr. Nehru, it is safe to say, has become far less sure of the inaccessibility and impregnability of his country since his co-signatory of the *panca-sila* of Bandung attacked his north-eastern frontiers and proved unamenable to reason or negotiation; and the Chinese depredations against Tibet have had widespread repercussions in the Afro-Asian bloc. During 1958 and 1959, a shift of mood was apparent among many of the neutralist countries. Burma, for instance, became much more anxious about the threat of China, as did statesmen in Indonesia. In the autumn of 1958, Burmese and Indonesian statesmen privately approved the U.S. attitude in the Formosa Straits, although publicly remaining true to the policy of non-alignment. It is true that recently Prime Minister U Nu of Burma met with Chou En-lai, signed a new border treaty and conferred on his guest the unprecedented rank of "Supreme Upholder of the Glory of the Great Love," awarding him a lavish gold and jade medal, and making many speeches about co-existence. But this does not necessarily weaken my point, for it was probably less a demonstration of faith in the old Chou En-lai of Bandung than an attempt to make another accommodation in the hope that it would postpone trouble.

NATIONAL INTEREST

There are other signs of growing sophistication among the new nations. The members of the Arab bloc, who used to respond eagerly and passionately to Nasser's evocation of the idea of Arab unity, have been more reluctant of late to subordinate their own policies to Nasser's. There has been a dawning realization that what Bismarck used to call sentimentality in foreign policy, and what we call ideological unity, does not always promise well. When the Syrian constitution was first drawn up, it stated that Syria was an indivisible political unity, but said further that "our people constitute a part of the Arab nation in their history, their present and their future, look forward to the day when our Arab nation is united as one state, and will tirelessly work to realize that sacred aspiration." It is doubtful that Syria is quite as enthusiastic about that ideal today. It is known that Iraq and Jordan are less so, and that both states suspect that the fulfilment of Nasser's ambitions (especially with respect to Israel) might well be disastrous for them.

And other Moslem nations and groups have been less responsive to the appeal to the ideal of Moslem unity than formerly. A recent attempt by Nasser to break up a trade pact between Israel and Nigeria (a state with a large Moslem population) was a miserable failure.

What we may be seeing here is the dawning in many of the new nations of a clearer appreciation of the realities of foreign policy in a divided world, and the beginning of a diplomacy based less on sentimentality or ideology or history than on state interest.

What can we do to promote this healthy development?

For one thing, we can continue to be tolerant of those actions of the new nations which are the natural expressions of their youth and inexperience, and we can stop thinking that they have a duty to side with us on all issues in which we take an interest. To regard every abstention or deviation from the Western line as a sign of communism and to say so publicly, as Secretary Herter did of Kwame Nkrumah at a press conference . . . , is not only naïve but dangerous, since it is calculated to alienate peoples who should be our friends. The sooner we stop thinking of neutralism as a dirty word the better. The world perhaps needs more neutrals than fewer.

In the second place, we should try to promote the ability of these states to be truly independent by increasing the magnitude of our economic aid and technical assistance programs (without becoming less circumspect about the conditions of aid) and by divesting them of military conditions, upon which we have sometimes insisted so vehemently that it used to be said wryly that, if you asked the United States for a tractor, you received a tank. Along the same line, it is high time that we began to match the Soviet cultural offensive in scope and imagination, in order to combat the unfortunately widespread notion (sedulously cultivated by Soviet propagandists) that we are the twentieth-century barbarians with nothing to export to the outside world but plumbing fixtures, Coca Cola and guns (the last of which are not as good as those manufactured in Czechoslovakia and the Soviet Union).

International Peril

In the third place, we can explore new areas in which representatives of the new nations can meet in fruitful collaboration with Americans. The Peace Corps plan is one encouraging example of this. So is the recently launched "Young Diplomats Program" of the Carnegie Endowment of International Peace, which brings promising young members of the diplomatic services or the foreign offices of the newer countries—men and women under thirty and with less than five years of service—to American universities for a year's work in fields of international relations, diplomacy, international economics and finance, and similar subjects, followed by three months' experience in UN headquarters or other international agencies located in this country. Such a program can hardly fail to be productive of many kinds of good.

Finally, the most important thing that Americans can do is to refrain from actions that obscure our position or our purpose in the world. It would be a tragic mistake if we should, by speech or posture or action, give the impression to the new states that we were beginning to adopt the methods and the principles of our totalitarian adversaries. When he gave the Stafford Little Lectures at Princeton . . . , Sir Hugh Foot, the former Governor of Cyprus, said that the fate of the world might well rest with the new states which have joined the United Nations since 1945. Whether this is true or not, it would be folly for the United States to forget the importance of those states and, by failure of understanding, lack of sympathy or mere indifference to their views, make them turn toward our enemies because they feel they have no other place to go.

2

*The New Cult of Neutralism**

Henry A. Kissinger

HENRY A. KISSINGER, *Professor at the Center for International Affairs at Harvard, also serves as a consultant to the United States Arms Control and Disarmament Agency. His books include* Nuclear Weapons and Foreign Policy (*1957*); The Necessity for Choice (*1961*); Prospects of American Foreign Policy (*1961*); *and* The Troubled Partnership (*1965*).

The problems new nations face in political and economic development are difficult enough in their own right. But they are further complicated by the fact that the new nations find themselves drawn into international affairs to an unprecedented degree. While building governments and seeking to realize the most elementary aspirations of their people, they are constantly being wooed, asked to make judgments or to assume responsibilities for which they are, in most cases, thoroughly unprepared.

Our own approach to the new nations has not helped matters. As in most other fields of policy, the United States has been going from one extreme to the other. For a time we acted as if the only political significance of the new nations was as potential military allies; neutrality was condemned and great efforts were made to induce new nations to join security pacts. Within a few years this policy has been replaced by its exact opposite. We now not only seem to find neutrality commendable; we have gone further and have conducted ourselves in a manner that may make our allies, at least those outside the North Atlantic area, doubt the wisdom of close association with the United States. The oversimplification that could see no political role for the new nations except as members of security pacts has been replaced by another oversimplification based on the premise that the "real" contest is for the allegiance of the uncommitted. We sometimes act as if we were engaged in a debate with the Communists in a sort of Oxford Union where the uncommitted or neutral nations act as moderators and award a prize after hearing all arguments.

We must ask ourselves, however, whether the new exaltation of noncommitment is not just as dangerous as the previous emphasis on alliance-building, and whether there is not an inconsistency between the desire of the new nations to be neutrals and their desire to be arbiters.

To begin with, there is a certain ambivalence, if not disingenuousness, in the sudden deference now being paid to neutrality. The principal difference between the Dulles approach to the new nations and that which urges America "to respect neutrality" often seems to be merely one of

* Pp. 329–339, *The Necessity for Choice*, by Henry A. Kissinger. Copyright © 1960 by Henry A. Kissinger. Originally appeared in *The Reporter*, under the title "The New Cult of Neutralism," and reprinted by permission of Harper & Row, Publishers.

method. Both policies are designed to bring the new nations somehow to our side. Secretary Dulles thought the way to do this was to castigate their neutralism. Many of those who see in the new countries the arbiters of international relations imply that the way to win their friendship is to respect their desire for noninvolvement. Both assumptions are based on an illusion.

For it is extremely doubtful whether, on many of the most important issues dividing the world, *any* policy can win the support of the uncommitted. A number of Americans seem to assume that the reluctance of the new nations to commit themselves is due in large part to our failure to "present our case properly" or to the fact that the new nations have certain positive views that we have failed to take into account. But this line of reasoning itself fails to take into account the fact that on most international issues, except those affecting them most directly, the new nations will invariably take a position somewhere between the contenders, regardless of their view of the intrinsic merit of a given dispute. To the new nations, neutrality seems more important than the issues involved in any particular dispute because both their image of themselves and their bargaining position depend on maintaining that neutrality. "Neither side has won us," said an African diplomat during the 1960 session of the General Assembly, "and we are determined that neither will."

The United States, of all countries, should be able to understand this state of mind. In the first years of our existence no conceivable British policy could have led to an American alliance or even to American support on policies outside the Western Hemisphere. Our desire not to become involved was stronger than any views we may have had on international issues, except those affecting the Western Hemisphere most urgently. Nothing Britain could have said or done would have induced us formally to take sides. If Great Britain in 1914 or 1939 had made its resistance to aggression dependent on American support, Germany would have overrun Europe both times without opposition. No British policy, however respectful of our neutrality, could have induced us to give up our noncommitment.

It is no different with the new nations. A grave problem arises when the laudable view that we should understand and *accept* their desire to maintain neutrality is transformed into an *exaltation* of noncommitment. Although it would probably have been wise to have avoided such groupings as SEATO (Southeast Asia Treaty Organization), it is surely going too far to seem to pay greater attention to neutrals than to allies. The realization that we should not press the new nations to join alliances should not be carried to the extreme of discouraging those who have made a different choice. When noncommitment becomes a cult, slogans such as "appealing to world opinion" can easily turn into excuses for inaction or irresponsibility.

The new nations will take a stand against dangers that they fear will affect them. But they are not apt to take a stand on problems that seem to them far away. The Chinese brutality in Tibet made an impression in India; the equally brutal Soviet repression in Hungary did not. Despite all moralistic protestations to the contrary, the reason for the difference in attitude was practical and not theoretical. Chinese pressure on India's borders was a concrete danger and the events in Hungary simply were not. Though it is true that our policy with respect to the new nations has often been maladroit, it does not follow that a different policy can change their nonalignment.

THE NEW JUDGES

To be sure, the new nations sometimes create the opposite impression because their own attitude toward noncommitment is at least as ambivalent as ours. All too often, they couple insistence on respect for their neutrality with an attempt to play the arbiter's role in international affairs. But the arbiter's role implies that they will support one of the parties if they can be convinced of the correctness of its position. It is an invitation to a courtship that encourages the very pressure which is said to be resented.

Many of the leaders of the new states are flattered by the rewards that fall to the uncommitted in the competition of the major powers. For many of them, playing a role on the international scene seems not only more dramatic but also much simpler than the complex jobs they face at home. Almost all of their domestic problems require patient, detailed efforts, and the results are frequently long delayed. Domestically, each action has a price. But on the international scene, it is possible to be the center of attention simply by striking a pose. Ambitious men can thus play the dramatic role that is often denied to them at home, or they can use foreign policy as a means to solidify their claim to national leadership.

Unfortunately, the same factors that make the international arena so tempting—being wooed, escaping from intractable domestic problems—also militate against the seriousness of the effort. It is the symbolic quality of international forums that is most attractive to many of the leaders of the new nations, as we have seen in the opening weeks of the present session of the U.N. General Assembly. The opportunity was welcomed to declaim general maxims that never seem to apply quite so simply at home or to the issues of foreign policy in which an uncommitted nation is directly concerned. But these same nations are much less willing to assume substantive responsibilities, particularly in areas not directly related to their immediate interests.

If the new nations are encouraged to arbitrate all disputes, the impact on international relations will be demoralizing. Noncommitment will thereby defeat its own object. It will be merely another reason for occupying a place at the center of all disputes.

The utility of common action for carrying out tasks in which a real world opinion exists is not at issue. But we must recognize that on many of the most difficult international problems there is no such thing as a meaningful world opinion. And it is simply asking too much of the new nations, which have barely achieved independence, to help settle such technically complex disputes as that over disarmament.

The argument has often been heard that one of the obstacles to a wise United States policy on arms control is the absence of adequate technical studies. Yet our sophistication in this field is incomparably greater than that of any new nations, most of which do not have even one person studying the problem full time. They have no modern weapons arsenal of their own to give them an understanding of strategic problems. They have no technical staffs to study the subject. What they do have is a volatile public opinion at home. In these circumstances, the new nations can easily fall prey to Soviet slogans which sound attractive but which in fact are disguised efforts to disarm the West. The uncommitted are in no position to form a responsible judgment, much less to develop a serious program.

The result of gearing all policy to the presumed wishes of the uncommitted is that many issues are falsified and many problems are evaded. Abstract declarations substitue for concrete negotiations, and diplomacy is reduced to the coining of slogans. Pressure for confrontations of heads of major states is exerted, but is not accompanied by any detailed programs. Peace is demanded in the abstract, but much less attention is given to defining the conditions that make peace meaningful.

Far from aiding the diplomatic progress that is demanded so insistently, such a process tends to thwart it. Far from "strengthening the United Nations," it may ultimately undermine it. Soviet negotiators will lose any incentive for making responsible proposals, since they will be constantly tempted by opportunities for cheap propaganda victories. The West will grow increasingly frustrated when it finds itself incapable of enlisting the support of the new nations no matter how moderate or reasonable its program. And the new nations will be induced to take positions on issues in which the very act of noncommitment proclaims their unconcern and with respect to which their judgment is often highly erratic. It is far from clear why nations that are in need of assistance in almost all aspects of their national life, many of which have difficulty maintaining order within their own borders, should be capable of dealing with the whole gamut of international problems.

Khrushchev's Shoe

Indeed, when neutrality becomes an end in itself, it can unwittingly lead the uncommitted to add their pressure to that of the Communist bloc. The tendency to seek a position separate from the two big blocs can be used by skillful Communist diplomacy to drive the West back step by step.

When countries as varied as India, Yugoslavia, Indonesia, Ghana, and the United Arab Republic form a "bloc," they are united above all by two motives: to stay aloof from the disputes of the major powers and to magnify their own influence. This desire is understandable. But we must not assume that they will be swayed from this course by the logic of our argument. Apart from domestic and Communist pressures, the internal politics of the neutral "bloc" will prevent it. Individual neutralist nations will not easily separate themselves from their partners even if they should disagree with them on specific measures. India, whatever the private convictions of its leaders, will not easily oppose the United Arab Republic lest it face a united Moslem opposition in its quarrels with Pakistan and also for fear of its own Moslem minority of forty millions. The United Arab Republic will be reluctant to disavow extremist African states lest it forfeit its claim to leadership in Africa. The tone of the whole neutral "bloc" can thus easily be set by the most irresponsible of its members. While we should have patience with these attitudes, we must understand also that on any given issue most of the new nations will seek a position between the two contenders regardless of the merits of the disputes.

As a result, a premium will be placed on Soviet intransigence. When Mr. Khrushchev spoke to the General Assembly in September, 1960, a considerable portion of the American press claimed that he "had overplayed his hand," that he had "alienated the uncommitted." His intemperance was contrasted with the sobriety and statesmanship of President Eisenhower. There is no doubt that Mr. Khrushchev was intemperate. It is less clear, however, whether in the long run his actions will not prove of considerable advantage to the Soviet Union. The very violence of the attack on Mr. Hammarskjöld served as a warning to the new nations of the fate awaiting them should they displease the Communist countries too much. In any given crisis, therefore, the urgings of the new nations may be directed against us not because they disagree with our position but because opposition to us carries few risks. Conversely, the virulence of Communist reaction to any criticism causes the uncommitted to behave with great circumspection in opposing Communist policies.

The speeches in the General Assembly of 1960 by such leaders as Nasser, Sukarno, Nkrumah, and even Nehru illustrate this point. The attacks on the West were pointed and direct, those on the Communist bloc circumspect and highly ambiguous. Almost every speech by these leaders attacked western imperialism. Not a single reference was made to the unprovoked Soviet threat against Berlin—not to speak of other Soviet policies in Eastern Europe. Nor did the uncommitted nations that were supposed to have been alienated by Mr. Khrushchev rush to the defense of the Secretary-General.

Further, if one considers Soviet relations with the neutrals from the point of view of bargaining technique, Communist belligerence may not have been nearly so foolish as was often alleged. Since the new nations are not likely to support the position of either side completely, regardless of what arguments are presented, it may in fact be good negotiating tactics to start from extreme proposals. Then even if the new nations support Communist demands only partially, the Soviets can in effect add the pressure of the uncommitted nations to that of their own bloc in order to realize at least part of their program. The requirements of maintaining formal neutrality force many leaders who have opposed the Soviet Union on one issue to support it on another. Thus at the 1960 session of the General Assembly, Mr. Nehru failed to support Mr. Khrushchev's proposal for a change in the U.N. Charter with respect to the Secretary-General. In return, he proposed organizational changes whose practical consequence came very close to meeting Mr. Khrushchev's aims. Soviet brutality, coupled with the desire of the uncommitted to remain neutral above all else, can establish the familiar Soviet diplomatic "rules" in the United Nations, according to which the only acceptable changes in the *status quo* are those which magnify Communist power or influence.

Conversely, by seeking to meet all the presumed wishes of the new nations, we may force them to move away from us to demonstrate their independence. It would be ironic indeed if in seeking to approach them too closely we drove them in the direction of the Communist position.

SLOGANS AND THE CONGO

World opinion is not something abstract that our diplomats must seek to discover and to which we then must adjust. We have a duty not only to discover but to shape it. World opinion does not exist in a vacuum. It is compounded of many factors, including the imagination and decisiveness of our own policy. Many a leader from the uncommitted areas would prefer a clear and firm United States position to the almost desperate attempt to make him share responsibility for our actions.

When we are convinced of the correctness of our course, we should pursue it, even if it does not gain the immediate approval of the uncommitted—particularly in fields such as disarmament and European policy, which are remote from both the understanding and the concern of the new nations. If the uncommitted are to act as intermediaries, there must be clear positions to mediate. Otherwise a responsibility is thrown on the neutrals or on the United Nations that they will not be able to bear.

The crisis in the Congo illustrates this point very clearly. Our objective of "keeping the cold war out of Africa" was desirable. But the measures adopted to achieve it were highly questionable. "Keeping the cold war out of Africa" is a meaningless abstraction unless at least a tacit agreement on some ground rules is established between the United States and the Soviet Union. Instead of throwing all the responsibility on Mr. Hammarskjöld, we should have come forward with a concrete charter of what we understood by the independence, the development, and the neutrality of the Congo. This could then have been negotiated with the neutrals and the Communists. Instead, we advanced vague resolutions and left it up to the Secretary-General to interpret them, putting him into the position of assuming personal responsibility.

Though in this manner we achieved temporary tactical gains, we may well have mortgaged the future position of the Secretary-General as well as that of the Congo. It may be argued, of course, that the Soviet Union was not interested in stability and would therefore not have accepted our charter. But quite apart from the fact that it would have been useful to make the Soviets' intransigence evident, the course adopted forced the Secretary-General to attempt to impose on the Communist countries a course of action that was highly distasteful to them. It was against all reason to expect them to accept at his hands what we thought they would not even consider if a formal proposal had come from us.

Moreover, by not defining our position, we deprived the Secretary-General of any real bargaining power. Rather than seeking to adjust conflicting views, he was forced to develop his own definition of stability. This had the practical consequence of exposing him to direct conflict with the Communist states and with some of the African countries as well. It is clear that the office of the Secretary-General cannot survive the determined opposition of the Communist bloc together with that of some of the neutrals. The Secretary-General should never be put into a position of being the sole originator of policy. For he will then either come under violent Communist attack or else will be forced into serving as a spokesman for a kind of neutralism that adds its pressures to those of the Soviet bloc or that uses the United Nations as a means to further national ambitions. Thus the Ghanaian and Guinean troops in effect have taken advantage of the mantle of the United Nations to pursue their own national policies in the Congo.

In short, in a situation where a great deal depended on the ability to be both specific and firm, our approach was uncertain and abstract. We proclaimed stability in circumstances where all criteria of judging it had evaporated, and we offered no others to take their place. The chief result was to sharpen the contest for Africa rather than to ameliorate it, and to raise issues about the structure and operation of the United Nations that would have better remained muted. The noble purpose of "strengthening the United Nations" is turning into a means for weakening it.

A Lonely Job

In dealing with the new countries, we obviously have to do much more than engage in a mere popularity contest for their favor. We must show sympathy and support for their efforts to realize their economic aspiration—to an extent considerably beyond our current contribution. We must respect their desire to stand aloof from many of the disputes that divide the world. On many issues we can work closely with the new nations, and on all issues they are entitled to our understanding and sympathy. But we must not expect that either our sympathy or our economic assistance will be paid for with short-term political support. Unpleasant as it may be, *some* situations are conceivable where we may have a duty to act without the support of the new nations, and perhaps even against the opposition of some of them.

Though we naturally prefer to be popular, we cannot gear all our policies to an attempt to curry favor with the new nations. We cannot undermine our own security for illusory propaganda victories, because the safety of even the uncommitted depends on our unimpaired strength—whether they realize it or not. As for the uncommitted, we must make it clear to them that they cannot eat their cake and have it too: they cannot ask us to respect their neutrality unless they respect our commitment. And they cannot remain uncommitted and expect to act as arbiters of all disputes at the same time.

We thus face two contradictory dangers: we can demoralize the new nations by drawing them into the political relationships of the cold war, but we can also demoralize them by making a cult of their noncommitment and acting as if only incorrect United States policies kept them from taking sides. The latter danger may be the more insidious because it is the more subtle. We have to face the fact that in major areas of the world, constructive programs as well as defense depend largely on us. Compassion, understanding, and help for the new nations must not be confused with adjusting all policies to their pace. The cult of noncommitment could doom freedom everywhere.

As the strongest nation in the West, we have an obligation to lead and not simply to depend on the course of events. History will not hand us the prizes we seek on a silver platter. A leader does not deserve the name unless he is willing occasionally to stand alone. He cannot content himself simply with registering prevailing attitudes. He must build opinion, not merely exploit it.

What is involved here is a question of style as well as of substance. Moderation, generosity, and self-restraint are all desirable qualities in our relations with the new nations. But one receives credit for these qualities only if an alternative is known to be available. If we seem forever on the defensive, frantically striving to stave off disaster, and if we give the impression that we use world opinion as a substitute for developing our own purposes, our policy will seem to be the result of panic rather than of sober thought. Regardless of what they may think of the individual measures we advocate, our constant defensiveness and our erratic behavior may merely convince the new nations that we are doomed.

Even more important than a change in policy, then, is a change in attitude. We will finally be judged not so much by the cleverness of our arguments as by the sustained purposefulness of our actions.

CHAPTER SIXTEEN

The Threat and Use of Force

Having dealt in an earlier chapter with elements of the military capability of states, we may now address ourselves to the use to which such capability can be put in international relations. Military force can be utilized in ways to constitute the essential backdrop to negotiations between states. It can be used to enable states to make threats and gain concessions. It can be used to deter other states from doing these things; and finally it can be used to wage war. Now we must deal more specifically with the last of these options that military force enables a state to exercise. Nonetheless, the other functions of force should never be overlooked; they may have become more important than ever before.

Of all the types of relationship which may exist between states, war is the least attractive and, quite possibly, the most significant, because it entails the possibilities of rapid changes in the structure of the international system. In recent times, the nature of war has changed drastically, primarily because of the changing technology of war, but also because of changing concepts about the purposes of war. In former times (e.g. the sixteenth through the nineteenth centuries) wars were, on the whole, fought with limited means—partly because no other means were available—and for limited objectives. The participants in an armed conflict took it for granted that, with minor rectifications and changes, the postwar environment would resemble the prewar scene. War, in other words, was important but not crucial; its outcome made a difference, but it did not usually make the difference between survival and extinction. With the coming of total war of, by, and against whole populations and for total stakes, previous concepts of war have become inapplicable, and the need for reevaluating war as an instrument of policy has become a pressing need.

In considering the use of force and violence and the institution of war in international relations, one is compelled to raise serious questions concerning not only its morality, but also its practicality as a method of conducting relations among states.[1] Yet, one must also admit that the threat of force and its use in war has been instrumental in achieving the present distribution of power and values, and that not all of its consequences have been detrimental to order and

[1] Cf. the introduction to Chapter 9 of this book, dealing with military power as an element in the capability of states to achieve foreign policy objectives.

progress. Nieburg, in the selection reprinted in this chapter, advances some extraordinarily discomforting thoughts on the periodic necessity for the use of violence in relations among states. The uncomfortable, almost tragic, fact is that without the threat—and, according to Nieburg, without the periodic use—of violence, a given status quo would tend to remain frozen. "The threat of violence and the fear of the breakdown of law and order act to moderate demands and positions, thereby setting into peaceful motion the informal political processes of negotiation, concession, compromise, and agreement." Nieburg's essay is a useful caution signal not to let our personal inclinations get into the way of our scholarly analysis.

There are many theories on the causes and occasions of war. Most of them leave much to be desired. Thus, we can identify a "who-done-it" theory of war, which assumes that there is a villain or group of villains who can be identified and properly and conveniently punished. These villains may be governmental leaders, the press and an inflamed public, the big businessmen, warlords, and munitions makers. The temptation to leave analysis at this level may be strong, but unfortunately the problem of war is too difficult to lend itself to such easy explanations and obvious corrections.

Another misconception that is often encountered lies in the idea that countries are either at war or at peace with one another. In this view, the presence of war is identified by a formal declaration of hostilities. But many armed encounters take place without such formal statements. The United States alone has been engaged in more than a score of undeclared wars, of which the Korean and Vietnamese conflicts are only the most recent examples. Also, the distinction between war and peace runs into difficulty in terms of "warfare" by means other than armed forces—such as psychological, political, economic, subversive warfare. The very term "cold war" indicates that the simple war-peace dichotomy is insufficient. It is probably more useful to think of relations among states as lying along a continuum where one finds complete amity and absence of violence on one end, and total violence without restraint on the other. Both extremes are seldom reached, but somewhere along such a continuum it may be possible to place specific inter-state relationships.

Among other dubious ideas about war, we find the Marxist-Leninist view which holds that wars are caused by economic motivations—more specifically, by capitalist countries at a certain phase in their development. Others believe that wars are caused by racial, religious, or cultural differentiations that give rise to frictions. The Marxist-Leninist thesis has been discredited by evidence that in many instances "capitalists" have opposed war as an undesirable disturbance of normal economic processes. Nor is there conclusive evidence to substantiate the view that inter-racial, inter-religious, or inter-cultural wars are more frequent than intra-racial, intra-religious, or intra-cultural ones.

More plausible is the idea that wars may be caused by individuals and groups who, for some reasons, desire it. The reason may be their genuine attachment to certain symbols, ideas, or ideals. It may be the fact that an incident has occurred, or a situation exists, for which war appears to be the only suitable remedy. Or the conclusion is drawn that in a particular conflict situation, the threat or use of force is a promising device to achieve stipulated goals. One also hesitates to discard altogether the idea that individuals may desire war as a means of escape from unsatisfactory conditions of everyday existence, although it should be said that popular enthusiasm for war has waned in recent decades. Yet, it has not thus far been possible to make "peace" as meaningful a symbol as war, in the sense that men are willing to work and sacrifice as much for one as for the other.

Emery Reves has advanced the thesis that the real cause of all wars has always been the fact that social units exercising unrestricted sovereign power come into contact with one another. He proposes that wars will cease the moment sovereign power is transferred from states to larger units. "War takes place whenever and wherever nonintegrated social units of equal sovereignty come into contact."[2] This may be the formulation of a necessary cause, but it is hardly in itself a sufficient one. It fails to explain 1. the incidence of civil wars, and 2. the existence of long-range amicable relationships between many "non-integrated social units of equal sovereignty."

In a sense it may be argued that the most obvious cause of war is war itself —or, rather, the expectation of war. Since states live in an environment approaching anarchy, and since wars have frequently occurred in the past, each state must consider the possibility that another war may occur in the future. Hence, it feels that it has to take steps to protect itself against such an eventuality. In taking these steps (examples: acquisition of bases, strengthening of armaments, concluding alliances, and so forth) other states may find their insecurity increased, and tension may reach a point of open hostility.

We must admit that we cannot formulate general statements as to the cause or causes of war. But we do know that war is, and always has been, a fact of international life. There are few among the older states in the world which have not engaged in war at one time or another. Nor is resort to violence specific to international relations. It occurs within states and other groups as well, albeit less frequently and on a smaller scale. The continuum from complete amity to unrestrained violence exists potentially within any community, except that within well-ordered communities the situation will more often tend toward amity, within a context of law, than it does in international relations.

Within the relatively brief history of the so-called Western State System (the system of independent sovereign states), there have been profound changes in the conduct of warfare. During the sixteenth and seventeenth centuries, warfare was usually conducted by hired mercenaries or small professional armies, not particularly anxious to take undue chances. It was only in the eighteenth and nineteenth centuries that wars began to involve large portions of the population. Frederick II of Prussia and more particularly Napoleon I of France relied on mass armies. To motivate conscripts, wars needed a "cause" other than selfish or dynastic gain. The ideological component came to be stressed more and more, and this trend has continued into our own day.

[2] *The Anatomy of Peace* (New York: Harper & Row, Publishers, 1945).

According to Professor Morgenthau, war has become total in at least four respects: 1. it involves total populations emotionally; 2. it involves total populations actively and physically; 3. it is conducted against total populations (i.e. saturation bombings during World War II, which killed more civilians than actual warfare killed military personnel); and 4. it is fought for total stakes, reflected in the insistence on unconditional surrender in World War II.[3] All of this has meant that total resistance and recourse to any and all means of conducting the war have become more important.

With the advent of weapons of total destructive capacity, attempts to reevaluate the role of war as a means of policy have assumed new significance in recent years. War is, after all, a means to an end, not an end in itself. The objective of war is not victory alone (even though victory may be a necessary precondition), but the establishment of conditions after the war that are either more congenial than those which had existed or, minimally, the establishment of conditions that are more congenial than those which would have existed had the war not been fought. Thus, to say that "in war there is no substitute for victory" is to posit, at best, an intermediate goal. The real question is what is to come after the victory has been achieved: will it be possible to establish (or reestablish) a world environment in which the "victorious" state can function?

The availability of new weapons of destruction has cast grave doubts on an affirmative answer to this question, because it is dubious whether "victory" in a nuclear exchange can provide meaningful possibilities for a new and better world order. Because this is so, more thought is being devoted to alternatives to total nuclear warfare—non-military contests (competitive coexistence, whose conflicts are conducted by diplomatic, political, economic, or psychological means) and limited or localized wars.[4]

Unfortunately it would be puerile optimism to assume that, since total war has become irrational, it has therefore automatically become impossible. The conclusion that what is unreasonable is impossible is the counterpart of the equally false notion that whatever is necessary is also possible. It assumes, in the first place, that men always act rationally, and that pathological behavior-patterns, such as those of Hitler, will never recur in international relations. But there are other reason, too, why wars—including major wars fought with nuclear weapons—may still be possible. Kahn, in the selection reprinted below, lists various possibilities. He attaches relatively low probabilities to any of them, but surely in a matter of such importance, even low probabilities are too high for comfort. One side or the other may miscalculate the likely effects of an aggressive action. It may believe that it can "get away with it" and may, in fact, achieve its goals through the use of force. Or one side may believe that the other side is about to launch a military action and that it is therefore essential to "get there fustest with the mostest," so as to at least minimize the effects of the enemy's action when it comes. This is the doctrine of preemption. The first blow in a nuclear exchange may not be totally decisive, but it is bound to

[3] *Politics among Nations,* Chapter 20.

[4] See Raymond Aron, *On War* (New York: Doubleday Anchor Books), pp. 70–71.

be important. A war may break out not because of a miscalculation arrived at by deliberation (however faulty), but simply by accident. This possibility may be remote, but it cannot be eliminated altogether from consideration. Or one side or the other may achieve a genuine technological breakthrough, in weapons, delivery systems, or defense capabilities. Either of such breakthroughs might drastically shift the present uneasy balance,[5] and might make war once again seem to be a rational policy choice. Also, just as the American monopoly on nuclear weapons soon gave way to an American-Soviet duopoly, and as the two states have since then been joined by Great Britain, France, and China as nuclear powers, other states may well be on the threshold of joining the "nuclear club." With the spread of nuclear weapons availability, the control problem will become constantly more difficult and quite possibly altogether insoluble. This relates to the final reason why one cannot be confident that another major war is totally impossible. Local, limited conflicts may grow in area and scope until they embrace major powers with nuclear capabilities. Even if one can imagine that nuclear weapons may not be used at the outset of a war, it stretches the imagination to assume that a country would prefer losing a war to using its full arsenal.

There is, then, no assurance that the use of war as a method of achieving goals in international relations has forever ended. But one is left with the inescapable judgment that wars—whatever utility they may have possessed in the past—are simply not functioning well in the present era and will not function well in the foreseeable future. The task of statesmanship, and of informed citizenship, therefore seems to be that of creating alternatives to a method of international relations which has become outdated.

[5] Albert Wohlstetter, "The Delicate Balance of Terror," *Foreign Affairs*, **XXXVII** (1959), 211–234.

1

*Uses of Violence**

H. L. Nieburg

H. L. NIEBURG *is in the Department of Humanities and Social Science at the Case Institute of Technology.*

* * *

The argument of this essay is that the risk of violence is necessary and useful in preserving national societies.[1] This specifically includes sporadic, uncontrolled, "irrational" violence in all of its forms. It is true that domestic violence, no less than international violence, may become a self-generating vortex which destroys all values, inducing anarchy and chaos. However, efforts to prevent this by extreme measures only succeed in making totalitarian societies more liable to such collapses. Democracies assume the risk of such catastrophes, thereby making them less likely.

Violence has two inextricable aspects: its actual use (political demonstrations, self-immolation, suicide, crimes of passion, property, politics, etc.), or its potential use. The actual demonstration of violence must occur from time to time in order to give credibility to its threatened outbreak; thereby gaining efficacy for the threat as an instrument of social and political change. The two aspects, demonstration and threat, cannot be separated. The two merge imperceptibly into each other. If the capability of actual demonstration is not present, the threat will have little effect in inducing a willingness to bargain politically. In fact, such a threat may provoke "preemptive" counter-violence.

The "rational" goal of the threat of violence is an accommodation of interests, not the provocation of actual violence. Similarly, the "rational" goal of actual violence is demonstration of the will and capability of action, establishing a measure of the credibility of future threats, not the exhaustion of that capability in unlimited conflict.[2]

. . . Within each system there are conflicting values among members which are constantly adjusted as roles change, maintaining a state of tension. Political systems have an objective, dynamic interrelationship,

[1] The role of violence in political organizations is vividly demonstrated by a recent event among a group of elks at the Bronx Zoo. A 4-year-old bull elk, Teddy, had his magnificent antlers sawed off to one-inch stumps. He had reigned as undisputed boss of a herd of six cow elks and one younger bull. But the breeding season was on, and he was becoming "a bit of a martinet." With his antlers off, he gets a new perspective on his authority and becomes a tolerable leader. A younger bull may try to take over as paramount leader of the herd, but if he does, the veterinarian will saw off his antlers, too (*New York Times,* September 26, 1962, p. 35).

[2] By "rational" here is meant: having a conceptual link to a given end, a logical or symbolic means-ends relationship which can be demonstrated to others or, if not demonstrable, is accepted by others (but not necessarily all) as proven.

* *Journal of Conflict Resolution,* **VII** (1963), 43–54. Reprinted by permission.

structured into the hierarchy of macrosystems. Within the latter, each subsystem has a role much like that of the individual in smaller constellations. Each subsystem may be part of several macrosystems, imposing conflicting demands upon it. Consequently, within macrosystems there is maintained a state of constant tension between subsystems. This objective tension, existing on all levels, is seen subjectively in terms both of competition and consensus, depending on the comparative degrees of collaboration and conflict which exist in the situation at any given moment.

Any two or more systems may appear as hostile at any given time. From the viewpoint of the participants, the conceptual framework of competition overrides underlying consensus. Decisions and policies of the rival elites are rationalized in terms of hostility to the values and leaders of the other system. However, if events conspire to place a higher value on a hostile tactical situation involving the macrosystem of which both smaller systems are a part, their relationship will be transformed quickly to a conceptual framework of consensus which will override and mute the unresolved competitive elements. Such an event may also bring about internal leadership changes in both subsystems, if the elites were too firmly wedded to the requirements of the now-irrelevant competitive situation.

Objectively, tension is always present among all roles and systems; that is, there are always present both elements of competition and consensus. The subjective emphasis which each pole of the continuum receives depends on the value which the tactical situation places on acts and attitudes of hostility or collaboration among the various systems at various times. Degrees of hostility and collaboration are structured by a hierarchy of values within and among all roles and systems all the time. All are involved in a dynamic process.

Conflict, in functional terms, is the means of discovering consensus, of creating agreed terms of collaboration. Because of the individual's personal role in the macrosystem of nation-states, he tends to view the Cold War in terms of competition. Similarly, because of his role in the subsystem of the family, he tends to view family problems in terms of consensus (until the system breaks down completely).

* * *

The commitment required by a credible threat of violence, able to induce peaceable accommodation, is one of a very high order. Not all individuals nor all political systems are capable of credibly using the threat of violence in order to induce greater deference by others to their values. There is general recognition by all of the kinds of values which can and cannot elicit the high degree of commitment required to make the threat credible.

By and large, all violence has a rational aspect, for somebody, if not for the perpetrator. All acts of violence can be put to rational use, whether they are directed against others or against oneself. This is true because those who wish to apply the threat of violence in order to achieve a social or political bargaining posture are reluctant to pay the costs or take the uncertain risks of an actual demonstration of that threat. Many incoherent acts of violence are exploited by insurgent elites as a means of improving their roles or imposing a larger part of their values upon a greater political system. The greater the logical connection between the act and the ends sought, the easier it is to assimilate the act and claim it as a demonstration of the threat available to the insurgents if their demands are ignored. The rapidity with which insurgent movements create martyrs, often from the demise of hapless bystanders, and the reluctance of governments to give martyrs to the opposition, are evidence of this.

* * *

The International Process

Many people blithely argue for law as a substitute for violence, as though there were a choice between the two. They call for international law and world government to eliminate war. This point of view reveals a blissful ignorance of the functions of violence in domestic legal systems. A viable system based on law protects the conditions of group action. Law always rests on violence. The threat of violence and the fear of the breakdown of law and order act to moderate demands and positions, thereby setting into peaceful motion the informal political processes of negotiation, concession, compromise, and agreement. Although there is no centralized police power in the international forum, the processes of mediation and negotiation operate in much the same way. The credible threat of violence in the hands of the nations has a similarly stabilizing effect, providing statesmen are attentive to maintaining their national capability for demonstrating violence, and providing their ambitions are commensurate to the bargaining position which their armaments achieve. More comprehensive legal codes and a world government may not improve the stability of the world community in any case, since the possibility of civil conflict exists in all political systems. Civil wars are frequently bloodier and more unforgiving than wars between sovereign nations.

In international politics, the threat of violence tends to create stability and maintain peace. Here the threat is more directly responsive to policy controls. The nation-state has greater continuity than the informal political systems that coalesce and dissolve in the course of domestic social change. The threat of violence can be asserted much more deliberately and can be demonstrated under full control, as in "good will" navy visits, army maneuvers near a sensitive border, partial mobilization, etc. Because of the greater continuity of these macrosystems, the national leaders must strive to maintain the prestige of a nation's might and will. If the reputation of a nation's military power is allowed to tarnish, future bargaining power will be weakened. It may be forced to reestablish that prestige by invoking a test of arms, as a means of inducing greater respect for its position from other nations. All strong nations are anxious to demonstrate their military power peaceably in order that their prestige will afford them the bargaining power they deserve without a test of arms.

Because the threat of violence is a conscious instrument of national policy, it generally lacks the random character which violence has domestically. This means that if the armaments of nations fall out of balance, if the prestige of nations is no longer commensurate with their ambitions, if the will to take the risks of limited military conflicts is lacking, if domestic political considerations distort the national response to external threat, then the time becomes ripe for the outbreak of violence, escalating out of control.

In general, the dangers of escalating international conflict induce greater, not lesser, restraint on the part of national leaders in their relations with each other. Attempts to achieve infinite security for the nation are as self-defeating as such attempts are for domestic regimes.

The functioning of consensus and competition between nations is not fundamentally different from that of domestic politics. The most striking difference is that in domestic politics the level of centralized violence available to the state creates a high threshold of stability against the threats brought to bear within the system by private groups. In the international forum, the closest approximation to such a threshold is the decentralized forces available to the Great Powers. A power interested in modifying the status quo must raise the level of its threat of violence, in order to induce other powers to choose between concessions to its demands or the costs and risks of an arms race. To the extent that the status quo powers are capable and willing to pay the costs and take the risks, their own levels can be raised, depriving the challenger of any political advantages from his investment. When all of the great powers are attentive to the equations of potential violence, no nation can hope to gain conclusive political advantages from an arms race. This situation makes possible international agreements for stabilizing arms and bringing about political settlements.

Diplomatic ceremonials, like the ceremonials of personal relations which we call "manners," serve to minimize the dangers of provocation and threat in the day-to-day relations between nations. Conversely, manners tend to minimize the dangers of provocation and threat in relations between people.

* * *

2

*The Arms Race and Some of Its Hazards**

Herman Kahn

HERMAN KAHN *was one of the founders and now serves as the director of the Hudson Institute. As a defense systems analyst he has served with the Atomic Energy Commission, the Gaither Commission on Strategic Warfare, the Stanford Research Institute of Non-Military Defense, and as a private consultant to defense industries. His books include* On Thermonuclear War *(1960) and* Thinking About the Unthinkable *(1962).*

PREFACE

It is easy to write graphically and persuasively of the dangers of the arms race, nuclear and otherwise. Such documents are often well received: the author's heart seems to be in the right place; he is for people and against the abominations science and technology have produced. Yet, this question remains unanswered: Why do nations in general, our own in particular, continue to play such a dangerous and pointless game?

* *Daedalus,* **LXXXIX,** No. 4 (1960). Reprinted by permission.

Here we hit on the nub of the matter: the game is indeed dangerous, but not pointless, since not to play it (even to reduce forces or submit to arms control) can also be dangerous: a Pearl Harbor or a Munich is all too possible. If we examine the whole range of possibilities, beginning with unilateral disarmament, surrender, appeasement, or accommodation, and ending with an accelerated arms race, preventive war, Mutual Homicide Pacts, and Doomsday Machines, we discover that there are no pleasant, safe, or even unambiguously moral positions for the individual, for a nation, or for civilization. Unfortunately the discussions that concentrate on one facet of our dangerous future tend to create a psychological atmosphere conducive to the neglect of the remaining problems of security. This is no reason for not discussing the dangers of the arms race (or any other dangers), but only for emphasizing the ultimate need for a balanced comparison of all the dangers. . . .

While the most important problems of the 1960's and 1970's may result from the arms race itself, rather than from the political and military dangers against which the arms race is supposed to protect us, those dangers exist. Today they are manageable only because the arms protect us from them; *ill-advised* measures to control the arms race can still reduce our security[1] We are trying to negotiate some very rough and dangerous terrain. While it is by no means clear that there are any "reasonable" routes to wherever we want to go, it is clear that there are precipitous and unscalable heights in all directions. Let us now examine some of this terrain.

[1] The possibility implied by the author's use of the word *still* in this sentence is to be noted.—Ed.

Various Ways in Which War Can Start

The major danger of the arms race lies precisely in the fact that the arms may be used; thermonuclear war may be unthinkable, but it is not impossible. Arms control can reduce the risks that ensue from the ever-present possibility of war by reducing:

1. The number of events, both international (tensions and crises) and technical (false alarms and misunderstandings), that could give rise to war.
2. The probability that an event of the kind that could cause war will actually result in war.
3. The damage of an actual war, not only by abolishing the use of certain weapons and controlling the use of others, but also by facilitating ahead of time the machinery by which wars are ended before they become overwhelmingly destructive.

There is no space here to expand on these possibilities. . . . However, it may be well now to discuss systematically how a war could arise and indicate some of the problems to be considered. I will begin by listing a number of possibilities, in a semi-technical jargon intended to categorize and describe them.

1. *Unpremeditated war* (human or mechanical error, false alarm, self-fulfilling prophecy, unauthorized behavior).
2. *Miscalculation* (game of "Chicken," rationality of irrationality strategies, escalation, overconfidence).
3. *Calculation* (Type II Deterrence situation; preventive war; pre-emptive war; world domination; solution to a desperate crisis).
4. *Catalytic war* (ambitious third nation; desperate third nation).

The items in these four categories are neither exhaustive nor distinct from one another. They are not exhaustive because our weapon systems are so new, and their impact, both on one another and on international relations, is so little known that it would not be surprising if a war started in some manner not heretofore thought of. However, I have made the list as exhaustive as possible; in doing so it has been convenient to list categories that occasionally overlap. This is probably better than to strain too much to prevent duplication or leave out some important possibility.

Unpremeditated war

The four categories are ordered by the writer's personal estimate of their likelihood of actually being a cause of war in the next decade or two. I have put unpremeditated war at the top of the list, the fearful possibility that a war may occur almost unintentionally. There is a widespread fear that this could occur; that a button may be pressed accidentally, an electrical circuit short, a relay stick, a telephone call or other message be misunderstood, an aurora borealis or meteor or flock of geese be mistaken for an attack, a switch fail, some ICBM's launched through some mechanical or human error, some stockpile weapons accidentally exploded, and so on. Such things have happened in the past and may happen again. However, unless one side or the other is careless enough to install a quick-reacting, nonrecallable strategic system, it is most unlikely that any single one of the above events would trigger off a retaliatory attack. It is just because radars do indeed occasionally give false alarms and accidents do happen that it is essential for both sides to install weapon systems that either have so-called "fail safe" or "positive control" features built into them, or that are large enough and well enough protected that they do not need to be "trigger happy" to survive. If a system can accept the enemy's attack and still strike back effectively, the decision maker has time to evaluate and decide—time to be careful. Such systems may use an ambiguous warning so as to take some temporizing measure that will reduce vulnerability to enemy attack or provide a better posture from which to retaliate. But the commander can then wait for further confirmation before making any irrevocable commitments.

There is a danger that the temporizing measures that are instituted on an ambiguous warning will remove some of the psychological, legal, and physical safeties that normally govern the strategic force, so that there is a greater load thrown on the remaining safeguards. For this reason several accidents in a row or even a simple accident during a period of considerable tension could be dangerous. Actually, the greatest danger is the possibility that a chain of "self-fulfilling prophecies" is set into motion. It is perfectly conceivable for one side's temporizing action to be observed by the other side and to be misinterpreted as being aggressive rather than defensive, thus causing the other side also to make some temporizing defensive move. This second defensive move can in turn be misread by the side originally alerted as confirming his suspicions, so he may make some further moves. It is then possible for reactions and signals to be set into motion which trigger off further reactions and signals by both sides until a point of no return is reached. This is one reason that it is necessary for each side not only to be cautious and responsible, but also to make sure that the other side also understands what is happening. In so far as any temporizing measures depend on doing things which raise apprehensions on the other side, it is important to be prepared to allay those apprehensions. This is possibly a very fruitful area for arms control.

The Soviets are completely aware of the problem. For example, in a Security Council debate of April 21, 1958, Arkady S. Sobolev made the following statement:

> American generals refer to the fact that up to the present time the American planes have taken off on their flights and returned to their bases as soon as it became clear that it was a case of false alarm. But what would happen if American military personnel observing their radar screens are not able in time to determine that a flying meteor is not a guided missile and that a flight of geese is not a flight of bombers? Then the American planes will continue their flight and will approach the borders of the Soviet Union.
>
> But in such a case the need to insure the security of the Soviet people would require the USSR to make immediate retaliatory measures to eliminate the oncoming threat. The Soviet Government would like to hope that matters will not go so far.
>
> In order to get a clearer idea of the extremely dangerous character of acts of the United States [that are] dangerous to peace, it is enough to ask the question what would happen if the military Air Force of the Soviet Union began to act in the same way as the American Air Force is now acting? After all, Soviet radar screens also show from time to time blips which are caused by the flight of meteors or electronic interference. If in such cases Soviet aircraft also flew out carrying atom and hydrogen bombs in the direction of the United States and its bases in other states, what situation would arise?
>
> The air fleets of both sides, having observed each other, having discerned each other somewhere over the Arctic wastes or in some other place, apparently would draw the conclusion natural under those circumstances, that a real enemy attack was taking place. Then the world would inevitably be plunged into the hurricane of atomic war.

In spite of their awareness of the problem, the Soviets have tended to emphasize disarmament almost, but not quite, to the exclusion of other aspects of arms control. For example, at the 1958 Surprise Attack Conference, they stressed larger issues and refused to discuss narrow technical issues although our own position may have been excessively narrow. To this writer it seems dangerous to wait for a settlement of the political issues before considering this problem, but in this kind of a problem it takes two to make an agreement. However, even informal implicit agreements or, on some aspects, unilateral concessions can be helpful.

It is also conceivable that some pathological or irresponsible person will deliberately try to start a war or crisis. The Soviets have made much of the possibility that a deranged or irresponsible American pilot on airborne alert would take it into his head to attack Russia alone. Not only are there many safeguards against this, but it is most unlikely that a single-plane attack would touch off a war. A much more ominous possibility is given in the book *Red Alert,* in which a determined SAC general, who, unknown to his superiors, is sick with an incurable ailment (and whose judgment and sense of discipline are thus affected), decides personally to end the Soviet problem once and for all. The most interesting part is the clever way he gets around the rather elaborate system set up to prevent exactly this kind of behavior.

I should make clear that I believe that, currently at least, the probability of unpremeditated war is low. The reason I put it on the top of the list is because I believe (assuming, perhaps optimistically, that both sides are careful, competent, and responsible) the other ways in which a war could occur should have an even lower probability. It is also clear that many of the methods recommended to reduce the probability of war by accident might very well result in increasing the likelihood of war from one of the other causes. After both these points are made, it must also be mentioned that nobody can estimate realistically what the probability of accidental war is. (There seems to be some tendency to underestimate the probability of war. For example, Wheeler-Bennett reports in his book, *Munich: Prologue to Tragedy*, that on January 1, 1939, Lloyds was giving 32 to 1 odds against war in 1939. This was three months after Munich and eight months before the war actually started. While it would be hard to convince me that it is as high as, say, 1 in 10 a year, still, if it were this high, the situation would be entirely unsatisfactory. Even if it were 1 in 100 a year, it would still be unsatisfactory, because the current state of affairs could not be allowed to continue indefinitely. One must eventually introduce a major change in the situation, or expect to get into a war anyway.)

The really dangerous intensification in the probability of unpremeditated war is likely to come in the future, partly as a result of increased alertness or dispersal of weapons carriers in the missile age, partly as a result of the increase in the number of buttons that can be pressed accidentally, but mostly as a result of the proliferation of independent nuclear capabilities to other countries, each with its own standards of training, reliability of personnel, and safety practices.

War by miscalculation

Nearly as worrisome as the possibility of unpremeditated war is the war which is more or less premeditated (perhaps as in the *usually uncalculated* "calculated risk")—but the decision maker doing the premeditating has miscalculated or misunderstood the risks or consequences of his actions. Many believe that the most likely way for this to occur is as a result of the use of a committal strategy. For example, one side may make it clear that it is going to stand firm in some crisis in the belief that "since neither side wants war," the other side will back down. If the other side does not back down, then war can result. A graphic if somewhat oversimplified example of such a situation is given by Bertrand Russell:

> This sport is called "Chicken!" It is played by choosing a long straight road with a white line down the middle and starting two very fast cars towards each other from opposite ends. Each car is expected to keep the wheels of one side on the white line. As they approach each other mutual destruction becomes more and more imminent. If one of them swerves from the white line before the other, the other, as he passes, shouts "Chicken!" and the one who has swerved becomes an object of contempt.

It is clear that if one side really wishes to win this game its best (rational) strategy is to commit itself irrevocably to going ahead. If one can convince the other side that one has done this, then the other side must back down. However, if the other side still refuses to back down after the irrevocable commitment has been made, it would be irrational to carry out the rationally made commitment. Since both sides will be attempting to use this strategy, it is also quite clear that the game may end in a disaster.

According to Bertrand Russell, the game is played by degenerates in America, and by nations everywhere. It is a caricature, because Russell ignores the fact that it is a major purpose of diplomacy to prevent a crisis from arising which can only be settled by the total and humiliating defeat of one side or the other. Most bargaining situations involve gains for both sides, and the major question is on the division of these gains and not the humiliation of the other side. However, the game of Chicken may occur. Barring enforceable adjudication, the less one is willing to play the game, the more likely it may be that one may end up having to play it. Life, liberty, and security may depend on being willing to play this dangerous game. As Russell states:

> Practical politicians may admit all this, but they argue that there is no alternative. If one side is unwilling to risk global war, while the other side is willing to risk it, the side which is willing to run the risk will be victorious in all negotiations and will ultimately reduce the other side to complete impotence. "Perhaps"—so the practical politician will argue—"it might be ideally wise for the sane party to yield to the insane party in view of the dreadful nature of the alternative, but, whether wise or not, no proud nation will long acquiesce in such an ignominious role. We are, therefore, faced, quite inevitably, with the choice between brinkmanship and surrender."

The game of Chicken is an extreme example of the use of "rationality of irrationality" strategies. Because these are so important it may be worthwhile to dwell on them briefly. In any bargaining situation, even the most innocuous, it can make sense to commit oneself irrevocably to do something in a certain eventuality, and at the same time it may not make sense to carry out the commitment if the eventuality occurs; if one could, one would revoke the "irrevocable" commitment. The analogy with the game of Chicken should be clear. It should also be clear that if both sides commit themselves to incompatible positions, there will be no bargain. But if the bargaining is carried on with skill, and if both sides are cautious, then the bargaining will take on the aspects of a normal commercial transaction in which both sides gain, the exact division of the gains depending on their relative skill, but in which neither is driven to the wall.

Unfortunately, in any long period of peace, there is some tendency for governments to become more and more intransigent. The thought of war may become unreal. Even more important, every government is likely to build up a background of experiences in which it did very well by standing firm and very badly when it displayed a flexible, reasonable, or conciliatory attitude. It is only when peace fails that the governments are likely to learn that standing firm on incompatible positions is not a feasible symmetrical strategy. One can almost confidently predict that unless arrangements are made for adjudication or arbitration, somebody is going to play the international analogue of Chicken once too often.

The rationality-of-irrationality war should be distinguished from one caused by the two sides having incompatible objectives which they are determined to achieve, no matter what the risks: in this case war must result. The rationality-of-irrationality war corresponds to a situation in which neither side really believes the issue is big enough to go to war over, but both sides are willing to use some partial or total strategy of commitment to force the other side to back down. As a result, they may end up in a war they would not have gone into, if either side had realized ahead of time that the other side would not back down, even under pressure.

A typical circumstance in which such a situation could arise results from the use of Type II Deterrence.* Imagine, for example, that the Soviets had done some very provocative thing, such as invading Western Europe with conventional armies, on such a large scale that we felt that we could not stop the invasion by any limited actions, and that we would not be able to rescue Europe at a later date. We might still not be willing to strike the Soviets with our SAC, in view of the terrible price we would have to pay to their retaliatory blow, even if we struck them first. However, we could evacuate our cities and place our forces on a super-alert status, and thus put ourselves in a much better position to strike first and accept the retaliatory blow. We might then present the Soviets with an ultimatum. We would in effect be presenting the Russians with the following three alternatives: to initiate some kind of strike; to prolong the crisis, even though it would then be very credible that we would strike if they continued to provoke us; or to back down or compromise the crisis satisfactorily. We would hope that the Soviets would prefer the third alternative, because our Type I Deterrence would make the first choice sufficiently unattractive, and our Type II Deterrence would do the same for the second; but we might be wrong, and they might take the first alternative. Or they might take the second alternative in the assumption that we would back down, and we might not.

Another method of getting into a war by miscalculation would be as a result of a limited move that appeared safe, but which set into motion a disastrous sequence that ended in all-out warfare. This increase is called escalation. One can imagine some sort of crisis which gradually increased in violence or scope until it triggered one of the reactions already discussed. This could occur either because the limits of a limited war are not being observed, or because more parties are being drawn into it, or because the issues themselves become fraught with significances that did not initially exist, or because of some unauthorized or accidental behavior by subordinates. It is difficult to supply a plausible reason for escalation (except, of course, as a move in the game of Chicken), when it is to everybody's interest to control things, yet almost everyone considers that it can and perhaps will happen.

Escalation is possible particularly if one of the two contending sides does not think through the consequences of its actions. To return to the Type II Deterrence situation discussed above: it is perfectly conceivable that the Russians, looking at the 60 million hostages we have in our fifty largest cities, might decide that it was safe to attack Europe, and that we would not attack them in retaliation. They might also vaguely realize that if they attacked Europe, we would probably evacuate the 60 million hostages; but they might not understand the full consequences of that evacuation, in terms

* As in my book, I would like to distinguish three kinds of deterrence. Type I is the deterrence of an "all-out" direct attack. Type II is the deterrence of extremely provocative acts, other than an all-out attack on the nation using the deterrence. Type III might be called a graduated or controlled deterrence: it is the deterrence of provocations by making the potential aggressor afraid that the defender or others will then take limited actions, military or nonmilitary, which will make the aggression unprofitable.

of the psychological stiffening of the backbone and the enormous decrease in the risks this country would be running if it went to war.

The possibility of escalation may actually play a useful role in deterring certain kinds of crises or limited wars. For example, it is quite clear that the nuclear-weapon systems we and the British have in Europe are on the whole fairly vulnerable to Soviet attack, so that they have little second-strike capability. Yet the Soviets might be afraid to destroy them in a limited European attack, for fear that the level of by-product destruction would automatically cause escalation into an all-out World War III. On the other hand, if the Soviets did not destroy them, the Europeans might use them, and this in turn would not only be damaging to the Soviets, but might also cause escalation into World War III. This means that lower than all-out attacks may be deterred for fear they will escalate. The same mechanism holds, for example, if we decide to open a route to Berlin by force if the Soviets or East Germans try to close it. . . . The purpose of the action is not to overwhelm Soviet countermeasures, but to make it clear to them that the stakes are large. It is clear that we might be willing to take a small but appreciable risk of an all-out war, even if we were not willing to go immediately into an all-out war. The action might be effective precisely because it was so dangerous. To the extent that various types of arms-control measures reduce the possibility of escalation, then to that extent the deterring effect of escalation on limited actions is decreased. The author finds this no reason for not carrying through such control measures, but he knows many Europeans who are antagonistic to any reliable limits on the use of violence, for the very reason that such limitations may increase the probability of a provocation at that limited level.

Another possibility of a war by miscalculation occurs when one side goes to war in the mistaken belief that it has a sufficient preponderance of force or a clever enough war plan to be able to win satisfactorily. The mistake can occur through some uncertainty being underestimated, some imponderable ignored, or sheer ignorance or recklessness. Given current beliefs in the West, it is almost impossible to imagine this happening to a Western government unless the decision makers have their judgment clouded by desperation or madness. The situation is less certain in the Communist bloc. The Chinese clearly underestimate the effects of nuclear war. Hopefully, it will be some time before they have the power to use nuclear weapons, and time may bring them greater wisdom. The Soviet estimates, as gleaned from their public statements, seem plausible, though whether this comes as a result of more or less sophistication than is prevalent in the West is hard to tell. They talk of the possibility of great destruction and suffering together with the likelihood of the "victor" surviving and recovering. The Soviets do not seem to be trigger-happy or reckless, one judges at this writing, so that it does not seem to be necessary to put much effort into attempts to educate them on the danger of being over-confident about the use of modern weapons. The Soviets may underestimate the need for collaboration in controlling the technological development and dissemination of new weapons and thus be unwilling to make the necessary compromises entailed in getting feasible arms-control programs accepted by both sides. If they go to war, however, it is as likely to be as a result of calculation as of miscalculation. This thought brings us to our next topic.

War by calculation

War could result from calculation. After due study, a nation might decide that going to war would be the least undesirable of its choices. Common belief, of course, holds just the opposite: that war could arise only as a result of miscalculation—but this is based on the unsophisticated view that all wars result in automatic mutual annihilation. This could happen, but in all likelihood it would not. One type of war by calculation could occur in the Type II Deterrence situation referred to above. If at that point we attacked the Soviet Union, the damage we received in return would be considerably reduced. We might well decide that our nation was better off to accept this retaliatory blow rather than let Europe be occupied, and also to accept the costs of living in the hostile and dangerous world that would result.

Or, to give another example, the Soviets suffered from 20 to 30 million casualties in World War II, and in addition they lost about one-third of their wealth. It is sometimes pointed out that this did not happen from calculation but was inflicted on a day-by-day basis: no alternatives were ever really put up to them. However, given the nature of the Nazis and their program, I would believe that even the average Soviet citizen (not to mention the government) would have been willing to accept the cost of World War II in order to achieve the position they have since won, as an alternative to Nazi domination.

Another war by calculation would be the so-called preventive war. This does not necessarily mean that one side believes the other is planning eventually to attack the first, which is therefore merely getting in the first blow. One side has only to feel that a war is inevitable—or so likely that it might as well get the disaster over with as soon as it gets a sufficient lead, so that it is safer to seize the opportunity than to wait. Such an edge is most likely to result from a technological change to which the other side has not reacted. The so-called missile gap illustrates how this problem could arise.

The United States SAC (Strategic Air Command) is supposed to be based upon about fifty home bases. If the Soviets happened to acquire, unknown to us, about three hundred missiles, then they could assign about six missiles to the destruction of each base. If the Soviet missiles had, let us say, one chance in two of completing their countdown and otherwise performing reliably, then there would only be 1 chance in 64 that any particular SAC base would survive a Soviet attack. There would be better than an even chance that all the bases would be destroyed, about one chance in three that one base would survive, and a small chance that two or more bases would survive.

A missile gap of the sort described is especially dangerous because missile attacks are so much more calculable than any other kind of attack. They are so calculable that many people feel that even a cautious Soviet planner might be willing to rely on the correctness of his estimates; that Soviet decision makers might find it the path of caution to attack while the opportunity was still available.

Actually the results of missile attacks are not mathematically predictable. There are imponderables and uncertainties with regard to such things as reliability of basic data, field degradation, intelligence leaks, and firing discipline so that the probability of something going wrong cannot be predicted. But so many laymen and professionals persist in regarding the reliable prediction of the results of missile attacks as simple problems in engineering and physics that it would be irresponsible to rely on Soviet caution and sophistication alone as a protection. And if such an attack were successfully carried out, it would truly be a war by calculation.

The need for a quick reaction to even "hypothetical" changes in the enemy's posture is likely to persist indefinitely, in spite of the popular theory that once we get over our current difficulties we will have a so-called minimum nuclear deterrent force that will solve the Type I Deterrence problem. (Some even maintain that it will solve all strategic problems.)

It should be noted that if a serious deterrent gap ever occurred, then, even if the Soviets were not willing, either out of caution or morality, to use their superiority, the situation would still be dangerous. They might well be tempted to a strong (even reckless) foreign policy, if they believed that their military technology entitled them to some gains, or that if they got into trouble they could use their missiles to rescue themselves. This kind of situation could be especially dangerous if the Soviets considered that they could not disclose their superiority, since if they did so, we could take remedial action (e.g., an airborne alert). Still, they might be willing to hint at their superiority, in the belief that this would be just enough to make us weak or uncertain in our response in a crisis, but not move us prior to a crisis to institute the airborne alert in time.

Another possibility for preventive war could occur if an arms-control agreement broke down and one side had a considerable lead, either because of its previous success in evading detection, or its greater ability to rearm. This side might well feel that, rather than see the world subjected again to all the dangers of an arms race, it would be doing a public service to stop the race, once and for all. And this could best be done by stopping the cause of the race—its opponent. It might be especially willing to start the war soon after the arms-control agreement terminated, because the risks, even if things went awry, would not be so great at the existing low level of arms than before the arms-control agreement had lowered the absolute level of the balance of terror. The rather high probability of war breaking out after the arms race had begun again (but before both states were fully armed) is often ignored. Most writers focus attention on the situation existing at the time of the breakdown, when the posture is still determined by the agreement and on the feasible violations of the agreement, rather than on the situation some months or a year or two later.

Then there is the idea of "pre-emption," or as Einstein called it, "anticipatory retaliation." Almost all authorities agree that at present the advantages of striking first are so great that if there seems a high probability that the other side is actually attacking, it may be better to take the certain risk of a relatively small retaliatory strike rather than the high probability of a much more destructive first strike. This calculated pressure for preemption is especially likely in one situation very similar to that of "self-fullfillment," previously discussed. Even if only one side suspects that the other may attack, each can easily become convinced that it should attack—not because it wants to, or even because it believes the other side wants to, but only because it believes the other side may attack simply to preempt a supposed attack by the first (which is itself being launched as a pre-emptive attack). Schelling has labeled this situation, "the reciprocal fear of surprise attack." As described, it is not a case of miscalculation, but a case of calculating correctly. This is clearly a situation in which each side has nothing to fear but fear, yet the knowledge that the other side is afraid fully justifies that fear.

Many things could touch off a "reciprocal fear of surprise attack" situation. The only reason I have put this possibility low on the list of possible causes of war is because of the belief that as long as decision makers are consciously in control of events, they are very much more likely to draw back from pressing buttons and accept any resulting risks, than to do something which would make war inevitable—particularly, if this war were to occur at a time and under circumstances not of their choosing. However, complicated and dangerous situations can occur. For example, suppose that one of our own Polaris submarines accidentally launched some missiles at our own country. Even if the submarine commander succeeded in informing us of what happened before the missiles landed, the accident could still cause a war. The Soviets might observe these missiles exploding and if they did know where the missiles came from, they might decide that it would be too dangerous to wait. Even if the Soviets knew that the missiles had not accidentally come from a Soviet submarine, they might not believe that we would wait to find out.

We might ourselves be under pressure to attack even if we thought the Soviets knew nothing about the incident because we could not be sure they did not know. It might appear safer to pre-empt than to let precious minutes slip away while we tried to persuade the Soviets that we knew they were innocent. The possibilities for trouble are almost infinite, and it would be wise to reinforce the natural caution of decision makers with explicit measures, both unilateral and multilateral, to facilitate communication and persuasion and to make waiting safe.

The line between preventive and pre-emptive war is sometimes very fine, and it is on this line that some of the most plausible war-making situations can occur. For example, let us imagine the Type II Deterrence situation discussed earlier, in which the Soviets were hypothesized as invading Europe, and we as evacuating our cities as a preliminary to delivering an ultimatum or otherwise exerting pressure. If the Soviets struck us at that time, it would not be a pre-emptive war, because very likely we would not have made up our own minds as to whether we would strike or not; in particular, we would intend to give them the option of backing down or compromising. However, we are so close to making up our minds that this cannot be labeled as a preventive war, either—a war to head off some generalized future threat. Similarly, if after evacuating our cities, we gave the Soviets an ultimatum, and the Soviets chose the alternatives of prolonging the crisis, we might decide to strike, even though we thought there was a big chance that they were going to back down eventually. We would not be sure, and if we had already evacuated our cities, the risks of going to war would have been sharply diminished.

There is also a possibility of going to war simply to achieve world domination. Most people (the author included) believe the risks involved in going to war are so great today that no matter how promising an attack might look on paper, the "imponderables" and other "uncertainties" are large enough so that not even a moderately irresponsible decision maker would go to war for positive gains—though one like Hitler might. However, if we ever disarm, either unilaterally or bilaterally, to the point where the available weapon systems do not present the awful potentialities present today, then, of course, this possibility reappears.

Even if decision makers are unwilling to go to war for positive gains, they may still be willing to go to war, if, in their opinion, "going to war" is less risky than not doing so. There are many situations in which this could occur. One could imagine an internal or external crisis getting out of hand, and one which was being aggravated by the opponent, perhaps merely by his very existence. One may then be tempted to go to war, not because it looks so tempting, but because it looks like the least undesirable alternative.

Catalytic War

The last possibility is the catalytic war. This is the notion that some third party (or country) may deliberately start a war between the two major powers for reasons of its own. As it is usually discussed, the concept holds that some power which is third, fourth, or fifth in the international hierarchy wishes to improve its position by arranging for the top two nations to destroy each other, thus moving itself up two notches. This is one of the major reasons why some people fear the dissemination of nuclear weapons to "ambitious" powers. However, there are several reasons why this particular concept is not considered plausible: 1. risks are so great for the triggering power that it is difficult to believe that one power could make and carry out such a decision, 2. more important, the United States and the Soviets will probably put into effect slow-reacting systems with a lot of stops in them before the decision for all-out war is reached. This means that it will be much harder for a third party to start a war than is often imagined, though if it tries hard enough and has a large enough capability, it is not impossible.

There is another type of catalytic war which I think much more likely and important: a desperate third nation thinks it has a problem that can be solved only by war. Let us imagine a war between India and China which the Indians were losing. The Indians might feel that if they induced the United States to strike at China and Russia, this would solve their problem, and any method they used to achieve this end was as good as any other. Conversely, let us imagine a situation in which the Chinese felt hard pressed (possibly over Formosa) and told the Russians, "We are going to strike the United States tomorrow, and you might as well come along with us, for they will undoubtedly strike you, even if you do not do so."

As stated, the situation may seem somewhat implausible, but one can devise hypothetical situations which make it seem more plausible than I have done here. One may wish to broaden the definition of catalytic war. Any method by which a nation uses military or diplomatic power to embroil larger nations or increase the scope of the conflict could be called catalytic. By this definition, World War I was a catalytic war, set off by Serbia and Austria, which also had some overtones of "reciprocal fear of surprise attack" and "self-fulfilling prophecy," because the side which mobilized first was likely to win. It means that even a defensive mobilization (by the Russians) touched off a defensive-offensive mobilization (by the Germans), in much the same way some believe that a badly designed, quick-reacting force can be touched off by defensive moves by the other side.

. . . .

3

*Deterrence and Power**

Glenn H. Snyder

GLENN H. SNYDER *is Professor of Political Science, State University of New York at Buffalo. His work in the field of national security, civilian-military relations and international relations theory have appeared in scholarly journals. His books include* Deterrence by Denial and Punishment *(1958) and* Deterrence and Defense *(1961).*

Anyone who comes to the study of military affairs from the field of international relations is likely to be struck by the discontinuity between the prevailing theoretical concepts in the two fields. One notes, for example, that, although a good deal of theoretical effort has been devoted to the idea of deterrence in the context of the problem of national security, it is still not clear where this notion stands in relation to the older concept of power, which also has been subjected to considerable analysis. One also wonders how the ancient idea of "balance of power" should be modified to take account of the idea of nuclear "parity" or "balance of terror."[1] The literature on national security abounds with such concepts as "active" and "passive" deterrence and defense, "counterforce" and "retaliatory" strategies, and alliance "burden-sharing," all of which have yet to be integrated into international relations theory. While this paper is chiefly concerned with probing into the nature and meaning of deterrence, I hope in passing to show the connection between this concept and the more general idea of power.

Conceived broadly, deterrence appears to be a species of "political power." Defining political power generally as the capacity to induce others to do things or not to do things which they would not otherwise do or refrain from doing, deterrence is simply its negative aspect. It is the power to dissuade another party from doing something which one believes to be against one's own interests, achieved by the threat of applying some sanction.

Deterrence does not have to depend on a threat and capacity to impose punishment. It may also be achieved by having the capability to deny the other party any gains from the move which is to be deterred.

[1] A remarkable pioneering effort to assess the impact of the new weapons on the classic balance of power was Arthur Lee Burns's article, "From Balance to Deterrence."

* *The Journal of Conflict Resolution,* **IV** (1960), 163–178. Reprinted by permission.

Thus we may speak of "deterrence by denial" as well as "deterrence by punishment." In military affairs deterrence by denial is accomplished by having military forces which can block the enemy's military forces from making territorial gains. Deterrence by punishment grants him the gain but deters by posing the prospect of war costs greater than the value of the gain.

Deterrence (like political power) does not have to depend on military force. We might speak of deterrence by the threat of trade restrictions, for example. When non-military means are used, deterrence may be accomplished by the promise of rewards as well as by the threat of deprivation. Thus the promise of economic aid might "deter" a country from military action (or any action) contrary to one's own interests. Or we might speak of the "deterrence" of allies and neutrals as well as potential enemies, as Italy, for example, was "deterred" from fighting on the side of the Dual Alliance in World War I by the promise of substantial territorial gains. Both deterrent capability and political power stem from the control which one has over another party's total value "inventory," whether the control takes the form of a capacity to increase or to decrease this inventory.

Robert A. Dahl has written that power consists of four basic components: *base*, *means*, *amount*, and *scope*. The power *base* is the material or attribute which provides the capacity to affect the value positions of others, for example, military force, economic assets, etc. The *means* is the method by which the power base is brought to bear, for example, by threat, ultimatum, or force demonstration. The *amount* of power is the degree of influence over potential actions. The *scope* is the range of potential actions by the other party which can be influenced by the threat or promise of applying the base. Degree of influence is expressed most precisely as a probability figure indicating the chances that the other party will do (or refrain from doing, as the case may be) the things which the power-wielder specifies in his threat or promise.

These categories can also be applied to the phenomenon of deterrence. Considering, for example, deterrence by "massive retaliation," the base is the capacity to inflict devastating punishment, the means is the threat of retaliation, the scope refers to the various forms of aggression the probability of which may be reduced by the threat, and the amount is the reduction in probability of each of these moves which results from the threat.

I would add two further components to the four suggested by Dahl: the *object values* and the *credibility* of a threat or promise. *Object values* are the values of the other party, which are subject to being decreased or increased by the actual carrying-out of the threat or promise. Object values are theoretically distinct from both power base and scope values. The scope of the power-wielder's power follows from the threat of deprivation of, or the promise of additions to, the other party's object values by application of a power base. Thus deterrence of an aggressive act (scope) may be effected by the threat of applying nuclear punishment (power base) to the aggressor's cities and population (object values).

The juxtaposition of deterrence and power helps one to recognize the importance of a sixth component, *credibility*, defined as the perception by the threatened party of the degree of probability that the power-wielder will actually carry out the threat if its terms are not complied with or will keep a promise if its conditions are met. The idea of credibility, so prominent in the literature on deterrence, really has application to all forms of political power. In domestic politics the person or group against whom a threat is directed may harbor doubts about whether the threatener "really means" it, and these doubts will affect the *amount* of power actually available to the threatener. A President may threaten to withhold patronage from a particular senator, for example, but, if the senator has some power of retaliation (e.g., by failing to support other aspects of the President's program) or if the withholding of patronage might adversely affect the President's political support in the senator's state, the President's threat may not be very credible to the senator, and his voting on the immediate issue may not be affected.

In short, the concept of power must take some account not only of the power-wielder's control over the value inventory of the recipient of the threat but also of the latter's capacity to affect the values of the power-wielder and, generally, of all the possible adverse consequences to the power-wielder from carrying out his threat. Political power, like deterrence, is a two-way street; A's power over B depends on B's power over A. A has little or no power over B, even if A possesses a "base" for inflicting deprivations on B, if B can inflict punishments of similar weight against A and can be expected to do so in retaliation with a high degree of credibility. Of course, if the credibility of B's retaliation is low, A may still have an edge in the "balance of power" vis-à-vis B, but the *amount* of his political power over B (defined as the probability that B will behave in the manner desired by A) must be discounted, in some sense, by the loss of credibility occasioned by B's recognition of A's recognition that B *might* retaliate and also by the size of the value loss which both know B can inflict in retaliation.

All that I have been saying is that the source of political power resides in two distinct elements: *capabilities* (or the capacity to affect object values by application of a power base) and the opponent's perception of the *intent* to use these capabilities if one's demands are not met. In the field of international relations, both in scholarly analysis and in actual practice, the intentions factor has often been given less attention than it deserved. What was always unreal, for example, about the argument for building up "situations of strength" in Europe to make the Russians more amenable to negotiations was that it seemed to be assumed by its proponents that "strength" by itself was sufficient to extract concessions from the enemy. It was overlooked that the strength would have to be accompanied by a willingness to use it, and, when one stopped to think about it, it seemed doubtful that the West was, or would be, so willing. Similarly, the United States was never able to extract much political power from the atomic bomb during the heyday of its monopoly because it was clear to all that there was no intent to use it except in response to the most serious aggression.

The advent of "nuclear parity," defined as a situation in which the recipient of an all-out nuclear strike would have the means to deliver completely unacceptable retaliation, has vastly increased the importance of the intentions factor in international power relations. In earlier ages the important calculation for the incipient aggressor concerned the balance of capabilities between himself and his opponent. Would he, or would he not, be able to win? It was rather certain that the defender, and, with somewhat less certainty, his allies, would respond with whatever force might be available. But now that the destructive power of military force has far outrun almost all conceivable interests or political goals, the response, and the severity of the response if it comes, is far less certain. What is certain for both sides is that the other has the *capability,* if he cares to use it, to exact costs which render insignificant any potential territorial changes. The critical calculation now concerns the *balance of intentions.* Each side must ask: What portion of his available destructive power will my opponent use in response to this or that move of mine? How willing is he to take steps which may increase the danger of unacceptable destruction for both of us? How does his willingness to run risks compare with mine? Is the opponent likely to act irrationally? How does *he* think we compare in "nerve," in "will power," in propensities to irrationality?

The Logic of Deterrence

Deterrence, like all political phenomena, is not likely to operate according to strict logic. However, it does have a logical core which is useful as a basis for analysis.

The object of military deterrence is to reduce the probability of enemy military moves inimical to one's self. If we postulate two states, an "aggressor" (meaning potential aggressor) and a "deterrer," the probability of any particular attack by the aggressor is the resultant of four factors which exist in his "mind." All four taken together might be termed the aggressor's "risk calculus." They are 1. his valuation of an objective; 2. the cost which he expects to suffer in an attack on the objective, as the result of various possible responses by the deterrer; 3. the probability of various responses, including "no response"; and 4. the probability of winning the objective with each possible response. These are the basic factors the aggressor must weigh in determining, on balance, whether a venture is likely to result in a net gain or a net cost.

The third factor in the enemy's calculus represents the "credibility" of various possible responses by the deterrer. But credibility is only one factor; it should not be equated with the deterrent *effectiveness* of a possible or threatened response, which is a function of all four factors, that is, the net cost or gain which a response promises, discounted by the probability (credibility) of its being applied. An available response which is very low in credibility might be sufficient to deter if it poses a very severe sanction (i.e., "massive retaliation") or if the enemy's prospective territorial gain carries relatively little value for him. Or a threatened response that carries a rather high credibility but poses only moderate costs for the aggressor (e.g., a conventional response) may not deter if the aggressor places a high value on his objective and anticipates a good chance of successful conquest.

The "credibility" factor deserves special attention, however, because it is in terms of this factor that the "risk calculus" of the aggressor "interlocks" with that of the deterrer. The deterrer's risk calculus is similar to that of the aggressor. If the deterrer is rational, his response to aggression will be determined (within the limits, of course, of the military forces he disposes) largely by four factors: 1. his valuation of the territorial objective and of the other intangible gains (e.g., moral satisfaction) which he associates with a given response; 2. the estimated costs of fighting; 3. the probability of successfully holding the territorial objective; and 4. the change in the probability of future enemy attacks on other objectives which would follow from various responses. Variations on, and marginal additions to, these factors may be imagined, but these four are the essential ones. The deterrer will select the response which minimizes his expectation of cost or maximizes his expectation of gain.

The aggressor, of course, is not omniscient with respect to the deterrer's estimates of cost and gain. Even the deterrer will be unable to predict in advance of the attack how he will visualize his cost-gain prospects once the aggression is under way. (Witness the United States response to the North Korean attack in 1950, which was motivated by values which apparently did not become clear to the decision-makers until the actual crisis was upon them.) Nor can the aggressor be sure the deterrer will act rationally according to his own cost-gain predictions. Because of these uncertainties the aggressor's estimate of credibility cannot be absolute. More than one response will be possible, and the best the aggressor can do is attempt to guess how the deterrer will visualize his gains and losses consequent upon each response and from this guess arrive at a judgment about the likelihood or probability of each possible response.

The deterrer, in his turn, evaluates the *effectiveness* of his deterrent posture by attempting to guess the values of the four factors in the aggressor's risk calculus. In estimating the credibility factor, he attempts to guess how the aggressor is estimating the factors in *his* (the deterrer's) calculus. He arrives at some judgment as to whether the aggressor is likely to expect a net cost or net gain from the aggressive move, and, based on this judgment and his degree of confidence in it, he determines the probability of aggression. Happily, the spiral of "guesses about the other's guesses" seems to stop here. In other words, the aggressor's decision whether or not to attack is not in turn affected by his image of the deterrer's estimate of the likelihood of attack. He knows that, once the attack is launched, the deterrer will select the response which promises him the least cost or greatest gain —at that point the deterrer's previous calculations about "deterrence" of that attack become irrelevant. . . .)

Part IV

The Struggle for World Order

CHAPTER SEVENTEEN

Peaceful Change and The Problem of Arms Control

For most states the outbreak of war represents a distinct failure of diplomacy and a retrograde step in foreign policy. But admitting this, what is that elusive thing called "peace"? Is it merely the absence of war? Hardly, as the term "Cold War" demonstrates. Is it no more than merely keeping things as they are? Hardly, for history has shown that in the course of politics and diplomacy, change is inevitable and "things will never be the same again." The test of statesmanship is to accept change, and preferably to direct its course, so not only the interests and well-being of one's own society are served and advanced but also the cause of world peace is promoted as well. Is peace, then, appeasement and surrender, since one way to avoid war is to refuse to fight? Hardly, for peace has never had a purely negative connotation, but clearly involves both the absence of violence and the preservation of social values. Failure on the part of statesmen to find peaceful solutions to international disputes may mean either a gradual escalation of conventional conflict into one that has the most serious implications for all mankind, or possibly even the sudden kind of Pearl Harbor-type catastrophe that so many foreign observers feel haunts those responsible for American national security.

The politics of peaceful change is as vital a subject for the analyst and practitioner of international relations as the assessment of the capacities of States to achieve their own particularized set of policy objectives. It is an unfortunate fact that the spokesmen for the powers, recognizing the universal *will* for peace, tend to cast their aims and objectives in the garb of peace, while at the same time claiming that the other side is deceitful and insincere in making analogous claims for its set of policies.[1] For example, one term frequently utilized in contemporary discourse, in a purely propagandistic context and as an instrument of power politics in disguise, is that of "reducing international tensions." Obviously, even the aggressive state may under certain conditions seek to reduce tension by making less powerful entities submit meekly to its will: when the proposed "victim" resists, "tension" occurs! In the other sense, however, tension exists not because of intentions to control and responses of resistance, but because of stereotypes, "images" and assumptions that, when fully and dispassionately examined, often prove to be exaggerated, inaccurate, or unwarranted.

Such scholars as Otto Klineberg, Professor of Social Psychology at Columbia University, see in the work of such agencies as UNESCO the first breakthrough in drawing into the decision-making process the findings and advice of specialists in the sciences of human relations.[2] Realists may disparage efforts to reduce tension, but Klineberg takes the position that the reduction of tensions can be approached directly, that tension itself creates further tension, and that it is therefore a political problem whose solution can have a significant impact upon political reality. Tensions and crises do occur because of a lack of understanding between statesmen, and perhaps even more fundamentally, between the peoples they represent. When the words of Archibald MacLeish, "since it is in the minds of men that wars begin, it is in the minds of men that the defenses of peace must be constructed," were incorporated into the Constitution of UNESCO, only a few tentative and modest steps had been taken to implement so noble a concept. Even the most sympathetic supporters of the so-called "UNESCO approach" tend to think in terms, not of years or even of decades, but of a century or more before the nature of politics at the world level can be expected to undergo changes of a very fundamental sort. Nevertheless, they fervently argue that a beginning must be made, if for no other reason than the expectation that, given the character of "advances" in weapons technology, the world cannot survive many more wars.

The hard-headed realist, needless to say, rejects the assumptions implicit in this approach, and contends that wars begin, if not in men's stomachs or their hearts, in the incompatible objectives of protagonists in the power struggle in a world devoid of legal and moral restraints. This has always been so, argue the realists, and *ipso facto*, it will always be so. From this viewpoint, "understanding" may produce *more* rather than less hostility as in the case of the later responses of the Western democracies to Hitlerism as they came to *understand* its implications for their own security, and the post-war "hardening" of free-world attitudes toward Russian and particularly Chinese Communists as their

[1] It was this phenomenon which prompted the great British political cartoonist, David Low, to portray a vast sea of peace-loving sheep ("the common people of the world") being addressed by their respective leaders (portrayed as tearful crocodiles) leaving an abortive meeting to resolve their differences: "My friends, we have failed. We just couldn't control your warlike passions." *The London Evening Standard,* May 23, 1934.

[2] "The United Nations," in *World Tension* (Englewood Cliffs, N.J.: Prentice-Hall, Inc., 1951), pp. 276–282.

aims have become more thoroughly comprehended by observers in the free world. Yet it is not so much in the sense of "knowledge" about the intentions of others that the idealist utilizes the term "understanding;" it is rather in the sense of sympathy for others' situations, their attitudes, their fears and hopes, the values they share in common with people everywhere.[3] By the same token, Paul Kecskemeti of The Rand Corporation has warned that merely to talk about reducing tensions does not reduce them. Since they exist because of fundamental differences of value and policy between powers, he argued that it is illusory to regard tension-reducing schemes as productive of any promising solution. If the policy differences were resolved, the tension they create would disappear of its own accord, but "we cannot make it vanish by incantation."[4]

By contrast, the contention of the Marxists (or at least some of them) is that tension, conflict and violence are but manifestations of the class struggle taking the form on the international scene of "a series of terrible wars" between the capitalist states themselves and then between them and the socialist states. To them, an international institution is nothing more nor less than another arena for the power struggle, and represents neither an alternative to it nor an amelioration of it. Wars tend to be regarded as creators of fluid, revolutionary situations that should be fully exploited.

Certain of the approaches to the problem of peaceful change that are drawing serious attention today (as seen in the selections below) are quite different from those which occupied the attention of scholars and policy-makers in the period following the First World War. Pacifism, for example, has little effect upon policy, even though it is true that as the war in Vietnam intensified, pacifist demonstrations in the United States increased. The pacifist pleads for love as the basis for all human relationships and practices nonviolence at every level of life, including international relationships. But the countervailing demonstrations in support of government policy reveal the public-opinion base of pacifism to be less prevalent or less broad today than it was, say, in Britain in the thirties.

While changes in the prevailing distribution of values *within* societies may be brought about relatively easily, or at least formally recognized, through normal legislative and judicial institutions and procedures, such institutions on the international level are largely left untried. Nevertheless, one frequently advocated approach to the politics of peaceful change is the institutional one. As Grayson Kirk has put it, "our policy must continue to do whatever can be done to strengthen all available mechanisms of international cooperation and peaceful adjustment of differences."[5] From this perspective, in order for States

[3] Masterly analyses of this whole perspective on the problems in the process of peaceful change is to be found in Professor Frederick S. Dunn's *War and the Minds of Men* (New York: Harper & Row, Publishers, for the Council on Foreign Relations, 1950) especially Chapter 1; and his earlier work *Peaceful Change* (New York: Harcourt, Brace & World, Inc., 1938).

[4] "Reducing International Tensions," *Commentary*, **XX** (1955), 517–521; this article was reproduced in part in the first edition of this book, pp. 359–363.

[5] "World Perspectives, 1964," *Foreign Affairs*, **43** (1964), 13.

and men to cooperate, methods and techniques, developed within the framework of organized international society, must be created and perfected for the promotion and expansion of their mutual interests. Among other places, this approach is formalized in Article 14 of the Charter of the United Nations, which calls for the "peaceful adjustment of any situation, regardless of origin, including situations likely to impair the general welfare or friendly relations among nations," and takes form in the multiple regional and functional agencies reflected in the subject matter of the next chapter of this book. The adaptability of the institutions that have been developed has been noted by Ernst Haas, a close student of international and especially of regional and functional organizations, in the following words:

> To the superficial observer, contemporary international organizations appear to be very frail institutions for stabilizing anything: their involvement in the exchange of propaganda broadsides and their failures in guaranteeing the firm military security of the member states receive such disproportionate attention. But if viewed against the background of the fundamental changes which the international environment has undergone since 1945, the organizations which make up the United Nations appear to be remarkably adaptive contrivances.[6]

In a world of competing value systems, Cold Wars, and escalating military operations, the process of peaceful change is more likely to emerge from innovative approaches to discovering how better to use what we have than it is from radical proposals for reorganizing the entire political base of world affairs. It is of course a truism to say that a static world is impossible, and that attempts, therefore, to rigidify or to render permanent any particular distribution of power among nations is bound, sooner or later, to fail. Change will occur, and must occur; as Prime Minister Wilson said in discussing the proliferation problem before the United Nations General Assembly, "if in 1966 we do not succeed in negotiating an effective and watertight treaty to stop the spread of nuclear weapons, the world may have passed the point of no return."[7] The possible consequences of the resort to force by the great powers have become so horrendous, in an age when weapons of mass destruction are capable of being projected across vast oceans and broad continents, that statesmen and other specialists in international relations have a more urgent mandate than ever before to come up with new methods and techniques of permitting existing power relationships to change, without the loss of core values and without the use of violence.

[6] "Toward Controlling International Change," *World Politics*, **XVII** (1964), 8.
[7] *The New York Times,* December 19, 1965, p. 39.

1

*Threat-Perception and the Armament-Tension Dilemma**

J. David Singer

J. DAVID SINGER *is Associate Research Political Scientist of the Mental Health Research Institute at the University of Michigan. His books include* Financing International Organization: The UN Budget Process *(1961), and* Deterrence, Arms Control and Disarmament: Toward a Synthesis in National Security Policy *(1962).*

In his famous treatise on military affairs, Vegetius advised his emperor: "If you want peace, prepare for war." Theodosius followed this advice, yet within a few years was embroiled in a series of bloody conflicts. This crude doctrine of deterrence failed to preserve the peace in the fourth century, did little better during the fifteen succeeding ones, and has thrice in this century failed to prevent mass bloodshed. Neither the evidence of history nor the application of logic would suggest that the *para bellum* doctrine holds out any peaceful prospects for the present; yet, as Madariaga sadly concluded, "its vitality is incredible." Clinging to the dogma as if in a trance, the Soviet and Western blocs are today engaged in a hypertrophic race for superiority in weapons technique and production: Like the Hobbesian "Kings and Persons of Soveraigne Authority," they find themselves "in the state and posture of gladiators; having their weapons pointing and their eyes fixed on one another; that is, their Forts, Garrisons, and Guns upon the Frontiers of their Kingdomes, and continuall Spyes upon their neighbors; which is a posture of War."

I. THE PERILS OF "PARA BELLUM"

The historical and logical inconsistencies implicit in this paradoxical doctrine of national security might be made more explicit by a brief examination of its application to the present bi-polar "balance of terror." No political canon can survive the centuries without some kernel of truth, and that of *para bellum* is no exception. Thus, given the persistence of certain ideal and specified conditions, there might well be some modicum of security in the pursuit of weapons parity or superiority. At the very least, today's military stalemate does make highly unlikely any calculated initiation of large-scale hostilities by either the Soviet Union or the United States. The capacity of each to mount a massive and punishing counterblow, does, in fact, provide a not insignificant deterrent. But any number of technological, diplomatic, or psychological developments could, with violent rapidity, reduce this precarious balance to a shambles. Several such possibilities will be alluded to here.

Perhaps the most dramatic illustration of the tenuousness of that balance is revealed in the recent Soviet

* Journal of Conflict Resolution, II (1958), 90–105. Reprinted by permission.

protest over SAC flights in the Arctic. Despite the patently propagandistic intent, it is difficult completely to ignore the fears expressed by Ambassador Sobolev during the Security Council debate: "But what would happen if American military personnel observing their radar screens are not able in time to determine that a flying meteor is not a guided missile, and that a flight of geese is not a flight of bombers?" Both the Secretary of Defense and the Chairman of the Joint Chiefs of Staff have tried to assure the world that the "fail-safe" turnback system is foolproof, but "foolproof" military techniques have been known to fail before; a repetition of the combination of human and mechanical error which laid waste Pearl Harbor could be far more disastrous today. Furthermore, the two hours or more now available for the making of a responsible political decision will, when the Soviet ICBM becomes operational, be reduced to approximately fifteen minutes. And when the Western missile systems are in readiness, there will be no "fail-safe"; once launched, the ballistic missile cannot be recalled. In addition to the dangers inherent in an erroneous reading of the radar scopes or a failure in communication later on, the identical train of events could also be set in motion by the crash of a nuclear bomber or the accidental discharge of its cargo. Before the source of the detonation, if such occurred, could be identified, the retaliatory signal might have been given. Despite considerable precautions and frequent reassurances, these perils cannot be ignored.

A second development which might upset the delicate strategic balance is that of a major technological breakthrough, particularly if it were in the field of defensive weaponry. Were either power or bloc to come up with the means of preventing, or markedly reducing, an effective and devastating counter-blow, it might certainly consider certain types of military adventurism and boldness which are now ruled out by the threat of massive retaliation.

Another possibility which might vitiate the stability of this precarious balance is the rise of "moral disarmament" in either of the camps. Certainty is the very essence of deterrence, and if at any time the willingness of either to make good on its promise of retaliation is called into question, the other might well be tempted to take certain military risks. That such ambiguity already exists in the West is undeniable, and further evidence of loss of "nerve" can only serve to increase the danger. Finally, with the United States administration pressing the Congress for permission to make available the techniques and materials of nuclear weapon construction to its allies, the "fourth-power" problem takes on grisly significance. Nuclear bombs and advanced delivery systems in the hands of certain trigger-happy military leaders is far from a comforting thought.

This represents only a sample of those developments, any one of which could set in train a sequence of events culminating in total war. Faced with such risks, particularly when added to them are a multitude of domestic political pressures, economic limitations, and other policy considerations, those who shape policy in Washington, Moscow, or elsewhere are provided with a powerful incentive to search for other paths to national security. The purpose of this article is to explore several of those alternatives paths, especially as they are affected by and might act upon the vicious circle of national armaments and international tensions.

II. The Question of Cause or Effect

In examining the present pattern of bi-polar hostility in search of a possible avenue of escape from its ominous paradox, one is insistently confronted with the armaments-tension phenomenon. That there is some sort of reciprocity between national military capabilities and international tensions would be difficult to refute, but the problem of illuminating this reciprocal relationship has proved consistently elusive. Positing the desirability of breaking out of this circle, the first question to arise is the old chestnut of "which comes first?"

One view is expressed by a former United States delegate to the United Nations, Benjamin V. Cohen; in addressing a meeting of the International Law Association, he stated that "if we knew of certainty that no nation was in a state of preparedness to undertake a war with any prospect of success . . . there would be a profound change in the climate of international relationships." In a more extreme form, this view is also expressed by some Quaker spokesmen, who are "convinced" that disarmament "in itself would so change the climate of world opinion that no power on earth could oppose it effectively."

At the opposite extreme is Sir Alfred Zimmern, who concludes that "armaments are not a cause of international tension; they are a symptom. . . ." Another Briton, Sir Alexander Cadogan, endorsed this stand when he told a meeting of the United Nations Commission for Conventional Armaments that "the reduction and regulation of armaments and armed forces depends primarily on the establishment of international confidence; the converse argument is misleading and dangerous."

Rejecting both these polar and mutually exclusive positions would be found most of those who follow closely the pattern of world politics and who are not required to defend any specific governmental policy. For example, in his recent thoughtful study of international organization, I. L. Claude takes the position that "this is a circular problem, in which causes and effects, policies and the instruments of policy, revolve in a cycle of interaction and are blurred into indistinguishability." The circularity view is also put succinctly by Governor Stassen's White House Disarmament Staff in an official publication: "World tensions and world armaments tend to reinforce one another. Each serves as a breeding ground for the other."[1] To summarize, it might safely be held that when students of international politics are in a position to observe dispassionately and are inclined to theorize, they will tend to describe the arms-tension relationship in predominantly reciprocal terms. Despite this, however, when pressed for an opinion, many will indorse either a tensions-first or arms-first approach, frequently to the exclusion of the other; concentrate on one, it is argued, and the other will take care of itself. Each of these broad approaches will be discussed presently, in light of the perceptual setting which is examined in the following section. . . .

A. The tensions-first approach

The recent Soviet-American cultural exchange agreement was hailed in its communiqué as "a significant first step in the improvement of mutual understanding between the peoples of the United States and the USSR"; the text then expressed the hope that the agreement would be carried out "in such a way as to contribute substantially to the betterment of relations between the two countries, thereby also contributing to a lessening of international tensions." To

[1] There is considerable evidence that this has not necessarily been the view held by other, and more influential, presidential advisers.

many, this sort of program illustrates the most fruitful approach to the arms-tension dilemma; cultural exchanges, educational and literacy programs, increased travel, and expanded trade are all viewed as the way to reduce or eliminate peoples' "ignorance of each other's ways and lives . . . through which their differences have all too often broken into war." The reasoning upon which this so-called "UNESCO approach" is based, though not always made explicit, is quite clear: provide the people of the quarreling powers with an opportunity to meet with and learn about one another; this will lead to increased mutual tolerance, understanding, and respect and a consequent reduction in tensions between them. This new set of attitudes will, in turn, influence governmental relations, and, once such inter-governmental tensions have commenced their downward swing, it is contended, the national elites will no longer see any need for the maintenance of expensive and dangerous arsenals. With this realization will come a willingness to disarm or at least a more tractable approach to multilateral disarmament negotiations. Until such a diminution of international tensions has occurred, national armaments will remain as their fearsome manifestation.

Without attempting any thorough diagnosis of the "UNESCO approach," two closely related questions raised by that point of departure will be examined here. First, if the approach is aimed primarily at the *people* of the separate states, what is the connection between popular attitudes and the readiness of policy-makers to engage in bellicose behavior? Second, what are the really effective forces at work in the shaping of those popular attitudes? Regarding the first question, the connection would seem to be unmistakably clear in this "century of total war." Whether it be limited or global, war today requires the fullest mobilization of a nation's resources—military, industrial, governmental, and psychological. Moreover, such mobilization must be undertaken long before the appearance of armed conflict; without preparedness, there can be little deterrence and, without deterrence, no security. The citizenry must therefore, in the name of national security, send its men into uniform, finance the ravenous military machine, adapt to new and dangerous levels of radioactivity, and acquiesce in the inevitable transfer of individual liberties to the agents of the evolving garrison state. That popular attitudes are an essential element of national preparedness would be most difficult to deny.

Less obvious is the answer to the second question; yet it is in the reasoning of the first that we find the answer to the second. If, as has been stated, the public's attitudes are so crucial to national preparedness, can it be reasonably expected that governmental elites will encourage, or even permit, more than token opportunities for the public to develop an image of the potential enemy in other than hostile and menacing terms?

Classically, public opinion is seen as a resultant of two general sets of factors. One of these is the sociocultural framework or national ideology; vague and amorphous, yet internalized and powerful, the national ideology provides the cognitive and affective setting within which specific attitudes on particular problems are formed. The myths and symbols associated with the ideology need only be tapped and manipulated by those who control the second set of factors: the presentation and interpretation of recent and immediate experiences. By the adept use of the appropriate cues, the elite can readily generate a menacing and hostile image of the potential enemy; given the high concentration of ethnocentrism in most national ideologies, the opinion-maker need merely single out and label the appropriate foreign target. Just as there are techniques for inducing pacifistic attitudes, there are those which are equally effective in creating an atmosphere of tension and bellicosity.

Thus there are three main conditions which come into play. First, there is the dominant preoccupation of the elite with national security. Next there is the urgent necessity for public support of any preparedness program. And, third, there is the relative ease with which this support may be induced. The implications of this three-way interaction are evident. The public's support is contingent upon its perception of a genuine threat to the nation's way of life and political independence; and, since the potential threat may rapidly become an immediate one, some marginal surplus of popular threat-perception must be maintained. Therefore, while tension-reducing programs are exercising some impact upon a selected few intellectuals, artists, farmers, or workers, little permanent headway is made. A visiting group returns from the other country, perhaps with considerably modified views (though this is by no means guaranteed), and disperses among its own citizenry. As the returnee attempts to recount his experiences and demonstrate the peacefulness (or other virtues) of his Russian or American counterpart, he runs headlong into the inevitable reaction from those who have not shared his experience. "Surely," it will be said, "many of those people are indeed peace-loving, but after all, they are not the ones who make policy. Our enemies are the fanatic Communists [or the war-mongering imperialists]. It is their aggressive leaders who drive them to war against us." Within this simplification there is the usual germ of truth. The attitudes of the masses may influence the policy-makers, but the setting within which the people form these attitudes is something less than objective reality. Their simplified and exaggerated definition of the situation is formulated for them to a considerable degree by those responsible for national security.

The logic of the process is inexorable. Each elite perceives the other's military capabilities in terms of aggressive intent. They transmit this perception to their people, and the tension between the governments makes impossible any reduction of tension between the people. As long as each nation retains the capacity to wage aggressive war, mutually perceived threat will continue to flourish, and tensions will be perpetuated and exacerbated, not eliminated. Disarmament based upon a prior elimination of tensions will be a long time in coming.

B. The political-settlement approach

As might be anticipated, not all adherents of the tensions-first school are convinced of the fruitfulness of any direct assault upon the "minds of men." Rather, while accepting the chronological precedence of tensions vis-à-vis armaments, some of them seek to back up a step and look for the indirect source of such tensions. In his *Politics among Nations*, Morgenthau traces them to the "unformulated conflicts of power," while Kennan discovers them as arising out of "substantive political differences and rivalries." Arguing that any direct search for disarmament would be placing the "cart before the horse," such observers stress that the "reduction of armaments must await the political settlement" and that disarmament is "impossible as long as there exist unsolved political issues which the participating nations regard as vital to themselves."

Proceeding from these premises, the political-settlement approach suggests that the first step is therefore to identify the areas of political conflict, define the interests of the protagonists, and then attempt the negotiation of a realistic settlement. As Kennan describes it, this process requires "taking the awkward conflicts of national interest and dealing with them on their merits with a view to finding the solutions least unsettling to the stability of international life." In order to achieve success in this diplomatic pursuit, national decision-makers are advised to *a.* arm themselves with "an attitude of detachment and soberness and a readiness to reserve judgment," *b.* rid themselves of "arrogance or hostility toward other people," and *c.* exercise "the modesty to admit that our [their] own national interest is all that we [they] are really capable of knowing and understanding." So prepared psychologically, the professional diplomatists may then actively engage in "the pursuit of the national interest," an activity which "can never fail to be conducive to a better world." Of course, in this reasonable pursuit of the national interest, each nation shall rely upon "physical strength, armaments, determination, and solidarity" and meet the other with "unalterable counter-force at every point where they show signs of encroaching upon" the former's conception of a peaceful and stable world. Within the context of this particular approach to world peace, both sides will pursue their respective national interests by the intelligent application of national power; this will eventuate in a series of negotiated political settlements, leading to a relaxation of international tensions; and, from such a tension-reduction, disarmament may legitimately proceed. It is little wonder that Professor Kennan refers to disarmament as a "utopian enthusiasm."

In addition to the inability of the political-settlement approach to get to the heart of the threat-perception problem by ignoring the role of weapons in that perception, it suffers from a further logical contradiction. In their writing and lecturing, Morgenthau and Kennan (with their colleagues of the "realistic" school) assume a sharp and identifiable distinction between political settlements and armament reduction; this distinction is made explicit in their demand that the one must precede the other. Yet this distinction is far from self-evident. In pursuing the national interest, an elite's primary instrument is national power, much of it in the form of military hardware; its other elements might be bases for the stationing of forces and the deployment of the weapons, accessibility to raw materials and industrial products, the strength and viability of the economies and political systems of one's allies, and perhaps the attitudes of the elites and masses in the uncommitted areas. The realist might argue that national power is a vast, complex, and all-inclusive phenomenon and that one cannot separate a single element, such as armaments, and deal with it individually. Yet Kennan has only recently stirred intellectual Europe by proposing a modified disengagement. Apparently the granting of significant politico-strategic concessions differs in some way from scrapping of military hardware. The reduction of bomb and missile stockpiles is "disarmament," but the surrender of the bases from which they might be deployed is merely "political settlement."

C. The armaments-first approach

Believing that no direct attack upon tensions themselves will be successful and that any political settlement which disregards the primary instruments of national power is doomed to failure, some students of international politics have begun to give serious consideration to the problems inherent in the disarm-by-disarming approach. Within this school there is a wide and complex range of alternatives, which, for the sake of clarity in analysis, will be divided into four general categories: (I) unilateral and complete; (II) unilateral but partial; (III) multilateral but partial; and (IV) multilateral and complete.

Alternative I is that espoused by the pacifist movement and is embodied in the proposals of such groups as the Fellowship of Reconciliation and the American Friends Service Committee; their position is based upon two primary and well-articulated assumptions. First, there is no genuine national security in adherence to the doctrine of *para bellum,* and, second, if one major power or bloc were to take the decision for unilateral and total disarmament, "it is entirely probable that other heavily armed powers would follow the lead."[2]

The first assumption has already been discussed here, but it should be emphasized that it is accepted not only by the critics of preparedness but by many of those responsible for the formulation and execution of that very policy. In testimony before the Disarmament Subcommittee, Secretary Dulles himself referred to the "constant menace of destruction," and Commissioner Murray observed that "it is by no means clear that a balance of terror furnishes an assurance that aggression . . . will not be undertaken. . . . A balance of terror is too easily upset." Similar reservations have been expressed, not only by those out of power such as Gaitskill and Ollenhauer, but by those currently responsible for their nation's security, such as Eisenhower, Khrushchev, Macmillan, and Nehru; there is today an almost universal recognition of the tenuousness of a peace or a security based upon either parity or superiority in military capability.

As to the second assumption, there is greater room for doubt. While it is true that spokesmen for both blocs continually protest that they arm only for self-defense and imply that their opposites need only demonstrate their peaceful intent by scrapping their weapons and they will immediately follow suit, several obstacles arise. Since it is, by definition, the *other* power which arms for aggression, *they* obviously must disarm first; who will take the first step? Even if one power agrees to begin disarmament unilaterally, how do the others know that the process has in fact been started? And, in addition, some powers will raise the question of "fulfilment of international obligations" (usually the United Nations Charter is invoked here) without military forces available. In the absence of an effective ethical or legal code assuring high correlation between promise and performance, it is difficult to expect a government elite to commence disarmament on the *hope* that its opposite numbers will do likewise. The responsibility for and preoccupation with the national security assures that such an act of faith will appear far too risky to even the most sanguine policy-maker.

Alternative II, however, is a somewhat different proposition, despite apparent similarities; whereas alternative I calls for disarmament which is both

[2] The quote is from the testimony of M. Q. Sibley, of the University of Minnesota, an active pacifist. It should be added that the pacifist begins from an even more fundamental premise: violence and the tools of violence are themselves immoral and under no circumstances justifiable. This aspect of pacifism will not be discussed here.

unilateral and complete, down to the last weapon of mass destruction, this requires only a partial reduction and, as a result, has many more adherents. It proceeds from the same first premise as I—the inability of weapons to assure any lasting national security—but it relies to a considerably lesser extent upon the likelihood of one power or bloc following the other in stripping itself of aggressive military capability. Rather, it views such an eventuality as possible, rather than probable, and therefore seeks a modification which might minimize the risks inherent in the unilateral and total scheme.

In fuller terms, the partial unilateral approach takes a less simplistic perspective of the arms-tension dilemma than does alternative I. Recognizing the grip which threat-perception has upon the minds of the decision-makers, the opinion-makers, and the general public, it proceeds to address itself to a relaxation of that grip. It appreciates that protestation and promise will not materially diminish reciprocally perceived threat and that concrete deed is essential to break the spell. For example, the Committee for a Sane Nuclear Policy, in a series of newspaper advertisements, has proposed that missiles and nuclear weapons be considered separately from other weapons and that all nations immediately suspend their testing and development. While the committee does specifically refer to the need for United Nations monitoring and control, it is nevertheless willing to see the United States take the first step unilaterally and unconditionally, prior to the establishment of any international control system. In this same category are the British Campaign for Nuclear Disarmament and the West German Fight against Atomic Death. Each of these seeks a bilateral or multilateral inspectable agreement prohibiting both the further testing of nuclear weapons and the stationing of delivery systems within their territories; but each is willing to engage in immediate and unconditional unilateral nuclear disarmament in the Western bloc. The assumption of all three movements is that, despite the genuine military risks inherent in such unilateral action, nothing less will suffice to demonstrate Western sincerity and diminish the degree of threat which the Kremlin infers from the NATO military posture.[3]

While it may be reasonable to expect that such deeds *might* reduce the sense of insecurity in the Soviet camp, it does not necessarily follow that diminution of threat-perception will lead the Soviets quickly to reduce their own arsenals. Their policy-makers may hail the action as "a welcome step toward the strengthening of peace," yet interpret it as *a.* a reflection of domestic economic, popular, or partisan pressures; *b.* a propaganda device; *c.* a shift in military or technological strategy; or *d.* a ruse to generate complacency. Concern for national security requires that each place the most cynical interpretation upon such a gesture. An excellent example of this array of reactions to a unilateral cutback is found in the American response to Soviet announcements of a troop reduction of 1,200,000 men in May, 1956. A *New York Times* article by Harry Schwartz carried the caption "Domestic Economic Pressure and Desire to Embarrass West Believed Involved," while another by Elie Abel was headed "Russian Arms Cut Laid to Empha-

[3] Obviously, there are other considerations behind these movements, such as fear of nuclear retaliation in a war "not of their making," costs, increasing fallout, and the search for domestic political issues, but these merely supplement, rather than negate, their basic reasoning.

sis on Nuclear Power." Any suggestion of a new Soviet peacefulness was quickly scotched.[4] The almost inevitable reaction to such a "tension-reducing" step is found in Prime Minister Eden's letter to Premier Bulganin: "My own feeling is that unilateral reductions of this kind are helpful. I do not think, however, that they are of themselves sufficient if international confidence and security are to develop as we wish." Unless unilateral cuts are followed up quickly on both sides by further reductions, any diminution of threat-perception will be of only the briefest duration. They might make preparedness somewhat less expensive, but they would not make it any less necessary. It might even be argued that if a unilateral reduction on one side were not promptly succeeded by a similar move on the part of the other, the originators might experience a sharp increase in threat-perception and return to the arms race with renewed vigor; thus the long-range effect of unilateral action might be to heighten, rather than reduce, international tensions.

Turning now to alternatives III and IV, we come across an element which was lacking in I and II—that of reciprocity, In the bilateral and multilateral approach, each sides makes its arms reductions contingent upon a similar reduction by the other. Such a reduction might flow from a negotiated treaty, agreement, or convention or possibly (and not to be excluded) a process of "tacit bargaining" proceeding out of a public exchange of conditional statements and communications. Whether such disarmament is partial or total, it is clearly contingent and reciprocal.

Alternative III (multilateral but partial) is that which has been most frequently pursued in the twentieth century. For a variety of reasons, the governments of the major powers might seek to enter into (but not necessarily conclude) negotiations on some measure of weaponry limitation or reduction.[5] Generally, such negotiations would deal with a specific category or type of weapon; during the interwar period of the 1920's and 1930's great importance was attached to the distinction between offensive and defensive armaments; Lord Davies' "principle of differentiation" was based on pre- and post-1914 hardware, and today's dichotomy tends to separate conventional from thermonuclear and chemical devices. In addition, implied is some measure of verifiability, either through reciprocal or third-party inspection of territory, bases, or such official records as budgets, which would reflect levels of military preparedness.[6] Such has been the nature of almost all disarmament proposals and negotiations since World War II.

The benchmark against which this type of arms reduction must be measured is the same as that applied to the unilateral alternatives: How effectively does it break into the arms-tension circle? Today there is under consideration a range of possibilities which includes the cessation of nuclear or missile tests, cutbacks in mobilized manpower, or withdrawal of all for-

---

[4] However, after the alleged cut had been negatively interpreted by Dulles, Wilson, and most of the press, Governor Stassen called a special news conference to praise the step as an "initiative we wanted them to take."

[5] Van Dyke asks "why states propose disarmament" and enumerates the following: to save money, to reduce tensions and the danger of war, and to achieve a propaganda advantage. "Of these, only the first is well reasoned and fully compatible with the . . . objective."

[6] Recent French proposals have emphasized the merit of this sort of inspection and verification.

eign forces from certain specified areas of central Europe. Let us suppose that one or more of these has been successfully negotiated, that an adequate inspection system installed, and that both sides have commenced the required action in accordance with a mutually acceptable schedule.

Such reciprocal and verifiable adherence to the arms-reduction agreement would certainly tend, despite the inevitably cynical interpretations, to produce a more relaxed atmosphere for some measurable period of time. The policy-makers on each side would have rather clear evidence that the other had actually diminished its capacity for armed attack, albeit to a limited extent; each could logically infer that such a diminution of the other's aggressive military capabilities reflected a corresponding diminution of aggressive intent. Furthermore, each would have concrete evidence that, under certain clearly defined conditions, the other would adhere to its commitments. Though such affirmative interpretations and results are by no means assured, the experience of the early interwar period suggests that they may reasonably be anticipated. Similar limitations and reductions were negotiated in 1922, 1930, 1936, and 1937 (this latter between Germany and Britain), and to some extent they resulted in a temporary reduction of mutually perceived threat and consequently of international tensions.

However, if such a first step were limited to inspected partial reduction (or merely aerial inspection to prevent surprise attack), the impact of the agreement would tend to decrease as time went on and no further reductions in striking capacity were negotiated—or undertaken unilaterally. The agreed and verified decrease in capability would be less and less interpreted as an indicator of peaceful intent and more and more in those cynical terms outlined earlier. Such was the final interpretation placed upon those agreements negotiated in the pre-World War II era, and such is the interpretation already being put upon the several disarmament proposals now being bruited back and forth across the Iron Curtain. Inability or unwillingness to go beyond some limited, partial agreement implies unwillingness to accept total disarmament, and when one side sees the other insisting on the retention of some military capability, it may reasonably assume that such weapons as are retained may be for other than purely defensive purposes. Referring to the reductions and limitations negotiated during the 1920's, Madariaga observed that "so-called disarmament discussions are in fact *armament* discussions, and that whatever the label, the commodity bought and sold in the market is power." Bilateral or multilateral partial disarmament may temporarily mitigate the mutual perception of threat, but to expect any lasting diminution of this ingredient of war is to overlook the transcending preoccupation of the decision-maker with the security of his nation-state.

Finally, we turn to alternative IV (multilateral and total) of the various arms-first approaches. Is there anything in this alternative which permits it to overcome the liabilities inherent in the tensions-first, political-settlement, and previous armaments-first approaches? It will be recalled that the crucial element in the latter's inability to break out of the circle was the failure to maintain, over any durable period of time, the temporarily decreased levels of threat-perception. Each time that a halt in the reduction of military capability was reached, the natural tendency was for a sense of national insecurity to reappear, with a commensurate reestablishment of the original levels of mutual threat-perception. The problem, therefore, would seem to be one of *continuing and perpetuating,* once commenced, the gradual diminution of military capability.

This, however, is precisely the core of the problem; two factors arise which might well paralyze this total reduction process even before it had begun. First, even with the establishment of a thorough inspection system, there would always be some possibility of evasion or the development of a new and unexpected weapon or delivery system which would make invalid the assumptions upon which any schedule had been negotiated. Given the pre-existing condition of mutual hostility and fear, each side must and would operate on the premise that such an evasion or development was quite possible, if not probable. Second, some power not covered by the agreement might secure enough military might to become an aggressor-by-proxy for one of the signatories.

While this latter danger might be avoided, in theory at least, by insistence upon universality, the first menace would be much less readily mitigated. Whereas in any partial disarmament scheme the risks of an evasion are significant but not tragic, in a complete and total disarmament program the hazard is almost intolerable. In the former, the nation has not denuded itself completely; its defensive or retaliatory power may be diminished, but it is not eliminated. In any complete disarmament schedule, there comes a time when each government is virtually incapable of self-defense and when, if another has successfully concealed any significant offensive weapons, it may be faced with the choice between surrender and annihilation.

It may safely be said that it is the awareness of this haunting possibility which will, in the final analysis, deter any national elite from agreeing to any total disarmament schedule of the nature described above, no matter how effective the inspection provisions may seem. They may perceive the continuation of the spiraling weapons race as a major gamble, pregnant with dangers, but the other alternative may well be discerned as an invitation to national suicide. Given the choice between the two sets of risks, national policy-makers will probably continue in the path, at least familiar, of their predecessors. It would appear, then, that, whereas unilateral or partial multilateral disarmament could not, if attempted, produce the necessary effect upon threat-perception, complete disarmament implies hazards so great as to preclude even its attempt. Thus, by themselves, none of these approaches would appear to offer a road out of the arms-tension dilemma. Each fails the acid test of national security; each seems incapable of meeting the rigid requirements of those responsible for national self-preservation.

CONCLUSION

Having analyzed the tensions-first, political-settlement, and armaments-first approaches, and finding them separately incapable of escaping the inexorable logic of the arms-tension dilemma, one might conclude that there is, in fact, no escape. Such a conclusion has already been reached by a staggering number of statesmen and students of international affairs, and much of the evidence, historical and logical, would seem to substantiate this gloomy judgment. Yet this writer cannot acquiesce in such a conclusion. Be it tender-minded optimism or ordinary human obstinacy, he is convinced that there exist, within the mind of man, the ingenuity and the persistence to discover a workable solution. Such a conviction leads him, despite the limitations of space and intellect, to hazard a few brief paragraphs suggesting those modifications and combinations of the separate alternatives which might possibly hold the promise of reprieve.

It will be recalled that each approach, considered separately, was ruled out by its inability to cope in any lasting way with the problem of perceived threat to national security. For example, the tensions-first and three of the arms-first approaches failed to provide anything more than a temporary mitigation of threat-perception, while the political-settlement approach, by attempting to ignore weapons entirely at the outset, failed to even initiate a trend in that direction; none seemed to produce a situation out of which might develop an increasingly permanent sense of national security. And the total multilateral approach, probably the most promising of the traditional alternatives, appeared to be doomed at the start because of the risks involved later.

Let us suppose, however, that a radical change in the concept of disarmament were introduced. In place of the traditional reliance upon the scrapping of weapons or their conversion to peaceful purposes, let us assume that certain specified national weapons were instead transferred—slowly, cautiously, but regularly and in accordance with a prearranged schedule—to previously designated United Nations depots, where trained members of an international gendarmerie were prepared to receive, account for, maintain, and man such weapons. Further, let us assume that this gendarmerie had been assigned certain clearly defined and limited, yet very real, legal and political responsibilities for their operation and deployment, such responsibilities extending to the protection of the signatory nations as their military capabilities approached inadequacy while those of the United Nations agency were gradually increasing. Might such a procedure not ultimately remove the greatest psycho-strategic barrier to the policy-makers' willingness to engage in any long-range and total arms reduction program? If it is true that the gamble of finding one's nation militarily denuded, while the potential enemy has managed secretly to preserve a part of his striking power, is in fact the single most paralyzing factor in the path of global disarmament, perhaps the substitution of an international agency, armed with the requisite legal, political, and military powers, might serve to eliminate the dread with which that gamble is contemplated.

This brief suggestion probably raises more questions than it answers, but the implication should be clear. No national statesman, Western, Soviet, or neutral, has yet proposed a disarmament plan that has any chance of lasting success, and it is unlikely that any will until the basic, crucial issue is faced squarely. In order to protect the people of a nation which has willingly surrendered its weapons, the United Nations will require a range of powers and a delegation of authority considerably greater than that now intrusted to it. To deal effectively with the arms-tension dilemma, the Organization will need certain of the powers which have come to be associated with those of a federal government. But that would imply an abrogation of traditional state sovereignty, and, as long as such transfer of sovereignty is perceived as a greater threat than thermonuclear obliteration, disarmament negotiations will remain as before—on top dead center.

2

*Disarmament: Theory or Experiment**

David Frisch

DAVID FRISCH, *who teaches physics at M.I.T., helped to establish the American Academy of Arts and Sciences committee on technical problems of arms control.*

The Government of the United States is conducting an intensive study of the problems and possibilities of disarmament. Along with the behind-the-scenes work of experts, there needs to be a great deal of public discussion of the vast array of arms-control topics ranging from unilateral actions to comprehensive international agreements.

Unfortunately for public discussion, the facts are shrouded somewhat in military secrecy and even more in widespread inability to comprehend the pace of technical developments. But even if the military and technical picture were crystal clear, the complexities of the political situation would remain staggering. It is all the more sobering, therefore, to consider that our evaluation of this Problem of Problems may be decisive for the survival of civilization over the whole face of the earth.

Since Stalin's death, as many ideas about arms reduction seem to have come out of the East as out of the West. But as we get deeper into disarmament problems, it is likely that the situation will change and we will have to think things through not only for ourselves but for the nations of the Communist bloc as well. While their goals and ours will increasingly have in common a dominating desire to escape the destruction of large-scale international warfare, the Communists will continue to be sharply inhibited, both by their suppression of public discussion and by their dogma, from examining the problem of disarmament as freely and imaginatively as we can.

When the dense verbiage is cleared away, several clear points of view on disarmament emerge.

One attitude is that we should have none of it. Instead, we should stay so far ahead of all other nations in all military and economic affairs that no one will ever dare threaten us. This peace - through - invulnerable - strength approach will possibly be that folly which marks the apex of man's journey up from the primeval sludge and rapidly down again. Almost every candidate for high public office in an alarming number of countries pays at least lip service to it.

Unfortunately, "invulnerable strength" is based on a dream, or rather a technical nightmare. A 50 per cent efficient defense would have been impressive against a World War II bomber attack with high explosive bombs aimed at our cities. In sharp contrast, even a 90 per cent efficient defense against a World War III mis-

* *New York Times Magazine,* July 30, 1961, pp. 8ff.

sile attack with H-bombs would leave us almost inconceivably devastated. By concentrating research on some particular technical aspect of missile offense, or perhaps on a comparatively new field, such as biological warfare, a future aggressor would have an easy time opening a lethal 10 per cent gap in any total defense system.

Proposed reliance on "invulnerable strength" often reflects a hypnotic preoccupation with Soviet aggressiveness, to the neglect of the problem of the instability of an all-out arms race among an ever-increasing number of nations.

If, for example, Asians and South Americans get into a full-scale nuclear war fifty years hence, U. S. superiority in, say, hypothetical Multiorbit Anti-Counter-Anti-Bacteriofusion Research (Project MACABRE) may not be able to keep the radioactive and biological fallout from devastating North America. Furthermore, United States "superiority" very probably won't keep the political fallout from such explosive world events from changing our way of life into just what we are so firmly resisting.

A second theory of how to achieve peace is that we should disarm unilaterally and completely and win the minds and hearts of any and all aggressors by nonviolent resistance. Instead of keeping significantly ahead of everybody else in everything technical forever, we would rely on superior moral strength.

It is tempting to patronize this pacifist position as being politically impossible, but a reasonable view as to the single most probable course of events is that after two or three cycles of nuclear and biological world wars and slow recoveries, an almost fatally crippled humanity will find that nonviolent resistance is a major component of all viable political organization.

There is no denying, however, that most of us are too frail in moral strength to be confident of practicing nonviolent resistance successfully. Because there has been no demonstration of its efficacy in preserving our present civilization against such tough customers as the Chinese Communists, nonviolent resistance has a negligible chance of commanding a working political majority in any democracy today, including even Gandhi's own India.

A third and less extreme approach toward disarmament is that, while keeping our present military stance, we should use whatever powers of persuasion and international moral pressure can be brought to bear to get the Communists to join us in recognizing a common conception of world order and law. For example, one serious student of disarmament problems writes: "If there can be no agreement to make the United Nations a responsible instrument of political accommodation and peaceful change, and an effective guardian of international order, I submit that we will make *no* progress in discussing the mere technique of inspection."

Every thoughtful person recognizes the dominant importance of the political environment in which technical treaties are made. But we cannot afford to postpone serious attempts at limitation of armaments until that happy day when the Soviets and the Red Chinese become deeply committed to the idea of an external authority to which a strong nation must submit against its immediate interests. Indeed, it is not clear how deeply we ourselves have accepted the inevitable loss of national sovereignty in the world of the future.

What can we do if there seems to be no clear approach which holds promise of real progress before it is too late? In order to limit the development and spread of weapons of mass destruction, do we really have to have formulated points of view which are clearly understood and agreed on by all parties to agreements? Do we have to seek master formulas which will unlock the puzzles of contemporary history and of future human behavior?

I submit that in such a difficult situation we had better *experiment* than theorize. Bold experiments in every field of human activity have ways of putting old ideas into much better perspective, of bringing out new ideas which have never been thought of or which have not seemed practical, and above all, by the very act of doing something new, of modifying the background circumstances which seemed previously to prevent any major changes.

What appears today to be immutable Soviet opposition to international control of nuclear stockpiles may soften after a few years spent helping to enforce even a fragmentary nuclear-test ban on unwilling Communist, Western and neutralist nations alike. What appears today to be Western inability to rely on other than nuclear deterrence may vanish after experience with demilitarized zones and with inspected reduction of the number of opposing long-range nuclear missiles.

Certainly we should not give up trying to solve the intellectual questions of the ultimate disposition of power in this extremely complicated world. But we are inescapably pressed by the rapid development of armaments to act on disarmament now. We must try many new arrangements, constantly re-examining them to be sure that we are not being booby-trapped. Yet at each stage of entering new agreements, we must also weigh our loss of security, if any, against the irretrievable loss that we are constantly sustaining by maintaining our present course.

What useful initial steps could we take? We should keep pressing for an inspected nuclear-bomb test-ban treaty with the British and the Soviet Union and, if necessary, a limited test ban even without the Soviets. Before giving up hope of bringing them in, however, we should be willing to give up all on-site inspections and rely entirely on the fixed detection stations and on conventional espionage to give verification of Soviet compliance in the megaton-bomb test region. The unreality of such a treaty with respect to inhibiting small bomb tests would be worth the price to us of starting some activity on Soviet soil so that they can see the workings of international law and order in controlling weapons.

This only partly inspected cessation of bomb testing may be worth the loss of privacy to the Soviets—great by their standards—if they get us to make the beginnings of a commitment to abandon nuclear weapons. It may mean to us, on the other hand, the beginning of a commitment by the Soviets to allow serious inspection of all kinds of disarmament arrangements. Neither side will really feel that it has made such a commitment, but neither side will be profoundly weakened by such a test-ban treaty. Both sides will learn a great deal from what will probably be the long, trying experience of setting up an international detection system.

Another partial step we might attempt soon, whether or not the Soviets accept any test ban, is to set up inspected troop limitations. All the countries represented in the Geneva ten-power negotiations have subscribed to the principle of limiting the total numbers of national military forces. It will take some thought and much negotiation to agree on a reasonable inspection system and to define military troops as opposed to civil police forces.

It might be wise to make an inspected troop-limitation treaty for all nations which wish to join, as the Soviet Union and Red China may refuse to come in at first, saying that they don't want to participate in piecemeal disarmament. Watching such an inspected troop-limitation system operate might be an important experience for Communist countries.

As a third example, consider that the Soviets have proposed destruction of *all* long-range missiles, aircraft and naval vessels. Whether this is to be accomplished in stages or all at once, there will remain a difficult problem of monitoring the movements and cargoes of civil aircraft and ships to ensure that they cannot be converted easily into long-range nuclear-weapons carriers.

No matter what the probability of all nations reaching such a stable inspected disarmed state, we can try now to formulate the outlines of a suitable international long-range civil-carrier agreement. When the Soviets hear details of such an agreement—even if only as listeners at conferences they refuse to take part in—they will have to take disarmament technology much more seriously than they have in the past.

As a fourth and last example, consider a much more difficult kind of step, area withdrawals. Probably Soviet and United States political expectations from inspected troop and weapons withdrawals differ widely, yet in my view we ought to try, for example, the Rapacki-Eden plan for demilitarization of the Soviet satellite countries and Western Germany. By pursuing the illusive alternative called "keeping the status quo" in Central Europe, we are in reality losing a race against time, since several of these countries can have their own nuclear and biological warfare capabilities a few years hence.

The question that arises immediately when we discuss the possibility of even partial disarmament arrangements with the Soviet Union is: Are Communists sufficiently responsive to the pressures of external or internal opinion to be at all reliable in any working agreement? This is a hard question, and one for which there is apparently no agreement on a simple answer.

But there is at least some evidence that the Soviets are sensitive to charges of legal correctness before the bar of world opinion, even more among their fellow Communist nations, and remarkably enough (as pointed out by Ithiel Pool in Donald Brennan's important collection of articles, "Arms Control, Disarmament and National Security") within the Soviet Union. But even if there were no present evidence of Soviet sensitivity to fixed legal standards, we would still have no alternative but to try to inculcate understanding and response in them by going ahead with working experiments in this field. Our ace in the hole is that they have at least as much fundamental motivation as we to change the present dangerous course.

A closely related question is whether partial measures can give substantial progress toward the goal of large-scale disarmament. Are the steps we have discussed so small as to be unable to prevent the spread of nuclear weapons? If it is true, for example, that a nuclear-test-ban treaty between the present nuclear powers will not help slow the development of nuclear weapons in other nations, then we are lost in any case. We have no choice but to try little steps when the big ones would involve changing our way of life so completely that we would rather continue to risk destruction than give up.

This brief review of a few disarmament possibilities suggests that there are many small initial steps to be taken, steps which might not necessarily require concordant approaches between East and West, but which might lead to new views on both sides. Whether or not the Soviet government really wants total disarmament—and my impression at the International Conference of Scientists in Moscow . . . was that their government undoubtedly wants to get rid of nuclear bombs and to avoid major wars—it will be an eye-opener both to them and to us if we take their disarmament proposals seriously and make serious proposals of our own.

There is much to be done, using all our energy and intelligence, for we face a common danger.

3

*The New Meaning of Arms Control**

Wesley W. Posvar

WESLEY W. POSVAR *is Head of the Department of Political Science at the United States Air Force Academy. A 1946 graduate of West Point, he has studied at Oxford, which he attended as a Rhodes Scholar, and at Harvard, which he attended while recently on leave on a Littauer Fellowship. A command pilot, Colonel Posvar has served as an instructor at the Military Academy and as a member of the Long Range Objectives and Programs Group at Air Force Headquarters.*

During the past decade, military strategy has become a major province of study by academic and quasi-academic scholars. This phenomenon is having an important effect upon the military posture of the United States. The studies, the books, the articles about arms policy are a good deal more than obscure professional discourses. They reach into the places where decisions are made and into the minds which make them. Nowhere is this influence more apparent and pervasive than in the area of arms control.

As a result of this scholarly attention, a distinction is now made between disarmament, with its discouraging history, and arms control. The former means the reduction or elimination of military forces and weapons. Arms control, on the other hand, includes all measures intended to reduce the likelihood and destructive consequences of war, especially nuclear war. This may or may not involve reduction of arms forces and weapons. It

* *Air Force Magazine,* June, 1963, pp. 38–45. Reprinted with permission from Air Force/Space Digest, official journal of the Air Force Association, 1750 Pennsylvania Ave., N.W., Washington, D.C. The views expressed in this article are the author's own and do not necessarily report official policy of either the Department of the Air Force or the Department of Defense.

may even require considerable increase in military expenditures. More importantly, it entails shifts in emphasis as to the technological characteristics of weapons and involves subtly different doctrines for their employment. A prime example of arms control in this context is the policy of deterrence itself.

Early arms-control studies were motivated by one particular aspect of our military security. This was the small logical loophole in the policy of deterrence of nuclear war, and the need to draw that loophole even tighter. The aim was not to subvert deterrence but to strengthen it by broadening the rational basis of our policy regarding nuclear war.

The loophole lies in the fact that the only practical way to avoid nuclear war has been to promote fear of its consequences in the enemy. This is deterrence. And yet, paradoxically, the greater the fear, the greater might be the risk of an irrational decision which could spell the failure of deterrence.

Most of the early discussion about arms control reflected real anxiety about this problem. The power of nuclear weapons makes essential a high state of mutual preparedness. If war appears inevitable or even likely, there is an incentive for striking first in the hope of reducing one's losses. The very awareness of this fact tends to exacerbate tensions, as well as increase cautions, on both sides. War is made more likely, at least in some small degree, through desperation or miscalculation. The first emphasis of arms control, then, was to develop a concept of relative stability between the military postures of both sides.

The search for stability led to a great deal of study about the difference between being prepared to strike first and being prepared to strike second (or retaliate) in nuclear war. Despite the strictly military advantages of striking first, an ostensible capability to do so could be very destabilizing. This was especially true if the United States possessed large forces, such as unprotected bombers on crowded airfields, which might be useful *only* in a first strike. The Soviets could develop quite a morbid desire to eliminate those forces. So the capability to strike second after surviving attack became more important, to enhance stability by reducing any enemy temptation to strike first. This kind of arms control proved expensive. It required, first, the program for ground alert of SAC aircraft, and subsequently greater dispersal of the bomber force, hardening of missiles sites, and increasing mobility of retaliatory forces, such as Polaris submarines.

Studies regarding stability also led to much better understanding of a bona fide need for a first-strike *capability* which would be credible to the Soviets in the proper circumstances. The need was described by Herman Kahn as Type II Deterrence. This kind of first-strike capability deters major provocations short of direct attack on the United States, such as an all-out Soviet attack on Europe. In these cases, United States ability—and willingness—to respond by direct attack on the Soviets provides the deterrent.

Greater stability was the aim of President Eisenhower's "open-skies" proposal. This would have provided, through aerial and ground inspection facilitated by exchange of military blueprints, warning of preparations for imminent attack. This approach has been weakened by the growth of missile forces, which don't require detectable preparations for attack. The whole question of reconnaissance and inspection will remain a difficult one on which to reach agreement, because of the inherent Soviet advantage in things as they are, through his access to our open society and the information available in our press.

So far, arms-control thinking had concentrated on reducing the likelihood of a premeditated attack, under either deliberate or desperate circumstances. This was the conventional aim of deterrence. The danger of accidental war soon became an added concern and was one of the motivations behind the surprise attack conference, on a technical level, between US and USSR experts in 1958. Although this conference, like all the others, failed, measures taken unilaterally against accidental war make sense anyhow. Many safeguards have been incorporated in US weapons systems; one is the "two-man rule" which requires at least two responsible persons to be present at every handling of a nuclear weapon and at every level of decision concerning its operation. General emphasis has been placed on more firm and foolproof command and control of nuclear strike forces.

Arms control was to develop beyond the simple concept of stability. But before examining the refinements of arms-control thinking, it is important to identify some of the divisions within it and some of the obstacles to effective arms-control programs.

There are two general schools of thought about arms control, and there is a great deal of misinterpretation of the difference between them. The one sees the underlying cause of international conflict as the clash between the interests of nations as they pursue their separate goals. Armed force is seen as a symptom, and there is little avail in treating the symptom while ignoring the disease. The members of this school can point to the sorry history of attempts to prevent war by disarmament alone, such as the Hague Peace Conferences before World War I, and the Washington and London Naval Conferences and the abortive efforts of the League of Nations disarmament commission before World War II.

Members of the other school still see in armaments themselves a serious cause of international tension. They rest part of their case on the history of arms races, particularly the one preceding the outbreak of World War I. They argue that to reduce armaments is to reduce the risk of war even in the absence of a settlement of political differences. In other words, they believe that disarmament in the historically understood sense is a worthy end in itself. They remind us that, since we are faced with the unprecedented threat of nuclear war, historical failure is not a sufficient reason for abandoning attempts at disarmament. While the first school tends to favor arms-control measures that preserve United States power and freedom of action, the latter school is more likely to produce schemes for general and complete disarmament.

Surprising as it may seem, these schools are often in agreement and seem to be moving closer together. There is scarcely a member of one who does not concede the validity of the recommendations of the other if proper safeguards are postulated. For example, the most hardheaded strategist will admit the case against an uncontrolled arms race. He will seek to avoid provocative national acts which might lead to an escalation of mutual fear of preemptive nuclear attack. The hopeful disarmer, on the other hand, more and more recognizes that the power of military coercion may be a permanent part of international politics. His plans for general and complete disarmament, therefore, now include the details of an international police force, to be built up step by step as disarmament progresses. Now that the United States government itself has presented an official proposal for general and complete disarmament, one might even question whether the term "schools" as applied to these groups should be abandoned in favor of something like "converging points of view."

But why should the growing agreement between these groups be surprising, as it surely is to many? Probably because there are popular conceptions of conflicting ideas about arms policy which bear superficial resemblance to these groups. There are the memories of prewar differences between preparedness (Churchill) and appeasement (Chamberlain). There is Hans Morgenthau's contrast between the realist, who upholds prudence as the supreme value in international politics, and the idealist, who believes in the perfectibility of man. On a subconscious level there is a dichotomy of war and peace.

So, in the popular view, thinking about arms control tended to be associated with historical antecedents. On one side were the advocates of power politics who believed that national survival, the highest goal, could be safeguarded only by national power, and who scorned the broken dreams of the "pacifists." On the other side were those convinced that the first step toward a better world was an ideal vision of that world.

Under the present-day threat of communism and nuclear war the choices are drastically narrowed, all the more so as the expert comes to feel a share in the responsibility for policy. Faced with the pressures daily brought to bear, everyone becomes a realist regarding international affairs, and prudence becomes a primary guide to action. Even Bertrand Russell has a realistic purpose in pressing for surrender. He wishes to survive, and he is willing to state the price. (Obviously, however, his underlying assumptions are quite different from most others who follow the course of prudence.) For the American strategy expert, and likewise for the government official, arms control has become a special avenue of prudence in the conduct of military policy.

On another level, there are differences of opinion which affect thinking about arms control. We refer to the controversies about military posture and strategy. The noise of debate about "massive retaliation" and "minimum deterrence" has long since died away, even as United States policy has moved beyond. The more recent arguments about "finite deterrence" and "counterforce" have been mostly stilled by the march of events and by more centralized direction of strategic programs in the Department of Defense.

Finite deterrence, it is recalled, takes a conservative or "finite" view of the need for strategic nuclear forces, in order that more resources can be allocated to forces to meet lesser threats; a variation, which emphasizes these lesser threats, is "graduated deterrence." Counterforce is a strategy for attacking only enemy military forces in general nuclear war, saving enemy cities as "hostages"; the concept applies for either a first or a second strike, at least to the extent of being an optional strategy.

Some of the aspirations of the proponents of finite deterrence have been satisfied by the expansion of the limited war forces of the Army and the Polaris submarine forces of the Navy. Secretary McNamara, moreover, announced . . . at Ann Arbor, Mich., the adoption of the "no-cities" doctrine of strategic targeting, which is an adaptation of the Air Force's counterforce doctrine. Echoes of the old arguments remain, however. The one group questions counterforce, claiming (without a very careful perusal of Mr. McNamara's speech) that it is an infeasible strategy of "victory." Air Force supporters openly express anxiety with the loss of weapons like the Skybolt and the RS-70 which they feel are needed for employment of the counterforce, or no-cities doctrine.

In these circumstances there may be an understandable tendency for military services to blame the influence of arms-control thinking for their current misfortunes in the programing of new weapons. Whether or not there is any validity in such a view, it is fair to point out that the RS-70 suffers, at least in part, for its high costs. Yet the counterforce strategy of which it is meant to be an element is itself an arms-control concept. There is little doubt that the influence of arms-control thinking helped pave the way for the adoption of counterforce as official policy.

There is another issue, which, though dormant, would likely become an active dispute if a plan for general disarmament is eventually adopted. That is, on which end of the conventional limited war-nuclear strategic war scale of forces should cutting begin? Quite apart from parochial service considerations, there are strong arguments on both sides from the standpoint of our security in a disarming world. If we cut nuclear forces first, we might leave the Communists at an advantage with their conventional forces; but if we don't, is the agreement really to be taken seriously?

Nevertheless, the most important deduction to draw from the differences of viewpoint about arms control —whether between international politics and military strategy, or civilian and military, or Army, Navy, and Air Force, or public official and expert—is that they are tending to converge. Even though there may be disagreement about particular means, there is agreement that arms control is a valid policy objective. This is an unprecedented reaction to an unprecedented danger. In the dismal context of the threat of Carthaginian destruction in nuclear war, it is a very promising development.

Arms-control measures, then, become in themselves functional measures of national security, designed to reduce the likelihood and destructive consequences of nuclear war. Skeptics should be reminded that no responsible military or civilian leader has made any greater claim than this for our military policy in the past ten years. They all accept the critical assumption that the USSR and Communist China continue to hold aggressive ambitions and that their long-run goals, if not impeded, involve the establishment of a world-wide Communist society. No agreement with Communist powers is possible except where it is in their own interest, and no agreement can be expected to survive conditions which become inimical to them. Likewise, the United States cannot tolerate any agreement that is based upon wishful thinking about the motives or actions of our antagonists. Accepting these assumptions of self-interest, we are limited to arms-control measures which fit into the security posture of this country and contribute to that posture.

Arms control takes this line of reasoning one important step farther. It is a step which is easy to misjudge, unless we keep in mind the above assumptions regarding self-interest. For arms control seeks to recognize a *common* interest between antagonists. In fact, this is an essential feature of arms control. It is the difference between measures designed to "reduce the likelihood and destructive consequences of nuclear war," and the classical view of pure conflict. In the classical view, "winning" a war could at least be conceived as improving the well-being and prosperity of the nation which won. One obvious common interest between the US and the USSR is the avoidance of mutual destruction in nuclear war. Upon this interest must be laid the groundwork for any agreement.

Even if ardent enemies have a common interest, one may ask, how can they reach agreement? On what could they cooperate? Here the modern theories of conflict, games, and bargaining are brought into service by the strategy experts. Ludicrous as it may appear, the relations between the US and the USSR are technically a game, because they do involve both shared and conflicting interests. There are rules of the game, arrived at by a tacit process of which little is understood. For instance, there is a tacit agreement for both sides to refrain (so far) from giving nuclear weapons away to allies. There is another not to assassinate one another's leaders, and another to take steps to avoid the accidental triggering of war. In Korea, the geographical limitations which were applied and the restraints which were imposed on the use of certain weapons and tactics were the result of tacit bargaining.

John T. McNaughton, General Counsel of the Department of Defense, and an arms-control expert himself, has publicly expressed the view that arms-control measures need not be negotiated. He asserts that security can be enhanced by reciprocal initiatives and unilateral acts, and says, "It may be that the one distinguishing characteristic of all arms-control measures is that of a design to achieve *mutual* improvement of security." He adds that it is wrong to assume that any gain in US security necessarily means a loss in Soviet security (in the jargon, he would be asserting a non-zero sum game). Nevertheless, it is clearly United States policy to negotiate as well as engage in tacit bargaining, regardless of the meager results obtained in either area so far.

Arms control, then, is more than a concrete set of proposals for altering the military posture of the United States. It is a way of thinking, a policy framework, a special approach to strategy based on the security environment of the United States at this time. It is in this form that we must seek its real impact.

This helps to explain the anomaly that most real arms control orginates in the Pentagon, despite the creation of the Arms Control and Disarmament Agency as a separate organization. While ACDA continues to negotiate at Geneva, the result is not to be measured in signed agreements, desirable as they may be. In the largest sense, the entire new budget of the Department of Defense is an arms-control program, even though it makes few open references to disarmament or arms control. The search for stability and the regard for armed forces as a preventive of general nuclear war have become dominant themes in all major defense programs. ACDA, moreover, by its very separate existence, probably serves as a spur and a continual reminder to defense officials that arms control is very much their own business too.

There are four major areas of investigation by arms-control experts. Two of these are mainly empirical—1. the search for stability and 2. the actual problem of negotiation and bargaining with the Soviets. Both are embodied in the actual events and measures to which we have already referred. The other two go beyond the realm of experience, and to them we now turn our attention. They are 3. an examination of conditions of disarmament—kinds of weapon limitations, inspections, safeguards, controls, and hazards; and 4. investigation of ways to limit the destruction of war when it occurs. Despite this simple classification, plenty of theoretical effort is put into the first two, and some practical evidence can be applied to the latter two.

Nevertheless, we have never experienced a real nuclear war, nor for that matter any kind of really effective disarmament. It is one thing to take those steps which obviously reduce the likelihood of war while preserving or increasing our power, like those which improve the second-strike capability. Beyond such steps, arms control moves rapidly into untested hypotheses, educated guesses, and open speculation. In considering later theories and studies of arms control, then, the decision maker must take such proposals with appropriate caution. He must also be reminded of another limitation of arms-control studies. This is the limitation of any expert advice that applies quantitative analysis to problems which require personal experience and judgment in final decision. For example, how can risks be compared? In a nuclear test ban, the final choice between the risk of being cheated and the more general risk of abandoning a control agreement can never be made by an expert. It must be made by a responsible official.

In area (3), the examination of conditions of disarmament, the question of weapons limitation and inspection receives the most attention. However, any real answer, if it is found, will probably be more the result of hard international bargaining than abstract analysis. There was a great deal of early study given to the possibility of disarmament and inspection by zones, with zones to be added step by step as mutual trust increased. On a scheme such as this the United States and the Soviet Union in 1957 probably came closer to agreement than any time before or since. There are a host of questions to be answered in any plan for limitation and inspection, and studies have been made of all of them. Should inspections be made of stockpiles, delivery systems, manufacturing facilities, or all of these? How often? To what extent could aerial reconnaissance substitute for ground inspection? How useful would be "nonphysical" inspection (interrogations, lie detectors)? Granted that total inspection is impossible, what scheme of random inspection would be suitable? (Surprise spot checks can produce surprisingly high statistical confidence for a relatively modest effort.) Appalling thought, what would be the danger of getting erroneous information indicating that we are being cheated? Is our whole concept too negative? Should we be trying to think of a system with built-in incentives for compliance?

The difficulties of limitation and inspection, and a partial answer to the last question, are illustrated in the "stable-deterrent system" hypothesis. This would hold each side to a given number of weapons, rather than incur special hazards of going down to zero. No inspection system for nuclear weapons is guaranteed reliable; hence, some degree of violation by the Soviets is possible and should be assumed. Therefore, as nuclear armaments are reduced toward zero, the military situation becomes potentially more unstable. If the prohibition were complete, a violation of only a few concealed weapons, say ten or twenty, would give a decisive advantage to the violator, even enable him to coerce the whole world. There is, therefore, a theoretical minimum figure for agreed mutual reduction of nuclear weapons which must be enough to render negligible the temptation to violate.

There has been some interesting analysis of the projected state of affairs in a disarmed world. What would be the incentives for and restraints against violating the disarmament agreement? Military security threats would still exist. A deterrent situation, similar to that now regarding nuclear war, would work against cheating and likewise against open rearmament if the disarmament agreement were broken. The consequences of failure of this deterrent would not be so immediately drastic as nuclear war. But the security of the West could be seriously threatened because democratic countries would be less likely than authoritarian ones to act decisively upon evidence of cheating and to rearm, particularly if the evidence were ambiguous. Even if the agreement worked, it is argued, there would be special dangers for the US. In a world in which nations had only internal security forces, large Eurasian states like the USSR and China could still intimidate their neighbors, even conquer them, without the US being able to intervene.

The most likely road to disarmament may lie in collective military action such as the United Nations Emergency Forces we have seen in recent years. Admittedly, the Soviet Union is far from supporting such forces, and we are very far from furnishing nuclear weapons to the UN. But the next decade will undoubtedly see the spread of nuclear weapons to Red China and others, and the "Nth Country Problem" will be upon us. The risk of nuclear war, according to the theory, will rise at an exponential rate. And so, we presume, will the sense of urgency to take preventive action. Ultimately all nations, in their common interest, may be driven to vest major military power in a collective organization. Then we shall have another problem: how to provide safeguards against an international police force becoming a tyranny.

The final category (4) is the latest object of arms-control study and shows promise of giving new meaning to arms control. This is the investigation of ways to limit the destruction of war when it occurs. At first glance this seems no different from disarmament or some of the measures for stabilization like dispersal and hardening of strategic forces. The difference is in potential applicability. Assume that the second-strike posture has been made as secure as possible, accidental war has been prevented to our best extent, and nothing more can be done about disarmament until the Soviets accept one of our proposals. What problem remains? The wars that do occur—or, we might say, "actual" wars. The United States has directly engaged in or provided critical support for more wars during the nuclear age than in all our previous history. Fortunately, all of these wars were limited. There will surely be more of them, as the pace of conflict quickens in the underdeveloped areas. Every such war and every sharp confrontation with the Communists short of war comprise the new challenge of arms control: how to keep "actual" wars limited.

The theoretical frontier of this problem is just being crossed by the strategy experts. Part of their attention is given to the limitation of "actual" general war, hypothetical as it may seem. Serious thinking in these terms is always desirable, for the subtle reason that general war must remain at least remotely possible in order to sustain the credibility of our deterrent policy. Soviet belief that we would not employ our power in any circumstance would mean the failure of deterrence. A complete preoccupation with the idea of stability should be avoided. There have been some bizarre studies of "limited strategic war," in which selective nuclear attacks would be made on specified targets in an enemy homeland as a punitive action. More realistically, the studies and plans for civil defense and for counterforce strategy, which are designed in part to improve stability, have the direct aim of reducing destruction in "actual" strategic war. In terms of "actual" war, good command and control means "controlled response," and the ability to limit and terminate hostilities when desired.

Suggestions are made to limit future wars by avoiding the development of new classes of weapons. For example, it is proposed that restrictions be sought against placing nuclear weapons in orbit. The arguments usually advanced are that space weapons are far less efficient than ICBMs anyhow, and that an arms race in space is such a grim prospect that it must be forestalled before it is too late. In an adroit dialectic, the case often employs at the same time, both sides of this contradiction regarding the lack of value and the highly threatening value of space weapons.

Interest grows in the problem of limiting local wars, because of their frequency and because of the danger of escalation. There is nothing hypothetical about the "actuality" of these wars. Interesting speculations have been made about distinctions in the size of weapons used in local war, so as to reduce the chance of escalation. At first, the concern was to separate tactical nuclear weapons from strategic nuclear weapons. Now, since nuclear weapons have still not been used in a local war, habit and tradition seem to make it easier to draw the line between conventional and nuclear. There have been studies of crisis decision-making, and talk of the need for steps to "tranquilize" crises. An attempt [has been] made to set up direct communication between Moscow and Washington for this purpose. Apart from these contributions, little has been accomplished. The idea of escalation has been a source of grave concern, but so far it has not become a rallying point for useful strategic concepts. Forthcoming books and articles may improve this situation. The challenge, in its importance, might be compared to the danger of experiencing a real missile gap, on the order of that which frightened us a couple of years ago, all compressed into the days and hours of every crisis.

A moral question creeps in when one discusses the possibility of bringing war under effective limitation and control. If we succeed in making limited war a safe and easy course of action, will we not have resurrected warfare as a profitable instrument of national power? The answer is that we are far, indeed, from realizing such success. Furthermore, we cannot seriously hope to reach it absolutely. Unless nuclear weapons are abolished from the earth, they will remain a deterrent in some degree against the smallest use of force in local situations. Thus, even the goal of complete nuclear disarmament has its moral paradox.

The new meaning of arms control may best be seen in relation to the whole conflict with communism. If we back off to look at this conflict in larger perspective, we might conclude that it is entering a new stage. This stage could be called the period of "full engagement." In the period immediately following World War II,

United States policy was mainly defensive; we established the perimeter of containment and held it by force in Asia and in Europe. Subsequently, recognizing the enduring nature of the threat, we established alliance systems and built a military establishment to serve us for the long pull. Still, we had room for maneuver. Communism was mostly confined to the interior of the Eurasian land mass, and our military power, when our nuclear weapons were taken into account, was predominant. We could afford the temporary luxury, in the policy of massive retaliation, of substituting nuclear power plus commitments to allies for a fuller panoply of military capabilities. We had sufficient elbow room to be able to depreciate our losses while taking seriously proposals for withdrawal and disengagement.

Full engagement, the condition we suggest exists or is approaching today, is a loss of elbow room. The signs of the past few years support this view. Virtually all of the underdeveloped areas of the earth are now involved somehow in the struggle between the free world and communism. United States freedom of action is constrained, on the one hand, by the need for reliance on a United Nations force to establish stability in the Congo, and by loss of its dominant UN voting bloc on the other. It is no longer possible to think with impunity about direct military action by the United States in many parts of the world. In fact, it is clear that many of our security challenges can be met, if at all, only by economic and political means. Few of these developments derive directly from the menace of general nuclear war, but they are all related to it and reflect the impression that the Soviets are "catching up" with United States military technology. Hungary and Cuba are striking examples of how either side will exercise the most painful restraint when it perceives that the vital interests of the other have become involved.

The problem of full engagement, then, is the need to serve the interests of the United States without the freedom of action or the second chances which history previously has generously provided us. The task it requires is to place all the ends and means of our security policy in better order and to employ them with greater care than ever before. Deprived of our accustomed margin of error, we must match every action to its objective and weigh it against its risks. In the military sphere, this means the ability to apply suitable and controllable elements of power as needed in the service of political objectives—just as Clausewitz emphasized but American political leaders themselves have forgotten at times in the past.

Ordering the ends and means of military policy is the emphasis which arms control places upon strategy in the nuclear age. It is by no means certain that we will meet with success in the long run, preserving our vital interests while avoiding nuclear war. The evidence of history is not reassuring on the prospect for securing permanent restraints against the use of best weapons in an environment of international hostility. If we do succeed, our intellectual resources applied to strategy and their prudent employment by our political leadership will have counted as one of our greatest assets.

the Anglo-Saxon "special relationship," has drawn away from its NATO commitments, and may seek fundamental changes when the scheduled reeaxamination of the entire relationship takes place in 1969. So even in the Atlantic world the regional concept has yet fully to mature.

The conception of "region" is even more anomalous on the other side of the earth. Several thousand miles separate Australia and New Zealand from the United States, its defensive partners in the ANZUS pact. American bilateral military agreements exist with Japan and Taiwan off the coast of Asia, but no arrangement for the Pacific analogous to the Atlantic Pact is in prospect. No Asian states other than Pakistan, the Philippines, and Thailand participate in the only organization in that part of the world that represents any attempt at the institutionalization of regional cooperation. The list of neighboring countries that are outside the South East Asia Treaty Organization is admittedly more impressive than those which are included, particularly when the largest powers in the area, India and Indonesia, are not only outside of but at times even hostile to the purposes of the organization. Indeed, at one time it appeared that a basic element of Indonesia's foreign and defense policy was to be a new "axis," based upon an alliance between that country and Communist China, which unlike the Warsaw Pact in Europe would cut right across the middle of the areas of the opposing states. Efforts in the Middle East to set up another arrangement analogous to the North Atlantic grouping proved abortive for a number of reasons, but principally because of its identification with essentially Western interests. Yet, at the same time, the truly indigenous Arab League has had an ineffectual and sometimes stormy existence. While it has lasted for several years, it has never had the internal strength to give it the requisite basis for viability, even if it has been held together (most of the time) by a common enmity toward the non-Arab irritant at the region's center—Israel. In Africa, impressive expressions of intentions by the leaders of the O.A.U. (Organization for African Unity) have yet to be matched either by demonstrations of effective unity or of structural permanence.[4] On the other hand, the Organization of American States, based upon the Rio Pact of 1947, but with historical precedents reaching back into the nineteenth century, is gradually developing its capacities effectively to deal with Western Hemisphere problems.

From the functional perspective, which involves organizing to facilitate the performance and coordination of economic and other kinds of activity, there are signs of lasting achievement, especially in Western Europe. Urgent commercial and industrial necessities on the continent have been met, even though there have emerged two distinct groupings in the form of EFTA (the European Free Trade Association) and EEC (the European Economic Community or Common Market). Whereas security organizations like NATO depend for their vitality upon the recognition of an external threat shared by a number of States none of whom would have the strength to resist alone, functional associations

[4] Clyde Sanger, "Toward Unity in Africa," *Foreign Affairs,* **42** (1964), 269–281.

depend for their vitality upon the degree to which they are able to promote the economic health and well-being of their memberships. Their impetus, in other words, is internal rather than external, so that given the shifting nature of the balance of power, there is every reason to expect that they might have longer lives than the purely military associations. Experience indicates that through efficient operation of practical programs and their implementing agencies, the unity of Europe has been brought closer to achievement than it ever could have been either by the mere continuation of a sense of military insecurity or through elaborate blueprints and theoretical planning. At the same time, it would be hard to overestimate the importance of the impetus given to European economic cooperation by the American initiative which led to the Marshall Plan, that had profound security implications as well as economic and genuinely humanitarian purposes.

The effective development of supra-national institutions of a functional and/or regional nature may be contrasted with the halting steps that have been taken toward organization at the world level. While the age of nationalism may be passing in some parts of the world, the age of globalism has not yet arrived, and one reason is that the age of nationalism may just be getting under way in other parts of the world. Yet it would be a grave error to conclude from this that the United Nations and its specialized agencies have had no salutory effect, and to accept the arguments either of those who discount the UN because it hasn't achieved world peace or those who condemn it because it has gone too far in bringing about internationalism. In assessing the value of the United Nations, one must endeavor to understand what the organization is and what it is not, for many of its critics blame it for not doing things it was never empowered nor intended by its founders to do. To be sure, their *hopes* can be found in the Charter, whose first Article sets forth the purposes of the organization as being:

1. to maintain international peace and security;
2. to develop friendly relations among nations based on respect for the principle of equal rights and self-determination of peoples;
3. to solve international problems of an economic, social, cultural, or humanitarian character, and to develop respect for fundamental human rights and freedoms for all persons;
4. to be a center for harmonizing the actions of nations in the attainment of these common ends.

In contrast to these hopeful ambitions stand two basic strictures of the Charter, which must be understood in order to comprehend the role and the limitations of the United Nations as a force in world affairs. First is the fact that the organization is "based on the principle of the sovereign equality of all its members," and the second is that nothing in the Charter authorizes intervention in matters "essentially within the domestic jurisdiction of any State." (Article 2, paragraphs 1 and 7.) Thus the United Nations, *as such*, can do little, if anything; only through its independent members or by their authority can it act.

The functions of the six organs which make up the organization are: for the General Assembly, to consider general principles of cooperation in the maintenance of international peace and security; for the Security Council, to accept primary responsibility for acting to preserve peace and security; for the Economic and Social Council, to deal with health, educational, cultural, social, and economic matters; for the Trusteeship Council, to give attention to the advancement of people in territories held by certain of the powers in trust under the international trusteeship system; for the International Court of Justice, the judicial organ, to handle cases in international law placed before it; and for the Secretariat, the international civil servants, to act for the organization (and not on behalf of any particular government) in the administration of organizational matters, particularly at its headquarters.

The United Nations reflects the realities of world politics (or at least some of them). Because of the Soviets' extensive use of the veto, the functions of the Security Council were for several years to some degree assumed by the General Assembly, particularly after passage of the "Uniting for Peace" resolution as a result of the Korean crisis of 1950. Certain observers in the West have viewed recent and probable future additions of members to the UN, that give more weight to the Asian-Arab-African bloc in the Assembly, as endangering the position of the Western powers in the United Nations. Actually, predictions of patterns of voting which are hostile or revengeful toward the Western powers (growing out of anti-colonialism) have not come true.[5] Nor have the alarms sounded often, particularly in the United States, that the UN would come to be dominated by Communist countries; Soviet-controlled votes have generally stood alone or merely followed the lead of other nations and blocs. For several years the basic intention of the leaders of the Big Five at San Francisco to control UN action in the crucial area of international security tended to give way to assumption of this role by the General Assembly. But even though these gradual transformations in turn resulted in decreased reliance upon the United Nations by the Great Powers in favor of the more traditional methods of diplomacy and of stronger regional arrangements, one authoritative American source has recently indicated that "if the nations of the world had been without a place to air their grievances and adjust their differences under a code of international behavior, our civilization might well have been destroyed in a nuclear war."[6] The United Nations *has* been useful in the political field, even if it has fallen short of the expectations of 1945.

In the long run, the organization may prove most effective through the extensive but usually unspectacular programs of the non-political agencies in solving economic and social problems which might otherwise lead to war. Here, as at the regional level, functionalism seems to be demonstrating its

[5] Inis J. Claude, *Swords into Plowshares,* 2nd ed. (New York: Random House, Inc., 1958), pp. 454–457.

[6] Francis O. Wilcox, "The United Nations: the Road Ahead," *Department of State Publication* 6712 (October, 1958), p. 20. Dr. Wilcox, who is presently Dean of the School of Advanced International Studies of the Johns Hopkins University, was then Assistant Secretary of State for International Organization Affairs.

practical utility. Coordinated through the Economic and Social Council, which has increased its membership to twenty-seven, these functions are performed mainly by Economic Commissions on four continents (Europe, Asia and the Far East, Latin America, and Africa), and by the specialized agencies, each with its own membership, budget, and set of operating principles.[7] Programs of these bodies are supplemented by an increasing number of agencies created by and working directly under the General Assembly, such as the Korean Reconstruction Agency, the Relief and Works Agency for Palestine, and the Committee on Information from Non-Self-Governing Territories. The activities of these bodies seldom make headlines but they may promote international collaboration in a manner never imagined by practitioners of the older diplomacy, nor indeed even by many earlier theoreticians of international organization itself.

Meanwhile the United Nations as an effective force fluctuates between the kind of paralysis that for a time characterized the sessions of the General Assembly, in which formal voting had to be suspended because of the financial crisis over Article 19, and the demonstration of real influence for peace in halting the bloodshed over Kashmir. Two facts need always to be kept in mind when assessing the place of the UN in world politics: one is that the UN can only be effective in matters affecting international peace and security to the extent to which the Great Powers agree, that is, when their interests happen to coincide; and the other is, as Professor Goodrich points out below, that the UN is a very different kind of body today than it was when it was founded.[8] With twice as many members, many of which are scarcely viable states by any criterion except that of sheer existence within identifiable boundaries, the Assembly increasingly seems to fail to reflect the hard realities of development and power. Yet what has recently happened in the UN has made this obvious weakness less telling; whereas the Uniting for Peace Resolution of 1950 had had the effect of transferring the peace-keeping authority of the UN from the Security Council to the General Assembly (where the role of the smaller states was thereby greatly enhanced), the financial crisis of the mid-sixties has put it back again, not perhaps where it belongs, but certainly back where the framers at the San Francisco Opera House intended it to be. This new phase represents a backward step if movement toward world order means developing the Assembly into a kind of world parliament with authority to make its members, whether they vote with the majority or not, pay for the implementation of its decisions. On the other hand, the decision to add to the membership of the Security Council and the Economic and Social Council is a step forward, if it will make those bodies more reflective of actual political and economic reality than ever before.

[7] These agencies are listed below in Director-General Maheu's article.

[8] See also Roberto Ducci, "The World Order in the Sixties," *Foreign Affairs*, **XLII** (1964), 379–380.

1

*The Triple Role of International Organizations Today**

René Maheu

RENÉ MAHEU, *formerly a professor at the University of Cologne, is currently Director-General of UNESCO.*

Whether the Jeremiahs like it or not, international organizations have become a recognized feature of our time. It is a fact that they exist, that they are active, steadily growing in stature and even increasing in number. And if this is so it is because they meet the real needs of the present-day world and are part and parcel of the most fundamental trends of this age.

Among these needs and trends, the most evident are those resulting from the growing complexity of international relations, itself due in part to the steadily mounting number of States in the world and in part to the increasing diversification of our civilization and hence of the exchanges to which it gives rise. This complexity of the relations between States and peoples plainly gives rise to problems of organization that can only be solved with the help of institutions as specialized and yet at the same time as universal as the problems themselves. It is for this reason that we have in the United Nations system, grouped around the nucleus of the United Nations itself, ten organizations known precisely as Specialized Agencies—the International Labor Organziation, which dates from the time of the League of Nations, the United Nations Food and Agriculture Organization, UNESCO, the World Health Organization, the International Bank for Reconstruction and Development, the International Monetary Fund, the International Civil Aviation Organization, the World Meteorological Organization, and those older bodies, dating from the late nineteenth century, the Universal Postal Union and the International Telecommunication Union. To these has been added the International Atomic Energy Agency, which has a special status. As their names indicate, each of these organizations deals with a particular sector of economic, social or cultural activity.

But it is perhaps in their approach, even more than in their actual purpose, that we can best appreciate the originality of these Agencies and perceive the true origin of their dynamism, and of what I do not hesitate to call their concordance with the general trend of evolution of our civilization. For these Agencies are at pains to approach the problems with which they deal from a universal standpoint, striving to find for each one a solution that shall contribute to the general organization of mankind. Thus, while

* Long extracts from an address delivered by the Director-General in Paris on 20 November 1963 at the formal reopening of the Institut Français de Presse at the Fondation Nationale des Sciences Politiques. *UNESCO Chronicle,* **X** (1964), 3–8. Reprinted by permission.

they are constantly concerned with specific situations and questions, each, of course, with a social and historical context of its own, their action tends to foster a universal way of thinking and to strengthen its hold on the minds of men in all parts of the world, while constantly refining and improving its methodology. That, to my mind, is the fundamental purpose of these organizations. That is their true mission, all the rest is a matter of technique, of the most effective ways and means of achieving the desired end. This it is that gives such promise to their future and it is in this perspective that we should view their present activities—which are no more than a humble beginning.

Generally speaking, there are three main aspects to the present activities of the international organizations, and of UNESCO in particular.

In the first place they provide *a setting, a meeting place and a means of coming together,* alike for the representatives of the governments of the Member States and for specialists in all the disciplines and techniques that lie within their compass. The conferences, meetings, symposia and seminars they organize on an international or regional scale provide an opportunity for exchanging information and comparing notes, and for joint deliberations, the fruits of which are embodied in reports and publications distributed the world over in several languages. By way of example I may mention that in 1962 UNESCO organized 119 meetings and subsidized 69 others. As for its publications, no less than 4,000 titles have been issued in various languages since the Organization was founded. UNESCO itself, in addition to its fourteen periodicals, brings out some fifty new titles per language each year, and the number of those published with its co-operation or under its auspices is almost as large.

Gradually, from these encounters ideas emerge which are of course world-wide in the purely geographical sense, but whose main virtue is their universality of vision. Based upon a series of international studies and a body of data which we endeavour to render steadily more comparable, this composite reflection on the main problems of our day is gradually bringing the individual States—not without occasional hesitation and even friction—to an awareness of their common interests and the consequent advantage, indeed necessity, of international co-operation, a co-operation whose purpose it is to lay the intellectual foundations of a truly universal modern civilization.

That is the first type of action by international organizations. It is the oldest and the most traditional, for it already existed, with its present structures and methods—though far more limited in resources and in scope—in the international institutions which preceded the United Nations system. Of these, the one most closely resembling UNESCO was the International Institute for Intellectual Co-operation, founded in Paris in 1924 under the auspices of the League of Nations and with the help of France. I have called this the most traditional type of international activity; I would add that—though no doubt the least spectacular—it is also the most fundamental, for everything else depends on the intellectual solidarity which it is the aim of this technical work to foster.

Since 1950, however, the United Nations system has had the merit of adding a new dimension to international work by embarking upon a kind of activity much more directly concerned with the hard facts of the situation in the various countries; I refer to what are generally called *operational activities.*

This second type of activity and its remarkable expansion, are the direct result of the admission of the less-developed countries to the international community, where they now constitute a majority. Their appearance on the world stage, where they at once began to play a very active part, drew attention to the inequality between peoples to which their geography and history have given rise, while the fact that this disparity is a constant threat to world peace and security was brought home to all not merely as something that should be known but as a call to action, and swift action at that. For the inequality to which I refer is growing steadily greater with every increase in the rate of technical progress.

It is upon the concept of *development,* that the thought of international organizations has come to be focused and it is to the task of assisting development that the greater part of their efforts is now devoted. This, as has often been observed, is a quite new departure, which, as the concept of development itself took on a more definite shape in our minds, has brought about a profound change in their methods of action.

Thus it was that the conventional concept of economic development, which was based on the experience of the industrial countries of Europe and North America in a different historical context, gave place about the year 1955 to a more comprehensive notion, better fitted to the circumstances and needs of other regions of the world—the concept of balanced economic and social development. Thus, too, though not without difficulty, the concept of planning—without which there can be no balanced development—has gradually won acceptance in the course of the last ten years. This has brought a certain unity and coherence into undertakings which at the outset, it must be admitted, were prompted by somewhat confused impulses of pragmatic humanitarianism. The resistance at first aroused by the idea of planning was due to its being regarded in some quarters as the first step towards a particular brand of economic and social system. This resistance has slowly melted away. The concept of integrated national development plans has shed its political implications and the plan has at last come to be looked upon as a mere instrument of development, based on the facts of the national situation.

Planning—I mean, of course, at the level of suggestion—has now spread from the national to the regional scale. By way of illustration I may mention that at three regional meetings organized under the auspices of UNESCO, the Ministers of Education of the African, Asian and Latin American countries have adopted long-term plans—ranging from ten to twenty years—setting up definite targets for the development of education at all its levels and pledging themselves collectively to reach these in equally definite stages.

Lastly, at its 1961 session, the General Assembly of the United Nations proclaimed a Development Decade with the aim of enabling every Member State, whatever its present level of development, to achieve by the end of the ten-year period an annual rate of expansion amounting to not less than 5 per cent of its total national income. This is the first attempt to fix targets on a world-wide scale for the development of mankind as a whole, targets towards which practical international action is being directed.

What is the nature of this action?

Firstly, each of the organizations in the United Nations system devotes part of its own budget either to activities undertaken at the request of its Member States on their own territory with a view to their having a direct impact on the situation there in accordance with the aims fixed by the Government concerned, or to activities carried out for the benefit of several States in the same region. But this operational action is also financed on a much wider scale under joint programmes in which the various organizations of the United Nations system participate. The oldest of these, dating from 1949, is the Expanded Programme of Technical Assistance (EPTA), the object of which, in accordance with the now well-known formula, is to provide States with the services of experts, with equipment and with fellowships. In 1959, ten years later, came the United Nations Special Fund which finances pre-investment operations, usually the setting up of institutions to train personnel of the country concerned. For example, of the fifty-six projects for which UNESCO is the executive agency on behalf of the Special Fund, fifty relate to institutions for training technical personnel at post-secondary and university level or to training colleges for secondary school teachers. The United Nations Children's Fund (UNICEF) and the World Food Programme, employing their own particular means and methods, also conduct activities with the technical help of the appropriate Specialized Agencies. After confining itself for a long time solely to child nutrition and health, UNICEF recently extended its interests to the education of children and this has led it to establish an active and most effective collaboration with UNESCO.

The International Bank for Reconstruction and Development and its offshoot, the International Development Association, recently decided to grant loans in spheres where they had never previously made banking investments; education was until quite recently one of those spheres. The first loan of this type was made last year to Tunisia for school building and this, it seems to me, marks a decisive step in the history of international organizations. Thanks to this investment policy which, from an economic point of view, will not show an immediate or even a short-term return but represents a vital factor in long-term development, international operational activities have acquired a new dimension which enables them to give of their full measure.

Yet, however considerable the efforts of the international organizations in this sphere may be, the aid administered by the international community cannot be compared in volume with the bilateral assistance programs and still less be regarded as their competitor. In 1962, the sums allocated by the industrialized countries for their bilateral programs of aid to development were estimated at $5,400 million. Compared with this figure, what are the $19.5 million total of UNESCO's annual budget for 1963–64, or the $132 million to which the combined EPTA and Special Fund budgets for the entire United Nations system amount for 1964?

It is a fact that, in the present state of affairs, owing to the marked preference which most of the great powers continue to show for bilateral forms of co-operation, this bilateral aid plays an essential and quantitatively preponderant part in furthering the development of the less-developed countries. It is a fact which the international organizations have to take into account in drawing up their multilateral programs, just as they take account of the recipient countries' own efforts—which are naturally the major factor.

Yet multilateral assistance, limited as it is, seems something irreplaceable to the peoples in the developing countries. The very nature of the international organizations guarantees that the assistance received from or through them will not fail to be strictly objective, that it will have no political or economic "strings" attached to it, and will be administered in consultation with their own responsible authorities with full respect for their right of initiative and free decision.

The essential purpose of the aid programs of the international organizations is to give the less-favoured nations, anxious above all to safeguard their independence—for the most part of recent date—the opportunity and the means of piloting their country's development freely and in full knowledge of the facts, of comparing their plans and experience, and of accepting aid of all kinds without the slightest sacrifice of their sovereignty.

The international organizations have already shown their Member States that they, and they alone, can provide the common ground where those same States can freely pool their efforts for the advancement of civilization on universal lines, thereby enabling those efforts to achieve their true significance.

The third aspect of the role of the international organizations is to *try to ensure that problems will be studied and conduct determined, on the basis of universal human considerations.* These organizations have to operate in a world in which deep differences are felt: inequality in development, diversity of cultures, ideological divergences. Their role must therefore be to prompt, to encourage, and to sustain by the lessons of their own experience, a process of fundamental thinking in both the moral and the technical spheres, on the ideals and standards which should inform international relations between partners whose equality of rights must be constantly reaffirmed in all aspects of their exchanges and of their practical co-operation.

Through these organizations, ideological conflicts can give rise to fruitful discussions, provided that the disputants keep to the dispassionate atmosphere and the strict methods proper to philosophical and scientific debate. In dealing with the practical problems that mankind has to solve in common, it is their part to try to find where interests converge or, at least, can be reconciled even if only pragmatically at first, for where peace is concerned, the first requirement is to be realistic.

We may be even more modest and say that, given the passionate antagonisms which rend the world today, it is already a great advance simply to recognize the possibility of mutual tolerance with a view to organizing on a lasting practical basis, peaceful co-operation between communities whose ideals and principles may differ and diverge but which are nevertheless engaged—and never before have we been so dramatically conscious of it—in the same adventure: that of the human species, with the grandiose possibilities for its future and the risks threatening its survival.

One of the major tasks of the international organizations, and in particular of UNESCO, is to assist, honestly and clear-sightedly, in bringing to light for all men a body of mental references, enabling them to understand one another, and the fact that they share a body of aspirations and motives, enabling them to work together.

The transformation of the world, and its economic and technical progress, would be pointless if man, the whole, real man, the unification of flesh and spirit, who is at once the agent through which the necessary changes are accomplished and the one who benefits from them, were not the object of all progress. Development, as a progress, can be only an instrument serving the end of human dignity.

In the last analysis, the real justification for the work of the international organizations is *ethical.* When, almost fifteen years ago, the United Nations General Assembly unanimously adopted the Universal Declaration of Human Rights, it not only threw down the greatest challenge of our time but also set an aim reflecting the deepest aspirations of peoples and of individuals.

2

*The Maintenance of International Peace and Security**

Leland M. Goodrich

LELAND M. GOODRICH, *one of the outstanding authorities in the field, participated in the meetings at San Francisco as an adviser to the United States delegation which helped draw up the Charter. He is the co-author of the definitive work,* The Charter of the United Nations: Commentary and Documents *(1949) and is a member of the editorial board of* International Organization. *At Columbia University he is Professor of International Organization and Administration.*

It is a truism that the text of the Charter gives a quite misleading picture of the United Nations as it is today. In no respect is this more true than in the working of the Organization in the maintenance of international peace and security. Those provisions of the Charter which were claimed by its authors to provide the new Organization with teeth that the League of Nations did not have either have never been used or have in practice been of little importance. New emphases and new methods have been developed through the liberal interpretation of Charter provisions. These have not always been equally acceptable to all Members, however. The process of adaptation and development continues, with great present uncertainty as to what the future has in store. . . .

NEW TRENDS IN PEACEKEEPING

The decade of the 1950's saw a new trend in thought and practice regarding the role of the United Nations in keeping the peace. This change was due to many factors no one of which was by itself decisive. The total impact of the Korean experience and the

* *International Organization,* **XIX** (1965), 429–443. Reprinted by permission.

ineffectual efforts to implement certain provisions of the Uniting for Peace Resolution were disillusioning. The balance of atomic terror came to be recognized as the effective deterrent of major power aggression while, with the death of Joseph Stalin, Nikita Khrushchev's emphasis on "peaceful coexistence" seemed to offer some reasonable prospect that the Soviet Union would find it in its interest to avoid war. The breaking of the membership deadlock in 1955, the consequent large increase in the total membership of the Organization, and, more particularly, the increase in the number of Asian and African states committed to "neutralism" in the Cold War struggle made it necessary to find a role for the United Nations which was consistent with the policies and aspirations of the new Members.[1] Finally, and this perhaps proved to be the most important factor, Dag Hammarskjöld's appointment as Secretary-General in 1953 brought to that office a person who soon demonstrated a capacity for performance that won for him the confidence of governments and led to their vesting unprecedented responsibilities in him.

The new approach to peacekeeping—new in the sense of contrast to the emphasis of the preceding decade, though embodying elements of earlier practice—can best be described in the words of Mr. Hammarskjöld. In a press conference on February 27, 1956, the Secretary-General was asked to tell what kind of "preventive action" the UN might be able to take in an area where war threatened or was "right on the verge of breaking out." After explaining his view in some detail in relation to the current situation along the Israeli-Arab border, he generalized as follows:

> In other words, the two lines of preventive action which I think are obviously indicated are, first, to stabilize the situation in the field on a day-to-day basis and to avoid the incidents which may lead to major friction, and, secondly, to be—you will excuse me for using the word—*quietly* helpful by being a third party with which the two conflicting parties can discuss matters and which may help them to bridge the gulf not by formal mediation but by working out a maximum of understanding which, I think, will increase as time goes on if the operation is wisely run.[2]

That these techniques were not new is obvious. In previous cases, the UN had sought to "stabilize the situation" by getting the parties in conflict to agree to a cease-fire, to withdraw forces from dispute areas, and to accept UN observation and report as a means of assuring respect for armistice or cease-fire agreements. Furthermore, the use of "quiet diplomacy" to achieve wider agreement had been practiced, though customarily through formal arrangements involving the appointment of a committee of good offices, a mediator, or a UN representative. The novelty of preventive diplomacy, as conceived and practiced by Dag Hammarskjöld, lay rather in the contrast to previous emphasis on methods of coercion and in the fact that he proposed to exercise or to accept personal responsibility as Secretary-General for initiating and for carrying out such preventive measures.

In the Middle East crisis of 1956, after Mr. Hammarskjöld's efforts to mediate the Suez and Israeli-Egyptian conflicts had been cut short by appeals to violence and after the Security

---

[1] See . . . Laurence W. Martin (ed.), *Neutralism and Nonalignment: The New States in World Affairs* (New York: Frederick A. Praeger, Inc., 1962).

[2] Wilder Foote, ed., *Dag Hammarskjöld: Servant of Peace* (New York: Harper & Row, Publishers, 1963).

Council had been prevented from taking decisions by the British and French vetoes, the General Assembly authorized the Secretary-General to organize a UN force "to secure and supervise the cessation of hostilities." The UN Emergency Force, in accordance with the Secretary-General's proposals, approved by the Assembly, was to be composed of contingents voluntarily contributed by Members, was to enter Egyptian territory only with the consent of the host state, was not to use force except in self-defense, and was to be under the executive direction of the Secretary-General. Furthermore, the permanent members of the Security Council were not asked to contribute military contingents. It was made clear by the Secretary-General that the Force was not to be used in any way to influence the political settlement which was to be the responsibility of the parties with such assistance as they might accept from the UN.[3]

Two years later, when the government of Lebanon complained of intervention in its political affairs by the United Arab Republic, the Secretary-General was authorized to dispatch an "observation group" to insure that there was no "illegal infiltration" of personnel or supplies of arms across the Lebanese frontier. While the UN Observation Group in Lebanon (UNOGIL) was not able to satisfy the United States in regard to the extent of infiltration and thus to forestall United States military intervention at the request of President Camille Chamoun, it did contribute to the eventual stabilization of political power in Lebanon. Furthermore, in this instance the Secretary-General established the important precedent that such a UN group should not interfere in the domestic politics of the host state.[4]

This technique of introducing the UN presence and seeking through it to stabilize the situation and assist the parties in reaching wider agreement received its most vigorous test in the Congo (Leopoldville). In this instance the Secretary-General used his powers under Article 99 of the Charter to bring the situation resulting from the collapse of law and order and the Belgian military intervention to the attention of the Security Council. His motive in part was, by interjecting the UN into the situation, to prevent what might be regarded as a power vacuum from being filled by the major contestants in the Cold War. By its resolution of July 14, 1960, the Security Council authorized the Secretary-General to provide the Congolese government with military assistance necessary to enable the national security forces to perform their tasks. The Secretary-General made it clear that he intended to follow the UNEF guidelines in the organization and conduct of the force. The Congo situation turned out, however, to be much more difficult to handle by techniques of preventive diplomacy than the Middle East or Lebanese situations since the UN Operation in the Congo (ONUC) had to contend not only with the unwanted Belgian and foreign presences but also with the disintegration of the recognized government and the attempted Katangese secession, aided and abetted by foreign influences. In the course of discharging his responsibilities under Security Council and General Assembly resolutions and the Charter of

---

[3] See Gabriella Rosner, *The United Nations Emergency Force* (New York: Columbia University Press, 1963); and D. W. Bowett, *United Nations Forces:* A Legal Study (New York: Frederick A. Praeger, Inc., 1964).

[4] See Gerald L. Curtis, "The United Nations Observation Group in Lebanon," *International Organization* (Autumn 1964), **XVIII,** No. 4, 738–765.

the UN, Mr. Hammarskjöld came under criticism from Congolese authorities for failure to give sufficient support to their political objectives, from the Soviet Union for failure to act with sufficient force to expel the Belgians and other foreigners, and from certain Western powers for excessive interference in the internal affairs of the Congo. Though Mr. Hammarskjöld's successor, U Thant, equipped with more adequate authority to use force, was able to bring the Katanga secessionist movement to an end, the financial crisis caused by the refusal of certain Members, especially the Soviet Union and France, to contribute to the expenses of the military operation made necessary its premature ending with the initial mission of the force still unfinished.[5]

Other peacekeeping operations since 1960 have been undertaken and arranged under the shadow of the financial crisis that the Congo engendered, with the Secretary-General adopting a more cautious attitude regarding the assumption of responsibilities, more particularly insisting that there be reasonable assurance in advance that funds will be forthcoming to cover the costs. In West Irian in 1962, through the United Nations Temporary Executive Authority (UNTEA), the United Nations provided a face-saving device under which the control of the disputed territory could be transferred from the Netherlands to Indonesia.[6] The mission of the UN Authority was determined by agreement of the parties, subsequently approved by the General Assembly. The Authority was supported by a military contingent of 1,500 men provided by the government of Pakistan, and costs were shared equally by Indonesia and the Netherlands. In 1963 the United Nations Yemen Observation Mission (UNYOM) was established by agreement of the United Arab Republic and Saudi Arabia to observe compliance with a disengagement agreement these two countries had entered into with respect to their military interventions in Yemen. The Mission was handicapped from the beginning by failure to get the full cooperation of the parties and the difficult physical conditions of its work. In this instance also, the parties directly concerned agreed to pay the costs.[7]

The most recent United Nations peacekeeping operation has been the UN Peacekeeping Force in Cyprus (UNFICYP), which is still in process. By its resolution of March 4, 1964, the Security Council called upon Member States to refrain from action that would "worsen the situation" in Cyprus and recommended the creation of a peacekeeping force

> to use its best efforts to prevent a recurrence of fighting and, as necessary, to contribute to the maintenance and restoration of law and order and a return to normal conditions.

It also recommended that the Secretary-General designate a mediator to promote "a peaceful solution and an agreed settlement" of the Cyprus problem. Certain features of the Cyprus operation differentiate it from the

[5] For good discussions of the Congo military operation, see Arthur Lee Burns and Nina Heathcote, *Peace-Keeping by U.N. Forces: From Suez to the Congo* (New York: Frederick A. Praeger, Inc., [for the Center of International Studies, Princeton University], 1963); and Bowett, Chap. 6.

[6] For a critical account see Paul W. van der Veur, "The United Nations in West Irian: A Critique," *International Organization* **XVIII,** No. 1 (Winter, 1964), 53–73.

[7] See *Annual Report of the Secretary-General on the Work of the Organization* (*16 June 1962–15 June 1963*) (General Assembly *Official Records* [18th session], Supplement No. 1).

UNEF and ONUC operations. A permanent member of the Security Council is a major contributor to the Force, the mandate runs for limited periods of time (three months), extension requires explicit action by the Security Council, and costs have been covered by voluntary pledges. It is too early to say what the success of the Cyprus operation will be; thus far it has succeeded in maintaining an uneasy peace with some difficulty.[8]

Lessons for the Future

UN experience with peacekeeping to date suggests that the detailed prescriptions of the Charter have in many respects proved to be completely unsuited to postwar conditions, that adaptations that have been developed by Member governments and the Organization in dealing with postwar situations have had some success but have encountered serious difficulties, and that the future is uncertain with various possibilities of future development now open.

Experience on the whole has shown that the emphasis of the Charter on peace enforcement was unrealistic; at least in the conditions that have prevailed since 1945, peace enforcement of the kind that was thought to give "teeth" to the Organization has only been possible, and then in highly modified form, in one case—Korea—and there with only limited success. But while peace enforcement has not been practiced, there has been ample demonstration that the assumption of the Charter-makers that peace enforcement requires concurrence of the Council's permanent members, especially the United States and the Soviet Union, and that such measures are not likely to be effective against a major military power is sound.

It has been possible, however, for the United Nations to play a somewhat more restricted role with considerable success. In a number of instances, with the agreement of the permanent members of the Security Council, or at least in the absence of positive disagreement, the United Nations has been able to achieve agreement of the parties in conflict to the cessation of hostilities, either through a cease-fire or a formal armistice agreement. Furthermore, the UN has assisted in securing the observance of such arrangements through various forms of UN presence, thus providing opportunities for observing, reporting, mediating, and exercising a restraining influence. The possibility of the Organization's playing a limited role of this nature was anticipated in Article 40 of the Charter but has been developed beyond the limits of purely provisional measures. It is important to note that many of the basic techniques that have been utilized in recent peacekeeping operations were developed and utilized early in the Organization's life, for example, in Indonesia and Palestine. Furthermore, Trygve Lie's proposal, which was not accepted, of a United Nations Guard envisaged the establishment of a UN military body with limited police functions.[9]

Limiting the role of the UN in the control of violence to the arrangement and supervision of cease-fires and armistices and to the performance of mediatory functions does not of course eliminate the possibility of UN activities having important political implications and effects. Sponsoring a cease-fire or being willing to assist in

[8] For the text of the resolution establishing UNFICYP, see UN Document S/5575. See also the periodic reports by the Secretary-General on the United Nations operation in Cyprus.

[9] UN Document A/656 (September 28, 1948).

implementing one and assuming responsibility for the establishment of internal order and stability, as in the Congo, involve taking decisions that are bound to affect the development of situations in which many states, including Great Powers, have serious interests. The discharge of such responsibilities must consequently be based on an adequate consensus of Members. The need of such consensus cannot be avoided by delegating authority to an international official pledged to impartiality and to placing the purposes and principles of the Organization ahead of national interest. To be more specific, the conclusion can fairly be drawn, from the Congo experience in particular, that vesting discretionary power in a Secretary-General who has demonstrated outstanding qualities as a public servant is not an adequate substitute for agreement of the major powers on critical issues.

In the light of experience, many questions arise with regard to the organization and direction of peacekeeping operations. We have had instances of such operations being initiated by decision of the Security Council, on the recommendation of the General Assembly, with the parties themselves sometimes making the initial request, and with the Secretary-General in some cases taking important initiatives. If the consensus of the major powers is considered important to the success of the operation, obviously the Security Council is in the best position to assure this agreement. Up to the present, there has been no permanent international force available for peacekeeping operations and there is little likelihood that such an international force will be established in the near future. Dag Hammarskjöld was of the opinion in 1958 that peacekeeping forces should be organized on an *ad hoc* basis because of the uniqueness of each situation.[10] Other studies that have been undertaken suggest that the establishment of an international police force with enforcement powers, such as has been envisaged in plans for a disarmed world, are far in the future.[11] In an address at Harvard University on June 13, 1963, Secretary-General U Thant gave a number of reasons why it seemed to him that "a permanent United Nations force would be premature at the present time."[12] These judgments appear sound. Nevertheless, there are obvious possibilities of advanced planning that would assure smoother and more efficient operations once the need for peacekeeping arises. These include the establishment of a planning staff and the assumption of advanced commitments to make properly trained and equipped units available when needed.[13] It should not be assumed on the basis of limited experience to date that the major military powers should necessarily be excluded from contributing military contingents to peacekeeping forces.

---

[10] See *United Nations Emergency Force. Summary Study of the Experience Derived from the Establishment and Operation of the Force* (UN Document A/3943, October 9, 1958).

[11] See William R. Frye, *A United Nations Peace Force* (Dobbs Ferry, N.Y.: Oceana Publications, 1957); Lincoln P. Bloomfield and others, *International Military Forces: The Question of Peacekeeping in an Armed and Disarming World* (Boston: Little, Brown and Company, 1964); and Bowett, *United Nations Forces.*

[12] *United Nations Review* (July 1963), p. 56.

[13] Canada and the Scandinavian countries have shown interest in these possibilities and the readiness to act. See Per Frydenberg, *Peace-Keeping: Experience and Evaluation* (Oslo: Norwegian Institute of International Affairs, 1965); and Lester B. Pearson, "Keeping the Peace," in Andrew W. Cordier and Wilder Foote, eds., *The Quest for Peace: The Dag Hammarskjöld Memorial Lectures* (New York: Columbia University Press, 1965), pp. 99–118.

The special considerations that dictated exclusion of major power contingents in the Middle East and the Congo will not necessarily be decisive in other situations where the UN is called upon to perform a "peacekeeping" function as Cyprus has already demonstrated. However, since the essence of the UN's task is likely to be that of persuading the major powers to stand aside rather than become more involved in a given situation, it can reasonably be anticipated that the practical requirements of preventive diplomacy in the future will be more commonly met by excluding the military contingents of major powers and using the forces of relatively uncommitted states to represent and implement the general interest in stabilizing many situations.

The measure of success that the UN has achieved to date in discouraging and controlling the use of armed force has not been accompanied by equal success in bringing about accommodation of the conflicting interests and demands that are the source of tension. Since the war we have had a progressive accumulation of situations in which serious tension and the danger of open violence continue to exist after initial outbreaks of violence have been brought under control. What is particularly significant is that old areas of tension tend to remain as new ones are created. The failure of the UN in its efforts to promote settlement or adjustment is in all likelihood due to a number of considerations. The major cause may well be the failure thus far to harness the influence and authority of the major powers in support of reasonable accommodations of conflicting interests. Efforts to achieve equitable settlements through the organs and procedures of the UN have thus far had limited success because the proposals of UN organs for peaceful settlement and accommodation have not as a rule been supported by necessary agreement among the Great Powers. Too often these powers have seen it to their advantage to give encouragement to one side or the other as a means of gaining advantages in their own power struggles or at least have so distrusted each other's motives as to be unwilling to join in promoting a result which each might otherwise consider desirable. Thus, in 1948, while both the United States and the Soviet Union supported the General Assembly's recommendation for the settlement of the Palestine question, they could not agree on using the Security Council as an instrument to implement that recommendation. Furthermore, the Cold War confrontation has permitted the parties in conflict to exploit the situation by playing one side against the other.

It is often maintained that the agreement of the permanent members of the Security Council is not as important to the exercise of its mediatory and conciliatory functions as to the discharge of its responsibilities under Chapter VII. The General Assembly has in fact recommended that permanent members refrain from claiming the right of veto in such cases. While there is much to be said for this point of view, it must be recognized that any UN recommendation that has the support of all the major powers is more likely to be accepted than one that might have the support of only a majority of them. Furthermore, it is clear that if the permanent members use disputes or situations before the UN for airing their own propaganda claims and introducing a major-power confrontation, the result cannot fail to be negative so far as the promotion of settlement is concerned.

The experience of the UN during the past twenty years suggests that those who wrote the Charter were not too far off the mark when they emphasized the need of agreement among the major powers if the Organization was to succeed in performing its peace-keeping function. New techniques have been developed, but these too depend for their effectiveness, as the current financial crisis demonstrates, on agreement among the Great Powers. The authors of the Charter recognized that in an international organization of sovereign states for keeping the peace, while there must be recognition of the interests and possible contribution of each Member, large or small, there must also be recognition of the special position that the major powers must occupy in any system based upon voluntary cooperation. Recognition of this truth may result in limiting the activities of the United Nations in the maintenance of peace but it will assure a more substantial success in what it undertakes.

3

*United Nations Use of Military Force**

Inis L. Claude, Jr.

INIS CLAUDE, JR., *a specialist in international organizations, is Professor of Political Science at the University of Michigan. He has written* National Minorities, an International Problem *(1955), and* Swords Into Plowshares, the Problems and Progress of International Organization *(1956) and* Power and International Relations *(1962).*

* * *

Two points are crucial to the theory of preventive diplomacy:

1. The kind of operation which is envisaged, designed to seal off a zone of trouble from the competitive intrusions of the East and the West, is dependent upon the active or the passive consent of both the major contestants in the Cold War. Hammarskjöld acknowledged this—perhaps not quite explicitly—when he described the UN's role as that of "providing for solutions whenever the interests of all parties in a localization of conflict can be mobilized in favor of its efforts." He hoped that the major powers would tolerate or even support UN ventures in preventive diplomacy because each would recognize its own interest in avoiding new confrontations that might disrupt their delicate relationships. The theory rests upon the assumption that conflict of interest breeds a limited community of interest, particularly in the thermonuclear era. Rival parties have a common interest in preventing their conflict from degenerating into uncontrollable violence. This common interest does not suggest that the conflict is unreal, or is not fundamental and deep-seated, or is diminishing in intensity. Quite to the contrary, it arises precisely be-

* From "United Nations Use of Military Force," *Journal of Conflict Resolution,* **VII** (1963), 117–129.

cause the conflict is a basic one; the community or mutuality of interest is a function of the intensity of the conflict of interest.

It is one thing to assert that the United States and the Soviet Union both *have* a stake in the avoidance of a military show-down, and thus in the encouragement of preventive diplomacy by the UN. It is another thing to assume that both great powers are *aware* of this common interest and prepared to act on the basis of that awareness. Putting Hammarskjöld's point negatively, we can say that the UN cannot hope to develop the function of preventive diplomacy successfully if the major powers do not share the conviction that their own interests would be served thereby. A UNEF or ONUC intervention is something that the UN can do *for* the great powers; it is not something that the UN can reliably do *against* the great powers, or either of them.

This immediately limits the field. It should be recalled that Hammarskjöld spoke of the possibilities of preventive diplomacy in areas *outside* of, or *marginal* to, the well-defined zones of the Cold War. He assumed, realistically, that neither of the major antagonists would look favorably upon UN intervention of the type under discussion within its own sphere of influence. Preventive diplomacy is applicable to the no-man's-land of the Cold War, the in-between area where both contestants may, on grounds of self-interest, give greater weight to the value of avoiding mutual weight to the value of avoiding mutual confrontation than to the hope of winning a competitive encounter.

2. The function of preventive diplomacy is essentially *neutralist* in character. It does not involve neutral mediation in disputes and conflicts between the Cold War blocs—that is also an important political potentiality of the UN, but it falls under a different heading, and it calls for diplomatic or legal techniques rather than military or quasi-military instrumentalities. Rather, preventive diplomacy as such involves neutral interposition between contestants, using military personnel under UN direction as agents for achieving the neutralization of a trouble spot—i.e., for insulating the area against the intrusion of Cold War competition.

Preventive diplomacy is neutralist in method as well as design. It promises to fill a vacuum with forces contributed by relatively uncommitted states; note that the exclusion of military units from the major powers or the states most intimately aligned with them has been a cardinal principle in the constitution of UNEF and ONUC. Thus, it treats neutralist states as the members of the organization uniquely eligible for service as agents of the UN in the performance of its neutralizing function. Preventive diplomacy provides the relatively uncommitted states (I use the qualification in recognition that neutralism is never absolute) with an opportunity and a challenge to make their neutralism positive and constructive; it invites them to use their limited military forces, on behalf of the UN, to do something for the great powers that the latter could not do for themselves, and thereby to promote their own interest in the survival of civilization. Preventive diplomacy, in short, places the major active responsibility for the military function of the UN upon the smaller and less involved states. The great powers must *permit* the UN to play the neutral role; the states that stand most aloof from Cold War alignments must *enable* the UN to play that role.

It might be argued that the UN should develop, for the performance of this role, a standing international force, conceived as a continuously available UNEF, an instrument of preventive diplomacy rather than an army dedicated to the defeat of aggressors. Thus equipped, the organization would presumably be emancipated from dependence upon the uncertain willingness of neutralist states to provide units for exercises in preventive diplomacy. I am not convinced that such a development is either necessary or desirable. Thus far, the record indicates an impressive willingness on the part of the uncommitted states to do the jobs which preventive diplomacy requires of them. Moreover, there is substantial doubt that a standing international force would necessarily turn out to be the most appropriate or most acceptable instrument for dealing with particular cases that might arise; it may be that every case will be so distinctive as to require a tailor-made UN force. In practical terms, a permanent force might be inordinately expensive, given the budgetary realities of the UN. In any case, I suggest that the UN will be able to carry out successful operations of preventive diplomacy only if and when there is wide-spread willingness among its uncommitted members to undertake the military burden, and there is little point in attempting to evade the implications of this reality.

Up to this point, at least, the major difficulty has had to do not with the willingness of neutralist states to serve, but with the willingness of the great powers to be served. The problem of securing the necessary consent of the great antagonists is intimately connected with the issue of the neutral character of the UN in its practice of preventive diplomacy. The great powers will tolerate or support UN action in this realm only if they *want* the neutralization of a given trouble spot and if they *believe* in the neutral character of the UN's activity.

Let us look first at the question of the will of the great powers. In the major cases that have arisen—UNEF and ONUC—the United States has welcomed neutralization. The American stake in the avoidance of new confrontations that might disturb the Cold War situation has been amply recognized. Nevertheless, it is not at all clear that either our public or our government is prepared to accept the general proposition that the UN can best serve us—or the world—by operating as a neutral force in global politics. We have valued the UN primarily as an instrument whereby Western victories have been won—or, at least, as a stage upon which Western triumphs have been enacted—and it is not easy to shift to the view that its value to us may be increased as our control over its operations diminishes. Yet, the point stands that the United States has approved and supported the neutralizing function of the UN in the Middle East and Congo cases.

The attitude of the Soviet Union has been different. In the case of UNEF, Soviet disapproval has taken the mild form of passive opposition—refusal to contribute financial support. One might make a case that this is really passive acquiescence. The Congo, of course, makes a much more interesting story. Why did the Soviet Union, after initially supporting the Congo operation, turn against it? A plausible answer is that the USSR did not want the UN to achieve the neutralization of the Congo, but preferred to have a free hand in undertaking to achieve the Communization of the Congo. The Soviet Union supported the UN initiative in the hope that it would contribute to the de-Westernization of the Congo—notably by ousting the Belgians—and then moved to enter its own Soviet elements into the situation. This analysis would suggest that the Soviets did not want to avoid the intrusion of the Cold War competition into the Congo, but welcomed such a competition in the expectation that they would win.

The second problem is that of great-power confidence in the impartial character of the UN: can the organization be trusted to function neutrally in the no-man's-land of the Cold War? The experience of the United States presents no difficulties for us. With considerable reason, we have normally regarded the UN as a pro-Western institution; at worst, it has appeared to function, or to be likely to function, neutrally. Again, the Soviet case is quite different. Starting with a deep-rooted conviction that it confronts a hostile world, the Soviet Union has had a virtually unrelieved experience as a perpetual minority in the UN; from the Soviet vantage point, the UN might, at best—but most improbably—function with genuine impartiality as between East and West. Note that the constant theme of the Soviet attack upon the conduct of the Congo operation is that ONUC is only spuriously neutral, that the whole affair represents the prostitution of the UN to the service of the Western powers. I am in no position to judge the sincerity of the Soviet assertions, although I must admit to some difficulty in believing that a Russian would not have serious doubts about the impartiality of the UN. We have not helped matters by our inveterate declarations that the UN does, and assertions that it should, serve the anti-Soviet cause—interspersed occasionally with appeals to the Soviets to recognize the "obvious" fact that the UN presides with majestic impartiality over the affairs of all the nations.

Indeed, the Soviets are not alone in interpreting the Congo operation as a move favorable to the West. Note what Ambassador Adlai Stevenson said in an address at Hofstra College on June 5, 1961:

> The Belgian withdrawal was followed by anarchy with which on the one hand the Belgians stepped back and on the other the Russians began to step in. In these circumstances, any direct intervention by the West would have been interpreted as an attempt to reimpose colonialism. Local opinion would have swung over to support the Communists, and the West would have been left in the impossible position of fighting a guerrilla war against a background of implacable local hostility . . . direct Western interventions tend of their very nature to produce a revulsion of local feeling which threatens the effectiveness of the intervention. . . . The result is that in situations such as the Congo, the Western World would be almost powerless if there were no United Nations force available to restore order, [and] check a take-over by an outside power. . . . Direct Western action would only hasten a communist takeover.

Mr. Stevenson went on to say explicitly that the UN had frustrated the Soviet plan to establish control over the Congo, and that the UN is "the only instrument by which the end of the Western system of colonialism can be prevented from opening the doors to the new imperialism of the East."

I do not mean to be critical of the UN's giving the West a victory which, according to Mr. Stevenson, the West could not have won for itself. My point is that if an official American spokesman can regard the UN's Congo operation as an intervention justified less by its helping both blocs to avoid the dangers of a confrontation than by its helping the West to contain the expansionist thrust of the Communist bloc, it is plausible that a Soviet spokesman should regard the operation as an instance of unneutral, pro-Western, UN activity. Moreover, if we regard the Congo action as a defeat inflicted by the UN upon the Soviet Union, it hardly makes sense for us to expect that the Soviets will refrain from opposing that action, or will help to pay for it, or will be inspired to assist in equipping the UN to act similarly in future contingencies.

The Congo operation has not yet been concluded, although it now appears likely to be brought to a successful conclusion. This possibility might be taken as an indication that preventive diplomacy can, after all, be effectively performed in the face of great-power opposition. Perhaps the Soviet attack upon the operation was never as determined as it was made to appear, or the Soviet hostility was mollified by the alterations of UN policy and personnel which occurred in the course of the operation. In any event, the Soviet Union refrained from carrying out the threat to wreck the organization because of its activity in the Congo. While the outcome of the Congo case may suggest the wisdom of testing the limits of Soviet toleration for operations of this kind, rather than surrendering to announced opposition, it ought not to stimulate the confident assumption that the UN can be regularly used to carry out the function of preventive diplomacy, with or without the support or acquiescence of such a power as the Soviet Union. The extreme difficulties which the Soviet reactions against the Congo operation posed, and the grave risks which the UN encountered in conducting that operation under the political circumstances which developed, should be taken as a warning against adopting that assumption. Regardless of the outcome of the Congo case, it seems, on balance, to confirm the general proposition that the UN can effectively perform the quasi-military role attributed to it under the theory of preventive diplomacy only if, and insofar as, the major powers are impelled by their perceptions of their own interests to welcome UN interposition as a means of helping them to avoid dangerous confrontations, and are convinced that the UN can be relied upon to act in a neutral manner in the exercise of this function.

It appears that the only significant military function which may reasonably be attributed to the UN is that suggested by the theory of preventive diplomacy—the conduct of operations, analogous to UNEF and ONUC, designed to assist the great powers in keeping the Cold War cold. This can be done for the great powers only if they are agreed in wanting it to be done, and only if each of them is confident that the UN will genuinely promote the neutralization of trouble spots, not act in the interest of the other. The outlook for the continuation and development of this role by the UN is discouraging, primarily because of the disaffection of the USSR. If the Soviet Union is not persuaded that it has more to gain from the containment of the Cold War, the prevention of its spreading into new and dangerously explosive situations, than from the waging of the Cold War competition wherever it may spread—and if the Soviet Union is not persuaded that the UN is capable of serving with genuine neutrality as an agent of preventive diplomacy—then it seems to me that it is a major task of American policy, inside and outside of the UN, to promote these convictions on the part of the Soviet Union. If the United States and the Soviet Union can join in accepting and even in valuing the performance of this role by the UN, it seems to me that the organization may contribute significantly to the stabilization of the global situation. If they cannot, the UN may yet contribute valuable services in other realms, but I see no important role for it with respect to the use of military force under international auspices.

CHAPTER NINETEEN

Toward a Rule of Law

Perhaps the first thing to recognize about the nature and functions of international law is that it is law *among* states, not law *over* states. The legal formalization of international collaboration should be thought of as serving and advancing the respective national interests of the participants, as a supplement rather than as an alternative to conventional diplomacy on their part. It recognizes the fact that certain of their interests can best, and indeed *only,* be served within the framework of law. In a world of sovereign states, international law should not be conceived of as something separate from an existing state system which it might in some way replace.

Authorities on the subject differ in their definition of international law according to the "stress put upon the sources from which they believe the law to be derived, the older writers stressing reason and justice and later writers emphasizing the facts of international life."[1] One definition, in broad terms, is that international law is "the body of general principles and general rules which are binding upon the members of the international community in their mutual relations,"[2] made up of numerous customary and conventional rules, presumably accepted by civilized states. The sources of international law are many and varied, but as indicated in Article 38 of the Statute of the International Court of Justice, they are regarded as being:

1. international conventions which establish rules which are recognized by contesting states in the case of disputes between them;
2. international custom as being evidence of general practices which are accepted as law;
3. the general principles of law which civilized nations recognize; and
4. judicial decisions and teaching of "the most highly qualified publicists of the various nations" as indicating the means whereby customs and legal principles may be determined.

While international law has traditionally been regarded as applying exclusively to the complex relationships of sovereign states, it has been argued that

[1] Charles Fenwick, *International Law,* 3rd ed. (New York and London: Appleton-Century-Crofts, Inc., 1948), p. 27 *n.*

[2] *Ibid.,* p. 27.

the individual himself should have a more direct place, in terms of his relations both with states and with other individuals in a modern law of nations.[3] Another stimulating and novel approach is represented by the "law of mankind" perspective set forth by Jones in the article reprinted below. Potentially significant as these approaches may be, most contemporary analysts of international politics find themselves less concerned with the place of the individual or with the universal implications of international law than with the degree of its impact on the actual conduct of foreign policy. As one writer has recently observed,

> The assumption that international law is or should be a coercive restraint on state action structures almost every analysis, no matter what the school of thought or the degree of optimism or pessimism about the effectiveness of the international legal system. With an intellectual framework that measures international law primarily in terms of constraint on political action, there is little wonder that skepticism about international law continues to increase while creative work on the level of theory seems to be diminishing.[4]

Indeed, since international law does not appear to restrain or even affect states in their actual pursuit of "vital national interests," which are often narrow and selfish, doubts are often expressed that *international* law is really *law* at all.

Prevailing assumptions about the relevance, efficacy, or potential utility of what we call international law tend to vary with the degree of stability in the international system. Before the turn of the century there was much more stress upon the universal efficacy of international law than there is today. The reason is clear: before the outbreak of war among the "civilized states" shattered the illusion, it was widely believed that there existed among the leadership of these Great Powers a consensus of values which could underlie the development of a rule of law. The Hague Conferences of 1899 and 1907 seemed to reflect and to broaden this consensus. In the words of one of the most influential authorities in the field,

> Problems of international public health, public morals, public safety were dealt with in a constructive manner, as if the nations were indeed a true international community. Statesmen and publicists in different countries began to have visions of a world of law and order based upon the voluntary cooperation of sovereign and independent states which had come to recognize so vast a body of common interest.[5]

After the First World War, interest on the part of those who believed that law had to rest upon the existence of community tended to concentrate upon the development of international institutions such as the League of Nations, until that body proved incapable of meeting the challenge of totalitarianism. The

[3] Philip C. Jessup, *A Modern Law of Nations* (New York: The Macmillan Company, 1948), pp. 15–16. Now a Member of the World Court in The Hague, Dr. Jessup was for many years Hamilton Fish Professor of International Law and Diplomacy at Columbia University.

[4] William D. Coplin, "International Law and Assumptions about the State System," *World Politics*, **XVII** (1965), 616.

[5] Fenwick, *op. cit.*, p. 19.

years immediately following the Second World War even more quickly saw the frustration of any possibility of erecting a world community on the basis of the wartime coalition. There emerged not just two, but several competing value systems in the world. In the wake of what Professor Hajo Holborn of Yale has called "the political collapse of Europe," the European system of values on the basis of which a structure of law seemed possible of achievement early in this century could no longer prevail. To speak of a world rule of law today assumes that among the several systems of value, particularly but not only between the main protagonists of the "Cold War," there is a high enough degree of consensus that a universal legal structure can be created. Such a consensus is difficult to locate in a situation in which each side tends to define error and illegality in terms of whatever the other side does.

It is this which has prompted many observers of the international scene sadly to conclude that international law simply does not exist. Their principal argument is that since leaders of one bloc reject the values of another bloc, they would hardly allow their states to be placed in a position of having to accept decisions of a tribunal whose values were not their own. They contend, in other words, that international law is not law because there is no way in which it could be enforced once it is violated.

Others, however, contend that international law does in fact represent reality, even if its functions fall far short of a world *rule* of law. Obviously, unless some state or combination of states succeed in creating a world empire whose legal norms will then become applicable to all mankind, the development of a world rule will be a gradual process rather than a sudden event. One step in preparing for its eventual acceptance is the creation of a climate of legal observance, insofar as this is possible under existing political conditions. Enforceability may be lacking, but as long as states, or even some states, obey the law —for whatever reason—then it is perfectly proper and essential to speak of the existence of an international legal system, limited though it may be.

In the words of a distinguished Dutch diplomat, Eelco van Kleffens, ". . . we feel in our heart and conscience it is right and useful that the law be observed. . . . We had the natural desire to see law respected precisely because it is law." As a spokesman for one of the smallest of states, he has urged that this "powerful weapon of defense" no longer be neglected, arguing that an appeal to international law will be "understood and admitted by all decent people, and evil-doers without hesitation branded as such," since the obligatory force of international law, like all law, is fundamentally based upon a sense of right and wrong.[6]

On the other hand, a leading spokesman for one of the most powerful states, John Foster Dulles, contended that the Communists have made observance of a rule of law impossible. In order to make more use of law in the kind of framework within which it could be expected to work, he believed that states *with*

6 "The Place of Law in International Relations," *United Nations Review,* I (1955), 20–23.

common standards should advance the rule of law by submitting *their* disputes to the International Court or some other tribunal.[7]

But Lincoln Bloomfield clearly brings out below how unrealistic it would be to make the assumption that if the U.S.S.R. did not have to be taken account of in international affairs, frustrations in the development of international law would automatically be overcome. Something which could be called a community would have to exist before a world system ruled by law could be established. No such community exists today, any more than the problems involved in the application of law to the conduct of international relations can be solved exclusively by the elaboration of attractive organizational and legal formulae. From the point of view of the facts of international life, it seems clear that until the Great Powers as well as the small agree to accept the limitations that a rule of law would impose upon their own actions, international law is unlikely to play a decisive role in world affairs. As Quincy Wright has observed, "international law remains subordinate to international politics."[8]

From the point of view of theory, however, it is still useful to examine the basis for the idea that international law is binding. One view is that states can, as an exercise of their sovereignty, agree to observe certain rules in the conduct of their relations with other states; "International law" is simply the body of these rules of conduct. According to this "consent theory" could not a state, still being sovereign, withdraw its consent to abide by these rules as well? If so, what happens to the *binding* character of law? A contrasting theory has it that, once consent is given, a rule of law is created which henceforth ceases to be a subject of repeal by states. But this view raises the further question of what the *source* of international law really is, if it is somehow beyond the state to decide whether or not to be bound by it. Fenwick and others argue that the theory of consent is inadequate and that law exists because without it there would be anarchy, and that the interdependence of states is a fact, "so that international law may be said to be based upon the very necessity of its existence, upon the very human beings in constant contact with one another under the condition of the present day."[9]

Be that as it may, it is difficult to contest the view expressed by Hans Morgenthau when he writes that to recognize that international law exists is not tantamount to saying that, as a legal system, it is as effective as the legal systems of states. Nor does it follow from the *existence* of international law that it is "*effective* in regulating and restraining the struggle for power on the international scene."[10]

[7] In "The Rule of Law in Peace," *Department of State Bulletin,* Series S, No. 79 (January 31, 1959), pp. 1–7.

[8] *Contemporary International Law: a Balance Sheet* (New York: Random House, Inc., 1961), p. 52.

[9] Fenwick, *op. cit.,* pp. 31–32.

[10] *Politics Among Nations,* 1st ed. (New York: Alfred A. Knopf, Inc., 1948), p. 211. See also on this point Percy E. Corbett, *The Study of International Law* (New York: Random House, Inc., 1955), esp. pp. 45–47.

1

*Law and the Idea of Mankind**

Harry W. Jones

HARRY W. JONES, *a lawyer, is a frequent lecturer on public and international affairs. He serves as a trustee of the Meyer Research Institute of Law. His books include* Economic Security for Americans (*1954*) *and* Legal Realism and Natural Law (*1956*).

In "the extremity of doom" let us consider what we expect law to do for mankind. For the idea of mankind, indeed the survival of that idea and of mankind itself, is inseparably linked to the idea of law. What are the distinctive tasks of law in society? How does law operate? Where do the points of tension occur in the functioning of a legal order? What special significance, if any, has the "idea of mankind" for law and legal philosophy?

Let us begin by considering the idea of mankind, as defined by the Committee for the Study of Mankind. "Today," reads the Committee's manifesto, "mankind for the first time is emerging as a communicating and potentially cooperating society. . . . We propose to study human society as a whole and to stimulate the rethinking of concepts and values in terms of the future of that society." I suggest that this is a new way of thinking about law in two respects. First and manifestly, the mankind idea challenges the idea of national sovereignty, which is the central concept of traditional international law and the assumption underlying both the public law and the private law of every existing legal system. A true mankind perspective would view the common good of mankind, not the established rules of nation to nation behavior, as the basic norm of a world legal order.

The idea of mankind is new for law in another respect—its greater inclusiveness. Legal philosophies, even the most aspiring ones, display a certain inevitable parochialism, the product of their social contexts and conditions. A mankind perspective is the best safeguard against parochialism in legal thinking, against our dangerous tendency to think that the American way—or the English or the French way—is the only true way of law, and that all others are misguided, primitive, or worse. And there is no jurisprudential parochialism that quite equals the Marxian version, according to which objective law is but deception and fraud and the legal ideas of other lands mere expressions of capitalist oppression. No one is more pessimistic than I about an ultimate reconciliation of the communist and noncommunist worlds, but their respective ideas about law might be made less jarring in their impact on each other by a resolute mutual determination to view the problems of international order in mankind perspective.

We recur, then, to the proposition

* *Bulletin of the Atomic Scientists* (1963), pp. 6–8. Reprinted by permission.

that "mankind for the first time is emerging as a communicating and potentially cooperating society." A "potentially cooperating" society? Yes, I suppose, if we do not confuse potentiality with reality, and if we are forever aware that any statement of social potentiality is less a matter of factual description than a declaration of faith. Lawyers, by vocation and training, are distrustful of enthusiastic claims that imperfect societies possess this or that happy potentiality. As a lawyer, I want to hear about means, not content myself with a statement of ends, however noble. Further, I offer two flatly dogmatic propositions concerning the affirmation that mankind is a potentially cooperating society: first, that this cooperating society will forever remain in the shadowland of "potentially" unless it is structured, governed, and ordered by law; second, that the accomplishment of a law-ordered society of mankind will require acts of legal construction bolder and more imaginative than any ever before undertaken by men of law. The legal systems of even the great nations of the world are but small scale models for the planning of a rule of law for mankind. But they are all we have. Our question becomes this: what has legal experience to offer that might conceivably illumine the problems inescapably involved in devising a law for mankind?

One of the most dangerous illusions of our time is that international law, the body of historical and logical doctrine developed over centuries of experience with the relations of states to each other, is a complete and definitive statement of principles that, once affirmed, will solve every problem of the twentieth century world. No international lawyer of competence makes that claim. An international lawyer works with the doctrines and precedents of traditional international law, uses these sources as tools of analysis and instruments of argument. But he knows that law and policy are interwoven and inextricable.

A law for mankind is not something to be found or deduced from preexisting precepts. It will have to be fashioned by responsible men working in a great tradition. Account must be taken of all we know about the conduct of men and particularly about possible ways in which to make group behavior less wayward and irresponsible than it is in a state of nature. For in human communities, whether they be tribes along an African river or great industrial societies like our own, the whole is likely to be something different—and usually something worse—than the sum of the parts. A man in a mob is incomparably harder to control by law than the same man is in his individual behavior at work or at home, and this is true to a far greater degree when millions of individuals are banded together in a "sovereign" civil society. It is a tragedy of our time that nationalism has become a compelling slogan again, that the charismatic leaders of the emergent countries of Africa and Asia are nationalists and rarely libertarians. In the perspective of mankind, nationalism, regionalism, and emotional patriotism are forces working against the possibility of an international rule of law.

I have of course been describing not mankind law but international law. This is a painful concession, but one that must be made if we are not to go off into sheer wishful thinking. No one could feel more strongly than I that the rights of man are far more important than the rights of nations. Some day, I devoutly hope, the rights of individual men will be fixed and guaranteed by a higher political authority than the nation in which each happens to reside. But in the time we have, drastic acts of creative construction must be performed on international law, for it is all there is to go on. We relinquish, for the time, the long-held dream of a law of mankind and settle for something short of that, a law of nationkind. International law is not mankind law, but international law may, if men are patient, generous, and lucky, secure mankind's survival.

Theoretically, an effective rule of law might be imposed by force of conquest, a modern Pax Romana, as would occur if any one of today's great powers were to overcome the others in open war or terrify them into surrender and acquiescence. But this is most unlikely, since the destructive power unleashed in a third world war would cripple winner and loser alike. What then is the prospect for world legal order by accepted consensus among the nations of the world or, at least, among the great powers? The answer seems plain enough. Assent to an international rule of law will become possible whenever the peoples of the world, or their governors, are brought to the conviction that law of almost any content is better than no law at all; that any settlement of a dispute is better than international violence; that in the long run any nation—every nation—is better off accepting an ordered system of international adjudication, arbitration, and negotiation than reserving the "sovereign" right to assert its claims by power and intimidation.

When an individual or a nation assents to an ordered legal system, he or it must take the bad with the good, must be prepared to bear inevitable disappointments with equanimity. Those who participate in the operations of a practical legal order must anticipate that they will never get everything to which they believe themselves entitled. They must be prepared to be cheerful about a .500 batting average, even to accept a majority of decisions adverse to national interest. The central consensus must be, above all, that someone must decide and that the decision shall be final. In an international legal order, there will be proper occasions for criticism of decisions, for vigorous assertions of national interest, but the decision must be accepted by the loser as binding upon it.

We find it hard to renounce the idea of self-help; we believe ourselves strong enough to look after our own interests, and so we may be. Would we make the essential concession that important American interests are to be judged, and with finality, by some supranational authority? Let us try a case or two. Suppose that a proposal were made to submit today's Berlin crisis, or the question of American treaty rights to Guantanamo, to a panel of five or fifteen judges or arbitrators chosen from neutral countries. (I mean genuine neutrals, of course.) Would we agree to be bound by any such decision? Can you conceive of the uproar in the Congress of the United States if such a proposal were seriously entertained by the President or the State Department? Yet a world rule of law is inconceivable if only the lesser powers are to be bound by it, or if decisional processes are restricted to minor and technical matters and true trouble cases reserved for self-judgment and self-help. If we would have an effective international rule of law, it is precisely the trouble cases, those which might lead to war, to which orderly processes of legal settlement must extend.

We need to be on constant guard against soft-mindedness in our discussions of the role of law in international relations, and Ambassador George Kennan has been a particularly useful devil's advocate in this connection. Kennan rejects the notion that law or the rule of law is the skeleton key to international order. He is scathing in his condemnation of what he calls the "legalistic approach" to international relations and states his central thesis (in *American Diplomacy, 1900–1950*) in flat and uncompromising terms:

> History has shown that the will and the capacity of individual peoples to contribute to their world environment is constantly changing. . . . The function of a system of international relationships is not to inhibit this process of change by imposing a legal strait jacket upon it but rather to facilitate it; to ease its transitions, to temper the asperities to which it often leads, to isolate and moderate the conflicts to which it gives rise, and to see that these conflicts do not assume forms too unsettling for international life in general. . . . For this, law is too abstract, too inflexible, too hard to adjust to the demands of the unpredictable and the unexpected.

I agree cordially with Mr. Kennan's statement of the functions of an international order. My difference with him is simply that I have a very different view of what law is and what it is capable of. If law were inescapably abstract, inflexible, and incapable of adjustment to the demands of the unpredictable and the unexpected, I would share Mr. Kennan's conviction that law cannot avail mankind at this critical point in its history. But the law men live by, the law that might provide a structure of order for a community of nations, is something far less formal—less majestic, certainly, and incomparably more pragmatic—than the idealized doctrine of Blackstone's dreams and Mr. Kennan's fears.

* * *

2

*A Pragmatic View of the New International Law**

John N. Hazard

JOHN N. HAZARD, *Professor of Public Law at Columbia University since 1946, is a recognized authority on Soviet law. Among his many books are* Law and Social Change in the USSR *(1953);* The Soviet System of Government *(1957); and* Settling Disputes in the Soviet Society *(1960).*

Let us be candid and pragmatic. What is this new international law of which so many are speaking? It is a philosophical construction which we have misunderstood, because we are not philosophically minded people. To the Communists it is new because in their book a legal system must be judged not by the norms it incorporates but by the ends it serves. They purport to see contemporary international law in the service of the exploiters and to anticipate the evolution of a new function for international law

* *Proceedings of the American Society of International Law* (1963), pp. 79–83. Reprinted by permission.

which will make it new. For them the new content must change the form as well, because form and content are in dialectical unity. Thus, a legal system composed of the norms we all know, with but a few changes, can be a wholly new legal system. That is what the Communists are talking about.

For the jurists of the newly developing states of Asia and Africa new international law is also largely the familiar norms, but applied with a new style. They argue that the dignity of men and of states has been degraded by colonialism. Men are not treated as equals, nor are the developing states yet treated as equals, and some are even still colonies. A new international law becomes under this approach a system of norms denuded of those that foster colonial domination. Yet these rules of the past are not many when related to the whole body of law. A new law becomes under this interpretation primarily a new attitude of statesmen in the chancelleries of Europe, an attitude that accepts former colonials as equals, not only in renunciation of the use of force to collect debts and protect materials, but, more importantly, in daily association around the green tables of diplomacy. An African can tell a handshake that is offered by a man who thinks he is being magnanimous in offering his hand from one who thinks nothing of it at all, but assumes that it is routine.

How can we know that our task is less complicated than we thought and that the changes we are being asked to accept are less sweeping than was supposed? The record in print proves it, as does association in the corridors of the United Nations and at scholarly congresses. No one is asking for the complete rejection of what we know as international law. No one is asking that the books be burned and that we start afresh in rejection of the lessons history has given as to the rules which minimize friction. If we approach the problem pragmatically in examination of specific suggestions for alteration of the rules, and avoid the philosophical conceptions of "new" law, we shall be able to proceed. This is our English heritage, and when combined with our American heritage of anti-colonialism, the two forces should facilitate our task as North Americans in reaching our goal of a system of law that can minimize frictions.

This is not to say that we can construct a legal system that will assure the peace if power-hungry statesmen with ample resources to overcome their neighbors turn to the sword. Reluctantly I have reached the conclusion that legal norms cannot perform this task at this moment in history, and we cannot expect either old or new law to save the world from the madman or the zealot or the reckless empire-builder. Yet, inability to assure world peace through world law is no reason to avoid doing what we can to minimize frictions that could lead to conflict of a lesser type, and the place to begin is at the conference table in review of the individual norms of international law against which complaint has been lodged.

Suppose that we begin with the Russians. Many have been suspicious of their aims, and we tend to see a Trojan horse in the innocent-sounding proposals that come from their jurists. But lawyers are used to this problem. Who has not learned in law school to look for advantages which the other side is trying to gain by innocent-looking proposals made in the negotiation of a contract? And when the hidden possibilities are discovered, experienced counsel determines whether to reject them, to counter them with alternatives, or to accept them in expectation that they can cut both ways.

Knowing this tradition of the Bar, we need not refuse to look at the proposal.

The legal adviser to the Soviet foreign office has set forth his concept, and, therefore, the concept of his government, of what is needed to improve the law. He divides the norms of international law into three groups: norms to be discarded, norms to be strengthened, and norms to be changed. Into the discard would go: spheres of influence, capitulations, consular courts, unequal treaties and intervention. No American statesman or jurist will object to these proposals. They are principles from the past, superseded by the practice of states and by the United Nations Charter.

To be strengthened as norms of the second category would be: respect for state sovereignty, non-interference in domestic affairs, equality of states and *pacta sunt servanda.* Here we move to a group of issues that have been much debated in the United Nations and elsewhere. No American objects to these principles, and many see in them only problems of interpretation. For example, we see sovereignty strengthened when utilized to join groupings of states organized to resist aggression, or to reduce tariff barriers in expansion of economies, or even to provide judicial assistance to foreign plaintiffs in the courts of the United States. We brook no interference in the domestic affairs of the United States and we propose none on our part in other countries as long as they do not threaten our existence. To us it seems that threat to existence goes beyond domestic affairs and becomes of moment internationally. The United Nations is creating from year to year a new jurisprudence establishing a definition of the seemingly domestic activities that threaten world peace. We can be content to let this process continue.

As to equality of states and *pacta sunt servanda,* we have no quarrels. We have relinquished our few colonies, offered to Puerto Rico complete freedom to choose her future status and begun a program of political education in the few islands we maintain as fortresses. We reluctantly supported colonial empires of allies when their loyalty in the alliance seemed jeopardized by our anti-colonial sentiments, but we sighed with relief when France and Algeria reached accord as to the latter's status. And who would reject the very principle on which law rests, the concept of *pacta sunt servanda?* We might be tempted to recall the 1920's when Soviet jurists argued that in principle Tsarist treaties were not binding, at least insofar as they created financial obligations. But we read that this period is over and that the U.S.S.R. is even more conservative in application than many others of the *clausula rebus sic stantibus.* Yes, we can accept *pacta sunt servanda* and demand that all nations adhere to it.

It is with the third group of norms to be established anew that we shall want to be most careful, as is any lawyer with concepts for which there are as yet no annotations telling us what the language means. This is the more so since some of these principles have been in discussion for years in the United Nations, and there has been no agreement on definition.

Here are the Soviet proposals for this category: prohibition of aggressive war within the meaning of the United Nations Charter, peaceful settlement of disputes, self-determination of nations, peaceful co-existence, disarmament and prohibition of war propaganda. No one knows what aggression means, since the United Nations committee seeking to define it has had to postpone its work until it thinks agreement possible, and it has not suggested recall of its members. No one knows what peaceful co-existence means, although efforts are being made both inside and outside the United Nations to define it. Everyone is for self-determination of nations and disarmament, but agreement cannot be reached on how these two concepts can be put into effect without increasing the threat of war. Only prohibition of war propaganda presents a case of rejection at the present time in keeping with the Western world's reluctance to silence freedom of speech unless there is a clear and present danger resulting from its use. And up to now, the majority in the West does not believe that the utterings of some military men and sensational journalists would really create such panic in the minds of responsible statesmen as to drive them to war against their considered judgment.

My point in reviewing the Soviet proposals is to show that they do not require rejection of international law in its totality, or in its major aspects. They are but moves on the chessboard of international politics which can be met calmly in preservation of an international law which has always seemed to Americans to be a dynamic discipline capable of change without loss of its identity.

Let us turn to the second group of states that are demanding new international law, namely, the states of Asia and Africa. The record in the Sixth Committee of the United Nations discloses what is desired. It is first and foremost a recognition of the dignity of individuals and states, regardless of previous condition of servitude, race and religion. This is the matter of "style" of which I have spoken, which requires little new in the way of law. The evil features of colonialism are on the wane, and only a few sore spots remain beyond the nearly one hundred small islands and enclaves for which solution must lie not in independence but in federation or union with neighbors with whom wealth and defense can be shared. The problem is not the break-up of the old empires, but avoidance of the creation of new ones. A candid man cannot look without alarm on some events in parts of Africa and Asia today which suggest that new Alexanders have aspirations out of keeping with the trend of the postwar years.

The details that the developing states wish revised are various. Some fear the use of consular immunities for purposes of espionage and ask that the privileges of the pouch be denied to all but diplomatic representatives. Some fear foreign warships severing communications between islands of an archipelago state. Some want established their right to subsoil resources now owned by foreign interests. Some demand that the former colonial powers return in expiation of their exploitation of colonial resources large sums of money in the form of grants and technical assistance so that economies may be improved. Some demand access to foreign markets currently protected by customs barriers.

The statesmen of the world are already meeting to consider these desires, and the International Law Commission is not only codifying but developing the law. This is an orderly procedure, and the forums are varied in which the claims can be discussed and met to the extent possible. The recently concluded Vienna Congress on diplomatic privileges and the . . . one on consular rights will resolve some of the issues. More will be heard on the law of the sea. The United Nations has just concluded adoption of a resolution on nationalization of resources, and the financial agencies of the organized world are filling economic needs. These measures probably fail to meet all the desires of the developing states, but no state can expect to obtain all of its aims immediately, and the new states are sophisticated enough to know that fact.

There is one avenue of change that has become popular with the developing states and for which the long-established powers have been slow to rally. It is the resolutions of the General Assembly. Admittedly, such resolutions are not sources of international law, although many speakers in the Sixth Committee from the small states have wished that they were, and some have even tried to pretend that they are such sources. Nevertheless, these resolutions are having increasingly persuasive importance in guiding the conduct of foreign ministers. If we Americans take into consideration that the great majority of states in the United Nations share the values, if not always the institutions, for which we have declared ourselves, we can hope usually for the statement of desirable guides to action in these resolutions. There are few states, after all, which evidence an expectation that they can lord it over the whole world, although some may talk of hegemony in philosophical terms as an ultimate desideratum of a social system for which they hope to be the teacher. We can expect a majority vote for independence as conceived by nationalistically oriented statesmen for the foreseeable future, and if we work with this majority we can share in strengthening concepts which meet our needs. If they are ill-conceived, as some surely will be, our function will be to point out the shortcomings for consideration by a world public opinion which is increasingly literate and experienced in distinguishing the wolfish aggressor, who seeks to cloak himself in the sheep's garb of peaceful propaganda, from the real peace-lover.

My point is simple. Face the future of international law fearlessly. No one can hope to rend the fabric, and very few seem to want to do so. We have only to attend to patching the garment or to weaving new parts. We are skilled in that process as pragmatic jurists. We know how to be wary and yet receptive of legitimate proposals. I cannot resist a melodramatic conclusion. Why be afraid?

3

*Law, Politics and International Disputes**

Lincoln P. Bloomfield

LINCOLN P. BLOOMFIELD, *a Harvard graduate, was a Naval officer in World War II. He served in the State Department for eleven years, most recently as Special Assistant, for policy planning, to the Assistant Secretary for International Organization Affairs. At the present time, Dr. Bloomfield is a senior staff member of the Center for International Studies, Massachusetts Institute of Technology. He has written extensively on problems of international relations, specifically in the area of international organization.*

Arnold Toynbee once wrote: "Life and law must be kept closely in touch, and as you can't adjust life to law, you must adjust law to life. The only point in having law is to make life work. Otherwise there will be explosions."[1] Men have worked hard in this century to adjust life to law, and it has not seemed to work. There has been no want of good motives behind the effort, and the extra incentive, if one were needed, has been the increasing unattractiveness of international life.

Some of the jurists stuck to their guns and proclaimed a universal, all-embracing legal order into theoretical existence, pausing only to minimize the political world about them as a superfluous irritant. Other writers were so carried away by the sometimes brutal and irrational behavior of men in political groupings, that they dismissed for all time the possibility that law could ever rule the international jungle, governed then, now, and forever by the "iron laws of politics."

But some spokesmen perceived the subtle grays in the web of civilized life, where ideals and passions, reason and unreason, and law and politics, are linked together, incessantly clashing, struggling for mastery but intimate and inseparable. This continuous process produces a rough equilibrium, and while it denies a "pure" role for the law, it is still an odd fact, as Pascal pointed out, "that there are people in the world who, having renounced all the laws of God and nature, have themselves made laws which they rigorously obey."

There can be little argument that the kind of consensus needed in order for law to play a fuller role in international affairs is profoundly lacking today, just as it has been in the past. As early as 1899, at the first Hague Conference, the delegate of Imperial Russia made the following statement setting forth a rigid concept of national sovereignty and reservation of unilateral national rights that has never

---

[1] "The Lessons of History," in *Peaceful Change—An International Problem,* C. A. W. Manning, ed. (New York: The Macmillan Company, 1937), p. 36.

* *International Conciliation,* No. 516 (1958). Reprinted by permission.

really been departed from since by any major power:

> There is no Government which would consent *in advance* to assume the obligation to submit to the decision of an arbitral tribunal every dispute which might arise in the international domain if it concerned the national honor of a State, or its highest interests, or its inalienable possessions.[2]

Fifty-seven years later the Soviet delegate to the United Nations General Assembly in an identical mood expressed the identical position, asserting that the decision to submit a matter to the world Court is part of a nation's "sovereign prerogative, and no State could be required to indicate such willingness in advance."[3]

It is both tempting and justifiable to cite the specter of the Soviet Union to support the conclusion that legal methods cannot work in today's world. The Soviet Union is a symbol of the sort of force—hostile, expansionist, sporadically revolutionary—that always seems to frustrate hopes for a legal world. The Soviet Union has so far displayed nothing but contempt for international legal institutions as conceived in the Western tradition, and efforts such as that of the United States to have the International Court of Justice adjudicate claims arising out of damages to United States aircraft and personnel at the hands of the Soviet bloc have been flatly rejected.

But it would be delusory to assume that, without the Soviet Union, the problem would disappear. There has also been a noticeable lack of effort on the part of the Western nations to translate into juridical deeds their verbal aspirations for a rule of law in the world. It is not at all clear that France, for example, would be willing to put at stake its legal position in Algeria. And undoubtedly, in the present political environment, the United States would simply have to defy a Court decision that Formosa legally belongs to Communist China. . . .

On the other hand, . . . Communist Albania, albeit reluctantly, did accept the Court's jurisdiction in the *Corfu Channel Case.* Colombia and Peru could be heard breathing a sigh of relief when, after two tries, the Court unhooked them from the dilemma of the protracted asylum of Haya de la Torre. And the United States did swallow the pill of the Advisory Opinion upholding the United Nations Administrative Tribunal awards to suspected Communists among Secretariat employees who were United States citizens. One can hope that Egypt's alleged right to exclude Israel shipping from the Suez Canal, as well as other legal aspects of the Arab-Israel situation such as international status of the Straits of Tiran, will be submitted to the Court for adjudication. But as a general rule of thumb, it seems depressingly true, at least in recent practice, that a government "may not subject itself to those supreme laws of renunciation and self-sacrifice that represent the culmination of individual moral growth."[4]

The process has been a regressive one in recent years. The United Nations Secretary-General in his report to the twelfth General Assembly noted regretfully that in the previous two

[2] *The Proceedings of the Hague Peace Conferences: Conference of 1899* (New York: Oxford University Press for Carnegie Endowment for International Peace, 1920), pp. 173–174.

[3] United Nations General Assembly, Official Records: 11th Sess., 6th Cmte., 488th Mtg., (3 Dec. 1956), para. 25.

[4] George F. Kennan, *Realities of American Foreign Policy* (Princeton: Princeton University Press, 1954), p. 48.

years the number of acceptances of compulsory jurisdiction of the Court had declined to a figure of 32 out of the 84 nominal parties to the Statute.

Some sober reflections on this score based on his experience as a judge in the International Court of Justice were recently set down by the distinguished Belgian jurist Charles De Visscher. They bear on the major themes explored in this inquiry. Regarding the distinction between legal and political disputes, he wrote:

> Recourse, to an international court implies that, and is only completely effective when, the dispute is completely separated from politics. . . . Ever-present politics blocked the effort of doctrine to give what it called a rational definition to the political dispute or to classify political and juridical disputes in sharply distinct categories.

Arbitral agreements, he wrote, "depend, on one hand, on a sufficient moral community between the contracting parties, and, on the other hand, on the condition of general political relations between them." Reservations in the arbitration treaties had a valid purpose: "Experience has shown that agreements accompanied by maturely thoughtful reservations are often those which are the most carefully observed." He concluded:

> There is no doubt . . . that a part of the present disappointment with regard to international justice is due to the survival of a state of mind which has exaggerated the possibilities of recourse to courts for the maintenance of peace.[5]

All history suggests that willingness to abide by law is the end product of a whole chain of social and political events, not the starting point. For nations consistently to act lawfully requires a generalized confidence—now lacking—that any losses they may suffer in one particular proceeding will be balanced out in the long run, as in any going legal order, by advantages based on the over-all protection and satisfactions a community would continuously furnish them.

If this is so, there is little sense in trying to "force" nations to submit disputes of vital political interest to judicial settlement as a general rule. This is not to argue that states cannot sometimes be persuaded to submit certain issues to adjudication. This is sometimes brought about by exploiting their vulnerability to public opinion, their sense of guilt, or their desire to "see the machinery used more frequently," or more concretely, by invoking the existing network of legal obligations in the United Nations Charter and other treaties. Perhaps such a development is the only practicable path to a more lawful world. Certainly its lack of lofty motivation only mirrors the pessimism that colors any analysis of recent experience.

Furthermore, if the limits of international law are not immutable, it does not necessarily follow that the axioms of politics are subject to drastic change. The experience of the past decades has shown that international problems of peaceful change more often than not involve factors no legal system could or should try to encompass. Even in domestic societies one does not legitimately expect municipal law ever to embrace completely those great areas of national life in which interests representing the plural power centers in the nation argue it out according to laboriously developed ground rules, generally without bloodshed, and ultimately through the process of legislation. Law must not be ex-

---

[5] "Reflections on the Present Prospect of International Adjudication," *American Journal of International Law,* L, No. 3 (July, 1956), 468–471.

pected to do internationally what law cannot do at home.

Domestic society, in order to keep change within peaceful bounds, requires the seamless web of mutual confidence and purposeful centralized strength without which no community could long endure. In this setting, we have long since recognized the existence of an effective and, in this sense, constitutional relationship between law, politics, and community. The great hope for international society is that men will learn to apply with perception such a constitutional conception. But the *sine qua non* is some form of consensus that can legitimately be called community. For if a true community, however modest, rather than an abstract and purely postulated community, comes alive, the judicial process can concomitantly grow and bear fruit. Such community could emerge as a mutual interest in reducing the threat of a surprise attack, or it could appear as a function of evolution in the structure of the Communist world, or in other ways.

Characteristically unwilling to wait for this necessarily slow development, we tend to become frantic, wishing away the obstacles, or conversely, betraying the disillusionment of the ex-Puritan who "has nothing left but a cynicism that clatters like invisible handcuffs tying his hands forever from any deep commitment or great purpose."[6]

While working to assist history in the creation of constitutionalism and community among the nations, we must be ever alert to the "backdoor" approaches to world law, and to their potential for growth and development. But nothing would be more fatal to the development of world community, or to the world law that will accompany its development, than to pretend that the process of politics has been, or can be, or even should be eliminated. For all our experience teaches us to assume that in that far-off world order under law, there will still be disputes that are predominantly legal and those that are political. It is only by accommodating itself to these verities of political life that law can be used to help make life work. The alternative is for the theorems of law and the facts of politics to remain locked in a meaningless and futile battle. In this battle, man is the loser.

[6] Margaret Mead, *And Keep Your Powder Dry: An Anthropologist Looks at America* (New York: William Morrow & Co., Inc., 1943), p. 204.

CHAPTER TWENTY

The Responsibility of National Leadership

In spite of the great gains that have been made in the development of international law and organization, it is still inescapably true that the responsibility for whatever degree or kind of world order may be forthcoming is that of the leaders of national states. It has been some time since the general response to an emergence of a new crisis on the world stage has been the question, "Why doesn't the United Nations do something?" It is coming to be realized that the United States, in particular, has assumed an enormous burden for the maintenance of world stability, and that this will require more sacrifice, more imagination, and more frustration rather than less of any of these qualities. Even the isolationists now accept the fact that there is no turning back the course of history, and no turning our back on the world.

The dimensions of this responsibility, and the stakes of those being led, are implicit in these words of the President of Columbia University, Grayson Kirk,

> . . . today the head of a nuclear-armed state, in his capacity as commander-in-chief of all the defense forces of his country, has literally in his own hands—unchecked by any legislative mandate—the power to plunge mankind into an unimaginable abyss. Such power did not exist in the old days of conventional weapons. Its mere existence is frightening, and it is sure to have some cautionary effect upon the selection of any head of government. We must assume, however, that leaders in this awesome position will be prudent, rational men, in which case the great-power diplomatic contest of the foreseeable future will be reasonably free from the possibility of any deliberate resort to the use of ultimate force as an instrument of state policy.[1]

Yet in a democracy it is not enough to assume that this kind of leadership will always rise to the fore. "Prudent, rational men" we have, but it is the responsibility of party organization, and ultimately of the citizen himself, to insure that these are the men in whose hands the destiny of the state will reside. If there were always a "foreign policy consensus," and it were always clear that this consensus was wise, well-informed, and far-sighted, then the bipartisan doctrine that "politics stops at the water's edge" would properly and effectively remove foreign policy from the arena of national political discourse and debate. But as

[1] "World Perspectives, 1964," *Foreign Affairs*, 43 (1964), 11.

the United States has become more deeply involved in world affairs, as the distinctions between domestic and foreign affairs have become increasingly blurred, and as the world outside our borders has come to have so much at stake in the course of American policy, the ability of the public—or at least of the "attentive public"—to take intelligent fundamental positions on international questions has become a matter whose ramifications reach far beyond our own shores. As one saddened Briton was heard to say when President Kennedy was assassinated, "in a way, he was our President too."

The problem is only partly one of information. The American people are, if not the best-informed people in the world, at least the most-informed. It is perhaps even more fundamentally a problem of outlook, insight, and wisdom. If the citizen cannot be expected to possess all these rare qualities, he owes it to himself and to the function of his country in the world to heed the words of those who do. It is for this reason that we are proud to bring to a close this volume with the words of highly respected authorities imbued with what Walter Lippmann has termed "the public philosophy."

1

*Statesmanship and Moral Choice**

Arnold Wolfers

Throughout the ages moralists have expressed horror at the way princes and sovereign states behave toward each other. Behavior which would be considered immoral by any standard can obviously be detected in all realms of life; but nowhere does the contradiction between professed ethical principles and actual behavior appear so patent and universal as in the conduct of foreign relations. Governments spy on each other and lie to each other; they violate pledges and conduct wars, often at the cost of millions of lives and untold misery. No wonder, then, that in western democracies if not elsewhere indignation over such practices should be voiced with vehemence. In our day it frequently expresses itself in wholesale denunciations of the multi-state system on the ground that sovereign states cannot deal with each other except by the use of immoral means, derogatorily called power politics. Some draw the cynical conclusion that morality has no place in international politics, while others would have men fulfill their moral duty by substituting world government for the present immoral political system.

This sweeping moral condemnation of foreign policy as pursued by all nations points to a striking and disturbing contradiction in our public life. Most of our statesmen claim to be

* *World Politics*, I (1949), 175–95. Reprinted by permission.

pursuing policies of peace and enunciate high moral principles upon which their policy is supposed to be based; they and many publicists praise the democracies for the moral superiority of their conduct of foreign affairs over that of aggressive and ruthless dictators. Yet at the same time many respected students in the field of international relations insist that all sovereign states alike are compelled by the "system" to play the evil game of power politics. The two positions would seem to be incompatible. Either our statesmen and their supporters are deceiving themselves and others or those who without discrimination condemn all power politics as immoral are overstating the case. In a country like the United States where moral passion tends to run high and where the question of morality in politics is a matter of genuine and wide concern, it is important to try to resolve this contradiction.

The idea that power politics are beyond the pale of morality is not new. Down through the centuries Machiavelli and Machiavellianism have stood for a doctrine which places princes and sovereign states under the rule not of ordinary morality but of the "reason of state," considered an amoral principle peculiar to the realm of politics.[1] German writers have been particularly insistent that ethical standards which apply to private individuals cannot measure the behavior of states which are said to be guided by necessity if not by a *höhere Sittlichkeit.*[2]

The English-speaking world, not seldom accused of comfortably ignoring or hypocritically denying the contradictions between ethics and international politics, has been unwilling on the whole to admit of any peculiar ethics of state behavior. Because states are abstractions, or at best fictitious personalities, it is not the state that decides and acts but always individuals, though they be statesmen. Should their behavior be judged differently from that of other individuals merely because they act for the state? To answer in the affirmative would mean accepting the hardly more palatable idea of a double standard of morality, according to which individuals when acting for themselves shall follow one set of moral principles while the same individuals when conducting their nation's foreign policy shall be bound by another and presumably less stringent code of behavior.[3]

[1] One might question whether Machiavelli meant to draw a sharp distinction between the ethics of state behavior, the behavior of "princes," which was his main concern, and the ethics of individual behavior. In the same Chapter XV of *The Prince,* in which he advises the sovereign to learn "how not to be good," he also speaks generally of the condition of man, saying that "whoever abandons what is done for what ought to be done will rather learn to bring about his own ruin than his preservation." He goes on to say that such a man "must necessarily come to grief among so many who are not good."

[2] Friedrich Meinecke's *Die Idee der Staatsräson,* Munich and Berlin, 1925, is a classic study of the relations between ethics and power politics as seen by Machiavelli and his continental disciples down to Treitschke. No similar study has been written on the views of their Anglo-Saxon contemporaries, though Gerhard Ritter, in *Machtstaat und Utopie,* Munich and Berlin, 1914, makes a suggestive beginning to such a study. He contrasts Machiavelli, "pioneer of the continental power state," with Thomas More, "ideological father of the English insular welfare state"—the former setting power above morality (p. 31), the latter seeking the "Ethisierung und Entdämonisierung der Macht" (p. 89).

[3] While Hans J. Morgenthau in *Scientific Man vs. Power Politics,* (Chicago: University of Chicago Press, 1946), declares that "No civilization can be satisfied with . . . a dual morality" (p. 179), William Ernest Hocking, *The Spirit of World Politics,*

At first sight the facts seem to bear this out. Do we not condemn and punish citizens for committing the very acts of violence, treaty violation or untruthfulness which we condone in international politics? Are we not constantly struck by the gulf that separates the relatively peaceful and humane life within the national borders of states from the events occurring on the international scene? It is this contrast—more apparent than true, as we shall see—that has led some to demand that statesmen be made to give up their sinful ways and to conform to the rules of behavior expected from individuals in an orderly community. Unfortunately, advice of this kind often proves so patently impractical that instead of inducing statesmen to mend their ways it provokes in them a sense of moral cynicism. What is the use of listening to moral advice, they ask, if statesmanship, capable of mastering the problems which present themselves in practice, is apparently incompatible with morality?

The fundamental discrepancy which seems to exist between the morality of "state" and private behavior would disappear only if it could be shown that politics conducted in a multi-state system is not necessarily any more immoral than average private behavior, or that the chief difference pertains not to the degree of immorality prevailing in the two spheres of human action but to the circumstances under which men are required to act. Much of what strikes people as immoral practices of governments may prove to be morally justified by the peculiar and unhappy circumstances which the statesman has to face and which, moreover, he may often be unable to change.

(New York: The Macmillan Company, 1932), writes that statesmen distrust public opinion in international affairs because the public "takes for granted that the codes (for individuals and for states) are the same." E. H. Carr, *The Twenty Years' Crisis* (London: Macmillan & Co., Ltd., 1940), in contrast to these authors, asserts that most people, while believing that states ought to act morally, do not expect of them the same kind of moral behavior which they expect of themselves and of one another (p. 199).

Any ethical perfectionist will be shocked at such a suggestion. He will deny that any action that would be evil under one set of conditions could be morally justified under another. If men are held to be morally bound to act in accordance with an absolute ethic of love such as the Sermon on the Mount, obviously no set of circumstances, even circumstances in which the survival of a nation were at stake, could justify acts such as a resort to violence, untruthfulness, or treaty violation. The concern for self-preservation and power in itself would have to be condemned as evil. This being the case, the ethical perfectionist can offer no advice to statesmen other than that they give up public office and turn their backs on politics. As a matter of fact, in order to be consistent, the perfectionist, as some have pointed out, must give the same advice to private citizens, requiring of them that they abandon their concern for their own welfare, for family or business. If, as Hans Morganthau holds, "the very act of acting destroys our moral integrity," only a life of saintliness could come close to satisfying perfectionist moral commands.[4]

We must address ourselves exclusively then to the non-perfectionist who demands of man, not that he follow an absolute code of ethical rules—what Max Weber calls the "natural law of absolute imperatives"—but that he make the best moral choice which the circumstances permit.[5]

[4] Hans J. Morgenthau, *op. cit.*, p. 189.

[5] See Max Weber's "Politics as a Voca-

But surely, it will be objected, no moralist, at least in our culture, could deviate so far from perfectionist standards as to condone even in wartime such inhuman practices as the torture of enemy soldiers or the shooting of hostages. One would wish that this objection would always be valid, but the fact is that the non-perfectionist cannot escape the conclusion that circumstances may justify what superficially appear to be the most despicable kinds of human conduct. Or would he condemn without careful prior investigation all the members of the French Resistance movement who, in the face of brutal Nazi tactics, are said to have answered their enemy in kind. What if they were unable to discover any other alternatives but either to stop in this repulsive fashion the horrors committed by the Nazis or else to leave their friends and their cause unprotected? This does not imply that circumstances morally justify every act of power politics from the violation of the pledged word to aggression and concentration camps; the chances are that in most instances they will not, whether because the cause is unworthy of such extreme sacrifices or because other means are available which will assure morally preferable over-all results. Nor does it mean that where circumstances do justify such acts men may not be guilty of having brought about these circumstances or of having failed to remove them.

There is nothing peculiar to international politics in this impact of circumstance. Our conscience revolts at the idea of men putting other men to death. Yet non-perfectionist moralists throughout the western world agree in condoning the acts of those who kill in self-defense, in obedience to an order to execute a criminal, in war, or possibly in the case of tyrannicide. In other cultures it has been considered morally proper, if not a moral duty, to put the first born, aging parents, or widows to death. One and the same act, then, will be judged differently depending on the context within which it is performed and depending also, of course, on the ethical standards by which behavior in general is judged.

This is not the place to enter upon the age-old discussion of what the standards of a non-perfectionist ethic should be, nor is such a discussion necessary for our purpose. However much non-perfectionists may disagree on ethical standards and thus on the nature and hierarchy of values, they hold in common the process by which they reach their moral judgments. They start with the conviction that there can be no escape from sacrifices of value whether, as theologians maintain, because of man's original sin and essential corruption, or because of the dilemmas of a world in which man is faced with incompatible moral claims. With this as a basis they hold that men, statesmen and private individuals alike, are morally required to choose among the roads open to them the one which under the circumstances promises to produce the least over-all destruction of value or, positively speaking, points toward the maximization of value.[6]

tion," in *From Max Weber: Essays in Sociology*, (New York: Oxford University Press, 1946), pp. 120 ff.

[6] Max Weber's "ethic of responsibility," (*op. cit.*, pp. 118 ff.) comes closer to what is here described as a non-perfectionist ethic of maximization of value than it might appear from some of his statements. Weber, it is true, declares that "from no ethics in the world can it be concluded when and to what extent the ethically good purpose 'justifies' the ethically dangerous means and ramification" (p. 121). He is here taking issue with the revolutionary fanatic who from the point of view of an "ethic of ultimate ends" considers every act of violence justified so long as it serves his ultimate end. But when

Moral condemnation, according to non-perfectionist ethics, rests not on the fact that values have been destroyed, however deplorable or downright evil such destruction may be judged. Instead it is based on the conviction either that the action in question rested on false ethical standards or that in terms of agreed ethical standards a less destructive choice could and should have been made.[7]

Thus a private citizen who breaks family ties in order to serve what he considers a higher cause may find himself condemned because his cause is not considered worth the sacrifice or because there were other less costly ways of attaining his end. Similarly a statesman who decides to break off diplomatic negotiations rather than to accept the terms of the opposing side may be judged wrong because he placed undue value on an increment of national prestige which was at stake or because he failed to appreciate properly the dangers involved in his choice of action. There is no difference either in the method of evaluation or in the ethical standards, whether the case be one of political or private behavior. In that sense the ethic of politics is but a part of general ethics. The question which remains to be answered, however, is why the sacrifices of value in international politics should be as widespread, continuous, and shocking in extent as they so obviously are. Is it because the circumstances under which foreign policy is conducted are so different and so unalterably different from those under which private citizens make their choices?

German writers on international politics have emphasized what they consider a unique and all-pervasive circumstance characteristic of inter-state relations. Writing in the heyday of German *Realpolitik* Ratzenhofer declared categorically that the relations between sovereign states are unalterably relations of enmity.[8] His assertion reminds one of the no less dogmatic Marxist proposition according to which the relations between capital and labor in a capitalist economy are relations of enemies engaged in a class war.[9]

If one looks at the facts of history and of the contemporary world, one cannot subscribe to this German view. Instead it seems as if the relations between sovereign states no less than the relations between other groups or individuals run the whole gamut from almost complete amity—take Canadian-American or Anglo-Canadian relations—to almost unmitigated enmity, as in the days of war. Amity and en-

Weber goes on to demand of men that they hold themselves responsible for the consequences of their acts, especially their acts of violence, he does not refute their moral right to "contract with the diabolic powers of violence" which as political men they must do, but implicitly calls on them to choose the road which will minimize the evil consequences for which they bear responsibility.

[7] Hans J. Morgenthau, *op. cit.*, following in the footsteps of Max Weber, also emphasizes the "ethical paradoxes" of politics. "Political ethics," he says, "is indeed the ethics of doing evil" (p. 202). Yet he too concludes that "it is moral judgment," meaning presumably the best a man can morally do "to choose among several expedient actions the least evil one" (p. 203).

[8] See Gustav Ratzenhofer, *Wesen und Zweck der Politik*, (Leipzig, 1893).

[9] Carl Schmitt, in *Der Begriff des Politischen*, (Munich, 1932), modifies Ratzenhofer's thesis by declaring that inter-state and, in fact, all truly political relations are in the nature of "friend-foe" relations. While he does not claim that relations between all states at all times are inevitably hostile, he maintains that nations always group themselves as friends and foes and that, there could be no such thing as statehood or politics if it were not for the existence of potential enmity, by which he means the possibility of deadly physical combat.

mity appear as the two extreme poles of a wide scale of human relationships. It remains true, however, and a matter of great political and moral consequence, that the multi-state system, for reasons which cannot be analyzed here, has a tendency to push relations between at least some states in the direction of enmity—and, for that matter, more so in our century than in the last. The Nazis certainly saw to it that this would be so. As faithful disciples of Gustav Ratzenhofer, Carl Schmitt and others, they not only believed in the inevitability of international enmity but true to their theoretical assumption conducted German policy in such a way as to arouse the fiercest kind of enmity in most parts of the world.

The concepts of amity and enmity can be usefully employed to shed light on the context within which statesmen are forced to make their choices. They stand for the two opposite and marginal extremes of human relationships. Behavior changes as the relationship approximates one or the other of these poles. The causes of enmity in interstate relations are significant to the moral problem only to the extent to which statesmen may be responsible for bringing about or for not eliminating enmity, and thus become responsible for the consequences of such enmity.

One can imagine a condition of complete enmity between states. There would be no trace of community between them, no sense of commonly held values or of common interest. Each individual state would have to be looked upon as an entirely separate entity operating in the social vacuum of absolute anarchy. There would exist a state of latent if not actual war all the time, turning diplomacy into warfare with other means. With good reason nations could consider themselves in a constant state of emergency with all the things gravely endangered to which they attached value. It would be a situation, as we know it from the experience of total war, in which the sheer quest for survival would justify almost any course of action. "Out-group morality" of the most extreme type would prevail.

Take the other extreme, that of amity or the "friend-to-friend" relationship. While there would be no complete identification, a sense of community would exist sufficient to eliminate mutual fear and suspicion. There would be no expectation of violence and therefore no need for preparations with which to meet the dangers of conflict. Despite the fact that each state would be sovereign, or rather because each state would be free to handle its own affairs, such friendly nations could behave toward each other according to the codes of "in-group morality" and live in peace with each other.

The more relations between states degenerate toward enmity the more nations are justified in fearing for the things they cherish and the more reason they have to make and require sacrifices by which inimical claims can be defeated. Greater enmity therefore increases the likelihood that Machiavellian practices will become necessary and morally justified. The degree of amity or enmity thus appears as a morally portentous circumstance. While in a state of amity, statesmen are likely to be able to choose between different avenues toward cooperation, compromise, and conciliation. Enmity, however, may preclude such choices and place before the statesman a different set of alternatives. He may be able to take steps which will promise to mitigate if not to eliminate existing enmity. Often, however, he will have to choose between efforts to deter his opponent, thereby neutralizing the effects of enmity, and efforts to defeat him.

This cannot be said to be a peculiarity of international politics or of the multi-state system. The same phenomenon can be found in the relationship between father and son, employer and and employee, white and colored man. There may be complete amity between them with no trace of distrust, no shadow of fear, no concern for self-protection, no awareness of conflicting demands or expectations. But here, too, relations may degenerate into fierce hostility for reasons too numerous to detail. Behavior then may change beyond recognition.

. . . .

It will be objected, and rightly so, that intra-state relations are less likely than inter-state relations to reach a degree of hostility that would call for the use of violence and other Machiavellian devices.[10] The state protects many of the values to which people are attached. The state can also prohibit the use of means to which society is opposed and can enforce its prohibition —though only by the very means which the components of that society have renounced for themselves. This holds true, however, only for well organized states where the government can marshal sufficient authority and police power to prevent family feuds and social or racial conflicts from breaking into the open and degenerating into violence and the use of other Machiavellian means. But while the pacifying influence of such a state and its influence on human behavior should not be minimized, exponents of world statehood tend to exaggerate the case for government.[11] The kind of government and therefore the kind of internal peace which this country enjoys at this time represents the exception rather than the rule. Our government operates under conditions, not wholly state-made, of widespread amity between most of the groups that are powerful enough to influence the course of domestic events. It is recognized as legitimate by practically everyone and is ordinarily obeyed not because it has the force of coercion but because its authority is freely accepted. If one looks at the performance of other governments either in the contemporary world or in past periods of history, one finds no lack of examples of governments operating under quite different conditions and with quite different results.

Some governments are strong and ruthless enough to suppress the hostilities that would otherwise break out between warring factions, ethnic, social, or religious, but they do so by means of suppression, often tyrannical or terroristic. Rather than eliminate Machiavellian practices, such governments merely monopolize them. To what extremes of behavior this may

[10] Some writers while agreeing that the ethical problems of political and private life are basically the same nevertheless stress the difference, if only quantitative, which makes international power politics the domain of evil *par excellence.* In his earlier works Reinhold Niebuhr stresses the peculiar selfishness and immorality of human communities including the state, as indicated by the title of his book, *Moral Man and Immoral Society,* (New York: Charles Scribner's Sons, 1936). Later, however, he places more emphasis on the fact that all life is a "contest of power" and that international war and conflict are but a revelation of the general character of human existence and human sinfulness. (See his *Christianity and Power Politics,* (New York: Charles Scribner's Sons, 1940), especially pages 11, 12, and 103.)

[11] Mortimer Adler, *How To Think About War and Peace,* (New York: Simon and Schuster, Inc., 1944), declares anarchy to be the only cause of war and defines anarchy as "the condition of those who try to live without government" (p. 69).

lead has been drastically demonstrated by the way modern totalitarian regimes have persecuted the "enemies of the people." Other governments are too weak to control the forces of internal enmity; then there are bloody revolts or civil wars. When that happens enmity often reaches a degree of fierceness which relations between states rarely approximate. Machiavellian practices of the most extreme kind become the order of the day.

Government or statehood, whether national or world-wide, is therefore no panacea against those aspects of power politics which are morally deplorable. The real evil is enmity and its threat to values to which people are devoted.

However, the moralist needs to be reminded of the fact that there is not only no sure way to eliminate the fateful circumstances of enmity but that [at] a given time there may be no way at all. Certainly the elimination of the multistate system itself, whether within a region such as Europe or on a world-wide scale is not one of the objectives statesmen are free to choose and therefore morally obliged to choose under all circumstances. Even if a radical change in the existing order were morally desirable because there was reason to suppose that a regional federation or a world government would create circumstances of greater amity than exist today, the psychological prerequisites for a concerted move of major nations toward such a goal are beyond the control of governments.

If it be true that statesmen cannot at all times choose to work for conditions of world-wide amity under world government, is it not their moral duty at least to promote amity at all times and at all costs? Once it is conceded that enmity requires and justifies sacrifices of value often of the most shocking kind, it would seem as if no price paid for amity could be considered too high. Yet statesmen would be rendered incapable of maximizing value if, without respect for the context in which they were forced to operate in a given instance, the quest for amity were taken as the sole measure of their actions. Amity is a condition passionately to be desired; but there are times when efforts to bring it about will lead to disaster. It takes two to make friends. An attempt to establish bonds of friendship may be interpreted as a sign of weakness; the result may be aggression. Again the demands of the opponent may call for sacrifices of value greater than those connected with continued enmity. Firmness and even resort to force may under certain circumstances require less loss of life, less human suffering, less destruction of faith and principle than the most sincere attempt to eliminate the causes of hostility by concessions.

This is not the same as saying that power politics generally preclude the opportunity for persistent and active pursuit of amity—or of justice for that matter. There are many occasions when disputes can be settled peacefully and when enmity can be eliminated or avoided, provided one side at least has enough courage, imagination and initiative. Sometimes a spirit of conciliation or even of generosity can do wonders in evoking a ready and sincere response. Whenever the lines of enmity are not irreparably drawn, there may remain room for moderation and self-restraint, for better understanding of each other's true designs and for fair compromise. While it is true that in the end it needs two to make friends, it is not always the other side which must take the first step.[12]

[12] Winston Churchill, *The Gathering Storm,* (Boston: Houghton Mifflin Company, 1948), p. 320, testifies admirably to these opportunities for statesmanship. He says

Only those who extol the value of national "virility" which is supposed to express itself in obstinate resistance to compromise, or those who are afraid of being the suckers will insist that the "necessity of state" is always on the side of toughness and unrelenting assertion of national claims. Harold Nicolson castigates Napoleon for being able to ascribe Castlereagh's "splendid moderation" only to treachery or corruption, ignorance or folly.[13] Whether moderation is politically practical or suicidal depends on the circumstances. Those who feel called upon to give moral advice to statesmen must be realists if they are to be true to the tenets of non-perfectionist ethics to demand restraint of power, charity and forgiveness in our situation, as when feelings of revenge and war passions run high, but to insist on a break with an opponent, if not on the use of violence, when weakness or procrastination threatens to bring on greater evils. If world government were not only practical but would, if established, temper enmities and help nations protect or attain what they rightly value most highly, it would be the moral duty of statesmen to seek to bring it about. As things stand today, however, lack of consensus among the major nations about the desirability of world government, as well as about the kind of world government they would accept is so obvious that any attempt to establish such a government today would be more likely to lead to war than to reduce enmity.

To the extent that enmity exists and cannot be eliminated at a given moment it would appear to dictate to the statesman a course of action that will often run counter to his moral preferences. Does this not mean that those exponents of *Realpolitik* are right who claim that the statesman, instead of being able to make moral choices, is left with virtually no leeway, having to bow to the dictates of the "necessity of state?"

It confuses the moral issue to state the case in this way. The "necessities" in international politics and for that matter in all spheres of life do not push decision and action beyond the realm of moral judgment; they rest on moral choice themselves. If a statesman decides that the dangers to the security of his country are so great that a course of action which must lead to war is necessary, he has placed an exceedingly high value on an increment of national security.

Necessities of a similar kind are known to private citizens. Parents may decide that in order to save the family business they must try to get their son to enter the family firm. Although they know that they are asking him to choose a career he abhors, they are ready to sacrifice his happiness to the "necessity of family." A trade union leader who calls a strike which he knows to be ruinous to patrons to whom he is devoted makes and requires a painful sacrifice for the "necessities" of the labor movement. In every such case conflicting values, interests and loyalties call for choices in which what is deemed to be the higher

"those who are prone by temperament and character to seek sharp and clear-cut solutions of difficult and obscure problems, who are ready to fight whenever some challenge comes from a foreign Power, have not always been right. On the other hand, those whose inclination is to bow their heads, to seek patiently and faithfully for peaceful compromise, are not always wrong. On the contrary, in the majority of instances they may be right, not only morally but from a practical standpoint. How many wars have been averted by patience and persisting good will!"

13 Harold Nicolson, *The Congress of Vienna*, (London, Constable & Co., Ltd., 1946), p. 236.

cause or value calls for submission to its necessities.

It is no play on words to say that the necessity or reason of state is but another of these necessities of life which become compelling only as a particular pattern of values is accepted. If the position of the statesman differs from that of private citizens it is because he must take upon himself the responsibility for sacrifices of value in order that others, as a nation, may protect or attain the things which they treasure. He may feel in duty bound to do so even though in a given instance he may disagree with the moral judgment of those to whom he is responsible. In that sense if in no other it may be justifiable to speak of the peculiar "demonic" quality of politics and public office, as Max Weber and other writers frequently do.

There is good reason why the controversy about the relationship between necessity of state and ethical standards should be rife in our culture. It points to a clash between two sets of ethical standards, one Christian or humanistic, the other nationalistic. Nationalistic ethics place what are called vital national interests—and not national survival only—at the very pinnacle of the hierarchy of values. The preservation or attainment of these values—territorial integrity, colonial possessions, *Lebensraum*, treaty rights or economic interests—are therefore assumed to justify the sacrifice of almost every other value whether it be life, generosity, humane treatment of others, truthfulness or obedience to the law. Especially, the interests of other nations count for little, if anything, on a nationalistic scale of values.

While those who adhere to nonperfectionist Christian or humanistic ethical views accept the fact that sacrifices of value are inescapable, as nonnationalists they may nevertheless, in the case of any policy decision, question whether a particular national interest is worth the sacrifices required or could not be protected by a less costly method. This may not seem to hold true when national survival itself is unquestionably at stake. It could properly be said that the multi-state system, since it rests on the co-existence of a multitude of independent states, is incompatible with any ethic which would forbid sacrifices necessary for national survival. Moral advice not to submit to the necessities of survival would not only be advice to commit national suicide but would tend to wreck the multi-state system itself.[14]

As a matter of fact, the controversy between exponents of nationalistic and non-nationalistic ethical standards in our culture is not over the moral right to pay the price of sur-

[14] It is not surprising that authors who believe that international politics is essentially a struggle for national survival should reach very pessimistic ethical conclusions. Thus, Nicholas J. Spykman, *America's Strategy in World Politics,* (New York: Harcourt, Brace & World, 1942), bases his case on the proposition that "the struggle for power is identical with the struggle for survival" and that states can survive only by constant devotion to power politics. Although the use of power "should be constantly subjected to moral judgments" (p. 12), Spykman concludes that the "statesman can concern himself with values of justice, fairness and tolerance only to the extent that they contribute to or do not interfere with the power objective," meaning the quest for survival. In his further statement that the quest for power is not made for "the achievement of moral values" he is taking issue with those exponents of nationalistic ethics who place supreme moral value on national survival. See also in this connection Mortimer Adler's statement that "so long as national self-preservation remains the dominant end for which prudence must choose means, the principles of morality cannot be reconciled with the counsels of prudence" (*op. cit.,* p. 78).

vival. None but the perfectionists or absolute pacifists deny a nation which is engaged in a life and death struggle the right to make and demand every sacrifice necessary for victory.

But this is not the same as saying that the non-perfectionist must capitulate before every alleged "necessity of state." Nations engaged in international politics are faced with the problem of survival only on rare occasions. How otherwise could it be explained that most of the nations which have attained independence in recent centuries have survived when surely most of them most of the time have been devoted to anything but an unrestrained quest for power? If ever any country did employ Machiavellian principles consciously and methodically it was Hitler's Germany, but with the result that she lost her independence as conclusively as few great nations have done.

As a rule, not survival but other "national interests" are at stake, such as the preservation of outlying bases and possessions, the protection of treaty rights, the restoration of national honor, or the maintenance of economic advantages. While it is a prerequisite of the system that nations attach a high if not the highest value to their survival, the same cannot be said of these other national interests. As a matter of fact, the moral dilemmas with which statesmen and their critics are constantly faced revolve around the question of whether in a given instance the defense or satisfaction of interests other than survival justify the costs in other values. Does the expropriation of American investments abroad, for instance, justify the choice of military intervention rather than of unpromising negotiations? Is it morally preferable to risk a loss of prestige with its possible dangerous consequences for the safety of the country rather than to insist on maintaining a position which threatens to provoke hostilities? In every case the interpretation of what constitutes a vital national interest and how much value should be attached to it is a moral question. It cannot be answered by reference to alleged amoral necessities inherent in international politics; it rests on value judgments.

Even national survival itself, it should be added, is a morally compelling necessity only as long as people attach supreme value to it. In that sense the multi-state system itself depends on a value pattern in which there is an element of nationalism. If at any time those who have the power to decide over the foreign policies of the major countries should come to attach higher value to the attainment of world government than to the preservation of independence, the psychological, though not necessarily all other practical, obstacles to world government would be removed.[15] Until that happens nations art likely to consent to all kinds of Machiavellian practices, however much they may abhor them, whenever they are con-

---

[15] R. M. MacIver, *The Web of Government*, (New York: The Macmillan Company, 1947), suggests that these basic value judgments may change as the old myths of national sovereignty and national interests lose their grip on people, while Arnold Toynbee, *A Study of History*, (New York and London: Oxford University Press, 1947), p. 299, passing moral judgment, denounces the "pagan worship of sovereign nation-states" calling it a monstrous product of the impact of parochialism on the Western Christian Church." See, in this connection, also Harold Lasswell, *World Politics and Personal Insecurity*, (New York and London: McGraw-Hill Book Company, 1935), who devotes Chapter XI, "In Quest of a Myth: The Problem of World Unity," to the problem of how, by the use of symbols, myths, and other practices, human value judgments might be changed in favor of world unity.

vinced that their independence can be saved in no other way.

International politics offer some opportunities and temptations for immoral action on a vast and destructive scale; they tend to present themselves in the guise of "necessity of state." Statesmen in command of the machinery by which public opinion can be manipulated may make it appear as if they were acting for the sake of objectives to which the people attach high value when in fact they are out to serve material personal interests or to satisfy personal ambitions for power. Where men wield as much power as they do in international politics there is room for an infinite variety of abuses for which the "necessity of state" can serve as a convenient cloak. Then again, statesmen may sincerely believe that a particular course of action is dictated by vital national interests; but judged by non-nationalistic standards of ethics they may be placing undue value on certain interests of their people or underestimating the value of things not pertaining to their nation which their policy would sacrifice.

While this makes moral criticism and self-criticism imperative, the difficulties which stand in the way of their proper use in international politics need to be emphasized. If it is hard for statesmen to make proper moral choices, it is not any easier for others to do justice to their conduct of foreign policy.

It is a baffling task, almost exceeding human capacity, to compare the value of an increment of national security with the value of human lives, or the value of a continued period of peace with the risks of a more destructive war in the future. Yet the statesman is faced with even more exacting and truly terrifying problems. Forced to make his choices whenever a decision is called for, he may have to compare the value of an uncertain chance of greater security with only roughly predictable risks of conflict and destruction. It may be easy with hindsight, and years after the event, to condemn a statesman for having failed to maximize value; but it also becomes increasingly difficult as time goes on to do justice to the inevitable lack of knowledge and foresight under which the decision-maker labored at the time. Yalta is a good example to illustrate this moral problem.[16]

The trouble about much of the moral condemnation of foreign policies and with much of the moral advice tendered to statesmen goes back to a lack of appreciation of the kind of knowledge required for proper and useful moral criticism in international affairs. From a non-perfectionist point of view the circumstances, however technical, have to be taken into consideration; moral conviction and high ideals, much as they are needed to guide moral judgment, cannot by themselves offer an answer. Nor is this true in international politics only. It needs some knowledge of economics to judge whether an industrialist is exploiting his workers; he may be paying the highest wages the traffic will bear. It needs psychological understanding to decide whether in a particular situation divorce represents morally the least evil choice.

Similarly, in international politics where the circumstances are no less involved and technical, moral convictions cannot tell what roads are open to a statesman under the specific conditions under which he is forced to act, nor can they reveal what the political consequences and therefore the

[16] See Rudolph A. Winnacker, "Yalta—Another Munich?" in *The Virginia Quarterly Review*, Vol. 24, No. 4 (Autumn, 1948), 521–537.

relative costs in terms of value of any one of several courses of action are likely to be. Will an alliance provoke war or will the failure to make a commitment tempt an aggressor? Will an appeal to the United Nations in a given case help bring about a peaceful settlement or instead create graver tension, perhaps even going so far as to destroy the organization? Disarmament may be morally the best choice under one set of circumstances; it may be downright evil in another in which it would place a nation—and small nations dependent upon it for their security—at the mercy of an ambitious conqueror. The same holds true for all the other panaceas or devices so dear to the heart of those who are most quickly ready to give moral advice to policy-makers or to condemn them for their actions. In one context it may be right to offer concessions whereas in another it may constitute "appeasement" with all of its evil consequences.

There might seem to be one exception to the rule that no general principle can guide non-perfectionist moral judgment on all occasions. It might seem proper to assume that the "defensive" side is always right and that every action is justified and justified only if necessary for the protection and preservation of values already possessed. Unfortunately, while individuals can disprove their guilt if they can rightly claim to have acted in self-defense, the case of nations is far more complex. Neither the nation's self nor its possessions are clearly circumscribed. May a nation defend as its self and its possessions only its territorial integrity and independence, or does the right of self-defense cover a way of life, national honor, living space, prestige, colonial possessions and economic rights abroad? *Status quo* powers whose main concern is the preservation of the values they possess and therefore the defense of the established order are prone to blame all Machiavellianism on those nations that seek to bring about change, whether it be revision of treaties, revolution of the social order or liberation from foreign domination. Yet, the "offensive" side may have a valid case for insisting that it has a vital need for things withheld from it and may rightly value them to a point where any means of attaining them become morally justified. Those who refuse to make the sacrifices of change or who, having brought about an unjust distribution of possessions and power are unwilling to correct it, may be guilty of provoking enmity and aggression. If the Moslems in India or the Zionists in Palestine resorted to violence, they were not defending an existing order but were seeking to establish new and independent national homes through changes in the existing order. They were not necessarily at fault merely because they wanted these changes so urgently or because they despaired of any means short of violence. The *beati possidentes* may be more peaceful and less inclined to initiate open hostility, but their guilt may lie in their self-righteous and blind devotion to the *status quo* or in the resentment which they evoke in others.

Despite the difficulties of doing justice to the statesman and of avoiding the pitfalls of politically dangerous as well as morally untenable condemnations, men who have non-perfectionist and non-nationalistic moral convictions dare not evade the task of moral judgment whether of their own political acts or of the acts of others. Where there is so much room for moral choices as there is in international politics and where the destiny of entire nations depends on these choices, attempts to evade, silence or ignore moral judgment merely play into the hands of those who relish the uncriticized use or abuse of their power. The Nazi leaders were helped by the climate of moral cynicism which prevailed in Germany. It made it easy for them to justify even the most brutal acts on the grounds of necessity of state or to glorify their freedom from any "decadent" moral inhibitions.

The world will not fail to suffer from the immoral acts of statesmen as of other men in the future as it has in the past, nor does it look as though nations would soon be freed from the bitter consequences of international enmity, or from the appalling sacrifices inflicted and justified in the name of national interest and survival. A single powerful government, engaged for whatever reasons, in a policy of aggression and aggrandizement may force all others into line with its Machiavellian practices, provided these others have the will to survive. In such cases moral exhortations and intentions will serve little unless the causes of such aggression and the dangers inherent in it are removed.

Yet international politics are not beyond the pale of non-nationalistic, non-perfectionist morality. Statesmen need not be fooling either themselves or others if they contend, as they frequently do, that in specific instances they have restrained their nation's quest for power; nor need they apologize if, on occasion, they choose a conciliatory or even a generous course of action, though a more egotistical policy would promise more tangible national benefits. Despite the continued strength of nationalist sentiment in all parts of the world, there is no reason to assume that people value national benefits only. They often attach a great deal of value to a good record of international collaboration and at times applaud a leader who takes risks for the good will, the amity or the interests of other nations—or seeks to keep his own conscience and that of his people clear.

This explains why under certain circumstances a national government might receive the backing of its people even in sacrificing national independence itself, particularly if it were done for the purpose of establishing a better international order, perhaps a world-wide federation. From the point of view of non-nationalistic ethics such national self-sacrifice for world government might appear morally justified if there was assurance of enough amity and all-round consent to permit the establishment and functioning of an orderly and humane government of the world; it might be condemned if it led to world tyranny or world anarchy. There are historical instances when such sacrifice of independence has justified itself in the eyes of almost everybody, as when the thirteen American states federated successfully.

Under the circumstances usually prevailing in a multi-state system painful limitations are set on policies of self-negation, generosity or restraint of power. It would be utopian to expect drastic changes in this respect. But to say that the field of international politics is reserved for selfishness, brutality, self-righteousness, or unrestrained ambition for power is not only cynical but manifestly unrealistic.

2

*The Problem of Incompatible Purposes**

Charles Burton Marshall

Charles Burton Marshall, *who holds degrees from the University of Texas and Harvard University, has a varied background. He has worked as a newspaperman, a teacher (at Harvard University and Radcliffe College), an officer in the U.S. Army during World War II, a consultant to the Committee on Foreign Affairs of the House of Representatives (1947–1950), and a member of the Policy Planning Staff of the Department of State from 1950 to 1953. Since that time he has published* The Limits of Foreign Policy *(1954), and has held positions with The Washington Center of Foreign Policy Research and The Carnegie Endowment for International Peace.*

In international affairs, as in other fields, simple terms are used to communicate about hugely comple, shifting, multifarious situations and relationships. There never would be time enough to think, to remember, or to discuss if one had always to describe fully the phenomena concerned. So to keep tabs on ideas, we put tabs on them. The tabs then tend themselves to become legal tender in the exchange places of ideas as if they had independent meaning and validity. This leads to a great deal of fallacy, and it becomes necessary from time to time to refresh comprehension of the processes for which the tabs are only symbols—in a shift of metaphor, to restore the edges of words dulled by ill usage.

A number of words and phrases in the common lexicon of international affairs come to mind as illustrations—*the cold war, balance of power, the rule of law, the battle for men's minds, containment, liberation, the free world, aggression, peace with justice, alliance,* and so on and on. Anyone can make his own list of the poster words which publicists, professors and practitioners use often with careless regard for the complex actualities.

Just now an overworked tab is *negotiation,* closely attended by *disengagement* and *relaxation of tensions.* It is to negotiation that I wish to give academic attention.

A catalogue of the vapid, inapposite things said with high solemnity . . . [about] negotiations on both sides of the Atlantic would be as long as your arm. I can deal here with only a few of them.

"What harm would there be in our talking to the Russians?" is a question put by a Midwestern newspaper. The same issue contained two long news items demonstrating that in fact our Government was doing just that already, and being talked to voluminously in turn. The idea that negotiation is necessary to cure Washington or Moscow of being tongue-tied is ob-

* *East-West Negotiation* (The Washington Center of Foreign Policy Research, 1958), pp. 68–73. Reprinted by permission.

viously specious. Has there ever been a time of fuller communication between adversaries than the present?

"Negotiation at least might lead to better understanding even if it did not produce agreements," a professor said at a dinner meeting. One hears this idea repeatedly. It is as if a reservoir of reconciliation were secreted in the rock waiting only to be smitten by negotiation, whereupon it would gush forth in abundant streams. The nub, I suspect, is that in fact our Government and the one in Moscow actually understand each other quite well.

One current notion about negotiation attributes to it qualities of an intercollegiate debate—an exercise in histrionics and logic, with the decision going to the side scoring best in presentation. It is as if at a certain point in the argument across the table [their man] might say to [our man], "All right, you've got me! I can't answer that one. So what are your terms?"

Another notion attributes to negotiation the characteristics of a one-shot business deal. Let us call this the haggling theory of negotiation—or the Yankee trader theory. One can imagine the American and the Russian arguing about prices and the quality of the goods—[our man] making for the door in feigned scorn with [their man] turning around with a shrug to put the fabrics on the shelf and then each turning back to renew the bargaining until at last the price is right.

A third notion conceives of negotiation in terms of a Quaker meeting—as if the spirit of togetherness descends upon a gathering, bringing new insights, new efficacy, and a new spirit of reconciliation through the interaction of souls in propinquity. This view of negotiation let us label as the inspirational theory.

In searching for illustrations of these views of negotiation, I happened to come across all three in one context. It is an item in a recent issue of *Saturday Review.* It refers to a speech by Alf Landon to a teacher's meeting in Kansas and characterizes him as sounding "more like a yeasty young liberal than a former Republican candidate for President." The article then quotes him as urging "that we should use our Yankee ingenuity in a summit meeting," continuing, "Instead of saying no-no-no to the Soviet's proposal for a summit conference, why don't we sit down and start arguing?" The quotation then goes on: "The Secretary of State says we can't trust them. Who wants to? Americans were famous once as Yankee traders who always got their money's worth. They didn't bother about the religion, the political philosophy, or sincerity of the other party, just so the deal suited them." The *Saturday Review's* writer endorses all that and adds on his own: "The time seems ripe for a fresh, imaginative, and inspired approach to international relations."

There we have the three—sit down and start arguing, get your money's worth and don't worry about sincerity, and finally get inspired.

According to my dictionary *negotiate* means "1. To treat for, obtain, or arrange by bargain, conference, or agreement. 2. To transfer for a value received, as a note, bond, or other written obligation. 3. To accomplish or cope with successfully, as to *negotiate* an obstacle. 4. To treat or bargain with others." Negotiation embraces then the process of talking about terms, the achievement of terms, and the terms.

Clearly we are already in the midst of negotiations, and long have been, if we mean only the process of talking about terms—at least about the terms for talking about terms. The Russians have been busily propounding the conditions for a spider's feast. [the American negotiators] have been assiduously—and properly—rejecting these. In this [Washington] has been accused of inflexibility—which is the pejorative word for firmness.

The reason why negotiations have not progressed to the achievement of terms (in this case even the achievement of terms for trying to achieve terms) is not a lack of inspiration or yeastiness. It is not even a lack of understanding.

We do understand the Russians.

Basically, and quite clearly, the Russians do seek world domination. A great many experts on Russia may deny this. They will point to the remoteness and theoretical character—and hence the supposed irrelevancy—of the ultimate aspirations of the Marxist ideology and contend that there is no active desire whatsoever in the Kremlin rulers really to subjugate Western Europe, etc. This is really not the point. The point is that the Russian rulers do set as their goal and actively pursue the condition that all problems exterior to Russia deemed important to them are to be settled their way. This does not mean that the Russian rulers aspire to see the Red flag over the Quai d'Orsay or Whitehall. It merely means paramountcy for Russian purposes when the issues are drawn.

On the other hand the Russians understand us quite well. I can state this only as a supposition. I cannot give personal assurance about it. Our own purposes and interests make unacceptable to us the condition of world relations coveted by the Russians.

This mutuality of understanding is what impinges upon negotiation in the sense of achievement of terms.

In a negotiation which advances to terms, each side seeks ends and brings means. Each side conceives its ends in terms of means to be tendered by the other. In a one-shot deal—the Yankee trading sort of negotiation—means and ends settle out in an exchange if the price is right, and the seller awaits other customers while the buyer takes home the goods or goes to other markets. This has no bearing on the sort of negotiation which the U.S. is being exhorted to undertake. The point at issue is the conditions for a continuing relationship. Whether at the summit or elsewhere the basic bargaining must be on how in broadest terms the entities concerned are to relate themselves to each other. If we wish to draw a metaphoric parallel, the most apt would be the sort of negotiation which took place between the U.A.W. and General Motors in 1937. Here the issue was whether the company and the union would thenceforth relate themselves to each other in a continuing bargaining relationship. That issue settled, the other elements in contention fell into place more or less readily.

The conditions of successful collective bargaining shed some light on the problem of negotiating with the Russians. In collective bargaining that works, the adversariness of the parties is limited by their recognized need of each other. Their ends are not the same. They may even be opposite, but they are compatible. Each side seeks satisfaction of its own ends at a minimum practicable expenditure of means to satisfy the ends sought by the other, but neither hates or fears *per se* the ends which the other seeks, and so neither feels compelled to suspect or distrust the use which the other might make of a success.

Between the Russians and us such conditions do not exist. Debate is not likely to convince either party to the contrary. A basis for Yankee trading is lacking. The inspiration of tête-a-tête is not likely to cause either side to forget the facts.

In this perspective the argument about locus—whether to negotiate at a mysterious summit or along even more mysterious corridors of professional diplomacy—becomes as derivative and arid as a question whether Neville Chamberlain or Nevile Henderson was the best man for doing business with Hitler. If a universe of discourse making for compatible ends were shared, negotiations at whatever level might be productive of the longed-for solutions. If this were so, moreover, the problems and dangers which men of good will wish to abate would not exist.

This brings us to the vaunted relaxation of tensions. One hears that the Russians harbor thoughts of bringing this about and need to be met only halfway. If by the phrase one means a sag along our side of the confrontation—a disengagement, an abatement of the challenge which we carry to Russian purposes—then the answer is that, of course, the Russians are ready for it and want it the worst way. If it means that the Russians are in a mood for modifying the intensity and constancy of their own desires, one can only answer that the mood is deeply concealed, and its existence a matter of guesswork.

This does not mean an endlessly static situation. The material relevancy of certain means may alter from one stage to another, and problems may move up or down in the scale of negotiability; particular impasses may become unblocked, as occurred, for instance, in the case of the Austrian Peace Treaty. The time when it will become possible to transform the situation by putting means of high importance in the bargain and to reconcile ends seems remote, however.

If there is to be relaxation of tensions otherwise than on terms of capitulation, it will be only in the inward sense: a reassertion of captaincy over our own spirits and resolving to live calmly in danger for a long time to come. I am not hopeful that this will be done easily. I can almost hear the yeasty throngs chanting:

> One-two-three-four
> Terminate the cold war!
> Five-six-seven-eight
> Hurry and negotiate!

The problem is how to restore balance to our side, how to dispel the beguiling notion that negotiation of itself is a means of redressing dangers and achieving harmony of interest, rather than merely an avenue along which one may proceed to success, impasse, or catastrophe, depending on the ratios of will and resources between the adversary parties. To counter the surge of demand for negotiation under conditions of high disadvantage to our side it will be necessary to abandon the secondary and unattractive propositions that clutter up the American case and to concentrate on a few basic and sound propositions: a proper insistence on the baleful character of the adversary, the necessity of American interposition, in fact and not merely in promise, on the continent; and the indispensability of NATO. Above all, it will be necessary to correct our imprudent strategic reliance on a thermonuclear weapon that frightens our friends more than it cows our putative enemies.

3

*History's Limitations in the Nuclear Age**

Reinhold Niebuhr

REINHOLD NIEBUHR, *one of America's outstanding theologians, is Professor Emeritus of Applied Christianity at the Union Theological Seminary in New York, and has been a Research Associate of the Institute of War and Peace Studies at Columbia. Among his many books are* Christianity and Power Politics (*1940*); Christian Realism and Political Problems (*1953*); *and* The Nature and Destiny of Man (*1965*).

We have now lived in the precarious peace of the nuclear age for more than a decade. Yet we have not comprehended its full scope, for the obvious reason that only historical perspective and artistic imagination can fully delineate the outlines and dimensions of a historical epoch. Immediate urgencies and emergencies produce a kind of experience, but not the kind which sets events in perspective.

History means two things. It means the actual course of events; and it also means historiography: what people think about these events and how they interpret them in the light of previous and subsequent events. Obviously, no generation can interpret its own experience in the light of the future, and harassed generations are too preoccupied with immediate perils and promises to interpret their current situation in the light of the past. That is why we must wait for historians and artists to tell us about the full quality of our experience. Every historian is something of an artist, for only imagination can piece together the multifarious and kaleidoscopic configurations which make up the "raw stuff" of history.

There are thus probably two reasons why we do not fully appreciate the unique and peculiar distinction of the "balance of terror"—the constant environment of the nuclear age—which forces us to live on the edge of catastrophe and to beguile our anxieties and apprehensions by preoccupying ourselves with such things as whether or not cars should have tail fins, or whether compact cars will displace their more ponderous competitors. One reason is that we are too technocratic. We lack the imaginative capacity to interpret the real meaning of the time in which we live. The second reason is of course our inevitable lack of historical perspective.

The first reason—lack of artistic imagination—may account for the fact that World War II did not prompt anyone to write a *War and Peace,* and thus illumine (as Tolstoy did with the Napoleonic period) one of the great enigmas of history: the problem of determinism and voluntarism, the relation of the purposes of the human agents in the historical drama to the

* *The New Leader* (1963), pp. 18–19. From *The New Leader,* February 4, 1963;

forces of history beyond their control. Instead it only prompted Norman Mailer to write *The Naked and the Dead,* a book contrasting the grim realities of war with the erotic fantasies of the men engaged in those realities. It was pathos in a minor key, touching neither the greater pathos nor the irony of a war which both fulfilled and negated all the hopes previous centuries had for the enterprise of man.

The second reason—lack of historical perspective—has deprived our generation of the full savor of the epoch through which we are bound to live in alternate stages of anxiety, great responsibility and irresponsible defeatism. For only future generations can fully measure the curiously ironic quality of an era in which the hopes of a global community have been fulfilled through the technical cohesion of the entire world and refuted by the realities of the cold war and the nuclear dilemma. In place of the expected "parliament of mankind and federation of the world," we have the precarious peace of the balance of terror, which prevents two hostile blocs from engaging in conflict lest that conflict bring about mutual annihilation.

There is, in short, an ironic quality to the experience of our generation that is not immediately discernible in the experience itself. And it requires artistic imagination and historical perspective to bring out the full irony of a culture and civilization which can penetrate the mysteries of the planets and lift the living standards of advanced nations to hitherto unimagined heights, but cannot settle a conflict between two blocs of nations—though it has sufficient prudence not to initiate an ultimate conflict that might leave the difference between victors and vanquished negligible.

The crucial question is whether our generation, immersed in escaping from thoughts too dreadful to think about, can grasp the full import of our situation. And even if we should fully realize our predicament, is there any escape from it?

Artistic imagination is always scarce, and it is particularly so in a technocratic culture. There was only one Cervantes to recognize fully the ironic quality accompanying the decay of chivalry. What is more important, historical perspective is a limited achievement. It is reserved for our children, who alone can measure the full dimension of our condition in the light of insights which only the passage of time can give.

Yet while men are creatures of time, they are not its prisoners. True, we cannot pierce the mysteries of the future; but a careful analysis of the present will furnish some valuable clues. The past is not exactly an open book; still, its pages can be scanned and rescanned until they yield some insights into the character of the present.

The chief insight to be gained by interpreting the present in the light of the past is to realize the ironic contrast between the hopes of the eighteenth and nineteenth centuries and current realities. From the early Renaissance to the nineteenth century, everything contrived to create an atmosphere of hope. The Renaissance freed human reason from the tutelage of church and state, and thus created the hope that evils due to ignorance, superstition and unfounded dogmas would be eliminated. The development of technical civilization held out the promise of emancipation from age-old poverty. The rise of democratic governments gave promise of relief from irresponsible government and tyranny. And finally, Darwin's discovery of the laws of evolution offered the hope that history would emulate nature in rising to higher and higher levels of human competence. Social Darwinism was in fact one of the many ingredients of the gospel of hope, though the concept of the "survival of the fittest" was hardly a good slogan for a human community which required greater and greater cooperation rather than conflict.

If we set the present under the light of the past we shall have a clue to the irony of our situation. Previous generations discovered an important truth, and they combined this discovery with a fantastic error. They clearly saw that, in the sense that the whole human enterprise is influenced by man's increasing power over nature, there is indeed progress. Their error lay in assuming that this added power and freedom would invariably be used for "socially approved" ends. On the contrary, the simple facts of history reveal that every increase in human power and freedom contains destructive as well as creative possibilities.

Our own nuclear age has discovered that this obvious fact has tragic and paradoxical overtones. For the same technical advances that created a potential global community also increased the destructive power of the weapons of warfare. These advances have brought us to the point where the fear of destruction is a more potent force for peace than the mutualities of community.

The knowledge of our predicament is not, of course, completely redemptive. But it may help a culture, and particularly a young hegemonous nation accustomed to grow from strength to strength, to realize that the simple victories of the past are no longer possible. It may also teach the lesson that any effort to bring history to a victorious conclusion by a final assault upon "evil" forces such as Communism could bring our whole civilization to a sorry end. Clearly, the slogan "there is no substitute for victory" is a snare and delusion, prompted by ignorance of the ironic qualities of our experience and obtuseness to the limits of the capacities of any nation, or culture or civilization in a day when the destructive abilities of mankind have reached their highest pitch.

In analyzing the present for clues to the future we may also discover some consolations for present burdens and the ominous years ahead. Could it be, for instance, that the rift in the Communist bloc might finally lead to a tacit partnership between Russia and America across the great ideological chasm, a partnership based on a common responsibility for avoiding disaster and a common "bourgeois" determination to guard present achievements against irresponsible fanaticism. The thought is horrendous, but it may be the "silver lining in the dark cloud shining."